Injustice

The Social Bases of Obedience and Revolt

Injustice #b

The Social Bases of Obedience and Revolt

BARRINGTON MOORE, JR.

M. E. Sharpe INC., WHITE PLAINS, NEW YORK

This book too is for E.C.M.

Contents

List of Tables   xi

Preface   xiii

PART ONE   The Sense of Injustice: Some
            Constants and Variables

Chapter 1.   *Recurring Elements in Moral Codes*
                1. Starting Points   3
                2. Authority and the Challenge to
                   Authority   15
                3. The Division of Labor   31
                4. The Distribution of Goods and Services:
                   The Permutations of Equality   37
                5. Concluding Observations   45

Chapter 2.   *The Moral Authority of Suffering and Injustice*
                1. Preliminary Remarks   49
                2. Asceticism   50
                3. The Untouchables   55
                4. Concentration Camps   64
                5. Stifling the Sense of Injustice   77

Chapter 3.   *The Rejection of Suffering and Oppression*

1. The Issues   81
2. Cultural and Social Aspects   83
3. Moral Autonomy and Human Personality   89
4. Freudian Interpretations   109

PART TWO   **An Historical Perspective: German Workers 1848–1920**

Chapter 4.   *Prologue*   119

Chapter 5.   *German Workers in the Revolution of 1848*

1. The Conflict of Principles in Modernization   126
2. Strains on the Guilds   129
3. The Proletariat   133
4. Articulate Diagnoses   144
5. Workers' Behavior in the Revolutionary Period   156
6. Nationalism and the Workers   167

Chapter 6.   *Social and Cultural Trends Before 1914*

1. Introduction   173
2. Size and Composition of the Industrial Work Force   175
3. Wages and Workers' Conceptions of the Wage Relationship   185
4. Elite and Masses among Workers   191
5. The Common Liability to Misfortune   196
6. Relationships with Superiors and Other Workers   202
7. Some Sources of Working-Class Culture   205
8. Images of the Future   208

9. Political and Economic Action   217

10. Identification with the Empire   221

Chapter 7.   *Militance and Apathy in the Ruhr Before 1914*

1. Significance and Character of the Ruhr   227
2. The Coal Miners   233
3. The Iron and Steelworkers   257
4. The Consequences of Different Historical Experiences   269

Chapter 8.   *The Reformist Revolution 1918–1920*

1. General Background   275
2. The Duel between the SPD and the Radicals   285
3. A Note on Councils and councils 1918–1920   313

Chapter 9.   *The Radical Thrust*

1. General Aspects   316
2. The Ruhr from War to Revolt   328

PART THREE General Perspectives

Chapter 10.   *The German and Russian Revolutions: Some Comparisons*   357

Chapter 11.   *The Suppression of Historical Alternatives: Germany 1918–1920*

1. Some General Considerations   376
2. A Crucial Non-Decision: The SPD and the Army   381
3. Was a Different Policy Possible?   385
4. Why Was Such a Policy Not Attempted?   391

Chapter 12.   *Repressive Aspects of Moral Outrage: The Nazi Example*
    1. The Issue   398
    2. Who Were the Nazis?   400
    3. Forms and Sources of Nazi Moral Outrage   411
    4. "Right" and "Left" Radicalism: Similarities and Differences   420

Chapter 13.   *Moral Relativism*
    1. Evaluative and Descriptive Aspects   434
    2. Rational and Predatory Authority   440
    3. Principles of Distribution   449
    4. Exploitation   455

Chapter 14.   *Inevitability and the Sense of Injustice*
    1. Introductory Observations   458
    2. Individual Personality   462
    3. Social Aspects   468
    4. The Problem of National Identity   484
    5. Cultural Definitions of the Inevitable   489
    6. Time and the Sense of Injustice   496
    7. The Expropriation of Moral Outrage   500

Chapter 15.   *Epilogue: Reciprocity as Fact, Ideology, and Ideal*   506

    References Cited   511

    Index   529

Tables

Chapter 5
1. Increase in Numbers of Workers: 1816–1846   137

Chapter 6
2. Industrial Workers in 1913, as Reported by the Factory Inspection Service   178
3. Trade-Union Membership: 1907, 1912, and 1913   182
4. Indices for Real Wages: 1871–1913   185
5. Workers' Hopes and Fantasies, According to Levenstein's *Arbeiterfrage*   214

Chapter 7
6. Distribution of Gainfully Employed Persons in the Three Main Administrative Districts of the Ruhr in 1907   229
7. Center Party and SPD Votes in the Three Main Administrative Districts of the Ruhr: 1898–1912   230
8. Principal Occupations and Numbers of Industrial Workers in the Ruhr in 1907   232
9. Coal Production and Numbers of Miners: 1800–1913   235

Chapter 8
10. Industrial Workers, as Reported by the Factory Inspection Service: 1913, 1918, and 1920   277
10a. Changes from 1913 in Numbers of Industrial Workers: 1918 and 1920   278

Chapter 9

11. Distribution of Gainfully Employed Persons in the
Ruhr: 1907 and 1925   329

12. Principal Occupations of Industrial Workers in the
Ruhr: 1907 and 1925   330

Chapter 10

13. Selected Occupational Groups Ranked by Proportion
of NSDAP Members, Based on 1935 Party Figures and
Official Census Reports   404

14. Social Composition of NSDAP in 1935   409

Preface

This is a book about why people so often put up with being the victims of their societies and why at other times they become very angry and try with passion and forcefulness to do something about their situation. For the most part, the book focuses on people at or near the bottom of the social order: those with little or no property, income, education, power, authority, or prestige. It tries to uncover how such people feel about and explain the circumstances of their lives. At the same time it searches for further reasons for their behavior. What are their notions of injustice and thereby of justice, and where do these ideas come from? Is there any central core of common or widely shared features in such conceptions, and if so, why? How and why have these conceptions varied among different groups of workers and what have been some of the most important historical trends that have affected them and can account for these variations?

For a time I thought of calling the book a study of moral outrage, making it an analysis of some of the social and historical conditions under which moral outrage did and did not put in an appearance. Many elements of this original concern remain in the book. But working through the evidence about the way people without much property or other social advantages actually felt and behaved led to a realization that the expression "moral outrage" failed to convey adequately what I was often finding. "Moral outrage" suggests too strongly the agonies of intellectuals trying to interpret, judge, and change the world. It smacks too much of the preacher. People of little education and refinement are certainly capable of feeling anger, but the word "moral" carries overtones of condescension and introspection that miss both the tone and concreteness of much popular anger. At the same time there is a clearly moral component to this anger. Hence "injustice," or the sense of injustice, captures the tone and content of these expressions more accurately.

Part One is a preliminary attempt to find out what central and recurring elements there might be in conceptions of injustice and to account for the most extreme variations in such conceptions. The first chapter examines as wide a range of human societies as possible, looking for recurring situations that people generally regard as unfair and unjust. The next two chapters search in two opposite directions for the greatest possible deviations from any such potentially universal sense of justice and injustice. Through an examination of extreme examples of the acceptance of degrading and unjust situations the second chapter tries to discover the psychological and sociological mechanisms that stifle the sense of injustice. The third and last chapter in Part One then, so to speak, reverses the field: it is an attempt to locate and identify those psychological and sociological mechanisms through which human beings come to resist injustice, or to define their situation as one of injustice and do something about it. While Part One contains a fair amount of historical material, it is not innocently ahistorical but explicitly so.

Part Two introduces historical dimensions and considerations. Though the time may be rapidly approaching when a comparative history of Western industrial workers—and not just labor movements involving a small minority of these workers —may be feasible and profitable, this did not seem possible to me at the time I began serious work on this book, more than ten years ago.* Most of the secondary literature consisted of books about what theorists *thought* masses of ordinary workers felt, or else were rather detailed blow-by-blow accounts of the history of national labor movements. There were occasional brilliant exceptions, such as E. P. Thompson's *The Making of the English Working Class* and Carl Schorske's *German Social Democracy 1905–1917,* which shed valuable light on selected aspects of the issues. But there were not enough such studies. Fairly soon it became apparent that at this stage there was the prospect of learning much by mining the available sources for *one* country in

---

*One scholar published such a study when I had nearly completed this book, Peter N. Stearns, *Lives of Labor* (New York, 1975). Because of the date of publication, I have been able to make only limited use of this book.

an effort to uncover the life situations of different kinds of ordinary workers and how they responded to them. Comparisons might then be possible for these different kinds of workers within the same country.

Once the decision had been made to stick to the literature on one country it was easy to choose Germany for a combination of compelling reasons. Without claiming that German working-class history is prototypical, one can see that some of the most important things that have happened to workers in other countries happened also in Germany, but in a more intense form. Guilds were far more important in Germany than elsewhere in Western Europe: their decay and the creation of new industrial forms of organization presented especially severe and revealing problems. In the second place, Germany before 1914 had created a powerful industrial establishment for its time and had managed to integrate its workers into the capitalist order to an extent that astonished radical Marxists. But there were obviously forces working against capitalist integration too. In addition, Germany had undergone two revolutionary experiences, that of 1848 and that of 1918–1920. Perhaps because both were unsuccessful, the prospects of learning something new seemed to me especially enticing.

Furthermore the primary sources on Germany, though far from completely satisfactory, are unusually rich in the type of data necessary for the problems at hand. There were more workers' autobiographies than apparently existed for England, the United States, France, and Russia, the other countries whose language I could read. There were several sociological investigations of factory life prior to 1914 and even one primitive, but in many respects highly revealing, investigation of workers' attitudes. Used with critical care, such sources can tell us a great deal about how a variety of workers actually thought and felt about contemporary issues, the categories and concepts through which they diagnosed their situation, the forms of cooperation and antagonism on the job and off it, and similar matters. To set such information in its general context and as a check on its representative character, I found invaluable the German census reports, supplemented by those of the factory inspection service, neither of which so far as I know has yet been the object of critical scrutiny and interpretation.

The explanation in Part One of central elements in conceptions of injustice, their relationship to recurring aspects of the division of labor, and of the range of variations in human willingness to put up with oppressive social relationships suggested many questions that should be put to the German materials and some of the possible answers. But I had no intention of forcing the facts of German history through a conceptual sieve in order to "test" hypotheses. Historical facts have a certain patterned relationship to each other that such a procedure would obliterate and destroy. It is the task of the investigator to elicit this pattern through careful and critical attention to the evidence. It is necessary to proceed delicately, patiently, listening for contradictory clues and signals, much as a skilled diagnostician tries to understand the state of organs and tissues in a live human patient while searching for patterns that will reveal a state of health or a specific disease. Dissection and hypotheses are necessary in both forms of inquiry at certain points. But they are nowhere near enough.

Furthermore it is a provincial and philistine notion of "relevance" which requires all worthwhile knowledge to be relevant to either political action or scientific theory or both. Historical inquiry can have other purposes without falling into mere antiquarianism or the manufacture and distribution of admirable ancestors for a usable past. One of these is to uncover and assess the main causal links in a unique chain of events that has had powerful consequences all over the world. What German workers tried to do during the nineteenth and twentieth centuries, and what they failed to do or were not even interested in trying to do, are a set of related events with consequences on this order of magnitude. These are important facts in their own right with their own patterns of causal connections, which carry vital implications for the issues discussed in this book. Finally, historical inquiry enables, indeed almost forces, one to perceive and raise questions missed by a static analysis.

German history during the period under consideration, from the Revolution of 1848 to the capture of power by Adolf Hitler in 1933, was a contest among the forces of conservatism —including eventually reaction in its mass form of National Socialism—liberalism, and revolutionary radicalism. As best I could, I have tried to understand and portray the changing lives of ordinary workers living through this contest, the extent to which they were and were not aware of it, and the nature of their contributions to it.

Part Three constitutes a return to the general issues raised in Part One, together with an attempt to cope with both the methodological and substantive issues that came to light through the introduction of an historical perspective. The shift to a higher level of generality is deliberately gradual. Chapter Ten investigates selected aspects of the Russian revolutions in 1917 to explain significant differences and similarities in the behavior of German and Russian workers in the crises that came at the end of the First World War. At this point the analysis raises the general question of suppressed historical alternatives by trying to discern what other possibilities were open in the German context of defeat and revolutionary turmoil between 1918 and 1920. Chapter Twelve uses National Socialism as an extreme example of repressive and aggressive tendencies in popular or mass conceptions of injustice, in an effort to analyze and comprehend the more general causes of these trends. Finally, the last three chapters, including the Epilogue, try to come to terms with the twin issues of moral relativism, or the denial of any generally valid conception of injustice, and how people come to perceive and struggle against injustice. This part of the discussion draws on evidence and theoretical considerations that have emerged so far in this book and also on whatever additional intellectual resources I could bring to bear.

Without concealing my own moral preferences or the reasons for them, I have tried throughout to construct arguments that would be open to refutation through an appeal to evidence and logic. About the intellectual position that governs the work as a whole it is enough to say here that I am as skeptical about catastrophe as the inevitable human fate as I am about utopia, and even more skeptical about catastrophe as the necessary prelude to utopia.

In writing this book I have refrained from the common practice of asking fellow scholars to read and criticize the manuscript, very likely to my cost as well as the reader's. But I had the sense that this practice was becoming burdensome. This does not mean that I wish to take full credit for whatever merits the book may have, responsible as I must be for its defects. There are certain scholars from whom I have consciously borrowed certain ideas and who I felt were looking over my shoulder in my struggles to make sense of the materials. (My colleague John Rawls has accepted with his usual wit and good nature my refusal to read his *Theory of Justice* until after completing my work on injustice, lest his rigorous philosophical categories unwittingly shape my attempt to perceive accurately the forms of untrained popular reactions to life experiences.) Partly because these debts are not always apparent from the citations I would like to acknowledge them here without implicating these writers in my shortcomings, or, as should be obvious to those who know their work, implying their support for views expressed in this book: Herbert Marcuse,

E. P. Thompson, George C. Homans, Robert Paul Wolff, Gabriel and Joyce Kolko. Without their stimulation and support I would never have attempted to write this book. Without that of Elizabeth Carol Moore I could never have finished it. That is only a part of what she has meant in the life of this writer. The rest, could I express it adequately, would not be for publication.

My good friend Adam Ulam, former director of Harvard's Russian Research Center, has generously given me valued moral support in the writing of this book—and of others that have had little or nothing to do with Russia. For more than two decades Rose Di Benedetto has accurately typed and retyped my manuscripts. Amid many other demands on her time she has been a source of constant cheer and varied help to my wife, to me, and · to my students.

As an author I have tried hard not to emulate the ways of Heraclitus, the famous Greek philosopher who served as an early inspiration for Marx. According to a distinguished modern authority, Heraclitus was an aristocrat in politics who wrote in a difficult style comprehensible to few. In his old age he retreated to the woods, having deposited his book of philosophy in the temple of Artemis. At least to me it seems that some of the more important differences between my ways and his are due to the efforts of Elizabeth Moore and Arnold C. Tovell, Editorial Director at M. E. Sharpe, Publisher. I wish to express my thanks to Joyce P. Tovell for her special care in copyediting this book and to my publisher for his willingness to publish this book without the guaranteed market of a textbook and in a format attractive to the general reader as well as usable by the scholar.

PART ONE

The Sense of Injustice

Some constants and variables

CHAPTER ONE

Recurring elements in moral codes

1. Starting points

Once upon a time in those happy days when students of human affairs were sure of their ground, it was possible to draw a sharp distinction between a political and social system based on force and fraud and one based upon rational authority and justice. Even if it might be rather difficult to find a convincing empirical example of a just society, this distinction appeared to be an elementary and obvious one, the foundation of intelligent political discussion. By the end of the nineteenth century this pleasant certainty had largely crumbled away under the onslaught of ideas that by now have become part of the intellectual fare conveyed in fifty-minute portions at many of our universities. Anthropologists shook our assurance by vividly exhibiting such a variety of human customs and beliefs as to make the notion of any single standard of moral and political judgment seem no more than a provincial rationalization for some brief phase of European history. Oddly enough it was the philosopher Herbert Spencer, in many ways the epitome of philistine Victorian provincialism, who culled the writings of anthropologists and historians to present in the opening pages of *Social Statics* (1850) one of the most spirited attacks on behalf of moral relativism. Though Spencer is now somewhat of an intellectual curiosity, from more acceptable sources the modern reader may learn that conflicts over values, or basic assumptions about good and evil in the ordering of human affairs, are issues that science cannot settle because science concerns the way things are, not the way they ought to be. Lest such a viewpoint have too corrosive an effect on traditional moral beliefs, one might add some saving clause to the effect that in a democracy one has the duty as a citizen to take a stand on political and ethical issues but should not make these claims as a scholar or scientist.

To recapture old certainties is then out of the question, at least in the form they once existed. Nevertheless there are grounds for suspecting that the welter of moral codes may conceal a certain unity of original form, as well as a discernible historical drift in a single direction, and that variations from this pattern of a single basic form undergoing prolonged historical modification are explicable in general terms. It is at least just barely possible that human affairs do make sense after all.

We can begin looking for sense by taking an example of the kind of situation this book will be analyzing throughout. It will be both a greatly simplified example and a hypothetical one. Let us suppose one man strikes another man hard enough so that it hurts. How will the victim feel? There will be some physical pain. On the other hand, we know that the ability to tolerate pain varies a great deal for all sorts of reasons that would bear looking into.[1] This book will not do that in any detail, but it remains an important point to remember. If the victim has reason to believe that the blow was for something he did that was very evil, he is rather likely to feel some sense of relief that he got off so lightly. There may or may not be some residue of anger as part of the response to punishments that are felt to be thoroughly deserved. Now let us change the example slightly and make it more concrete to see a different kind of feeling.

The man who strikes the blow is a white policeman in an American city. The victim is an educated black man who has been doing nothing more than minding his own business in a perfectly peaceful fashion. In that situation the black man is almost certain to feel moral outrage, because, as far as he can see, the blow and injury were totally unjustified and undeserved. In what sense was the blow unjust? What does the word really mean? Simply put, it means that the white policeman had no right to do what he did. If the episode happened in an ideal racially integrated community, everybody else would agree with the black man. There is only too much reason to fear that no community is like that, though some may approach it. In most American cities the black man would feel angry because the policeman had violated

[1] Cf. Ronald Melzack, *The Puzzle of Pain*.

a rule that the former felt with all his heart *ought* to be the one that governed decent social relationships.

Evidently social rules and their violation are crucial components in moral anger and a sense of injustice. Essentially it is anger at the injury one feels when another person violates a social rule. There are two distinct possibilities here. One can be angry because one feels that the existing rule is itself wrong and that a different rule ought to apply. In real life such situations frequently take the form of disagreements about what the rule actually is. But for the sake of simplicity we can set this situation aside for the present. Without rules governing social conduct there could be no such thing as moral outrage or a sense of injustice. Likewise, awareness of social injustice would be impossible if human beings could be made to accept any and all rules. Evidently there are *some* constraints on the making of moral rules and therefore on the possible forms of moral outrage. There is also a great deal of variety. How can both be explained?

To the extent that there are any recurring or constant features in moral outrage, they would have to derive from the interaction between more or less constant aspects of human nature and equally recurring imperatives that stem from the fact that human beings must live with each other, that is, in human society. There are formidable difficulties in the way of spelling out any general characteristics of human nature and human society in a fashion that is both scientifically tenable and nontrivial. There is a great risk of being either wrong or banal or both. Nevertheless the risk is worth taking because the position taken on these issues, consciously or unconsciously, is likely to have a powerful influence on the way other questions are asked and through them on the findings that emerge.

The first difficulty stems from the fact that it is impossible to observe anything that can be called pure or innate or biologically determined human nature uncontaminated by social influences, or at least any form of such behavior that would be very relevant to understanding moral outrage and the sense of social injustice.[2] Nevertheless, it is obvious that human beings do have something that can be called innate needs. They are not simply blank slates upon which it is possible to impress any kind of

---

[2]The behavior of small infants, as yet hardly exposed to social influences, would not be very useful even if we could be certain that social influences had not intruded through such factors as the kind of nourishment available to the mother during pregnancy. Nor would the few instances of human beings who have somehow managed to survive without human care provide useful information, because such persons have obviously not had the opportunity to acquire the capacities necessary for living in human society.

personality, as many parents of even very small children will testify with some vehemence.

To deny any possible knowledge of what appears as obvious as all this—the existence of innate human nature—seems in the end a curious counsel of scientific perfectionism. One way to get some clues is by noticing human wants or needs that are common to most known societies and inferring that they have their origin in innate human nature. Therefore let us first ask a very simple question: What is generally noxious to human beings? Since our general problem is to account for situations in which anger does *and does not* occur (or is present to a very low degree) as a response to injuries, it will be helpful to have at the start a working notion of what things actually are injurious to human beings.

Failure to satisfy certain physical requirements is quite obviously harmful. Roughly in order of their importance these requirements are air, water, food, sleep, shelter in the sense of protection against extremes of heat and cold, sexual gratification. Failure to meet these needs will cause suffering for any human being. Except in the case of sexual gratification extreme deprivation produces death. And without heterosexual reproduction—until or unless a satisfactory substitute takes hold—human society will die out. Disease and physical mistreatment, such as torture, are clearly harmful, though, as will appear shortly, human beings under certain conditions inflict torture on themselves.

Moving away from these physical needs, which are always satisfied in culturally elaborated fashions, psychologists and anthropologists would be likely to agree that the lack of love and respect from other human beings is also harmful to the individual. Indeed, there is a wide range of favorable responses whose absence can be in some way damaging. Here I will mention only one: distinction. I suspect that the desire for distinction is universal because so many cultures either invent and embellish ways to envy other human beings, while other cultures condemn or try to suppress envy. Another noxious situation that has not yet received the attention it deserves is sheer boredom.

Finally, the inhibition of aggression against dangerous targets (natural or human) is certainly harmful, since the inhibited person is thus rendered vulnerable, an easy victim. There is little profit in trying to settle the issue of whether or not aggression itself is some form of an innate human instinct. All that we need to notice for the present is that (1) there is no known human society in which aggression does not appear in some form; on the other hand, (2) the scope of its expression and damage to other human beings is extraordinarily wide, ranging from the hostile glance to the obliteration of whole populations. Because of this range of possible effects, it does not seem to me very useful to discuss aggression in terms of an instinct. Rather it appears more useful to think of it as some sort of human capacity that is set in motion in a great variety of ways with equally many different consequences that depend on specific circumstances. Therefore the social causes have far greater explanatory power than the elastic biological capacity. Again, that is not an issue that has to be settled here.

As a working hypothesis, I propose a conception of innate human nature, innate in the sense of being *prior* to any social influences but not necessarily immune to them, for which not only physical deprivations are noxious but also psychic ones: specifically, the absence of favorable human responses, boredom, and the inhibition of aggressions. To the extent such a conception is valid it implies the existence of a "natural morality" in the sense that *some* moral preferences, particularly negative ones, are not merely the consequence of social training and conditioning. Generally human beings will try to avoid these situations anyway. And on a closer look one can see that it does not make much difference whether one describes the behavior in terms of negative avoidance or a search for positive goals. In addition to the satisfaction of physical needs, we could say, human beings seek some degree of variety and challenge in their lives, favorable responses (including distinction) from other human beings, and opportunities for the discharge of aggression, a human capacity which, if not instinctive, is aroused by such a variety of frustrations that it is bound to find expression somehow. Up to this point it has been possible to avoid the use of the slippery and loaded term "healthy." But it is plain that successful aggression against real danger deserves to be called healthy and the suppression or inhibition of such aggression a form of pathology. After all, the human animal does possess remarkable powers of logical thought and can use them in the pursuit of any goal.

The main value of any conception of natural morality lies in the implication that moral codes, moral anger, and hence a sense of social injustice have some very important roots in human biology. Human biology not only sets limits on what forms moral codes can take, but also gives them a certain direction and impulse. The political optimist believes that it is possible to create a social order based almost entirely on natural morality. A pessimist, of which Freud is the best-known though not necessarily the most convincing example, believes that this hope is illusory. This is scarcely the point at which to resolve such an issue; I hope that the book as a whole will clarify some of the relevant considerations. But it is worth drawing attention to the issue in order to keep before us the prospect that it may not be at all possible to have completely healthy human beings and still have society at all. Some aspects of human society, it could turn out, are bound to be noxious for some human beings.

If human society is noxious for anybody, why then does it exist? The obvious and banal answer is that by means of the division of labor, possible only in and through society, human beings enormously enhance their capacity to adapt to and control their environment. And even if it is obvious and banal, it is also true. Without the invention of human society, *Homo sapiens* might well have become extinct long, long ago. As a biological specimen man's individual capacities to cope with the environment are quite unimpressive, while the collective capacities of human society have now reached the point where they may be able to destroy all forms of life. By any criterion, that is quite a remarkable achievement. Nevertheless there have been costs all along, and far from equally distributed. Living and working with other human beings generate their own demands on human behavior and human feelings. It is one thing to be a solitary hunter completely dependent for survival on what one can kill with one's own hands and a few simple tools. It is something else again to be a member of a primitive hunting tribe with its set of rules about who beats the bush to drive the game, who takes the risk of killing ferocious wild animals, how the catch is to be divided up, and so on. The need to cooperate with other human beings produces a new and distinct system of causation for human behavior. Social causation will not work without some of the qualities and capacities that innate human nature provides. But it has to be understood in its own terms. Together with biological or innate factors, social causation—a very shorthand and inadequate way of expressing the fact that there are lots of other human beings in the world with whom it is necessary to come to terms—creates the actual human nature we can see and study. It is in this sense that the fact of living in society generates moral codes. To say that "society" generates moral codes can be misleading, because it is actually concrete individuals who create the moral codes. A very large part of the time some individuals create moral codes for their own particular advantages and to the detriment of others in the society. Nevertheless there is a sense in which everybody in any society has to hang together or else each will hang separately.

To elaborate slightly, certain problems always arise wherever and however a number of human beings attempt to live together and reproduce their kind. These problems can be lumped together under the general notion of the problem of social coordination. In turn this problem can be broken down in several ways. There is the problem of authority. In very small and simple societies it amounts to hardly anything more than who is going to make suggestions and who is going to follow them. There is the problem of the division of labor: who is going to do what work and when and how. Then there is the problem of allocating the resources available to the society and distributing among its members the goods and services that they collectively produce. *Pace* Marx, or at least some readings of Marx, the social relations of production and exchange will not always determine the system of authority that prevails. The lines of causation can run in both directions.

In a sense these three divisions of the problem of social coordination (authority, division of labor, and allocating goods and services) have about them an air of Cartesian arbitrariness. In many a nonliterate society the three aspects flow together in such a way that it is easy to misunderstand how the society works by being too precise about the distinction. Nevertheless I would maintain that the problems do exist in any given society and that for its members it is imperative to find *some* solution. Otherwise the society would cease to exist. It is in this sense legitimate to speak of social imperatives leading to moral imperatives and through these to moral anger and a sense of social injustice. By using the words "social needs" or "social imperatives" one is not necessarily concealing a selfish class or group interest under the cloak of a spuriously objective language. Failure to meet a genuine social need or imperative has the consequence that *all* members of the society suffer severely even if the suffering is not distributed equally.

Nevertheless the expressions "social need" and the stronger version "social imperative" are simultaneously so slippery and so essential in reasoned discourse about human affairs, even when other words are used to express the same general ideas, that it is necessary to pause briefly to comment on what they imply. As far as I am able to discern, "social need" contains three essential elements. The first element is a notion of causation with the ordinary temporal order reversed: something very unpleasant is bound to happen in the future if the need is not met. There is likewise and secondly an element of inevitable choice. The society can meet the need or fail to meet it. If it does meet it, there may be more than one possible way to do so. One way of meeting the need may satisfy some people in the society and another way will satisfy another group. Both groups are likely to claim that their way is meeting the "real" need of the society as a whole. This is, in a somewhat simplified form, the commonest source of ideological distortion. Finally, if an investigator continues to press the question "why does this particular need or imperative exist for this particular group or this particular society?" the answer will at some point include an ethical judgment.

Take, for example, the proposition that in all industrial societies, including socialist ones, it is essential to set aside a high proportion of the goods and services produced by the society as a reward for the managerial function. For the sake of showing the structure of the argument let us assume that the proposition is true and that it is possible to demonstrate empirically what the word "high" means—naturally a quite dubious assumption. Nevertheless, *if* the opponent of high rewards for management were forced back this far, it would still be possible to assert a preference for a society without industry. That is an ethical judgment. It is still possible to debate this judgment rationally, because one could ask whether by any ethical criteria the costs of setting up such a society now might not be too great in terms of human suffering.

It is a counsel of perfection to assert that those who use the phrase "social need," or some similar expression, keep all these considerations in mind all of the time. But it is worthwhile remembering that they exist, and that all sorts of empirical and philosophical presuppositions are hidden behind any possible use. The best way to be on guard is to make sure that we know as clearly as we can just what human beings are under consideration whenever the idea comes up.

With this warning in mind it is possible to go back to, and amplify slightly, the statement that people living in any society must solve the problems of authority, the division of labor, and the distribution of goods and services. They do this partly by working out rough-and-ready principles of social inequality and teaching each other, with widely varying degrees of success, to accept and obey these principles. They create, as they go along, an implicit and sometimes explicit social contract. There are many ways to do this. Fear, force, and fraud are not the sole basis of any human society, even if their role has been decisive throughout the known history of the species. Nor for that matter are human societies simply more or less elaborate systems of exchanges. They are mixtures of both coercion and exchange. The proportions of the two ingredients vary tremendously from case to case. They are not the same in the Trobriand Islands as in a modern industrial society. The ways of extracting a surplus from the underlying population and turning it into culture with the consent, if not necessarily the advice, of the lower orders is very different in the two cases.[3] Just to make matters even more complicated, human beings have a way of changing the value they put on the items they contribute to the system of exchanges. They can teach each other that the value of a man's contribution has something to do with the color of his skin. Then they can teach each other that this is not the case. In both kinds of teaching there is a generous dose of coercion. There are limits to which this process of mutual education can go. But it is not very easy to pin down what the limits are.

Even the simplest known societies display in at least a rudimentary form some principles of social inequality. They appear, for example, in the division of labor by sex. It might be just barely possible to disprove this proposition by finding a society in which the work of men and women, though differing, was ranked equally in every one of its possible forms, from gathering fuel and finding food to cooking meals. But it is highly unlikely that such a society can be found.[4]

This is not an appropriate point to enter into a general discussion of what these principles might be or their possible varieties in time and place. Several principles might very well be discernible in the workings of any one society, even a quite simple one with a rudimentary technology. In a larger and more complex society it would be natural to expect that different sectors of the population owed allegiance to different principles, and that there were huge differences in the extent to which various people were consciously aware of these principles or could put them into words. In this chapter the discussion will focus on the issue of whether there might be any discernible recurring themes in *complaints* about the existence of these principles or the way they work out in practice. No presupposition is possible in advance about whether recurring complaints exist or about whether they are in some sense justified. Human societies may or

---

[3]On the extraction of a surplus in nonliterate societies, even those without hereditary systems of social stratification, see Paul Radin, *Primitive Religion*, chap. 3, as well as the critical observations by Raymond Firth in *Primitive Polynesian Economy*, 171–172.

[4]An instructive if old general survey of the anthropological data may be found in Gunnar Landtmann, *The Origin of the Inequality of the Social Classes*, chaps. 1–3.

may not have common features that are both intolerable, or nearly so, and inevitable.

The word "society" has come up several times already, and it will also be helpful to say something about the analytical pitfalls that can be hidden in its usage. There is hardly any difficulty in agreeing that ancient Athens was a society and so was ancient Sparta. The inhabitants of each of these city-states lived under an easily identifiable set of institutions that were quite distinct from each other. Not all the inhabitants knew each other personally by any means. But they had dealings with each other on a continuing basis which, if frequently charged with conflict, only occasionally erupted into open violence. That is the sense in which the word "society" has been used so far and the way to be followed in subsequent discussion so far as possible. Thus a society refers to the largest body of inhabitants in a specified territory who have a sense of common identity, live under a set of distinct social arrangements, and do so most of the time at a level of conflict well short of civil war.

By this meaning, classical Greece was *not* a society, though it is useful to think of it as a social system—something quite different from a society—composed of competing city-states with its own internal dynamics. Even in doing this it is necessary to be careful and think of the "needs" of quite concrete groups of politically active groups in Athens, Sparta, and other cities. All the same there are quite good reasons for holding that the system of Greek city-states imposed political, and here we should say *amoral,* constraints on the political actors in these city-states.

The point that emerges is that in any society, except perhaps a few completely isolated ones, the working rules of morality do not derive from that society alone, but from a larger context which includes other societies. This fact can at times lead to conflicting pressures and ambiguities that require consideration. William Graham Sumner is justly celebrated for his distinction between the in-group and the out-group. It is a useful one but rather gross. In a number of situations different individuals in the same society can draw the boundary in different ways. How does an American citizen who is a powerful executive in a multinational corporation draw the boundary and in connection with what decisions? I confess ignorance about the answer. In some nonliterate groupings afflicted with numerous internal feuds it can be even harder to decide how and where these people draw the distinction between "them" and "us" and on what grounds.[5]

[5]For a good theoretical discussion see Marshall Sahlins, *Stone Age Economics,* chap. 5.

any means free of them. Societies without scarcity still have a great many quarrels and bitter disputes. Up to a point it is possible to keep them in bounds by a variety of social devices such as scolding, shaming, or temporarily isolating any person who threatens to become disruptive. In a great many such societies, on the other hand, what peace and order exist are highly precarious. A group or an individual can become so angry as to kill another person or persons. The outcome is likely to be a powerful demand for vengeance. Its institutional form is the blood feud, found over many parts of the world.

The cry for vengeance—suppressed here, encouraged and elaborated there—has echoed through a huge portion of human experience. Vengeance means retaliation. It also means a reassertion of human dignity or worth, after injury or damage. Both are basic sentiments behind moral anger and the sense of injustice. Vengeance is a way of evening things out, and of course one that never works completely. There is no such thing as a complete restoration for injuries once inflicted. Vengeance may be the most primitive form of moral outrage. But if primitive, it is also highly contemporary. It can be found in social orders of all sorts: those under political authority, influencing what authority does (or despite authority), as well as in cultures that are practically without authority.

So far I have refrained from an attempt to define authority on the grounds that we were talking about situations where it did not exist. In general, authority is one of those things we notice most easily after seeing situations where it doesn't exist or, more precisely, where it hardly exists at all. The blood feud with its perpetual round of vengeance is a good example. Blood feuds continue because there is no authority to stamp them out and provide other solutions to the problem of social order.

Authority is a reflection of the fact, mentioned earlier, that human society is in part a set of arrangements through which some human beings manage to extract an economic surplus from other human beings and turn it into culture. Authority is also a reflection of the fact that the extraction of a surplus is not all there is to human societies, and that it is not the only source of culture. Authority implies obedience on the basis of more than fear and coercion. It is necessary to see what the "more" amounts to in practice.

Though traditional theories about the social contract seem rather disreputable nowadays to hardheaded social scientists, they do contain a significant insight supported by abundant evidence that is attracting increasing attention.[8] In any stratified society—the kind we shall be talking about mainly from here on—there is a set of limits on what both rulers and subjects, dominant and subordinate groups can do. There is also a set of mutual obligations that bind the two together. Such limits and obligations are not set down in formal written constitutions or contracts, though in societies that have such paraphernalia, some of the provisions—not necessarily the most important ones—may be set down in this fashion.

To assert that there is an implicit rather than an explicit social contract, an unverbalized set of mutual understandings, does not quite convey the situation accurately. This way of making the point sounds as though there existed somewhere a sort of Platonic charter to which all members of the society except the socially obtuse and politically deaf would agree; any good anthropologist or sociologist would then be able to elicit fair copies of the charter from a variety of informants. What takes place, however, is a continual probing on the part of rulers and subjects to find out what they can get away with, to test and *discover* the limits of obedience and disobedience. No one knows exactly where the limits are until he finds out by experience, although both parties may have reasonably accurate anticipations beforehand. The more stable the society, the narrower the range within which this testing and discovering take place. The less stable the society, the wider and more diffuse the limits. But some limit is always there. Otherwise there would be no society.

In this sense the terms of the social contract are always being renegotiated. Rulers know that there are certain bounds to their power beyond which they cannot expect compliance. (This was true even in the Nazi concentration camps.) And to remain rulers, they require subjects. Meanwhile standards of approval and condemnation exist among the subjects and form the source of these limits. In due course we shall come to the question of how and why popular standards of condemnations arise and change. For the present it is sufficient to note that these mutual obligations and limits exist, and that their existence is both manifest in and discovered by intermittent testing of each other's reactions.[9]

Rulers and subjects are here rather general, simple, and overly abstract terms for individuals and, more often, for groups

---

[8]As an example see E. P. Thompson, "The Moral Economy of the English Crowd in the Eighteenth Century."

[9]Explicit conceptions of social contract occur in myth and tradition at widely separated points in space and time. To choose at random an African example, Max Gluckman, *The*

of individuals. At one end of a spectrum—say, a modern industrial state—they are vastly more differentiated and complex than the terms usually denote. For the other end of the spectrum—say, a nonliterate society without the institution of chiefs—the terms seem, on the other hand, too complex to denote a differentiation into those who command and those who obey, a distinction that does not exist in any permanent form. I have no desire to stretch the English language out of recognizable shape for the sake of creating pseudo-social uniformities. These differences do exist, and somewhere nonliterate societies do slide off the edge of the range of phenomena to be discussed now. As indicated at the beginning, their kind of social contract can work with almost no authority. Nevertheless it is clear that a social contract in the form just described exists at numerous levels of authority within the modern state. It is apparent in employer-employee relationships and many others. It also exists in many a society where there is no formal state but some activity that requires fairly sustained organization and cooperation, as in some types of hunting parties, and even more clearly in the practice of temporary war chiefs.

There are common provisions shared by a large number of societies, and subsocieties such as those just mentioned, in this form of social contract. Systems of authority generally specify (1) why persons who hold authority have that status and (2) how they obtain it or enter into it. Very often there is some ceremony, in the case of political rulers generally quite an elaborate one, to signify a person's entrance into that status. The modes of selection of course vary enormously, all the way from hereditary kingship to selection by lot. In this sense the social contract resembles a blank form, such as a job application or an income-tax form, into which it is possible to insert a limited range of values or data.

Ideas in Barotse Jurisprudence, 29–30, reports that, according to the Barotse creation myth, kingship was established by the people who undertook on their own the obligation to render tribute. According to Gluckman, there is an "idea of a contract between king and people" in this myth. In an interpretation of ancient political theories and social institutions on the Indian subcontinent, Charles Drekmeier, *Kingship and Community in Early India,* 245, asserts that "The Hindu governmental contract, like the Buddhist, was in essence an exchange of taxes for protection, and the king's authority was limited by sacred law." One text goes so far as to describe the king as the salaried servant of the people. Occasionally other texts indicate the subject's right to dethrone an unjust or irresponsible king, though such statements are rare. Such explicit and organized conceptions, however, are not universal. It would be hard to claim anything of the sort for the Greeks. In Homer, especially the Odyssey, we find a series of sharp deals between specific humans and specific gods, often directed against other gods, for quite limited and specific purposes. There can be an implicit social contract in the sense of a set of rules by which most people live, without these rules finding expression in a charter myth.

In any society a violation of prevailing procedures for the selection of authorities is likely to stir up anger. Attempts to present a new principle in the place of existing ones generate profound moral indignation and political turmoil. Also new principles may be introduced by attempts to correct violations or alleged violations in existing practice.

There are certain mutual obligations that generally link rulers and ruled, those in authority and those subject to authority. They are obligations in the senses (1) that each of the parties is subject to a moral obligation to carry out certain tasks as its part of the implicit social contract and (2) that failure of either party to perform the obligation constitutes grounds for the other to refuse the execution of its task. Each party finds moral justification and support for its own sense of outrage and anger in the alleged failure of the other to do its job properly. Charles I of England accused his parliamentary opponents of violating the laws of England and tried to set himself up as the protector of the liberties of the subject; the parliamentary leaders accused him of failing to carry out the obligations of kingship and unjustly abusing his subjects. Meanwhile some raised the issue of whether England needed a king at all. In Imperial times Chinese rebels accused the Emperor of failure in the performance of his task, of thereby losing the Mandate of Heaven. If they won, the Mandate of Heaven descended upon them; if they lost, they went down in the history books as brigands who had tried to seduce the population away from its obligations to the Emperor. Although at least one rebel leader went so far as to treat the Mandate of Heaven with surprising cynicism as a racket to hoodwink the masses,[10] prior to the intrusion of Western ideas no Chinese rebel took the radical step of asking whether they needed an Emperor at all. Though the preindustrial Chinese did not carry their challenge as far as the preindustrial English, in both societies and many others we find a reasonably clear sense of existing mutual obligations, a sense that emerges most vividly at a time of challenge that arouses moral passions on both sides.[11]

In broad outline these obligations break down into three distinguishable though related sectors. The first, perhaps most

---

[10]Vincent Y. C. Shih, "Some Chinese Rebel Ideologies," 214–215.

[11]In nonliterate societies the obligations of those in authority are often very strong. Max Gluckman observes that generally in tribal societies the chief is expected to succor directly all in need in a way very different from the impersonal help given through modern welfare agencies. Among the Barotse in Africa, whom he studied, the king's weightiest obligation is to provide at least a residential site and some arable land for all his subjects. See his *Barotse Jurisprudence*, 6, 80. As to what happens when an authority fails to

essential, obligation of the ruler is protection, especially protection from foreign enemies. This obligation applies not only to the head of a state but to much lower levels of authority. In this connection it is worth drawing attention to the widespread sentiment that the ruler should be in some sense a member of the same group: such a person should have enough cultural traits in common with the subjects to permit them to identify with the ruler. There is no reason to attribute this sentiment to anything resembling a herd instinct or innate aversion from what is strange. Foreigners are usually conquerors who have oppressed "us" or persons whom "we" have managed to oppress and exploit—slaves, immigrants, or victims of "our" conquest. If the foreigner is more of an equal, as in the case of refugees with socially useful skills, such an individual is a potential competitor. Though there are instances of seeking a powerful foreign protector, for subjects that is a sign of weakness and an inherently disagreeable situation.

From the standpoint of the present inquiry the most interesting of the ruler's obligations concern the maintenance of peace and order. The heart of this function is to settle the quarrels that arise among subjects and between subject and ruler in a manner that all parties will regard as basically fair.[12] The crux of the issue that interests us is whether or not there are any cross-cultural and transhistorical conceptions of fairness, or whether such conceptions are so historically specific and culturally limited as to render generalization impossible or fruitless. Shortly I will give some reasons for holding that there are some general conceptions of unfair and unjust behavior, and by implication therefore of the proper behavior of rulers. They are likely to make better sense, however, if we look at the relevant situations in the context of the full range of mutual obligations between ruler and ruled and the forms and consequences that violations of these obligations may take.

The third obligation of the ruler is to behave in such a way as to contribute to the material security—to say material pros-

---

live up to obligations or expectations, I have been unable to find much in anthropological accounts; however, Leopold Pospisil, *Kapauku Papuans and Their Law*, 244–245, reports a striking case, to be discussed more fully in a later connection, where there is evidently an obligation to kill a leading individual who does not live up to social expectations.

[12]In response to the centralizing efforts of Shih-huang-ti (Ch'in dynasty), builder of the Great Wall of China, a rebel in the year 206 B.C. gave as part of his program what may be a minimum definition of legality and fairness: "There will be only three items of law: he who kills shall die, and he who hurts other people, or steals from people shall be subject to retribution. All the rest of the Ch'in law shall be abrogated." See Shih, "Rebel Ideologies," 159.

perity would imply too great an emphasis on the accumulation of wealth—of the subjects. The forms this obligation can take vary all the way from the magic of the Lovedu rain queen, a secret and mysterious ruler over one of the Bantu tribes, to the efforts of American presidents to ward off a depression. The nineteenth-century notion that society bore no responsibility for the welfare of the population, that it was both especially futile and quite immoral to expect the chief of state to take effective action countering threats to popular welfare, now looks like a minor historical aberration. In England, where the idea received its clearest expression, it was not taken very seriously in practice.

Thus the ruler's expected contribution comes down to security: security against foreign and domestic depredation, supernatural, natural, and human threats to the food supply and other material supports of customary daily life. In return, the obligations of the subject are obedience to orders that serve these ends, contributions toward the common defense (lacking in those few societies where war is unknown), material contributions toward the support of the rulers who do not as a rule engage in straightforward economic production. Finally, subjects are generally expected to make some contribution through their own social arrangements toward keeping the peace.

That there are numerous variations on these themes and the extent to which they are elaborated goes without saying. There are also strong grounds for skepticism about any view to the effect that these mutual obligations usually sort themselves out into a general system with an equality of burdens upon those in authority and those subject to it and a harmonious relationship among the parts and functions of the social order. Nevertheless it is worthwhile observing that for very many human beings, especially the mass of human beings at the bottom of the pyramid in stratified societies, social order is a good thing in its own right, one for which they will often sacrifice other values. They detest violent and capricious interference with their daily lives whether it comes from brigands, religious and political fanatics, or agents of the powers that be. People will generally support, even if partly frightened into it, a political leader who promises peace and order, especially when he can do so under some color of legitimacy as defined in that time and place.[13]

[13]A famous account of an ancient Chinese utopia, given in the Book of Rites and cited by Jean Chesneaux, "Les Traditions égalitaires et utopiques en Orient," 90, asserts that it was an age when thiefs and brigands did not appear and the outer doors of houses were left open. Historians of Europe stress the sufferings of French, German, Spanish, and other

Although the social contract inherent in relationships of authority is always undergoing testing and renegotiation, and in revolutions may collapse almost completely,[14] I shall argue here by way of hypothesis, that there are certain forms of violation of this contract that quite generally arouse moral anger and a sense of injustice among those subject to authority. Where we do not find this anger, we will usually find certain repressive mechanisms at work, a type of situation to be examined in the next chapter. In authority relationships the archetypal situations are ones in which the ruler does not do his (and more rarely her) job properly, that is, does not provide security, or seeks personal advantage at the expense of the social order.

Before proceeding to somewhat more detailed analysis some additional comments by way of qualification and clarification are in order. Popular sentiments are not inclined to hold rulers to strict accountability. If anything, there is a noticeable tendency to dislike and distrust authority that rules too much by the book.[15] The positive image of authority is more likely to be that of the gruff, stern father figure, whose rare fits of rage reveal his power to protect and intimidate "our" enemies, but whose human foibles also promise some prospect of forgiveness for "our" transgressions.

The root of this paternalist conception of authority and the source of its frequent recurrence probably rests in the experience of childhood. Since the child begins life as totally dependent on the parents, the authority of the parents, who are at first the source of all gratifications, is likely to have a very benign component. Parental authority is also likely to range over the whole of a child's daily activities: the forms and times of eating,

---

populations during periods of anarchy and religious warfare, and their willingness to support a strong power to put an end to such suffering. As Eric J. Hobsbawm shows in *Primitive Rebels,* the brigand who gains some local support does so *against* a capricious and weak central authority. Insofar as a political leader working in a chaotic situation organizes his own armed bands, he of course partly frightens the population into supporting him. A great deal of revolutionary support by "the people" is obviously synthetic and the result of sheer bullying. But the revolutionary's program can make an enormous difference in gaining popular support when his competitors are much worse bullies.

[14]Local networks of authority of either the *ancien régime* or the revolution generally manage, however, to maintain themselves precariously until the new order is established.

[15]There are some grounds for the thesis that *Homo sapiens* is essentially an anarchist or at the very least an old-fashioned liberal. Even where authority appears to be completely legitimate and accepted, there is likely to be some sign of distrust or hostility. The Barotse, according to Gluckman, *Barotse Jurisprudence,* 38, say that "everyone loves a prince till he is made king; then everyone hates him." Authority always implies some degree of restraint and hence frustration. On the other hand, as we noted earlier, it is also a source of security. Thus human beings always want authority at the same time that they reject and distrust it.

excreting, playing, and sleeping. Functionally specific authority, that is, authority limited to a specific sphere of life, is something the child encounters later if at all. Indeed it is only in some aspects of modern industrial life that this form of authority has been developed to a high degree.[16] Nowadays the authority of the employer over the employee is more and more strictly confined to working hours and to behavior strictly related to the job; such authority produces moral indignation in many cases when it extends to hair styles, dress patterns (which may reflect an intrusion of sexuality into the formally desexualized sphere of work relationships), and of course skin color and religious beliefs. But this rationalist and individualist current toward personal autonomy runs against powerful impulses derived from childhood experience, the demand for completely enveloping authority and the security that this authority is supposed to provide. If this demand for a diffuse, paternalistic authority stems from the experience of childhood that would help to explain why it is often so terribly difficult for human beings to believe that the prevailing authority is inherently cruel and evil, as in the case of Job or the behavior of many a victim of Stalinist terror. There is of course considerable variation on this score, not of all of which is likely to be explicable in terms of differing childhood experiences. For the present we need do no more than take due note of a widespread human tendency to interpret the clauses of the implicit social contract for the rulers' benefit and some of the reasons for this tendency.

If these very general observations help us a little way along the road toward understanding popular and plebeian conservative tendencies, what about the opposite response—that of regarding the behavior of superiors as unjust and to be opposed? Obedience implies the control of impulses, and it is a reasonable working assumption that the control of impulses always involves some degree of unpleasantness and, in more severe cases, real pain. It is a safe prediction that minor forms of subversion can be found in the most placid forms of human authority. The general situation is one of limits to obedience beyond which the acts of authority appear capricious, oppressive, and unjust. Popular attitudes toward authority are understandably shot through

[16]For a good discussion of one instance of diffuse paternalist authority see J. J. Maquet, *The Premise of Inequality in Ruanda,* 161–162, 168–169. Acceptance of inequality insured internal peace for many years. In recent times, however, the system broke down in massive slaughter by the dominant stratum, probably due to the effects of encroaching Europeans and increased competition for resources. Accounts appear in *The New York Times,* May 31, 1972, and June 6, 1973.

with ambivalence, and in many cultures—not all—there is evidence for a powerful undercurrent of egalitarianism, of resistance to and suspicion of all forms of subordination of one human being to another.[17]

Now we can turn to specific violations of the social contract. Derelictions in the duty of protection by authorities are fairly obvious and need not detain us long. Treason by subjects is another violation, and can take place in any form of struggle, from straightforward military acts to the union leader's "sellout"—real or alleged—in modern economic conflicts. When severe, and there are of course all sorts of gradations, the penalty for the ruler is forfeiture of the right to rule and for the subject the rights of membership in the society—if not worse. There is no reason to belabor the sense of injustice that it provokes. Chinese rebels under the Sung used the payment of tribute to the barbarians in an effort to discredit the dynasty, all in a manner that would be perfectly understandable in Western society. More generally, rulers who cannot protect their own society, whose ill success in war discredits them, are liable to forfeit the right to rule. On several occasions military reverses or sheer incompetence have been the prelude to revolutionary outbreaks.

The consequences are more varied and puzzling in cases of the rulers' failure or inability to control their own instruments of power as well as their deliberate misuse. It is a reasonably safe assertion that no population lacks resentment and outrage at acts of plunder by its own troops, another recurring theme in Chinese rebellions. But it by no means always happens that such plunder and looting produce a strong reaction. There was surprisingly little to all the abuses and brutality of Europe's Thirty Years' War. Likewise the feeling that those in authority ought not to punish those subject to authority except for a definite crime appears quite widespread. It too occurs in China, as well as in the West. On the other hand, as everyone knows, arbitrary punishment has occurred very widely, not only in modern dictatorships and their concentration camps. Though fear and helplessness may well account for the absence of overt resistance, we need to understand more clearly what factors produce this sense of helpless fear. Overt and overwhelming terror in the hands of the

---

[17]The propaganda appeal of another Chinese rebel sums up nicely the demands of many a preindustrial population: "Li Tzu-cheng does not kill, he does not love wealth; he does not insult women, he does not loot; and he will buy and sell in fairness and relieve the people of all taxes; he will redistribute the money of the rich among the people." As Shih, who quotes this passage in "Rebel Ideologies" (208) remarks, it is no wonder the Ming government found him very hard to deal with.

authorities does not appear to be a sufficient explanation because human beings in such situations do from time to time undertake objectively hopeless acts of resistance. At the moment, however, these issues do not concern us. The point to be made is that despite a wide range in the degree of sensitivity, every culture seems to have *some* definition of arbitrary cruelty on the part of those in authority.

Misuse of the rulers' instruments of violence against their own subjects is an extreme violation of the obligation to keep the peace. A principal part of that obligation, we have seen, is to compose quarrels among the subjects. This obligation, which includes the administration of justice, but is broader insofar as it extends far beyond the formal arrangements usually associated with this term, is part of legitimate authority wherever it exists. One normal task of a shop foreman in industry, a noncommissioned officer in military services, or an administrator in any bureaucratic hierarchy is to straighten out disagreements and spats among subordinates. More generally, the right to intervene in disputes is one of the most eagerly sought and jealously guarded of the prerogatives of authority, whether bureaucratic or otherwise.

There is a perpetual tendency for those in authority to twist this process to their own advantage, and a corresponding tendency on the part of the subjects to resist, evade, or oppose authority.[18] At this point in our inquiry the main issue is whether any recognizable common standards underlie this opposition. Offhand it seems unlikely that one has to have grown up in the Graeco-Judaic tradition or to have been subject to the influence of Roman law to feel that one has had a raw deal. The common theme in conceptions of a raw deal, I suggest, is a violation of reciprocity. The authority obtains an advantage, causes harm to the aggrieved individual, without any real justification in terms of gains for the society as a whole. When David, in order to take Bathsheba to wife, sent her husband to certain death, he acted out the paradigm of this situation, possibly one reason it is so famous. Even if the form is much more abstract and less dramatic, it is easy to recognize the same essential elements in the complaints of Chinese rebels that high ministers use their offices to impeach their enemies and advance their relatives,

---

[18]One source of this opposition, especially in stratified societies, is the tendency of groups subject to a higher authority to perpetuate traditional ways of handling their own disputes, or to develop new ones. Gluckman, *Barotse Jurisprudence*, 212, gives a vivid example which shows how such interference can produce outrage. In one case of a killing, the Barotse king intervened, ordering the dead man's kin to accept compensation

while crime goes unpunished due to personal connections.[19]

A similar violation occurs when rulers impose severe material privations upon the population for purposes the latter do not accept, generally because such purposes are remote from their own way of life and interests. A Chinese rebellion under the Sung, mentioned earlier in another connection, found its justification in terms of the insufferable misery imposed by the ruler's efforts to obtain at any cost certain rare plants and stones.[20] A hostile Chinese account of the rebellion reports one episode that has the ring of universality:

[Fang-La, leader of the rebellion] then, taking advantage of (the feelings) of the people who were suffering the unbearable, secretly gathered the poor and impoverished and the idlers, and gave them alms to win them. When he was sure of their support, he had bulls butchered and wine strained, and called together over one hundred particularly wicked ones for a feast. After a few rounds of wine, La rose and said: "Basically, there is a single underlying principle for state and family. Suppose the young were to plough and weave, slaving the whole year through, and when they have some grain and cloth accumulated, their elders take everything and dissipate it and flog them for the slightest offence, showing no mercy in torturing them even to death. Would you like that?"

"Certainly not," all replied.[21]

The ring of universality comes from the likelihood that any set of subjects will have certain ideas about the proper tasks and obligations of the rulers, the proper purposes of authority, whose flagrant violation will produce a sense of moral outrage and injustice.

One further comment on popular attitudes toward a special form of the misuse and misappropriations of resources: bribery. The dictionary defines bribery as a gift or promise of reward in order to corrupt judgment or conduct. As such it probably exists in all human societies, including nonliterate ones without formal political institutions, since all human societies have moral rules,

---

because the killing was accidental. The father of the dead man refused the compensation and tried to kill the wrongdoer. At this point the king ordered the execution of the victim's father, who, however, managed to escape. *Pace* Durkheim, it is by no means generally the case that the reaction of moral outrage serves to restore social order. One has to take account of whose order is at stake. By and large, it appears that the efforts of subordinate groups to work out their own rules for settling internal disputes represent attempts to maintain some degree of independence in respect to superior authority.

[19]Shih, "Rebel Ideologies," 197.

[20]Shih, "Rebel Ideologies," 179.

[21]Shih, "Rebel Ideologies," 183.

whose existence implies at *some* point the rendering of judgment against the wishes of a member of the society. Here again investigation and reflection turn up revealing ambivalences. Bribery is a morally disapproved way of reconciling the irresistible force of X's will with the immovable object of Y's objection to that will. In the formula, X and Y can stand for either rulers or ruled. In pre-twentieth-century China alleged corruption and bribery were recurring themes in rebellions. In nineteenth-century American cities, under boss rule, bribery was a way through which the lower classes and immigrants mitigated the rigors of the law. It was a weapon in their hands rather than something about which they were expected to become outraged. Bribery has been called the American substitute for the class struggle.[22] In the world at large, moderately honest government is a relatively recent historical innovation. Thus although the moral attitudes toward bribery and the participants vary greatly in time and space (social as well as geographical), there appears to be a common core of negative attitudes toward it.

To conclude this part of the discussion I will raise one more general issue: do human beings quite generally have a sense that certain forms of punishment are unjust? An unjust punishment we can define as one that arouses revulsion either because it is undeserved or because it is excessively severe or cruel, or some combination of these two reasons. In the light of the variety, ingenuity, and cruelty that human beings have displayed in punishing and torturing each other, at first glance it may seem almost bizarre to argue that there could exist anything remotely resembling a universal conception of unjust punishment. But there are grounds for holding that this variety may be reduced to a few simple yet related principles.

This time it may be best to begin with a concrete example and work outward toward generalizations. Among the Kapauku Papuans the worst thing that can happen to a person, they think, is to be put into a white man's jail. Asked by an astute anthropologist what was wrong with jail, a native answered that in jail a man's vital substance deteriorates and he dies.

"We used to kill only very bad people, but now one may get into prison simply for stealing or even fighting in a war. One dies if shot by an

---

[22] Perhaps this aspect has been romanticized. In the nature of the case, bribery must have taken the form of extracting small sums from the poor for petty favors, such as granting pushcart licenses, or leniency after minor brushes with the law. This kind of bribery looks like extortion from the extremely poor by those somewhat less poor, an arrangement that saved the plutocracy the trouble of governing.

arrow, but in jail one has to suffer before death. One has to stay in one place and has to work when one does not like it. Jail is really the worst thing. Human beings should not act like that. It is most immoral."[23]

From other abundant evidence presented by this anthropologist, who learned their language and became an accepted member of their community, it is clear that the essence of humanity for the Kapauku Papuans is autonomy, independence, freedom, and the opportunity to acquire wealth and influence. Any severe restriction on this independence, such as the white man's jail, appears to them as a violation of this humanity.

In the spectrum of recorded conceptions about humanity the Kapauku Papuans, like nineteenth-century American capitalists, are probably somewhat extreme in their emphasis on individualist qualities at the expense of cooperative ones. For the problem at hand, that is unimportant. The instructive and revealing aspect of this example is the close connection between a specific conception of humanity and convictions about the injustice of certain forms of punishment, convictions that if violated evidently produce moral outrage. In this society there are certain punishments that one ought not to inflict on other human beings because they are too painful and degrading.

Such sentiments are very widespread. The punishments that are rejected vary in accord with varying conceptions of humanity. In many societies with class and caste systems there exist codified systems of punishment appropriate for each caste or class, because each level is supposed to represent a different degree or form of humanity. In general, the less "human" the victim, the more cruel and painful is the justifiable punishment. The upper classes represent "true" humanity while those at the bottom, such as slaves, are the furthest removed. Such codes also regulate and punish aggressive behavior between individuals from different strata, inflicting heavy penalties on members of the lower strata who attack their superiors and light penalties for the reverse. Cruelty toward the lower strata finds its justification on the grounds that they are in some sense not really human beings. Similar principles are at work in warfare. Where the enemy is defined as somehow inhuman or inferior, the severest cruelties may appear morally justified and arouse no revulsion. Aristocratic codes, on the other hand, may define at least the enemy's leaders as fellow aristocrats who ought so far as possible to be spared. Homer portrays the behavior of Achilles in drag-

[23]Pospisil, *Kapauku Papuans*, 77.

ging the body of Hector through the dust before the walls of Troy as a repulsive act that is the consequence of his rage at the death of Patroclus, his closest comrade. In our own times morally sensitive individuals feel outrage and revulsion at the cruelties inflicted by American troops or by American courts and prisons on blacks and poor people because the assumption has become widespread that all human beings do share some essential qualities.

The reasons for changing social definitions of what is and is not human, and the various gradations in between, are too complex and poorly understood for any attempt to unravel them here. It is sufficient to suggest that most and perhaps all human societies have some definition which reflects their particular social order, and that the character of this definition sets limits on the forms and especially the severity of punishment that the members of this society hold to be morally appropriate. Once again it is necessary to emphasize that the limits are liable to be exceeded, and that in any large society more than one definition is likely to be current. Nevertheless, transgressing these limits is likely to produce a reaction of moral outrage and sense of injustice.

Whether a particular punishment is deserved or undeserved is not the same question as whether or not it is cruel, inhuman, or excessive, though modern Westerners would be likely to apply the term unjust in both instances. Persons subject to authority may accept a given rule and believe that punishment for its violation is deserved, while at the same time they regard a specific form of punishment as something that no human being should inflict on another. Or they may reject the rule itself.

It is possible to distinguish two basic forms of the latter situation. Either the authority imposes punishment in violation of a rule or norm that is accepted by those subject to authority, or imposes punishment in accord with a rule that is no longer fully accepted by those subject to it. Basically both situations are part of the continual testing of the implicit or explicit social contract that takes place wherever authority exists. Because this process goes on all the time and is familiar to the most casual observer or participant in human relationships, there is no need for extended discussion. Since those in authority can seldom control every aspect of the way a task is performed, subordinates work out their own practices, which with the passage of time acquire the moral authority of precedent. A challenge to the moral authority of precedent, to accustomed ways of behaving that subordinates have created to protect their own interests vis-à-vis superiors as well as the integrity of their own social group, will generally produce a reaction of moral outrage. (That is also true when the challenge comes from a member of the subordinate group itself, as in the case of the worker who is a "rate buster" and exceeds informally set norms of output.)

In England during the sixteenth century, peasants often became angry because their lord broke the custom of the manor and challenged ancient rights. Among town dwellers during the eighteenth and nineteenth centuries there was much angry turbulence as craftsmen perceived in the advance of capitalist industry an attack upon traditional rights and privileges. Since any society that is not absolutely static will by definition display changing rules, there is at this point little to be gained by adding more recondite illustrations from other times and cultures. For the moment it is sufficient to suggest that in the absence of quite powerful contrary mechanisms a reaction we can recognize as a judgment of social injustice will occur whenever a punishment (1) violates the prevailing conception of what a human being is or ought to be; (2) violates a rule or norm accepted by those subject to the authority that inflicts the punishment; or conversely (3) takes place in accord with a rule or norm that those subject to authority have come to regard as no longer valid or in effect. If the argument just sketched is correct, we can conclude that every human society does have a conception of unjust punishment and a specific way of deciding why the punishment is unjust.

3. The division of labor

Every known human society displays a division of labor. In some nonliterate societies the division is mainly one between the sexes with very little specialization along occupational lines. So much one can learn from many a textbook in anthropology and sociology. Though the textbooks are not likely to add that in no human society is the division of labor completely satisfactory for all its members, it is safe, I believe, to accept this proposition too as a starting point for the analysis. Even in a nonliterate society with a very simple economy and abundant resources, not all tasks are equally attractive all of the time. Under more complex economies the differences, of course, become very striking. Thus, in the division of labor, as in systems of authority, we are again concerned with an implicit social contract subject to perpetual testing and renegotiation.

This social contract serves to regulate an inherent and unavoidable conflict, though one whose intensity varies greatly in time and space. This is a conflict among (1) the demands and requirements of the individual worker or household for food, clothing, shelter and a share in the amenities and pleasures of life; (2) the needs of the society as a whole;[24] (3) the demands and requirements of the dominant individuals or groups.

There is not only a conflict of interests between the individual and the requirements of the social order plus those of the dominant class. There is also some degree of harmony, without which it is unlikely that the social contract would work. In fact some of the most significant social devices are those through which the larger society manages to make the individuals shape and define their own interests in such a way as to bring them into congruence with the social order, to accept with pleasure their part of the bargain in the social contract when the straightforward material compensations are very slight.

It is possible to arrange the main known forms of social contract regulating the division of labor on a rough scale according to the degree of compulsion and persuasion inherent in the arrangement. Presumably the greater the degree of compulsion the less successful the arrangement, the less there is of a genuine contract, which denotes the acceptance of reciprocal obligations by free and rational human agents. By this reckoning, chattel slavery in its severe forms in mine and field would belong at the bottom of the scale. Sheer compulsion is the overwhelming aspect of this relationship. There is not much less compulsion where a person has the choice between starvation and taking a job at very low wages and exhaustingly long hours, the classic situation in at least some factories in early nineteenth-century England or on American cotton farms after the end of slavery. In much of the economically backward part of the world today the situation is similar but there is nevertheless a significant difference: there is some possibility of escape via the labor market and migration. Going backward in time to ancient Greece, we might place close to the top of the scale the situation of a man like Eumaios, the swineherd who greets Odysseus on his return to Ithaca in the guise of a beggar. Homer portrays Eumaios as carrying out a responsible task, proud of his master and completely identified with his master's interest. In today's world the situation of the highly skilled worker is similar, except that the identification and pride derive more from the task itself.

[24]On difficulties in the use of this term, see above, pp. 9–14.

Behind these variations and permutations it is possible to detect certain recurring features. There is a pattern to the way societies widely separated in time and space evaluate different kinds of work.

High political, religious, and military officials rank somewhere near the top in all stratified societies of Europe and Asia, and also in several nonliterate stratified societies of the new world and Africa, such as the Incan and the Dahomean. Economic power also generally brings high status, though more grudgingly in some cases, such as Imperial China. In preindustrial societies generally, wealth is mainly a by-product of high position derived from other activities, political, religious, and sometimes military. Though the commercial and industrial revolutions did much to reverse the relationship, during the twentieth century there has been a strong tendency for the older relationship to reassert itself once more. What is common to all these positively evaluated tasks is, first of all, control—mainly though not entirely of the activities of other human beings—and, to a lesser extent, skills, particularly mental skills.

Negatively evaluated tasks and social functions contrast with these in that they involve (1) lack of control over other human beings and, in its place, subordination; (2) lack of any but the most rudimentary and rapidly acquired manual skills; (3) toil: that is, labor that is repetitive and therefore uninteresting, as well as physically arduous; (4) in a number of cases, work requiring contact with excrement, decay, dirt, and death. For someone of high social status the performance of such tasks generally constitutes a degradation or a powerful insult. Only if the punishment is believed to be just—in other words only if that person has already undergone degradation and accepts responsibility for the act that brought it on—will such an individual be unlikely to display some extreme form of moral outrage, of injured *aretē* (or innate sense of one's excellence). This type of situation seems relatively unproblematic. How about people in the lowest positions, our main concern in this study? Do they have their own version of *aretē*?

I think that the anger, or at least discontent, is latent here whenever it is not openly expressed and shall so argue as a hypothesis. In the negative (and positive) evaluations of different tasks there are grounds for suspecting a reflection of innate human nature: that nobody really wants to do these jobs, that these tasks constitute a violation of some innate sense which human animals have about what they want to be. The main reason behind this suspicion is that human beings generally avoid these tasks when they can, and perform them only under some form of compulsion. At the same time these tasks have been "socially necessary" in a wide array of societies, and there has been no small measure of "voluntary" compliance. In the next chapter we shall analyze one extreme form of "voluntary" compliance, that of the so-called Untouchables in the Hindu caste system, in an effort to comprehend more clearly what factors produce "voluntary" compliance. As indicated earlier, the discovery of any case in which the compliance was truly voluntary would disprove the hypothesis. Genuine voluntary compliance could be presumed only where there was no indication of resistance to undertaking such tasks, and where there were no indications that socializing people to be willing to undertake them involved pain for such individuals.

Two other aspects of the division of labor are capable of arousing moral outrage and a sense of social injustice. They appear to be universal or nearly so: conceptions of property and sanctions against the idler. In every society there has to be *some* sort of relationship among human beings to govern their access to and use of the means of production, i.e., land and other natural resources, as well as the tools or other physical means of working upon them.[25] It is safe to assert that none of the relationships so far invented has been completely satisfactory to all persons concerned, and that some degree of conflict has been present in all of them. In turn a violation of such a relationship is likely to seem unjust, arousing anger and outrage on the part of the injured party. An attack on this connection between human beings and the means of production constitutes an attack on the person, whether the person is an individual or a collective body such as the capitalist corporation or the socialist state. The socialist state is in fact a fierce and primitive defender of property—that is, socialist property.

---

[25]Modern anthropologists are inclined to de-emphasize the significance of property rights among nonliterate peoples on the ground that in simple societies land, food, water, tools, weapons, ornaments, indeed just about everything are, as Morton Fried remarks, "either immediately open to all or so mobile as to obviate problems of possession. Equally clear is the obviation of theft. . . . Actually in a simple egalitarian society the taking of something before it is offered is more akin to rudeness than to stealing." See Fried, *The Evolution of Political Society,* 74–75. This assessment, though supported by some evidence, appears to be an exaggeration. Cf. Gluckman, *Barotse Jurisprudence,* 151, 162, 163, on property rights and status relationships in Barotse society. In a large collection of miscellaneous cases presented by Edward Westermarck, one of the last of the evolutionary school of anthropologists, there are several from quite simple societies where it is plain that very severe sanctions, including in some instances death, attach to theft from fellow tribesmen. See Westermarck, *The Origin and Development of the Moral Ideas,* II, 4–12.

If we confine our attention to the lower classes, who of course have less favorable property rights than the elites (even in socialist societies in practice), we find very frequently the notion that every individual ought to have "enough" property rights to play a "decent" role in the society. Both "enough" and "decent" are defined in traditional terms. A peasant should have enough land to support a household and enable its head to play a respectable role in the village community; a craftsman should have property rights over the tools of his trade and enough custom (or customers, as we say today) to play his assigned role in the urban community. Wherever an increase in commercial relationships has threatened this type of independence, it has produced an angry sense of injustice, usually directed at creditors. Hesiod's complaints about "crooked judgments" have been echoed through the ages. Such complaints can be found among small businessmen and farmers pushed to the wall under capitalist expansion, and can take on a "right" or "left" coloration, depending upon immediate circumstances. It is important to realize that there is much more to this anger than straightforward material interest. Such people are morally outraged because they feel that their whole way of life is under unfair attack. It is hardly necessary to add that this form of moral outrage is by no means always politically effective. Often enough it runs out into futile despair, with or without elements of rage.

Probably in all cultures the confirmed slacker and sponger, the individual who refuses to do his or her part of the common task and who lives off the labor of others, constitutes a negative social model, *if that person is poor.* This is true even in such a society as the Lovedu of Africa, who display about as noncompulsive an attitude toward work as is possible to imagine.[26] The person who is being deprived of his or her property by impersonal social forces is often the one most eager to apply severe social sanctions against the idler, even though both of them may be suffering from the same set of impersonal social forces.[27] That is quite understandable: the small property owner, or even the employee working furiously to hang onto a job (and possession of a job is popularly regarded as a property right), both resents and fears the prospect of falling into the ranks of the unemployed, and eventually the unemployable. With wealth, on the contrary,

[26]Eileen J. Krige and J. O. Krige, *The Realm of a Rain Queen: A Study of the Pattern of Lovedu Society,* 53–54, 284.

[27]On this situation and its recurrence in different forms at several points in European history see Svend Ranulf, *Moral Indignation and Middle Class Psychology.*

idleness may be an object of envy or mild derision if it is not simply ignored.

Among the Kapauku Papuans the negative character is very close to his counterpart in a small nineteenth-century American community. He is the man who doesn't work, cheats on his economic obligations, and violates sexual mores to boot. Such a ne'er-do-well among the Kapauku Papuans can arouse the violent moral outrage of the community to the point where "leading citizens" ask for the death penalty when he repeatedly violates some norm.[28] At first glance the North Alaskan Eskimo appear very different. In times of food shortage the successful hunter and his family might go hungry since in his generosity he gave away whatever he had in hand. Meanwhile the lazy and shiftless could beg their way through life. But to do so they would have to fly in the face of public opinion. Here too "the greatest sin was idleness," and continual dependence on others painful and degrading.[29] Although the range of sanctions against the slacker is very considerable, such individuals are to my limited knowledge never positive social models as such. Where, as in India, beggars constituted socially approved models, they have been expected to perform religious functions. Even egalitarian theories and practices include some notion to the effect that every individual ought to pull an oar in the ship of state or at least go through the motions of making the effort.

This widespread hostility to the idler does not contradict the thesis that in general human beings dislike work. Instead it reflects the universal necessity to work that has characterized human society up to now, and the ways in which this necessity has been internalized to become part of the moral personality in most individuals. One of the most powerful sources of moral outrage is to see someone else getting away with breaking a moral rule one has undergone great pains to make a part of one's own character.

[28]See the vivid account in Pospisil, *Kapauku Papuans*, 223–224.
[29]Robert F. Spencer, *The North Alaskan Eskimo*, 164–165, but note 130–131, 142, 155.

4. *The distribution of goods and services: the permutations of equality*

In any society the methods in use for allocating resources, goods, and services among its members are closely related to the prevailing division of labor and the methods of production. It is by no means clear that the latter always determine the former, though the available methods of production can set limits on possible forms of distribution. In Western feudalism, for example, production was organized around ways to assure a supply of goods and services for the fighters. This consideration governed land tenure and the cultivation of the land and, through these, many other aspects of the social order.

In systems of distribution generally one can usually come upon evidence for the existence of the two contradictory principles we have seen in connection with the division of labor. One is a general notion of equality based on what consumer units need: a sense that every person or household should receive "enough." The other is a principle of inequality based upon some ranking of the value of different tasks and social functions. Attempts to reconcile them take the form of notions of distributive justice in which the extra reward comes from the extra investment of effort, skill, or some other quality that performance of the task requires. Thus in the end some conception of equality, of evening things out, seems to prevail. But before jumping to this conclusion it will be well to take a closer look at forms of equality and inequality and their justifications as well as their degree of popular acceptance. Violations of any of these can be a source of moral anger, a breaking of the social contract.

Equalitarian ideas and practices are likely to flourish in situations where supply is precarious and any given individual is liable to face an unpredictable shortage. Rationing systems in modern societies are one example. At the other end of the technological scale, tribes that live by hunting often have a rule that the catch be shared equally within a specified group. For example, among the Semai, an aboriginal tribe in the Malay Peninsula, the successful hunter receives no extra portion of catch, not even thanks. The game animal is divided up into portions that are as nearly equal as possible.[30] Though equality seems to work quite smoothly in this and other societies, that is by

[30]Dentan, *The Semai*, 48–49.

no means always the case. Among the Siriono, a tribe in eastern Bolivia with a rather poor hunting technology, the distribution of meat is ordinarily confined to the extended family because the supply is seldom abundant. Usually someone feels cheated. Men especially accuse the women of hoarding meat, of eating it when the men are not around, or of consuming more than their share. Quarrels are frequent, and the bigger the catch the more sullen the returning hunter.[31]

Equality does make very good sense as a form of group insurance. Any hunter knows that hunting is chancy, that an empty-handed return is only too likely, in which case it is good to know there might be another source of supply. But, as we have just seen, these arrangements are often subject to strain. Among the Maori, where it was customary to divide up the fish catch when the fishermen hauled their nets ashore, during the general excitement poor tribesmen were inclined to slip extra fish into the folds of their garments. Better-off members of the community regarded such behavior as vulgar and immoral. It is hard to imagine a more vivid illustration of the perpetual renegotiation of the social contract.[32]

Equality as a form of social insurance displays similarities to a very widespread set of beliefs and practices we can conveniently group together and label as the taboo on the dog in the manger. The essence of the taboo is the belief that personal and private retention *without use* of resources that are in short supply and needed by others is somehow immoral and a violation of the higher rights of the community. Among other things this belief or sentiment is behind the widespread hostility to the hoarder and speculator. In some form it exists in numerous nonliterate societies.[33] Probably any American who has walked the streets desperately in search of housing and comes upon a vacant apartment or house that is being kept off the market will recognize this sentiment.

Both the taboo on the dog in the manger and the less widespread rule of equality as a form of general social insurance against misfortune depend for effectiveness upon the possibility of identifying oneself with the person in need. Where social

---

[31]Allan R. Holmberg, *Nomads of the Long Bow: The Siriono of Eastern Bolivia,* 154–155.

[32]See Firth, *Polynesian Economy,* 285.

[33]For some examples see Raymond Firth, *Primitive Economics of the New Zealand Maori,* 148; Firth, *Polynesian Economy,* 149; Krige and Krige, *Rain Queen,* 68. Pospisil, *Kapauku Papuans,* 181–182, describes an especially interesting concrete case, in which kinship rights gave the owner the right of refusal to allow cutting a tree for canoe-making. But the actual exercise of the right was considered unethical.

circumstances render such identification difficult or unlikely, as in some aspects of the master-slave relationship, the sentiment is liable to be weak or absent. In this Edmond Cahn appears correct in his stress on the significance of empathy for the sense of outraged injustice.[34] What makes the taboo on the dog in the manger widespread is that some form of shortage is very likely to occur from time to time in almost any society. Even very sheltered individuals from among the dominant classes are at some point in their lives likely to undergo this experience.[35]

It would be a manifest error to maintain that all forms of social waste arouse moral indignation. Veblen in his most famous book, *The Theory of the Leisure Class,* has called attention to a variety of forms of social waste by upper classes that apparently receive general approbation. In the well-known institution of the potlatch there is a deliberate destruction of valuable property for the sake of validating high social status. Veblen's prime example was of course the United States, which had plenty of resources to waste. The potlatch too occurs in an area of abundance. The taboo on the dog in the manger applies to scarce resources. That scarcity is partly a matter of social definition and partly objective fact quite independent of social perception goes without saying.

Justifications for inequality generally rest on some special capacity or function that the privileged group possesses and that is presumably both scarce and valuable to the society as a whole. These capacities and functions may include rainmaking, dealing with the gods and unpredictable, frightening aspects of the environment, or take more diffuse forms of moral and mental superiority supposedly suitable for a governing class. For these reasons the dominant stratum claims rights to a larger share, very often the lion's share, of what the society produces.[36] Most

[34]See his article "Justice," *International Encyclopedia of the Social Sciences* (1968), Vol. 8, 346–347.

[35]The writer began the reflections that led to this book after watching in a Maine coast harbor a bitter exchange between two owners of small cruising boats. One skipper was steaming into the harbor to reclaim his mooring—a facility in short supply in this harbor—after leaving it unused and vacant for a long time, during which period the other yachtsman had picked it up. Only after vividly expressing his sense of injustice did the "squatter" relinquish the mooring. Local sentiment, as far as I could judge, was not on the side of private property in what was otherwise a citadel of this belief.

[36]It would be worthwhile to have more accurate figures on the distribution of the social product in a variety of preindustrial societies if it is really feasible to work them out. I suspect that the results would show a much larger proportion of the preindustrial social product flowing into the hands of the dominant classes than we usually think, because most of us have imbibed modern egalitarian notions. In studying comparative agrarian history I soon noticed that nearly every specialist on a particular country believed that the ownership or effective control of the land was unusually highly concentrated in the country about which he had written.

of the time so far in human experience this extraction of a surplus has taken place without overt objection. It is just taken for granted. But the absence of overt objection does not mean that the acceptance of inequalities in distribution is enthusiastic or even willing. There are signs of an undercurrent of resistance in popular attitudes even toward the Brahmans, beneficiaries of what is probably the oldest, least coercive, and best entrenched among the world's systems of organized inequality. An Indian proverb has it that there are three bloodsuckers in this world: the flea, the bug, and the Brahman.[37]

Inequalities of wealth are quite common in nonliterate societies and, where they occur, part of the accepted order of things. The wealthy person is generally expected to perform some socially useful function and to be what we would call magnanimous. Rather that present a scattering of examples it will be more useful to summarize the evidence from one that is especially revealing. Among the Kapauku Papuans the acquisition of wealth is a major focus of human activity. On this score they are rather unusual for a nonliterate society with a quite simple technology. As mentioned before, they are also as individualist as the best model of economic man. Cooperation is at a minimum. "Two people cannot work together because they have two different minds" is their justification for private ownership. But once capital (mainly in the form of pigs) has been accumulated, social obligation takes over. "The only justification for becoming rich is to be able to redistribute the accumulated property among one's less fortunate fellows. . . ." Generosity is the highest value in the culture. A man who fails to live up to the ideal of generosity offends against the community and is subject to ostracism and boycott—and even death. In especially flagrant cases the obligation to kill the offender falls preferably on his son, brother, or paternal cousin.[38]

The anthropologist Leopold Pospisil reports a case of execution where villagers persuaded several relatives to kill a man who had failed to lend out his property in proportion to his fortune. The son was promised a pig and some cash for his participation in the act and was the first to shoot bamboo-tipped arrows into his father's body. After the execution the relatives built a scaffold for the corpse and smeared ashes and soot on their faces to express grief over their necessary act. To avoid the vengeance of

---

[37] L. S. S. O'Malley, *Popular Hinduism: The Religion of the Masses,* 191.

[38] Pospisil, *Kapauku Political Economy,* 152–153 on individualism; on generosity, see Pospisil, *Kapauku Papuans,* 79–80.

the dead man's departed shadow they took the precaution of sleeping for two nights in the bush. After that they killed one of the dead man's pigs and distributed the meat to all comers. Then they divided the dead man's property among themselves.[39]

This particular case shows how a high degree of inequality may not only be acceptable but even regarded as very desirable, as long as in the end it somehow contributes to the social good as perceived and defined in that society. The same connection appears in a variety of plebeian and popular responses to magnificence and display among the dominant classes in more clearly stratified societies. Nearly every ruler and practically every governing class, including newly arrived revolutionary ones, have made use of pageantry and display. This is curious. Such display amounts most of the time to a ritualized affirmation of inequality, of pomp, circumstance, dignity, and even many times of beauty: those things that separate some human beings from others.

Two factors appear to be significant in making such display not only acceptable but desired. In the first place, the masses have to believe that the elites whose display they enjoy are serving a purpose of which they themselves approve. If the purpose is approved, I suggest, then so will be the pageantry. Otherwise, not. Though display can to some extent create approval, its power is limited. Thus, as English power began to lose its authority in India, it became necessary—or at least seemed advisable—to curtail the pomp of English royal visits. Nor can a government, even a modern government, conceal the effects of serious military defeat with victory parades and triumphal arches.[40] The other condition appears to be some form of vicarious identification with the elite; people perceive the display as a manifestation of the greatness and achievement of *their* society.[41] Here one has to be cautious because there is not much reliable information (and quite a bit of romantic nonsense) about the ways ordinary people actually felt about such display in times prior to our own. Yet there is some evidence. From the days of Pericles—and no doubt before—dominant groups and rulers have used art and pageantry for the explicit purpose of creating this form of vicarious identification, and it does not seem quite credible that they

[39]*Kapauku Papuans*, 78, 80, 244–245.

[40]An old but still very valuable survey of the social role of spectacles in the Roman Empire is in Ludwig Friedländer, *Roman Life and Manners under the Early Empire*, II, chap. 1.

[41]I omit here any consideration of display as an attempt to overawe, since the problem under consideration is not one of fear, but of moral approval versus anger and negative judgment.

would have devoted so much energy to this effort without some indication that the effort was politically worthwhile. There also exist a few fragments of precious testimony from "little people" themselves which do indicate a collective pride in the architectural achievements of their community.[42]

Where the rulers have failed in their task, mainly one of providing security and protection, and where the possibility of identification with the social order through the rulers evaporates —something that can happen for many different reasons including but not limited to changes in the social relationships of production—display seems to arouse a maximum of anger. The *sansculotte* image of the aristocrat during the high tide of French revolutionary radicalism provides the best example. With some degree of assurance one can perceive during the course of the revolution both the discredit of the monarchy (and its moderate revolutionary successors) as well as the evolution of a substantial portion of the French nobility into figures that were likely to appear as either parasitic or exploitative, or both, to members of the lower classes. It is also worth recalling that the *sansculottes* directed much of their venom at speculators and hoarders, the classic version of the parasitic upper class in the popular mind, one without any of the redeeming features of a paternalist system.[43]

In this connection it would be worthwhile to explore the degree of variability and historical changes in popular conceptions of "real" work, as opposed to amusement, unproductive labor, ceremonial display, and the like. The constant element in all likelihood would involve productive hand labor for others. Attitudes toward manual skill vary considerably, however, as shown by differences in the status of the smith: an outcaste in some African societies and a god, though a lame one, among the Greeks. As the medieval European term "mystery," meaning "craft," shows—and indeed the two meanings of "craft" itself— there is an undercurrent of fear along with respect (and among the upper classes its opposite: contempt) for unusual manual skill. Governing does appear to involve "real" work from the standpoint of the subject, or if not real work, an acceptable form of activity as long as it produces the results of security and protection.

The upper strata, it is important to remember, always enjoy huge advantages in putting forth claims to perform socially necessary functions. To a great extent they are the ones who define what is socially necessary. These claims can be true at one

[42]See, for example, Alain Lottin, *Vie et mentalité d'un Lillois sous Louis XIV,* 209–211.
[43]Albert Soboul, *Les Sans-culottes parisiens en l'an II,* 412–413, 421–423; on hoarders see Albert Mathiez, *La Vie chère,* espec. 520–522.

time and false at a later time, when, for example, a specific form of military skill may become obsolete. Quite independently of their truth or falsehood such claims may win acceptance or encounter rejection among the influential segments of other strata. Once human beings have learned to take certain social arrangements for granted as part of the way the world works, it is evidently quite difficult for them to change. The emotional satisfaction that the belief in a specific social function imparts can for long periods of time override the truth value, which is often very difficult to determine anyway. How can one ever be sure that bureaucrats, capitalists, party officials, military officers are not performing socially necessary labor? Only when the obsolete character of a dominant group becomes blatantly obvious through failure in competition with another society and culture is it liable to lose its legitimate right to appropriate the surplus extracted from the underlying population. That is what happened to the Tsarist bureaucracy, the scholar gentry of China, and the armed knights of medieval Europe.

Popular notions of distributive justice constitute an attempt to resolve the inherent conflict between demands for equality and inequality. Examining human reactions to the distribution of rewards in a wide variety of contemporary situations, George Homans has formulated what he holds to be the common man's working rules of distributive justice. In the language I have used, these rules would constitute the basic terms of the implicit social contract. The central element is all that requires discussion here. It is, as Homans puts it, "a curious mixture of equality within inequality." Human beings, he argues, seek proportionate relationship between what they invest in a task and the rewards they receive for performing it. The difference between what they invest and what they receive he calls "profit" or net reward from a particular action. As long as rewards or *rates* of profit are roughly equal within a group, people will feel that they are receiving just treatment. The person who makes a big investment should get a big reward, whereas the person whose investment is small has no right to expect more than a small reward. Anger occurs when the rules of distributive justice are violated. Resentment arises very easily when persons doing roughly the same kind of work see that their co-workers are receiving higher rewards.[44]

The thesis that human beings have a strong inclination to develop a rough conception of the just and proportionate relationship between what they invest in a task and the profit or

[44]See George Caspar Homans, *Social Behavior: Its Elementary Forms,* espec. 30–31, 247–250, 252–253.

benefit they ought to get from executing it is a highly plausible one. Frustrated effort can be a source of powerful moral anger, as already pointed out, and there will be many occasions later in this book to recur to this theme. But in societies that live by hunting wild animals this kind of anger makes little sense. The behavior of the quarry is too erratic. As we have seen, in such societies there is a tendency to develop straightforward egalitarian principles instead, as a form of insurance. In some other societies, such as the Lovedu, the very notion of calculating a connection between effort and rewards would strike its members as rather meanspirited. By itself such evidence is not decisive, because over the long run any great departure from distributive justice might also strike them as somehow savoring of exploitation. But I rather doubt it. The attitude that prevails rather widely in stratified literate and nonliterate societies is some rather vague, customary standard of magnanimity attached to a particular status relationship. Close bargaining over such matters on a wide scale is a modern development, though it is certainly possible to find cases of it in earlier forms of society. The development of handicrafts and some degree of trade may be a prerequisite for the appearance of this moral assumption as a dominant theme.

Even in modern Western society the notion of distributive justice may not always arise spontaneously. I have come upon one revealing instance where exactly the opposite happens. It is to be found in an investigation of a Norwegian correctional institution whose findings, not all of which concern us here, have implications that transcend this very limited situation. The inmates of this institution receive quite mild treatment with enlightened therapeutic objectives. Nevertheless and understandably enough they very much dislike their situation. They take out their resentment in the form of continuous complaining about their treatment at the hands of the custodial staff. *Any* standard of criticism that they can draw upon from their previous experience will serve as a basis for complaints, with the usually justified expectation that the complaints will find an echo among the staff and be somewhat wounding because the staff shares with the inmates the same set of general norms and values.

If some inmates get advantages for making progress toward rehabilitation, there will be criticism based on a standard of absolute mechanical equality which compares the correctional institution unfavorably with life in a regular prison. Life was more just in a regular prison, an inmate will claim, because everybody was absolutely equal. At the same time there are complaints that the correctional institution provides no rewards for achievement, that signs of good behavior are not taken into account.[45] In this situation a generalized resentment prevents the adoption of any one criterion that could make the behavior of those in charge of rewards and punishments appear just and equitable. It would be hard to maintain that such situations are confined to Norwegian prisons.

As Homans stresses, notions of distributive justice, even if widely held, do not by themselves provide a basis for the peaceful and rational resolution of disputes over the distribution of the social product. As he puts it: "Even if [people] concede that reward should be proportional to investment and contribution, they may still differ in their views of what legitimately constitutes investment, contribution, and reward, and how persons and groups are to be ranked on these dimensions." For instance, as he points out earlier, to be a black or a woman as compared with a white man, can in some groups lower the value of the former's investment. Only when persons agree on the value of what they invest in a task, by comparison with others, can they agree on the scale of rewards.[46] In other words, the basic principles of social inequality are themselves at stake a considerable part of the time. Disputes over these principles are a major source of moral anger and sense of social injustice.

5. Concluding observations

If there is so much disagreement over the principles of distribution, what happens to any concept of moral universals? In an effort to make sense of human affairs it might seem wise to abandon this whole line of thought because, even if uniformities existed, they apparently could not serve to settle serious issues. Whatever uniformities turned up would be intellectually trivial. That move, however, would be premature. What, after all, are some of the reasons for the variation and disagreement that Homans has so effectively and forcefully pointed out? Why, for example, have blacks and women been willing to place a lower value on the effort they have invested in a task? And how willing were they? It is not necessary to be a modish radical to recognize

---

[45]Thomas Mathiesen, *The Defences of the Weak: A Sociological Study of a Norwegian Correctional Institution*, 154–157.

[46]See Homans, *Social Behavior*, 250–251.

the significance of repressive and especially self-repressive mechanisms of the type to be examined in the next chapter. There is no reason to challenge the fact of variation. But the reasons for variation have important bearing on the validity of any conception of universality.

Before discussing these reasons further let us take a brief backward glance at the kinds of moral anger and social judgments our soundings have turned up in a wide variety of times and places, in order to see if the evidence does fall into some kind of an intelligible pattern. Are there some underlying themes from which it would be legitimate to infer a tendency toward a pan-human sense of injustice?

In those aspects of social life selected for investigation here, there is a good case to be made for the recurrence of certain problems and issues arising out of the basic fact that human beings with certain innate propensities have to live together somehow. Even if the problems of authority, the division of labor, and the distribution of goods and services differ enormously from one age to another, there is enough of a recognizable similarity to enable us to speak of a common pattern of issues. But how about their resolution? Is there really a range of resolutions likely to make human beings angry?

There are indications that failures of authority to meet its express or implied obligations to provide security and advance collective purposes arouse something that can be recognized as moral anger at being treated unfairly. Vengeance appears as a motive prior to organized authority, serving a similar collective purpose. Vengeance is also a motif that occurs under organized political authority. It influences the form that authority may take, as in the demand for "appropriate" punishment. Some of the more important failures of authority are failures to control the instruments of power, failures to keep the peace, demands and exactions that run counter to or exceed the prevailing definition of collective purposes, and punishments that violate a sense of what human beings are or ought to be. In the division of labor we have found indications that there is a considerable area of agreement across time and place about what constitutes desirable and undesirable forms of work. While it would be far too much to claim that there is always moral anger at having to do unpleasant forms of work, the basis for this kind of reaction appears to be present wherever such work exists. In such situations there appears to be a latent form of moral anger that social and psychological mechanisms may either suppress or arouse. Then there is the widespread moral indignation at the slacker, though this indignation too varies a great deal in its intensity. Finally, at the point where the division of labor connects with the distribution of the social product there are indications of a widespread feeling that people, even the most humble members of society, ought to have enough resources or facilities to do their job in the social order, and that there is something morally wrong or even outrageous when these resources are unavailable. (Different notions apply to those defined as not actually members of the society and who merely perform labor for it, such as slaves, though the working conceptions of this status are notoriously varied and hazy.) In the distribution of a society's resources, material products, and services there exist principles of both equal and unequal sharing. The violation of either one can be a source of anger. So too is the violation of what I have called the taboo on the dog in the manger. Perhaps there is more regularity here than meets the eye on a preliminary survey, insofar as different principles might apply to different circumstances or reveal some regular connection with historical changes.[47]

This summary of the types of situations that lead to moral outrage and a sense of injustice displays no great architectonic beauty. That is not surprising. Ordinary human beings are not philosophers trained to draw out the implications of first principles and draw consistent conclusions. In the course of searching for recurring forms of moral anger and what ordinary people regard as socially unfair, evidence repeatedly showed the existence of contradictory requirements that moral codes had to meet, along with signs of fundamental ambivalence toward social rules and regulations. There are perfectly good reasons why human beings cannot have their cake and eat it too. But there is no reason why human beings cannot *want* both. Hence there is likely to be an undercurrent of grumbling and opposition to just about every moral code, a discontent that is at least a potential source of variation and change.

The sources of similarity and recurrence we can provisionally attribute to similarities in the types of situations that human beings face in their rarely satisfactory efforts to live together. Our soundings have revealed a tendency for negotiations over the social contract to oscillate around arrangements where roughly equivalent values are exchanged. For example, subordinates want security and protection in return for the grant of legitimate authority to their betters. Major sources of variation

---

[47]On this aspect see the suggestions in Ephraim Yuchtman, "Reward Distribution and Work-Role Attractiveness in the Kibbutz," 592–594.

come from the way people define and perceive the worth of what they contribute to a social relationship and what they get out of it. Through certain social and psychological mechanisms, not all of which derive from the fact of domination, human beings can teach each other, and more significantly teach themselves, to put a low value on their own worth, to accept pain and degradation as morally justified, even in some cases to choose pain and suffering. Whole societies can at times teach themselves an ethic of submission. The Semai have made a virtue of timidity. For them it has worked so far, because it has turned out to be an effective way to cope with encroaching and stronger neighbors. Through the analysis of a variety of extreme examples I shall in the next chapter try to specify some of the main forms and causes of this self-devaluation, this embrace of the moral authority of suffering. Reversing the focus of interest I will then try to specify the processes through which human beings try to overcome self-devaluation, to redefine upward the worth of their actual and potential contribution to the social order as well as what they deserve from society. At that point, after we have worked our way toward some general conception of a recurring social contract and the main forms and reasons for deviations from this contract—including efforts to tear it up and write a new one—we shall in Part Two look for some of the historical components in the way human beings define and redefine acceptable and unacceptable treatment by their social superiors.

CHAPTER TWO

The moral authority of suffering and injustice

1. Preliminary remarks

The preceding chapter investigated constant features in human responses to injustice and suggested some reasons for the observed range of variation. In this chapter and the next we shall try to understand some of the things that happen at each end of the range of variation: moral outrage and moral submission. During the turmoil in the 1960s and early 1970s a number of books appeared in the United States with variations on the title *Why Men Revolt.* The emphasis in this chapter will be exactly the opposite: on why men and women do not revolt. Put very bluntly, the central question will be: what must happen to human beings in order to make them submit to oppression and degradation?

To pose such a question may seem the height of moral irresponsibility. Except for torturers and secret-police officials who wants more of such knowledge today? There is, I believe, a very good answer. Until and unless we understand why people acquiesce in such situations it is impossible to understand how they can resist or help them to resist. Behind this immediate and practical concern there lies a more general one. From the standpoint that human beings generally recognize pain and avoid it so far as they can, the behavior we are about to examine is at the very least bizarre and puzzling. Evidence that seems to challenge such a basic assumption is not something to ignore.

Because the issue is a different one in this chapter, the method of investigation will also be quite different. Instead of taking soundings into a number of societies in search of recurring situations, this task requires the analysis of a specific kind of human behavior. That one can do best by scrutinizing several particular manifestations of this behavior in some detail, examining the context and the responses themselves from various viewpoints until explanations emerge that illuminate the general issue. Each of the three examples chosen presents a prima facie challenge to our assumption. Ascetics deliberately choose a life of pain and suffering. Many Hindu Untouchables appear to take pride in their servile status and degrading work rather than resent their situation. Some concentration camp victims identify with their tormentors. A larger number of prisoners in this and similar situations resent and punish fellow prisoners who attempt to resist the authority of the guards. A common thread ties these examples together: suffering and submission come to these people with such a powerful aura of moral authority that they take pride and pleasure in their pain. As such, the psychological dynamics will not, however, be our central concern.[1] Instead we shall try to understand the social and cultural factors that create these feelings.

2. Asceticism

In analyzing ascetic practices it is important to notice first of all that the suffering is primarily physical. It is definitely not psychic suffering in the form of degradation or damage to the individual's self-esteem, as can happen among the Hindu Untouchables. The practitioners of asceticism are the objects of veneration and curiosity, not to say notoriety. Also, unlike the role of the Untouchable, that of ascetic is self-chosen. In general, human beings become ascetics "voluntarily," though in the case of Christian monasticism in its earlier or purer forms, social pressures surrounded and supported the individual in such a way as to sustain the role.

To a modern Westerner the self-tortures of Hindu ascetics appear extraordinary indeed. Evidently the practice of asceticism in India is quite ancient, since the Laws of Manu contain a long, vivid quotation on ascetic practices, which, however, may be recommendations rather than a description of actual be-

---

[1]Partly because what is known or suspected about this aspect has become familiar through the deservedly well-known work by Anna Freud, *Das Ich und die Abwehrmechanismen.*

havior.[2] Among more familiar and recently observed forms are lying or sitting on spikes, wearing sandals lined with spikes, holding an arm rigidly aloft until it becomes atrophied, keeping a hand clenched until the fingernails grow through it, hanging the head downward in the smoke of a fire, and sitting between "five fires." In the last form the ascetic sits among four fires, one at each quarter of the compass, with the fierce sun overhead making the fifth flame.[3] What must be one of the most extreme forms was the performance of a phallic worshiper of Siva reported by an English observer in the early nineteenth century. This worshiper had vowed to "fix every year a large iron ring into the most tender part of his body" and to suspend a chain therefrom many yards long to drag along the ground. At the time when he was observed, the worshiper had just put in the seventh ring. Because the wound was recent and painful, he carried the chain on his shoulder.[4] The author just cited also reports having actually seen an ascetic who lived on a bed of nails. From time to time he was hung upside down over a fire and rocked gently back and forth by his attendant like a pendulum, on the occasion observed by the author for a total of exactly twenty-seven minutes. Other Indian ascetics merely lead very austere lives, giving up property, choosing an absolutely minimal diet, and going about the country begging. Still others choose to live in one place. As wise men they become the focal point for pilgrimages. Female ascetics are also quite common, though the sources have much less to say about them. Examples of extreme self-torture appear to be confined to males. As the reader may have suspected, there are some clues suggesting an undercurrent of faking. Thus Oman reports from a hostile source the story that one ascetic who sat on a bed of nails had cleverly fitted iron plates onto his buttocks. On the other hand, Oman reports having seen himself one ascetic's wooden shoes "bristling inside with a close crop of pointed nails."[5]

Though the examples just mentioned are especially striking, they exemplify in intense form themes that occur in all forms of asceticism, including Christian ones. One theme is the escape from the routine burdens of life through the repression of desires and instincts. In Christian asceticism this aspect is so familiar as hardly to require comment. In India it took the form

[2]James Hastings, editor, *Encyclopaedia of Religion and Ethics*, II, 89–90.

[3]L. S. S. O'Malley, *Popular Hinduism: The Religion of the Masses*, 208.

[4]John Campbell Oman, *Mystics, Ascetics, and Saints of India*, 99–100.

[5]Oman, *Mystics*, 45–46.

of an effort to escape from the endless cycle of birth and rebirth. Indian asceticism was an attempt to cut loose from the hopes, fears, afflictions, and desires of earthly life.[6] In contrast with Christianity the notion of expiation of sin, on the other hand, appears to have played little or no part in Indian asceticism.[7] In the context of the caste system, the notion of escaping from the routine demands of the social order had equalitarian consequences. Thus there was one important ascetic sect which all Hindus, even Sudras and outcastes, might join. During the spring saturnalia, low-caste individuals became members of this sect temporarily, for the duration of the festival. At this time they would inflict such tortures upon themselves as passing thick metal skewers through their tongues. All members of the sect might eat together, accepting food from any Hindu. They discarded the outward symbols of Hinduism such as the sacred thread and the tuft of hair.[8] According to the Laws of Manu, on the other hand, the privileges of an ascetic were confined to the twice-born.[9] This piece of evidence indicates that asceticism was not a form of renunciation imposed on the lower classes by the dominant ones. Common to both Christian and Hindu asceticism was the avoidance of unpleasant social burdens inherent in marriage and property.

Another theme, especially prominent in Hindu asceticism, is aggression against the self for the sake of vengeance and control over the outside world. According to one Western scholar, asceticism constitutes for individuals "the way to conquer the powers of the universe itself, the macrocosm, by subduing completely their reflection in the microcosm, one's own organism. . . . What it represents is an expression of an extreme will for power, a desire to conjure the unlimited hidden energies that are stored in the unconscious vital part of human nature."[10] In Hindu legend and tradition there are many indications that ascetics were regarded as dangerous. When an ascetic met his death, "all nature was exceedingly relieved and rejoiced." According to another tale from the *Mahabharata,* one ascetic acquired a fierce craving for vengeance on account of wrongs suffered by his ancestors. He set out to subject himself to the most dire penance by his resolve to destroy single-handedly every creature in the

[6]Oman, *Mystics,* 170.

[7]Oman, *Mystics,* 21, 100.

[8]Oman, *Mystics,* 153–154.

[9]Hastings, *Encyclopaedia of Religion and Ethics,* II, 89.

[10]Heinrich Zimmer, *Philosophies of India,* 400, note 102.

world. Only the intercession of the souls of his forefathers persuaded him to desist. In much of Hindu legend rigid austerity, self-denial, and suffering constitute the most effective way to obtain what one covets. In this manner it is possible to compel the will of even the Supreme Being. This aspect of asceticism resembles primitive magical practices found all over the world and may derive from them. In a rough parallel to the story of the crucifixion, the Hindu Supreme Being himself endured self-inflicted penances for thousands of years in order to obtain sovereignty over all created things. Ascetic demons were supposedly able to terrorize the universe through their practice of self-inflicted mortification.[11]

At least one component in this aggressive current was a fear of sexuality. Sexual temptation interfered with asceticism and was a major threat to the ascetic. Whenever Indra, the jealous king of the gods, sensed a threat to his cosmic sovereignty from the increase of some ascetic's spiritual power, he sent an unbelievably beautiful, heavenly damsel to intoxicate the senses of the spiritual athlete. If the damsel succeeded, the saint in a sublime night or aeon of passion poured away the whole charge of physical force that he had spent a lifetime striving to accumulate.[12] In Christianity too, there occurs the scene of castration for the sake of salvation to bring about the return of God.[13]

There are, to be sure, some striking contrasts between Christian and Hindu asceticism. In the case of Saint Francis of Assisi, it is difficult to speak of any overt aggression or search to control the universe. Likewise, in Christian asceticism the effort to alleviate the misery of others through charity plays a prominent part that appears to be absent in Hindu asceticism. On the other hand, charity was a prominent virtue in the main current of Hindu religious tradition.[14] Nevertheless both Christian and Hindu asceticism stress the rejection of the ordinary routine burdens of human society in favor of an active search for the most unpleasant and painful type of human experiences. Even

[11]Oman, *Mystics,* 21–23, 25–26. It is worth noticing that these extreme forms of aggressive asceticism aroused criticism within the main current of Hindu tradition; see Zimmer, *Philosophies of India,* 399–400.

[12]Zimmer, *Philosophies of India,* 536–537. Here Zimmer also points out that Indian epics and romances were full of accounts of holy men who exploded irritably at slight annoyances.

[13]See the discussion in Peter Nagel, *Die Motivierung der Askese in der Alten Kirche und der Ursprung des Mönchtums,* 48–50.

[14]On the abandonment of property out of love for one's fellow man in Christianity, see the comments of Nagel, *Die Motivierung der Askese,* 75–76.

Saint Francis forced himself to endure close contact with lepers for whom he had earlier in life developed a special detestation.

Three related themes emerge from this survey of ascetic practices. One is the renunciation of or escape from routine social obligations. A second is aggression against the self, including the repression of sexuality, for the sake of some larger objective such as personal salvation or personal control over the powers of the universe. The third theme, especially prominent in Christianity and from which the word asceticism (Greek *askesis* = exercise, practice, training) derives, is preparation for painful experiences that the individual can expect to encounter at some later point in time. (Here asceticism verges on rites of initiation, some of which, especially in primitive warrior societies, are especially painful and mutilating. Initiation rites, however, are hardly voluntary in societies where all normal young males are expected to submit to them at a certain age.) The common element in all three themes is an effort to cope with generally unavoidable or apparently inevitable suffering by the deliberate infliction of pain on oneself.

It is obvious that asceticism presupposes a distinct social and intellectual climate. In a secular age with powerful technology human beings are unlikely to turn to ascetic practices until or unless it appears that technology fails to satisfy human wants.[15] Self-inflicted suffering is one possible response to a high level of frustration produced by uncertainty about the natural and social environment, and the inability to control it. Asceticism is also likely to spread first within the classes that are not at the very bottom of the social order. Despair about the possibility of happiness on this earth and a general religious environment that encourages such despair would also appear to be further basic prerequisites. Still another part of the intellectual environment may be a distinction between the soul and the body, which, however, is very widespread in popular beliefs at all levels of civilization.

With its emphasis on the return to older and simpler forms of life, its anticommercial and antiurban animus, asceticism may be seen as a characteristic though not inevitable reaction to social change and strain in preindustrial times. Asceticism is a negative form of utopianism, an escape from life by the suppression of desire instead of its satisfaction. It exists also as part of utopianism even in its modern forms, perhaps out of the aware-

---

[15]This may be one reason for the incongruous mixture of hedonism and asceticism in some leftist circles as, for example, in certain food fads.

ness that desires can never be wholly satisfied. It formed a significant current in nineteenth-century anarchism, particularly in the Spanish variant, and, as already noted, even in the modern youth revolt, where it has shed the aspect of sexual repression. In its rejection of the routine obligations of social life, asceticism displays affinities with modern revolutionary movements. The same is true about the notions of rigorous training for future crises and self-denial as a source of control over the world. At the same time asceticism is a functional substitute for revolution since it accepts suffering as inevitable in this life and directs the hostility produced by suffering inward against the self instead of outward against its social causes.

3. The Untouchables

Ascetics imposed their own sufferings upon themselves. Their misery was their own choice in pursuit of larger goals. Exactly the opposite has been true of the Indian castes known as the Untouchables.[16] There is no element of choice. An individual is born into an Untouchable caste, and membership is hereditary. Nevertheless there is in the whole arrangement a revealing element of pseudo-choice. The dominant castes have tried to make the status of Untouchable appear as the result of individual acts. But the individual is one of the Untouchable's ancestors who failed to treat a high-caste person with sufficient respect and whose soul therefore undergoes punishment in the form of reincarnation as an Untouchable. For injustice to be acceptable evidently it must resemble justice.

In apt if colloquial terms the task then becomes one of describing what the Untouchables must put up with, and the more difficult task of accounting for the extent to which they actually do put up with it.[17] Essentially the Untouchables perform the

[16]Apparently there is no name that does not carry wounding overtones or implications. "Harijans" is patronizingly offensive. "Scheduled castes" may be the least offensive, though that too is a piece of patronizing bureaucratese. I shall therefore use the term "Untouchable," which has the virtue of describing a situation that unfortunately still exists.

[17]An outcaste suffers disabilities very similar to those of an Untouchable. In some modern accounts, as well as in older ones such as Crooke's in Hastings, *Encyclopaedia of Religion and Ethics,* the two are sometimes lumped together. But, strictly speaking, one *becomes* an outcaste through violating the taboos of one's caste and paying the penalty, usually inflicted by a caste council, of being ejected from the caste into which one was born. In the Hindu social order both Untouchables and outcastes are

most disgusting tasks in Indian society, as well as a great deal of the most severe toil. They clean the latrines and cart away the excrement, a task that often means climbing down into the places where the excrement is dropped and carrying it off in the form of head-loads. They are also the village sweepers charged with cleaning the streets. They remove the carcasses of dead animals. By extension it appears they are often also leatherworkers. At an earlier point in history these scavenging functions may have been their primary ones. For a long time, however, Untouchables have also made a heavy contribution to the supply of agricultural laborers. Though there is considerable variation in their treatment, depending upon both local practice and the exact occupation that a particular Untouchable caste pursues, the following account published in 1920 is not particularly exaggerated.

The Chamars, Untouchables who are most numerous in north central India but exist also in other parts of the country, occupy utterly degrading positions in village life. Higher castes regard them with loathing and disgust. The Chamars' quarters abound in all kinds of abominable filth. Their foul mode of living is proverbial. Except when absolutely necessary a clean-living Hindu will not visit the Chamars' section of the village. The very name connects them with the carcasses of cattle. Chamars not only remove the skins from the cattle that have died, but also eat the flesh. The defilement and degradation resulting from these acts are insurmountable.[18]

In this connection it is worth noticing that although there are cultural differences in the definitions of cleanliness and pollution, as shown, for example, by the different treatment of leatherworkers in Western and Hindu civilization, there is also a very substantial common core of agreement. There will be occasion shortly to show more clearly just what the Hindu concepts of disgust and pollution mean in concrete, human terms.

In the attempt to explain why the Untouchables put up with their situation, we can exclude military and police force or the application of overt terror. There is no hint of these sanctions in the sources. What other social and psychological mechanisms, then, produce their overwhelmingly compliant behavior? A partial explanation emerges from some evidence that the Un-

---

close to nonpersons. Untouchables are born to this status and outcastes fall into it. Outside India there are similar groups, such as the *eta*, an outcaste stratum in premodern Japanese society. As the literature on the Untouchables is somewhat superior, I will confine the discussion to them.

[18]Paraphrased and slightly abbreviated from George W. Briggs, *The Chamars*, 20.

touchables have accepted and absorbed the dominant Hindu beliefs (Karma) about fate and the transmigration of souls. There is rather more evidence that they have accepted Hindu beliefs about pollution, an essential basis of the caste system.

For present purposes the primary conceptions in the famous set of Hindu beliefs about human destiny and transmigration of souls may be described as upward social mobility for good behavior, with the upward mobility postponed until the next life. Conversely, the sanction for evil behavior, defined very largely as failure to show proper respect to superior castes, is downward mobility in the next life. Thus evil and misfortune in this life are due to transgressions, particularly transgressions against the Brahman, in the preceding life. If, on the other hand, according to these beliefs, the individual accepts fate patiently and fulfills the duties of caste, the reward will be to be born into a higher caste in the next reincarnation. There are grounds for skepticism about the extent to which Untouchables actually believe these notions, especially since they are to such a large extent excluded from "higher" Hindu culture. On the other hand, there is some evidence of the acceptance of these beliefs.[19]

More convincing evidence about the internalization of the moral standards of the society whose victims they are comes from practices among Untouchables in connection with pollution. Belief in pollution is one of the most important pillars of the entire caste system, reinforcing economic and political distinctions, though it does not coincide exactly with them. The Hindu caste system is organized ideally and, to a marked extent in practice, as a series of status gradations between the polar concepts of purity or holiness, on the one hand, and degradation and uncleanliness, on the other hand. In Hindu society as elsewhere pollution is a political as well as a religious category: it refers to "matter out of place" or something to be avoided. Thus pollution serves to conceal unpleasant aspects of the social order from the dominant castes and to enforce these aspects for the latter's benefit.[20]

Among the Untouchables themselves there are sharp divisions setting off various subcastes. These divisions distinguish various grades of uncleanliness or potentiality for pollution.

---

[19]Briggs, *Chamars*, 200–201, states flatly that the Chamars accept the doctrines of transmigration and of Karma. Hazari, *Untouchable: The Autobiography of an Indian Outcaste*, 4, 16, 18, 33–34, 36, 65, gives a variety of concrete references to the acceptance of these beliefs. Yogis were one source for transmission of such doctrines to Untouchables (see 18, 36).

[20]Cf. Mary Douglas, *Purity and Danger: An Analysis of the Concepts of Pollution and Taboo.*

Members of the separate Untouchable castes will not eat together nor take water from each other nor allow intermarriage. As late as 1960 the Indian government found it necessary not only to construct separate wells for Untouchables in the villages, but also to construct separate wells for Untouchables *within* the Untouchable castes.[21] Likewise, some Untouchable castes try to improve their status by mimicking the customs and taboos of the higher castes. In parts of India this form of collective self-improvement has led to a situation where above the impure Untouchables are the pure Untouchables who have given up beef and other such polluting diets. Pure Untouchables are regarded as polluting only by their touch.[22] Although these practices demonstrate the acceptance by the Untouchables of at least some of the major moral standards of the dominant society around them, the effort to move up the caste ladder shows that acceptance of moral standards is not the same thing as contentment with their application in practice.

By itself this set of beliefs is insufficient to explain why Untouchables accept their position. It would be most enlightening to know how these beliefs arose in the first place and even more how the Untouchables were made to accept them. To these questions we shall almost certainly never have answers, which by now are lost in the depths of history.[23] On the other hand, a substantial body of evidence reveals the concrete sanctions through which these beliefs—or at least the appropriate behavior—are inculcated and sustained among the Untouchables. One major purpose of these sanctions is to prevent individual Untouchables from acquiring any sense of self-esteem that could challenge the authority of superior castes. Like old-fashioned military regulations, the etiquette of relationships among castes serves to draw the line between permissible and forbidden actions at a point well before what is realistically dangerous for the dominant groups. The size of this margin of safety in relationships with Untouchables is in itself an indication of the potentially explosive nature of the situation.

In earlier times Untouchables over many parts of India could

[21]Harold R. Isaacs, *India's Ex-Untouchables*, 29, 52.

[22]G. S. Ghurye, *Caste, Class and Occupation*, 228.

[23]We do know that the caste system, including Untouchability, existed in a form not very different from that of modern times as long ago as the Laws of Manu. For some textual quotations from the Laws of Manu that strongly support this view, see Hastings, *Encyclopaedia of Religion and Ethics*, II, 95; III, 234. The thesis of the antiquity of Untouchability has been hotly, but so far as I can see incorrectly, challenged by many Untouchables today.

not enter streets and lanes used by caste Hindus. If they did, they had to carry brooms to brush away their footprints in the dirt behind them. In other places, Untouchables could not contaminate the earth with their spittle, but had to carry a box around their necks to keep pure the ground reserved for the spittle of caste Hindus. In still other parts of India an Untouchable had to shout warnings before entering a street so that the purer folk could get out of the way of his contaminating shadow. Again, in other areas there were strict sumptuary rules limiting the type of house in which Untouchables could live, as well as the styles of dress and undress they had to use. Prohibitions against their entering any Hindu temple or caste Hindu's house or other establishment, and against using water from the common village well were very widespread.[24]

In interpreting the meaning of these sanctions for daily life, it is necessary to be cautious. Merely listing the sanctions, especially the more colorful ones, from all parts of India, could give an exaggerated impression. In his autobiography Hazari, an Untouchable, expresses acceptance of his "station in life," without signs of resentment, at least in his early childhood.[25] Only halfway through his life story does he report the first episode that he himself regards as humiliating.

One morning, as I was going through this very narrow street, I saw a few high-caste Hindu children coming toward me; but, as soon as they saw me, they stood up against the wall, and one of them shouted to the others to keep clear of the Untouchable. This distressed me deeply, perhaps because I was weak from illness, and, for the first time, I became aware of real anger within myself.[26]

Though there is not nearly as much information about caste etiquette for Untouchables as has now been collected for slavery in the Western hemisphere, I would hazard the guess that the etiquette did not sear the consciousness of inferiority into the personality in as painful a way among Untouchables as among the slaves.

Unenviable though their status certainly was, the Untouchables were not slaves, or at least as a rule not in most parts of India. In rural India, which is to say for the overwhelming majority of India's population in premodern times, Untouchables were

[24]Isaacs, *India's Ex-Untouchables,* 27–28.

[25]See *Untouchable,* 41, 51, 66, 69.

[26]Hazari, *Untouchable,* 91. It is impossible to determine the exact age when this episode occurred. From the context it appears that Hazari was then a young adolescent.

hereditary servants. Hazari, who as a member of a scavenging caste, had swept roads, cleaned latrines, and salvaged dead animals, gives a good concrete account of relationships with those for whom his caste worked. His father's family had served a limited number of landlord houses from generation to generation, purportedly for centuries. According to unwritten law, if his family wanted to move out of town, it would first have to find another Untouchable family to take its place. The high castes had no choice as to who should work for them. If Hazari's family had wished, it could have sold the family's right to work in their street to another family of the same caste. But these sales were rare because they meant losing one's birthright and family reputation.[27]

Such was, and in many respects remains, the economic system in which the etiquette was embedded and which it served to uphold. Each village constituted a largely independent system of exchanges of goods and services regulated through the caste system. Though there has been some scholarly debate on the matter, it is, I believe, appropriate to designate this system as a form of exploitative reciprocity. It was exploitative because the main burden of the obligations fell upon the lower castes, especially the Untouchables, and the main benefits of the rights flowed to the dominant caste. Nevertheless, it was a system of rights and duties that was regarded as legitimate by its victims. There were Untouchable caste councils which punished individual Untouchables who failed to live up to their obligations under their own systems.[28]

Although evidence of the impact of these sanctions upon the personality of individual Untouchables is fragmentary, there is enough to support two tentative generalizations. The impact of the system was profound, in the sense that Untouchables *did* accept the legitimacy of their low status and of the obligations that they had to perform. Yet it seems highly likely that they never did so fully and completely. There are many indications of ambivalence and aggression to be discussed in a moment. To be sure, such data are in a sense contaminated. With modernization traditional norms have decayed. Foreign influences and in-

---

[27] Hazari, *Untouchable*, 5, 8–9.

[28] For a systematic review of the literature see Pauline Mahar Kolenda, "Toward a Model of the Hindu Jajmani System," 11–31. Edward B. Harper, "Social Consequences of an 'Unsuccessful' Low Caste Movement," in Silverberg, editor, *Social Mobility in the Caste System in India,* 37–65, gives an instructive historical analysis of the relationship between an Untouchable caste and its employers in southern India from the early nineteenth century down to the present day.

creased economic pressures have evidently generated among more and more individual Untouchables a set of unbearable psychological pressures. Nevertheless by discounting the obviously modern features and combining what remains with known facts about earlier times it is possible to glimpse the social and personal meaning of being Untouchable.

Hazari's father in advice to his son at one point sums up the traditional "good servant's" ethic: "Never steal, never gamble, never tell lies that might hurt other people, never despise any work however dirty, never take another man's wife, drink only in moderation, and always thank God, even if you have only a piece of dry bread and a cup of water for a meal."[29] To dismiss this type of statement as mere camouflage or rhetoric would be a grievous error. There *is* such a thing as pride in resignation. What else could make their situation tolerable? As Harold Isaacs's account shows in revealing detail, similar attitudes have remained very widespread even in urban areas, though modified and challenged under new conditions. He observes that great masses of legal ex-Untouchables remain Untouchables not only in fact but in their own minds, living, in the words of a high ex-Untouchable politician, "in psychological cages." A Brahman friend told Isaacs of his return from school one year as a youth, all fired up with enthusiasm for India's emancipation from its dead past. He found an old Untouchable standing outside the gates of his home. "Come in!" the boy urged the old Untouchable. "Come in the house!" The old man stood there and looked at him sternly. "*You* may have given up your religion, young master," he said, "but *we* have not given up *ours.*"

Nor is the source of these attitudes even among the young difficult to discern. In another passage Isaacs cites an interview with a twenty-three-year-old rather lively young man who had moved to the city from his village. In his youth he had been able to move freely with other students, but was still not allowed to enter their houses. Untouchables, the young man reported, could climb the stairs to the verandas of upper-caste Hindus, but could not go inside or drink water. His family had instructed him: "Do not touch. Do not go. Do not do this. Do not do that. They might get angry. You might get beaten. Better keep quiet." In all of his travels, Isaacs came upon only one person who had been pushed by the humiliating and offensive circumstances still surrounding the life of Untouchables into a condition of violent and openly expressed anger. It is of some piquant interest that

[29]Hazari, *Untouchable*, 153–154.

this episode occurred when Isaacs was attending a meeting with a group of students. On this occasion a young man burst out, "The Congress party is making fools of the Scheduled Castes! We need to revolt against the whole caste system! Half of all the caste Hindus must be killed, immediately! I can't tolerate it!"[30]

In a reasonably diligent search of the literature, I have been unable to find any trace of open revolt among Untouchables. In the absence of any severe repressive apparatus—there was certainly nothing resembling the infamous *krypteia,* the Spartan secret police used to hold down the helots—it appears reasonably certain that what psychologists call the internalization of the norms of Hindu society must have taken place. In this instance, at any rate, it would be more accurate to speak of an acceptance of the moral authority of the oppressors. If there was a definite trace of ambiguity in this acceptance, that is true of all morality.

There are several clues to the existence of hostile feelings. Hindu texts mentioned in an authoritative handbook reflect fears of what might happen if Untouchables became too powerful.[31] In north central India Untouchables were popularly regarded as poisoners of cattle. They had a bad general reputation for crime, a reputation that one author regarded as exaggerated. In turn this reputation for criminality was one of the main reasons why the Untouchables were despised.[32] Here we glimpse the tragic, vicious circle in which circumstances generate just enough hostility among an oppressed group to make their situation worse. Elsewhere there existed such standard reactions by Untouchables as careless and inefficient work, feigned ignorance and incompetence. Again, such behavior reinforced the stereotype held by the dominant caste about the character of the low-caste persons.

A sign of the coming of modern times has been the refusal of the Untouchables to compel an individual member to perform his duties. Such reactions are, of course, perfectly compatible with the continued acceptance of the prevailing order as such. They represent one form of the familiar demand within this order for treatment that provides a measure of self-respect.[33] Since the prevailing order is the only one they have ever known, it would be unreasonable to expect them to feel otherwise. In an

[30]Isaacs, *India's Ex-Untouchables,* 33, 60, 161.

[31]A. L. Basham, *The Wonder That Was India,* 145.

[32]Briggs, *Chamars,* 235.

[33]Harper, "Social Consequences of an 'Unsuccessful' Low Caste Movement," 48–49, 60–61.

illuminating vignette Isaacs mentions the case of a young Untouchable who, in the 1920s, got into schoolboy fistfights when called by his caste name. In recent times among other, primarily urban Untouchables, there has arisen a response that is undoubtedly new: insistence on one's rights, big and small, and at times being openly resentful of contempt or insults. Caste Hindus describe such an individual as being "proud of being Scheduled Caste."[34]

Circumstances and historical trends can obviously alter the balance between the acceptance of the moral authority of the oppressor and various forms of aggression. The latter do not necessarily culminate in a rejection of this moral authority though they are probably an essential ingredient in its rejection.

In closing this sketch of the Untouchables, it is well to recall some more general institutional aspects of the situation that they have faced and which may help us to understand their response. As a minority, even if a large one scattered through all parts of India, they had scarcely any realistic prospect of overturning the social order, of replacing priests and landowners with latrine cleaners, even if the notion *had* occurred to them. In the literature known to me there is no sign that such a notion appeared spontaneously. When it does occur, as perhaps in the case of the angry young student mentioned by Isaacs, the chances are overwhelming that it is the consequence of foreign contact. Among these low castes, resources for more peaceful political bargaining were also extremely limited. Like others in similar positions the only resources they commanded were the services they performed. They could deliver these grudgingly and inefficiently, and in more modern times on occasion engage in collective efforts to withhold them. But the obstacles to concerted action were enormous and the prospect of gain uncertain.

Just how much of an awareness of these broader institutional factors sifted down into the consciousness of individual Untouchables we cannot know. Still, even if we could know, this knowledge would not be decisive. The lack of realistic prospect for success, a form of realism that can never be more than very approximate, has by no means always prevented oppressed groups from revolting. (The revolt in the Warsaw ghetto against the Nazis is a very clear, recent example.) Hence we are forced back toward the explanation that for some reason the spirit of revolt could *not* arise in these specific social and historical circumstances. Either it could not occur to the Untouchables spon-

[34]Isaacs, *India's Ex-Untouchables*, 43, 133.

taneously or it was beaten out of them, or some combination of the two. Such an explanation is likely to be offensive to the victims of historical misfortune, and especially offensive to those who are now engaged in militant action to undo this misfortune. If the explanation is a valid one, however, the grounds for offense disappear, because to take offense implies the existence of moral opportunities that simply were not there.

4. Concentration camps

In asceticism suffering appears as a self-imposed choice due to an inability to cope with a dangerous and unpredictable environment. Among the Untouchables suffering has not been a matter of choice but of fate. In contrast to the situations of both ascetics and Untouchables, prisoners in concentration camps have cruelty and suffering imposed upon them with a maximum of violence and coercion. Under such circumstances one might expect that the suffering would seem most unjust and would have no moral authority whatever. Such is not the case. To paraphrase Shakespeare some men seek suffering; others are born to suffering; still others have suffering thrust upon them. In each case a sizable number of the victims feel that the suffering comes with moral authority. What is or appears to human beings unavoidable must also somehow be just.

Under the Nazi regime *some* concentration camp inmates came to accept the moral authority of their oppressors through quite complex processes that I shall now attempt to explain.[35] In certain camps this acceptance sometimes reached the point where some inmates tried to achieve identification with the SS, copying its style of dress (to the limited extent possible) in a manner that would be ludicrously comic had not the circumstances been so tragic. Though most of the inmates did not go this far, the degree of acceptance is surprising. How and why did the different responses develop?

A focus on the social aspects yields a twofold answer, almost a dialectical one. In its operation of the camps the SS deliberately tried to break up all social ties among the inmates and reduce them to an atomized, homogeneous, and helplessly degraded

[35]Though my explanation and use of these data differ from the well-known comparison between plantation slavery and the concentration camp in Stanley M. Elkins, *Slavery: A Problem in American Institutional and Intellectual Life,* 104–115, his work made me aware of the potential theoretical relevance of this human experience.

mass. To a great extent they succeeded. But the SS could not carry this policy of atomizing the prison's population through to its logical conclusion. They needed some minimal cooperation from the prisoners in order to carry out the day's routine of getting them to the dormitories, feeding them, and making them work. Furthermore, there were aspects of prison life about which the guards did not want to bother. Hence there were ways in which informal networks of cooperation could and did spring up among the prisoners to mitigate at least some of the rigors of a Hobbesian war of all against all. The synthesis of these two opposing tendencies toward atomization and cooperation was, as we shall see, its most horrible aspect. The SS was able to pervert to its own cruel purposes the networks of social cooperation that did arise spontaneously, and that otherwise might have formed foci of opposition to, or disintegration of, camp society. Finally, different individuals, marked by different historical and social experiences, displayed their own sharp variations in their capacity to survive, as well as in their choice or rejection of strategies for survival that camp society created.

Upon entering the camps the prisoners faced "welcoming ceremonies" of a thoroughly brutalizing nature, a set of experiences that was to continue during the rest of their stay.[36] As we shall see, however, most of the brutalization came from the behavior of other prisoners in the same situation. These traumatic rites of passage had two closely related effects. The first was straightforward degradation, the destruction of the prisoner's self-respect, the obliteration of whatever individuality and status he or she may have enjoyed in the outside world.[37] Second, the camp officials "processed" the prisoners to make them as much alike as possible by issuing them uniforms and numbers after confiscating all personal possessions.

These actions were the beginning of a regime that deprived the prisoners of all but a minimum of food and a minimum of sleep. As soon as possible, camp officials put the prisoners to exhausting work. The officials controlled nearly every moment of the prisoners' waking life, even to the point of giving them only very limited and selected periods of time for urination and defecation. One consequence, of course, was to make the prisoners almost completely dependent upon the camp officials. From

[36] For a vivid description of these ceremonies, see Eugen Kogon, *Der SS-Staat: Das System der deutschen Konzentrationslager*, 72–79. There is a more psychological interpretation in Elie Aron Cohen, *Human Behavior in the Concentration Camp*, chap. 3.

[37] For similar processes in other contexts see the well-known description of admissions procedures in "total institutions" by Erving Goffman, *Asylums*, 14–35.

psychologists' experiments on animals it is safe to conclude that this regime of extreme but not total deprivation also increased hunger, and perhaps other drives, in such a way as to speed up the processes of adaptive learning.[38]

From the moment of entry then, the prisoner was subject to a regime of acutely painful deprivation and fear for life and limb. Aside from intermittent savage beatings by the SS if one happened to attract their attention, the prisoner might be killed for relatively minor infractions of arbitrary and uncertain discipline. Is fear of the guards, then, enough to explain the prisoner's behavior, and was the acceptance of SS morality—when it occurred—no more than simulation?

The answer, I believe, is no. As details to be mentioned in due course will show, the behavior of at least many prisoners went beyond believable simulation. Conditioning, as we know, *can* change attitudes. There are two additional considerations. In the first place the prisoners became used to fear. Brutalization dulled their senses. Furthermore, even if SS power and influence were pervasive, the SS often appeared like a hurricane and disappeared. To the extent that fear was a significant component, most of the time it was not fear of the SS. It was fear of other prisoners. According to a common saying in the camps, the prisoners were their own worst enemies.[39]

One of the milder forms of the prisoners' mistreatment of each other was stealing. Due only in part to competition for scarce resources, there was a widespread breakdown of social ties. Cohen quotes the assessment of a female prisoner: "Will you survive or shall I? As soon as this was at stake, everyone turned egotist."[40] Since survival itself often required some degree of cooperation among the prisoners, social disintegration was by no means complete. For a great many prisoners, however, the complete lack of privacy, the absolute impossibility of being alone, made the situation even less bearable. Forced

---

[38]Cohen, *Human Behavior,* 135, mentions the case of Allied officers taken prisoners by the Japanese who sometimes found it impossible to hold to their refusal to work for the enemy when they were promised an extra ration of rice. This is conditioning or co-option in its rawest form. In the concentration camps, however, it does not appear to have been quite so simple a matter, even though a small amount of additional food was a crucial reward.

[39]Kogon, *SS-Staat,* 372; Bruno Bettelheim, *The Informed Heart,* 186.

[40]Cohen, *Human Behavior,* 123–124. See also 136. There are striking similarities here to the behavior of the Africans who had lost their traditional hunting grounds, as reported by Colin M. Turnbull, *The Mountain People,* 135–154.

intimacy may be an enemy of solidarity and cooperation.[41]

Thus the prisoners' fear and hostility toward each other were by no means just a consequence of any direct intervention or deliberate policy on the part of the SS. Another factor was the fact that ordinary criminals made up a fair proportion of the concentration camp population. In American prison populations there is the same fear and suspicion. The presence of only a small number of "outlaws among the outlaws," in effect, bullies willing to take advantage of other prisoners and steal from them, is evidently enough to create this atmosphere.[42]

In addition to internally generated pressures, the heterogeneity of the prison community rendered cooperation and solidarity and hence resistance almost impossible.[43] The camps contained prisoners of both sexes, all ages, and all social statuses from members of the highest nobility to the lowest ordinary criminals. There were also prisoners from different ethnic backgrounds between whom there was often violent hostility, even among Jews from different nationalities. In Theresienstadt Czech Jews frequently hated German Jews. At one point the Czech Jews said, "Now the Germans will see what 'transport' means!" (Transport was the euphemism for shipping prisoners out to an extermination camp.) Czech Jews also fought with the Zionists.[44] Neither repression nor misery was sufficient to unify those who came to the situation with very different backgrounds and expectations.

These variations in social and cultural background had very important consequences in determining an individual's response to concentration camp life and hence ability to survive despite all official efforts to grind the prisoners down into an atomized mass. Apolitical individuals of middle-class background, including assimilationist Jews, were the most likely to disintegrate and succumb. Though unjustly imprisoned, they dared not oppose their oppressors even in thought, as Bettelheim observes, though it would have given them a self-respect they badly

---

[41]The same effect occurs sometimes in youthful communes, I have been told. It may be strongest among persons from a middle-class background.

[42]Gresham M. Sykes, *The Society of Captives: A Study of a Maximum Security Prison,* 76–78, 90–91. Similar atomization and lack of prisoner solidarity occurs under the very much milder regime of a Norwegian prison analyzed in Thomas Mathiesen, *The Defences of the Weak,* espec. 124, 132, 141. There the situation appears to be due much less to competition for scarce resources, such as food, than to a generalized reluctance of the prisoners to identify with each other because *all* of them are labeled as needing psychiatric help. No one wants to associate with someone who bears this stigma.

[43]Cohen, *Human Behavior,* 208–209.

[44]Hans Günther Adler, *Theresienstadt 1941–1945,* 123, 303.

needed.[45] Many of them were inclined to think it was all a horrible mistake, a reaction that is perhaps characteristic of privileged individuals.[46] For many a German middle-class person the disappearance of all "social corsets," the comforting etiquette and titles of respect and status, was a traumatic shock they could not withstand.[47] For some, the feeling of being innocent, and yet having to suffer, aroused self-pity and deprived them of the energy necessary for survival.[48]

The German Jews who came to Theresienstadt in the summer of 1942 displayed an extreme form of this reaction. They were elderly and brought up with a blind faith in law and order. Now they could not see that this law and order had thoroughly rotted. Unable to understand why they were in the concentration camp, they put blame for camp conditions less on the SS than on "misunderstandings" or on failures of the internal management which in this case was in the hands of other Jews. In manner they were often stiff, pedantic, and tragicomically correct.[49]

Among middle-class prisoners generally another factor that fatally weakened their powers of resistance and adaptation both inside and outside the camps was a tendency to cling to the security of familiar routines. Bettelheim makes some penetrating criticisms of the once very popular *Diary of Anne Frank,* showing how the Frank family's effort to continue with their usual private life brought them to destruction. In Buchenwald Bettelheim asked many German Jewish prisoners why they had not left Germany beforehand because of the utterly degrading conditions to which they had already been subjected in 1938. Their answer was to the effect that they could not leave because it meant giving up their homes and places of business. "Their earthly possessions had so taken possession of them that they could not move; instead of using them, they were run by them."[50]

The same tendency could develop even inside a camp. In Theresienstadt there was once a short period of "normalization" that even included the opening of a coffeehouse. Shortly afterward there followed a brief cessation of the transports to the

---

[45]Bettelheim, *Informed Heart,* 120.

[46]Alexander Weissberg, a distinguished Soviet physicist, had the same reaction to his imprisonment in the Soviet Union. See Weissberg, *Conspiracy of Silence,* 84, 103, 217.

[47]Kogon, *SS-Staat,* 367.

[48]Cohen, *Human Behavior,* 144.

[49]Adler, *Theresienstadt,* 107, 304.

[50]Bettelheim, *Informed Heart,* 253, 258.

extermination camps. The consequence was a wave of optimistic self-deception among the prisoners which Adler aptly attributes to "die gefährliche Macht der Gewöhnung," the perilous capacity for getting used to things.[51] There could hardly be a more grisly illustration of the lethal potentialities of this very necessary and highly developed trait of *Homo sapiens.*

It might be more accurate to characterize the middle-class responses just described as a form of capitulation to the moral authority of the oppressor rather than its acceptance. The most extreme form of capitulation was that of the "Moslems," walking corpses who had given up any effort to assert themselves against an overwhelming environment. First they had abandoned all action as utterly pointless, then they gave up feeling, because feeling was mainly painful or dangerous or both. In the later stages they still obeyed orders in the sense that they moved their bodies when told to do so, but ceased to do anything on their own. When the other prisoners recognized what was happening, they separated themselves from these marked men because further association with them could lead only to their own destruction. Finally, these men ceased to act altogether and just died. This attempt to withdraw completely into the self and to shut off all external stimuli, along with the decline in instinctual drives (in the later stages they stopped eating) displays suggestive similarities to some forms of asceticism.[52] In the case of the "Moslems" the self-destructive process went further. Asceticism was an attempt to control an unmanageable environment. Among the "Moslems" the attempt was abandoned as impossible.

At the opposite end of the spectrum all accounts agree that those most likely to survive were persons with strong religious or political convictions. Jehovah's Witnesses, who were arrested as conscientious objectors, stood an excellent chance. Both more numerous and more important than the Jehovah's Witnesses by far were political prisoners with strong leftist convictions. The concentration camp, instead of undermining their convictions, as happened with apolitical prisoners with their firm belief in law and order, confirmed the beliefs and expectations of the leftist prisoners by "proving" that such persons were really dangerous to the Nazis and that the Nazis took them seriously. Indeed they

---

[51] Adler, *Theresienstadt,* 128–129.

[52] There are also strong similarities to the famous phenomenon of voodoo death in which a frightened victim of magic just gives up and dies. For an explanation of the physiological aspects see Barbara W. Lex, "Voodoo Death: New Thoughts on an Old Explanation," 820–821.

took pride in their imprisonment.[53] Criminals were in an inter-mediate situation. Like the political left they had rejected bourgeois society and had no reason to make pathetic efforts to cling to its outward symbols. For criminals the jungle world of the concentration camp was not totally unlike that which they had known beforehand. The concentration camp had the fur-ther spice of putting them on an equal footing with bankers, lawyers, and aristocrats.

Among the political prisoners the Communists played far and away the dominant role. Though their convictions were essential to their survival, the Communists by no means owed their survival to their convictions alone. They formed a cohesive group and managed in some camps to take over much of the camp administration including two key functions; the allocation of work details and the assignment of prisoners to other camps for extermination.

All this was possible because, as is usual in such situations, the officials could not control, through fear or other sanctions, abso-lutely every detail of the prisoner's life. Some areas of autonomy, or at least pseudo-autonomy, have to be left to prisoners in order to get them to do such simple things as march to their eating and sleeping quarters at the appropriate moment. This grant of partial autonomy provided an opening that the Communists did their best to seize and expand as a bridgehead for their own power. In so doing they had to compete with other informal groups of prisoners, particularly those among the common crim-inals. In this way severe factional struggles developed among the prisoners. The Communists used their position to punish their enemies and reward their friends and allies with safer jobs, better food, and exclusion from the list of those to be sent to the extermination camps. Enemies in turn they placed on these lists. The Communists and those who worked with them willingly accepted the guilt inherent in decisions to condemn many to death in the hope of saving a few and purportedly improving conditions in the camp as a whole.[54] As Bettelheim remarked, they generated in this manner the typical justifications and social blindness of a ruling class.[55] Nevertheless they created the center of what resistance there was and could be within the camps,

---

[53]Bettelheim, *Informed Heart*, 188–189. Under other circumstances this sense of pride may be very difficult to maintain. Goffman, *Asylums*, 57, quotes a revealing passage from an imprisoned conscientious objector who expresses "the curious difficulty I have in feeling innocent, myself."

[54]Kogon, *SS-Staat*, 308, 310–315.

[55]Bettelheim, *Informed Heart*, 184–186.

organizing covert propaganda, the distribution of news, and doing what they could to undermine the confidence and morale of the SS. As Kogon, a non-Communist member of this prisoner elite, confesses, they could not affect real policy: they could not prevent the death transports. As informal camp managers, their activities required at least a minimum degree of collaboration with the SS. In this manner they became the core of the camp elite (*Prominenten*) in Buchenwald and other camps.

In time a segment of the camp elite, including even the politicals, became thoroughly corrupt. Chests of food from camp supplies were smuggled out and sent to the families of the prisoner elite. In the latter stages of the war some members of the prisoner elite paraded around the camp in tailor-made clothes with little dogs on a leash; this at a time when the SS no longer wore high boots but only ordinary army shoes. All this occurred in the midst of the chaos of misery, filth, illness, hunger, and death.[56] Thus the concentration camps forced the revolutionary activist into a highly ambiguous "reformist" role. Even if such individuals never accepted the moral authority of their oppressors, while fighting against it they became tainted by it.

Resistance was mainly an affair of the prisoner elite. The mass of the prisoners formed or was caught up in other social networks. Such networks grew up around common membership in the same dormitory or assignment to the same work detail. In both situations the SS gave people tasks to perform that were beyond the powers of most human beings to carry out, particularly human beings in a semistarved condition. For the failure of one prisoner the whole unit would receive punishment. This situation generated enormous hostility to any prisoner who by failure or weakness attracted the attention of the SS to his or her unit, an attitude perhaps intensified by the fact that it was impossible for prisoners to direct their hostility where it belonged, against the SS itself. One symptom of this high level of hostility was continual verbal rudeness, and a complete end of such familiar lubricants of daily social intercourse as "please" and "thank you." When a newcomer used these phrases, he usually received a hail of obscenities.[57]

Each morning, for example, the prisoners had to "build" their beds correctly, that is, restuff the straw mattresses so that they were flat as a table, and align the coverlets so that the pattern

---

[56]On the camp elite see Bettelheim, *Informed Heart*, 183–186; Kogon, *SS-Staat*, 315, 317, 322, 347, 374–376; Adler, *Theresienstadt*, 309–312.

[57]Bettelheim, *Informed Heart*, 136, 168, 212; Kogon, *SS-Staat*, 372.

of checks on the coverlets was in perfect alignment. Sometimes the SS used yardsticks and levels to make sure that the beds were built correctly; others shot their guns across the beds to see that they were absolutely flat. All this the prisoners had to do, as well as go to the toilet and wash, in a strictly limited period of time. The result was generally frantic chaos, tension, anxiety, fightings, and beatings among the prisoners. As Bettelheim reports, "Cooperation between a few friends, which existed in most units, was ineffectual against the ferocious disorder that reigned among the majority. Those sleeping in the top row messed up the mattresses of those below and those alongside of each other frequently did the same thing."[58]

Hostility was especially strong against the newcomer. Old prisoners had a pride in their own toughness at having survived and become an "old hand," which played some part in this hostility. But the main reason was that a newcomer endangered the group because he or she did not know the ropes. A newcomer was liable to be clumsy and to bring down the wrath of the SS upon the group. There was the same hostility toward weaklings who were also felt to be liable to turn informer.[59]

From the standpoint of the present inquiry the most significant aspect of the prison camps' social organization was the way it worked to inhibit any action that smacked of heroic resistance. (Its effect on the Communists, who are inclined to be contemptuous of heroic gestures other than their own failures, has already appeared.) The SS, Bettelheim observes, was usually successful in preventing martyrs or heroes from being created. "If a prisoner tried to protect others and it came to the guard's attention, the prisoner was usually killed. But if his action came to the knowledge of the camp administration, the whole group was always punished severely. In this way, the group came to resent its protector because he brought them suffering."

Bettelheim gives a concrete example. Two brothers were marching back to the camp as part of a column that had been on an outside detail. They encountered an SS officer who ordered the members of the column to throw themselves down in the muddy road several times, a relatively harmless "sport," according to SS custom. One of the brothers lost his eyeglasses in a water-filled ditch beside the road. He asked for and received permission to look for them and dived into the water-filled ditch. He came up without them and dived again, but then was ready to

[58]Bettelheim, *Informed Heart*, 213–216.
[59]Bettelheim, *Informed Heart*, 170–171; Kogon, *SS-Staat*, 375.

give up. But the SS man forced him to dive again and again until he died, either by drowning or heart failure. This piece of sadism appears to have been somewhat out of the ordinary, perhaps because a German civilian witnessed the scene and reported it in disgust to some official. There was an investigation into the death. The whole column was brought before the commander of the camp and asked to tell what they knew about the episode. Each member stated that he had seen nothing and could give no information. Only the brother of the victim felt obliged to do what was possible to avenge his brother's death and told the truth. Later that evening the brother was called to appear before a subordinate SS officer. By then he was in utter despair. It was clear that his statement had not only endangered himself but all his comrades in the same labor group. All members feared not only the vengeance of the SS but also that their labor command, which was a relatively soft one, might be dismissed, which would be a disaster for all concerned. Having lost his brother that day, the man had to fear for his own life, for his labor command, and the reproaches of his comrades. But it was too late to recant and alter his testimony. Several days later his corpse came into the morgue under strange circumstances. In a few more days other members of the column died, having been killed by injection. In about three months the entire command and all possible witnesses had been eliminated.[60]

Similar pressures toward rejecting the role of heroic resistance exist in American prisons and indeed may be part of the "natural" human response to oppression. In one maximum security prison, for example, any man who engaged in hopeless defiance of the guards and asserted his dignity in the face of insult, was known as a "ball buster." Only to a very limited degree did the other prisoners regard him as a welcome symbol of courageous opposition. More often they treated him as a fool, as one who upset the delicate system of compromise and corruption that was the basis of prison society. To other prisoners he appeared as one who sacrificed the well-being of the inmate population as a whole, for the sake of childish emotional outbursts.[61]

Similarly, Jews both in and outside the concentration camps were afraid that behavior that could be identified as Jewish might tend to increase anti-Semitism.[62] Bettelheim reports a

[60]Bettelheim, *Informed Heart*, 141–145.

[61]Sykes, *Society of Captives*, 100.

[62]Cohen, *Human Behavior*, 188–190.

moving case from German civilian life, one that is typical of many others. A young girl in a non-Jewish family had a father who was a convinced anti-Nazi. From her adored father, she at first drew the moral strength to resist the Nazi regime. Then under pressure from her age-mates she began to give in on small and presumably harmless matters. At school she had to swear allegiance to the Führer and to give the Hitler salute repeatedly. Under these pressures she began to resent her father as a source of disagreeable moral conflict. Later, as part of her schoolwork, she had to make a census of families in the town, on the surface apparently a harmless task. But then she came upon some Jewish families, and with a shock realized the meaning of what she was doing. She realized that these Jews saw her as a symbol of the regime and hated her. Her resentment against them, she also realized, was exactly what the regime wanted her to feel. She also hated herself for helping to send Jews to their death. What resolution there may have been to this dilemma we are not told.[63]

At this point in the analysis we can begin to understand how identification with the SS took place. The superficially bizarre and paradoxical acceptance of the moral authority of the oppressor is explicable in terms of three sets of causes. First, a substantial number of prisoners, as "patriotic" Germans, already shared certain values with the SS. When Bettelheim in 1938 asked more than a hundred old political prisoners if they thought the story of the camp should be reported in foreign newspapers, many hesitated to agree that this was desirable. Nearly all the non-Jewish prisoners, he asserts, believed in the superiority of the German race and took pride in the so-called achievements of the National Socialist state, especially its policy of expansion through annexation.[64] In the second place, as we have just seen, there existed powerful social pressures on the individual against heroic resistance because such acts threatened the survival of the group to which he belonged. Among the mass of the prisoners it seems clear that tendencies toward resistance were effectively crushed. The Communist organization could not and did not counter such pressures. Any *act* of resistance drew not moral approval but moral condemnation from the group. Thought and *sub rosa* talk were different matters. Finally, the entire situation stressed toughness as a model of behavior that did not differ greatly from the brutality of the SS itself.

Therefore it is not surprising that some of the older and

[63]Bettelheim, *Informed Heart*, 291–293.
[64]Bettelheim, *Informed Heart*, 169–170.

more thoroughly conditioned prisoners aped the SS. Older prisoners were at times instrumental in getting rid of so-called unfit new prisoners, an act perhaps necessary for their own survival, but nevertheless modeled after the SS. Likewise, although self-protection required the elimination of traitors, the way in which they were tortured for days and slowly killed was copied from the SS and Gestapo. When prisoners were in charge of other prisoners on work details, the old prisoners, and not merely former criminals, often behaved more cruelly than the SS itself. Old prisoners, as mentioned earlier, tended to identify with the SS even in appearance, although this was forbidden. They tried to obtain for themselves old pieces of SS uniforms, or to mend or sew their prison garments until they resembled the uniforms. Again, certain old prisoners felt great satisfaction if, during the daily counting of prisoners, they had stood well at attention or given a snappy salute. Quite often the SS would for a brief time enforce some nonsensical rule originating in a momentary whim. Generally the rule was quickly forgotten. Some old prisoners, however, continued to observe it and tried to enforce it upon other prisoners long after the SS had lost interest. For example, the SS once ordered prisoners to wash their shoes inside and out with soap and water. As a result the shoes became as hard as stone. Though the order was never repeated and many prisoners did not even carry it out the first time, some old prisoners not only continued to wash the insides of their shoes every day but cursed all those who failed to do this as being negligent and dirty. Such prisoners, Bettelheim reports, believed firmly that all rules set down by the SS were desirable standards of behavior, at least in the camp.[65]

As emphasized above, such behavior was not universal. Some prisoners held exactly the opposite attitude and regarded all SS regulations as ludicrous.[66] Although this acceptance of and identification with the SS seems to have occurred in only a minority of cases, it is all the more revealing for our purposes because, unlike that which took place in indoctrination centers and "brainwashing" camps for American civilian prisoners of war in Korea, it came about quite unintentionally.[67]

[65]Bettelheim, *Informed Heart,* 170–172.

[66]Cohen, *Human Behavior,* 137–138.

[67]The similarities and differences between concentration camps and indoctrination centers for war prisoners are instructive. In the indoctrination centers there was the same deprivation of food, sleep, and privacy though perhaps not to the same degree. It served the same purpose of raising the level of "drives" to produce quicker learning. Brutality, although it existed, was very much less. The first stage in getting a prisoner to change his

Whether this identification with the Nazi aggressor went so far as to preclude all hostile feelings toward the SS is not clear from the available data, though it seems rather unlikely. In another context Bettelheim observes that, in general, "weakness and submission are often charged with greater hostility than open counter-aggression."[68] Most prisoners, it is clear, hated the SS though not quite in the way one might expect. They often felt deeper and more violent anger against the SS guards for minor acts of cruelty than they felt against those whose acts were much more vicious.[69]

Another account mentions a widespread absence of deep hatred; to many inmates the SS seemed more ridiculous than hateful.[70] Understandably the desire for revenge was powerful. But for the most part this desire took the form of fantasies. Many camp victims gave themselves over to vague and unrealistic plans for a revolution that would leave nothing in the world untouched, once they were able to get out.[71] Their reactions recall those that have been common in the beginning stages of various revolutionary movements.

As a whole, then, the concentration camp appears as a horrible but only too easily recognizable caricature of many a "civilized" society. There is the same class hierarchy, the same competition for crumbs among individuals in the lower strata, the same emergence of a reformist and arrogant elite among those in principle opposed to the regime, and a variety of mechanisms that produce in the subordinate strata an acceptance of the values of the rulers. As will appear in due course all

---

beliefs was intensive interrogation and questioning about his past life in order to challenge his old assumptions about himself and, if possible, to impart a sense of guilt about his past and present behavior as an "enemy of the people." Prison authorities managed to manipulate the informal groups to which prisoners belonged in much the same way as that which took place in the concentration camps, making them exert pressure on the individual to adopt a new set of political assumptions. The new prisoner was surrounded by other prisoners who had already made considerable "progress" in adopting the new viewpoint. In later stages the prisoner was forced to hunt around for "genuine" answers that his interrogators sought, without being quite certain what they wanted, a device that according to some experimental evidence is remarkably effective in establishing new forms of behavior. There were also the usual social and material rewards for conforming to the new doctrine. On the other hand, the treatment appears to have been generally ineffective unless the individual returned to a social environment that confirmed or sustained the new outlook. See Edgar H. Schein *et al., Coercive Persuasion.*

[68]Bettelheim, *Informed Heart,* 249.

[69]Bettelheim, *Informed Heart,* 129.

[70]Cohen, *Human Behavior,* 197–199.

[71]Kogon, *SS-Staat,* 379–380, 384.

of these social processes are to be found in the history of the German working classes and are by no means confined to that country.

5. Stifling the sense of injustice

It would be a serious error to raise the concentration camp to the level of a general model of repression. That is especially true for the problem now at the center of our attention: the forms and mechanisms of self-repression. Because the concentration camp uses the most force there is good reason to regard it as the least effective of the three forms just sketched.

The preceding chapter presented evidence for the view that there *is* such a thing as a recurring, possibly pan-human, sense of injustice, which arises from the combined requirements of innate human nature and the imperatives of social living. Stipulating in advance that it was possible to stifle the demand for justice and the end of human suffering, the discussion has in this chapter sought to uncover the ways in which this stifling can occur. Each of the three extreme cases reveals certain aspects of this general process of self-repression.[72] Let us now try to see what some of the most important ones are.

To begin with the concrete individual human being, it would be a mistake, I suggest, to view the process as mainly one of the destruction of self-esteem. Self-esteem is something that has to be created even if the desire for it may be innate. In our own society with its emphasis on achievement self-esteem requires perpetual renewal in the course of the life cycle. From the standpoint of a dominant group the important task is to inhibit any potentially dangerous form of self-esteem and to deflect any such innate tendencies into sentiments like pride in doing humble work[73] that will sustain the prevailing order. In the etiquette of caste as it applies to the Untouchables it is possible to see quite clearly how such feelings can be created. A diffuse and informal

[72]It is, I hope, plain that this analysis is quite distinct from contemporary critical interpretations of the consumers' society under advanced industrialism, where there is hardly any straightforward physical suffering of the kind accepted and endorsed in these three examples.

[73]Not all such pride, incidentally, deserves to be labeled as unjust repression until and unless one is prepared to argue seriously that all hierarchical forms of the division of labor have become historically obsolete. On this issue see the discussion of rational authority in Chapters One and Thirteen.

variety of coercion that begins in early childhood may be the most effective device for this purpose.

Etiquette is a form of inhibition through teaching people to know their place. Unless individuals are willing to learn, no amount or manner of teaching can be effective. Here material deprivation, originally in the form of hunger, comes into play. Modern prisoners of war who cannot resist the temptation to serve their captors for the sake of increased rations reveal the essence of the relationship. Hunger increases alertness to cues from the social environment about ways to behave that will reduce the pangs. Though there is considerable variation from one individual to another, the effect is to make people eager to learn how to please those persons in charge of the environment. When drives have been aroused, simple withdrawal from the situation becomes much more difficult. A critical rejection of the source of gratification seems almost impossible. The result is an acceptance of the social codes and standards held by those in control of the situation. It is the elementary form of co-option.

These considerations show that it is necessary to take into account cultural definitions, the ready-made pointers to danger, and formulae for coping with it that individuals acquire from the social lore and practice around them. If every human being had to figure out every situation afresh, human society would be impossible. These cultural formulae define socially acceptable and unacceptable needs, the meaning and causes of human suffering, and what, if anything, the individual can or should do about such suffering. In asceticism, Hindu caste, and to a lesser extent the concentration camps, it is possible to discern a general pattern of cultural explanation that stifles the impulse to do anything about suffering. The explanation produces this effect by making the suffering appear as part of the cosmic order, hence inevitable, and in a sense justified. Even more significantly the form of the explanation helps to turn aggressive impulses that suffering and frustration produce against the self. This turning inward of aggression is most noticeable in the case of asceticism. But it is also true of Hindu beliefs about caste in general: failure to show respect to superiors in this life will lead to penalties in the next one. In the concentration camps the same mechanisms appeared among those inmates previously conditioned to accept German law and order without critical questioning who explained their current plight as due to misunderstandings or mistakes in the way this law and order had been applied to their particular cases.

Thus the available cultural definitions of social reality limit the range of possible responses to this reality. On the basis of these three examples it is also possible to distinguish four types of social processes that serve to inhibit collective efforts to identify, reduce, or resist human causes of pain and suffering. It is hardly necessary to add that effective action against the social causes of suffering must be collective. Individual efforts are not to be dismissed, and are certainly better than no effort at all unless they occur at the expense of other victims, as unfortunately is often the case. But individual solutions that help only a minority by definition do not change the situation.

To this sociologist the most striking set of facts to turn up in these examples is the way solidarity among an oppressed group forms readily *against* an individual protester or protector. This social mechanism appears not only in the concentration camps but also in ordinary prisons. In the less overtly threatening form of the Hindu caste system it occurs in the fully institutionalized form of lower-caste councils who punish their own members for the infraction of caste rules. The reasons for this solidarity are clear enough: any single act of defiance runs the risk of retaliation that threatens the whole group. Thus the group's spontaneous efforts at defense can easily and almost unavoidably serve to perpetuate and even intensify its submission.

The other three social processes are so much a part of common knowledge that few comments are necessary here. One of them is the destruction of prior social ties and habits among the sufferers to the point where individuals are left without social support from other human beings. That can happen as a result of the deliberate policy of an oppressor as in the concentration camps, or as a consequence of more diffuse social processes that bring about the disappearance of traditional ways of gaining a livelihood. Since the crucial role of a minimum of social support for any act of criticism or resistance will appear clearly in the next chapter, there is no need for further discussion here.[74] Nor is there any need to elaborate further at this point on co-option since its essential psychological elements have just been discussed in connection with social learning. The last social process, perhaps best labeled as fragmentation, does, on the other hand, deserve some brief comment.

Fragmentation characterizes the situation of an oppressed or subordinate population whose previous historical experience has left it divided into two or more competing groups with their

---

[74]It is worth noticing, however, that asceticism can occur as both an individual and a collective reaction to stress.

own distinct ways of life. Such divisions along class, ethnic, religious, and occupational lines often interfered with even minimal cooperation among the prisoners in the concentration camps. Similar forms of fragmentation have been an obstacle to wider forms of cooperation in other contexts such as ethnic divisions among industrial workers in the United States or the problems of minorities in the Austro-Hungarian Empire. This kind of fragmentation is the opposite of the process of atomization just mentioned. Fragmentation generally implies the intensification of prior social bonds instead of their destruction. An inherited network of obligations and hostilities encapsulates the individual victim of misfortune or oppression to the point where it is impossible to break out and form ties with other human beings in the same plight. Too much social support, or social support unsuited to the circumstances, can render a person as ineffective—and perhaps cause as much pain—as no support at all.

All of the psychological, cultural, and social processes just reviewed work together or separately to create the sense that 'pain and suffering come with moral authority, indeed that these experiences are to a degree morally desirable. The experiences themselves also appear as unavoidable or even inevitable. Perhaps, therefore, the conquest of inevitability constitutes the core of the issues under consideration. If so, there has to be a conquest in the real world as well as in human emotions, perceptions, and reasoning. Though the clue seems promising, there will be obvious limits to any exploration until after our examination of the historical dimension. In the meantime we may reverse the focus of this chapter to consider the social and psychological mechanisms that human beings have used or tried to use in overcoming hopelessness in the face of adversity.

CHAPTER THREE

The rejection of suffering and oppression

1. The issues

In terms of the argument presented in the first chapter, to overcome the moral authority of suffering and oppression means to persuade oneself and others that it is time to change the social contract. Specifically, people come to believe that a new and different set of criteria ought to go into effect for the choice of those in authority and the manner of its exercise, for the division of labor, and for the allocation of goods and services. That is a rather mouth-filling and complicated way of putting the point. Fortunately those who actively seek to bring about changes usually express matters much more simply. They say something like "Workers of the world, unite!" "A fair day's pay for a fair day's work!" "Land to the tillers!" "Liberty, Equality, Fraternity!" Otherwise probably nothing would have ever happened. But as soon as one tries to discern what actually did happen, as well as what political leaders were trying to accomplish, and the differences between these two things, it becomes necessary to use more complicated terms. These will serve as a useful opening reminder of what it really means to overcome and change an oppressive social system.

To put the main issue just a bit more technically, in this chapter we are looking for general processes that occur at the level of culture, social structure, and individual personality, as groups of people cease to take their social surroundings for granted and come to reject or actively to oppose them. The main process of cultural transformation amounts to an undermining of the prevailing system of beliefs that confers legitimacy, or at least naturalness and some degree of correspondence with ordinary expectations, upon the existing social order. In the area of social structure this is the creation of an effective political presence, some form of organization to counter organized authority, such as Third Estate, Black People, etc. As part of the new political identity, there appear new diagnoses for human miseries and new standards for their condemnation. In some cases this innovation may amount to the recognition and discovery of unhappiness, something quite different, however, from its invention. Psychologically there is the infusion of iron into the human soul to give it the power to judge and to act. The process culminates in the taking of power, or more accurately, a decisive share in power, and the eventual establishment of a new kind of society.

The process may be more or less peaceful and gradual or relatively violent and abrupt, though it has never been completely one or the other. Nor is it something that occurs at all times and in all places. I have come upon hardly any trace of it in nonliterate societies.[1] The near absence of critical thought and action of the type just sketched is quite striking even in those anthropological monographs that penetrate well below those cultural norms about which natives tell strangers to what actually happens. Hence it is more likely that this kind of social process does not put in an appearance until mankind has reached a more complicated level of civilization. Nor does it by any means appear everywhere at that level. Until the twentieth century it was mainly a feature of what is loosely called Western civilization. To locate it more accurately in time and space is a larger claim than the argument requires at this point. We are at a stage similar to that of a naturalist trying to find out if giraffes exist. The problem of their exact habitat can be set aside.

Before proceeding, it is necessary to indicate one further limitation on the scope of the discussion. I shall not have anything to say about the actual process of taking power in either revolutionary or nonrevolutionary situations, partly because the historical analysis in Part Three will consider two revolutionary situations in concrete detail. Nevertheless it is appropriate to make one brief general remark here. There is a tendency, I believe, to overemphasize the underlying long-run social trends behind revolutionary outbreaks as well as dramatic peaceful

---

[1] For one instance, where an informant took a very detached and critical view of the workings of his own society, see Napoleon A. Chagnon, *Yąnomamö: The Fierce People*, 17, 93–96, 137.

changes, and to underestimate the importance of control over the instruments of violence—the army and the police—and the significance of decisions taken by political leaders. The long-run trends merely provide temptations and opportunities for political leaders and set outer limits on what is possible in terms of thought and action. Those who have made revolutionary history in the name of Marx apparently recognize this to be the case rather more clearly than many Marxists writing about history.

At this stage of the exposition the best procedure will be to discuss how cultural and social obstacles are overcome in a reasonably systematic fashion. In this portion the objective will be to maintain the analysis at a sufficiently high level of generality so that the more important considerations come to light and fall into place without taking off into meaningless abstraction. Part Three will return to many of the same issues after an examination of how some of these processes worked themselves out during a decisive slice of modern Western history. Therefore the treatment of these topics will be deliberately tentative, sketchy, and general. When we arrive at the psychological aspects and what it really means to put iron into the human soul, we enter new and difficult terrain, at least for this author. The vexed issue of moral autonomy comes plainly into view. So does the question of what psychological processes lie behind the acquisition of independent moral judgment. Those who have studied these matters empirically have done so from quite different standpoints and have not always reached the same conclusions. I have chosen the strategy of viewing and reinterpreting this evidence as the one most likely to yield worthwhile results. Therefore the exposition and interpretation of the psychological processes will be much more detailed and extensive.

2. *Cultural and social aspects*

Just how and where the process of overcoming the moral authority of suffering and oppression gets started is very hard to state, partly because the beginning is unlikely to be very visible. Likewise it is hard to see any logical or empirical reason for conferring an aura of causal hegemony on changes taking place in any one of the three areas conventionally, conveniently (yet not too clearly) designated as culture, social structure, and personality. What is clear is that the degree of change in one area is limited by the degree of change in the others. Industrial revolutions don't come off without changes in human nature, and intellectual revolutions remain fads or playthings in an unfavorable social setting. Hence it does not matter very much where the investigation starts. Since we began by observing that somewhere near the beginning of the process some concrete individual has to have doubts about the legitimacy of the suffering that does prevail, it will be profitable to look first at the nature of legitimacy.

In the case of stratified and civilized societies it is possible to distinguish certain types of rule that are connected with the kinds of ruling strata in these societies. There is of course no such thing as a pure form of any specific variety of ruling stratum. Nevertheless variations in emphasis are reasonably clear, and the categories theocracy, military elite, plutocracy, and welfare bureaucracy not only correspond with observable reality but appear, with the usual allowance for mixed and overlapping cases, to cover the actual range of variation that human experience has so far provided. Pursuing this line of thought,[2] we can see that each specific type of ruling group is liable to display its specific form of vulnerability to critical attack. Each type of dominant stratum can be expected to have its own form of social contract based upon its own specific principles of social inequality. These in turn stress the importance of whatever social functions that dominant stratum performs or claims to perform.

Hence one main cultural task facing any oppressed group is to undermine or explode the justification of the dominant stratum. Such criticisms may take the form of attempts to demonstrate that the dominant stratum does not perform the tasks that it claims to perform and therefore violates the specific social contract. Much more frequently they take the form that specified individuals in the dominant stratum fail to live up to the social contract. Such criticism leaves the basic functions of the dominant stratum inviolate. Only the most radical forms of criticism have raised the question whether kings, capitalists, priests, generals, bureaucrats, etc., serve any useful social purpose at all.[3]

In societies with a strong theocratic emphasis a characteristic

[2]Derived of course from Gaetano Mosca, *The Ruling Class.* In his terms I am suggesting that each type of political formula has its specific weaknesses.

[3]Marxism, it is worth recalling, sets the main forms of dominant strata in an evolutionary sequence where each one is driven from the historical stage after it has performed its task of carrying humanity through a specific phase on the road to greater freedom. Through its conception of historical obsolescence Marxism tries to counter the charges of unrealism and softhearted idealism, leveled against more static utopian notions and their claim that it is possible to dispense with social inequalities.

popular criticism has been that priests exact too much in the way of material goods for the benefits they claim to produce. Only at a much later stage are there likely to be skeptical comments to the effect that their rituals are ineffective in making the crops grow, fish and game abundant, curing sickness, and putting enemies to flight. In a tight situation people are reluctant to give up anything that might work. Generally, as Sumner and Malinowski have pointed out in different ways, priests manage those aspects of human existence that are beyond human control. They may be actually beyond control or just socially defined as uncontrollable. As long as either situation exists, the priestly function in some form will probably continue to exist.

A military elite or aristocracy is the easiest of all to judge and condemn when its members fail to bring about victory or protection; violation of the social contract is plain for all to see. On the other hand, if the regime can manage to hang onto control over the means of violence, it may be the hardest of all to dislodge. The extent to which the obstacles depend on modern technology is problematical. On the basis of an analysis of the Zulu despot Shaka, who established one of the most effective regimes of terror on record without the use of gas chambers, machine guns, or a guillotine, the sociologist E. V. Walter claims that it is not the instruments of violence as such but the techniques of social control that are decisive.[4]

Radical attacks on a militarist society take the form of attacks on the military and heroic ethic. From Adam Smith through Herbert Spencer and Thorstein Veblen it is possible to trace a current of thought that singles out materialism and rationalism as the enemies of the military and heroic ethic. Contemporary social critics often reverse this argument. They draw a connection between materialism, rationalism, and the drive to dominate and exploit. With the decay of preindustrial elites and the intensification of violence and oppression in the twentieth century the basic principles of modern industrial society itself have, as every literate person knows, come under increasing attack.

Unlike military aristocracies and for reasons that are obscure, plutocracies have a hard time justifying themselves strictly in their own terms. It is hard to make the accumulation of wealth an end in itself. Perhaps because it can serve almost any purpose, wealth, unlike holiness or wisdom, has to be an instrumental value. Attacks on riches and the demand that they be put to socially approved uses are as old as the human record. This

[4]Eugene Victor Walter, *Terror and Resistance*, 110–111.

does not mean that plutocracies are unavoidably vulnerable: witness the case of Venice, a stable plutocracy if there ever was one. But it suggests that they are the least likely to exist in a pure form, and that in a secure plutocracy the extraction of an economic surplus has to be indirect and not, as was the case in turbulent Florence, dependent on an underlying population. Otherwise, plutocracy may be the form of social order whose legitimacy is most liable to challenge. At the same time because wealth is a solvent of other values through making it possible to purchase the good things of life, a great many societies ostensibly based on other principles display a marked tendency toward turning into plutocracies.

Welfare bureaucracies are a novel and quite recent historical development. They are really variants of plutocracy since they accept the same materialist goals but claim that they can reach them more rapidly and with greater equity. And concepts of equity are liable to clash sharply with a plutocratic ethic even when veiled in paternalism. At the present historical juncture there are two variants of welfare bureaucracy. One is a modernizing elite in an economically backward country thrown up by a revolutionary upheaval, and so far made up mainly of communists or socialists with a strong savor of national patriotism. Critical responses to this elite can take the form that the modernizing leadership is not bringing welfare to the population but keeping it for itself and becoming a new dominant stratum. There may also occur a somewhat more leftist criticism that the elite is not modernizing effectively or rapidly enough. In both cases the accusation is that the regime is betraying the ideals of the revolution.

The other variant occurs in advanced industrial states. Here the main impulse is toward equitable distribution of the social product. No fully developed case has so far arisen though Sweden approaches it, while New Deal and labor governments have been attempts to move in this direction. Since modernization as such is in these cases no longer an issue, the main popular criticisms can only take the form that distribution is not equitable enough. In both forms of the welfare bureaucracy the only rationalist critique has to be an instrumentalist one: to the effect that the regime is not doing the job properly. Under these circumstances a more fundamental critique must reject the ethic of accumulation and the ethic of work.

There are grounds for holding that all possible forms of this rejection face a serious risk of running into a blind alley. The leftist form of criticism turns easily into an apolitical religion of brotherhood and love. Other fundamental criticisms turn out to be generally unacceptable variants of conservatism. One is the effort to revive an heroic and military ethic. Fascism shows where that leads. A more moderate version holds that welfare bureaucracy in an advanced industrial country is essentially unworkable because in the end the country cannot afford it: the system destroys initiative, provides insufficient rewards for skill, is inflexible, and will destroy or weaken production to the point where the country will lose its markets (domestic as well as foreign) and hence the high standard of living that is a prerequisite for the whole system. These arguments are not to be dismissed as sheer rhetoric. They amount to saying that a combination of institutional pressures forces any given modern society to accumulate wealth and retain the work ethic, and that the penalties for failure to do so are widespread misery vastly beyond what happens when a few people lose morally suspect luxuries. Any political and intellectual leader able to solve these problems would deserve the gratitude of modern mankind, and might even get it.

These observations on different types of legitimacy and their social bases indicate the range of openings available to oppositional groupings and the structural sources of such opposition. For any oppressed group the primary task is to overcome the moral authority of the sources of their suffering and to create a politically effective identity. For analytical purposes it is useful to distinguish three significant social and cultural aspects of this process. One is to reverse the kinds of solidarity among the oppressed that aid the oppressor. Examples of this kind of solidarity are the hostility to the "ball buster" reported from American prisons and similar behavior in the concentration camps where prisoners discipline each other to carry out the will of the guards or the SS. To reverse this kind of solidarity and direct antagonism outward against a common enemy is no easy task because even the solidarity that aids the oppressor constitutes some protection for the victims. Nor do all the obstacles to collective action against the dominant groups come from the acts and policies of the authorities. In modern societies, as we shall see in Part Three, the fragmentation that arises from a complex division of labor is especially important.

The second aspect of the process is cultural rather than social: the creation of standards of condemnation for explaining and judging current sufferings. As the preceding chapter has shown, human beings can learn not only to accept but even to choose pain and suffering. If there always remains some biological substratum of resistance to painful experiences, as I strongly suspect is the case, it is nevertheless quite possible to overcome such instinctual tendencies through various forms of conditioning. As pointed out earlier, this human capacity to ignore and accept suffering is essential to human survival. Therefore any political movement against oppression has to develop a new diagnosis and remedy for existing forms of suffering, a diagnosis and remedy by which this suffering stands morally condemned. These new moral standards of condemnation constitute the core identity of any oppositional movement.

As part of this new identity based on a new perception of evil there develops a new definition of friend and foe. In any but the most isolated society, where far-reaching social change is in any case highly improbable, the redefinition of friend and foe has to apply to neighboring and often competing societies as well. This process of redefining the foreign enemy is sufficiently difficult and important to warrant attention as a separate aspect of the creation of an effective political identity by oppositional movements. The Jacobin surge of patriotism at the time of the French Revolution and the failure of international working-class solidarity at the outbreak of the First World War come to mind as famous examples of such attempts to redefine the foreign enemy. The issue is by no means confined to modern times. In the history of Greek city-states the domestic conflict between rich and poor, oligarchy and democracy, was inextricably intertwined with the conflict among different types of city-states. At other times and places the great world religions and sectarian movements within them have contributed heavily to the definition and redefinition of the foreign enemy.[5]

Rather than elaborate on these three sociocultural processes at this point in the discussion it will be better to keep them in mind for the historical investigation to come in Part Two. They are matters about which we should be alert in examining concrete materials and clues to possible meanings for facts that would otherwise pass unnoticed. After working through the historical materials we may come upon other processes that are obviously important and will be in a better position to explicate those just sketched.

[5] A word of caution is appropriate here about the modern tendency to find economically based forms of social protest behind all such movements. It is nearly always possible to find an economic aspect in any social movement. But such a discovery cannot justify the claim that economically based protest constitutes the most important part of the explanation. To discover what is important it is necessary to ascertain all the forces at work, to assess on the basis of specific evidence their relative importance and relationship to each other. In the absence of experimental procedures that is far from easy.

One general aspect of the whole process does, however, require comment before attempting to analyze what happens to individual human beings. Put crudely, the issue is this: do the lower strata really give a damn about the reigning principles of legitimacy in their society? How much do they actually know or care about such matters? Obviously the answer will vary considerably from case to case. For stratified preindustrial societies, with a dominant stratum whose way of life is sharply distinct from the peasants', life in field, village, and hamlet proceeds very largely according to its own social and mental rhythms. It is very hard indeed to ascertain how such people thought and felt, though there is more information about how they actually behaved. About the lower strata in the towns before comparatively recent times we don't know a great deal more. But from what anthropologists tell us about nonliterate societies, and what can be gleaned from historical studies, there can be hardly any doubt that the behavior of preindustrial peasants and artisans conforms to *some* principles of social organization that can be spelled out in some reasonably satisfactory fashion. Put differently, there are principles of legitimacy. It is also reasonably plain that these have to mesh somehow with principles prevailing among the dominant strata, and that the nature of the mesh will have significant consequences for the forms and character of social discontent. Furthermore, a rigid distinction between the dominant strata and the mass of the population is by no means the universal situation in preindustrial societies. On this score eighteenth-century Russia and Japan were very different. Thus, to complete this very quick reconsideration, an attempt to gauge the significance of principles of legitimacy leads at once into issues that have to do with the social networks and relationships that link, or fail to link, dominant and subordinate groups in the population.

3. Moral autonomy and human personality

At all points in these complex processes, concrete human individuals have to act and act in certain ways. What is it then that gives them the courage to break wholly or partially with the cultural and social order in which they are embedded? This is the issue we face now.

The answer that common sense gives is that the pain of

suffering sooner or later leads to an act of desperation. It is hardly a satisfactory answer. By themselves pain and suffering do not provide an adequate explanation. As the preceding chapter pointed out, the pain can be anesthetized and there are situations that lead human beings to inflict pain on themselves. In other situations action may be or seem futile or threaten even worse suffering.

Some "iron in the soul," as hinted earlier, appears to be a necessary ingredient. But what does iron in the soul really mean and how does it get there? At this point I plan to discuss what answers modern psychology can and cannot give to this question. First, however, it is necessary to try to be somewhat more precise about what the question itself can mean.

Ready answers might be moral autonomy or moral courage. Neither concept is really satisfactory. By itself at any rate the term moral courage will not describe the qualities we are looking for. Human beings can have the courage of their convictions and be willing to stand up to overwhelming social pressures at the same time that they are behaving in a cruel and oppressive fashion. Since this issue will come up in a wider context when we examine the behavior of rank-and-file Nazis facing public hostility and even at times the blows of the police under the Weimar Republic, there is no need to discuss it further here.

Upon even the briefest reflection the concept of moral autonomy presents even more complicated problems. Can moral autonomy exist in a universe supposedly governed by universal causation? Is the closely associated concept of moral autonomy no more than an illusion?[6] This issue too will recur in a wider context in the course of an effort to test the conception of suppressed historical alternatives in the concrete context of a critical turning point in German history, indeed the history of modern Western society: the failure to establish a viable liberal regime in Germany after the defeat and revolution of 1918. At that point I shall try to sketch a sufficiently tenable position to justify the inquiry. For the present task it may be enough to suggest certain things that moral autonomy cannot mean.

To put the main points bluntly, moral autonomy cannot mean either self-indulgence or a painless recognition of some huge overarching necessity. It is not an act of moral autonomy to refuse to learn the rules of arithmetic, at least not in the modern world. The talk about "authenticity," "finding yourself," and

---

[6]Cf. Robert Paul Wolff, *The Autonomy of Reason: A Commentary on Kant's Groundwork of the Metaphysic of Morals,* espec. 194–222.

"developing your own potentialities" that began to gain popularity in the mid-1960s has hardly anything to do with moral autonomy (or social and political change) because this current of thought fails to confront seriously and concretely the issue of what constraints are necessary on individual human beings for the sake of living in society, or on its fringes. The very word "autonomy" is suspect on the grounds that it tends to obliterate these admittedly variable but still inevitable constraints. At the other end of the scale there is a distinguished intellectual tradition which recognizes inevitable constraint but defines human freedom as the recognition of necessity. Somehow it seems inappropriate to call submission to any restraint, no matter how necessary or beneficial, autonomy or freedom. One has the right, indeed, the intellectual and moral obligation, to be even more suspicious whenever it turns out that the recognition of necessity turns out to imply heavy sacrifices for somebody else and a privileged position for those somehow wise enough to recognize the necessity.

Nevertheless it seems impossible to excise the notions of moral autonomy and moral courage from our thought and vocabulary. Everyday experience shows us that some human beings have these qualities and others lack them. Therefore the best thing to do at this juncture is to try to describe these qualities very briefly. Even with only a crude sense of what one ought to look for, progress is more likely than it is from prolonged philosophical discussion of how to look.

As a more realistic way to begin I will therefore posit three distinct if related human qualities or capacities that might add up to "iron in the soul." We shall also seek whatever explanations for their existence psychologists of varying persuasions can furnish. The first quality we can still call moral courage, in the sense of a capacity to resist powerful and frightening social pressures to obey *oppressive or destructive* rules or commands. The second quality is the intellectual ability to recognize that the pressures and rules are in fact oppressive. This recognition can take the form of moral awakening in terms of existing but largely suppressed standards of behavior. The third capacity, moral inventiveness, is much rarer, and I shall not have much to say about it. It is the capacity to fashion from existing cultural traditions historically new standards of condemnation for what exists. In their different ways Jesus and Martin Luther were moral innovators. Presumably this capacity can exist in some ordinary human beings to a much lesser degree.

Upon turning to the psychological literature for assistance in explaining this set of qualities, one point becomes clear that perhaps should have been obvious beforehand. Whatever moral autonomy may mean, it is something that exists in varying degrees and under more or less specifiable conditions. Psychologists using different procedures and starting with very different general assumptions have generated findings that tell us a great deal about where this quality comes from, the circumstances that promote its development in the human personality, and perhaps even more about those circumstances that can prevent its appearance or even utterly destroy it. In what follows I shall review and interpret some of these findings.

An outsider searching through the literature for enlightenment soon notices that some psychologists emphasize the significance of concrete circumstances and specific situations as the main determinants of human behavior. They expect most people to behave the same way in similar situations. Many of these investigators use laboratory techniques to elicit their findings. Others stress what laymen would call character and personality in distinguishing among the ways different human beings perceive and respond to similar external circumstances. For the latter group of psychologists, circumstances enter the stream of causation as influences on the formation of character and personality. Since the explanations of the former group are both relatively simple and quite striking, it will be best to begin with them.

Two sets of experiments have become justly famous outside professional circles, because they present frightening demonstrations of how easy it can be to create and manipulate group pressures on the individual in such a way as to suppress not only humane inclinations but even the unambiguous evidence of the senses. The essence of both sets of experiments was to place an ordinary American adult in a contrived experimental situation where social pressures forced this individual to make a decision against his or her "normal" or expected rational and humane inclinations. The burden of the findings is to the effect that most people do indeed give in to such pressures. Both experiments give information, however, about *some* individuals who did *not* yield to the contrived pressures of the experimental situation. The experiments also report on the conditions under which this minority did not yield, and under which the general results of the experiment were reversed. This is the aspect of special significance for our purposes because it provides significant clues about those conditions under which moral autonomy can overcome severe obstacles. To make this aspect comprehensible, however, it is necessary to say something about each experiment as a whole.

In S. E. Asch's experiment, which was designed to uncover some effects of group pressure upon the individual's powers of judgment,[7] individual subjects were asked to match the length of a given line with one of three unequal lines. The subject sat in a room along with a group of other persons, all matching the same lines and identifying them out loud. Ostensibly also subjects in the same experiment, the "other persons" were actually all confederates of the experimenter. The experiment was carried out several times on different subjects.[8] In the midst of this rather monotonous task of matching lines the subject suddenly found his judgment unanimously contradicted by the other members of the group, the experimenter's confederates. On the average, 32 percent, or just short of a third, of the estimates of the subject became incorrect due to this majority pressure.

In these cases individuals denied the plain evidence of their senses in order to conform to the opinions of their fellows. It would be enlightening to know if the subjects gave in to the opinions of others because they thought the issue was trivial, and whether they would behave quite differently in a situation that seemed to them one where the consequences of a decision mattered more. Yet it is impossible to find out everything at once. And the results are enlightening enough, especially when the experimenter made some alterations in the experimental conditions. In one variation, when *two* naïve subjects were placed in the group, the proportion of promajority errors in judgment dropped to 10.4 percent. In another instance when the real subject heard a confederate of the experimenter announce the correct answer *before* the real subject could speak, while the remaining confederates gave wrong answers, the proportion of promajority errors dropped to 5.5 percent.

If the experiment reveals the very considerable power of group pressure, it also reveals what dissolves this pressure. A single ally can provide sufficient support to enable a person to make a correct judgment, at least in this simplified situation.

---

[7]See Asch, "Effects of Group Pressure upon the Modification and Distortion of Judgments," in Harold Guetzkow, editor, *Groups, Leadership and Men*, 177–190, espec. 185–186.

[8]To carry out such an experiment it is of course necessary to conceal its true purpose from the subject. It is also customary to explain the true purpose immediately afterward or as soon as practicable and to discuss the experiment freely and fully with the subject or subjects. Some experiments, such as the next one, raise serious ethical issues. This one by Asch, so far as I can see, was quite benign.

When the emperor is naked, we might infer, he must be able to count on the unanimous imagination of his subjects to supply him with a suitable wardrobe. Naturally it would be unwise to draw too optimistic a conclusion on so small a basis. Though I know of no experimental data, there is good reason to suppose that the relationship will work equally well in reverse: an individual already predisposed to wrong judgments, and especially wrong judgments on matters important to this person, would very likely need no more than one ally to confirm this incorrect opinion.

The purpose of the second series of experiments, carried out by Stanley Milgram, was to discover at what point and under what conditions human beings would cease to obey legitimate authority when its commands became obviously cruel. In the basic experiment volunteer subjects were recruited by advertisements in the local newspaper and direct-mail solicitation from a variety of occupations and educational backgrounds. They included men and, later, women.[9] First, the subjects received instructions that as volunteers they were to administer or receive electric shocks, in order to acquire scientific information about the connection between punishment and learning. On the nature of this connection they received a simple and clear briefing. This briefing was part of the deception necessary to the experiment. Then each subject entered a very realistically staged laboratory in the company of another "volunteer," who was actually a trained actor. His role would be to play that of the "student" to whom the real subject in the role of "teacher" would administer increasingly severe electric shocks. The subject also was introduced to an "experimenter," suitably dressed in a white coat. The "experimenter," also a confederate of the psychologist, was to play the role of the figure of legitimate authority. The main piece of equipment in the laboratory was a very realistically constructed panel of electric switches. The panel was of course a dummy. There were thirty switches ranging from 15 to 450 volts. At intervals along the panel there were indications of the severity of the shock. In eight steps they rose from "Slight Shock" at 15 volts to "Danger: Severe Shock" at the seventh step with 375 volts; after that point the rest of the panel up to 450 volts was simply marked "XXX." The whole setting effectively conveyed an aura of scientific seriousness.

---

[9] I find convincing the author's arguments to the effect that the sample was sufficiently representative for the purposes of the inquiry and that those who did not volunteer probably would not have behaved in a manner sufficiently different to affect the general results. See Milgram, *Obedience to Authority*, 170–171.

Shortly after entering, the subject, through a rigged drawing of lots, found himself seated before this apparatus. He had drawn the role of "teacher" while the actor had drawn the role of "student." At this point the "experimenter" instructed the "teacher," that is, the real subject of the real experiment, to administer increasingly severe shocks to the "student," as the latter made "mistakes" in learning pairs of words. The "mistakes" of the "student" were deliberate and an important part of the real experiment. Meanwhile the "experimenter" in the white coat in a neutral manner instructed the "teacher" to continue the experiment by increasing the severity of the shocks after each mistake. The "student" actor evidently played his part extremely well. As the severity of the shocks increased, he gave increasing signs of pain, finally twisting and writhing in his seat, calling out for the "experiment" to be ended and the like. (There were some variations in different forms of the experiment.) The "experimenter" appears to have played his role equally well, and both roles were standardized to avoid influencing the results. When the actor "student" began to show increasing signs of discomfort or pain, and the naïve subject as "teacher" showed signs of reluctance to continue increasing the shocks, the "experimenter" told him that the experiment *required* that he continue to administer shocks, adding that "although the shocks may be painful, there is no permanent tissue damage, so please go on."

The subjects playing the role of "teacher" quite clearly believed that they were inflicting real pain on a total stranger for the sake of a scientific experiment. Milgram's purpose was to see at what point the subject would break off the pseudo-experiment by refusing to obey the orders of the "experimenter" to administer increasingly severe shocks. On the basis not only of general information but also of prior interviews asking a variety of people, including a panel of psychiatrists, how far they expected other people to go in this situation and how far they themselves would go, Milgram confidently expected that most subjects would break off and disobey at a quite early point in the administration of the shocks. Instead, to his legitimate surprise and evident horror, most subjects in most variations of the experiment went all the way or nearly all the way to the full strength "XXX" shocks.[10]

In order to discover if obedience to the authority of the

---

[10]Afterward the experimental staff undid the deception and in the course of extensive discussion informed the subjects about the real purpose of the experiment. These discussions and other forms of following up the subjects' views of their own behavior yielded some of the most valuable data.

"experimenter" was the real cause for this collapse of autonomy,[11] Milgram conducted a number of variations on the basic form of the experiment as I have summarized it here. His evidence that the situation of authority produced this obedience is very convincing. While important in its own right, it is not what we are looking for right now. Instead, we are trying to find out about disobedience, and especially principled disobedience. The variations did create situations in which compliance with the "experimenter's" instructions declined considerably or disappeared altogether. This is the aspect of the experiment most important for our purpose.

Before analyzing these variations it is worthwhile to point out that there was at least one case of a refusal to go through with the basic experiment that appears to have been based on principled objections to the infliction of suffering. It happens that the individual was a woman, a medical technician who had grown up in Nazi Germany and recently emigrated. Not much can be made of either of these facts, piquant though they are. The behavior of the women subjects did not differ significantly from that of the men.[12] There are plenty of Germans who did not acquire an aversion to cruelty due to their experiences under the Nazi regime. Even this woman did not stop until about halfway through the experiment at the point of "Very Strong Shock." Nevertheless, her refusal to go on despite an explicit command from the experimenter was a calm and firm refusal to accept responsibility for the infliction of harm no matter what the "experimenter" required. Rare though it may be, morally autonomous behavior is evidently possible.

In the standard form of the experiment the individual was absolutely alone in confronting authority. In American culture this authority, that of science, especially a form close to medical science, is one widely defined as benign. (The experiments took place in 1960–1963. If conducted on a population of college students in the early 1970s the results might have been very

[11]See *Obedience to Authority,* 133, for his use of the term "autonomy." Unless I have missed something, he does not use the term *"moral* autonomy." Instead, in other passages he writes of "moral judgment." These matters are unimportant: the experiment is a highly imaginative investigation of the human capacity for independent moral judgment and action, the issue under analysis here. There is one difference from situations in real life that deserves attention. As Milgram himself stresses (175), the experiments did not study the coerced obedience of the oppressed. His subjects were paid volunteers. But the distinction is not as great as his disclaimer states. There were coercive elements for the individual subject in the experimental situation, and in real life oppressed groups generally accept in some degree the legitimacy of their oppressors.

[12]Milgram, *Obedience to Authority,* 63; for the individual case, 84–85.

different.) Presumably Milgram's subjects felt that science was generally benign or they would not have volunteered for the undertaking. Finally, they were assured that the shocks "caused no permanent tissue damage." To resist authority alone, and even more so an authority one defines as essentially benign, is an extraordinarily difficult task for any human being. With social support, on the other hand, it becomes vastly easier.

Milgram demonstrated this point nicely in one variant of the basic experiment. He provided the naïve subject with two additional "teachers" who were actually confederates. At selected points first one confederate and then the other refused to go on obeying the "experimenter's" order to administer increasingly severe shocks. With this example before them, or to use Milgram's own terms, with the support of their peers, most subjects willingly rebelled against the authority of the "experimenter." Among all the variations in the basic experiment, the provision of social support was by far the most effective one in undercutting the "experimenter's" authority.[13]

With support from peers, the naïve subject's suspicion that he or she might be doing something wrong can come to the surface and form the basis for action. In some cases too, as the subsequent interviews revealed, the very idea of disobeying came to the naïve subject from watching someone else disobey. It is appropriate therefore to ask whether such behavior really represents moral autonomy.

The facts, insofar as they are revealed by the experiment, may be interpreted as follows: pure moral autonomy in the form of lone resistance to an apparently benign authority is very rare. With support from peers, on the other hand, the same kind of resistance increases enormously. These facts correspond to what it is possible to observe in the real world and shed much light on why it happens. What the data reveal is the significance of social support for correct moral reasoning.[14] Even with social support, on the other hand, the individual has to recognize the correct nature of the reasoning and to act on it.

Another set of ingenious variations on the basic experiment varied the extent to which the subject administering the shock would be aware of the "victim's" suffering and complaints. At one extreme the "victim" was out of sight in an adjacent room.

[13]Milgram, *Obedience to Authority*, 116–121, espec. 118.

[14]Correct as long as one accepts the premises of humane rationality. It is of course perfectly possible to reject them on logical grounds: to assert that human beings ought to be stupid and harm each other. Obviously they do that often enough. Whether that is good for them is not a logical but an empirical question.

His answers flashed silently before the "teacher" on a signal box. But at 300 volts the laboratory walls resounded as the "student" pounded the walls in protest. At the other extreme it was necessary for the "teacher" to press the "student's" hand onto a dummy shock plate. There were two intermediate steps that I shall not stop to describe. Compliance with the "experimenter's" orders dropped sharply as the physical proximity of the "student-victim" increased. With the "victim" out of sight 65 percent of the subjects were obedient. When it was necessary to press the "victim's" hand onto the shock plate only 30 percent obeyed. Similarly the intensity of the shock the subjects were willing to administer dropped off sharply.[15]

Interpreted in terms of situations in real life, these data show that a willingness to obey legitimate but oppressive orders is likely to decline rapidly if the situation permits or requires an awareness of the "victim's" suffering. Then the possibility of identification with the "victim" arises. That in itself is far from surprising. Those charged with keeping order in a hostile population generally see to it that their subordinates have a minimum of contact with those whom they are supposed to control. The thought-provoking aspect of the material lies rather in the way it demonstrates the very great power that this empathy may have under appropriate circumstances. It is necessary to recall that disobedience in these variants of the experiment was still a lone act taken in opposition to a figure of authority defined as benign, for whom the subject had undertaken an obligation by volunteering to take part in the "experiment," and who reassured the subject that the "victim" was undergoing no real harm. The more one thinks about the situation, with the very unfair advantage of hindsight, the more surprising it becomes that disobedience did occur at all, and even more that it occurred on such a large scale. Evidently empathy under the right conditions can break through some very powerful obstacles. Combining the results just discussed with the material on the consequences of peer rebellion in undermining authority permits an interpretation of the experiment as a whole very different from Milgram's emphasis on the dangers inherent in the human tendency to obey.

That, however, is an issue that far transcends this limited if outstanding experiment. Here it is appropriate to comment on only a few aspects. In the artificial situation of the laboratory the empathy that was effective required close physical contact and almost certainly many other factors difficult to specify accu-

[15]Milgram, *Obedience to Authority*, 32–36, espec. table 2.

rately. Everyday experience is enough to show that close association with another person—not to mention physical contact—is hardly effective by itself in creating sympathetic identification. Furthermore, it is alarmingly easy to destroy the awareness that another human being suffers from an experience in the same way that we would. The widespread practice of torture is enough to demonstrate that. Finally, even if knowledge did exist about the variety of conditions that created and destroyed sympathetic identification with other human beings, it would not be very helpful. By itself, love, sympathetic identification, empathy, or whatever one chooses to call this elusive emotion or series of emotions, is nowhere near enough to hold together any large human society and make it run. Under certain conditions it can be very powerful. But it won't get food and water into the cities and garbage off the streets.

The other variations in Milgram's experiment concern limitations in the quality and degree of authority. Since they bear only indirectly on the problem of overcoming the moral authority of oppression, it will be possible to comment on them briefly. The most significant variation has important bearings on the notion that human beings are innately cruel and aggressive. At one point in the course of the experiments the suggestion cropped up that the subjects might just enjoy inflicting shocks on a helpless victim. Two variations tested this notion. In one the "experimenter" in the white coat left the room to give his instructions by telephone. When the "experimenter" was absent, obedience dropped sharply. In the other variation the "experimenter" gave instructions that permitted subjects to choose whatever shock level they wished. In this situation the great majority of the subjects chose the lowest possible shock level on the apparatus.[16] Clearly these subjects were not—with some individual exceptions—inclined to inflict harm on a helpless person. A representative of legitimate authority had to be physically present and give explicit orders to make them do it. Left to themselves, if they *could* be left to themselves, human beings might very well behave in a more or less humane and rational manner toward each other.[17] The other variations point toward a similar

[16]Milgram, *Obedience to Authority,* 59–62, 70–72.

[17]The representativeness of the sample has a bearing here. Milgram, *Obedience to Authority,* 170–171, reports that the experiments were repeated in Princeton, Munich, Rome, South Africa, and Australia, yielding in general somewhat *higher* rates of obedience. It is not clear whether the variations just described were part of the experimental procedure carried out in the course of repetitions. But there is enough evidence from other sources of humane and rational behavior as a general practice in secure and relatively isolated societies to warrant the generalization.

conclusion. Compliance fell off in varying degrees, sometimes quite sharply, when the institutional trappings of authority were altered, when two authority figures gave contradictory orders, and when authority was transferred to an "ordinary person" instead of an "experimenter" in a white coat. In the last-mentioned variation a number of subjects rose valiantly to the occasion and either threatened or used physical violence to defend the "student-victim."[18] While thought-provoking in many of their details, these findings do not run counter to ordinary expectations about human behavior to anything like the degree that is true of other findings.

I have reported and reinterpreted Milgram's work at some length because it was the most relevant to the issues under consideration. In terms of a capacity to define the issues and to devise a procedure that would yield pertinent evidence this work was also in my judgment outstanding. On careful examination this set of experiments in social psychology, together with those by Asch, indicate that there are just about as many ways to dissolve an oppressive social atmosphere that stifles moral autonomy as there are ways to create such an atmosphere. Purely human capacities and their technical manipulation appear to be about neutral. The obstacles to moral autonomy come rather from the fact that the opportunities to control this atmosphere are unequally distributed in hierarchically organized societies. For other reasons the opportunities are also very slim in the few remaining societies that lack hierarchy and social stratification.

To a good many critics of modern industrial society the assertion that the opportunities to control the social atmosphere were "unequally distributed" would be a grotesquely comical understatement. According to a familiar critical tradition, modern technology and mass media have made possible the manipulation of human attitudes on a scale heretofore unimagined. In this way they have supposedly helped to destroy the very possibility of independent moral and political judgment in advanced industrial societies. Let us glance briefly at what the researches of contemporary social psychologists may have to tell us about this issue.[19]

The main impression that such studies convey is that the American population is neither dominated nor brainwashed by the media. By and large, most people pay no attention to what the media have to say if they are not interested in the subject to

---

[18]Milgram, *Obedience to Authority,* 93–99, 66–70, 105–107.

[19]For a challenge from another viewpoint see Walter's *Terror and Resistance.*

begin with, as is very frequently the case. The research findings about popular misinterpretation of the messages of the media, and lack of attention to such messages, reinforces the impression that ordinary people form their ideas from their immediate experiences, not from mass media, or not to any great extent. Similar data on the lack of "political" attitudes also indicate that people have *no* ideas, or very random ones, on areas remote from their immediate day-to-day concerns. Dramatic events, to be sure, such as the assassination of President Kennedy, do catch their attention. Then, however, people interpret these events in quite personal terms. Over and over again investigators of the effect of the media stress the importance of the audience's prior emotional and intellectual predispositions, their intellectual equipment in the sense of store of knowledge, conceptual framework, and mood.[20]

In other words, it is impossible to infer the effect of the media from the content alone. Information on the attention given to political campaigns in the United States does not support any strong notion of selective exposure to political messages. People, if they are interested in politics at all, do pay considerable attention to messages opposed to their prior opinions. This finding suggests that radical and nonrespectable views filter through, at first attracting attention on the fringes of respectability. The capacity to accept (or perhaps ignore) contradictory ideas comes out very vividly in one study of a sample of union members who were mainly Catholics. The union leaders were, on the other hand, Communists. The local newspaper supported the church view of American-Soviet relations, while the local union weekly and the union leaders supported the Communist line. Rank-and-file union members who were unconcerned about political issues were not even aware of these contradictions.[21] Presumably they would have reacted quite differently on a "hot" local issue.

---

[20]For a general review of the literature see Walter Weiss, "Effects of the Mass Media on Communication," in Lindzey and Aronson, *Handbook of Social Psychology*, V, 77–195. For evidence against the notions of selective exposure to the media (i.e., widespread avoidance of contrary or threatening views) and absence of evidence in favor of any persuasive effect by the media see William J. McGuire, "The Nature of Attitudes and Attitude Change," in *ibid.*, III, 218–219, 227. For evidence that large numbers of people lack any coherent political concern or opinions, and some data on the purported tendency of the media to reinforce prior general dispositions, see David O. Sears, "Political Behavior," in *ibid.*, V, 330–331, 349–351, 365. The reported absence of political concerns, it seems to me, might be a reflection of the interviewers' definition of "political," stressing national and international concerns. People are likely to have at least a crude diagnosis and remedy for painful pressures that they feel directly. Excellent data on this point are available in Robert E. Lane, *Political Ideology*.

[21]Walter Weiss, "Effects of the Mass Media," 87–89, 114–116, 159, 161.

Thus these findings cast considerable doubt on the Orwellian image of modern industrial society as culturally and intellectually managed from one or a few central points. The obstacles to moral autonomy, we may infer, derive from more material causes such as the unequal distribution of wealth and power.

When one turns from these concerns with group and institutional pressures on the mature individual to studies of how the human individual *becomes* mature and acquires a character or personality, the first impression is liable to be one of hopeless disagreement among different schools of psychology. It is at this point that the stress on external circumstances as the determinant of moral behavior at any given point in time becomes most apparent—as well as the limitations on an atemporal approach limited to the techniques of the laboratory. At one pole the sympathetically curious reader will find extreme skepticism about the possibility that anything resembling moral autonomy could possibly exist. The chief reason behind this skepticism is a belief in the overriding importance of specific and concrete situations with their rewards and punishments as the prime determinants of all human behavior, including any that might be labeled moral.[22] This is an important issue. If there were no continuity and no discernible pattern to the behavior of most human individuals, there really could not exist anything resembling moral autonomy.

There is something suspect about this heavy emphasis on the force of discrete circumstances, powerful though circumstances certainly are. Common observation of the lives of people we have known for a long time usually reveals a characteristic pattern to the way they react to circumstances. Some people rise to challenges and try to overcome them. Others avoid them. Some persons are inclined to tell the truth even when it is embarrassing. Others try to lie their way through minimally difficult situations.

This commonplace knowledge is deeply embedded in language in the terms used to describe human character and personality. To be sure, common knowledge can be one of the most dangerous guides to serious thought about human beings. It is full of prejudices, false inferences, stereotypes, mystifications, and the like. Nevertheless, efforts at scientific precision for the purpose of overcoming these defects can impose their own

[22]John Finley Scott, *Internalization of Norms; A Sociological Theory of Moral Commitment,* espec. 35–38, but note 116, where the author treats moral courage as real and explicable in terms of learning theory.

blinders and limit the accuracy of our vision. I suspect that (1) the resistance to such concepts as the internalization of norms (hardly an elegant addition to the English language) and (2) the stress on circumstances as *the* determinant of human behavior may come from an over-immersion in the atmosphere of the laboratory or an unwarranted faith in the laboratory's power to account for human behavior.

In the laboratory it is possible to create artificial situations that do limit very severely the possible ways in which a subject can react. It is necessary to do exactly that in order to test a theory. The experimentally inclined psychologist wants to limit the range of possible forms of behavior in order to be able to find out what causes what: whether cruelty comes from obedience or from some other factor such as innate aggressive tendencies, as in the experiments by Stanley Milgram discussed above. But one cannot confuse the artificial and necessary simplifications of the laboratory with many situations important in real life.[23] Furthermore, in the laboratory the investigator can only observe a tiny segment of an individual's behavior and only over a short span of time. In a laboratory there is no way to observe processes of growth that last for several years. It is likewise impossible to use laboratory techniques to control and vary the conditions that influence these processes. Hence the requirements of the laboratory can obliterate continuities and similarities that exist over long periods of time. Human and other realities are not necessarily arranged in such a way as to be most easily accessible to the most precise forms of verifications. A definition of scientific truth that overstresses the method of verification can be as misleading as any mystical conception of truth, i.e., as something attained only by gulping gobs of the Infinite during moments of ineffable bliss.

At the opposite pole from this skepticism about the very possibility of moral autonomy there are psychologists who argue for the conception of an innate tendency toward moral autonomy displayed in varying degrees by all human beings. Two distinguished traditions have converged on this claim. One derives from the work of Sigmund Freud and applies his categories albeit with considerable variations and modifications. The other tradition appears in the work of Jean Piaget, and those who have endeavored to extend and refine his theories. Investigators

---

[23]Even in laboratory research the results are generally statistical. There are nearly always exceptions to the relationships discovered. If the statistical results are ambiguous, the findings are generally disregarded. It might be useful to find out more about why they are ambiguous rather than discarding them.

working in each tradition have by now developed a considerable body of empirical findings.[24] Before discussing the findings it will be helpful to set them in their theoretical context by showing the main points at which these two theories converge.

For both theories the focus of interest and inquiry is upon certain processes of human growth and psychological maturation. Though Piaget and Lawrence Kohlberg have little to say about infancy, their general position is consistent with the Freudian image of the human infant as a morsel of self-centered protoplasm. It is the end point that is strikingly similar. Both schools see human development as heading toward, though by no means always attaining, a morally autonomous character structure and personality. When and if human beings reach their full potentiality, they are capable of giving and receiving affection. They also perceive and accept moral rules not as something handed down by superior authority, whether divine or human (though in the Freudian view this form of obedience never completely disappears), but as a body of rules freely and rationally accepted as well as subject to rational criticism and change for the sake of living together in human society.[25] Both traditions stress the capacity for rational and critical choice as the basis for principled obedience and disobedience as a final stage of development, and place more emotional forms of disobedience and obedience at specific stages along the route of maturity. The Freudian tradition devotes more attention and provides more insight into the emotional acceptance and rejection of authority. Piaget and those who apply his concepts stress the more strictly cognitive aspects.

Though the final stage of moral autonomy sometimes sounds in these writings more like an ideal than a reality, writers in both traditions do on occasion adduce enough evidence to suggest a reasonable approximation to reality. For the purposes of our inquiry the route is in any case more important than the final destination. For all investigators the route is a series of stages. The number and description of the stages vary greatly according to the interests of different investigators and the considerations

[24]The convergence is most striking in Robert F. Peck *et al., The Psychology of Character Development,* a largely Freudian study (with some references to Piaget) of adolescent character development among high school students in a small American city, and Lawrence Kohlberg, "Stage and Sequence: The Cognitive-Developmental Approach to Socialization," in David A. Goslin, editor, *Handbook of Socialization Theory and Research,* 347–480, an attempt to apply Piaget's theories in a cross-cultural context.

[25]See the concept of "Rational-Altruistic Morality" in Peck *et al., Psychology of Character Development,* espec. 166, 171–174, and Kohlberg's Stage 6 of moral development, that of "Conscience," or principle orientation, in "Stage and Sequence," 376.

they wish to emphasize.[26] The common feature in the conception of stages is the thesis that each phase of growth builds on the achievements of the preceding one or is hindered by failures to complete preceding phases. By no means do all human beings complete all stages. Limited reversals and regressions are possible and the process as a whole can be arrested. Stunted or deformed growth is in fact much more common than a successful passage to maturity. Nevertheless those who work within this tradition argue that the processes of psychosexual and moral maturation do display universal characteristics. These emerge from the interaction between unfolding human needs and capacities and universal experiences derived from living in human society.

In turning to more specific themes and studies we can begin with a well-established thesis about childhood, one that also provides an especially illuminating negative instance. It is evident that a childhood environment where affection is absent and punishment brutal, frequent, and erratic can damage the human psyche to a degree liable to be beyond repair. For the person who grows up in such an environment, moral autonomy is a highly unlikely prospect. In *Children Who Hate,* Fritz Redl and David Wineman give a vivid and at times moving account of an attempt to rehabilitate a group of such children taken from a slum background. These youngsters exhibited frequent and uncontrollable bursts of hostility toward each other and toward the adults, obviously very warmhearted and understanding persons, who were doing their best to take care of the children in an experimental environment that was as mild as the children's previous backgrounds had been harsh.

These bursts of hostility arose from the circumstance that these youngsters had almost totally failed to acquire anything more than the merest semblance of control over their impulses and desires. Whenever any impulse was frustrated, the child lost its temper. Even the mildest frustration of the sort inevitable in ordinary living, such as having to pause in traffic for a red light, would set off a wave of tantrums. At the same time the children had managed to acquire a vocabulary of obscenity rich enough to do credit to an adult with wide experience of the world. They also displayed remarkable ingenuity from time to time in tormenting the grown-ups who were taking care of them.[27] It is

[26]Kohlberg, "Stage and Sequence," 377, gives a tabular listing of the stages proposed by ten studies, done from a variety of viewpoints between 1908 and 1966.

[27]Redl and Wineman, *Children Who Hate,* espec. chap. 4. Colin M. Turnbull, *The Mountain People,* reports a similar inability to induce self-restraint and regard for others, including

hardly necessary to point out that the opposite treatment of complete indulgence for all impulses and whims is neither practicable nor likely to lead to desirable consequences.

Other studies confirm and extend these findings by providing evidence on the kind of upbringing that favors moral autonomy and the kind that tends to produce what has become widely known as the authoritarian personality. The rational-altruistic character described by Robert F. Peck was the product of consistent, highly trusting, and affectionate upbringing. (Shortly we shall see some reasons for believing that this study may have overemphasized consistency.) The parents firmly and unmistakably reserved the right to make final decisions when they believed it was necessary. On the other hand, as the child grew up and became more competent in its judgments, the parents encouraged and expected it to make an increasing number of decisions on its own responsibility. These families were not, in other words, "child centered." (In families that were "child centered" the children generally failed to develop beyond a morality of simple expedience.) Punishments occurred. But they were relatively lenient and never constituted a direct or disguised expression of the parents' hostility. Where this hostility was more frequent and more freely expressed, a likely consequence was to hold back moral development to an earlier stage close to the authoritarian type of personality. The main characteristic of this type is a heavy dependence on external sources of conventional authority combined with punitive attitudes toward "weakness" and immorality.[28]

That punishment itself can be a powerful spur to learning is, in contrast with earlier received doctrines, now part of the accepted corpus of psychological doctrine, with a substantial amount of experimental support, not to mention that of persisting human common sense.[29] There are also indications that

---

their own children—left by the doorway to die of starvation—among the Iks, an African tribe whose social organization distintegrated with the loss of their hunting grounds.

[28]Peck *et al.*, *Psychology of Character Development*, 177–178; see also 170 on the conforming personality and its similarity to the authoritarian personality as described and interpreted in T. W. Adorno *et al.*, *The Authoritarian Personality*. A good recent study that presents findings similar to these is David Mark Mantell, *True Americanism: Green Berets and War Resisters*, espec. 48–49, 60, 71–73, for similarities between the family climate among war resisters and the rational-altruistic personality. Since the historical and social sources of punitive authoritarian attitudes will appear in connection with popular support for the Nazis and rightist radicalism in Chapter Twelve, there is no need for further discussion here.

[29]Justin Aronfreed, *Conduct and Conscience: The Socialization of Internalized Control over Behavior*, 60–67, 295–296.

directly punitive forms of discipline, based on direct physical and verbal attacks, are less likely than a combination of the withdrawal of affection together with explanation of the reasons for its withdrawal, to induce an autonomous control over behavior in young children. The explanation offered for this finding stresses the role of anxiety. Anxiety produced by a parent's withdrawal of affection is less dependent on the parent's continued presence or physical proximity, and is therefore more likely to become a part of the personality than is anxiety created by the parent's direct physical punishment.[30]

It is somewhat more surprising to come upon evidence to indicate that strict consistency in the application of punishment and rewards may not be at all the most effective way of teaching any particular pattern of behavior. A response is more likely to become firmly established, to become what we would call part of the personality, if the rewards for this kind of behavior are somewhat erratic.[31] Upon reflection it is not too difficult to discern how what a layman would call firmness of character might arise from intermittent rather than consistent reward. To put the matter simply, the former process is biologically more adaptive. An animal that seeks water from a water hole that occasionally runs dry receives intermittent and erratic rewards for its behavior. If it ceased to visit this particular water hole after one or two occasions when the hole had run dry, its behavior would clearly be maladaptive. It is also worth noticing, however, that human beings apparently exhibit a strong preference for having the rewards and punishments under their own quite clear control.[32]

The role of sheer intelligence in moral autonomy receives strong emphasis in the work of psychologists of very different persuasions. Aronfreed attributes moral capacity in large measure to the human child's striking cognitive capacities.[33] There are a number of studies that purport to demonstrate the role of "sheer cognitive power in the operation of conscience."[34]

Kohlberg, who has extended Piaget's conception of stages of moral development by cross-cultural investigations, makes some particularly thought-provoking claims on this point. In all the nations studied, he claims, there are social-class differences in the direction of a higher level of moral development for the

[30]Aronfreed, *Conduct and Conscience*, 316–317.

[31]See Aronfreed, *Conduct and Conscience*, 22–26.

[32]Aronfreed, *Conduct and Conscience*, 36.

[33]Aronfreed, *Conduct and Conscience*, 66–67.

[34]Aronfreed, *Conduct and Conscience*, 265–266.

middle class. In *each* class, the older and more intelligent children have moved further along the general line of moral development. "If the 'retardation' of the lower-class child were to be explained as due to a different adult sub-cultural value system, the older and brighter lower-class children would have to be more 'retarded' than the younger and duller lower-class children, since they should have learned the lower-class value system better."[35] That is not what the findings show.

The whole procedure of using Piaget's categories in cross-cultural testing has been the object of severe criticism in recent times.[36] On both technical and general philosophical grounds the critics conclude that the procedure manifests an inherent bias in favor of modern Western conceptions of rationality that unjustly minimize the capacity for rationality among non-Western peoples and the lower classes in our own society. The technical criticisms are in my judgment well founded. Essentially they hold that testing situations are very frequently artificial from the standpoint of the persons tested and fail to elicit or record their true capacities. Thus a black adolescent may seem inarticulate and incapable of logical thought in a testing situation. Observed in his natural surroundings, the same young black person may display an unusual capacity for manipulating language and a disconcerting logical flair for puncturing white hypocrisies.[37] I do not find this aspect of the criticism convincing. Human cultures do vary greatly in their emphases and attainments. It is one thing to deny that non-Western cultures are inferior in the sense that they never can match or even supercede the attainments loosely known as Western rationality. It is quite another thing to deny that the differences exist, or to deny that they are very important. Though cross-cultural research in the tradition of Piaget may have overemphasized differences between modern and traditional modes of thought as well as class differences, and failed to do justice to ways in which these distinctions may change, it does draw attention to currently existing differences in the attainment of moral autonomy that are very important indeed. Combined with other theories, it helps to explain how these differences come about and how they may change in the future.

[35]Kohlberg, "Stage and Sequence," 375.

[36]Patricia Teague Ashton, "Cross-Cultural Piagetian Research: An Experimental Perspective," 475–506, presents a useful summary of the literature.

[37]On the limits of testing and a powerful critique of the concept of cultural deficit that nevertheless recognizes cultural differences see Michael Cole and Jerome S. Bruner, "Cultural Differences and Inferences about Psychological Processes," 867–876.

4. Freudian interpretations

If the supposedly "hard" evidence of the laboratory and test turns out upon critical examination to be at times rather spongy, we may be less ready to dismiss out of hand the reconstructed life history of Freudian tradition as a way of understanding psychosexual development and its bearing upon moral and even political judgment. According to psychoanalytic theory the most important influences on the human personality occur in the first few years of life. This is also the period about which it is most difficult to get reliable evidence. Just to make matters even more uncertain, one of the few comparative studies of major historical figures who have turned against the prevailing system of authority reports that early childhood experiences were sufficiently variable to indicate severe limitations on the explanatory power of these variables.[38]

If this were solid evidence, it would explode the central tenets of Freudian theory and cast severe doubt on the whole conception of a revolutionary personality. But it is very far from solid evidence and can yield more than one interpretation, as we shall see shortly. Hence it is better strategy to retain the notion of a revolutionary personality in the sense of a strong inclination to resist authority. Very likely the inclination displays a variety of forms and has a variety of causes. Within this variety, on the other hand, there are also likely to be some significant common features. Let us therefore put this query to the empirical literature derived from Freud: what are the important ingredients in the type of human personality capable of resisting oppressive authority?[39]

One ingredient that makes excellent sense on general grounds is self-confidence, or to use the neo-Freudian term, basic trust. To be daring and courageous, to be willing to stand up to oppressive social pressures, the individual must have a strong sense of security or faith in *some* aspect of his or her social

[38]E. Victor Wolfenstein, *The Revolutionary Personality: Lenin, Trotsky, Gandhi,* 303–304, reports the absence of clear patterns for the oral and anal phases of his three subjects.

[39]One study with a very promising title, Peter Seidmann, *Der Mensch im Widerstand,* was mainly a disappointment. For me the historical essays on Socrates, Erasmus, and the resistance of the White Rose group to Hitler were unenlightening, while the theoretical portions on the concept of resistance seemed no more than pretentious word juggling. On the other hand, one section (159–171), where the author draws on his clinical experience to show how and why individuals may prefer to put up with intolerable situations rather than risk the familiarity and slight gains of their neurotic adaptation, is very rich and suggestive.

surroundings. Freudians tell us that the model experience in the development of such confidence is the mother's feeding and treatment of the infant during what is known as the oral phase of human development. An affectionate and reasonably dependable gratification of the helpless infant's needs is supposedly of crucial importance in developing this basic trust. Apparently the experience need not take the form of total gratification, and the element of affection appears to be more important than merely mechanical meeting of biological needs.[40]

There is also evidence to show the possibility of considerable variation on this score. Lenin, whose credentials as a revolutionary are beyond dispute, had a quite suspicious and distrustful personality. Often, though by no means always, this suspicion was a politically useful trait.[41] Certainly this suspicion is a common enough revolutionary trait, as is a supreme self-confidence. That the experiences of early infancy are likely to be powerful forces in the development of such qualities seems highly probable. If specific Freudian applications are open to question, the theory nevertheless directs our attention to significant variables.

The second quality, which develops later, we can call orderliness and self-discipline, including the ability to control instincts and impulses in pursuit of larger and more distant goals. Again according to Freudian theory, the child acquires some of the basic elements for these qualities through the discipline of toilet training in the anal phase. Overly strict toilet training supposedly creates a cramped, miserly, and pedantic form of character. In Erikson's formulation, to "hold on can become a destructive and cruel retaining or restraining" in later life, while its opposite can be either an equally inimical release of destructive forces or a relaxed willingness to "let pass," "let it be."[42] Some form of training in between these two extremes is likely to yield an effective type of self-control. The acquisition of control over impulses continues beyond the anal phase. The process culminates in the child's incorporation into his or her own personality of standards taken from the parents or other adult models.

[40]Erik H. Erikson, *Childhood and Society*, 219–222.

[41]Wolfenstein, *Revolutionary Personality*, 303. Wolfenstein, who includes no Russian sources in his bibliography, does not mention Lenin's confidence in police spies. According to Bertram D. Wolfe, *Three Who Made a Revolution,* 535, a book that is listed in Wolfenstein's bibliography, there were at least three such spies close to Lenin in addition to the most famous one, Roman Malinovsky. Perhaps Lenin had more than his share of basic trust after all.

[42]*Childhood and Society,* 222.

Here we reach the third and most important ingredient in the type of personality under investigation. "Conscience" is the general layman's term, "superego" the Freudian term. The problem at hand, however, is not to explain the superego in general, but a particular type of superego. We need to understand the development of moral standards that condemn significant aspects of currently accepted social practice.[43] Persons with these standards not only deny the legitimacy of prevailing custom; they devote a large part of their lives and energy to active resistance and attempts at changing existing practices.

How exactly does all this come to pass? From infancy onward, we are told, social limitations on the child's wilfulness and demands to satisfy its own desires inevitably create doubt about the justice and benevolence governing relationships among growing and grown-up human beings.[44] Though this conflict takes on special forms and supposedly becomes especially intense during the phase of the Oedipal conflict, it is by no means confined to that. Evidence from the biographies of revolutionary leaders and other data strongly suggest that relationships with *both* parents continue to form and influence the human personality well into young adulthood. The factors that presumably impel a child toward resistance and some forms of social criticism are these. First of all, the ambivalence of the Oedipal conflict is unusually intense. Secondly, the child reaches young adulthood without a satisfactory resolution of this conflict. If other conditions are favorable, that is, if the social and historical opportunities exist, the individual is likely to try to escape the burdens of Oedipal guilt and ambivalence by carrying the conflict with authority into

---

[43]It is worth noticing that according to the Freudian schema resistance to social restraints can come from three sources in the human psyche with quite different consequences: (1) from the id an elemental rebellion against any form of constraint combined with an imperious demand for immediate gratification; (2) from the ego a cool, realistic, and rational critical assessment; (3) from the superego a passionately uncompromising moral condemnation. Presumably it should be possible to formulate the type of family situation and socialization process that leads to an emphasis on each of these three.

[44]Cf. Erik H. Erikson, *Young Man Luther*, 255. In what follows I have tried to extract and synthesize those theoretical points that seem to me applicable to lower-class people from this book and also from Wolfenstein, *Revolutionary Personality*, as well as two books by Kenneth Keniston, *The Uncommitted* and *Young Radicals*. Appendix B (306–310) of *Young Radicals* is very helpful in contrasting the etiology of alienation and commitment. I have also drawn on Richard H. Solomon, *Mao's Revolution and the Chinese Political Culture*, which has a great deal of information about how a socialization process can simultaneously implant moral justifications for authority, strong inclinations to resist this authority, and fears of the possible dangers in such inclinations. The study by Robert Coles of young blacks and whites under the stress of the civil-rights movement, *Children of Crisis*, is especially relevant but requires separate discussion.

the social and political realm.[45] At this point there are several possibilities. The young adult may reject the father's mode of life because it seems to represent too many compromises, but try to put the father's ideals into practice.[46] Or the father may be rejected in favor of some other adult model. Finally, if there is no strong paternal model against which to push, a situation some claim to be increasingly characteristic of modern Western society, the consequence is likely to be mere disorientation and inability to form any commitment.[47]

The luxury of an identity crisis at this stage of the life cycle is not generally available to the poor and oppressed, or just plain poor. For them there is little or no choice about their identity. If their parents have not taught them their place in the social order from infancy on, their identity can suddenly overtake them in a rush. This is a real crisis instead of the pseudo-crisis of the modern, overprotected child of advanced middle-class intellectuals. A brusque parental command to give up reading and dreams of grandeur in order to get a job in the neighborhood workshop or factory can shatter a child's hopes for the future. It is an event frequently reported in the autobiographies of nineteenth-century German·workers. Or a child can suddenly become aware of the parents' status through a snub or deprivation whose meaning illuminates social reality like a flash of lightning.

In the study by Robert Coles of the reactions of young Americans, black and white, to the burgeoning civil-rights movement of the early 1960s we fortunately possess a considerable body of information on how young people, mostly from very poor backgrounds, actually do acquire the courage to stand up to oppressive authority. Partly due to his training as a child psychiatrist, Coles asked precisely the questions most relevant to this part of our inquiry. He is also a gifted and cautious observer, whose reluctance to give flat answers to these questions deserves respectful attention.

The answers that he does give often fall outside the Freudian tradition. At times they are at least implicitly critical of it. From my reading the main message that the book conveys is this: a

[45]Wolfenstein, *Revolutionary Personality*, 306–308.

[46]The attempt to put the father's ideals into practice can only be a motive force for change where these ideals are in significant respects critical of the established order. It is, for example, difficult to see how such ideals could have a subversive impact under the good-servant ethic of the Hindu Untouchables.

[47]Cf. Keniston, *The Uncommitted* and Alexander Mitscherlich, *Auf dem Weg zur vaterlosen Gesellschaft*, 420–421.

remarkable number of blacks grow up with very strong characters, quite able to stand up to oppressive authority, despite theoretically most unfavorable and indeed damaging conditions in childhood. Toward the end of his book he raises the question "Why do not all Negro men become schizophrenic?" Without knowing the cause or causes of schizophrenia, he continues, there is reason to believe that consistently disorganized, brittle, tense, fearful parents in some ways influence its development in their children. "It does not seem fatuous, therefore, to inquire why *all* Negro men are not schizophrenic." The answer is that they are not, even if many live impoverished lives in a social and cultural climate that commonly rejects them, and in families frequently unstable and split apart. Somehow millions of Negroes survive these special strains, "if not handily, at least with no crippling mental disease." To be sure many are tired, apathetic, and listless, though even these show a surprising capacity to come to life when exposed to the currents of social and political change.[48] Still others whom he has described earlier show a remarkable resilience that deserves the appellation "healthy" by any definition. Where then does this courage and resilience come from? What experiences help to produce and sustain it?

In the first place, black people have not had to go through any complicated emotional and intellectual experiences in order to learn that they were unhappy and why. The white man thrust the blacks' identity on them in brutal and direct fashion by dragging them from their homeland and making slaves of them. They did not have to become angry; they had to learn how to contain their anger.[49] Practically from babyhood onward black children learn that life will be hard in the white man's world, that they have to be ready to withstand this hardship. This training and background helps to explain how a six-year-old black girl can walk past a threatening mob of whites who scream obscenities and threats of poisoning day after day as she enters a newly desegregated school.[50] If the family had prepared the child in a general way for harsh and degrading experiences at white hands, the older family members also gave the children warm support and understanding when they actually faced them.

Though the elements of cultural preparation and social sup-

---

[48]Coles, *Children of Crisis*, 346–347. Italics in original.

[49]Cf. Coles, *Children of Crisis*, 322.

[50]Coles, *Children of Crisis*, chap. 4. Threats of poisoning did temporarily disturb one child's eating habits.

port through the family are clearly important, it is also quite apparent they are far from the whole story. The parents had no real idea about what would happen. (Probably nobody knew for sure. The uncertainty of all actors is one of the most significant and neglected aspects of historical crises, great and small.) They had no ideological zeal and definitely no intention of making televised martyrs out of their children. They thought desegregation meant that it was "for all the colored" to go to school, and had no inkling their child might have to face the mob alone. If they had known, as they told Coles after he had won their trust, they would never have signed up. In other words, circumstances catapulted the child into an heroic role. Faced suddenly with this obligation all sorts of black children with different personalities and backgrounds just did the best they could. Most evidently succeeded.

In the case of the young civil-rights activists, black and white, there was a much larger element of free choice in the adoption of this role. A large variety of experiences and feelings influenced the individual to choose this role. Among black youngsters a limited degree of success within the white-dominated system could lead to guilty rejection of one's own privileges, especially when they were tied to the father's compromises. The way out was joining the movement.[51] In other cases too there was a conflict between parental warnings not to get involved and other models urging positive action, all played out against the background of a pervasive sense of injustice. The rejected model might be a brother who could not stand the strain and took to drink and drugs, as was true of a young man who came "down from Chicago."[52] In this example the positive model was a moderately militant teacher, whom the young man respected. In another case a young Alabama farm boy claims to have been quite satisfied with life until his path accidentally crossed that of a very different model, a militant young preacher with the local reputation of being "funny in the head," who was brutally murdered by the local police. The murder acted as a catalyst to bring the young farm boy into the movement.[53] In the case of these young militants it may well be correct to speak of an identity crisis resolved through political commitment. The part played by psychosexual maturation is not clear, though it may well be there. On that aspect Coles provides very little data. In any case it

[51]Coles, *Children of Crisis*, 174–187, espec. 178.
[52]Coles, *Children of Crisis*, 217.
[53]Coles, *Children of Crisis*, 203–209.

is reasonably clear that the processes of psychosexual maturation could not by themselves yield a specific political commitment. They can very likely favor such an outcome. But the outcome requires specific models and an historical situation favorable to that choice.

The lives of these young activists were extremely demanding, often very dangerous, frequently frustrating and discouraging due to the fear and apathy of those whom they were trying to help, and on occasion very rewarding. To sustain this commitment required both moral courage and resourcefulness of a very high order. So far as Coles could see, no one kind of young person typified the activist. Nor did he feel able to explain the difference between those who were able to stand up to the strain and those who collapsed.[54] But he does give some clues worth pursuing. Contrary to the evidence reported from the concentration camps, Coles reports that the most ideological were the least successful in coping with the strain. The difference might possibly be connected with the existence of a greater range of choices in the more open situation, compared with concentration camps. Or it might have something to do with the emotional yet uncertain commitment of youth as compared with older people. In both the concentration camps and this type of situation, on the other hand, the more ideological displayed a tendency to keep out of trouble themselves and persuade others to make the necessary physical sacrifices.

The author gives us somewhat more detail on the psychological mechanisms for coping with danger successfully. They amount to paying cool and careful attention to the details of the business at hand, and avoiding any tendency to dwell on the general aspects of danger. The fact that danger was shared, that social support existed, was obviously helpful. In order to *make* this helpful, on the other hand, people avoided talking about it except for sharing odds and ends of practical advice. "We try to keep the talk oriented to real problems and what we can do to solve them. There's plenty to keep us busy, without hitting at one another with 'observations,' and as a result falling apart."[55] This, I suggest, is a general and even pan-human collective response to danger, one to be found among sailors working furiously to "save the ship" in a storm, mountaineers concentrating on making their way down a dangerous slope, knots of soldiers under fire on the battlefield. Heroism consists of forgetting about heroics.

---

[54]Coles, *Children of Crisis*, 224, 226.

[55]Coles, *Children of Crisis*, 226–229.

If Freud, to my knowledge, never said this specifically, it is still consistent with the tone of sour sobriety that colors so much of his work.

If the burden of the preceding chapter on the sources of human submission seemed depressing, the evidence in this one serves to correct that impression. There are as many identifiable mechanisms on the one side as upon the other. A very small degree of social support, as we have just seen, is sufficient to shatter the mystique of oppression and deception and permit a critical response to surface. Furthermore, modern industrial society does not, according to this evidence, have the brainwashing effect that some critics have attributed to it.

At the level of individual tendencies and responses there are evidently grounds for belief in an innate human tendency toward moral autonomy, manifesting itself through the processes of psychosexual maturation. Variations in innate intelligence will evidently limit how far the process can go in any given individual. Differences in upbringing can have powerful effects in releasing and inhibiting this potential. The acquisition of self-confidence from affectionate maternal care, we are told, plays a decisive role. Parents and their surrogates can teach most effectively through the withdrawal of affection, though the occasional resort to stronger punishment is not something to fear. It is important to give the child responsibility as soon as it is capable of accepting it. The child in turn acquires both self-discipline and standards of judgment through resistance to loved parents. Above and beyond all this the most encouraging evidence is that which shows how moral courage can take root and flourish despite theoretically harsh and unfavorable conditions.

PART TWO

An Historical Perspective

German workers 1848–1920

CHAPTER FOUR

Prologue

Up to this point the analysis has been deliberately ahistorical. It has tried to uncover recurring elements in the diversity of moral codes through an interpretation of the interplay between innate human nature and the universal problems that derive from the necessities of living together in human society. In a similar manner it has attempted to isolate the more important social and psychological mechanisms that produce both submission to socially imposed hardships and resistance to such pains. Now we are ready to try to understand the historical dimension of these variations.

But I do not intend to bind the historical investigation to these issues or to use history merely to test hypotheses. Social history has its own patterns of causation and its own messages that can be discerned only through deciphering these patterns. To discover the connections and to interpret their meaning, in the sense of what they convey about changing conceptions of injustice and the causes of these changes, will be our central task in Part Two of this book.

In what follows I shall try to show how these processes worked themselves out among the German workers during the transition from the artisans' way of life to that of advanced industrial capitalism. For reasons already mentioned, the treatment will concentrate so far as the data permit on the lives and feelings of ordinary workers and neglect the history of organized political and economic movements except insofar as they reveal what was happening to such people. It will also not be in any sense a complete history. Instead, the interpretation will concentrate on three periods of important crisis. This is justifiable, because in the life of societies, as well as of individuals, crises illuminate the essentials of so-called normal behavior, especially when one looks for both the antecedents and consequences of the crises.

The first crisis is the Revolution of 1848, which reveals the contest between precapitalist and capitalist ways of thinking and acting. The second is the outbreak of the First World War, an event that brings into sharp relief the forces favoring and opposing the integration of the industrial workers into the specific variant of advanced capitalism that had grown up in Germany by 1914. The third crisis is the revolutionary one after the First World War. At this point a portion of the German workers gained political power. But the policies their leaders adopted, along with other factors, drove a substantial segment of the industrial workers into open revolt, the closest approximation to a proletarian revolution that has yet occurred in an advanced industrial country. For the crises before and after the First World War I have provided separate chapters on social trends in the Ruhr, Germany's industrial heartland. Without some understanding of what was taking place there, it is impossible to make any assessment at all of German working-class life and politics.

For a backdrop to the changing life of German workers in the nineteenth and early twentieth centuries I would like to have the reader step backward with me into the late eighteenth century and make the acquaintance of Ulrich Bräker, author of one of the earliest poor man's autobiographies that I know. Born in the tiny Swiss Alpine village of Wattwil in 1735, Bräker started life as a peasant and became by turn a forced recruit in the armies of Frederick the Great, a laborer in a saltpeter works, and a weaver under the putting-out system. Thus he underwent experiences common to many other central European rural folk in the very early stages of the industrial revolution. His experiences and reactions were by no means necessarily typical. In fact we do not really know what typical could mean in this connection. Nevertheless his reactions are especially important for the purposes of this inquiry because they show how felt hardship in this particular historical and social context did *not* generate any hostile or critical reaction to the social order. From the way Bräker reacted to hardship and suffering it is possible to infer some of the things that would have to happen to people in the lower classes before they would even want to react in a hostile fashion to the world around them.

It is not necessary to recount all the adventures, natural and unnatural, of "the Poor Man of Tockenburg," as Bräker became known to posterity.[1] Instead I will draw attention to some of his own explanations for his various misfortunes and his own responses to them. Despite all the misfortunes and injustices that he encountered and recognized as injustices, nothing remotely like the thought of revolution seems to have entered his shrewd and almost incurably cheerful as well as deeply religious Swiss head.

Close to the beginning of the story of his life, Bräker asserts with great pride that among his ancestors and relatives, despite severe poverty, there were no thieves, criminals, blasphemers, debauchees, slanderers, cursers—or other such models of misbehavior for which his repertoire of epithets is indeed extensive. Bräker was no carrier of a counter-culture or counter-morality. There is scarcely a hint of the picaresque in his life history, though during his forced service in the army of Frederick the Great he must have been thrown with very picaresque characters. Perhaps this contact is part of the reason for his vehement rejection of what he felt was the immoral riffraff beneath him. (The term proletariat would not gain currency for a long time to come.) Quite clearly he was afraid, and with good reason, of falling into the riffraff, the rejects of mid-eighteenth-century society. He perceived this prospect as a moral disaster as much as a material one.[2]

Though heavily intertwined with the vagaries of nature, the main factor that determined whether such a disaster would occur was the working of the market through debt. This situation prevailed even in this remote Alpine hamlet. As a boy, suffering for Ulrich Bräker took the form of frequent hunger and unremitting hard physical labor on his father's farmland, which in winter was covered with deep snow. But the social aspect of misfortune was there too. His father had to sell his property

---

[1] His autobiography was originally published in Zürich in 1789 as *Lebensgeschichte und natürliche Ebentheuer des Armen Mannes im Tockenburg* (Life History and Natural Adventures of the Poor Man of Tockenburg), shortened in later editions to *Der Arme Mann im Tockenburg*. The Reclam edition published in Stuttgart, 1965, is the one I have used. For further background material consult Rudolf Stadelmann and Wolfram Fischer, *Die Bildungswelt des deutschen Handwerkers um 1800*, espec. 25–26, 133–136. Bräker's experiences differed from those in more thickly populated areas near Zürich described by Rudolf Braun, *Industrialisierung und Volksleben: Die Veränderungen der Lebensformen in einem ländlichen Industriegebiet vor 1800*.

[2] As will appear in the next chapter, this fear was quite common among nineteenth-century guild members in Germany. But in Bräker's case it did not stem from experience in a guild, for there were none in Wattwil. The fear of being cast downward was quite widespread in any case. It had a strong religious tinge and probably some religious origins.

for debts and move to another location. For the boy the social and physical aspects were scarcely distinguishable, as was indeed the case. Illness in the family, which meant an unproductive mouth to feed, or among the livestock, or a bad crop due to poor weather could spell ruin. The only response that promised a way out was to work even harder and to tighten belts even farther.

The boy Ulrich Bräker somehow learned this lesson quite early. At one point he persuaded his father to let him have a small piece of land, to see what he could do on his own. Good-naturedly his father let him try. Though the experiment failed, it was an indication of the youngster's independent spirit that was to bring him through severe trials in adult life. His marriage represented a carefully planned economic strategy and was successful in those terms if not in those of human companionship, a cost-benefit calculation he foresaw clearly and whose consequences he accepted cheerfully enough.

As Bräker matured, the social aspects and causes of good and bad fortune became much more salient, though the natural and physical causes by no means disappeared. There is nothing to be gained in recording all the ups and downs of his economic career. Only a few general points deserve our attention. One is the general attitude toward debt prevailing in this community. Bräker has some very vivid accounts of the way neighbors kept themselves informed about each other's debts while hypocritically pretending to be each other's best friends. Bräker felt badly indeed when he tried to collect debts owed to him and learned that his debtors had hidden their valuable possessions. The Wattwiler were evidently linked to each other through a network of debts about which it was necessary to remain informed. Hence the perpetual gossip about the economic condition of other inhabitants.

Debtors and creditors were essentially alike. Indeed, the absence of any figures of authority or persons of higher or lower status in this community is quite striking. Given the intermingling of physical and social causes of misfortune, the sheer physical necessity for very hard work to survive, and finally the very indirect way in which outsiders extracted a limited economic surplus from the community—a matter to be discussed in a moment—it is scarcely surprising that there is no odor of revolt or subversion in Ulrich Bräker's babbling and philosophizing. If he had been born a peasant in a fertile rice-raising part of the world subject to rapacious tax gatherers or landlords, this enterprising and rather prickly individual might have had a very different view of life.

As matters turned out, the intrusion of market relationships was eventually a blessing for Ulrich Bräker. More accurately, he was able to make them into a blessing. Home weaving under the putting-out system, which he took up in place of his job in the saltpeter works because the labor there was too dirty and arduous, provided a crucial source of extra income that enabled him to get married and set up an independent household. At other points in his career, the "Grain Jews" (*Kornjuden*) along with bad weather drove up food prices, as Bräker saw it, and he encountered severe debts and credit problems of his own. On these occasions his fantasies turned to escape, to a world that had nothing to do with cotton textiles. Then in 1779 he took on the job of weaving cotton fabrics for a *Fabrikant* in Glarus, through which his economic situation cleared up rapidly. But in 1785 a French edict forbidding the importation of cotton fabrics dealt him another hard blow. By this time, four years before the outbreak of the French Revolution, the "world economy" of advancing capitalism had reached the isolated, snow-ridden hamlet of Wattwil and changed the life of Ulrich Bräker—as well as thousands like him.

Ulrich Bräker did not spend all of his life in the relatively egalitarian hamlet of Wattwil. During his essentially involuntary visit to the outside world he encountered both the harsher as well as the gentler patriarchal forms of eighteenth-century authority. How he coped with these is both sociologically and psychologically revealing. The basic attitude toward authority acquired through his relationship with his parents, and especially his father, appears to have been one of warmth and considerable confidence, tinged with a touch of rebellious emulation, as shown by the episode of the plot of land. He also had no experience of the ways of the larger world.

His departure from home as a youth took place very reluctantly. It came about because his family was in dire economic straits. Some fellow villagers talked Bräker's father into sending his nearly grown-up son along with them on a journey where they would show him how to make his fortune. Actually they were planning to sell him to a recruiting agent for Frederick the Great's armies. That was Bräker's first disappointment while away from home. But the blow was not too serious, at least not at first. The recruiting agent, a nobleman—or one who lived like a nobleman—took a liking to Bräker, and kept him to be his lackey, a job complete with uniform, lodging, and food. Bräker rather enjoyed this situation. He was treated fairly well and had an opportunity to learn the pleasures of upper-class city life as refracted in that of a lackey. These pleasures he claims to have rejected by and large, which might even be partly true, and is in any case of no consequence, because the semi-idyll soon came to an end. Pressed to deliver the goods in the form of live recruits, Bräker's master broke his promise to retain Bräker and turned him over to army officials. They soon put him under military discipline and started to train him as a soldier.

For Bräker the experience was traumatic: the simple peasant lad who had never completely overcome his homesickness, even in the pleasant life of a lackey, now found himself in a strange garrison and subject to the brutal discipline of the Prussian army. On first realizing his fate his immediate response was to appeal to authority. He thought he could appeal first to the King of Prussia, then to the major, his superior officer. Fantastic as the idea may seem to us, it makes some sort of sense. Escape at that moment did not seem possible. What experience he had had with authority so far had generally been favorable. Under these circumstances appeal to some presumably shared standard of justice and morality emerges as a natural if mistaken response, one that has occurred many times before and after the days of Ulrich Bräker. When he finally learned that his fate was set, he merely concluded that such was the way of the world. "The bigwigs fix up such soups," he reported, saying to himself, "and the small fry have to eat them."

Shortly afterward he managed to locate and have an interview with the "nobleman" who had sold him into the Prussian service. His reaction then was ambivalence personified. He could not bring himself to express his anger at a figure of authority who had betrayed him but had also treated him with paternal kindness. In miniature he revealed the classic block against a revolutionary response.

While his experiences as a soldier are most interesting, we must pass over them quickly. Naturally he had not the faintest notion of what the war was about, nor any reason to learn and care. The discipline was harsh; camp life and battles he describes vividly from a standpoint that rarely finds its way into the historical record. His one concern was to find a chance to desert and return home to his beloved Wattwil. In the course of the battle of Lobositz on October 1, 1756, he succeeded in deserting the troops. From there he somehow was able to find his way on foot to Prague and from Prague home to his native hamlet in the company of some other Swiss. All this he did on foot, his only mode of travel, and in the uniform of a Prussian soldier. There is nothing in his account to suggest that this must have been a rather remarkable feat. The tale serves as a vivid reminder of what has been after all throughout the centuries one of the common man's most frequent and effective responses to oppression: flight.

At this point we may take leave of Ulrich Bräker by asking what would have to happen in order to turn an Ulrich Bräker into a revolutionary. First, the idea of doing it would have to be available, that is, be part of the cultural repertoire of ready responses with which he was familiar. Secondly, the causes of his misery would have to appear as concrete human beings rather than as aspects of a more or less inevitable order of things, as did the mixture of market forces and physical nature that Ulrich Bräker confronted. In order to act, two more conditions would have been necessary. First, the prospect of flight and escape to a traditional form of security would have to appear impossible. There would also have to be experiences along the way enabling him to overcome his affectionate dependence on paternalistic authority, or creating in him a very different attitude toward figures of authority.

No doubt there are other factors that could be uncovered by further analysis of his case and others. But this will do for the present. Even if he happened to be a German Swiss, Ulrich Bräker was a historical ancestor of many a poor German townsman of 1848. By that time, several of the necessary conditions for revolt had put in an appearance in the course of the years that had passed since Bräker had deserted from the colors of the Prussian King. By 1848 a great deal of human misery seemed to German townsmen to have identifiable human causes, bitter though the arguments might become as to what the causes actually were and what should be done about them.

CHAPTER FIVE

German workers in the revolution of 1848

1. The conflict of principles in modernization

The making of modern industrial capitalist society in Western Europe generated changes in the implicit social contract that were the outcome of a conflict between the carriers and spokesmen of old and new principles of social inequality. This conflict was one between principles of social ranking based on birth and ascription and principles based on certain forms of merit and achievement.

In Western and Central Europe the main feature of the old regime was the system of orders or estates (*états* in French, *Stände* in German). Like most systems of social inequality its traits were clearest at the apex of the social pyramid, composed of two of the main estates: the clergy and the nobility. The third estate of commoners was a residual category trailing down in an indefinite fashion toward a vague line that separated respectable members of society from those who were not respectable. In German-speaking parts of Europe, however, the organization of society into distinct orders appears to have reached further downward. In addition to the familiar tripartite and conventional distinction among the three orders of those who fight, those who teach, and those who provide sustenance for these two (*Wehrstand, Lehrstand, Nährstand*), German writings frequently refer to the *Bürgerstand* or full citizens of the towns, the *Bauernstand* or peasants, and in more recent times an *Arbeiterstand* or order of workers.

Even in theory the European system of estates was not a

purely ascriptive one, where each individual was born into a group whose male members performed a social function. One was not born a member of the clergy; one became a member, even though in practice access to the higher ranks was for the most part limited to persons from noble families. But the emphasis was heavily ascriptive in the sense that an individual was born into a social group whose male members were expected to perform some functions and not others. Though these functions were not equal in rank or general esteem[1] each social function was deemed indispensable to the body politic and received its own distinctive form of honor and esteem. That appears to have been especially true of German areas, where the sources speak frequently of status-honor (*Standesehre*). Here "honor" meant pride in fulfilling one's specific social function even if a relatively lowly one. Honor also implied a proper style of life, especially in matters of housing, dress, food, manners, but also ethics and general social character. Indeed the purpose of economic production, whose laborious aspects were the task of the lower orders, was to supply the goods and services necessary to support each style of life and the form of social honor it manifested to society as a whole.

Though some mobility existed, strong sanctions were in effect to keep the individual from trying to perform social functions appropriate to a different order. Such an attempt was a violation of status honor. There was as much pressure to prevent downward as upward movement, the sanctions coming from the members of one's own estate as well as from superiors and inferiors. The adoption of an inferior's occupation by an individual from a higher order was both a form of unfair competition and a violation of the order of nature. Indeed, the two were hardly distinguishable notions among large segments of the German population as late as the middle of the nineteenth century. Such sentiments were part of the popular current of moral outrage that exploded in the revolutions of 1848.

A full-blown system of estates or orders is only compatible with a quite static economy. This is true even though all societies, including both capitalist and socialist variants of industrialism, display very visible tendencies to move in the direction of a system of estates. These tendencies derive from the efforts of organized groups to slow down the rate of social changes and alter their forms, in order to ward off threats to their position in

---

[1]The extent to which the rank order received general acceptance in practice among the population is a difficult problem over which we need not linger.

the social order. Dynamic economies, on the other hand, continually generate new occupations and new forms of wealth that upset the prevailing arrangements of social ranking. The bureaucracies of royal absolutism, that uneasy compromise[2] between medieval and modern principles of social and political organization, provided a considerable impetus in this direction, only to succumb in turn to revolutionary movements. In Germany royal absolutism did not give way until the debacle of 1918. Even then its defeat was incomplete since the bureaucratic apparatus survived with very little change on into the Weimar Republic. Though royal absolutism made an important contribution to the victory of the new principles, the main impulse came from the commercial and manufacturing classes and more specifically their intellectual spokesmen.[3] In the eighteenth and early nineteenth centuries "bourgeois" moral outrage derived from (1) pride in the exercise of relatively new social functions; (2) contempt for older social functions such as war, dynastic politics, and the whole "parasitic" aristocratic way of life, a pair of attitudes that appears clearly in Adam Smith; (3) anger at obstacles to the performance of new functions and the alleged failure to reward them sufficiently, an attitude more prevalent in France of the old regime. The individual, clothed with the rights of man and freed from all "artificial" fetters of status inherited from the past, was to compete with other individuals and seek the fortune he deserved. Social position remained essentially a matter for competing males, from whom females derived their status by marriage and descent. In a word, merit was to determine status, not birth.

If not without antecedents, this new morality, the new basis for social order, was in its scale and method of application a genuine historical novelty. It was the consequence of a new capacity for meeting the needs and problems of living in human society and would in turn generate new and anguishing imperatives of its own that are very much with us today.

---

[2]For a most illuminating study of the Prussian variant and its efforts to reconcile the conflicting principles of merit and inherited status, see Hans Rosenberg, *Bureaucracy, Aristocracy, and Autocracy, 1660–1815.*

[3]By the time the manufacturing classes had appeared on the scene in full strength it is anachronistic to refer to this impulse as bourgeois. Originally bourgeois referred to the elite of the medieval commercial cities. Though it would help to have a new word for their historical descendants, I shall not try to invent one.

2. Strains on the guilds

By 1848 in response to these changes and challenges a considerable segment of the lower orders in German towns became politically articulate for the first time. To understand the ways in which they perceived themselves and the society around them, and how they diagnosed their own misfortunes, it is necessary to understand what had been happening to the social arrangements under which they were living. At that time by far the most important ones in the daily life of townsmen and city folk were the guilds.

The guilds were part of the old order of estates. Though under attack from advanced royal bureaucrats and of course right-thinking spokesmen for the commercial and manufacturing classes—then a tiny, fragmented, but growing sector of German society—the guilds were very much alive in 1848. Indeed, one ironic consequence of the Revolution of 1848 was a not so temporary and perhaps not altogether "artificial" prolongation of their existence.

The guilds amounted to a series of local monopolies. In each city or town all the members of the same trade, such as butchers, bakers, tailors, shoemakers, belonged to the same guild. Each master was expected to have a limited but sufficient number of customers. Actually matters seldom worked out that way, since a number of customers sufficient from the master's standpoint might not be the number that could receive goods and services adequate from their standpoint as consumers. There was therefore a considerable degree of potential conflict built into the system of guilds from the start. On the other hand, a substantial proportion of any one master's customers would also be guild members, a situation that promoted rules of live and let live or solidarity for the benefit of all.

Two rules applied with particular force. No guild member could trespass on the economic territory, functions, or prerogatives of another guild member. No person who was not a guild member could exercise within the limits of the town any economic function that belonged to a guild. Such actions aroused the most vehement moral indignation among guild members. Their perpetrators were known by a variety of picturesque epithets: *Bönhasen* (literally, ground rabbit, interloper, bungler), *Pfuscher* (bunglers), *Störer* (intruders, disturbers). The rationale for this vehemence was that such intruders lowered the quality of workmanship and thereby threatened the honor (*Ehre*) of proper guild members. The vehemence behind this opposition to intruders was much more than purely economic. Guild honor implied a sense of moral decency and purity, while the intruder carried an odor of pollution, and therefore of evil that had to be stamped out. There were also many other ways in which the honor of a guildsman might be offended, such as the imputation of sexual misbehavior on the part of female members of his family, or by more direct methods such as hurling a dead cat into another man's work bucket. Not all of them are understandable to a modern reader.[4] Nevertheless it is plain that notions of pollution played an important role in the life of guild members.

Indeed, manual work was not merely and perhaps not even primarily a way of earning a living. Work was suffused with all sorts of ethical rules and prohibitions. Thus hard work and moral conduct requiring strict control over human impulses were by common consent, though not necessarily by universal practice, the essential prerequisites for success and social esteem. As in many a primitive society the significance of these qualities received heavy emphasis during rites of passage from one stage in the life cycle to the next. There were three stages in the guildsman's life cycle. The first was that of apprentice, the second that of journeyman, the third and final one that of master. Only by arduous and honest labor could the aspiring young man presumably expect to pass successfully through these stages and become as a guild master an honorable and honored citizen of the urban community. No doubt there were many departures from this norm. But the departures aroused resentment, moral outrage, and a sense of injustice, especially if someone else engaged in them.

Thus the traditional morality of the guilds came into sharp conflict with the new morality of the impersonal marketplace that began to flood across the frontiers in an ever more threatening fashion after the end of the Napoleonic Wars. To be sure, there was some common ground in the stress on hard work and self-control as routes to success and esteem. There, on the other hand, similarity ended. The ethos of the guilds was vehemently opposed to competition and to free entry into occupations subject only to the sanction of supply and demand. Furthermore, guild ethics were collective ethics. The new capitalist ethic was an

---

[4]See Wolfram Fischer, *Handwerksrecht und Handwerkswirtschaft um 1800: Studien zur Sozial- und Wirtschaftsverfassung vor der industriellen Revolution,* 52–53.

individualist ethic. It stressed above all the virtues of competition, free movement in and out of occupations. An individual's social esteem was to be earned or refused on the basis of his performance in the market. To many a guild master such notions were immoral and rather ominous.

As mentioned before, the guilds were part of a set of social arrangements that could only work in a relatively static economy. In effect this meant an economy where the production and consumption of basic necessities were largely a local matter carried on in a series of roughly independent units. It was also an economy in which exchange over long distances was limited to a few commodities and these, in the main, luxuries. In some respects, such as the growing of grain for export by the Junkers, these conditions had begun to disappear as early as the sixteenth century. By 1848 they had eroded heavily.

In comparison with contemporary England, Germany was a very backward, sleepy conglomeration of petty states or principalities, plus Prussia and Austria. Her national identity was yet to be decided. But in comparison with her own past, which is what mattered to most people, large and important changes were stirring. These are traceable to three related causes; a rapidly rising population, the intrusion of the factory system both in the form of the establishment of German factories and the diffusion of English-made factory goods in competition with domestic production, and, finally, government policies. Thus there was mixed support for some economic aspects of modernization with attempted repression of any signs of its nineteenth-century political counterparts: constitutional monarchy, representative government, freedom of expression. These political issues, however, concerned mainly the educated and articulate classes.

What concerned working men and women, in addition to imports, was legislation aimed at breaking up the monopolistic power of the guilds and opening up opportunities for the individual to choose his own occupation without guild approval or going through the stages of apprentice, journeyman, and certified master. On this score, policy varied from one German state to another and shifted back and forth in a confusing manner. Attempts to limit guild powers occurred as early as the seventeenth century. But the first real breach in the old system came about as a consequence of the French Revolution and the French occupation. After that and even in Prussian territories the legal situation did not become uniform. *Gewerbefreiheit* or free entry into trades existed in many areas but not in all. In 1845 *Gewerbe-*

freiheit began to be restricted once more.[5] In this connection it is important to recall that some occupational choice existed under the guild system, since a young man could apprentice himself to any guild master who would accept him and with whom his parents could agree on the arrangements and fees. All in all it is likely that the main consequence of legislation favoring *Gewerbefreiheit* was to provide an easy explanation and target to blame for whatever seemed to be going wrong with the economy under the pressure of new and often incomprehensible forces.

Important distinctions between old and new social formations among the workers in the towns had begun to attract the attention of contemporary observers before 1848. Theoretically the divisions within the guilds into apprentices, journeymen, and masters represented age grades, or stages in the life cycle rather than anything we could call social classes. To a very important extent this was still the case in 1848. Yet for reasons we shall come to in a moment the situation was changing in the direction of class distinctions, especially for the journeymen. Then there were growing up new forms of work relationships and expansion of old ones, both outside and in competition with the guilds.

One of these was the factory, *Fabrik*, as it was called. In 1848 F. W. C. Dieterici, chief of the Prussian statistical services, defined factories as establishments in which goods were worked up in large plants and *also* those in which workers were *not* brought together in large units but worked in different places under the direction of a *Fabrikant* or factor, receiving from him raw materials and turning over to him finished goods.[6] Thus a factory could be anything from what a modern person would recognize as such, through a small workshop with a half-dozen employees, on down to an example of what economic historians inelegantly but lucidly describe as the putting-out system. What distinguished factories from guilds was the use of hired labor, a distinction that, on the other hand, began to blur by 1848 as the relationship between masters and helpers altered quantitatively and qualitatively.[7]

---

[5]For a brief summary see Rudolf Stadelmann and Wolfram Fischer, *Die Bildungswelt des deutschen Handwerkers um 1800: Studien zur Soziologie des Kleinbürgers im Zeitalter Goethes,* 107–108. Covering a longer time period and hence very helpful is Heinrich August Winkler, *Mittelstand, Demokratie, und Nationalsozialismus,* in which see espec. 40–43. On early guild-state relationships see Kurt von Rohrscheidt, *Vom Zunftzwang zur Gewerbefreiheit.*

[6]Dieterici, editor, *Mittheilungen des statistischen Bureau's in Berlin,* I (1848), 150.

[7]Cf. Karl Abraham, *Der Strukturwandel im Handwerk in der ersten Hälfte des 19. Jahrhunderts und seine Bedeutung für die Berufserziehung,* chaps. 1–4.

In addition to the intrusion of capitalism the rise in population had important consequences on the guilds. The number of journeymen was rising and doing so most rapidly in the most modern areas, such as the city of Berlin. In the kingdom of Prussia as a whole, between 1816 and 1843 the ratio of masters to journeymen and apprentices combined dropped from 100:56 to 100:76. By 1846 the ratio for Berlin had reached 100:205.[8] The change meant a reduction in the opportunity for journeymen and apprentices to become masters in Berlin and other large industrial centers. The top of the ladder of advancement was beginning to disappear and with it the purpose of much hard work.

Though it is necessary to beware of romantic images of the past, there are also grounds for believing that the old patriarchal relationship between the master, his wife, and the journeymen as well as apprentices had suffered considerably. Formerly the journeymen had been part of the master's household, and the master with his wife had been responsible for their moral indoctrination as much as their education in matters of technique. The increase in the number of persons under the master's supervision, the loss of motivation due to increased difficulty in attaining the rank of master, and finally the precarious position of the master himself in many guilds must have undermined the sense of dedication and the willingness to curb a desire for immediate pleasures. Population increase and capitalism were demoralizing the guilds. Guild life itself was beginning to resemble that in the factory, and some similar conflicts of interest had begun to appear.[9]

3. The proletariat

As a consequence of both the natural increase in population and the intrusion of capitalism there appeared a mass of people in both town and countryside whom traditional social arrangements could not absorb in the old way. This was by no means a totally new historical situation. Similar problems had seriously plagued Elizabethan England, and earlier medieval society both in England and on the continent clearly had a substantial

[8]For 1843 figures see Abraham, *Strukturwandel*, 56. For 1846 see Dieterici, *Mittheilungen*, I (1848), 70.

[9]Abraham, *Strukturwandel*, 76, 90–94. Dieterici, *Mittheilungen*, II (1849), 6–7, comments on how guild and factory were becoming alike.

residue of the poor and unfortunate. Still there is hardly any reason to doubt that the problem was more acute in the years before 1848 and displayed historically new elements of decisive importance. In the 1840s the term "proletariat" was just coming into use as part of a confused awareness of these changes. Its usage was vague and elastic enough to serve a variety of polemical purposes.

Nevertheless the following characteristics would be likely to form the core of usage and perceptions current around 1848. First of all, proletarians could be dwellers in the countryside as well as in towns or cities. Almost certainly the bottom layer of the rural population was much larger than that in the towns. In the second place, proletarians were uprooted and lacked any recognized, or at least any fully recognized, place in the existing status system. Occasionally they were referred to as the Fourth Estate. That is perhaps one reason why an acute contemporary observer of Berlin included in his definition of the "pure proletariat" those who had given themselves over to scholarship, art, or education in an effort to realize some modest hopes. Others whom he included were day laborers, journeymen, marginal independent craftsmen, and small tradesmen.[10] Marginality was another important trait. They were marginal in the sense of somehow appearing to be extruded from the traditional status order and also in the sense of being very poor. In another sense of the word, a narrow margin also separated them from very severe economic distress. But they were *not* marginal in the sense of playing no significant role in the economy. The upper classes depended on them to perform a whole variety of tasks essential to the workings of the economy. These tasks were at the same time poorly paid and required little or no skill. Finally, proletarians were obviously poor. They had little or no property—in most cases in the towns very likely none at all. They did have to live from poorly paid labor. In all likelihood their employment was highly irregular and depended on the ups and downs of a very unpredictable business cycle.

The main variations in definitions and conceptions of the proletariat had to do with their potential political threat in the form of a revolutionary urban mob, and whether this threat was the consequence of the growth of factories. In educated discussions of the "social question" there were many persons who

[10]Friedrich Sass, *Berlin in seiner neuesten Zeit und Entwicklung,* 249; see also 259–260. On 284 he estimates the proletarians to be 150,000 or "about half" the total population of the city. His estimate and proportion of total population seem high. See Dieterici, *Mittheilungen,* II, 4, where the total population of Berlin is given as around 408,000 for 1846.

stressed the growth of a rural proletariat and the absence of any direct connection between industrial growth and the appearance of a new social stratum.[11] On the other side were those such as Dieterici, who in a brief discussion denied that there was a real proletarian danger in Germany. A real proletariat could arise, in his opinion, only where there were large numbers of workers in a factory and these engaged in a work stoppage.[12] Dieterici's emphasis on the connection between the factory and the proletariat is significant for showing that this conception was by no means limited to Marx and indeed was current in the most respectable circles.

Contemporary discussions of the proletariat, the propertyless, and allied issues were a reflection of the fact that during the first half of the nineteenth century a "surplus" population had made its appearance in German society. It was surplus to that particular social order and that particular level of technical development at that specific stage of historical development. Later in the nineteenth century there was a much bigger increase in population without serious social strains. Nevertheless most of the surplus in 1848 was the consequence of ordinary biological increase. At this juncture there are not many signs of the kind of institutional stresses and changes, such as the English enclosures of the eighteenth and nineteenth centuries, that threw people out of their accustomed places in the social order. Rather the basic German situation at this time was one where there was getting to be less and less room in the accustomed places at the bottom of the social ladder for a rapidly increasing number of people. As yet nowhere near enough new places had put in an appearance to take up the slack. That was not to happen until industrialization acquired its full momentum after the founding of the Empire in 1871. Thus one could say that industrialization solved the problem of the proletariat rather than created it. There is more to the issue, as we shall see when we discuss the political and social upheavals of 1918–1920. But it is correct to say that industrialization was a solution

---

[11]Carl Jantke and Dietrich Hilger, editors, *Die Eigentumslosen: Der deutsche Pauperismus und die Emanzipationskrise in Darstellungen und Deutungen der zeitgenössischen Literatur,* present a large selection of contemporary discussions.

[12]Dieterici, *Mittheilungen,* II (1849), 10–11. High tariffs and other measures of artificial encouragement to manufacturing that ran counter to the natural flow of capital, he continued, would produce a proletariat. Businesses that grew up "naturally" would never do so. His whole position is a curiously eclectic one, to the effect that guilds were doing satisfactorily and would continue to do so if they were neither aided nor hindered by the government, all to the general peace and contentment of Germany. This in 1849! The argument amounts to using Adam Smith to defend the traditional economy.

of some kind to the problem of the early and preindustrial proletariat.[13]

In the territory that was to become the German Empire in 1871 the population rose from nearly 25 million in 1816 to a little more than 34 million in 1845, that is, by more than one-third. During another 29-year period, 1881–1910, the population rose again, by 42 percent from around 45 million to about 65 million, this time without serious talk of overpopulation and of course without a revolutionary crisis. By the second period Germany had become a modern industrial country.[14]

In the earlier period the sharp rise in numbers produced severe suffering, whose impact varied in accordance with geography and social structure. In southwestern Germany, where the impact was most severe, a peasant might find that his land could supply food for no more than five persons when there were seven in the family. Then he would be likely to cut back or even eliminate expenditures for goods and services offered by artisans in the towns. At this point if not earlier the local shoemakers would find that there were too many shoemakers for the markets they could reach and hold. Meanwhile textile manufactures would be in trouble, due to competition either from English goods or from Prussia, whose agricultural interests had encouraged the growth of a transportation net and the consolidation of a low-tariff region, the *Zollverein*. For those close to the bottom of the social heap the escape hatch of emigration was beyond their reach. Mack Walker has put the general problem neatly: in one sense there were too few factories; in another there were too many.[15]

If there were too few factories, how big then was the urban proletariat?[16] It is not an easy question to answer, though there are some fairly good indications. To get a sense of proportion it is best to look first briefly at the statistical data on the working classes as a whole.

At least for Prussia, overwhelmingly the largest state in Germany with a population of more than 16 million in 1846 against a total of 34.4 million in 1845 for the territories that were to

---

[13]See Werner Conze, "Vom 'Pöbel' zum 'Proletariat,' " espec. 123–128.

[14]Data from *Statistisches Jahrbuch für das Deutsche Reich*, Vol. 35 (1914), 2.

[15]Mack Walker, *Germany and the Emigration 1816–1885*, 47–54, espec. 52–53.

[16]If one defines proletariat to mean *all* the workers, and then adds those who lived a marginal existence with some very minimal property inadequate to support a secure "*bürgerlich*" or peasant existence, the result would include at least 50 to 60 percent of the population, according to Conze, "Vom 'Pöbel' zum 'Proletariat,' " 122. For reasons to be given I do not think it is possible to include all the workers.

become the Empire,[17] it is possible to gain an approximate conception of the size of the various components of the working classes and their rates of increase for the thirty-odd years prior to the outbreak of the revolution.

Table 1.

Increase in Numbers of Workers   *(in thousands)*

	1816	1846	% Increase
Factory workers of all kinds	187	554	196
Guild masters plus self-employed persons	284 (1822)	410 to 449	44 to 58
Journeymen and apprentices	179	346 to 379	93 to 112
Unskilled common laborers (*Handarbeiter*)	880	1,470	67

SOURCES: F. W. C. Dieterici, editor, *Mittheilungen des statistischen Bureau's in Berlin,* Vol. I (1848), 83; on p. 70 Dieterici gives the higher figure for "Guild masters plus self-employed persons" for 1846, without explanation. Cf. Vol. II (1849), 4, 13, 16.

The most striking features of Table 1 are the slow rate of growth of the guild masters and the rapid rate of the factory workers. The number of journeymen and apprentices, in practice often hard to distinguish from workers in what was then called a factory, was also rising rapidly at about double the rate of guild masters and self-employed, but not as fast as the total number of factory workers. These changes show quite clearly in what direction the currents of social change were setting.

Nevertheless they do not give us very satisfactory information about the actual size of the proletariat or marginal and impoverished sector. Dieterici (*Mittheilungen*, I [1848], 77) defines the sector here called unskilled common laborers (*Handarbeiter*) as persons living independently from common labor, such as day laborers, woodchoppers, workers on roads and railroads, seamstresses, washerwomen, and the like. They are the largest group in the table and most of them would probably qualify as proletarians in the sense of not being fully absorbed into the traditional economy.

Workers in the factories present a more difficult problem. According to Dieterici (*Mittheilungen, I* [1848], 84), their wages, at least in Berlin, were superior to those of day laborers and they enjoyed relative security of employment. Elsewhere the workers

---

[17]Dieterici, *Mittheilungen,* I (1848), 70; *Statistisches Jahrbuch,* Vol. 35 (1914), 2.

in machine-making shops, in actuality a sort of centralized hand-icraft affair, constituted in terms of pay and social prestige an elite among the workers. But among factory workers there were sharp distinctions both by region and type of industry. In tex-tiles, where the number of women and children was especially high, the workers were drawn from rural areas where they had been engaged primarily in domestic industry. In mining and steelworks the recruitment was again mainly rural, in this case from former serfs and rural day laborers.[18] Karl Abraham cites figures on wages and hours for Berlin in 1846–1847, a period of extreme misery, which show that of all male workers, those in factories were the lowest-paid group of all.[19] The most accurate judgment might be that the factory workers as a whole were being absorbed into the new social order but at close to its bottom rung.

One good piece of evidence on who were the proletarians comes from official Prussian tax data. It is rather surprising to learn that what amounted to a progressive income tax existed in Prussia at that time. The tax was divided into twelve steps. Even day laborers, whom Dieterici estimates to have earned on the order of 100 *Thaler* a year, evidently paid this tax.[20] The bottom or twelfth class wus composed entirely of persons without prop-erty. In their case the tax wasmleveled on individuals, not on households. In 1848 there were reported to be about 3.4 million such persons.[21] Surely these were proletarians by any definition. With a total population of about 16 million, they would amount to slightly more than one-fifth. But it is hardly likely that even the Prussian bureaucracy was able to locate and tax *all* the pro-letariat. Thus the number was probably considerably larger. It might easily have been 5 million, though that is no more than a guess. Looking back at Table 1, it is not too hard to find 1.5 million very possibly 2 million as the number of the proletariat likely to be working in cities and towns.

These are very rough approximations indeed. On the other hand, they are enough to establish that a very substantial propor-tion of the German population was both very poor by the stan-dards of the time and socially uprooted. Werner Conze has stated that more than half was in this category. My calculations

[18]Wolfram Fischer, "Soziale Unterschichten im Zeitalter der Frühindustrialisierung," 427–428.

[19]Abraham, *Strukturwandel*, 136–137. Seamstresses, knitters, and milliners received about half the wages paid to male factory workers.

[20]*Mittheilungen*, I (1848), 105.

[21]*Mittheilungen*, I (1848), 111.

suggest that less than a third belonged to this group, and that the urban portion may have been somewhere between an eighth and a tenth of the total population. Hence the urban proletariat by any definition was a small minority in the total German population. On the other hand, the great majority of manual workers in towns and cities not only suffered material hardship; they were the victims of the various forms of social dislocation described above.

There are some clues to the changing material situation of the very poor. Dieterici provides a list of the annual per-capita consumption of several important items of food and clothing, giving the amount consumed and the price for the years 1822 and 1846. In 1822 total expenditures on these items of customary consumption came to more than 18 *Thaler*; by 1846 they had risen about 44 percent to over 26 *Thaler*.[22] Dieterici's conclusion that the general state of welfare increased by this percentage is patently absurd. For each item consumed the amount remained nearly constant, according to his own data. Only the prices increased. The per-capita consumption of grain products was the same in 1822 and 1846, but the price approximately doubled. The per-capita consumption of meat rose only slightly from 33 to 35 pounds, but the price rose from 2.5 silver groschen to 3.25 silver groschen a pound. Beer consumption oddly enough dropped, though the price also dropped. Sugar and coffee consumption increased noticeably with a slight drop in price. These, however, were a small item in the budget. The only important item whose consumption increased very markedly with some drop in price was cotton goods. For 1822 the annual consumption was 7 ells at 8 silver groschen an ell. In 1846 the annual consumption was 14 ells and the price had dropped to 6 silver groschen per ell. Other items fluctuated within relatively narrow limits in regard to the quantity consumed and the price.

Due to the relatively crude methods for gathering statistical data in the early nineteenth century it would be foolish to take these figures very literally. Nevertheless one can draw some general inferences. Food prices went up markedly. If average annual consumption remained constant, it is still highly unlikely

---

[22]*Mittheilungen,* II (1849), 12. Rudolph Strauss, *Die Lage und die Bewegung der Chemnitzer Arbeiter in der ersten Hälfte des 19. Jahrhunderts,* 252, mentions 2 *Thaler* a week as characteristic pay for *Erdarbeiter* (ditchdiggers, etc.). Thus Dieterici's estimate of 100 *Thaler* a year income for a day laborer seems a reasonable approximation which would mean that somewhat over a quarter of one's income would be required for the necessities of food and clothing.

that the consumption of the very poor did so. Real purchasing power declined, and the very poor had the least purchasing power with which to cope with the decline.

Unfortunately no biographical or other similar firsthand materials of the type that are fairly abundant for later in the nineteenth century exist for the German urban proletariat around 1848. Therefore we lack any direct insight into their life situation or how they felt about it. All that we have to go on are general analyses of the economic and social situation in secondary authorities and a very limited number of observations by persons from higher social classes. Though there was considerable discussion in educated circles of the "social question" and of the situation of the proletariat, most of it appears to have been highly theoretical and general, without a basis in direct observation.[23]

The only contemporary sketch of proletarian or near-proletarian urban existence with the ring of actual experience behind it comes from the writings of a representative of the east German landed nobility, Herrmann Graf zu Dohna.[24] Though his report on the situation among young urban apprentices is saturated with conservative bias, it is also sociologically acute in the way it stresses the connection between social situation and personality or character. Through the bias it is not difficult to discern what was taking place. His report is especially valuable for the light that is sheds on the way the world of the artisan was becoming that of the proletariat. It will be useful therefore to present an extended summary and paraphrase of his observations.

The Count zu Dohna focused his observations around characteristic conservative concerns: the apparent decline of a commitment to hard work and the loss of respect for authority among the lower classes. But he did not simply lament the situation. He tried to explain it. At the present time, he observed, it is much less common for the guild master to keep the apprentice with him in the household. Instead he often gives the apprentice money for his room and board, paying attention only to the apprentice's work, not to his personal welfare. Under these circumstances it is naturally rare that the apprentice grows

[23]Wolfram Fischer's "Soziale Unterschichten" provides a very useful interpretive summary of the available information about their situation and way of life. See Jantke and Hilger, *Die Eigentumslosen,* for contemporary statements showing the varied perceptions current among the educated classes.

[24]See his "Über das Los der freien Arbeiter" in Jantke and Hilger, *Die Eigentumslosen,* 244–245.

up to be an orderly and capable (*tüchtig*) journeyman. Nor is there much the master can do about this. If he is struggling with competition, the master has to use all his strength on his own work and can't afford to pay much attention to the apprentice. How the apprentice spends his evenings and Sundays is something the master cannot know.

Even if the apprentice has received a good upbringing in the home of the master, he may enter the world as a free worker at an age when he does not know how to use his freedom. The apprentice needs company. His isolated position forces him to join up with somebody. He doesn't have enough money to live by himself. Therefore he must find a place to sleep with several other journeymen. Among the journeymen all packed together in this fashion there are bound to be some bad ones. The weaker characters will follow the examples of the bad ones. The small group of well-behaved good journeymen becomes smaller and smaller, isolates itself from the others, and thereby loses its influence on the others.[25]

For the journeyman it is very hard to plan out his expenses sensibly ahead of time, because he never knows exactly what his income will be. That is true even when the pay is enough to last out the year. Apparently the Count zu Dohna has in mind here both the uncertainty of present employment as well as future prospects. On this account, he continues, the journeyman has a strong tendency to enjoy the moment. As a consequence, many go under; they are no longer in a situation of freedom. A week's pay is for the most part consumed on Sunday. The rest of the week he has to get along with a minimum of food. On account of the poor food the journeyman lacks sufficient strength. Pushed around from one place to another, watched by no master, loved by no one, the journeyman often takes up thievery. If at this point he marries, he is liable to find that family obligations are both expensive and terribly demanding. He may take refuge in brandy. Once again he is liable to be pushed into crime, and his children will be brought up in crime. Such a worker is not accustomed to look forward to a real and permanent improvement in his position. He has only the prospect of remaining a worker into his old age. Why then should he not use his pay to enjoy immediate pleasures? Accustomed to living from hand to mouth, he leaves the problems of tomorrow to God. All these

---

[25]These observations are confirmed at a later date in several autobiographies by socialist leaders who started out life as artisans. They contain vivid pictures of the filth, heavy drinking, and coarse talk in journeymen quarters.

observations, it is worth noticing, apply to twentieth-century blacks in American cities as well. The conservative Count zu Dohna must have been among the first to discern the effects of modern poverty on the human personality.

Some workers go back to the land in the wintertime, he observes. If, however, they can earn a little money by cutting wood or something similar, the pay is so small in comparison to what they got in the summertime that they prefer not to work at all and give themselves over to the excesses they had learned in the summer. In the first days of spring they go back to get jobs in various kinds of construction work. But in the spring they have neither strength nor morality left. These are the ones who go in for drinking, gambling, and other excesses. Losing their jobs, they increase the number of wanderers, beggars, criminals. Hence those public works that the state pushes with all its strength in order to give jobs to those without bread actually multiply the number of poor and criminal individuals. They are seedbeds for the poor and criminal.[26]

The Count zu Dohna's observations put into sharp relief some of the reasons why a considerable sector of the population was reluctant to discipline itself for hard work at this historical juncture. The most important cause appears to have been the lack of reward, or even prospects of reward, for self-control in the new situation. In such a situation the experience of personal defeat in an effort to succeed through one's own hard work can be quite shattering. The frustrations of such an existence can easily lead to escapes in fantasy, alcohol, sex, and blustering talk that alternates with cringing behavior. Group sanctions enforce this behavior. Those who would behave otherwise run the risk of rejection by their only possible associates. These sanctions resemble those against the defiant hero in the concentration camps and jails. Their purpose is basically similar: to preserve and validate for the group the minimal satisfactions (alcohol and the like) that are realistically available to it. The role of dependence is likewise significant. There is no obvious need for self-discipline if someone else is nominally responsible for what one does. Even if the superior's responsibility has become minimal, and the satisfaction it produces for the dependent equally small, the dependence itself is very real indeed.

Such considerations help to explain a set of facts that at first glance may seem quite paradoxical. By far the largest part of the German working classes in the cities was suffering severe mate-

[26]Herrmann Graf zu Dohna, "Über das Los der freien Arbeiter," 244–249.

rial hardship. They were also undergoing a process of social uprooting on a wide scale. Yet, with occasional exceptions, they were politically inarticulate. Those who suffered the most had the least to say about and against their sufferings. To say that they were inarticulate does not mean that they did nothing. From time to time they must have manned some of the barricades (rare in the German variant of the turmoil of 1848). But they created little if anything in the way of an independent diagnosis of their own situation. Nor did they manage at this point to develop any sustained organizations of their own with which to combat or change this situation. On this score their behavior is of course anything but unique. In the history of working classes in other countries those who are the worst off are generally the last to organize and make their voices heard. Those at the bottom of the social heap are generally the last ones to hear the news that there has been a change in the capacity of human society to cope with the miseries of human existence.

Some further reasons for the absence of any spontaneous and clearly articulated awareness of their position among this sector at this time deserve our attention. As uneducated persons, proletarians and near-proletarians in the first half of the nineteenth century had very little experience of the written or spoken word as a political weapon. Amid the fountains of words that are part of every revolution they probably felt uneasy, and possibly a bit contemptuous, as did their historical descendants on some occasions. In their own daily life blows and threats were common enough, but not just words strung together in complex patterns and drawn out into long speeches, unless these could take the form of good theater, as did occasionally happen. Songs are another matter and would deserve separate investigation. There the images that formed their picture of the world, a diagnosis and remedy for their condition, might well come together in a coherent whole and serve as Durkheimian collective representations for at least a temporary surge of social unity.

The famous song of the weavers during their revolt in Silesia in 1844 comes to mind as a significant example. It expresses a bloodthirsty hatred of the new capitalists and their exploitation, which in this case took the form of the putting-out system. The title was *Das Blutgericht* (literally blood judgment), and it was sung to the melody of *Es liegt ein Schloss in Österreich*. The final stanzas attack the *Fabrikant* for taking on the airs of the aristocrat. Evidently the new form of exploitation was condemned in the popular mind on the basis of standards of social relationships derived from past experience. This is hardly the first or the only

143

case in which past experience, filtered through folk memories, provides a standard of condemnation to be used against the present. Often quoted, a few stanzas are worth reproducing once more:

Ich sage, wem ists wohl bekannt
Wer sah vor 20 Jahren
Den übermütigen Fabrikant
Mit Staatskarossen fahren?

Sah man dort wohl zu jeder Zeit
Paläste hoch erbauen?
Mit Türen, Fenstern, prächtig weit
Ists festlich anzuschauen![27]

4. Articulate diagnoses

If the proletariat was politically inarticulate, that was not the case with workers who still had a recognized status in the preindustrial order. Under the stresses of encroaching capitalism, the guildsmen, both masters and now even journeymen, found their voices. Still the proportion of those who participated in the formulation of complaints, programs, demands, and requests —revolutionary acts in Germany at that time—was very small. The records of the Congress of the German Artisans that took place in Frankfurt between July 14 and August 18, 1848, provide important information on the numbers who became active and their perceptions of the current situation. This Congress met at the same time as the Constituent Assembly in Frankfurt. As matters turned out the Congress was an unsuccessful effort to put pressure on the Frankfurt Assembly for the sake of the guild masters.

There were in 1846, as the reader may recall from Table 1, somewhere between 410,000 and 449,000 guild masters and self-employed in Prussia alone at that time. They had behind them generations of organizational experience in resisting the pressures of governments and exerting in turn their own forms of counter pressure. They were the best educated and most articulate sector of the German working classes at that time. If

---

[27]The song is reprinted at the end of Wilhelm Wolff, "Das Elend und der Aufruhr in Schlesien," in his *Gesammelte Schriften*, 38–63.

widespread "democratic" participation in drawing up their grievances could be expected of any group, it could be expected of them. The Congress of artisans tried to present itself as a representative spokesman for at least all the masters. But there were only 116 names appended to the draft proposals upon which the Congress agreed after much discussion.[28] Of these at least 6 names are recognizable as not those of masters or not associated with identifiable guilds. That leaves 110 persons politically active at a crucial historical juncture, out of the better part of half a million in only part of Germany. To be sure, this Congress was not the only one organized by the guild masters, though it was the most important. There were also numerous individual petitions sent by guild masters to the Congress, which dutifully submitted them to the National Assembly.[29] Even with these qualifications it is apparent that the active spokesmen for guild interests were a very tiny minority.

The debates at the opening session of the Congress show an awareness of this problem and shed further light on its character. Those present were quite concerned about their own legitimacy and political identity. At the same time some at least felt that these issues should be pushed into the background lest the opportunity for decisive action slip by, a characteristic revolutionary dilemma. One of the first speakers commented with concern on the small number of delegates who had arrived on the scene. To this observation there came the reply that it was important to get down to business: it was not the numbers involved but the spirit (*Geist*) of the discussion and conclusions that counted. Further limits to representation appear from the proposal that the motion of only six delegates should be enough to shut off debate on any motion. There were objections that southern Germany was underrepresented because news about the forthcoming Congress had become public only on July 9, a few days before it was to be held. Northern Germany was supposedly overrepresented.

Even more significantly, the delegates were at least in the beginning unsure of their political identity and just whom or what they *did* represent. Though the merchant, and especially the *Fabrikant*, were eventually to emerge as major villains in the German economic drama, there was some serious discussion

[28]*Entwurf einer allgemeinen Handwerker- und Gewerbe-Ordnung für Deutschland, Berathen und beschlossen von dem deutschen Handwerker- und Gewerbe-Congress zu Frankfurt am Main in den Monaten Juli und August 1848*, 23–24.

[29]For details see P. H. Noyes, *Organization and Revolution: Working-Class Associations in the German Revolutions of 1848–1849*, chap. 7.

whether such persons could reasonably be excluded from a congress called to find answers to the "social question." (As we have seen, some guild masters had come to resemble factory owners. Some too were active in trade.) The issue of whether or not to include the journeymen produced still more extended and sharper debate. As one delegate observed tartly later on: what do the journeymen do except ask for more money and shorter hours? Others spoke of the apprentices as in effect persons working for the capitalists and therefore ruining the guilds. Still others took the position that it was unjust and improper to exclude apprentices who were also an integral part of the guild system. The solution adopted followed the proposal of a delegate who said: "We should tell the deputies of the journeymen to go home quietly and wait for written news; furthermore that they should wait reassured that the masters will take care of their interests." Only 13 out of the 49 delegates then present at this crucial decision voted for the admission of the journeymen.[30]

Especially in times of political crisis a very important part of the way people decide who they are is to decide who their enemies are. This was certainly true of the guild masters. If one reads through the first twenty-odd pages of their proceedings at Frankfurt and makes a list of who and what they agreed were their enemies, the result will include all sectors of German society with the important exception of the peasants: Merchants, Capital, the *Fabrikant,* Journeymen, Bureaucrats, and that bugaboo abstraction, the domination of money. Anyone who seemed able to make money without doing hard physical labor was automatically suspect, a very ancient idea. As noted in the opening chapter, the speculator, as the person who kept possession of valuable resources but did not use or consume them, has aroused moral indignation in a wide variety of cultures.

The draft program (*Entwurf*) drawn up in response to these discussions and presented to the Frankfurt Assembly put this miscellaneous collection of enemies into a more theoretical context in the form of a diagnosis of the ailments supposedly afflicting German society (actually of course mainly the masters) and proposed some remedies. Here the main evils or enemies appear as three. The first, not surprisingly, is competition (*Concurrenz*). The masters conceded that there was such a thing as legitimate competition. Evidently the current of modern opinion was too

[30]*Verhandlungen des ersten deutschen Handwerker- und Gewerbe-Congresses,* 19, 22–23, 40, on the apprentices; for other matters mentioned in the text see 1, 5, 10, 13.

strong for them to dare a frontal attack. But there was also dishonest competition, which was continually winning out more and more over the honest variety. (Conceivably this is something that all businessmen believe throughout modern times. Exactly the same idea crops up in the early days of the American New Deal.) Nevertheless it was a point about which the guild masters felt especial bitterness. The capitalist who committed usury with the labor power of the people was responsible for the creation of the proletariat and overpopulation. In the meantime statesmen, by encouraging freedom of entry into trades *(Gewerbefreiheit)*, stimulated production for its own sake without realizing, in their commitment to false theory (false theorists were not yet called eggheads), that consumption was not a necessary consequence of production and that when the majority of citizens became poor, consumption ceased, and everybody suffered. It is quite apparent that the guild masters, or at least very many of them, felt that both the *Zeitgeist* and the government were encouraging their enemies and encompassing their ruin, and that the middle-class leaders who might replace them would probably be even worse.

From their standpoint this was a quite realistic assessment. What they wanted in the way of remedies was therefore much greater power in the state, measures to preserve their social and moral role as well as their economic one—a harking back to the precapitalist situation with a certain amount of idealized window-dressing—and measures to restrict the number of apprentices and tighten up access to the guilds. This aspect of their remedies follows very naturally from their diagnosis as well as from their general situation and scarcely requires comment. That they asked for high tariffs for all products of German industry is also hardly surprising, though it is worth drawing attention to the fact that on this score at least they would have had significant capitalist and "theoretical" allies. What is rather more surprising is to find, among their list of measures to raise the status of the German artisans, several extremely "modern" proposals: a progressive income and property tax; a fundamental improvement of the educational system with free education; a common system of weights and measures and money for Germany; the obligation of the state to see that all able-bodied persons could find work in public enterprises such as railroads, roads, canals, etc.; and likewise the obligation of the state to take care of citizens who lacked means due to illness or accidental mutilation and had thereby become unable to work.

It would be a long time before modern industrial states accepted these obligations, which indeed are not fully accepted even today. Hence it is both unfair and incorrect to label the guild masters' program as purely reactionary and selfish. There was a great deal in it that could arouse a sympathetic reaction even among factory workers, though it is also true that the program was suffused with a mixture of nostalgia and self-interest. Caught between two historical epochs, the upper ranks of the artisans wistfully looked back to the one that was disappearing and sought to soften the impact of the one that was taking shape around them.

Excluded by the masters, the journeymen held their own congress in Frankfurt from July 20 to September 20, 1848. The delegates were heavily weighted toward southwestern Germany, but enough finally appeared to give some justification for their claim to speak for "a general German workers' group." The discussions that led up to their statement have not survived. Nevertheless the statement itself is especially interesting because it represents a spontaneous overlay of revolutionary optimism on basic despair, both unalloyed by any of the Marxist ideas that has been imported into Berlin by Stephan Born.[31]

Not surprisingly the diagnosis of what has gone wrong with history shows some resemblances to the views expressed by the guild masters. There is a similar complaint about the arbitrary domination of capital *(Willkührherrschaft des Capitals)*, the same distress about the inalienable rights of labor and to an honest living. These rights, the journeymen claimed, had been sacrificed to usury, games, and deceit, and honest work must regain the honor *(Ehre)* it deserves.[32] Free trade, competition, and the whole individualist ethic of modern capitalism, in which the palm of victory allegedly goes to enterprise and merit, were no more palatable to the journeymen than they were to the guild masters or, for that matter, the majority of the proletariat outside the ranks of a few relatively favored factory workers.

At the same time the journeymen evidently did not look back on a golden age of the guilds in the same way as the masters. For the journeymen the historical epoch that capitalism was destroying was the age of monopoly in which there had been a thousand obstacles in the way of anyone who wanted to earn an honest living by the diligent industry of his hands. In many places the number of masters was subject to artificial restrictions, the right to mastership hereditary or tied to the use of certain buildings.

---

[31]For background see Noyes, *Organization and Revolution*, 204–207.

[32]*Beschlüsse des allgemeinen deutschen Arbeiterkongresses zu Frankfurt am Main, gefasst in den Monaten Juli, August, und September, 1848.* See espec. 444.

The right to a master's status was only in theory to be won by examination and producing an example of the craft's work *(Meisterstück)*. Due to the expense involved, only the rich could actually become masters. All these criticisms, it is worth noticing, had long been common coin among progressive officials and "bourgeois" theorists. As people reached an awareness, the document continues, that they were born with the same rights but that monopolies were created by deceit and brute power, they decided to throw off their chains.

Instead of freedom, the results, however, were unrestricted competition, the unfreedom of work, a situation in which the rich became richer and the poor became poorer. The *Mittelstand* was brought to the ground, the *Arbeiterstand* to the beggar's staff.[33] Not freedom but a caricature *(Zerrbild)* of freedom appeared, in which the working rule was "To him that hath shall be given and from him that hath not shall be taken away even that which he hath." Hence the journeymen refused to identify with a *Liberalismus* that sought to impose a serfdom even worse than that of the age of guild monopoly. While rejecting liberalism, they rejected with equal vehemence the equalitarian notions that had begun to circulate from French and German socialism and communism. The grounds are revealing. Under an equalitarian system the slothful would receive as much reward as the hard worker. Unrewarded effort appears as a central concern for the journeymen, as it does for other groups.

This concern comes out even more clearly in their image of a desirable future, which follows their diagnosis of an evil past and present. Its main feature was to be that not *Kapital* (here with a *K*) but diligence and skill should determine the successes of the entire productive *(schaffenden)* population. There seems to be an echo here of the distinction between productive and unproductive labor that had become widespread in other parts of Europe as a polemical weapon against both speculators and parasitic aristocrats.[34] In the end they wanted the best of both worlds: a

---

[33]This is just one indication of the extent to which the notion of estate or order still permeated German categories of speech and thought. In the workers' document cited, *Stand* can appear in the same sentence with the term *Klasse*. This linguistic mixture reflects the historical situation in which hereditary order was still intermingled with economically determined social classes, or in which people were changing from one principle of social inequality to another.

[34]See *Beschlüsse*, 450–452. They also give the standard objection to equality, that it would lead to dull uniformity and that human needs are in any case different. The *sansculottes* too were especially vehement in their attack on speculators and aristocrats. But the distinction between useful and useless activities was much more widespread in the eighteenth century and is undoubtedly older.

society in which success depended on industry and skill, yet one that provided freedom of movement *(Freizügigkeit)* and the end of special concessions and privileges, along with one that assured to every member of civil society a guaranteed sphere in which to earn a living and one appropriate to his ability to work *(einem jeden Glied der bürgerlichen Gesellschaft die seiner Arbeitskraft angemessene Erwerbsphäre gesichert)*.[35] It may have been these hopes that enabled the journeymen to proclaim that the new general workers' organization they hoped to create would be open to any person over eighteen years of age who was willing to take on the task of raising the position of the working class and restoring the status of the *Mittelstand*.[36] Here *Mittelstand* obviously does not refer to the prosperous capitalist bourgeoisie. Rather, both *arbeitende Klasse* and *Mittelstand* appear to be vague general categories that include all people engaged in honest labor. As a separate category, all those from all estates sympathetic to labor and its aims were to be allowed and indeed encouraged to join, such as artists, scholars, merchants, artisans *(Handwerker)*, and even *Fabrikanten*. It may also have been this respect for work and desire for social reconciliation that enabled the journeymen, like the masters, to advocate certain "modern" forms of social welfare, such as public works, the elimination of involuntary poverty, an adequate minimum income, and free education.[37]

How were these somewhat utopian aims to be achieved? The *Beschlüsse* go into almost painful detail about the structure of the proposed general workers' organization, details that we may neglect as the organization remained on paper, though Stephan Born was able to start another one that did exist for two years. His, however, had more limited and more strictly working-class objectives. The other proposals by the journeymen were for a neo-anarchist form of federalism, as well as for the representation of labor in the organization of the state. But they were not altogether unrealistic. They stressed the difficulty of the task ahead and awareness that nearly everybody would be opposed to them.[38]

To point up the unrealistic aspects of the program would, however, not only be an unwarranted condescension but also in itself a form of unrealism. The statements of both the guild masters and the journeymen reveal a widespread *prise de consci-*

[35]*Beschlüsse*, 455.

[36]*Beschlüsse*, 449.

[37]*Beschlüsse*, 456.

[38]*Beschlüsse*, 452–453. Born's role is discussed below.

ence against the ugly, repressive features of the new capitalist society growing up all around them. Just how far these ideas were their own spontaneous creation is very hard to say. The main elements in the conceptual framework that the guild masters and journeymen used, especially the attack on competition, the role of the guilds in organizing economic production and exchange, had evidently been in use among educated people for some time. They were part of the polemical currency of the day.[39] It seems rather likely that the journeymen and masters borrowed the conceptual tools. But the borrowing was selective and it was their own experience that had provided the raw material for the concepts in the first place.

The rejection of competition amounted to a wholesale onslaught on the market as the main mechanism for determining the fate of human beings. Competition suited those ambitious sections of the bourgeoisie who had the means with which to compete and were resentful of special state help to certain forms of economic enterprise (not those that were useful to them such as railroads) and also of state interference. Competition had little to offer workers whose main fear was being pushed down into the proletariat either as factory workers (except for some who were doing reasonably well) or the much larger majority of day laborers and the unskilled. The attack on competition, encouraged later by intellectuals, was to gain wide currency among the workers and, as capitalism ran into difficulties, among the capitalists themselves. Ideas derived from the experiences of simple journeymen were to find wide and effective political echoes though not in their own time or intellectual costume.

To put the point in a wider historical context, we can now perceive that this counteroffensive against competition and the sufferings produced by the new capitalism—even if it had thoroughly selfish motives and was by no means the expression of the interests of those most severely affected—was a very significant attack on the new explanations of suffering, the new morality, the new "inevitability" of competitive capitalism. Earlier we have noticed that breaking the appearance of inevitability is crucial to overcoming the moral authority of oppression. That is exactly what the German artisans were doing.

The task had been rendered somewhat easier by their predecessors, the ones whom they were now attacking. By providing

---

[39]To cite just two examples, see the striking analysis of *Concurrenz* in Sass, *Berlin,* 261–263; see also the extended discussion by Dieterici, *Mittheilungen,* II (1849), no. 1, where the chief of the Prussian statistical service tries to present a statistical refutation of the masters' complaints and their explanation of the current troubles.

an essentially secular explanation of worldly success and worldly misery, earlier spokesmen for individualism and capitalism had helped to shatter any possibility of defending the prevailing distribution of human misery in terms of an unalterable and divine order of the universe. Before then, in medieval and early modern times, social diagnosis had been based on the Bible and had taken the form of arguments about what the divine order actually was. For Thomas Münzer, so often cited as one of the first radical social critics, political and social issues appear to have been peripheral matters. Most of what he was talking about was theology. In Münzer's day a direct attack on social problems based on the premise that they were amenable to popular demands and a popularly supported public policy was as yet hardly conceivable. The best one could hope for was a utopian escape into a "genuine" community constructed according to what the Bible "really" said. This current of thought still lingered on in the utopian socialists who had flourished in France shortly before 1848. German artisans tried to make their break with inevitability in a very different way with an almost entirely secular diagnosis and an equally secular remedy. None of that would have been possible had not their capitalist enemies forged the tools for them.

In stressing the importance of a secular analysis we must not lose sight of its moral component. The artisans felt moral outrage at an attack on their rights as human beings. The loss of allegedly ancient rights constituted the core of their grievances. In their view these rights were at the same time based primarily on their secular contribution to the social order: what they had been producing and the ways in which they had carried out this production. The same sense of injustice was behind their efforts and those of other workers to find new ways of obtaining rights and respect as human beings, both within and against the prevailing social order.

Such were the diagnoses and remedies that the historical record indicates were circulating among the artisans during the crisis of 1848. What reasons are there for regarding these ideas as more than the spoutings of a few agitators? Where did the ideas come from, and to the extent they did gain currency among artisans and wider working-class circles, how did that come about?

To answer these questions it is necessary to begin by reviewing the general situation. The urban working classes were divided into a series of groups, some more clearly defined than others, such as masters, journeymen, apprentices, factory workers, and several varieties of unskilled workers. Individuals in these groups faced many similarities in their life situations. Some situations, such as lack of public esteem, were common to many persons. Even guild masters were esteemed more in some forms of public rhetoric, mainly conservative, than in actual public policy (and especially the prospective policy of middle-class revolutionaries). Thus, the guild masters too were an outside group and certainly a discontented one. Any public statement that sharply contradicted these facts of daily experience was hardly likely to be effective. Furthermore, the authors of statements and programs were representative in the sense that they were elected at least by some rough-and-ready procedure and had a politically effective following. They either came from the ranks themselves or paid careful attention to popular sentiments. In this fluid situation they would not or could not put their names to statements that made no sense to their followers. If they did, they would not remain leaders. Or if their views were acceptable to some followers, and not to others, as very often happened, the movement that they led would split.[40]

On these grounds it is appropriate to take such statements as *articulations* of the various streams of urban working-class thought and feelings. They are articulations in the sense of putting together in a coherent form the vaguely and sometimes intensely felt sentiments and explanations of masses of ordinary people. Obviously they were put together in a way that was meant to be effective, to rouse people to action by making them say in effect, "That really hits the nail on the head. That fellow really knows what he's talking about. He sees what's hurting us, and sounds like somebody who'll do something about it." To believe otherwise is to believe that men trying to be popular leaders were deliberately ignoring what people wanted. At times they no doubt miscalculated, and no doubt details are frequently far from dependable. Exaggerated claims certainly existed. But it seems quite justified to take frequently expressed themes as reliable indicators of popular diagnoses and remedies for genuine grievances.

At times the mechanics of the relationship between spokesmen and followers in these turbulent times come to light in a revealing way. Stephan Born, later the leading spirit behind the

---

[40] In this connection it is worth noticing that even at the height of popular participation in Paris during the French Revolution, attendance at the meetings of the *sections* was very low. Albert Soboul, *Les San-culottes parisiens en l'an II,* 585–586 reports that most of the time it ran around 4 to 7 percent of the membership, rising only to 19 percent or less than one member in five at times of great excitement.

short-lived *Verbrüderung* (Brotherhood), a working-men's association, describes in his memoirs how in the early days of the
revolution he was asked to take the chairmanship of groups from
all over Berlin: trade unions about to establish a constitution,
freethinking clubs, and the like. The child of a lower middle-
class Jewish family whom misfortune had pushed into the working class, Stephan Born became an apprentice and later a com-
positor in the printing trade. Studying at every free moment, he
educated himself and learned to express himself in a strong
exhortatory style, a skill recognized by the workers who chose
him to articulate their sense of injustice and crank up the
machinery of social change to better their lot. Born was interested in improving the workers' immediate situation just as
much if not more than in the long-term goal of a socialist society,
about which he had learned from Marx.[41] During the period
prior to March 1848 there was a ferment of excitement among
the Berlin populace and much competition for their allegiance
from a variety of speakers. Born appears to have won out rather
easily against more radical opponents, including fiery student
demagogues.[42]

The different sectors of the urban populace took their ideas
where they could find them. Long before 1848 there had been a
very considerable diffusion of German high culture downward
into artisan circles.[43] Their own immediate experience and
situation determined what they could and would take, as well as
what they would make of it. Outsiders in the form of intellectuals, on the other hand, determined to a great extent what
was available for the taking and for reworking. There is little indication of independent creative activity. Self-educated thinkers like Wilhelm Weitling appear to have had little general influence. Nevertheless as a consequence of the historical experiences of Germany as a whole, the main "modern" ideas of the
nineteenth century—Nationalism, Liberalism, and Socialism—
were not unknown among artisans and peasants.[44] Socialist and
Communist ideas, on the other hand, made only very minor
penetration into proletarian circles. As already noted, the proletariat was too fragmented into groups with widely differ-

[41]See Stephan Born, *Erinnerungen eines Achtundvierziger,* 135–136 and Noyes, *Organization and Revolution,* 51–54.

[42]Noyes, *Organization and Revolution,* 78–80, 101–103, 136.

[43]Stadelmann and Fischer, *Bildungswelt,* 17–19, explain some of the ways in which this
took place.

[44]Stadelmann and Fischer, *Bildungswelt,* 202.

ing experiences and too imbued with a traditional outlook.[45]

The main popular group among which Marxist and other radical notions took hold was the journeymen. For this there were several reasons. In the course of their required *Wanderschaft* or "wanderings," a customary period of traveling about, during which the men were supposed to learn new techniques and widen their experience of the world, they often visited France and Switzerland where they came in contact with these ideas. Furthermore, notions about changing the world often had an appeal for those who as yet did not have a firm place in the occupational structure, whose prospects in it were uncertain, and who as yet had not been impregnated with the ethical values of their occupation. (For this reason too students were disproportionately likely to be recruits to radical circles.) Even if journeymen constituted a large proportion of those who got into trouble with the police for revolutionary activities, radicals were still an infinitesimal fraction of German journeymen as a whole.[46] Finally and perhaps decisively, the repressive aspects of the Prussian bureaucracy hit journeymen *and* professional intellectuals the hardest.[47] That was one of the important factors that by March 1848 made possible for a brief time a unified revolutionary opposition, stretching from capitalists through intellectuals, to guild masters, journeymen, factory workers, peasants, and some elements of the proletariat. At no time of course did the revolution draw on all individuals in any of these groups. Only a very small minority played an active part. As each group sought to formulate its own objectives, to estimate risks, and to seek its own political identity, they came into conflict with each other, and the revolution dissipated.

[45]Jacques Droz and Pierre Ayçoberry, "Structures sociales et courants idéologiques dans l'Allemagne prérévolutionnaire 1835–1847," 223, 227–228.

[46]Stadelmann and Fischer, *Bildungswelt,* 52, 56, 223.

[47]Droz and Ayçoberry, "Structures sociales," 221.

5. Workers' behavior in the revolutionary period

By themselves the various strains of incipient modernization, as social scientists euphemistically call them—they are really causes of acute human suffering—were probably insufficient to generate a revolutionary outbreak in Germany of the 1840s. But on top of them, beginning in 1845, there came a series of blows to which a society at this stage of economic development was especially vulnerable. In 1845 there was a potato famine. In 1846 and 1847 there were serious grain failures. Then in 1847 a trade crisis spread from England to the continent, adding fears if not the bitter actuality of unemployment.[48] Already in April of 1847 there were sporadic uprisings in Berlin and other Prussian cities, hinting at more serious events to come.[49] By the spring of 1848 the worst economic distress was over, and food prices had actually begun to drop. But then came the news that on February 24th Louis Philippe had fled in the face of a popular uprising in Paris. News still traveled slowly and erratically, and it took time for exciting events to have their effect. Not until March 15, 1848, did the barricades go up in Berlin.

So much one can learn from any good standard account. The sequence of events gives the impression that deep-running currents of misery finally stirred the mass of the population into revolutionary actions. There may be a bit of a problem with the chronology of misery, and Louis Philippe's abdication has to be brought in as an historical crank to get the locomotive of history, or at least German history, going along the right track. Yet that seems no more than a minor difficulty with the logic of the explanation.

Actually, the impression is false. Misery there certainly was, and in new and disturbing forms as well as old and familiar ones. But the main fact is simply this: the overwhelming majority of those whose "objective" situation would qualify them as being somehow the victims of injustice took no active part in the events of the period. As far as it is possible to tell now, they just sat tight, tried to make do in their daily lives, and waited for the outcome. Although in the twentieth century, the degree of popular participation has undoubtedly increased, I strongly suspect that doing nothing remains the real form of mass action in the main

---

[48]Noyes, *Organization and Revolution*, 32–33.

[49]Droz and Ayçoberry, "Structures sociales," 230.

historical crises since the sixteenth century. That is not to deny the decisive importance of occasional popular outbursts, which, however, can never draw on more than a tiny fraction of the population.

In addition to avoiding any kind of activity that might find its way into the historical record, there were three other forms of popular behavior during this period. One was flight in the form of emigration. Another was a series of attempts to organize and indeed create historically new forms of organization for economic and political objectives. The third was revolutionary violence. Before discussing each in turn it will be well to remark that sociological categories and modes of explanation do not provide anything like complete explanations of these differences in behavior. Especially in the case of revolutionary violence, quite immediate and unique historical circumstances played an important role. This warning against sociological imperialism need not be a matter for deep epistemological concern. As every competent statistician knows, though not Macaulay's schoolboy, it is better to explain some variation rather than none.

With these observations let us turn briefly to emigration. After fluctuating at around 20,000 a year for a decade, emigration from Germany rose sharply in the mid-1840s to reach four or five times that number in the crisis year of 1847.[50] According to Mack Walker, the emigrants came mainly from the lower middle class, that is, small property owners. In the towns these would have been mainly guild masters. In German society at that time this was the sector, as we have already seen, that looked backward for a solution to its discontents and grievances, thus contributing heavily to the revolutionary outbreak. Like the rebellious artisans who stayed behind, but unlike the revolution's articulate middle-class leaders, the emigrants wanted to stop the clock or turn it backward. Published statements by emigrants about reasons for their departure express the same nostalgic hostility to capitalism and the power of money, the same bitterness about the loss of respect for honest hard work that appear in the statements by representatives of the guilds during the revolution.[51] The emigration did not include apprentices or unskilled laborers. Proletarians did not emigrate as a rule, since proletarianization meant final failure that precluded even escape. Likewise, the unemployed or underpaid industrial workers of Saxony and Silesia were seldom able to scrape together

---

[50]Walker, *Emigration*, 79–80.

[51]See Walker, *Emigration*, 130, and 155 for some quotations from emigrants.

enough money to move. On the other hand, independent village shopkeepers and artisans did emigrate. In accord with the general pattern there was next to no emigration from the larger towns and cities. Those who left were persons who relied on their own skills, who wished to do so in the future, and who had some property that could be turned into cash.[52] From this evidence it is hard to estimate the net political effect of the emigration. Though it may have removed from the scene a good many people who were fundamentally conservative and in this way had an unsettling effect, I rather suspect that the main consequence was to deprive the discontented, who were for the most part discontented for conservative reasons anyway, of a corps of energetic supporters and potential leaders.

Turning to the efforts of the manual workers to organize, we find that these too could have done little more than skim an activist cream. The most successful organization in terms of numbers was the *Verbrüderung* (literally, bringing together in brotherhood), an attempt led chiefly by Stephan Born to recruit all workers into a national organization. For this goal the *Verbrüderung* waged a vigorous campaign during the autumn and winter of 1848–1849. In December of 1848 it held a congress in Saxony where elected delegates represented approximately 3,800 workers in various parts of the kingdom. There are no accurate figures about the number of members the *Verbrüderung* managed to win at any one time during the two years of its active existence. Contemporary figures vary from as low as 12,000 to as high as 800,000, the latter one perhaps from a police spy anxious to justify the usefulness of his profession. A reasonable modern estimate gives 18,000.[53] That is a very tiny proportion of the more than 550,000 factory workers to whom it directed its main appeal, not to mention the near million and a half unskilled laborers in Germany at that time.

Over the long haul the most important right that the workers had to obtain was the right to strike. Though precedents of a sort existed in more or less spontaneous actions, in mid-nineteenth century Germany this right still had to be discovered. It would take a long time to make it both effective and a recognized aspect of the social order, something not fully accomplished until 1918. In all countries during the early phase of capitalism, combinations by workers to enforce economic demands smelled to employers like sedition and revolt. Against it they used a combi-

---

[52]Walker, *Emigration,* 47, 51.

[53]Noyes, *Organization and Revolution,* 290–291, 298, 306.

nation of traditional and liberal arguments. Workers ought to obey their masters and leave to them the responsibility for their welfare. That was the traditional and patriarchal argument against unions and strikes. According to liberal conceptions, collective action was a violation of the individual worker's freedom of contract and right to seek and determine his own fate. This argument gave moral sanction to strikebreaking. Generally the power of the state enforced these views. Strikes and combinations were illegal, though to the extent they could not be prevented, their legal status was shadowy.

In his memoirs Stephan Born recounts an episode about a bookprinters' strike in Berlin some time after the March 1848 outbreak that sheds as much light on the situation at that time in Germany as many a monograph loaded with statistics. Among the Berlin workers of that day the printers were, according to Born, along with the machine makers, the pacesetters, perhaps even the aristocrats of the working classes. Their pay nevertheless was much less and their hours longer than those prevailing in Paris with whose conditions Born, himself a printer, was familiar. (Clearly standards of justice were in part set by what it was possible to get elsewhere, one way in which the conception of changing human capacities develops.) At their first meeting the printers elected Born chairman and agreed on a decision to put forth some wage demands, with the threat of a strike behind them. In the police state that had existed prior to 1848 all that would have been out of the question. But the situation had changed . . . somewhat. As chairman of the printers, Born had the inspiration to call in person upon the Minister of Commerce to tell him that a work stoppage would occur shortly. The Minister of Commerce was a pure Manchesterite who had long outgrown patriarchal notions about the relationship between employers and workers. For him the proposed strike was nothing out of the ordinary. He received Born in a very cordial manner, telling him to sit at one end of the sofa while he sat at the other end, to discuss the situation. After a few moments the Minister of Commerce gave an order to bring in an official known as the Secret Chief Court Bookprinter. This gentleman rapidly appeared and bowed far more deeply to the Minister of Commerce than young Born was accustomed to doing. The Minister introduced Born and explained the reason for Born's visit. The Secret Chief Court Bookprinter was as utterly startled as if Born had fallen through the clouds, and could only stammer a few incomprehensible words. Perhaps, as Born put it, the high official had expected to receive a huge order for his printing establishment. Obviously furious, the Court Bookprinter nevertheless refrained from making a totally negative response to the printers' demands.[54] The workers did go on strike. But for reasons that need not concern us here, they did not succeed in either this or subsequent attempts to gain their objectives.[55]

Since Noyes has presented a first-rate account of the workers' efforts to take care of their own interests during the revolutionary years of 1848 and 1849, further discussion of this point may be limited to a few general observations based on his work. A series of workers' meetings in Berlin following the March uprising revealed the pattern of demands and tactics that the workers were to follow. Essentially they sought both government aid and working-class organization. Political recognition meant government support for the demands that had suddenly become (more or less) legitimate after the March events; simultaneously, on the other hand, these workers sought to create associations that would have the power and prestige once possessed by the guilds.[56]

The term "proletariat" aroused great resentment when applied to these workers. A journalist who used it at one of the meetings was shouted down and made to retract the expression.[57] Indeed, what these workers feared most of all was that they might be forced down into the proletariat. What they sought was self-respect—which in practice means the respect of others—and a rate of earnings that would sustain self-respect. One sign of the importance of self-respect that rather outraged old-fashioned conservatives was that workers now wanted to be called *Sie* instead of the familiar *Du* (used like the French *tu*, with intimates but also for servants and children). While intellectual radicals looked forward to the time when all mankind would use a comradely *Du* or its equivalent, these workers were insisting on the respectful *Sie*.[58]

From the point of view of our inquiry certain characteristics of the movement require emphasis. First of all, the numbers involved were quite small, usually a few hundred, though in the case of the *Verbrüderung* mentioned earlier it reached several thousand. At no time did more than an infinitesimal proportion

[54]Born, *Erinnerungen*, 122–127.

[55]Noyes, *Organization and Revolution*, 133, 199–202.

[56]Noyes, *Organization and Revolution*, 77–78.

[57]Noyes, *Organization and Revolution*, 74.

[58]Noyes, *Organization and Revolution*, 127–128. Leopold Haimson has informed me that a similar desire for decent human treatment and the use of the respectful second person plural was prevalent among Russian factory workers before the Revolution of 1917.

of German workers take part actively. In the second place, most of those who did were evidently members of the labor aristocracy, though Noyes records at least one case where unskilled calico workers took the lead in demanding higher wages, shorter hours, and limitations on the use of machinery.[59] The line between guild and factory workers was very blurred; at times both joined in strikes, óften against their immediate and not so prosperous superiors—guild masters or small employers. Some of the strikes had anti-Semitic overtones. In this historical context anti-Semitism appeared as a form of folk anticapitalism inasmuch as the strikes were generally directed at rather small establishments, thought to be owned by Jews. Finally, as might be expected in Germany, there was a scrupulous and almost pathetic attention to the details of organizational structure. Though the organizations were ephemeral, they established a pattern that was to be followed as industrialism took hold with greater force in subsequent decades.

Perhaps the most striking feature of all of these movements for self-help among the German workers in the 1840s was the absence of any consideration for the needs of the mass of unskilled labor, the growing proletariat, and even more so, the lack of any articulate or organized response by the proletariat itself, either to this neglect or its own general situation.[60] As already noted, the stratum that Marx posited as the spearhead of revolution was in fact the most quiescent of all.

Who then did engage in revolutionary action and what did the word mean in this historical context? The reader who has followed the argument of this book up to this point hardly needs to be reminded that in the human repertoire of responses to deprivation and injustice an aggressive counterattack is scarcely the one to anticipate as automatic and somehow "natural." Ordinary lower-class German townsmen in the middle of the nineteenth century had severe obstacles to overcome before they would perform revolutionary acts. In Germany at that time, as well as earlier and later, there was a widespread and deeply rooted tradition of loyalty and submission to constituted authority, especially authority with patriarchal overtones.[61] In German

---

[59]Noyes, *Organization and Revolution,* 129.

[60]Cf. Noyes, *Organization and Revolution,* 220, on the Berlin Congress of August, 1848, perhaps the most important of these gatherings attended mainly by skilled workers in trades.

[61]The historical origins of this trait are obscure, at least to me. The rise of the Junkers and Hohenzollern absolutism probably played an important role. The earlier disaster of the *Bauernkrieg* in the sixteenth century may also have contributed.

towns there were almost no indications of the popular turbulence that was quite widespread in seventeenth- and eighteenth-century France.[62] In the 1830s, to be sure, there were some cases of rioting and machine breaking, particularly in the Prussian Rhineland. But far more characteristic of the expressions of the workers' temper up until 1844 was the petition of the handicraft workers of Cologne to the newly crowned Frederick William IV urging him "from the wisdom of his majesty" to remove the threat of poverty that went with freedom to enter a trade.[63] Even after the excitement of the March Days of 1848 had moved close to its violent peak in Berlin, there circulated among the workers a lithographed handbill in the form of a petition that began "Most Serene Royal Highness the King . . . *(Allerdurchlauchtigster König)*" and ended "In deepest humility we remain . . . *(In tiefster Untertänigkeit verharren . . .).*" The content was in keeping with these traditional formulae. It asserted that the state flourished only when the people could satisfy its necessities through work and asked that a ministry be set up, composed of only employers and workers, to remedy the current situation. Still, for the day this was a rather daring step, and is quoted in full by the major East German historian of the workers' movement in 1848 to show the degree of political and intellectual independence the workers had already reached.[64]

The workers' attitudes varied a great deal in response to quite local circumstances. The *Fabrikant* was frequently an object of hatred because, as a newcomer, he seemed to be both the cause of the breakdown of traditional ways of life and the person who was taking greedy advantage of this collapse at the expense of the poor. But this situation by no means prevailed everywhere. Particularly in the Rhineland the new economy itself displayed strong patriarchal overtones. In the case of the miners the patriarchal relationships were a heritage from their past relationship with the state.[65] In some parts of the Rhineland these patriarchal barriers to sedition and revolt appear to have held through the revolutionary period. On the whole, however, they

---

[62]See the excellent study by Mack Walker, *German Home Towns: Community, State, and General Estate 1648–1871,* espec. chaps. 1, 2. On France note the remarks in Pierre Goubert, *Louis XIV et vingt millions de Français,* 33–34; George Rudé, *The Crowd in the French Revolution,* 20–25; Charles Tilly *et al., The Rebellious Century 1830–1930,* 18–19. I am not familiar with the monographic literature.

[63]Noyes, *Organization and Revolution,* 35.

[64]Karl Obermann, *Die deutschen Arbeiter in der Revolution von 1848,* 122.

[65]For some contemporary accounts see Pierre Guillaume Frederic Le Play, *Les Ouvriers européens,* III, 99, 101, 102–106, 111, 112, 127, 129; Thomas Charles Banfield, *Industry of the Rhine: Series II, Manufactures,* 41, 46, 74–78.

were not very effective.[66] In Berlin the *Fabrikant* was not the target of the first outbreak of violence. There the enemy was the reactionary bureaucrat and especially the military. These were targets about which many advanced *Bürger* felt angry as well. Finally, the violence of the March Days was in any case extremely limited. Only in Berlin and Vienna were barricades erected and shots fired.[67]

Somehow then through a mixture of provocations, an increasing sense of resentment at what was in their eyes neglect and mistreatment, and above all stimulated by news of the events in Paris, a substantial number of workers at last did turn to violence. Peasants took part too. This violence was to continue intermittently until the clear defeat of the revolution in the summer of 1849. Among the town and city dwellers, artisans and workers were without doubt the main recruits to revolutionary violence. But what does revolutionary mean here? In what sense were at least some German workers revolutionary? Which workers? What circumstances drove them to it, and what were their objectives?

It will be best to give some negative answers first. No distinction appears possible between the lower ranks of the guilds and factory workers. In the course of disputes that eventually erupted in violence, factory workers might make demands about grievances that arose only for persons working in the context of guild arrangements.[68] During the March Days of 1848 the machine workers in Berlin took a leading part in the revolutionary events. Later they were to come out for law and order and still later endeavor to play the thankless role of mediator and pacifiers.[69] Indeed, it is possible to find among the urban lower classes striking examples of just about every kind of behavior, from calls to law and order,[70] through plain marauding and pillaging, on to what one can justifiably call revolutionary risings. In my judgment it would be a waste of time to try to spin out sociological categories and distinctions to explain these differences between one kind of behavior and another. There is no

---

[66]Miners are a special case to be discussed in more detail later. Apparently they did not partake in any of the revolutionary upheavals. Droz and Ayçoberry, "Structures sociales," 191, mention examples where the patriarchal barriers seem to have worked. Carl Schurz, however, in *Lebenserinnerungen*, I, 173, reports widespread violent outbreaks in the main Rhineland areas in May of 1849.

[67]Noyes, *Organization and Revolution*, 57.

[68]Strauss, *Chemnitzer Arbeiter*, 261–262.

[69]Obermann, *Arbeiter*, 124; Noyes, *Organization and Revolution*, 155, 273, 278.

[70]As issued by the Berlin Workers' Congress. See Noyes, *Organization and Revolution*, 218.

recognizable tendency toward any particular form of behavior that is somehow especially characteristic of the urban workers beyond rather obvious (but still important) ones. They displayed many resentments and had a great deal to resent. At one time they behaved one way, at another time differently, all in response to concrete and immediate circumstances.

These circumstances, on the other hand, do fall into a pattern that makes its own form of sense. The outbreaks that were part of the opening period of the revolution continued in a sporadic and spontaneous manner in the summer and on into the autumn of 1848. Some working-class marauders were reported to be lurking in the forests of Mecklenburg-Schwering, raiding local estates, demanding ransoms as high as 13,000 *Thaler*, burning houses and opening wine cellars, behavior that would scarcely endear them to the property-owning classes. In Baden there was so much sabotage of the railroads that they were put under public protection. Cities were even more unsettled. Riots occurred with the slightest excuse or without any excuse at all. Many of the brawls, according to one newspaper account, were among the workers themselves.[71] Once the lid was off, so to speak, old scores were settled between dominant and subordinate groups and within the working classes themselves. New causes for anger and revenge were simultaneously being created as the social order disintegrated. Meanwhile the main forces of the old order, the army, had retired temporarily from the scene to regroup. Eventually they would return and crush the revolution.

Some of these riots had more obvious and long-range goals; there was an especially important popular outbreak against the Frankfurt Assembly, on the occasion of its acquiescence in an unpopular peace, which will require fuller discussion when we try to assess the significance of the nationalist component in the movement of the lower classes. In Chemnitz the workers rioted in September, 1848, after their expectations of economic relief (especially from unemployment) had been aroused without being satisfied and when, on top of that, two of their number had been kept in prison and mistreated by the police and judicial authorities.[72] These disturbances appear to have been the high point of political violence used by the workers for distinctly working-class objectives. There were scattered revolts in Berlin on October 31, 1848, that broke out for somewhat similar reasons.

[71]Noyes, *Organization and Revolution,* 256–257.
[72]Strauss, *Chemnitzer Arbeiter,* 290–307.

These riots marked the final failure of the workers to support the democratic or left liberal movement and constituted the first major break with them.[73]

Subsequent violence was a defense against reaction. On the 10th of November, 1848, General Wrangel entered Berlin with the regular army and shortly afterward declared a state of siege. There was only very limited and ineffective protest, in which two special workers' corps, formerly of the civil guard, joined.[74] In April, 1849, Frederick William IV of Prussia felt strong enough to challenge the whole work of the National Assembly in Frankfurt by refusing the Imperial crown offered by the new Germany. The refusal set off a small-scale and brief civil war in which Prussian armies emerged victorious.

Some workers rallied to the defense of the bourgeois constitution, as the armed uprisings got under way in early May of 1849. According to Carl Schurz, there was an outbreak in the factory districts of Cologne following the king's refusal, despite overwhelming military force to oppose them. Similar outbreaks occurred in Iserlohn, Düsseldorf, and Elberfeld. The *Landwehr*, or local defense force, proved unreliable in these areas.[75] In Chemnitz, working-class elements were the most eager to form military defense units and come to the aid of the insurgents whose center of resistance was in Dresden. Propertied elements cooperated at first but soon began to reconsider and find excuses for delay.[76] Thus workers, including artisans, provided a great deal of spontaneous support for the revolution and constituted some of its main troops. Nevertheless, according to Noyes, the majority of the workers had at this point become disappointed with revolution and turned inward. Despairing generally of political action, those who were active at all turned toward what remained of the organizations they had created in the hope of salvaging what they could from the events of 1848–1849. The master artisans had by this point gained the legal protection they sought—but from the old established authorities, not from the Frankfurt Assembly. Meanwhile unsatisfied journeymen and the poorer workers had come to despair of getting anything out of either the established governments or the revolution.[77] With

[73]Noyes, *Organization and Revolution,* 270–271.

[74]Noyes, *Organization and Revolution,* 279.

[75]See Schurz, *Lebenserinnerungen,* I, 173–174. Made up of farmers, artisans, factory workers, and tradespeople, the *Landwehr* often refused to abandon families and jobs in order to put down insurgents with many of whom they warmly sympathized.

[76]Strauss, *Chemnitzer Arbeiter,* 309–320.

[77]Noyes, *Organization and Revolution,* 316, 322.

such a limited basis of support it is hardly surprising that the rally in defense of the constitution failed. With its failure there ended what chance there was that Germany might enter the age of industrial society under the auspices of constitutional liberalism. The next major impetus in this direction was not to come until defeat discredited the Kaiser's regime in 1918.

On looking over the whole record it becomes difficult to regard the workers' resort to violence as revolutionary. To be sure, there were quite a number of sporadic attacks on property, the fundamental basis of both the old order and the one that was being born. There is also clear evidence that the situation of both artisans and factory workers put them to some degree in opposition to the capitalist entrepreneur. But that is hardly revolutionary, in the sense of using violence to replace one political mechanism with a different one in order to assure the authority of a new social class or coalition of social classes. Even at times of high political tension the demands put together by working-class meetings, some of which were indeed quite large, reflected a complete acceptance of the prevailing social order. What they sought was fair treatment as subordinate members of this order: in the sense of jobs, enough pay to live on at a traditional standard, protection against the arbitrary authority of the employer, and to be treated with ordinary human respect by guild masters and *Fabrikanten.*[78] There is no sign of desire on the part of any organized group composed mainly of artisans or factory workers, or both, to take over the power of the state and rule Germany in their own interests. Since they were a small minority, that is scarcely surprising. But together with the peasants they would have constituted a large majority. I have come upon no trace of any such proto-Leninist conception. That too is hardly surprising in the light of the way German towns through their guild structure had long cut themselves off from the countryside except for essential economic exchanges.[79]

For the sake of accurate understanding of urban popular sentiments and demands in Germany at this time it would be helpful to reduce the notion of revolution to a much less salient

---

[78]Strauss, *Chemnitzer Arbeiter,* 260–269. On 266 he mentions a meeting attended by 4,000 persons. All crowd estimates, including modern ones, are highly unreliable. But it is safe to conclude that by the standards of the time this was a very large gathering. This account by an East German author is especially useful because it indicates that there was a minimum of influence by intellectuals at these particular gatherings. In the Chemnitz meetings the chairman is described as a nonworker, a petty-bourgeois democrat.

[79]Walker, *German Home Towns,* 112–119. The townsman's refrain was "No shit-hens fly over the wall."

position. Among articulate artisans and factory workers alike, the goal was acceptance in the social order. Acceptance meant enough esteem from others and a secure enough economic base to permit honest self-respect. Becoming a member of the proletariat was what all of them feared. Notions about how these objectives were to be achieved varied roughly in accord with social and economic status. For the guild master the big issues were prices and competition; and the proper solution, state aid. State aid meant that society should provide new services. For some workers the main issue was wages, a true sign of the advent of modern times. There was a large shadowy world in between, that of journeymen and apprentices, who were not yet factory workers in the modern sense and in their own sphere had little realistic prospect of becoming guild masters. Their concerns were mixed, and as yet they were hardly aware of the contradictions.

The varied demands of guild masters, journeymen, apprentices, and factory workers could be called revolutionary only to the extent that it was impossible to meet them within the framework of existing social arrangements.[80] In advance of the event it was very hard to tell what force would be necessary to renegotiate the social contract. On their own, the urban lower strata showed very little inclination to use violence for that purpose. This does not mean that they were incapable of anger and violence. Where violence did occur on a fairly wide scale it was the violence of those whose hopes had been raised and then disappointed, as in the uprisings of 1849. For the urban lower strata in Germany, to the extent that the crisis was a revolution at all, it was a revolution for the sake of respectability.

6. Nationalism and the workers

I have already drawn attention to the connection between a changing awareness of human capacities to do away with socially produced miseries and corresponding changes in the definition of friend and foe both at home and abroad. Some redefinition of the meaning of German and non-German was evidently taking place among the urban workers as early as the Revolution of

---

[80] The main line of cleavage was between the new commercial and industrial leaders—the new capitalist bourgeoisie, and *all* forms of manual labor, from the guild master seeking protection to the casual laborer employed for very low wages.

1848. In a thought-provoking study two distinguished historians have argued that in 1848 a strong current of nationalism had already set in among German workers.[81] It is very difficult to discern, however, just what was taking place below the level of occasional rhetoric by articulate leaders.

The riots in September, 1848, against the National Assembly in Frankfurt for its failure to uphold German claims against Schleswig-Holstein provide the best point of entry for an effort to understand the connection between German nationalism and social alignments during the revolution. Indeed, the September riots were not only a crucial turning point in the revolution; they were a miniature version of the whole revolution, and one during which the redefinition of self, friend, and foe took place with brutal clarity. By the time they occurred, reactionary forces in the German-speaking lands had already begun a strong recovery from their confusion and disarray at the beginning of the revolution. The organizations of democrats and workers in southern Germany had fallen under police bans. In Vienna at the battle of the Prater (August 23, 1848) workers protesting a reduction of wages in the public works had been routed, with 30 dead and 282 injured.[82]

At this point there occurred one of those major crises in foreign affairs, so frequent in German nineteenth- and twentieth-century history, that provided an opening for both radicals and conservatives to try their weapons in the domestic political arena. Prussian arms under the Prussian King had been unsuccessfully promoting German claims to Schleswig-Holstein, then under Danish sovereignty. Under pressure from England and Russia, pressure that added to the element of national "humiliation," the Prussian King accepted terms favorable to the Danes and unfavorable to the Germans. The terms were set out in the Truce of Malmö. The Frankfurt Assembly now faced the choice of accepting or rejecting the Truce. The Assembly, which had originally commissioned Prussia to send troops into the provinces, now found itself in the position of having to accept a loss of territory that many Germans, rightly or wrongly, held to be an integral part of the new Germany that was struggling to be born. The Prussian King was dictating the loss to them, and in turn was accepting dictation from foreign countries.

The Assembly was in a dilemma. The news of the Truce reached it on September 4, 1848. In a mood of disenchantment

---

[81]Werner Conze and Dieter Groh, *Die Arbeiterbewegung in der nationalen Bewegung*, 32–40.
[82]Noyes, *Organization and Revolution,* 258–259.

and dismay, and after a reminder by the speaker of its earlier commitments to defend German honor, the Assembly in the evening of the 5th refused to ratify the Truce. But without military forces under its own command there was next to nothing the Assembly could do. On the 16th of September the Assembly reconsidered and accepted the Truce by the narrow margin of 21 votes, 258 to 237.[83] The consequence was a massive popular uprising, complete with barricades. In its course two conservative leaders of the Assembly were murdered as traitors. The conservative senate of the city of Frankfurt called for troops to protect the Assembly, a call that the reactionaries—the only sector of society that had troops at its proposal—were more than happy to answer. Street fighting lasted for three days before Prussian and Austrian troops were able to restore order.[84] The respectable elements had thrown themselves into the hands of the reactionaries for the sake of order and property—and not for the last time in German history. In the future, respectability and nationalism, not to say chauvinism, would march happily together. In 1848, on the other hand, respectability was antipatriotic, albeit reluctantly.

Was the other side of the coin, the radical movement, at this juncture an upsurge of spontaneous popular and plebeian nationalism? From some accounts it looks that way. But Valentin's detailed account of the uprising and its background provides no support for such an interpretation. There may have been a fair dose of nationalism among the radical democrats, who enjoyed widespread support in southwestern Germany at this time. For a brief moment the news of the Truce of Malmö drove the radically democratic sector of the bourgeoisie and the mass of the plebs together, a potentially dangerous combination for the Assembly. But the radical democrats were reluctant to go beyond words to revolutionary action. When the plebeian elements—"masses" as they appear in several accounts—turned to insurrection, this coalition evaporated.[85]

The insurrection itself had been brewing since before 1848. Frankfurt was the crossroads and center of southwest German politics where radical currents were especially powerful. Nearly

[83]Veit Valentin, *Frankfurt am Main und die Revolution von 1848/49*, 310–311, 313–314.

[84]See the brief account in Obermann, *Arbeiter*, 302–305. Valentin, *Frankfurt*, chap. 4, provides a detailed account upon which I have mainly relied. Valentin, *Geschichte der deutschen Revolution von 1848/49*, II, chap. 3, draws on his earlier work and does not add any information relevant to the problems considered here.

[85]Valentin, *Frankfurt*, 314–315; see also 292–297 on the Democratic Congress held earlier.

every left-of-center orator came at some time to Frankfurt, where he could count on a noisy and sympathetic audience. The main recruiting grounds for such an audience were discontented working folk of low status. Here and there among them a voice spoke out in the language of the future calling upon the proletariat to rise and smash their oppressors. Gymnastic associations *(Turnvereine)* were the special sources of subversion, out of which the workers' union *(Arbeiterverein)* grew in March of 1848. Well before the Truce of Malmö the city of Frankfurt had provided large audiences for antiparliamentary radical speakers of various shadings and persuasions.[86]

This antibourgeois and antiliberal current among the lower classes in towns and cities made its first all-European appearance in the Revolution of 1848. In the Puritan Revolution and even the French Revolution the main thrust of popular demands had expressed itself in and through parliamentary assemblies. Though for a time this popular current flowed along with that of radical bourgeois democracy and sometimes intermingled with it, in Germany the September riots in Frankfurt put an end to their cooperation. The reason of course was the inability or unwillingness of the Frankfurt Assembly to meet popular demands.[87] This antiparliamentary current far overshadowed any nationalist element in the popular outburst and constituted its real historical significance. The excitement over the Truce of Malmö merely supplied the spark that enabled popular sentiment to turn from rhetoric to insurrection. Although the chairman of the *Arbeiterverein* on September 16th did tell his audience that the right wing of the Assembly was guilty of treachery to the German people,[88] there was hardly any mention of the Truce in the speeches of those who stirred up the masses in and near Frankfurt just prior to the uprising.[89] In the Germany of 1848 fanatical popular nationalism still lay hidden well over the historical horizon.

By this observation I do not mean to imply that workers did not show an interest in the character of the state. They certainly did. Earlier we have noted the journeymen's rather pathetic

[86]On the *Turnvereine* and their social composition, see Valentin, *Frankfurt,* 277; on contemporary use of the term proletarian, 278–280; on origins of the *Arbeiterverein,* 283; on antiparliamentary radicalism, 285–287.

[87]A point documented extensively in Noyes, *Organization and Revolution,* 221–261.

[88]Obermann, *Arbeiter,* 303–304.

[89]Valentin, *Frankfurt,* 345–346. On 353–354 in his final assessment Valentin speaks of the Truce as an "external" cause for the uprising that had long been brewing for "internal" reasons.

rejection of all prevailing political currents in favor of some form of federalism. This they symbolized by a rejection of all political flags and an attempt to promulgate one of their own. Again in the twelve-point program of the Chemnitz workers of April 22, 1848, and the fifteen-point program of Leipzig workers of March 27, 1848, there are several demands that have to do with the character and policy of the state. But only the first point of the Chemnitz program, a demand for an end to tariff barriers within Germany and for tariff barriers around Germany, has anything to do with Germany's relations with other countries. It is nationalistic in the sense of putting German interests ahead of any others. On the basis of these programs, mentioned because they seem to be more spontaneous expressions of worker interest, including both factory workers and artisans,[90] than others upon which I have been able to find information, it is also quite clear that the articulate sector of the German working classes did indeed have a strong interest in getting a unified German state. But they wanted such a state because of what they felt it could and should do for them. (The same was true of course of the bourgeoisie.) Their attention was firmly fixed on domestic issues. Indeed it is probably safe to say that domestic issues attracted something like 80 to 90 percent of what attention the workers could and did give to politics.

To be sure, articulate workers, if pressed in argument, might have agreed that these domestic objectives—or "social democracy," to use the term floating through all of Europe at that time, though it was yet to become a formal designation for an organized movement in Germany—could in the European context of the time be achieved only through and within a powerful state. But nobody seems to have pressed them. Furthermore, since for good reasons workers were utterly hostile to the existing standing armies and wanted to replace them with a people's militia, their leaders would have been in somewhat of a quandary about the means with which to achieve this state. Or perhaps they would have tried to parry the dilemma with the optimistic assertion that all nations and peoples would be brothers as soon as their social program had become reality. The essential point remains, however, that partly due to their powerlessness, workers did not have to face these problems. The most one can assert with confidence therefore is that the seeds for a working-class

[90]See Strauss, *Chemnitzer Arbeiter,* 260–262, 268–269. Significantly the manifesto of another group, quoted by Strauss on 249, where artisans and workers joined up with entrepreneurs, intellectuals, and bureaucrats, adopted a much more nationalist stance. It demanded a unified, powerful representation of German interests abroad.

nationalism, as well as its contradictions and dilemmas, were already present. They would have plenty of time to grow.

Even if one accepts at face value the reports of massive working-class participation in the excitement over Schleswig-Holstein, there is no sign of a messianic expansionism among German workers during this period. There is nothing remotely comparable to the burst of popular energy in the French Revolution (and was it really so popular?) that at first rallied to the defense of the revolution and then carried "liberation" across the European continent. From Christianity through socialism the great liberating movements of Western civilization began as pan-human ideals and became corrupted as agents of new repression in the course of becoming attached to specific governments. The transformation is visible in the Papacy, the Napoleonic Empire, the British Empire, the USA, Russian Communism, and Chinese Communism. In 1848 the German working classes had barely embarked on this trajectory.

CHAPTER SIX

Social and cultural trends before 1914

1. Introduction

Like their class comrades in France and England at the outbreak of the First World War, German workers marched off to the carnival of slaughter in perfect order. Up to the last moment there were doubts that this would happen: fears that it might not in upper-class circles, hopes that it might not in working-class circles. The event itself created a shock whose tremors still reverberate beyond the circle of professional historians. To some the event proves that workers were giving up revolutionary illusions and rhetoric. Under the influence of advancing industrialism they were learning the virtues and imperatives of political bargaining to the point where they were becoming good liberal democrats. For moderates the tragedy lies in the fact that this process of democratic integration could not be carried through in time to prevent a second and even worse tragedy: the rise of Adolf Hitler. For those with revolutionary sympathies, on the other hand, it was precisely this integrative process that first of all allowed the First World War to happen and then prevented the possibility of any effective resistance to Hitler.

Despite their differences intelligent moderates and intelligent revolutionaries tell essentially the same story. It is a story of the taming of the proletariat. Behind both versions there is the implicit assumption that a large industrial proletariat existed, and that at some point this proletariat represented, at least potentially, a serious revolutionary threat.

But do we really know for sure that there was a proletariat to be tamed? More specifically, was modern industry creating at any

173

time before 1914 a larger and larger mass of workers with sufficiently similar life conditions and sufficiently acute grievances to push them in the direction of becoming revolutionary tinder? Or, from a different viewpoint, was the industrial working class getting big enough so that it threatened to overwhelm the propertied classes by sheer force of numbers if it demanded and obtained the vote? Clearly it would be a mistake to accept either leftist boasts or conservative complaints as very good evidence on this issue. Both sides have too obvious an axe to grind. Occupational and other statistics, for all their limitations, ought to reveal more accurately the basic contours of the situation.

Whatever the statistics to be discussed in a moment show, at this stage of the inquiry it will be wiser to drop or at least bracket the term and concept "proletariat" with its overtones of potential revolution. The conception is one to be proved, not assumed. Furthermore, preoccupation with this conception can prevent us from seeing and asking more interesting questions. We ought not to spend all our time trying to decide whether or not the workers had revolutionary inclinations. To do that would be to force the workers' feelings and behavior into predetermined categories that may have little to do with their real lives and concerns. Instead we ought to try to discover what these concerns were. They may have had very little to do with politics and revolution. So far as possible we need to learn how they viewed their own lives, what they saw and felt as misfortune and good fortune, justice and injustice, and in what terms they explained these matters to themselves. In searching for answers to these questions it is important to remember that the history of the Social Democratic Party of Germany (SPD) is not the history of the German industrial workers.

Among their concerns we especially want to learn their hopes and fears about the future, including the historically created stereotypes and cultural lenses through which these images of the future were refracted. Obviously it would be a mistake to assume that all industrial workers were alike in the experiences they underwent and the feelings they shared, though it is reasonable to expect that some experiences and feelings were very widely shared. Even to speak of a working class in any sense beyond that of a gross statistical aggregate based on a certain type of employment requires evidence about shared experiences. The differences may be just as important or more important than the similarities. Hence one of the major tasks will be to locate and account for the principal lines of cleavage.

2. Size and composition of the industrial work force

In 1907 the German Empire carried out a large-scale occupational census whose results were published in several volumes during the years that remained before the outbreak of the First World War. With their numerous tables and extensive commentary these sober volumes constitute a unique if little-used source of basic facts about the structure of German society. Another quite useful source of quantitative and qualitative data about the industrial workers is the set of annual reports of the Factory Inspection Service (*Gewerbeaufsicht*). These data, supplemented here and there from other sources, make it possible to draw the preliminary statistical contours of the subject matter.

In 1907 the total population was 62 million. The occupational breakdown was as follows (in thousands):

Agriculture and forestry	9,883
Industry and mining	11,256
Commerce and transportation	3,478
Miscellaneous wage earners, including servants	472
Free professions	1,087
Total (excluding army)	26,176

To these should be added:

No occupation reported	3,405
Rentiers	1,792
Total	5,197
Grand total	31,373[1]

Since the occupational breakdown accounts for 31 million or half of the population, we may assume that the other half was made up of those persons who were not or could not be part of the labor force (such as the old and infirm, young people, non-working wives, etc.).

Of those engaged in industry and mining the occupational breakdown was as follows (in thousands):

Independent proprietors	1,977
Office workers	686
Workers and helpers (*Mithelfende*)	8,593
Total	11,256

---

[1] *Statistisches Jahrbuch*, Vol. 35 (1914), 2, 14–15. Small discrepancies here and elsewhere in the totals are due to rounding.

We see then that the total number of workers and helpers is 8,593,000 or about 27 percent of the occupationally accounted-for population.[2] With workers in industry and mining only slightly more than a quarter of the economically accounted-for population, it is clear that the industrial proletariat, no matter how defined, was still in 1907 a very small minority of the German population.

How small it was depends on the general conception one has of the proletariat. Two characteristics are likely to receive emphasis in any general discussion.[3] The type of industry might provide one criterion. On this score it is possible to make rough distinctions between types of industry characteristic of an advanced modern economy and those more typical of an earlier stage of historical development. Another and very similar criterion would be to define as characteristically proletarian those workers who live in big cities and are employed by giant firms. Let us find out what "big" and "giant" meant in 1914 and follow up each of these criteria in turn.

[2] *Statistik des Deutschen Reichs* (cited henceforth as SDR), Neue Folge, Band 211, Berufsstatistik, Abteilung X, 175, 176. For a markedly different set of totals for workers just before World War I, see Waldemar Zimmermann, "Die Veränderung der Einkommens- und Lebens-Verhältnisse der deutschen Arbeiter durch den Krieg," in Rudolf Meerwarth *et al., Die Einwirkung des Krieges,* 285. For 1913–1914 Zimmermann gives the total "working class" (*Lohn- und Gehaltsarbeiter*) as around 23 million. With family members they came to 44 million persons or 66 percent of the total population, then around 67 million. Zimmermann's working class, however, in addition to workers in industry and mining included argricultural laborers and wage earners in commerce and transport. Over one-fourth of such persons in commerce and transport were *Angestellte* or white-collar workers, with whom our study is not concerned at this moment.

[3] One can search out all the references to the term proletariat in the three volumes of *Das Kapital* without coming upon a concise definition. The closest Marx comes to such a definition is in n. 70, I, 645: "Unter 'Proletarier' ist ökonomisch nichts zu verstehen als der Lohnarbeiter, der '*Kapital*' produziert und verwertet und aufs Pflaster geworfen wird sobald er für die Verwertungsbedürfnisse des 'Monsieur Kapital,' wie *Pecqueur* diese Person nennt, überflüssig ist." (Economically speaking, a proletarian means nothing more than a wage laborer who generates capital and is thrown out on his ear as soon as he has served these purposes and is superfluous for Monsieur Capital as Pecqueur calls this person.) According to the relevant articles in the *Bol'shaia Sovetskaia Entsiklopediia* (2nd edition) proletarian describes *any* wage laborer who through his labor power creates surplus value for the capitalists or bourgeoisie. See *s.v. Proletariat,* vol. 35, 23; *Rabochii Klass* (working class), *ibid.,* 436; and *Pribavochnaia Stoimost'* (surplus value), vol. 34, 459. But in its more extensive discussion of "working class under capitalism," vol. 35, 437, in a reference to the enormous increase of the proletariat during the nineteenth century in several countries, only workers in industry and transport are included. If the definitions as such are not very helpful, one can hardly expect them to include what was supposed to happen as capitalism matured. For that one has to consider Marxist theory as a whole. On the other hand, it is precisely on this point that there has been the greatest controversy. Since I am not writing intellectual history, and since our present task is to find out what happened and not what Marx or his followers and critics thought was happening, I have cut the Gordian knot by working out my own conceptions of what the term could mean.

For the numbers of workers in different types of industries it will be best to use the figures collected by the Factory Inspection Service for the year 1913. They cover only firms with ten or more employees. For that reason they omit on the order of one million out of eight million workers. On the other hand, the workers in these small shops are not the ones that are relevant at this point. It will be useful to group these occupations into three main sectors. The first corresponds to what became the war industries. If one includes mining, as I think we should, this sector is quite clearly the most characteristic of an industrial society at that point in time. The second is an intermediate group, and the third a primarily civilian set of industries. The last, or most civilian, sector served mainly consumer interests. Before the First World War it contained by and large the least technically advanced sector. Table 2 below presents these data.[4]

Table 2 shows about 44 percent of the industrial workers to have been in the modern sector, as against 55 in the two sectors I have grouped as less modern. It is also in the modern sector that the largest concentrations of workers in similar occupations occur. Metals and machinery together were occupations for 25 percent and mining for 16 percent. Together they account for 3,050,000 workers. Other concentrations of 10 percent or over were to be found in food and textiles. These account for 1,670,000 workers. By the most generous estimate therefore it would be possible to include 4,720,000 workers, or about 64 percent of all the workers, as belonging in the category of modern industrial proletariat.

That number, however, is more impressive for its size than its meaning. The next chapter, on the Ruhr, Germany's industrial heartland, will discuss conditions among miners and metalworkers in some detail. Here it is enough to say that the political behavior of miners and metalworkers was very different in the prewar period. It is just one of many indications that the total figures, even when broken down by occupational categories, lump together persons whose circumstances and ways of life were very distinct and led to quite different political attitudes.

Many of the most important differences occur *within* a given occupational category. The machine industry is an interesting example. The 1907 occupational census provides some insight into the varieties of work lumped together in this category.

---

[4]Here I follow Gerhard Bry, *Wages in Germany 1871–1945*, in many respects, but I include mining in the first sector. For more details and fuller citations see my discussion in Chapter Eight, Section 1.

Table 2.

Industrial Workers in 1913, as Reported by the Factory Inspection Service

(in thousands)

Industrial Categories	Number of Workers	Percentage of Total for All Industries
WAR INDUSTRIES		
Metals	680	09
Machinery	1173	16
Chemicals	181	02
Oils and illuminating materials	82	01
Mining	1197	16
Total for war industries	3313	44
INTERMEDIATE INDUSTRIES		
Wood	454	06
Paper	199	03
Leather	121	02
Stone and clay	648	09
Building	277	04
Miscellaneous	18	—
Total for intermediate industries	1717	24
CIVILIAN INDUSTRIES		
Food	714	10
Clothing	431	06
Textiles	956	13
Printing	200	03
Cleaning	56	01
Total for civilian industries	2357	33
Total for all industries	7387	100+

SOURCE: *Statistisches Jahrbuch für das Deutsche Reich,* Vol. 42 (1921/22), 96–97; I have been unable to locate the original factory inspection reports for 1913 in American libraries.

NOTES: The Factory Inspection Service reported only on establishments with 10 or more employees. Slight discrepancies are due to rounding.

There were 469,000 makers of machines and tools, the largest of the subcategories. Then there were 107,000 wheelwrights and carriage builders, in addition to almost 90,000 makers of electrical apparatus. There were only 21,000 workers in automobile and bicycle plants together. The list proceeds on downward in a total of 15 subcategories or *Berufsarten der Maschinenindustrie,* through the makers of timepieces (41,000), musical instruments, pianos, and organs, down to the women who made incandescent mantles for lamps (2,000). This is still the world of the artisan. If anything, the demand for special skills has increased. It has little or nothing to do with the world of the big factory and its monotonous machine-tending, requiring a minimum of skill. That, of course, existed. But one should be careful not to exaggerate its influence. It was likely to occur in textiles and some of the new automobile plants, although the latter were barely starting up in the last years before the war.[5]

The size of the proletariat shrinks a great deal more if one thinks of looking for it in the big city. Germany in 1907 had 42 cities classified as "big cities" (*Grossstädte*), a term for towns with a population of 100,000 or over, a very small figure by contemporary standards. If we set 500,000 as an appropriate figure for the megalopolis of prewar Europe that Oswald Spengler viewed with such foreboding, Germany had five: Leipzig with 505,000, Dresden with 512,000, Munich with 533,000, Hamburg with 827,000 and Berlin with 2,005,000. Furthermore, by no stretch of the imagination could the mass of the inhabitants of the big cities be called an industrial proletariat. Out of every 10,000 inhabitants of all the big cities—most of which we would today call towns—only 2414.5 were engaged in industry, mining, and construction.[6]

Within the industrial sector in the big cities only the following occupational categories contained more than 300,000 persons and are therefore proper candidates for an industrial proletariat:

Metalworking	332,000
Machine industry, instrument making	359,000
Clothing manufacturing	483,000
Construction	419,000
	1,593,000[7]

If the proportion of the wage earners to the total number of persons in the occupation was 76 percent, as it was for Germany as a whole, that would yield a total of 1,211,000 persons. These persons could for the most part be considered the working members of the urban industrial workers. They come to only 10.7 percent of all industrial workers (11,300,000). If each had a spouse and two children, we can conclude that with their family members they totaled about 3,633,000. At less than 4,000,000

[5]SDR, N.F., Bd. 211, Abt. X, 126.
[6]SDR, N.F., Bd. 220/221, Abt. VIII, 97 (Gewerbeabteilung B).
[7]SDR, N.F., Bd. 211, Abt. X, 140.

this estimate works out to an industrial proletariat that came to less than 6 percent of the total population.

The data on employment in giant firms yield an even lower estimate, roughly half the size of this one. Giant firms at that time were defined by the census as furnishing employment for more than 1,000 persons, including not only wage earners but also the proprietors and administrative and clerical personnel. It is impossible to tell how many of these giant firms were in big cities, though it seems likely that many if not most of them were. The number of persons making their living in such establishments was 1,378,000 in 1907. Three industrial categories accounted for the overwhelming majority of these persons:

Mining, smelting, etc.	600,000
Machine and instrument making	326,000
Textiles	112,000
Total	1,038,000[8]

If 76 percent of these were wage earners, the total would come to 789,000. The strictest definition of modern industrial proletariat yields the lowest figure. But that is not all there is to the story. The census cited notes that the three industrial categories above were a rapidly growing sector, nearly doubling from 563,000 in 1895, the year of the preceding census. To this point we shall return.

If the industrial workers in the most powerful industrial state on the continent were not in the big cities, where were they? German industry before the First World War was, as a whole, still very much a small-town affair even by the standards of the day. All persons in industry, not just workers, were distributed as follows:

In rural areas	2,879,000
In small and middle-sized cities	5,569,000
In big cities	2,807,000[9]

By itself this fact goes a long way toward explaining the provincial and small-town atmosphere of German prewar labor politics.

So much for crowding into the cities. To the extent that becoming proletarian means a reduction in the significance of skill, the census data indicate that this process too had not gone very far. Among the nearly 8.6 million industrial workers, just

[8]SDR, N.F., Bd. 220/221, Abt. VIII, 65.
[9]SDR, N.F., Bd. 211, Abt. X, 140.

short of 5 million were classified as skilled and 3.5 million as unskilled. The division by sex was approximately 7 million men and 1.6 million women.[10]

Male skilled workers predominated in metalworking, machine building, woodworking, clothing, food production, construction, printing and allied trades. These were the occupations, where, according to the census, the work required a substantial dose of training in handicrafts. Unskilled males predominated in mining and smelting, stone and earth products, chemicals, illuminating materials, and the paper industries. These were among the main industries run by large firms and, for the times, marked by a high division of labor. Thus the process of proletarianization was quite visible here. Finally, the women performed unskilled tasks in nearly all industrial occupations. In addition there were substantial concentrations of more than 100,000 women (skilled and unskilled) in firms making textiles, clothing, and foodstuffs.[11]

We may close this part of the discussion with a brief survey of the statistical evidence concerning the degree of economic and political organization among the 8.5 million industrial workers. Of these two forms, let us fix our attention on the unions, since they had a more important influence on the daily life of the workers. The Free Trade Unions, associated (not always amicably) with the SPD, were by far the largest and most powerful unions. But they had competitors. These represented attempts to influence the workers, undertaken under religious, political, and employer auspices. The Christian Unions were essentially Catholic; the Hirsch-Duncker *Deutsche Gewerkvereine* had associations with the Liberal party. Employer unions, which had important local successes, also usually called themselves *Gewerkvereine,* whereas the Socialist and Catholic organizations called themselves *Gewerkschaften.* (In mining *Gewerkschaft* has a special meaning reflecting earlier corporate traditions.) Since the number of members fluctuated considerably in the course of a year as well as over the years and in addition the reports on membership come from the organizations themselves, it is necessary to treat membership figures with considerable skepticism. Nevertheless they do tell us something about the degree of organization among the workers. Table 3 gives membership figures for certain selected years.

The figures on membership show a rapid growth of the Free

---

[10]*Statistisches Jahrbuch,* Vol. 35 (1914), 15; SDR, N.F., Bd. 211, Abt. X, 178.

[11]SDR, N.F., Bd. 211, Abt. X, 251–253.

Table 3.

Trade-Union Membership: 1907, 1912, and 1913

(in thousands)

Year	Free Trade Unions	Christian Trade Unions	Deutsche Gewerk-vereine (H.D.)	Independent Unions	Economic Peace Unions	Protestant Unions	Total	Free Trade Union as % of Total
1907	1873	285	109	127	59		2453	76
1912	2583	351	109	303	231	156	3733	69
1913	2525	342	107	318	280	154	3726	68

SOURCE: 25. *Sonderheft zum Reichs-Arbeitsblatt: Jahrbuch der Berufsverbände im Deutschen Reiche,* 79.

Trade Unions between 1907 and 1912, after which there was a slight decline. They also reveal, however, a decline in the Free Trade Union's share of organized workers: it dropped from three-quarters to slightly over two-thirds in this period. The main gainers were unions in one way or another associated with employer interests. It is also worth noticing that in 1913 at most one worker in three belonged to a union with some nominal Marxist coloration. Somewhat less than half of the industrial wage earners belonged to any union at all. There was still a large reservoir of unorganized wage earners behind the best organized working class in Europe.

By 1912 wage contracts covered about two million wage earners, less than a quarter of the industrial workers. Wage contracts by themselves, however, were not an accurate index to union strength at that time. As, for example, among the coal miners, unions might have considerable influence and include a substantial part of the work force, but the employers still continued to refuse to engage in collective bargaining. Free Union strength remained concentrated in smaller firms where conditions remained similar to those of a workshop in a handicraft. That situation, on the other hand, was very widespread. Before the war the Free Unions had made hardly any inroads into heavy industry, iron and steel, or chemicals.[12] In other words, the Marxists had yet to gain a foothold in the core of the modern industrial proletariat.

The Social Democratic Party claimed to be the main spokesman for workers' interests and was, of course, the chief carrier of Marxist doctrines. As a proportion of the wage earners, its membership, though increasing rapidly, remained very small. In 1907 it claimed a membership of 530,466, which would have worked out to about one worker in sixteen if all members had been workers; it is quite clear they were not. Many were intellectuals. By 1913 its membership, on the other hand, had nearly doubled to almost a million, 982,850.[13]

A more meaningful indication of the SPD's influence, on the other hand, was its power to win votes. By 1890, it is worth noticing, Engels was waiting to learn election results just as eagerly as any election buff today and gave August Bebel detailed instructions on how to telegraph results by election districts without using too many words or spending too much

---

[12]Hedwig Wachenheim, *Die deutsche Arbeiterbewegung 1844 bis 1914*, 565, note 2.

[13]William Maehl, "The Triumph of Nationalism in the German Socialist Party on the Eve of the First World War," 24, table 6.

money.[14] The census year 1907 happened to be the year of a severe electoral setback for the SPD. In that year it polled 3,259,000 votes, nearly 29 percent of the votes cast. In 1912 it polled 4,250,000 votes, almost 35 percent of the votes cast.[15] That would come to about half of the industrial workers. But to judge from the union figures just cited, which show about 1.2 million workers affiliated with nonsocialist or antisocialist unions (some of whom may, however, have voted socialist anyway) there is reason to suspect that as many as a quarter of the SPD votes came from outside the ranks of the industrial working classes. Whatever the actual situation, the figures show once again that the history of the SPD is very far from being the history of German workers.

To sum up the statistical evidence, the more one looks for a modern industrial proletariat and the more carefully one defines the term, the smaller the species becomes. German industry before the First World War was still mainly a provincial and small-town affair. The world of the artisan lived on in many areas alongside, and even inside, the factory. Still that is not quite the whole story. There are a good many signs in the figures that the cutting edge of industrial advance was creating a modern industrial proletariat, by any reasonable definition. If it was an infant rather than a threatening giant, it was a rapidly growing infant. And just how the infant was going to act as it grew up was a matter about which only doctrinaires could be really sure. On balance then the weight of the evidence falls heavily on the side of skepticism about the existence of any massive reservoir of potentially revolutionary sentiment, either in the form of a pre-industrial proletariat or modern industrial one. I have no intention of doing a statistical juggling act in order to make a supposedly significant historical actor disappear from the stage. It will be necessary to take another look for this actor in the coal mines and blast furnaces of the Ruhr, where, if ever, such a collective appearance should be visible. But, to repeat, the task is to find out what sort of workers felt angry and in what situations—not what they were supposed to feel according to some theory. The basic situation for the workers was of course the wage relationship.

---

[14]But Engels kept his sense of humor, expressing to Bebel the fear that the SPD would get *too* many seats in the Reichstag. Other parties, he continued, can have a certain number of jackasses and do stupid things and nobody says boo ("Kein Hahn kraht danach"). We, on the other hand, are supposed to have nothing but geniuses and heroes. See *August Bebels Briefwechsel mit Friedrich Engels,* edited by Werner Blumenberg, 379–380. Eleven years earlier Engels had written to Bebel that the only thing he wanted from the SPD was that it leave him in peace so that he could finish his theoretical works (75).

[15]Maehl, "Nationalism in the German Socialist Party," 23, table 2.

3. Wages and workers' conceptions of the wage relationship

The available data on real wages indicate that as industrial growth gathered rapid headway after 1871, the workers' material situation improved. Several studies written from quite different viewpoints agree in conveying this general impression. Table 4 shows their calculations for indices of real wages for selected years. The amount of variation from one estimate to another, however, warrants caution. It is also important to remember what average real wages do *not* reveal: variations due to unemployment; the effect of a spouse's or children's earnings —or lack of such earnings—on the material situation of any given household; and, perhaps most important of all, variations from one kind of industry to another and those within an industry, due to skill or other reasons. Workers' households did not live on average real wages. They lived on the wages they could actually earn at a given time and place. Nevertheless, when all these qualifications are taken into account, the agreement on a general rise of between 26 points in the lowest estimate and 59 points in the largest for the period as a whole (1871–1913) does remain impressive. As a working-background assumption for the discussion that follows it is safe therefore to infer that for most industrial workers the material situation was getting better rather than worse.

What, then, were the workers' own ideas about the "proper"

Table 4.

Indices for Real Wages: 1871–1913

Year	Bry 1913=100	Desai 1895=100	Kuczynski 1895=100	Phelps Brown-Hopkins 1895=100
1871	74	66	82	72
1880	70	79	79	77
1895	89	100	100	100
1900	98	111	110	108
1905	98	114	108	104
1910	99	119	110	106
1913	100	125	112	109

SOURCE: Dieter Groh, *Negative Integration und revolutionärer Attentismus: Die deutsche Sozialdemokratie am Vorabend des Ersten Weltkrieges,* 40, 85.

---

level of wages? Naturally not all workers had the same notions on this issue. Nevertheless it is not difficult to discern certain widely recurring conceptions of desirable and undesirable forms of payment, what was and was not a just and sufficient wage, and finally those forms of inequality that were acceptable, or even just and desirable. Behind these conceptions the industrial workers had their own forms of reasoning. At some points their notions of justice coincided with those of their employers. At others the two came into conflict.

The most important point to grasp at the outset is that, for the workers, wages were a manifestation of their dependence on other persons and hence a limit on their autonomy. How much they earned, and whether they could even earn anything, was the central fact of their lives. That is the reason why getting a job in the first place, and then keeping it were such crucial issues. There were differences here that had to do with both skill and the life cycle. Casual laborers, especially in construction, did a great deal of wandering. They could hardly expect jobs to last, and a worker often stumbled into them through a chance acquaintance. They expected to be out of a job from time to time. Nevertheless the experience could be painful. Older workers at all levels faced the specter of unemployment as strength and skills waned. Dependence on wages is also the reason why a strike over a few cents an hour could so easily become an event that aroused powerful passions. These few cents an hour, multiplied by the number of hours in a year's work, could make the difference between penury and respectability.[16] Likewise, for an employer close to the margin it might make the difference between profit and loss.

It is possible to distinguish between the workers' feelings about the amounts they received and the ways in which these amounts were calculated and paid out. In one of the early questionnaire studies, very valuable for the information on workers' attitudes presented in their own words, around two-thirds of the workers expressed strong hostility to piece rates. "Piece rates are plain murder" (Akkordarbeit ist Mordarbeit) is a common refrain in their answers. The main reasons they advanced were that this method drove them too hard, creating a sense of often unbearable rush and tension. Simultaneously it produced all sorts of petty rivalries and quarrels, particularly in getting access to raw

[16] August Springer, Der Andere das bist Du, chap. 5, espec. p. 60. On the sense of dependence see also Adolf Levenstein, Die Arbeiterfrage: Mit besonderer Berücksichtigung der sozialpsychologischen Seite des Modernen Grossbetriebes und der psycho-physischen Einwirkungen auf die Arbeiter, espec. 133–140, 147–154.

materials that would work up properly and easily into the finished product. Yet this feeling was not universal. There was a substantial minority who felt that piece rates enabled them to earn more, unencumbered by the inadequacies or plain laziness of fellow workers. Though the evidence is too weak to support the generalization firmly, on the basis of reading through the protocols I suspect that unskilled workers, who were paid by the day as a rule, were more likely to prefer piece rates as they could earn more in that fashion.[17] The difference in attitudes toward piece rates and time rates reflects a deeper conflict between a desire for security and for open opportunity that permeates all of capitalist society, including a substantial portion of the working classes.

Very often workers did not know in advance of payday what they were actually earning, because the system of piece rates and deductions for spoilage was too complicated for them to grasp. At least that is what the trade-union literature claims. It is also quite possible that they understood the deductions perfectly well but resented them and feigned misunderstanding.[18] For our purposes the difference does not matter a great deal, because in both cases the deductions somehow seemed unfair. Furthermore the workers had no voice either individually or collectively in determining what the rates of pay were to be. Arrangements of this type were common in the big iron and steel plants of the Ruhr, but existed elsewhere as well. In such plants there was little or no discussion about wages when the worker was hired. The employers simply announced what they were going to pay and the basis for the various rates, very often by a notice posted on a bulletin board. Wage cuts—or what the workers took to be wage cuts because the notices were often rather complex as well as peremptory and the workers were understandably suspicious —were announced in this manner too. A worker who did not like the arrangement had in practice two choices: he could quit or not take the job in the first place.[19]

On this issue too, it is important to notice, the workers' attitudes were by no means uniform. Only the more politically

---

[17]See Levenstein, *Arbeiterfrage,* 19–44. Karl Fischer in his autobiography, *Denkwürdigkeiten und Erinnerungen eines Arbeiters,* frequently expresses distress at being forced to go on day laborer's rates when he ran into trouble with his superiors or when work was slack (see espec. 308–317).

[18]As Eric Hobsbawm has observed, "The refusal to understand is a form of class struggle." Quoted by Daniel Field, *Rebels in the Name of the Tsar,* 33, from Hobsbawm, "Peasants and Politics," 13.

[19]*Die Schwereisenindustrie im deutschen Zollgebiet, ihre Entwicklung und ihre Arbeiter,* issued by the German Metalworkers Union, 327–329, with sample notices quoted *verbatim;* see also 633–634.

and intellectually "advanced" workers raised articulate objections. Others, probably those whose experience of harsh authority in east German peasant life was more recent, accepted the arrangements in a docile manner, much to the discouragement of union organizers, who were unable to obtain collective bargaining rights in the big iron and steel plants of the Ruhr until after the First World War.[20] In other words, many workers had to be told what their rights were, and there had to be a fair chance that they could actually put them into practice, before they would believe in these rights and make them into their own standards of justice and injustice.

It is hard to imagine a clearer demonstration of the point that the sense of injustice can be an acquired taste: a learned response and an historically determined one, not an automatic and instinctive human reaction. At the same time we must not lose sight of the more elementary and perhaps even biological substratum. There is no reason to suppose that the autocratic treatment by the employers was painless for the workers. What the workers had to learn was not to feel pain, but how to stop feeling that the pain was just an inevitable aspect of their existence.

Workers' conceptions about justice and injustice in the amount of their earnings likewise make reasonably good sense while reflecting ambiguities and contradictions characteristic of this particular historical period. If a German worker at this point in time were asked what constituted a sufficient wage, he would be likely to make the following points: it should be enough so that he as the principal breadwinner could see to it that he and his family were not hungry, not cold, and had clothing suitable to their status. By this he meant clothing that was not ragged nor dirty, but also not "*vornehm*" or too elegant, appropriate to persons in high station. (These points recur frequently in autobiographical accounts.) This was an age, as we shall see later in more detail, where there had only begun to appear the faintest hints of the society of mass consumption. It was an age still marked by sharp social distinctions, not all of them by any means the object of resentment. Implicit in this conception of a sufficient wage was a notion of security of employment and of course the lurking fear of unemployment. What is rather surprising—unless I have missed something in a large body of evidence—is the absence of any strong signs of fear of *technological* unemployment. The most that

[20]The authors of *Die Schwereisenindustrie*, 329, comment ruefully that the foundry capitalist will be able to maintain the attitude of being the boss in his own firm (*Herr im eigenen Hause*) as long as the ideas of the modern labor movement have not gained entry among the foundry workers.

one encounters along these lines are rather general statements by elite workers or Social Democratic spokesmen to the effect that the fruits of technology should belong to all of the people and not to the wealthy capitalists alone. To sum up, the workers by and large had a clear conception of a minimum wage which they defined in negative terms as sufficient to avoid the more frequently recurring personal disasters of working-class existence.

Though there was a strong belief in, or perhaps better a strong desire for, a floor under earnings, the workers were by no means egalitarians. They made a clear connection between effort and reward. Perhaps it would be more accurate to say that they perceived and accepted a connection between what the worker invested of himself in a task and the payment that they deemed just, even if they might well have had trouble putting the relationship into an unambiguous mathematical formula. A worker ought to be paid more, they felt, if the job called for greater effort, a higher degree of skill, or exposed the worker to greater danger. Likewise, greater seniority called for greater reward. Taken together these considerations boil down to a notion that what the worker put of himself into the job *over time* ought to receive its just reward. In this sense a belief in the labor theory of value was almost second nature for the workers. What made them angry was not inequality as such; it was inequality that bore no obvious relation to these criteria and which therefore seemed highly arbitrary and unfair. It was this visible kind of inequality, a variety of witnesses testify, that really hurt.[21]

The system of four to five grades of pay, customary in steel rolling mills, pointed up such inequality, according to the trade-union authors of the report on the iron and steel industries cited. Workers in the steel mills felt that the system was unjust because those in the lower grades did more and harder work for less pay. On the other hand, the trade-union observers stated that it would not have been easily possible to eliminate such a system because a large number of foundry workers had no interest except in moving one step up the pay ladder. Hence this would appear to be a situation where in the eyes of the worker the potential gains for him as an individual outweighed the injustice of the system as a whole. It seems likely that such situations were widespread.

In some directions the workers' vision appears to have been quite acute. Thus there were intermittent objections to the

---

[21]See Paul Göhre, *Drei Monate Fabrikarbeiter und Handwerksbursche*, 49, 115–116; *Die Schwereisenindustrie*, 305, 331–333.

Lohndrucker, ordinary rate busters as they would be called in English. More frequent were complaints about workers of "foreign" origin (who were quite often simply from another part of Germany where they spoke another dialect), imported by the employers to work for lower wages. In other directions their vision to modern eyes may seem at first glance rather less than piercing. Women constituted a substantial part of the labor force, and when the war came, were able to replace the men in surprisingly large numbers. The notion that women deserved the same pay as men for doing the same work was supported, but only verbally, by top leaders of the Metalworkers Union in 1916.[22] Under ordinary conditions before the war women did not enter the industrial labor force except as an interim activity en route to marriage and motherhood. The worker's wife was expected to be a hardworking helpmate at home, especially valued for her ability to manage the family budget. Possibly the fact that this expectation had considerable correspondence to reality at that time explains the limited interest in and support for agitation for women's rights among the mass of the workers, an agitation that appears to have been carried on mainly by a small handful of women.[23]

The attitudes toward rate busters, foreigners, and women are of course consistent with two assumptions: first, that at any given moment there can be only a limited number of jobs to go around, and second, that workers individually and collectively had no control over what that number would be. On balance the reasoning displays a logic and realism which many a sociologist today might envy.

Thus in regard to the ever-vexed issue of the justifications for human inequality the workers did give some allegiance to the modern conception that these inequalities ought to be based on individual effort, demonstrable individual qualities, and not upon birth or inherited status. But this allegiance was limited. They wanted a secure floor put under wages, and displayed little sympathy for the law of supply and demand according to which a worker's wages were determined by his contribution to the

[22]See the report on women workers in heavy industry in 1915-16 in *Der Deutsche Metallarbeiter-Verband im Jahre 1916, Jahr- und Handbuch für Verbandsmitglieder,* espec. 21, where the union declares its unswerving support for the principle: "The same pay for the same job" (*Für die gleiche Arbeitsleistung den gleichen Lohn*). Coupled with this meritorious stand was the realistic worry that low pay for women could depress wage rates for men.

[23]For a vivid account of this situation as perceived by a woman of proletarian origins see the latter portions of the anonymous *Die Jugendgeschichte einer Arbeiterin: Von ihr selbst erzählt,* with introduction by August Bebel, espec. 77 ff.

employer's capacity to meet and follow the demands of the market. To be sure, they were not unaware that if their employer's business did badly, they would be the ones to suffer most. Yet even in the early twentieth century they show little more love for *Concurrenz* and the virtues of free competition and personal achievement than their predecessors did during the upheavals of 1848. For that matter neither did the capitalists themselves, and before 1914 many German workers learned the same lesson as the capitalists: that organization and political pressure could do much to mitigate the uncomfortable rigors of a society ostensibly based on merit alone.

4. Elite and masses among workers

After a relatively brief immersion in the autobiographies and prewar sociological investigations of German working-class life, an investigator will notice the existence of an intellectual elite among the working class with a somewhat patronizing stance toward what it regards as the mass of the workers. In modern times this is often the case with subordinate and oppressed groups, whose leaders are often unsure whether the masses will be up to carrying the burden that historical destiny has supposedly laid upon their shoulders. In Germany at this time the distinction was mainly between an articulate upper stratum of workers and a much larger stratum of inarticulate or possibly deliberately silent ones. Most though not all of the information that is available about the inarticulate comes from the articulate.[24] To learn what we can about the mentality of the inarticulate it is necessary to have as clear a conception as possible of the biases and predilections of the articulate. Otherwise the investigator runs the risk, well known to anthropological and sociological field workers, of swallowing the half-baked interpretations of professional "good" informants, anxious to let the social scientist in on the hidden secrets and laws of motion that govern their part of the social order. Nevertheless this group's relations with and attitudes toward the rest of the workers tell us a great deal indirectly about the character of the industrial working class as a whole.

August Springer provides a good introduction to this elite in

---

[24]To my knowledge there are no direct studies comparable to Elliot Liebow's *Tally's Corner;* William Foote Whyte's *Street Corner Society;* or Lee Rainwater's *Behind Ghetto Walls.*

his recollections of his first contact with the socialists, which took place when he was a young man working in a shoe factory in a small Bavarian town. There he met a man with bitter features, deep-set eyes, who seldom spoke, but then did so in a powerful manner. When other workers appeared childish and their chatter without sense or reason, the socialist refused to join in with them. To young Springer he appeared very manly, with sharp clear judgment, obviously a model for future behavior, even though Springer never became a socialist. Other workers feared the socialist because he would expose their silliness with a sharp word or a pointed question, poking holes in the bubbles of their slogans or phrases.

At a later point Springer describes how intellectually alert workers always sought out each other's company. Sometimes they would find one another at a big meeting, at other times in a doctor's waiting room. Then other workers would look on either in wonder or with ironical smiles as these members of the workers' intellectual elite discussed Gerhart Hauptmann, Émile Zola, Heine, Schiller, and many others. Though it is safe to infer that ordinary workers frequently felt uncomfortable and resentful in the presence of this elite, Springer points out that at least the convinced Social Democrats in this elite tried to be very patient with their more backward comrades. In its popular version Marxism provided both an explanation of this backwardness and a manner for coping with it. As described by the sympathetic but nonbelieving Springer, Marxism underpinned a complete faith in the automatic creation of more and more recruits to their party through the working of impersonal economic processes. Mechanization would show the skilled worker that he was no longer irreplaceable. Crises would become more severe and reveal ever more clearly the way capitalism destroyed human beings. As soon as the worker grasped these processes in the very marrow of his bones, he would struggle in order to preserve his own humanity. Therefore one must be patient with fellow workers who go after small advantages, who try to escape where no escape was possible, where in fact there was no hole to crawl through to get out of the position of wage worker.[25]

With a hint of envy of the Social Democrats, Springer confesses that at times he found it terribly hard to love his fellow workers. His own picture of the world bore a strong imprint of

---

[25]Springer, *Der Andere das bist Du*, 39, 150, 134–136. The events described probably occurred around the turn of the century, since the author had been active in politics for some time by the outbreak of the First World War, in which he served.

Protestantism, and he wondered if the failure to love came from some radical evil in his own nature. Yet he was able to perceive quite clearly some of the historical and social reasons for the stolidity and intellectual laziness of the mass of German workers in the provincial towns where he himself worked: the peasant and petty-bourgeois backgrounds of a large portion of them, as well as the conditions of factory life with its long hours and low wages. These left little time or energy for concern with anything more than just getting by somehow.[26]

If some of the convinced socialists were able to be patient with their more backward fellow workers, that was scarcely the case with all members of the workers' intellectual elite. Evidence on this point comes from a quaint but precious source of information on working-class attitudes, a mine of sociological data that has been the object of minimal exploration so far: Adolf Levenstein, *Die Arbeiterfrage,* published in 1912. Levenstein had been a foreman (*Werkmeister*) and over many years maintained close connections with a number of Social Democratic workmen.[27] Apparently he conceived quite on his own the idea of making what would now be known as an attitude survey using open-ended questions. He asked workers whom he had known to distribute the questionnaires. *Die Arbeiterfrage* contains the results of 5,040 questionnaires from miners, textile workers, and metalworkers. The bulk of the book consists of verbatim extracts from replies, complete with misspellings, colloquial remarks, and occasional passages of high-flown prose. Here we have a sounding into German working-class mentalities that almost permits us to hear *some* German workers speaking in their own words. It is the articulate who dominate the talk, though there are occasional revealing and tantalizing remarks from the others.

Before commenting on the substance of the reports it will be worthwhile to draw attention to some of Levenstein's difficulties in gathering his material—upon which he reports fully in a way that is more valuable than many a modern study's technical comments on measures of statistical significance—because these difficulties not only reflect the distinction between intellectual elite and masses among the workers but also shed light back upon the character of this distinction.

Levenstein divided his respondents into four types, of which only one need concern us at the moment. Unlike the other three

[26]Springer, *Der Andere das bist Du,* 134–135, 149.

[27]Wachenheim, *Arbeiterbewegung,* 520.

types who wrote lengthy replies to many of the questions, and sometimes long letters besides, those in the *Massenschicht* or mass type answered most questions with a simple yes or no, or with an occasional derisive answer (such as the reply to the question: "What would you get yourself if you had more money?"—"Four women"). At the end of his characterization of the mass type Levenstein burst out in frustration to say that these might better be called the type with dead souls, people who take an apathetic stance toward all expressions of human life, who might as well be put in a cage and fed.[28] That is elitism with a vengeance, and none of his working-class respondents go quite that far, though they approach it. Well over three thousand of his respondents, 64 percent or nearly two-thirds of his sample, he placed in this *Massenschicht* category.

By itself all that this proves is that a large number of workers did not want to fill out a questionnaire, even when asked by a fellow worker (who obviously had gotten ahead of them). Normal working-class suspicion of inappropriate nosiness could account for the result.[29] But there are good reasons to think that there is more to the situation than mere suspicion. Anyone who has had even minimal contact with uneducated persons knows that many of them *do* have considerable difficulty putting their feelings in words (though a minority may display a striking natural eloquence). Any social scientist worth his salt knows at least some of the reasons: lack of opportunity or even more a set of life conditions that is basically stultifying. Alfred Weber, one of those in charge of the *Verein für Sozialpolitik*'s inquiries into working-class life, asserted in 1912 that the man tied to the machine was the one who had lost the power to complain.[30] Now even the person who has lost the power to complain—in the presence of strangers or on paper, we must remember—is hardly a person who has lost the capacity to feel, even though there is likely to be a considerable degree of resignation, a certain damping down of feelings that would otherwise be too painful. This is exactly what the pattern of responses in the Levenstein report suggests. Members of his mass type do answer simple questions about the forms of pay (piecework versus hourly wages) fairly often; they are almost totally silent when he tries to

[28]Levenstein, *Arbeiterfrage*, 11.

[29]One question had to do with the use of alcohol. When some workers saw this, they slammed their fists on the table, shouting, "Now they even want to take liquor away from us!" Levenstein, *Arbeiterfrage*, 7.

[30]Alfred Weber, "Das Berufsschicksal der Industriearbeiter," 394.

tap working-class hopes and aspirations. Hence we come to the question of whether it is possible to use the information about the feelings of articulate workers as evidence about those for the inarticulate. If one makes allowance for lowered aspirations and probably a considerably lesser degree of self-confidence and self-esteem, I believe that one can insofar as their situations are generally similar. Since the inarticulate do have feelings, it is a reasonable inference that the articulate ones in many cases express the latent and perhaps not so latent sentiments of the rest. In the course of this chapter I shall draw on such evidence for that purpose. But first it will be wise to glance briefly at the elite's own attitudes.

At least some members of this elite were what an outsider would call snobbish to the point of outright contemptuousness. One Berlin metalworker, who had traveled considerably, commented on his fellow workers in these words: "They are all masses! And I hate these habit-ridden thoughtless people, dallying back and forth between work and pleasure. For the most part I have lost faith in their wish and will to carry on an evolutionary struggle, far less a revolutionary one."[31] Perhaps this critic lived to be surprised when the Berlin metalworkers formed the heart of the revolutionary movement there after the war. But the sentiment is one that crops up frequently. Several complain about the lethargy, ignorance, voracious egoism of the masses, and express in one fashion or another doubts about the prospect that they will ever learn to understand their situation. It is likely that these members of the working-class intellectual elite were frustrated party or trade-union activists.[32]

Paul Göhre, the Protestant pastor who worked on the shop floor of a Chemnitz machine tool factory and has left us one of the first field studies of working-class life reports the same situation. His account is more sympathetic to the mass of the workers and shows some of the causes for their behavior. He described them as persons with no political and social convictions of their own, who made no effort to earn the right to such convictions, but still considered themselves to be Social Democrats. Such persons seldom looked at a Social Democratic newspaper and rarely went to an SPD meeting. But they swore by the program. Within this group he noticed two general types. One, which he thought most deserving of pity, was too oppressed and too full of care to concern themselves with SPD politics. The others were

[31]Levenstein, *Arbeiterfrage,* 108.

[32]Levenstein, *Arbeiterfrage,* 218–219, 297, 317.

too incapable, thoughtless, or lazy; here young persons between the ages of sixteen and twenty were the commonest. The reasons he saw were the youngsters' love of pleasure and the easy possibility for satisfying their inclinations. They spent their time in dance halls or out walking with their girls. Political concern was more likely to arise after marriage and the necessity to face life in a serious fashion.[33] From this evidence it is apparent that many ordinary workers were in a situation where self-restraint was not much of a paying proposition. Furthermore, circumstances imposed enough frustrations for such people to be unwilling to add more on their own. There were signs of this among the apprentices before 1848. There, as in other times and places, the common reaction was to get what one could out of life in short-run pleasures. Very likely the somewhat priggish hostility of the worker elite to the masses "dallying back and forth between work and pleasure" comes from their own efforts to control exactly these impulses.

Such angry frustration is not, however, the only reaction. One miner, regarded by Levenstein as unusually intelligent, remarked that the party and trade-union movement had taught him how to understand his situation, and through this understanding had injected him with an honest hate of God's world and the property-owning class. "And the man who can hate honestly can also hope. Otherwise I would have talked my way free of both movements out of contempt for my class comrades." Finally, here and there one comes across a sensitive personality, perhaps with frustrated artistic inclinations, who finds the gross and rough manners of his fellow workers offensive and wounding.[34]

5. The common liability to misfortune

Besides this distinction between elite and mass there were many lines of cleavage among industrial workers. Religious differences were quite marked in some areas, especially in the Rhineland but also in parts of Bavaria. Often there was a line between workers born in the town or city and migrants into the city, the latter usually crowding into the less desirable tasks.[35] Occupa-

---

[33]Göhre, *Drei Monate Fabrikarbeiter,* 135–136.

[34]Levenstein, *Arbeiterfrage,* 287, 174.

[35]Springer, *Der Andere das bist Du,* 14–15, 21; see also Weber, "Berufsschicksal," 381.

tional differences we have already discussed at some length. Even a very modern factory in prewar Germany was likely to have a work force with numerous gradations of rank and status, each symbolized by a special costume.[36] Yet despite these distinctions there was a series of calamities and misfortunes to which all wage earners were liable. This common liability to misfortune becomes quite apparent on reading biographical accounts. To be sure, not all workers were equally exposed. Perhaps a majority never suffered the worst calamities. Nevertheless, the nature of these calamities does more to distinguish industrial wage earners as a group than any other single factor. To the extent that there is a justification for speaking of an industrial working class distinct from other classes, this is the reason.

In comparison with the situation around 1848, in the rapidly changing pre-1914 years there had been a marked increase in "specialization of misery," roughly corresponding to the increasing division of labor. Among the new industrial workers there are few echoes of the complaints about the squeeze on the small producer that were still a major theme in the journeymen's laments of 1848. By 1914 the belief that it was possible to *do* something about poverty and misfortune had seeped down much more widely. The notion of doing something about it through cooperation across class lines had by no means vanished. The patriotic and religious unions, as well as much of the actual practice of the SPD and SPD-affiliated unions, provide much evidence on that score. But there was a new intransigence against property-owners and employers. The workers were going to have to do things for themselves and to the rest of society. If there was an increased specialization in the causes and remedies for misery, corresponding to an increased division of labor, the human manifestations still did not seem very different. Fears for the loss of earning power and its chain of consequences in hunger and the erosion of self-respect were not, so far as I can see, very different in 1913 from what they had been three and four generations earlier.

From the workers' own point of view there appear to have been two main forms of misery: calamities and more or less "normal" suffering. The main form of calamity was the loss by the breadwinner of the capacity to earn a living. As the situation appeared to the worker, the calamity was liable to occur for three reasons: accident, illness, or more gradually from severe al-

[36]Marie Bernays, "Berufswahl und Berufsschicksal," part I, 162–163. For an earlier instance see Springer, *Der Andere das bist Du*, 35–36.

coholism. When any of these things happened, other members of the household had to pitch in and supplement its earnings in any way they could. Sickness and accidents appear in the main as events that just happen. There is usually very little in the way of explanation. The events are merely reported, along with the immediate causes.[37]

In the background, however, there appears a public institution that eased the shock. As far back as in the account of Karl Fischer, born in 1842 and who, as an unskilled or low-skilled worker wandering from one job to another, lived through the transition from handicraft to factory, it was possible for an ordinary worker to present himself at a local hospital and receive apparently gratis or for a nominal fee within his means very decent and humane treatment. To judge from the biographical accounts, workers knew about this possibility and took it for granted. Nevertheless free hospital care did nothing for the loss of earning power. If the worker did not recover his (or occasionally her) earning power quite rapidly, the household might be reduced to a situation close to starvation. There is no indication that the workers dwelt on this prospect. Very likely the ordinary problems of making a living kept them from thinking about it a great deal. Still every worker must have known others to whom this had happened. In this sense the possibility of disaster lurked constantly in the background.

Attitudes toward alcoholism varied. Occasionally other members of the family might be aware of the disappointments and pains that drove the head of the house to alcohol in excess and express understanding forgiveness despite their own suffering. In other instances the wife resented the husband's taking sorely needed money to spend in the tavern. Then there would be violent scenes witnessed by terrified children. In such cases the explanation of disaster would appear as a simple moral one: the wife accuses the husband of immoral behavior that hurts her and the children. A certain amount of heavy drinking was taken for granted. Many workers claimed that the work was so exhaust-

[37]For some examples of reporting traumatic events without emotion and without explanation see August Bebel, *Aus Meinem Leben,* I, 1–20; the anonymous autobiography of a woman, *Die Jugendgeschichte einer Arbeiterin,* 1, 5, 6, 23. Moritz Th. W. Bromme, *Lebensgeschichte eines modernen Fabrikarbeiters,* 65 ff., tells how his father's going to jail forced the family down into proletarian status. There is an explanation, but it is so involved and personal a story of minor embezzlement as to be scarcely comprehensible. An interesting contrast occurs in Franz Louis Fischer, *Arbeiterschicksale,* 44–45. There a miner, forced by illness to retire, successfully petitions twice for a pension (the second time to the Kaiser). But as we shall see in Chapter Seven, the miners' situation and traditions were very special.

ing that they could not stand it without a heavy shot of liquor. Springer reports an interesting ethical dualism in the workers' judgment of alcohol. Several of the best workers he knew were very heavy drinkers, evidently just because they enjoyed themselves that way. They retained their prestige as workers but lost in general social esteem. Trade unions carried on a vigorous propaganda against alcoholism, telling the workers that if they wanted decent and respectful treatment from their superiors they could not appear like drunken pigs.[38] Thus, even if heavy drinking was taken for granted, there was an undercurrent of uneasiness and social stigma about the practice. The reason appears obvious. Heavy drinking, whatever the cause, could easily be the first step along the road to disaster for the individual and those close to him. In this area the women appear in their traditional role as the main guardians of morality.

Losing one's job might be a severe blow, but did not turn into a disaster unless it turned out to be impossible to get another job for a long period of time. Some of the saddest and most moving parts of the workers' biographies are accounts of the search for work that met with perpetual failure.[39] On this score there was evidently an important difference between the unskilled and skilled or semiskilled workers. An unskilled worker, especially in construction, one of the biggest areas of employment, expected that any given job would probably be temporary. What mattered most about this kind of work was how much it paid. That would determine whether one had a margin to buy some cheap clothes and manage somehow while moving on to a new job.[40] Skilled and semiskilled workers, on the other hand, were tied to a particular kind of work. They moved around from one factory to another, doing very much the same kind of work in each factory. A contraction in their particular line of industry might therefore be disastrous. There are, however, indications that such an eventuality did not play a major part in the regular expectations of prewar German factory workers. At the last prewar Congress of the Social Democrats in 1913 one speaker cited with horror an official statistical report indicating an unemployment rate of 0.66 percent for Germany as a whole, and the local example of Munich's construction industry with an unemployment rate of 8.8 percent as an example of how bad the situation could get. To Americans who can recall the estimate of one worker in five out

---

[38]Springer, *Der Andere das bist Du,* 107.

[39]*Jugendgeschichte einer Arbeiterin,* 21, 30–31, 37–42.

[40]Karl Fischer, *Denkwürdigkeiten,* 134 and *passim.*

of a job at the height of the Great Depression of the 1930s these figures seem very small, though one must beware of differences in measuring what is in any case very difficult to measure accurately.[41]

Among "normal" miseries, fear of what would happen in old age appears as the overriding one. Workers in the large factories that formed the heart of the capitalist system reached the peak of their earning power at about forty years of age. After that, their earnings were liable to drop precipitously. By forty they were too old to stand the pace, which required not so much brute strength as the ability to pay attention under monotonous yet endlessly demanding conditions. As Alfred Weber pointed out, the career line of the factory worker contrasted sharply with that in other occupations. A factory owner or manager generally was just beginning to reach the climax of his career at forty. At that age a bureaucrat was entering the highest posts he would reach. Even an artisan could look forward to many more years of productive work and social esteem. For the factory worker, on the other hand, just at the point when his needs were likely to reach their maximum and he faced some twenty more years of hard work, he was used up and ready before long to be thrown on the scrap heap.[42] From the day he started on the job the worker was aware of this, though many must have repressed it in a happy-go-lucky fashion. "Getting ahead" for the worker amounted to a brief devouring intoxication of youth. At life's high noon there came short rations, to end perhaps in collapse.[43]

Though the contrasts were sharpest for the moderately skilled factory worker, they were present for all, and certainly no less intense in occupations with serious health hazards, such as

[41]See report by Joh. Timm on unemployment measures in *Protokoll über die Verhandlungen des Parteitages der SPD . . . 1913*, 390, 386. His figure for Germany as a whole was quite out of date, being based on the 1895 occupational census. On the other hand, the 1907 census did not appear in print until 1913–1914. The absence of up-to-date statistics on unemployment is in itself significant and cannot be taken as evidence that the problem did not exist.

[42]In the worker's life cycle the appearance of offspring and extra mouths to feed could be a traumatic blow, especially for the mother if the father was a mediocre breadwinner. The autobiography of Moritz Bromme, *Lebensgeschichte,* is particularly revealing about the strains on personal relationships that exist under poverty, even though his particular situation was probably an extreme one. For men and women, marriage, he remarks, was almost always a misfortune (206). His wife, a basically kind woman, at one point expresses vehement anger at the children because they take so much time, energy, and money. One day, after reading in the newspaper that someone's child had died, she burst out, "These people are really lucky, they have it fine! Now for them their child is already dead" (240–241). See also pp. 224–225 for similar reactions.

[43]Weber, "Berufsschicksal," 388.

mining. Alfred Weber saw the workers' career line as the main reason for a deep pessimism and alienation from the existing social order. This pessimism was certainly there and colors nearly all the workers' statements in Levenstein's interview materials. It was, however, a pessimism about their own personal fate that was partly offset by a mixture of hopes about a better world in the future. These hopes could be for a new social order or for their children's advancement within the prevailing system.[44]

If there were deep fears about the future, there were plenty of anxieties about the present. Biographical accounts are full of reports of periods of hunger, inadequate shelter in the form of whole families crowded into one room, sometimes without heat, and other penuries. There can be no doubt that these were painful and common experiences, especially in the big cities. While these experiences were very hard to bear, by themselves they do not appear as the source of resentment or moral outrage. Until and unless some form of spiritual awakening occurred, such as through exposure to socialist propaganda, these experiences evidently appeared to those who suffered them as part of the natural order of things. Like bad weather they were to be endured. If anything was to be done about them, the solution was to try for a better job. Especially the younger members of the family were expected to make superhuman efforts to relieve the plight of the household if they were at or near an age when they could earn something.[45] Still even if these experiences do not appear as a specific source of resentment, it seems likely that they contributed to a general undercurrent of dissatisfaction with the workers' place in the social order, a theme to which we shall recur in other contexts.

---

[44]Levenstein found majorities of about three to one among textile workers who were willing to express hope for the future and somewhat less than two to one among metalworkers. But in both cases the number who did not answer the question was very large. See *Arbeiterfrage*, 311, 322. On upward mobility for the children of skilled workers—which was at least *felt* to be a real prospect—see Bernays, "Berufswahl und Berufsschicksal," part II, 910.

[45]For some examples see the anonymous *Jugendgeschichte einer Arbeiterin*, cited above. The early portions are especially instructive about the daily life of proletarian women.

6. Relationships with superiors and other workers

Relations between workers and their superiors in the workplace were another matter. There resentment of injustice could often boil to the surface—for two closely connected reasons. From practical experiences on the job the workers developed certain conceptions about the proper way to execute their task, that is, what were good and bad materials (there are many complaints about having to work with materials that would not "work up" properly), how to combine them, the timing of operations, and similar matters. These reactions occurred among unskilled workers too, who certainly knew the difference between hacking at hard clay and stone and digging through sandy soil.[46] Then as now these informal work rules were probably a mixture of rule-of-thumb maxims about efficient and effective procedures for doing the job, rules for protecting the work group against increased demands from the employer,[47] customs governing the proper rates of reward for each task. Work rules were (and are) part of the implicit social contract governing the relationships among equals and superiors in the workplace.

In most German factories at that time the work rules were in theory entirely the prerogative of the management. That was rather a sore point with the workers, who were not supposed to have any part in their formulation but were to give complete obedience to them. Actual practice, on the other hand, often softened the antagonism. What the rules said and what happened might be two quite different things. The personality of the director was often a decisive factor. In the factory where Paul Göhre worked the director was very strict—almost military, but also human and understanding, and very just. Furthermore the foremen enforced the rules in such a mild and shrewd (*klug*) manner that their severity was not felt as very painful. When the director introduced new work rules about methods of produc-

---

[46]For social relations in the place of work see Springer, *Der Andere das bist Du,* 105–109; *Jugendgeschichte einer Arbeiterin,* 34–37, 46–48 (on sexual exploitation by superiors); F. L. Fischer, *Arbeiterschicksale,* 90–98 (on miners); Göhre, *Drei Monate Fabrikarbeiter,* 45–54, 76–86, 102 (on a machine tool factory). The material is also scattered through other sources, especially the autobiography of Karl Fischer (not to be confused with F. L. Fischer above) and the investigations of Adolf Levenstein, to be drawn on again in more detail later.

[47]Restriction of output by common agreement is mentioned by K. Fischer, *Denkwürdigkeiten,* 264.

tion, hours, or methods of payment, the majority of the workers held back timidly and uncertainly until the word was passed around and "public opinion" appeared as formed. The makers of this "public opinion" were a few respected Social Democrats, even though political propaganda was strictly forbidden within the factory gates. (In one case, the director had said, in a colloquial German that for once reproduces well in our tongue: "Social Democracy is all the same to me: outside you fellas can paint yourselves as red as you want. Here inside, no. Here I'm in charge. Whoever *does* anything flies right outa here." Even if several workers did not like "public opinion" and even if it went against their interest, it was a power that other workers respected and against which they rarely raised objections.[48]

As pointed out in the first chapter, the implicit social contract is usually subject to continual testing and renegotiation, and not all participants may regard all of its terms as equally binding. Subordinate groups are especially likely to feel resentment and moral outrage whenever those in authority attempt changes to their own advantage *and* at the same time appear incompetent according to the subordinates' work rules.

The important point in these considerations is that in the work situation resentment and moral outrage can arise quite spontaneously, that is, without the help of "outside agitators." In the workplace there are visible and concrete human beings who appear responsible for injustice because of their individual behavior. They are unjust because they violate the social contract that grows out of the nature of the work itself. This aspect distinguishes such situations from the more general distress of hunger and bad housing discussed a moment ago.[49] The spontaneous nature of these processes in an age before collective bargaining had established itself, and the rage that can arise out of them, appear so vividly in the pathetic autobiography of Karl Fischer that it is worthwhile recounting some episodes here.

Karl Fischer is likely to strike a modern reader as an individual somehow unusually impervious to feelings of moral outrage. The fact that his father periodically stole money out of his savings box when he was a boy is just one of many from his life

---

[48]*Drei Monate Fabrikarbeiter,* 75–76, 102. See also 80–81 where Göhre notes that skilled workers got nowhere if they barked orders at their helpers.

[49]Nevertheless it is curious not to find complaints about grasping landlords. The situation closest to that comes mainly from an earlier period: the complaints of the apprentice who lives in the master's household and is forced to perform numerous domestic chores that have nothing to do with learning the trade.

that he reports in a flat factual manner.[50] The shy, beaten child of a tyrannical father, he stumbled through most of his life from one crushing experience to another. But eventually he did reveal that he was capable of feeling unjustly treated when the shop foreman did not pay him according to the time he had actually put in on a job. Likewise when he felt that the shop foreman and the other workers were trying to gang up on him and get rid of him—by this time he was getting old for the job—he finally lost his temper and shouted them all down.[51]

Another time, on learning that the director of the establishment knew how to perform his own small task, Fischer's respect for the director suddenly shot up.[52] Turning to his relationships with other superiors, it is a surprise to discover that Fischer, along with the other workers, did not seriously object to having the engineer reduce their piece rates. They could all still earn enough by working hard. But when the bookkeeper set the rates, the reaction was very different, since the bookkeeper came in only once a year at inventory time and in Fischer's words "understood as much about the job as a cow does about Sunday." Furthermore, people were just a "side issue" *(Nebensache)* to the bookkeeper, at least as Fischer perceived him.

In all the episodes so far, Fischer displays no sign of a generalized hostility toward his superiors or "bosses." All that he reports are a series of personal instances of bad treatment. Ultimately, however, the effect turns out to have been cumulative. Toward the end of the autobiography we find him praying to God in despair. God tells him to slam the cast he was making down in front of the master and shout, "I want to earn a hundred marks a month. Everything is out of line here *(Hier ist keine Ordnung)*!"—a revealing cliché that usually has conservative implications. For this performance he got fourteen-days' notice to quit. But he felt much better. The remark *"Hier ist keine Ordnung!"* reveals his feelings of outrage at what he felt were rules not appropriate to the proper operation of the place of work. Though his rage shortly afterward became even more towering and dramatic, that was as far as it went in substance.

After getting his notice to quit, he had fantasies of telling the engineer and the director off, even of taking over the factory.

[50]*Denkwürdigkeiten*, 76–77.

[51]*Denkwürdigkeiten*, 277, 281–282.

[52]*Denkwürdigkeiten*, 268. But see also 355, where the director appears as a figure from afar who asks foolish questions and gets in the way of work and the possibility of earning the day's pay. Both images of the director reflect the same grounds for respect or its absence.

Eventually, after waiting at the director's door for three hours, he managed to get in and ask the director *why* he had been fired. He received a curt answer and was shown the door. Outside the door, he reports: "With a voice of thunder I uttered the judgment . . . you [in the familiar *Du*] want to fire people who have worked here so long, and whom you don't even know! Who made you the director? Whoever did that will have to answer for it!" Some masons nearby, who happened to hear Fischer loudly berating the director, beat their tools in time with his words.[53] At this climax the account ends.

Karl Fischer's account is especially useful because there is no trace in it of Marxist doctrine, or indeed of any other intellectual influences of a critical or subversive sort that could have colored or focused his experiences. In that sense it was purely spontaneous. In Fischer's oxlike submission to his life situation and his moment of rage against it the biography reveals both what the Marxists had to contend with and the forces that they could harness. There must have been thousands of Karl Fischers, not only during the transition to the factory system but long afterward. Like many before him (back at least to the 1840s) and many who followed him, the essence of Fischer's cry, even in his moments of near frenzy, was for decent human treatment (*menschliche Behandlung*). It will be possible to see more clearly just what this meant and its political consequences after exploring other aspects of working-class culture and the forces that shaped it.

7. *Some sources of working-class culture*

Among the forces that had shaped this culture, standard accounts generally stress three: the change from the patriarchal rule of the workshop and small factory to the more impersonal and bureaucratic world of the giant firm, the tyranny of the machine, and the dependence of the worker on the wage system. These are, so to speak, the sources of the workers' misery seen through the detached eyes of the economic historian rather than through the workers' own eyes. Workers' perceptions of these processes, to the limited extent we know about them, are similar enough to make it obvious that both workers and historians are talking about the same thing. Beyond that point, there is much more

[53]*Denkwürdigkeiten*, 375–378, 388–390.

variety than might be anticipated and some reactions one would not expect.

There *was* a transformation from a patriarchal to a more bureaucratic management, and it *was* perceived by at least the more intelligent workers while it was taking place. Yet many workers did not see the transformation as one that hurt them. Interviewers at both the Daimler automobile factory and a large textile works discovered that many of the employees had deliberately moved to these establishments because their previous place of employment was unpleasant and "too small," evidently in the sense of being somehow confining.[54] When August Springer moved to the new type of factory, he found that the proprietor in his impersonal way did not care at all about the political opinions of his workers as long as they did their jobs. The consequence was that the establishment became a refuge for Social Democrats.[55]

As for the effect of the new machines, Levenstein's inquiries turned up a large majority of articulate workers who did feel enslaved and exhausted by them. Yet there was also a minority who actually enjoyed the rhythmic workings of their machine. Some felt that the machine liberated them from toil in a way that allowed them all sorts of pleasant daydreams.[56] The evidence also shows the need for strong reservations about the familiar notion that the introduction of the machine forced the worker to concentrate on one tiny operation in the process of production to the point where the worker lost any sense of the meaning of his work or identification with the final product. What machines frequently required was concentrated attention, hour after hour and day after day. Safety equipment and regulations were probably very primitive in comparison with those that exist now. As Paul Göhre observed on the basis of his own experience in a factory, factory work put as much demand on a human being as the most exacting intellectual work. The necessity to pay close attention to a dangerous job amid noise, bad air, and using all one's physical strength for eleven hours a day could be frightfully exhausting. Nevertheless in the factory he observed, a

[54]Bernays, "Berufswahl und Berufsschicksal," part I, 162.

[55]Springer, *Der Andere das bist Du,* 103. As noted above, Paul Göhre encountered a very similar situation.

[56]Levenstein, *Arbeiterfrage,* 45–49, 68, 75, 104–106. Bernays, "Berufswahl und Berufsschicksal," part I, 161–162 reports that the workers paid very careful attention to their machines "so that [the machines] wouldn't feel hurt." In textile factories the women felt very much in charge of a little "kingdom" at their regular working spot with its machine. "People want to know where they belong" was a comment frequently encountered as an explanation.

relatively modern machine-tool factory, all the workers had a strong sense that they were working together to complete a single complicated task. Each individual from the most skilled to the most unskilled was aware that the prompt, accurate, and intelligent performance of his job was important for the whole product. Hence any worker who botched his job was the object of vehement reproaches from his fellows. Indeed, because the workers on the shop floor had little or no contact with other parts of the establishment, such as the sales force, engineers, and draftsmen, the manual workers felt that they did the "real work," that they were the creators of the machines they were building and truly represented the factory.[57] The assembly line was not the predominant model of factory life for prewar Germany. The situation recreated attitudes associated with the age of the artisans even in its most modern sector of machinery and metals.

Some of the most enlightening information turns up as the result of Levenstein's admittedly crude effort to distinguish between the workers' sense of material deprivation, due to low wages, and a more general unhappiness, due to the alleged loss of freedom and autonomy under the factory system. Levenstein asked the rather involved question: "What oppresses you more: the small wage or that you are so dependent on the employer, have so few prospects to get ahead in life, that you are unable to offer your children anything?" A modern reader can feel a good deal of sympathy for those workers among his "mass type" who replied laconically, "Everything oppresses me." Very likely this is an accurate report in the sense that the situation as a whole "got them down." At least one of the members of the "mass type," however, tried to elaborate (with almost every word misspelled): "It gets me down a lot that I can make too little money, and I don't want to be any kind of a patriot."[58]

The more articulate workers tried to express their complicated feelings in considerable detail. Two themes run through their responses. One is bitterness at the prospect that neither they nor their children were likely to escape their fate as workers. They were, as the expression now has it, "locked in." That, however, was a secondary theme.[59] The main theme was resent-

<hr>

[57]Göhre, *Drei Monate Fabrikarbeiter,* 74, 54, 117.

[58]Levenstein, *Arbeiterfrage,* 137. Appeals to nationalism had become fairly frequent in government circles by this time, and this is only one of several expressions of resentment at them.

[59]This evidence should also be set alongside that of Bernays cited above, about the feeling of skilled workers that the children would (and in many cases did) move up out of the class of factory workers. The attitudes reported by the two studies are not altogether

ment at the lack of autonomy, the feeling that it was necessary to sell oneself body *and* soul (for too low a price) in order to earn a wage, and that the employer just didn't care. (In the statistical summaries of the replies, which should be taken with salt and reserve, objections to dependence were just about as numerous as objections to the low wage.) As a Berlin plush weaver put it: "At seven in the morning the factory siren begins to whistle. It's the whistle of my bread master. So I'm whistled at, the way the master whistles for his dog. Five minutes later the factory gate is shut, or the time-ticket machine locked, and there I am, inside the jail."[60] Or as another worker put it: "If only I got more decent attention. But the *Fabrikant* doesn't even say good morning," a complaint that, according to Levenstein, runs with all possible variations through the replies of all the workers.[61] Once again we encounter the workers' plea for decent human treatment, a theme that recurs in their hopes and fears about the future.

8. *Images of the future*

A great deal of light on what industrial workers felt as painful deprivations comes from the richest section of Levenstein's study, on their fantasies, hopes, and fears for the future. His questions here were both broad and simple. They amount to asking what would you do if you had enough time and money, and what are your hopes and desires? In addition to showing what the workers felt they lacked, the replies also reveal the limits on what they *could* conceive as a happy life, limits that were the consequence of their present situation and past history. It is tempting to see in many of the replies evidence of an historically crippled imagination. Yet there are overtones of unwarranted condescension in such a judgment. It would be very difficult to prove that even professional intellectuals have as a rule been any less provincial in their images of a desirable future.

In any case, among these prewar German workers there were three main components in their images of a happy life. The first

---

consistent, even though Bernays was here discussing only skilled workers. Furthermore, the wording of Levenstein's question invites a complaining answer. These technical matters, on the other hand, are really secondary. Human beings often hold contradictory attitudes. Circumstances will determine which ones will come to the surface in either speech or action.

[60]Levenstein, *Arbeiterfrage*, 133.

[61]Levenstein, *Arbeiterfrage*, 131.

component was simply a vision of the present stripped of its painful aspects. The second was a future couched in terms of an idealized rural past, or else an idealized version of what they had seen or heard about contemporary life in the countryside. This was a counter image, a reversal of life as they knew it. Finally there was the imprint of socialist ideas. The proportion of these components varied from individual to individual. In some replies only one of these three elements appears; in others all three may be combined—or jumbled—as in a dream.

Here is a characteristic reply from a twenty-two-year-old miner with two children, making comparatively good wages. It is written in a colloquial German with numerous misspellings, and the flavor is hard to capture in English. It comes from the heart, without fancy decorations in imitation of educated tastes: "When I got back from the shift I'd eat myself full up and then go for a walk in the woods, drink a swig of beer then take a rest in bed so I could be in a good mood for the next shift—I'd build myself a nice house so that I could live in something *I* owned."[62] The idea of different work, or not working at all, does not occur to this miner. What he wants is very simple—and very necessary and very human—enough to eat, a decent night's sleep, the little luxury of a glass of beer, and a place to live that he can call his own. With these matters arranged, life could go on as usual and very happily. I would hazard the guess that this young man spoke for the majority of German workers in his day, and, allowing for differences in taste and idioms, even for most of mankind at all times. It is also very likely that in his simple statement we hear the authentic voice of those workers "dallying back and forth between work and pleasure" who were the despair of the slightly priggish working-class elite.

Statements very similar to those of this miner crop up intermittently in the replies. Here is one from a twenty-seven-year-old weaver, earning only two-thirds of the miner's wages. He worked a ten-and-a-half-hour day (against the miner's nine). For him it was also impossible to write correct German: "Sleep a bit longer in the morning, work from 8 to 1, after dinner sleep a bit till 4 o'clock and then go for a walk till supper. I'd build myself a little house, feed pigs, geese, chickens, doves for my own use and set up a nice vegetable garden which I would want to cultivate real nice so I could always be able to eat my fill."[63] Though in this instance the delights of simple rural life appear mainly gas-

[62]Levenstein, *Arbeiterfrage*, 176.
[63]Levenstein, *Arbeiterfrage*, 189.

tronomic, from other replies it is plain that the appeal was also aesthetic. Other workers, as might be expected, wrote about buying clothes so as to look more like a human being or just respectable.[64]

There is one case where hopes of owning a little piece of property and doing more for political organization are incongruously juxtaposed. Another man displays the imprint of radical notions mixed with others in what is probably a characteristic hodgepodge: "Take care of cultivating myself. (1) Stenography, which pleases me specially. (2) Writing and figuring! (3) Reading scientific books! A revolver with everything that goes with, in case we have to defend ourselves. Everything that is necessary for a human existence."[65] We may close this selection with the appealingly brief statement of one more worker, a twenty-nine-year-old father of two: "Take my wife by the arm and go for a walk. Go get myself a fila [villa] and a nice garden."[66]

In addition to these hopes for the satisfaction of simple material wishes, enough to eat, fresh air, a good night's sleep, a nice house and garden (similar to the Detroit auto worker's goal of a "nice little modern house"),[67] many workers expressed strong desires to satisfy a thirst for knowledge and what we would conventionally call cultural needs. Due to Levenstein's bias and procedure it is likely that this type of response is heavily overrepresented in the replies that he printed. Much of this alleged evidence about a thirst for knowledge and cultural satisfaction reads to me like a collection of New Year's resolutions put together for the approval of one's "betters."

There is support for this interpretation in a recent study of the reading habits of prewar Social Democratic workers, so far as these can be ascertained from the records of workers' lending libraries and from the sales records of books known to appeal to the working-class intellectual elite. Bebel's *Die Frau und der Sozialismus* (1879) was the only work about politics and society that enjoyed substantial popularity, running through fifty editions by 1910. It was also the main source of ideas about socialism. Even this book and similar popularizations appealed only to an elite within an elite. Workers' libraries were used only by a minority. In 1911 the library for the 28,000 members of the Berlin woodworkers loaned out only 228 books in the social

[64]Levenstein, *Arbeiterfrage*, 180, 195.

[65]Levenstein, *Arbeiterfrage*, 190.

[66]Levenstein, *Arbeiterfrage*, 178.

[67]Ely Chinoy, *Automobile Workers and the American Dream*, 126.

sciences. As there does not appear to be any significant difference between what workers borrowed from libraries and what
they bought, it is impossible to claim that the workers bought the
serious books and borrowed lighter fare. It appears that the
majority of the socialist workers, in itself a minority, was an
absolute stranger to socialist theory and showed no interest in
the Party's scientific literature. Nor is there evidence of more
than spotty interest in more general works.[68]

To leave the matter at that nevertheless would be both unjust
and inaccurate. Even New Year's resolutions reflect wishes, in
this case wishes that the harsh pressures of daily life made almost
impossible to carry out. To put the point more positively, there is
no sign of anti-intellectualism among the German industrial
workers, not even anything that would correspond to "ouv-
rierisme" among French workers. From handicraft times onward there had been, at least as a model to be imitated, a powerful current of interest in history, literature, the arts, and sciences.
Futhermore, at least a few workers managed by almost superhuman efforts to acquire a very respectable degree of familiarity
with major landmarks of human thought. One of the common
traits in the autobiographies, and of course a trait that shows
their authors to be atypical workers, is the appearance at an early
age of a voracious appetite for books.[69] Such workers were likely
to reach leading positions in the labor movement and exercise an
influence far out of proportion to their numbers. There are also
scattered indications of a widespread interest in music and the
theater as well as a resentment against the bourgeoisie for its
efforts to maintain a monopoly on high culture.[70]

Finally, in interpreting the prewar German workers' attitudes toward free time it is important to remember that this was
an age before mass culture and consumer durables. There was
none of the modern apparatus of mass leisure in the form of
television, movies, and radio. What took their place were news-

---

[68]Hans-Josef Steinberg, *Sozialismus und Deutscher Sozialdemokratie: Zur Ideologie der Partei
vor dem 1. Weltkrieg*, 129–142, espec. 130, 137–138, 141. See also for a somewhat more
favorable view the observations in Bernays, "Berufswahl und Berufsschicksal," part II,
911–912 where she expresses the judgment that skilled workers were at a higher cultural
level than the petty bourgeoisie.

[69]Springer, *Der Andere das bist Du*, chap. 4 contains a striking account of the effects on a
young mind not protected by the defenses of a broad education of reading a book on the
French Revolution and especially of reading Dante. The consequences were a romantic
intoxication and a break, largely permanent, with what seemed trivial and petty
bourgeois in his surroundings and the formation of critical standards with which to judge
the world about him.

[70]Carl Severing, *Mein Lebensweg*, I, 82, 87.

papers and trashy novels (*Schundliteratur*). Also attractive to workers were the cheap taverns, which were not necessarily better for the workers' health or cultural development. There were other opportunities too that do strike a modern reader as reflecting "unspoiled" tastes. The love of nature appears quite genuine. The very few happy pages in Karl Fischer's autobiography describe Sunday walks in the woods or a few hours of peaceful fishing—until he was chased away by a noble proprietor's gamekeeper. "Just to go for a walk in the woods," often elaborated on with real feeling, recurs as a major theme in Levenstein's answers.[71] As the majority of German workers lived in small towns and were still accustomed to using their legs as a means of transportation, it seems likely that a good many did have occasional access to woods and fields.

There are, to be sure, a few hints of the world of mass consumption that still lay far in the distant future and of the demands that could fuel it. Here and there workers expressed a desire for a watch, a bicycle, decent clothing, and even a bathroom. These at least some workers had begun to see as part of the equipment for a decent human existence.[72]

Sleeping, eating, going for a walk, a home of one's own, even reading a book and going to a concert are in modern Western culture regarded as personal and private acts and concerns. What then were the workers' public concerns? To what extent did workers *have* public concerns, in the sense of definite feelings about actions the society in which they lived ought to take and ought not to take? What did they perceive as public, as society, and what were its boundaries? Was it just the neighborhood and the factory? Did it include all of Germany? The workers of the world? All of humanity? And how did their public concerns fit together with private ones? Was the pull of private concerns stronger than public ones? If we knew the answers to these questions, we would have a right to claim an understanding of the German workers. But of course we don't know the answers. All that we have are glimpses, like those that come when someone shines a flashlight hurriedly about a strange room in a strange house. Still glimpses are much better than total darkness, perhaps enough to make one's way around with some confidence.

On this issue it is worthwhile to draw on some of the statistics

---

[71]Levenstein, *Arbeiterfrage*, 354–381, devotes a whole section to the workers' walks in the woods and their thoughts on such occasions.

[72]Levenstein, *Arbeiterfrage*, 181, 186, 190, 193, 195.

compiled by Levenstein on the basis of his questionnaire. The results are sufficiently striking to override many doubts about the reliability not only of questionnaires as an instrument but also his rather primitive use of this instrument. Table 5 below contains slightly condensed versions of his own summaries of the replies received to questions tapping the hopes, fears, and fantasies of industrial workers.

In interpreting Table 5 it is best to confine our attention for the most part to themes that draw very large and very small numbers of responses. In those cases it is likely that the questionnaire reflects actual social processes. The very large number of private concerns is obvious on inspection. A good many of these are rather "proper," that is, they are what a member of the working-class intellectual elite could be expected to say to a stranger. After concentrating on this bias several times there is no need to elaborate further. On the other hand, the workers chose these themes themselves. The questions were completely open-ended. Workers were not asked whether they preferred educating themselves to political agitation. This was their own way of categorizing these experiences. The large number of miscellaneous replies, presumably answers that somehow seemed unique to Levenstein or at least did not fall readily into patterns of thought apparent from reading the others, testifies to the variety and diffuse nature of hopes and desires within even this restricted sector of the working class.

The first point to notice, then, is that the workers spontaneously mention private concerns overwhelmingly more often than they do public and political concerns. Not only do they mention them more often; they mention a lot more of them; or more precisely they use many more categories in reporting on private life than on public affairs. Private life is rather clearly what concerned these people most. On that score, I doubt that they were in any way unusual.[73]

In the area of public affairs large numbers do express a hope for the victory of Social Democracy. But in two out of three occupations even more workers expressed the hope that they would earn more. From the texts of the answers it is clear that many workers drew a clear distinction between hopes and wishes. Hopes were expected to be at least somewhat realistic. About wishes or fantasies they felt they could let themselves go.

---

[73]But we will never know for sure. What would a similar but more incisive study of fifth-century Athenians have revealed about the much vaunted public concerns of ordinary Greek citizens?

Table 5.

Workers' Hopes and Fantasies, According to Levenstein's *Arbeiterfrage*

(1) *What would you do if you had enough time for yourself every day?*

	Metal-workers	Textile Workers
Give time to the family	416	143
Visit nature	108	209
Agitate for the Party or trade unions	177	111
Educate myself further	489	344
Paint	117	87
Miscellaneous	292	183

(2) *What sort of things would you get yourself if you had enough money?*

	Metal-workers	Textile Workers
Good clothes	141	199
Library	342	86
Enough to eat	65	188
Good housing	194	151
Piece of land or house with land	357	187
Miscellaneous	500	266
No answers to one or both questions	214	76

SOURCE: Levenstein, *Arbeiterfrage*, 198, 212, 213, 222–223, 232–233, 241–242.

NOTE: The list of replies differs slightly for each occupation. A blank indicates the absence of this reply from the list of those given for the occupation.

Hence it is all the more interesting that earning more and the victory of Social Democracy are the only two hopes or wishes that emerge spontaneously in large numbers—and in that order.[74]

One result that deserves comment is the small number who want to settle accounts with the capitalists. The number of those who had either the hope or the wish to earn more is several times larger. It would be dangerous to infer from these figures that there was little or no latent reservoir of resentment against the

[74]Looking through the answers as a whole gives the impression that the miners were substantially more pessimistic about the future than either of the others. It seems highly likely that there were quite significant variations on this score from one kind of work to another and at different points in time. But the data are inadequate to support assertions about these variations.

(3) *What hopes do you have?*

	Metal-workers	Textile Workers	Miners
None	65	26	253
Victory of Social Democracy	431	518	438
Earn more	550	471	590
Miscellaneous	481		680
To be happy (*selig*)			123
The victory of virtue		41	

(4) *What wishes do you have?*

	Metal-workers	Textile Workers	Miners
None	65	26	453
Decent human existence	267	136	198
Better life for the children	147	123	236
Settle accounts with the capitalists	132	75	87
Die soon			33
Eat till really full			72
Earn more		328	440
Better future society and state	202	148	262
Wife does not have to work in factory		48	
Prohibition of alcohol	92	42	
Miscellaneous	338	40	304
Happiness for all	118		
Be independent	170		
No answers to one or both questions	276	187	0

propertied classes that might boil to the surface in a crisis. The tone of a great many of the excerpts from the replies suggests that there was. At one point, in commenting on the replies, Levenstein remarks that otherwise quiet and intelligent workers would often go utterly wild in their correspondence with him when he criticized their strong language and extreme expressions of hate.[75] Probably such replies came from a small segment of the articulate minority, with whom he conducted an extensive and lively correspondence in the course of conducting his inquiry. Even if these were only a minority, there seems to have been a nerve here that had been rubbed raw in daily experience

[75]See *Arbeiterfrage*, 283.

and that, if stimulated, might set off an explosive reaction. What the figures do suggest is that in quiet times this response did not surface spontaneously with any great frequency: individual concerns about making a go of it in day-to-day life overrode this tendency easily.

In this connection it is worth noticing the rather small number who wished they could have more time to give to Party and trade-union affairs. Except for a small core that was quite angry, these workers did not sound vindictive or threatening as long as the world around them continued in its routine fashion. They hoped for the eventual victory of some vague entity called socialism or a better world in the future. But they were not planning to do very much about it on their own. That was somebody else's job. They were too busy making ends meet. What they would really like was enough money so that they *could* make ends meet, have decent clothes, enough to eat, and—well, one might as well dream—a nice little house in the country.

Pain and suffering must have some purpose. Human beings, as all the great religions reveal in different ways, find it very difficult to tolerate the prospect that most human suffering does not lead to happiness, however defined. For these German workers the theodicy apparently ends with a nice little place in the country. That would be the end of the exploitation of man by man.

Or was the house in the country a symbol for and a reflection of something deeper? Was it a crude but concrete image of the security that belonged to a world where workers received decent human treatment—a world still marked by sharp inequalities, but where the edges of these inequalities were smoothed by the superiors' recognition that workers were human beings? As human beings, did they not deserve the minimum of respect and consideration required by a shared humanity, enough material rewards for their hard labor to enable them to carry out their jobs without pain from hunger and cold? Could they not expect some indulgence for an occasional burst of fun and sheer animal spirits? Bringing together all the evidence from the questionnaires and the biographies, it seems to me that this simple conception of decent human treatment underlies them all, that it is the implicit (and often explicit) assumption that ties them together.

9. Political and economic action

If we ask what German workers did about achieving this goal, the plain answer given by statistics is that just about half of them did nothing and a large majority of the remainder did nothing more than pay dues to an organization. The main organizations were of course the SPD and the unions. Since there are several excellent analyses of the organizational aspect of working-class life, I shall limit myself to a few brief observations. That the SPD faced a dilemma in choosing between its formal long-range goal of socialism and the necessity of making day-to-day gains in order to attract and hold a following is too well known to require elaboration here. On the other hand, it is worth pointing out once more that the evidence discussed so far fails to reveal the existence of any massive proletariat of the "classic" type whose interests the leaders came to ignore. In the light of evidence about the occupational and geographical composition of the industrial working class—its provincial character still flavored by the artisans' traditions—as well as what evidence we have been able to muster about the workers' life situations and the way they felt about them, the SPD leadership with its cautious policies and occasional outbursts of rhetorical anger at the propertied classes appears reasonably representative. For the prewar years at any rate it is difficult to imagine just what else they might have done. A revolutionary policy would have lacked a popular basis and would have been easily crushed.[76]

The prewar SPD leaders were bureaucrats and politicians. But they were bureaucrats and politicians with an ear to the ground. The notion that they ignored or failed to provide the proper leadership for a huge revolutionary mass is merely a polemical exaggeration. There was a mass as yet beyond the reach of SPD and trade-union leadership, indeed a very considerable mass, about which both the unions and the Party leaders at times expressed uneasiness. Within it—for it was by no means a single undifferentiated whole—there were large bodies of workers whose reactions and lack of reactions from time to time forced the hand of the labor movement's leaders. The relationship between leaders and those they were attempting to lead appears, so to speak, in miniature in the autobiographical ac-

[76]The evidence supports Scheidemann's assessment at the last SPD Congress before the war, made in the course of a debate on the tactic of a mass strike: "The workers want a breath of air once in a while, they want to give some time to the wife and kids once in a while, and also get a good night's sleep now and then." *Protokoll . . . SPD 1913,* 334.

counts of important labor leaders. It is a cameolike miniature whose details reveal essential characteristics of the interaction between ordinary workers and their leaders, and especially the experiences that formed the views of working-class leaders about their actual and potential following. Since this relationship became increasingly important during and immediately after the First World War, it will be useful to take a careful look at it now.

By the end of the nineteenth century the flow of unskilled workers to the new machines in the great factories gave, at least in some areas, a powerful impulse to the German variant of industrial unions as opposed to older forms of organization along craft lines. The fact that large masses of workers were thrown together in the new factories did not necessarily make these workers easier to organize. Often the factories were very noisy places where the machines absorbed all the workers' attention and permitted no opportunities for conversation. There the worker while he was on the job was far more socially isolated than under most handicraft conditions. The situation varied of course from industry to industry. At the opposite end of the scale from a noisy textile factory was the cigar factory with its hundreds of workers quietly busy while a *Vorleser* or reader read aloud to the group. Since the *Vorleser* often read materials with an educational and propagandist slant, cigar workers took an early lead in the labor movement.[77]

Whatever the variety of situations, the workers' only resource in any form of struggle with the employers remained the fact that if they acted as a unit they could refuse to sell their labor power. (By this time unions and strikes, while of doubtful legality, were accepted facts of life.) To be effective, enough workers had to join the strike to force the plant to suspend operations. What was even more important, enough workers had to be willing and able to carry on the strike until the employer came to terms. In turn that meant unions needed funds to support the workers while the strike lasted. Though these are simple and obvious conditions, they were not always obvious in their detailed and practical application to specific cases, especially for rank-and-file workers in the heat of passion or the depths of despair. Certainly the conditions were not always easy to meet.

Strikes could break out among a crucial section of the workers, enough to shut the plant down, over a variety of issues. One might be news that the plant was making large profits. More

---

[77]Severing, *Mein Lebensweg*, I, 3, 30. But note signs of identification with the Empire, mentioned by Moritz Bromme and discussed below in Section 10.

often a strike broke out in reaction to some specific act of injustice to a few individuals. In the beginning stages there was a good deal of euphoria and excitement. But the end was often failure and disenchantment.

Carl Severing, at that time working in a sewing-machine plant with three thousand employees, gives some examples. In one the euphoria was such that the decision to strike preceded the formulation of the strike's demands. Only about ten percent of the plant was organized. In a short time the strike collapsed due to the withdrawal of support by the unorganized in near panic. The latter had been confident that they had enough to get by on somehow and could hold out. In their heady enthusiasm the organized workers had believed the assurances. When put to the test, all this optimism evaporated.[78] Such experiences must have taught the crucial significance of organization to many an intelligent young man like Severing, committed to the workers. There is no doubt that he learned the lesson. By the time of the next strike he had become a union officer. His detailed report on that event is a vivid account of how and why he found it necessary to break off the strike against the demands of angry union members. Realistic considerations of the relative strength of the union and the employers, and of the consequences for the union of continuing the strike, made it necessary, he believed, to sacrifice a few members, even though their cause was perfectly just. For the sake of longer-run objectives he was willing to argue down a hostile crowd, to face a period of unpopularity.[79]

Experiences such as those recounted here, likely to recur in any labor movement, produced in many of the German leaders an almost instinctive distrust of mass enthusiasm, a willingness to face unpopularity, and a contempt for noisy demagogues. *Lasst schwatzen* (Let them yak) became a byword among trade-union officials.[80] In both the leaders and a leading sector of the workers such experiences also bred a faith and pride in discipline. Discipline meant the ability to sustain a strike when a strike had been started. Discipline meant the capacity to get people to show up in imposing numbers for a public demonstration. Finally, discipline meant the capacity and willingness *not* to strike or even *not* to demonstrate when the conditions were unpropitious. To decide whether or not conditions actually were propitious required persons with knowledge of economic conditions not only in

[78]Severing, *Mein Lebensweg*, I, 41–47.

[79]Severing, *Mein Lebensweg*, I, 94–100.

[80]*Protokoll . . . SPD 1913*, 296 ff.

specific industries but also in Germany as a whole and, in some cases, such as industries with an important market for exports, even on an international scale. These requirements created a role for specialists and theorists. Furthermore, to keep the mass of the workers informed, willing, and able to act at the proper time, special newspapers and a whole apparatus of information and indoctrination became necessary. These efforts were not uniformly successful, and there were some rumblings of discontent from ordinary workers who felt that strategic considerations made on high ignored their interests.[81] On the other hand, these centralizing trends received considerable support from the awareness among workers that in the end their jobs depended on the prosperity of German industry. As a union official, Severing was anxious to protect the good name of his firm at a time when competition from Singer Sewing Machines was becoming serious.[82]

Partly due to these trends the leaders of the German labor movement began to take on some of the characteristics of army generals or the heads of any large bureaucratic organization. The end result of a general distrust of mass enthusiasm is of course a Stalin. To their credit the German Social Democratic and union leaders never traveled down that road.

Nevertheless the consequences were fateful enough. Like many a good general, SPD and union leaders were reluctant to risk their troops in a battle whose outcome was uncertain—and the outcome of most battles is in some degree uncertain. After the defeat of 1918 and during the chaos that followed, the leaders' suspicions of mass enthusiasm inclined them to see the main dangers as coming from the left and helped to blind them to those dangers from the right which before long were to prove far more serious. That, however, is to run ahead of the story. In the years before the outbreak of the war they backed away from any frontal attack on German militarism for fear that such an attack would provoke reprisals by the German government and the destruction of all that they had labored so carefully to build. With this refusal by the stronger of the working-class movements there came to an end whatever prospect there may have been for preventing the war through the action of the working classes.[83]

[81]Some instances among the Ruhr coal miners will come up in the next chapter.

[82]Severing, *Mein Lebensweg*, I, 89. He also expressed anger that French sewing-machine manufacturers were telling potential French customers not to buy German machines because they would be giving money to the victors of Sedan.

[83]For their failure to confront German militarism head on and their generally cautious policy the German working-class leaders and the German working class as a whole

10. Identification with the Empire

But how real was such a prospect in Germany itself? Could the German working-class leaders have acted differently in 1914? How much difference would it have made? The questions are in the end as unanswerable as they are tempting. Nevertheless it is possible to discover something about the extent to which the German working classes did and did not identify with the German Empire—and some reasons why they felt and acted in the way they actually did.

For the articulate stratum of the workers there were several powerful and obvious reasons for hostility toward the Empire. The Empire represented the success of conservative and reactionary forces in bringing about the unification of Germany after the disintegration of liberal and popular attempts in 1848. The leaders of the labor movement had reacted to this victory by proclaiming their sympathy for the Paris Commune, which for the respectable elements in German society—and by no means only German society—symbolized everything that was frightening and revolutionary about the lower classes.[84] In turn the Social Democratic Party was stigmatized as a body of enemies of the state. Bismarck had tried unsuccessfully to crush the Party with the Socialist Laws (1878–1890). After Bismarck's departure from power, the government's policy remained essentially hostile and suspicious, despite the new Kaiser's brief flirtation with the labor movement. Hence, for the working-class elite the kind of nationalism incarnated in the Empire, and especially the military expenses it required, appeared for the most part as a crude and dangerous manifestation of the selfish interests of dominant classes.

On the other hand, this hostility did not mean that the German working-class leaders lacked their own conceptions of German patriotism, which from time to time they put forward to

---

have been the object of severe criticism inside and outside Germany. To ask them to commit what looked like the prospect of revolutionary suicide in a way that could do no more than set an example for the future is to ask a great deal of any mortals. It is also a request that runs against a powerful current—though not the only one—of political realism and cool calculation of the possibilities in any actual situation that runs through the writings of Marx and Engels. After the war the situation was different and some of the criticisms appear, at least to me, justified.

[84]Werner Conze and Dieter Groh, *Die Arbeiterbewegung in der nationalen Bewegung*, 86–104, report the differences in the socialist movement during and after the Franco-Prussian War. They regard this event and especially the Commune as the point at which the labor movement separated itself from the nationalist movement.

counter the accusation that the SPD was essentially a seditious movement.[85] From the point of view of our inquiry there is the more important question of how far down into the working classes themselves had the leaders' hostility to the Empire penetrated. It is not an easy question to answer. But as a beginning two points can be asserted with considerable confidence. Among the workers, as we have seen, there was considerable antagonism to the dominant classes, but it was antagonism to their domestic policies insofar as these affected the daily lives and material interests of the workers. Foreign affairs as such were remote from their concerns. Second, a large though steadily diminishing segment of the working class was quite apolitical. Karl Fischer's only mention of the Franco-Prussian War, which occurred when he was thirty years old, is a passing remark about his boss having been a soldier in France and one up on him (*darin war er mir über*) for that reason. Earlier he had expressed his total lack of interest in and understanding of politics. He did not read a newspaper and mulishly resented pressure on him to vote in a Reichstag election along with the rest of the employees. To judge from his comments on the other workers, who were willing to be feted and vote the way the boss told them to, Karl Fischer was more than usually apolitical, even for the 1870s.[86] Nevertheless there must have been many like him. A great deal would have to happen before ordinary workers could understand the reasons for SPD hostility to militarism.

Moritz Bromme, who was born in 1873, and whose family read socialist papers at home during the period of the antisocialist laws provides some revealing glimpses of the incongruous mixture of ideas circulating among the workers before the turn of the century. In one of the rooms in his home that was rented out to boarders there hung pictures of Kaiser Wilhelm, General von Moltke (the hero of the Franco-Prussian War), and of course Bismarck. But there were also pictures of Bebel, Liebknecht, Marx, and Lassalle. He tells how frightened he was

---

[85]Thus Philipp Scheidemann in 1911: "For us . . . the Fatherland is the home to which we cling with love; for us it is the bond that holds us together as members of a great cultural community. . . . We know and love our Fatherland. But directly because we know not only its natural beauties but also its ugly institutions—for that reason we are Social Democrats. . . . And as such we are eagerly striving to arrange matters in our Fatherland so that all of the country's children not only have enough to eat but also, as fellow countrymen enjoying equal rights, can take delight in the Fatherland and in its culture. That is national policy in our sense of the word, and whoever wants to accomplish national work in this sense will join the Social Democrats." Quoted in Ursula Schulz, editor, *Die Deutsche Arbeiterbewegung 1848–1919 in Augenzeugenberichten*, 358.

[86]See his *Denkwürdigkeiten*, 307, 291–292.

on the occasion of a big noisy party for fear that the police would come in and arrest everyone for blasphemy and lese majesty.[87] Later on he mentions the patriotic songs about the Franco-Prussian War that the cigar workers sang at their work in the early 1880s.[88] Evidently the *Vorleser* did not have a monopoly on their attention.

With the establishment of the Empire as a going political concern there also came into play a series of forces attaching the workers to the prevailing social order. The educational system laid a heavy stress on patriotic virtues and apparently had considerable effect, even on the workers. In his autobiography Carl Severing, whose parents were factory workers, recounts the episode of his presenting a picture of the Hohenzollern family to a favorite teacher, asserting that as a student he took the lead in making the arrangements for this festive occasion.[89] August Springer mentions the patriotic festivals and parades, including that of the battle of Sedan (which the SPD tried to counter with the celebration of the anniversary of the Commune), as the pride of the citizens and joy of the youngsters in his youth. Reflecting on popular sentiment at the outbreak of the war, he attributed the patriotic spirit to the schools, as well as such festivals.[90] War scares and news about the affairs of rulers and the nobility could also induce a surge of patriotism among workers untouched by Social Democratic doctrines.[91]

In Chemnitz, according to Paul Göhre, the German *Vaterland,* the Kaiser, and the army were the objects of very friendly sentiments among the workers. Chemnitz was a town where SPD influence had permeated everything, to the point where it was a common remark to say that "Here even the machines are Social Democratic." Nevertheless many workers had military pictures, evidently something like crudely colored postcards, pasted up on their workboxes near their work station. (Today they would have pinups.) Göhre spoke about military matters on purpose with a large number of workers, including Social Democrats. His account reproduces many details of the conversation. They show the workers' pride in the military, their enjoyment of their period of military service, and the favorable impression made by parades, uniforms, and the like. The only person he encountered

[87]Bromme, *Lebensgeschichte,* 23, 60, 71–72.

[88]Bromme, *Lebensgeschichte,* 115.

[89]Severing, *Mein Lebensweg,* I, 11. The episode took place in the late 1880s.

[90]Springer, *Der Andere das bist Du,* 14–15, 239–241.

[91]*Jugendgeschichte einer Arbeiterin,* 57–58.

who was hostile to the military was, in his terms, a typically rabid Social Democratic leader from whom no other opinion could be expected. One major reason for this favorable attitude was simple: for the workers, military service was the longest, most complete and splendid relief from the boredom of factory life.[92] Social Democratic propaganda about the brotherhood of all nations fell on totally sterile ground in Chemnitz. Some special reasons existed. The border with Bohemia was not far away, and there were many Czechs among the workers. Native Germans looked down on these to the point where even Czechs of German origin suffered from this prejudice.[93]

Though the external influences that produced this identification with the Empire were certainly important, there are grounds for concluding that the most important sources of identification arose quite spontaneously within the workers' own ranks. Their longings converged in the demand to be treated like human beings, to be able to live like human beings. For them this demand, which we encounter as early as 1848, was what political and social struggle was all about—insofar as they took part in it at all.

Concretely and specifically, decent human treatment meant that minimum of respect and concern due to all members of the national community. This they felt their superiors owed them. Decent human treatment meant a minimum of security in old age: that the factory worker would not be cast on the social dump heap as his strength began to fail and his human demands and family responsibilities reached their peak. It meant further that wages should be high enough to satisfy material wants at a traditional working-class level, plus perhaps, at least in hopeful fantasy, a little place in the country, or more realistically a shack and garden plot on the edge of the city. Finally, it meant political equality in an old-fashioned liberal sense. That in turn required an end to the Prussian three-class franchise system, which helped to secure the predominance of Junker and business interests in Prussia and hence indirectly in Germany as a whole. There was no notion of taking over the factories by the working class, at least not yet, and certainly no notion of a dictatorship of the proletariat. The SPD leaders, aware that the workers were a minority, insisted on democratic political procedures, claiming correctly that it was their opponents among the dominant classes who had strong inclinations to resort to authoritarian measures.

[92]Göhre, *Drei Monate Fabrikarbeiter*, 117–122.

[93]Göhre, *Drei Monate Fabrikarbeiter*, 129.

Hence the demand for decent human treatment amounted to a demand for acceptance in the existing social order, for its modification in the direction of greater equality, but certainly not its revolutionary overthrow. From the demand for acceptance into the social order it could only be a very short step to a positive willingness to defend this order when a foreign enemy loomed on the horizon.[94]

The brevity of this step and its fateful consequences were apparent to no one at the time. Certainly not to the ordinary workers, and not to the socialist leaders who took it. It was not even clear to those who courageously and relentlessly opposed it. They misperceived the power of the demand for decent human treatment and suffered from the illusion that they had the masses behind them. Later, as the destructiveness and sufferings of the war had their impact on German society, it would become possible to mobilize a substantial body of working-class support in favor of ending the war. That was not to be in 1914. Nevertheless it is unfair to use the far from absolutely reliable wisdom of historical hindsight to belabor the actors in the drama of 1914 for failing to realize that the longings of the downtrodden could be met only within the framework of a concrete national state and that a world of independent national states was liable to be a world of wars and preparation for wars. After all, neither modern revolutionaries nor modern liberals have done more than barely acknowledge the dilemma—far less anything to resolve it.

From the wisdom of hindsight it would also be a mistake, I think, to hold that the patriotism of the German working class in 1914 was an absolutely foregone conclusion, the smooth culmination of underlying social trends. Up to the last moment there were countercurrents: mass demonstrations in Stuttgart, a *Vorwärts* extra on July 25, 1914, proclaiming "Down with the war! Hail to the international brotherhood of peoples!"[95] The tension was high, not only in the leading circles of the SPD, and of course the government, but also among wide sectors of the public, including many workers. After the Social Democratic fraction had come out in support of the government, the tension snapped. A wave of tremendous relief swept much of the nation

[94]For articulate workers the Russian threat was far and away the most important one. In Russia they saw both a threat to German cultural achievements and a despotic regime that would crush the socialist movement. On these issues their spontaneous ideas were not necessarily at variance with the Marxist tradition, which recognizes and indeed applauds the efforts of a socially advanced group to defend itself against attack by reactionary forces.

[95]Schulz, *Arbeiterbewegung 1848–1919*, 373–374, for excerpts from the editorial.

and affected many ordinary workers. The sharp pain of divided loyalties had come to a close. At the same moment—if only for a moment—the workers seemed to have achieved the dream of full acceptance into the social order. August Springer comments on the rapid change of mood. Shortly after the mass demonstrations against the war in Stuttgart, all the people in a trolley car in a "red" area sang "Deutschland, Deutschland über Alles!" The sentiment was very widespread that Germany was morally in the right and its very existence threatened. The most striking feature, mentioned in other accounts as well, was an almost drunken sense of belonging together with everybody else in one huge social body: Germany. Finally, there was great relief at the apparently sudden disappearance of the daily demands of a rather boring existence. Such a sense of relief and belongingness resembles closely the "disaster euphoria" that modern investigators have observed to be the result of the temporary suspension of social routines and obligations in the wake of sudden disasters like floods, tornadoes, and hurricanes.[96]

This was neither the first nor the last time in human history where an exalted sense of human brotherhood has had murderous consequences.

[96]Springer, *Der Andere das bist Du*, 239–241. For some other contemporary impressions, mainly from leading SPD figures, see Wachenheim, *Arbeiterbewegung*, 593–595. The agony of conscience over the necessity to betray either principles and comrades or one's country expressed by the former radical Konrad Haenisch and the joyous relief at finally being able to let himself go and join the furious singing of "Deutschland, Deutschland über Alles," were no doubt extreme manifestations. But it seems reasonable to infer that the excitement took this general form and spread well beyond local militants to engulf substantial numbers of rank-and-file workers.

CHAPTER SEVEN

Militance and apathy in the Ruhr before 1914

1. Significance and character of the Ruhr

By this time, if not before, skeptical readers may be asking themselves the same questions that have occurred to the author. Perhaps the reason why no mass of potentially revolutionary workers has appeared is simply because we have not been looking for them in the right way. Taking all of Germany as the object for investigation runs the risk of obliterating decisive regional concentrations of industry and industrial workers. To some extent the analysis has already covered this point in the data on big cities and big factories. But, one could still ask, where is the Ruhr with its teeming masses of miners and workers in the blast furnaces? Has it just vanished? And a reader familiar with German history might well ask about the bearing of the huge uprising in the Ruhr that occurred shortly after the First World War, complete with an indigenous Red Army that captured some of the major cities. Since that important event will play a part in the story to come in the next two chapters, there is no need to say anything about it here beyond the remark that the uprising is hard to square with any conception of proletarian revolution. If coming events cast their shadows before them, it is almost impossible for the social historian to discern their traces in the social world of the Ruhr before 1914.

To anticipate a bit, if one looks only for a massive industrial proletariat in the Ruhr before 1914, one faces a disappointment that, so far as I can see, no amount of statistical ingenuity can overcome. If, on the other hand, one scans the evidence for what the workers in this area actually did and did not do, the results can be most revealing about the workers' sense of injustice. More precisely, this evidence can tell us a great deal about the historical and social conditions under which this sense of injustice can come to the surface and take on effective political forms and— perhaps even more interesting—the conditions under which these things do *not* happen.

Within the general category of industrial workers there were sharp contrasts. The coal miners did develop acute feelings of injustice about their particular situation. Furthermore, they worked out forms of collective action to remedy their grievances on a scale remarkable for the years before 1914. Their grievances, nevertheless, remained essentially coal miners' grievances. Both their definitions of injustice and their capacity for collective action are clearly traceable to preindustrial practices specific to German mining.

Workers in the iron and steel plants behaved in almost the opposite fashion. There were no strikes of any consequence and no independent organization. Company unions flourished here far more than in any other part of Germany. The iron and steelworkers of the Ruhr were at that time very docile, to the despair of labor leaders. Yet the "objective" grounds for complaint in mining and the big metal plants were very similar. What accounts for the differences in the behavior of these two groups of workers, neither of whom behaves in the way familiar theories or even general knowledge would lead one to expect?

When one first looks at the Ruhr, there do seem to be good reasons to expect to find large concentrations of potentially radical workers. Indeed, the Ruhr appears to be the most likely place to find them in all of Europe. Between 1910 and 1914 Germany produced on an average about twice as much iron and more than twice as much steel as Great Britain. By 1900 the Ruhr was not only driving English steel goods from the European market; it was encroaching on the market in England itself.[1] The Ruhr was also the main center of German coal mining. In both mining and the metal industries there were huge firms. In both fields, management was widely felt, and not only by workers, to be autocratic and unresponsive even for the standards of the time. In several instances the same firm or a closely related one operated in both mining and metals. Here therefore one might expect to find masses of workers jammed together in such a way that they would perceive their novel fate to be a common one that would require a common and probably revolutionary solution.

[1]David S. Landes, *The Unbound Prometheus*, 269; Norman J. G. Pounds, *The Ruhr*, 97.

But most of that would be an illusion. Hence it will be wise to begin with at least a brief sketch of the social structure and political climate of the Ruhr.

The occupational statistics for this area, as given in the census of 1907, reveal the main contours—and some surprises. There were changes between then and 1914, of which the most important appear to be a rise in the number of miners and especially workers in heavy metals, some of which will be reported in the course of subsequent discussion. Unfortunately there do not appear to be overall occupational statistics for the last year of peace. However, postwar statistics, to be presented in a later chapter, show that the changes were hardly fundamental and that those for 1907 will serve. They appear in Table 6.

Table 6.

Distribution of Gainfully Employed Persons in the Three Main Administrative Districts of the Ruhr in 1907

	Number (in thousands)	% of Grand Total	% of Total in Industry
Agriculture	373	14	
Commerce and transportation	309	12	
Public service and professions	109	04	
Other (servants, no occupation, etc.)	295	11	
Industry, mining, and construction			
a. owners, managers	161	06	11
b. administrative staff	99	04	07
c. workers	1258	48	83
Total for industry, mining, and construction	1518	58	
Grand total	2605	100	100+

SOURCES: Computed from *Statistik des Deutschen Reichs*, N.F., Bd. 204, *Berufs- und Betriebszählung vom 12. Juni 1907*, Abt. III, 507 (Regierungsbezirk Düsseldorf); 442 (Regierungsbezirk Arnsberg); 411 (Regierungsbezirk Münster). These are the administrative districts listed *s.v.* "Ruhrgebiet" in *Der Grosse Brockhaus*, Vol. 16 (15th ed.), 191. Slight discrepancies are due to rounding.

Table 6 shows that the entire industrial working class in the Ruhr made up less than half (48 percent) of the gainfully employed population. Industry as a whole provided the livelihood of 58 percent of the labor force, though the figure rises to 70 percent if we lump industry together with commerce and transportation. Fourteen percent were still making their living from agriculture, and this in the most highly industrialized area of Europe. On the other hand, the purely industrial bourgeoisie was quite small with only 6 percent of the gainfully employed being owners or managers and another 4 percent administrators and office workers of various sorts. Within industry itself the workers made up 83 percent of the total. It is true, then, that a great many toiled—and toiled very hard—for very few.

Some good indications of the political climate in these Ruhr districts are available from the votes in elections to the Reichstag from 1898 through 1912. Between them, the Center Party, a stronghold of Catholic interests, and the Social Democratic Party (SPD) won between 65 and 70 percent of the votes. Table 7 presents their combined performance in the same three districts from which the occupational statistics for 1907 have been drawn. The table shows the SPD to have been making steady progress against its dominant rival whose share of the total vote steadily declined. Nevertheless in an area where nearly half of the population were industrial workers and where many more in commerce and transportation were accessible to the SPD, this working-class party did not manage to attract quite one-third of the votes. The most likely inference is that many workers did not vote.

Table 7.

Center Party and SPD Votes in the Three Main Administrative Districts of the Ruhr: 1898–1912

Years	Total Votes Cast	Center Party	%	SPD	%
1898	711,533	319,887	45	143,149	20
1903	931,807	377,573	41	266,485	29
1907	1,126,502	454,817	40	308,546	27
1912	1,289,403	463,792	36	412,239	32

SOURCE: Computed from Kurt Koszyk, "Die Sozialdemokratische Arbeiterbewegung, 1890 bis 1914," in Jürgen Reulecke, editor, *Arbeiterbewegung an Rhein und Ruhr: Beiträge zur Geschichte der Arbeiterbewegung in Rheinland-Westfalen,* 150.

Within the SPD itself there is little sign of any radical pressure from its rank-and-file membership, which numbered 48,190 in the beginning of 1914. Since it was scattered over the Party's lower Rhine district, an area larger than the three districts generally if not universally regarded as the Ruhr, it is impossible to compute what proportion of the workers were SPD members, though it is clear that the proportion must have been very small. To be sure, there are some signs of leftist pressure from below in the fact that most of the delegates to the Party's Congress in Jena of 1913 voted with the left wing and against the SPD leadership on the issues of taxes and the mass strike. But when the far more significant issue of war credits came up in August, 1914, the SPD representatives elected from this area to the Reichstag behaved very differently. In the meeting of the SPD fraction that preceded the public vote *all* representatives from Rhineland-Westphalia, Germany's industrial heartland, voted in favor of supporting the motion for war credits. To the end of 1915 the workers gave the war full and disciplined support, despite reductions in pay and many discharges, to the point where even the owners in the area praised it as a model.[2]

That is sufficient for the general economic structure and political climate. But one could go astray by stopping there if one wants to understand the workers. It is deceptively easy to acquire a mistaken impression of the place of miners and foundry workers among the industrial workers of the Ruhr. From general economic studies of Germany and even specialized works on the Ruhr itself one is likely to come away with the notion that together these two occupations accounted for the bulk of the industrial workers. This is not the case at all. Their importance rested on their strategic role in the economy, not on their numbers, which were surprisingly small. Once again a search through the occupational census shows the size of the advanced industrial proletariat in Germany prior to 1914 to have been quite tiny. As a preliminary sounding we may look at Table 8 but with the warning that it includes under metalworking many workers besides those in the giant iron and steel mills.

All miners and foundry workers together, category III in the 1907 census classification, made up only 31 percent of the industrial workers. Other forms of heavy work with metals may be hidden in categories V and VI. We shall look for them in a moment. At this point more general observations are appropriate.

Particularly in categories V and VI, but also in others not reproduced in Table 8, there are signs of a still vigorous artisan culture. For example, the subcategory *Schlosserei* (B 34 in census reports), which I have translated as "miscellaneous mechanical work" rather than the older "locksmithing," designates a wide

---

[2]Jürgen Reulecke, "Der Erste Weltkrieg und die Arbeiterbewegung im rheinisch-westfälischen Industriegebiet," in Reulecke, editor, *Arbeiterbewegung*, 208, 212, 214.

Table 8.

Principal Occupations and Numbers of Industrial Workers in the Ruhr in 1907 *(in thousands)*

Census Categories	No.		% of Total No.	
	Subgroup	Group	Subgroup	Group
III. Mining and foundry, total ..		389		31
Of which				
B 1. Iron mining	9		01	
B 2. Foundry	87		07	
B 4. Coal & other mining	292		23	
V. Metalworking, total		211		17
Of which				
B 28. Iron pouring, etc. ..	48		04	
B 34. Misc. mechanical work	61		05	
B 35. Hand tools, weapons	19		02	
VI. Machines & instruments, total		72		06
Of which				
B 40. Apparatus makers	62		05	
IX. Textiles		144		11
XIV. Clothing		59		05
XVI. Construction		163		13
Other (not in above categories) ...		220		17
Total		1258		100

SOURCE: Computed from *Statistik des Deutschen Reichs*, N.F., Bd. 204, *Berufs- und Betriebszählung vom 12. Juni 1907*, Abt. III, 507–512 (Regierungsbezirk Düsseldorf); 442–447 (Regierungsbezirk Arnsberg); 411–416 (Regierungsbezirk Münster). Roman numerals and subcategories are in source.

variety of skilled work with metal. In the census categories, as in real life, the twentieth century still rubbed shoulders with the eighteenth, even in the Ruhr. In a moment we shall try to separate some of these groups lumped together in the census categories. Beforehand it is worthwhile noticing how many of the industrial workers are in no sense specific to the Ruhr. Workers in textiles, clothing, and construction turn up in large numbers all over Germany. They, together with those in the category labelled "Other" (makers of pots and pans, leather-workers, saddlers, printers, woodworkers, and the like), included 46 percent of Ruhr workers. They are the forgotten men and women of the Ruhr working folk. Except for their appearance in the census it would be difficult, if not impossible, to take them properly into account. As far as I am aware, their fortunes and misfortunes have not found their way into tales of workers' struggle against oppression or into celebrations of the power and energy released from the bowels of the earth by coal, iron, and steel. To bear one's fate silently is no way to get into history books, even obscure and dull ones. With some regret—and unsatisfied curiosity—it will be necessary to leave them aside in the rest of this account.

Instead, our emphasis will be on workers performing heavy labor in mining and metalworking. It was mainly on these that German industrial supremacy rested. As indicated in Table 8 (categories B1 and B4) miners of coal and iron ore, etc., came to 301,000 in 1907. Foundry workers and iron pourers (categories B2 and B28) add up to 135,000. Together these 436,000 heavy workers made up only 35 percent of all workers in the Ruhr and no more than 17 percent of the total number of gainfully employed—hardly an overwhelming portion of the population in this most industrialized area of the European continent. Miners outnumber the iron and steelworkers by more than two to one. In the six years between the census and the last year of peace, 1913, about 91,500 miners were added to the employment rolls in the Ruhr, an increase of 30 percent.[3] Though I have not been able to find comparable statistics for the iron and steelworkers, it is likely that the rise was similar or even greater. But even at that rate of increase they would have remained a minority within the total number of gainfully employed.

2. The coal miners

Down to at least the middle of the nineteenth century the coal miners remained embedded in the system of corporate paternalism that had so aroused the enthusiasm of the famous conservative sociologist Le Play just before the Revolution of 1848. During the turmoil of 1848 the miners stood aloof or were even hostile to reform. A compilation of labor disturbances for the half century that culminated in the revolution does not mention

[3]Max Jürgen Koch, *Die Bergarbeiterbewegung im Ruhrgebiet zur Zeit Wilhelms II. (1889– 1914)*, 139.

a single one among the miners. The immediate cause for this peaceful behavior was their pride and sense of honor as members of a corporate body with a recognized status in the German social order. On the other hand, they would scarcely have been able to keep on feeling this way had it not been for the concrete material benefits that this still vigorous and essentially preindustrial order conferred upon them.

Subject directly or indirectly to the disciplinary paternalism of the highly status-conscious mine officials *(Bergbehörde)*, the miners were granted exemptions from certain taxes and feudal dues. Their working conditions were under state protection. According to prevailing legislation, "loyal and obedient mining *people*" (*not* "workers": a term that when used later was regarded as an insult) were to have their names inscribed in the *Knappschaftsregister* and had the right to receive from a collective fund specified amounts in case of illness or accident. There were also payments for the widows and orphans of miners. Both the mine management, in effect the state at that time, and the miners themselves contributed to the fund. In the usual manner of preindustrial guilds, membership was restricted. So were the benefits. Day laborers had a separate fund distinct from the *Knappschaftskasse* to which only miners of the first and second class belonged. Thus the *Knappschaft* was a concrete manifestation of the exclusive miners' community and its place in the larger social order. Wearers of special uniforms designed to protect the body in their dangerous and somewhat mysterious task, German miners were expected by law as well as by custom "to bring honor to the miner's estate and seek the confidence of superiors through good moral conduct, orderliness, industriousness, and obedience."[4]

The more idyllic aspects of this corporate paternalism require a close skeptical look. Both conservative and Socialist sources, upon which modern descriptions rest, had the same axe to grind in praising the corporate paternalism of the good old days and damning the machine age that followed. The miners were probably not as contented as these claims imply. Nevertheless there is strong testimony to the effect that they were not among the disturbers of the peace. And for the purposes at hand that is what counts.

In the 1850s their situation began to deteriorate with the

---

[4]Gaston V. Rimlinger, "The Legitimation of Protest: A Comparative Study in Labor History," 337–338; Gerhard Adelmann, "Die soziale Betriebsverfassung des Ruhrbergbaus vom Anfang des 19. Jahrhunderts bis zum Ersten Weltkrieg," 43–46.

advent of Prussian liberal legislation in regard to mining. Legislation passed between 1851 and 1865 withdrew most but not all of the state's supervision over coal-mining operations. The mine owners became free to conduct operations largely as they saw fit, guided primarily by considerations of profit. The miners ceased to be guildlike workers attached to a particular mine. With the grant of freedom to change employers and the advent of the "free" labor contract between individual employer and individual miner, miners found themselves at the not so tender mercies of the laws of supply and demand in a free market.[5] Though some of the miners themselves may have been happy to see the corporate "fetters on production" destroyed because the changes enabled them to earn more, there is reason to suspect that most miners lost out.

With the removal of preindustrial limits on production and the advent of capitalist social relationships in mining, the output of the coal mines shot up in a nearly classic textbook example of what free enterprise could accomplish. Though there were some technological changes, it is important to notice that their main effect was to make coal lying deeper under the surface more accessible. Mining was to remain a form of hand labor, with important social consequences. Hence the increase in output required a huge expansion in the size of the labor force. Table 9 shows this increase for the period under consideration.

Table 9.

Coal Production and Numbers of Miners: 1800–1913

Year	Production in Tons	No. of Miners	Per-Capita Production in Tons
1800	230,258	1,546	149
1850	1,665,662	12,741	131
1860	4,365,834	29,320	149
1870	11,812,528	51,391	230
1880	22,495,204	80,152	281
1890	35,469,290	127,794	278
1900	59,618,900	226,902	263
1910	86,864,594	345,136	252
1913	110,811,590	394,569	281

SOURCE: Computed from Max Jürgen Koch, *Die Bergarbeiterbewegung im Ruhrgebiet zur Zeit Wilhelms II. (1889–1914),* 139.

[5] Adelmann, "Betriebsverfassung," 51–62. The most important area in which the state maintained supervisory rights was that of the *Knappschaften,* which became the basis of a system of compulsory insurance. About this aspect it will be necessary to say more below.

Per-capita production was no higher in 1860 than in 1800. Between 1860 and 1880 it almost doubled, but afterward it merely fluctuated. The number of miners in 1913 was, on the other hand, over thirty times larger than in 1850.

The fact that mining expanded by increasing the size of its labor force had decisive consequences for the character of the mining community and for social relationships within the mine. After the Franco-Prussian War in 1871 the mine owners began to import labor on a large scale from East Prussia, Poland, and other parts of eastern Europe. Between 1871 and 1905 the number of Ruhr inhabitants who had been born in these eastern areas rose from 11,000 to 254,000, with the greatest increase occurring in only three years between 1898 and 1901. Such workers accounted for about half of the increase in the size of the work force in the mines.[6] In 1906 only 58 percent of the Ruhr miners reported German as their mother tongue.[7] Statistics on this point, however, fluctuated wildly in response to nationalist pressures from both the Germans and non-Germans.[8] Figures for the mining district of Dortmund in 1905 show only slightly more than a third of the miners as immigrants from the East. At the same time the concentration in several of the big mines was very high, running between nearly two-thirds to just short of 90 percent.[9]

Whatever the exact figures, it is plain that the immigration created what modern Americans would call an ethnic problem. Native Germans lumped Germans from the east, who spoke a dialect more or less incomprehensible to the local inhabitants, along with all the others as "Polacks." As might be expected, the old native stock resented the flood of newcomers, which with the advance of industrialism was transforming their remote and isolated villages into teeming towns and cities. To native miners the newcomers seemed like a rough lot. Crime rates rose, as did problems of health and housing.[10] Natives reacted with antagonism, contempt, and a touch of fear.[11] All this is hardly surprising since many of the new workers were vigorous young

[6]Koch, *Bergarbeiterbewegung*, 20.

[7]*Meyers Lexikon*, II, *s.v.* "Bergarbeiter."

[8]Hans-Ulrich Wehler, "Die Polen im Ruhrgebiet bis 1918," in Wehler, editor, *Moderne Deutsche Sozialgeschichte*, 440–443.

[9]Koch, *Bergarbeiterbewegung*, 20–21.

[10]Cf. Wehler, "Die Polen im Ruhrgebiet," 445.

[11]Some data are in the useful local study by Helmuth Croon and Kurt Utermann, *Zeche und Gemeinde: Untersuchungen über den Strukturwandel einer Zechengemeinde im nördlichen Ruhrgebiet*, 18–28.

bachelors, though later immigrants did bring their families. For them the wages and hours in the mines, harsh though they may seem to a modern reader, constituted, we are told, a definite improvement over their previous situation. Most of them had been peasants subject to severe and at times brutal authority.[12]

With its mutual antagonisms and especially the native attitudes of suspicion and contempt for newcomers who seemed to lack adequate self-control and be the bearers of crime and disease, the whole configuration of events brings to mind what happened in the United States in recent times when blacks migrated into northern cities, and the earlier British reactions to similar Irish immigration. But the surprising and important fact is that in the Ruhr before 1914 matters turned out on the whole quite differently. There are no reports of severe violence or anything comparable to racial and religious riots.[13] Almost certainly the immigration intensified existing cleavages along religious, political, and cultural lines. Yet somehow the miners managed to overcome these cleavages. On occasion they were able, as we shall see, to turn the turbulence of the unorganized, most of whom were probably of immigrant stock, to their own advantage in putting pressure on employers. Some of this turbulence they must have also tamed, since the miners won a great deal of public sympathy and praise, on occasion even from highly reactionary government officials, for their self-discipline and orderly behavior in major strikes. As far as I have been able to discover, no one has yet investigated the relative success story of immigration into the Ruhr, one that could throw a great deal of light on comparable problems elsewhere. While the shared economic fate of all miners must have by and large overridden the causes of mutual hostility, that hardly happens automatically and easily.

The fact that mining operations expanded mainly through an increase in the size of the labor force had its most important consequences in the way it affected social relationships in the place of work. The size of the work force in the mines increased

[12]This seems to be the standard judgment: see Croon and Utermann, *Zeche und Gemeinde,* 20–21; Koch, *Bergarbeiterbewegung,* 23; Wehler, "Die Polen im Ruhrgebiet," 438.

[13]The absence of racial differences in the Ruhr cannot by itself be the main reason for the difference, because American history contains numerous examples of violent outbreaks where whites fought against whites. In Richard Hofstadter and Michael Wallace, editors, *American Violence: A Documentary History,* part IV, Religious and Ethnic Violence, out of the twelve episodes reported there are five where it seems to me that the same ingredients were present in Germany. These are the Philadelphia Nativist Riots, 1844; the Pentecost Riot in Hoboken, 1851; that in Louisville, 1855; the Orange Riots in New York of 1870–1871; and the Anti-Italian Riot in New Orleans, 1871.

from about one hundred, a number small enough so that miners and supervisory personnel could know each other personally and patriarchal and paternalist relationships could exist, to a thousand and more. With new demands on the miners and this increase in size, paternalism ceased to be effective. In order to meet the requirements of the market the mine owners tried to impose more rigid and bureaucratic controls and alternated overtime shifts with unpaid layoffs. All this created resentment. More generally the mine owners superimposed some of the new features of a modern industrial plant on preindustrial social relationships without by any means destroying the latter. For the miners the consequence was to generate anger born of uncertainty, a feeling that discipline was often harsh and capricious, and a resentment at the loss of control over their social and physical environment. Unlike the workers in the iron and steel plants, where a new technology and new social relationships sprang up like hardy weeds, the miners carried their past with them into the new age. That appears to be the crucial distinction between the two types of workers: the miners had living standards from the past with which to condemn the present. To understand what this means concretely it is necessary to see how miners went about their daily tasks.

In the late nineteenth century and in the twentieth century up until the great rationalization movement of the 1920s, social relationships in mining remained heavily impregnated with forms and traditions inherited from the era of handicrafts. That was due to the nature of the task, in which inherent danger played no small role. The social network in the mines, which displays an interesting mixture of cooperation and antagonism, along with strong patriarchal traits, will be easiest to grasp by starting at the bottom with the miners themselves and then working part way up the hierarchy of authority and responsibility.

In the latter part of the nineteenth century and after the transition to mining by deep shafts the miners generally worked in teams of four to ten men known as *Kameradschaften*. The name, which means literally comradely groups, is in itself significant. They worked together under the supervision of a foreman called *der Ortsälteste*. Literally he *was* the senior in the workplace. *Ort* means not only place, but specifically in mining the place of work, and also the end point in a mine gallery, a cut that runs off more or less horizontally from the vertical shaft. Essentially the *Ort* is the main point at which the coal is mined. The senior's role was similar to that of the lowest noncommissioned officer in a military organization. He was responsible for the work done by his men and for their safety. Therefore he had to have their confidence, and ideally all the members of the group should have confidence in each other for the sake of smooth working relationships under arduous and dangerous conditions.

The senior was also responsible for representing his men in the process of striking the bargain of the wage contract known as *Gedinge,* a time-honored term that distinguishes the work relationship in mining very sharply from that in the rest of industry. The existence of the *Gedinge* long antedates the advent of the unions. I strongly suspect that it constitutes one reason why the unions were able to establish themselves quite firmly in mining before 1914 whereas they were unable to do so in the giant iron and steel plants. There, as mentioned earlier, the employer simply set the wage rates to be paid in a particular shop on his own authority, frequently just by posting a notice.

The *Gedinge* was a form of payment by results or a piece rate. But because the character of the coal seams may vary a great deal in thickness, pressure, and other characteristics, affecting from day to day or week to week the ease and difficulty with which seams can be worked, and also because other conditions such as temperature likewise vary, it was impossible to render uniform either the labor itself or the materials upon which the labor was to be expended in a manner comparable to a large factory.

The coal mine *could* not resemble the assembly line, at least not with the technology of that day, advanced though it was in many respects. Therefore the *Gedinge* was a bargain that had to be struck over and over again. The miners under the guidance of the senior had an interest in maximizing the difficulties of the task. The employer's representatives on the spot of course had the opposite interest. That this was a point of recurring tensions is obvious. The advent of large-scale mining and a more complicated administrative structure to oversee the activities of a thousand-odd miners instead of a hundred intensified the tensions and must have rubbed nerves raw. Particularly in the period 1851–1889, the apogee of relatively uncontrolled private ownership, it was fairly common practice for one of the higher supervisors to annul a *Gedinge* because the rates agreed upon were too high. On occasion, however, they also evened out rates that were too unfavorable to the workers.[14] It seems unlikely

---

[14]Adelmann, "Betriebsverfassung," 85. See also the discussion in Otto Hue, *Die Bergarbeiter,* II, 161–168. Hue, writing from a trade-union standpoint, may, however, overemphasize the employers' ability to manipulate the *Gedinge* to their own advantage.

under the circumstances that on balance their interventions were on the side of higher pay for the miners.

The employer's representative was called the *Steiger,* a term that goes back at least to the fifteenth and sixteenth centuries. The word literally means "climber" and derives from the frequent use of ladders in an earlier day. By the middle of the nineteenth century this officer's function had become subdivided into underground and aboveground tasks done by different sets of officials. The one responsible for underground work, the *Grubensteiger,* had to be thoroughly familiar with the construction of the mines and the technical operations conducted in them. He exercised a somewhat general supervision over the miners, going through the entire area and visiting each place where the miners were working, at least once in the course of the shift. He also had the task of taking a roll call before and after each shift, and presented his superior, the shiftmaster, with the figures necessary for accounting purposes. Theoretically at least, he was responsible for the observance of police ordinances concerning safety measures as well as for the general security of mine properties. As the main representative of the employer, it was on this official that the workers' antagonisms focused.[15] But it is also apparent that he was somewhat of a father figure, charged with special attention to the miners' safety. This task was evidently taken with considerable seriousness, as indicated by the further subdivision of the *Steiger*'s role, just beginning at this time, into special officers for observing the state of the air in the mines, important because of its connection with potential explosions; another in charge of the problem of accidents itself; still another in charge of the use of explosives; and one more still, in charge of the instruction of young persons in the working of the mines.

If the miners were indeed proletarians, it was a proletarian existence softened in some ways and hardened in others by the survival of practices from an earlier age. This survival was not some form of cultural inertia or mysterious historical momentum. Preindustrial and guildlike practices and attitudes survived because it was not yet possible to reduce mining to a series of completely mechanical operations.[16]

---

[15]On this intermediate role in both mining and the iron and steel industry see Elaine Glovka Spencer, "Between Capital and Labor: Supervisory Personnel in Ruhr Heavy Industry before 1914," 178–192.

[16]This interpretation of the miner's working life and situation is based primarily on Carl Jantke, editor, *Bergmann und Zeche: Die sozialen Arbeitsverhältnisse einer Schachtanlage des nördlichen Ruhrgebiets in der Sicht der Bergleute,* espec. 33–36, 44–45, 81–82, 97–99. It is a first-rate sociological field study of mining in the Ruhr with much historical background.

I have already suggested that the survival of these preindustrial practices and traditions, such as the habits of teamwork and simple collective bargaining, may have helped miners adapt to and struggle against their new proletarian existence. They inherited from the past certain tools useful in the effort to regain at least some control of their social and physical environment. For industrial workers generally, in the modern world getting higher wages has of course been the main method used in order to obtain this control.[17] In a world where goods and services are bought and sold, to increase one's power in the market is, after all, just about the most sensible and natural strategy to adopt. This was a very prominent aim among the miners. But it was not the only one. Indeed, in their case it would not be easy to sustain the thesis that wages were their most prominent concern. Greater control over their situation at work and decent human treatment by their superiors were of very great concern as well. In this sense higher wages were an indispensable *means* to attain a decent human existence, decent according to the definition that prevailed in this group at this point in history.

Certain other themes stand out too in the prewar history of the miners' efforts to understand and struggle against their situation. One is the persistence of faith in the benevolence of political authority, a faith understandable not only in terms of the general considerations advanced in earlier chapters of this book, but also as a consequence of the continuation of preindustrial social forms and traditions just mentioned. These traditions were both a handicap and an advantage in the miners' long efforts to discover and create effective forms of collective self-help, the strike and the unions. The miners' stubborn steps in this direction form the second theme of their prewar history. The surprisingly wide degree of rank-and-file participation in such efforts and the miners' insistence on sticking closely to their own concrete grievances were striking aspects. They had important consequences for the character of the German labor movement as a whole. A third theme is the set of recurring attempts by external political groups, mainly the Catholic Center Party and the SPD, to use the miners' grievances for their own purposes, efforts that at times exacerbated the internal divisions among the miners. Together these three themes blend into a minor epic of the creation of a modern industrial labor force and its struggles

---

[17]With the decline of the market as the central mechanism for allocating goods and services and the rise of political authorities, the strategy changes. Under socialist regimes the workers have a very difficult time resisting the "historically necessary" sacrifices demanded of them.

to achieve an awareness of new rights, and to make these rights effective, as part of a larger effort to create a new social contract in a new historical situation.

The first stirrings reach as far back as 1867, two years after the introduction of the Prussian legislation that did so much to remove the legal obstacles to the capitalist expansion of mining. In that year what appears to have been a small group of mining "people"[18] from Essen addressed a petition to the King of Prussia, their "Supreme Mining Lord" (*Oberster Bergherr*), with a series of complaints that were to be echoed in almost the same terms for more than the next half century. These had to do with the excessively long hours, compulsory overtime, and insufficient pay. The King was expected to correct injustice, and while the complaints were modern, the grievances were felt as injustices in the sense of violations of traditional rights and status. The authorities' reply must have been educational as well as disappointing: the complaints in the petition were examined and rejected as unfounded.[19]

Partly because of the unsympathetic response of the mining authorities, the miners turned more toward their own resources in the first good-sized strike, which took place in 1872. On this occasion many more people took part and did so from the beginning. Some five to six thousand, it is claimed, met in Essen to elect a "Committee of the United Mining People of Essen and Vicinity" to present demands to about twenty of the mining companies in the area. At the height of the strike, 18,000 miners ceased work, a very respectable portion of their rapidly growing numbers; 51,000 in 1870, they had risen to 84,000 by 1875. (No figure is available for 1872.) If the statistics are accurate, perhaps one miner in three went out on strike. The issues that stirred them were the same as those in the petition, together with certain new ones that were to recur over and over again. If anything, the new grievances were even more closely tied to the miners' specific way of life and work than those in the petition. One was that they should receive their own allowance of coal for domestic fuel at lower prices. Another had to do with regulations about filling the coal carts. Miners for decades to come were to continue complaining that they were not properly paid if the wagon was not full of coal of the required quality or if it spilled its contents on the way to the surface. Here once more we come upon resentment at what looks to the worker like unrequited

[18]One of the first grievances had been that under the new liberal legislation miners had been designated as "workers," not as mining folk (*Bergleute*).

[19]Koch, *Bergarbeiterbewegung*, 28, note 1.

effort, even if the wagons with coal of the wrong quality, or no coal at all, were hardly useful to the employer. Another demand was for a 25-percent increase in the normal shift wage for work apparently not covered by the *Gedinge*. Despite the numbers participating, the strike disintegrated within six weeks.[20]

The failure of the 1867 petition apparently taught the miners that they would have to strike, and the failure of the strike of 1872 taught them that the next time they would need better organization, though the lesson was slow to emerge. It came about partly through inherited institutions. Toward the end of the 1880s the enforcement of the antisocialist edict became milder, allowing workers with socialist inclinations to become more active in their agitation as members of the *Knappenvereine*, successors to the *Knappschaften*.[21] The liberal legislation of the 1850s and subsequent years had transformed the traditional *Knappschaften* into "voluntary" *Knappenvereine* in a manner that many miners felt was disadvantageous to them. Their main complaint was that with the coming of the "free labor contract" and "voluntary" membership in a new form of benefit association the employers had managed to shift most of the burden of payment onto the miners in the form of dues. In addition, the employers allegedly used the *Knappenvereine* as a device to discipline and hold workers by threatening to withhold benefits from those who changed jobs or went out on strike.[22] In using their rights of representation in the *Knappenvereine* and objecting to these transformations, a small group of active workers was able to appeal to traditional standards of justice (*das alte Recht*) and make use of institutions inherited from the past to create the solid beginnings of a collective will and an effective political presence.[23]

All this agitation was a prelude to the great miners' strike of 1889, which turned into a major political event. Fundamentally, the strike was a reaction to the transformation in social relationships brought about by the advance of the big mining firm and its new technology, together with the changes in the labor force produced by the advancing wave of immigration.[24] Once the strike got under way, the issues connected with the *Knappen-*

---

[20] Koch, *Bergarbeiterbewegung*, 28–29. On 139 the author provides statistics on the number of miners for selected years between 1792–1913 from which all such figures will be taken in the account of subsequent strikes.

[21] Koch, *Bergarbeiterbewegung*, 33–34.

[22] Hue, *Bergarbeiter*, II, 85, 94, 96.

[23] As noted in Albin Gladen, "Die Streiks der Bergarbeiter im Ruhrgebiet in den Jahren 1889, 1905 und 1912," in Reulecke, editor, *Arbeiterbewegung an Rhein und Ruhr*, 118.

[24] Adelmann, "Betriebsverfassung," 109.

vereine disappeared in favor of a demand for a 15 percent increase in wages, an eight-hour shift, abolishing overtime, and better protection from some of the hazards and discomforts of the new forms of mining.[25]

The strike itself was a highly spontaneous affair and gives the impression that a large segment of the workers, mainly the young and the new immigrants, were seeking by trial and error to discover a strategy and set of tactics with which to combat their new situation. In this fashion the actions of those not integrated into the traditional order supplemented and extended the behavior of those who were. Disturbances among workers in other industries in the neighboring region of the lower Rhine served as a spark that ignited a "prairie fire" in the Ruhr. A full shift would appear at the mine, change its clothes, and prepare to go to work. Then one or two workers would say they did not want to work. A few would agree and then suddenly the entire shift would refuse to go down the shaft. In as orderly a fashion as they appeared, they would simply go away. If a manager asked why they did not want to work, they would either refuse to answer or say they wanted "more," that is, better pay.[26] The willingness of some managers to make concessions helped the strike to spread. By the 10th of May, 1889, 81,000 miners in the Ruhr were out, more than 70 percent of the 115,000 miners in the area.[27] Only at this point did the strikers manage to set up a central leadership, a central strike committee chosen from deputies that had been elected by the striking workers at the separate mines.

Not all miners, it is worth stressing, went out on strike. Generally, those who refused were in mines where a more personal and paternalist relationship between management and workers existed and where the workers were themselves old-time miners long settled in the community. Those who did not want to strike were of course under considerable pressure from militants. At the same time there is evidence that many workers made use of this pressure and even invented incidents to prove its existence in order to play safe in a tense situation. In this way they could both demonstrate their solidarity with other workers by going out on strike and do something about keeping a good reputation with their employers as fundamentally loyal to the plant.[28]

By means of the strike the miners were seeking specific and

[25] Koch, *Bergarbeiterbewegung,* 35.
[26] Adelmann, "Betriebsverfassung," 101–102.
[27] Gladen, "Streiks der Bergarbeiter," 126–127; Koch, *Bergarbeiterbewegung,* 139.
[28] Adelmann, "Betriebsverfassung," 101–104.

limited gains, a wage increase and amelioration of working conditions. It is easy enough to say after the fact that these objectives were within the framework of capitalism as it existed in Wilhelmine Germany. That is not, however, the way the situation appeared to all interested parties at the time. Both the miners' objectives and ways of pursuing them were novel, at least in the sense of being on an unprecedented scale. The miners were obviously trying to change the terms of the prevailing social contract. Whenever that happens, the disputing parties are forced to act in a shadowy area where there is no generally accepted boundary between morally approved and reprehensible behavior. In this particular instance the concerned parties were the Imperial government, the employers, and that amorphous force we can loosely call educated public opinion. The miners were struggling to work out for themselves a new conception of justice, a new definition of the rights and duties of management and worker in the mines, and simultaneously to win public acceptance for this new conception. In the meantime the reaction of the other parties to their efforts had important and varied consequences for this attempt at self-definition.

The main expression of educated public opinion was the press. There the miners gained a surprising degree of success in arousing sympathy for their grievances. The sympathetic publicity given to their demands in wide sectors of the press served to convince the miners of the justice of their cause. At the same time bourgeois newspapers tried to tone down the elements of conflict and push the workers toward peaceful negotiations. The employers' reactions had contradictory consequences. Their willingness to make concessions on wages at the beginning of the outbreak likewise encouraged the miners and probably contributed to the spread of the strike. But the mine owners refused to engage in any form of collective bargaining with the strikers' representatives, treating the whole notion of collective bargaining as an infringement on the free labor contract and on the essential prerogatives of management. The consequence, we are told, was to make many a miner feel that he was a rebel, or at least not an acceptable member of German society.[29] Toward the government, the miners, or some of their articulate leaders, maintained their traditional attitude of deference toward the fount of justice. On the 9th of May, 1889, when more than half the miners were already out on strike and the day before a central committee was to go into action and proclaim a general

---

[29]Gladen, "Streiks der Bergarbeiter," 123–125; Koch, *Bergarbeiterbewegung,* 44.

strike, a gathering of miners in an inn decided to send a deputation to the Kaiser. Whether this was a shrewd tactical maneuver or a reflection of traditional beliefs that their King would help them in their struggle for "rights inherited from their fathers" is an issue about which the sources disagree. Probably both elements were present: the gathering ended with a traditional "Hoch!" to the Kaiser. The proposal attracted public attention which led to a famous audience with the Kaiser. He admonished both the workers and the mine owners.[30]

In the short run the degree of sympathy and legitimacy that the miners had won brought no tangible benefits. Though the mine owners felt themselves deserted by public opinion and the government, it was they who had the material resources to hold out until the strike ended. After complicated and distrustful negotiations involving the government, the mine owners, and the miners, the great strike petered out of its own accord. By the beginning of June it was already over.[31] Nevertheless, with its revealing mixture of old and new forms of struggle the strike did have permanent consequences. It brought to an end the period of the owners' maximum autonomy in the management of the mines. The state was forced to return partway toward its role of paternalist supervision. By itself that was no inconsiderable achievement that the workers had won, mainly by their own efforts. As we have seen, the strike broke out against the wishes of the workers' nominal leaders. In fact, a temporary leadership was only patched together at the height of the struggle.

More significantly the strike finally convinced many workers of the importance of organization for the achievement of their aims. Out of the contest came the Socialist and Catholic unions. We may now turn to certain aspects of their history for the light they throw on the situation and feelings of ordinary workers.

In 1889 the Catholics had some support among rank-and-file miners while the SPD had practically none. That was partly due to the antisocialist laws that were still on the books, even if weakly enforced, until 1890. Hence the Catholics had a head start in union organization, at least in the preliminary stages. The organizational history of the founding of the unions is one of those characteristically tangled webs of intrigues, personal and sectarian quarrels that have occurred from the days of the Twelve Apostles to those of Mao, Castro, and Guevara or whenever

---

[30]Koch, *Bergarbeiterbewegung*, 37–38. See also 41–43 where the author points out that higher officials were more likely to be sympathetic to the miners than those on the spot who identified more closely with the mine owners and managers.

[31]Koch, *Bergarbeiterbewegung*, 40; on the owners' sense of isolation see 51.

human beings have tried to organize in order to improve their lot. There is no need to inflict the details of this history on the reader. On October 20, 1889, the Socialists were able to establish formally the Union for the Protection and Advancement of Miners' Interests in the Rhineland and Westphalia, known to history as *Der Alte Verband*. Catholic efforts at formal organization succeeded in 1894, with the founding of the *Gewerkverein christlicher Bergarbeiter für den Oberbergamtsbezirk Dortmund*.[32] Formally interdenominational, Catholics predominated overwhelmingly in the *Gewerkverein*. A similar situation prevailed in *Der Alte Verband*. Welcoming Catholics and anybody else they could find, SPD leaders sought to advance SPD interests.

Thus, as has happened very frequently, the impulse toward organization came from "outsiders" who had their own interests to promote and their own conceptions of what the workers ought to want. The ups and downs in the organizations' history give us a good clue to what the miners actually did want. Quarrels among the leaders over religion and politics nearly strangled the infant socialist organization at birth, though in time it was to become the much stronger organization of the two. Miners evidently had very little patience with religious and political quarrels. As the record shows on this and subsequent occasions, large numbers of them did have quite deep-seated religious and political convictions. Actual and aspiring leaders would offend these sentiments to their cost. On the other hand, what the miners wanted in a union, if they were to have one, was an organization to defend and promote their shared economic interests as miners. When leaders tried to promote other interests, the miners just refused to follow.

At first the leaders of *Der Alte Verband* made the mistake of trying to promote socialist ideas. These were offensive to the Catholics, while the mass of the miners showed themselves indifferent or hostile. Membership, beginning with 58,000 in 1890, dropped to 5,000 by 1895.[33] The Catholics, who had joined up in the founding of *Der Alte Verband*, had withdrawn almost immediately afterward, in 1890. But that is not enough to explain the catastrophic decline. During this early phase the *Verband*'s newspaper fell into leftist hands and became for a brief time more and more radical in tone. At an international miners' congress in Paris in March of 1891 one of the leading officers of

[32]Koch, *Bergarbeiterbewegung*, 48–49, 51, for the early history of *Der Alte Verband*; Adelmann, "Betriebsverfassung," 114, on the Catholics and the *Gewerkverein*.

[33]Koch, *Bergarbeiterbewegung*, 53, 142.

the *Verband* laid a wreath on the grave of the Communards in the name of the German miners.[34] At about the same time it sponsored what appears to have been a poorly prepared strike, in which only a small number of workers—estimated at about 20,000 out of the 139,000 miners in the area—took part. The Catholics opposed the strike, which rapidly collapsed.[35] In addition to the political gestures that at the very least failed to arouse the miners' enthusiasm, this experience very likely persuaded the miners that this particular organization was unlikely to accomplish much for them.

The organization might have died had not the leaders fallen victim in 1895 to a politically motivated prosecution based on shaky evidence, an event that aroused the sympathy of a large segment of the general public unconnected with Social Democracy. The persecution set off a wave of solidarity among the miners who raised more than 62,000 marks for its victims. A week later *Der Alte Verband* reelected the chief victim to the position of first chairman.[36] He was the same man who had laid the wreath on the Communards' grave in Paris. If the members showed by their behavior a lack of interest in such general gestures, an unjust attack on one of their own was something many of them understood and to which they responded warmly with concrete personal sacrifices.

The situation began to improve in 1895 when Otto Hue took over the editorship of the newspaper. Under his leadership the union adopted the policy of trade-union neutrality: political and religious issues were not to be discussed within the union; the union as such was not to take a stand on such matters. Membership figures began to rise: in 1900 they were back to 36,000. By 1912 they were up to 114,000 (as against a rise from 5,400 in 1895 to 78,000 for the competing Catholic *Gewerkverein*).[37] In 1912, then, *Der Alte Verband* had brought under its wing 29 percent of the 394,000 miners in the work force. That is a very respectable percentage, though somewhat below the overall proportion of industrial wage earners, around one-third, organized in SPD unions. Evidently a substantial segment of the miners, presumably the politically most "advanced," felt that it was worthwhile to belong to a union at least nominally socialist.

The general political consequences deserve emphasis and

[34] Koch, *Bergarbeiterbewegung*, 53–54.

[35] Koch, *Bergarbeiterbewegung*, 55.

[36] Koch, *Bergarbeiterbewegung*, 56–57.

[37] Koch, *Bergarbeiterbewegung*, 142.

attention. Up to 1894 Otto Hue, like other leading Social Democrats engaged in trade-union affairs, had regarded unions as little more than a recruiting ground for the SPD. Also like other leaders, he feared that the trade unions might produce a "bogging down" (*Versumpfung*) of Marxist doctrine. After 1894 he changed abruptly to become one of the most prominent leaders of the conservative trade-union wing of the SPD, a sharp opponent of Rosa Luxemburg and even Karl Kautsky.[38] When the issue of the mass strike as a political weapon of the proletariat became acute in 1905, Otto Hue was one of those union leaders who argued vehemently against the whole idea.[39]

Now Hue had evidently been more radical and come to his conservative position on the basis of experience. In his case experience meant running one of the three biggest unions affiliated with the SPD. (The other two were the unions of metal and textile workers.) Furthermore, his was not a union of relatively skilled workers living mainly in small towns, as was predominantly the case with SPD unions—such workers were a major source of the antiradical and reformist impulse in the SPD.[40]

From these considerations the conclusion emerges that rank-and-file pressure from the "proletariat" pushed Hue to the right and forced him to drop any talk that put socialism on the immediate agenda. Certainly his own assessment of the miners' needs and attitudes impelled him in that direction. It is a conclusion worth pondering in any assessment of the revolutionary inclinations or potential of the most advanced industrial state in Europe at this time.

We may turn to the strike of 1905, the largest and most famous of the prewar miners' strikes, to see what it reveals about rank-and-file sentiments and behavior. The background supports the thesis that wages as such were not the miners' major concern. In the big strike of 1889 the issue of wages had been added as an issue only after the strike had started. In 1905, according to Koch, they were not an issue. One reason may have been that for some time pay rates had been rising much faster

[38]Koch, *Bergarbeiterbewegung*, 57–58.

[39]Koch, *Bergarbeiterbewegung*, 104–105. The author points out that the miners' situation was somewhat special because the Catholic union was openly opposed to the concept of the mass strike. But so in actual fact were the leaders of practically all socialist trade unions.

[40]Cf. Carl E. Schorske, *German Social Democracy 1905–1917*, 108–110, and the data presented above in Chapter Six. If the mass of the miners was not in some meaningful sense proletarian by the turn of the century, it would be better to abandon the term altogether, a semantic decision that has much to recommend it.

than food prices.[41] Instead the background causes appear to have been an intensification of long-standing grievances connected with the system of arbitrary discipline. Fundamentally they were due to the rapid expansion of production. This was the time when the tide of immigration reached its maximum flood. Exasperated and hard-pressed supervisors were liable to be especially harsh with unskilled and undisciplined immigrant workers. The housing shortage was acute. The Coal Syndicate's decision to close down several mines threatened some 10,000 of the better-off miners who had their own cottages and plots of land.[42]

On top of all this, there appeared the frightening disease known as "worm sickness" (ancylostomiasis or hookworm). It was due to an intestinal parasite that flourished in the warmth, dampness, and dirt in the mines, causing debilitating anemia, at times ending in death. Though usually curable in the early stages, an attack required painful therapy and loss of earnings. In 1901 there were about 1,000 cases. In 1903 there were more than 29,000, after which the epidemic began to subside. Mining was in any case a dangerous occupation, and the accident rate had mounted as unskilled workers poured into the mines, and production shot upward.[43]

Offhand it seems no wonder that the miners were reported to be in a generally excitable state before the 1905 strike broke out. Though the blows were probably hardest on the immigrant sector, all miners were affected or at least subject to threat. Still it would be unwise to make too much of all these blows. With the exception of the worm sickness, all of these conditions had, as we shall see, close parallels among the iron- and steelworkers, who never did go out on a massive strike. And frightening though the worm sickness certainly was, it is difficult to see it as the central cause of the strike because the worm sickness took the apparent form of a natural disaster.

The comparison with the iron and steelworkers becomes even more thought-provoking when we notice the immediate cause of the miners' strike. It broke out when one of the Stinnes mines bluntly announced by posted notices an increase in the amount of time the miners would have to spend traveling underground in order to reach their place of work. As pointed out

---

[41]Koch, Bergarbeiterbewegung, 79.

[42]Gladen, "Streiks der Bergarbeiter," 134.

[43]Koch, Bergarbeiterbewegung, 83–86; more detail in Bruno Heymann and Karl Freudenberg, Morbidität und Mortalität der Bergleute im Ruhrgebiet, 108–113.

in the previous chapter, this was exactly how the managers of the big iron and steel plants in the Ruhr changed the work rules from time to time with impunity. Steel and ironworkers disliked the practice, but evidently regarded it merely as part of a bad system. For the miners the situation appeared in a very different light. Such an arbitrary decision by the management violated a paragraph of the Mining Law *(Berggesetz)*, according to which any changes in work rules were not to be introduced without consultation with the older workers. On this occasion the miners refused to work, and a wildcat strike spread rapidly.[44]

In other words, the miners struck because they saw that the employer had violated their legitimate rights. This time they were not defending traditional rights inherited from their ancestors. Instead, they were defending a right recently won in the course of a bitter struggle: the *Berggesetz* had been amended in their favor in 1892 as a direct consequence of the great strike of 1889.[45] If in a sense newly won, the rights for which the miners fought in 1905 were still intertwined with tradition. Even during the period of the mine owners' greatest freedom from state interference, the *Berggesetz* was by no means wholly in abeyance. Miners felt that there was a legitimate authority to whom they could and did complain.[46] The *Berggesetz* gave a legitimacy to the miners' demands—a sense that they had a right to act, and therefore could and should take collective action—that was at this time wholly lacking among the iron and steelworkers.[47] Yet it was not an unmixed blessing. The belief that they were in the right gave the miners the courage to appeal to public opinion and public authority. Though they did this to good effect, they also became the prisoners of public opinion and public authority. In 1889 one consequence of respectable support in the press had been to push the miners toward peaceful negotiations out of

[44]Koch, *Bergarbeiterbewegung*, 88–92.

[45]Gladen, "Streiks der Bergarbeiter," 135. According to Wolfram Fischer, *Wirtschaft und Gesellschaft im Zeitalter der Industrialisierung*, 157, the *Novelle* of 1892 required the existence of public work rules *(Arbeitsordnungen)* in the mines. But it did not specify what the content of the rules should be. Only after 1905 did the validity of the rules, according to still another *Novelle*, become dependent upon the agreement of an elected committee of workers. Evidently the prevailing "social contract" was ambiguous, which probably contributed to the bitterness of the struggle. At bottom the issue was one of who was to determine regulations governing work: management or the workers.

[46]See Adelmann, "Betriebsverfassung," 59, for a general discussion and 61, 87, for specific instances of complaints; also Wolfram Fischer, *Wirtschaft und Gesellschaft*, 158–160.

[47]The importance of the *Berggesetz* and the *Gedinge* as the sources of legitimacy and organization in the Saxon mines emerge very clearly in the autobiography of Franz Louis Fischer (not to be confused with Karl Fischer), *Arbeiterschicksale*, 89–96, 104–108.

which they got nothing in material gains. In 1905 at the height of their strike, reports began to circulate that the government was considering another favorable modification of the *Berggesetz*. As a result the strike began to disintegrate rapidly. Quite possibly there was nothing else that the miners could have done under the given circumstances. But that is not the point. Rather the point has to do with the inherent limitations on a form of protest that derives its legitimacy from the standards prevailing within the established order.

Even more than in 1889 the outbreak of 1905 was the result of anger and pressure from below. The unions, which had in the meantime gained very considerably in membership, for once dropped their differences and in urgent tones warned the workers against a strike.[48] Their strategy was to use the excitement among the workers to recruit members while trying to avoid a direct confrontation with the employers, for which they judged the moment unpropitious. The behavior of union leaders recalls that of the great mercenary generals of the Thirty Years' War who often sought big armies as a basis for power and prestige, but tried to avoid battles because they were expensive and dangerous to this very basis. At the same time union leaders were caught in a dilemma. If they did not take advantage of the excitement, the movement among the workers would "run into the sand" with even more serious consequences.[49]

Therefore the leaders sat down and worked out rather hurriedly a set of demands for presentation to the employers. In the list of fourteen points presented we can see, as Koch observes, all the issues that had troubled the workers for the past twenty years and on which they had obtained no satisfaction. Because they do reveal the issues very clearly it is worthwhile to set them down, at least in summary paraphrase:

1. Eight-hour shift including time to and from the seams, with six-hour shift in especially wet or hot areas.
2. No overtime or Sunday shifts except for emergencies such as rescue work.
3. End of the system of no payment for improperly loaded carts—known as the system of "zero wagons."
4. Secret elections for the job of load inspector.
5. A minimum wage for all categories of workers.

[48] Koch, *Bergarbeiterbewegung*, 89.

[49] For some enlightening details of how these considerations worked out at the local level see Adelmann, "Betriebsverfassung," 134.

6. Creation of a workers' committee to present and settle disagreements with management over wage differentials and other complaints and abuses.
7. Introduction of a system of mine supervisors elected by the workers.
8. Reform of the benefit system.
9. Coal for household use to be delivered at cost in sufficient quantities to miners and their families.
10. Elimination of the frequent and severe penalties.
11. One month's notice instead of fourteen days for vacating housing units run by the mines.
12. Humane treatment of the workers. Penalties and discharges for all officials who mistreat or verbally abuse the workers.
13. No penalties for participation in the strike.
14. Recognition of the unions by the employers.[50]

The most striking feature of these grievances is that they are strictly miners' grievances even if several of them, such as the demand for decent human treatment, were widely shared among industrial workers in Germany at that time—reflecting a desire for acceptance as a human being with dignity and rights within the prevailing social order. At the same time they represent an effort to squeeze out within the framework of this order just a bit more elbowroom in order to give miners more control over their situation at work.

The aspects of this situation that they felt were unjust stand out very clearly: long and irregular hours over which they had no control; penalties that in their eyes deprived them of payments due for hard work they had performed (one more instance of a sense of injustice at the failure to receive a reward commensurate with the effort invested); the general atmosphere of arbitrary authority combined with personal abuse; the lack of a secure minimum below which their wages would not fall (yet another instance of the popular belief that one should have "enough" material goods to live out one's assigned social role on a secure basis). If set strictly in a miner's context, the grievances still reflect a recognizable common pattern, the echoes of a potential universal code.

That of course was not the way the demands looked to the employers. Once again they rejected the demands as an intolerable infringement on the prerogatives of management. The

[50]Koch, *Bergarbeiterbewegung*, 90–91.

refusal set off a general strike, proclaimed on January 16, 1905. More than a third of the miners were already out on strike, whether organized or unorganized it is now impossible to determine.[51] With the official proclamation of the strike after the owners' blunt refusal, participation shot up to heights unknown in the miners' previous history, and to my limited knowledge, in the history of workers' movements generally. The next day two-thirds of the mining labor force went out on strike. The day after that, more than three-quarters were out. Participation remained at that level, or even slightly above, for the next three weeks.[52] Presumably not every miner who went out on strike agreed with all of the fourteen points. Yet it would be hard to believe that these points were hammered out by leaders ignorant of what was on the minds of the mass of the miners, or that the miners ran the risks of a strike for sheer fun and excitement. The high participation in the strike, which again became a national cause célèbre, demonstrates rather impressively the resonance that these demands produced among the mass of the miners, including those outside the unions. Around three-fifths of the miners then belonged to one of the four competing unions, while, as we have seen, participation in the strike remained for some time at a level of more than three-quarters.[53]

Through the strike the miners did not succeed in extracting a single concession from the employers. On the other hand, this form of collective action, through the public sympathy it aroused, was almost certainly responsible for further changes in the *Berggesetz* that went a considerable distance toward meeting the miners' grievances. Reports that legislation was under active consideration contributed to the rapid disintegration of the strike in early February, 1905. Introduced after a dignified delay on July 14, 1905, the new legislation (1) provided that time spent traveling within the mine was not to exceed an hour—any time over this was to be paid for and counted as part of an eight-hour day; (2) abolished the rule of nonpayment for improperly loaded carts; and (3) established workers' committees with advisory and mediating functions.[54] Against the will of the employers the government had gone a considerable distance toward meeting the workers' demands. It had eliminated a decade-old source of conflict in the system of "zero wagons,"

[51]Koch, *Bergarbeiterbewegung*, 91–92, 107; Gladen, "Streiks der Bergarbeiter," 136–137.

[52]Koch, *Bergarbeiterbewegung*, 143.

[53]Koch, *Bergarbeiterbewegung*, 107.

[54]Koch, *Bergarbeiterbewegung*, 100.

given the workers a foot in the door to management's prerogatives over labor discipline, and done something to make sure that
the workers did not pay the full freight of extra costs arising
from the fact that man was tunneling ever deeper into the earth
to sustain his new industrial civilization.

The miners themselves indicated that they felt the victory
worthwhile and the methods more or less appropriate by flock-
ing into the unions. In 1904, 48 percent of the miners had
belonged to three unions, with 30 percent in the nominally
socialist *Alter Verband,* 16 percent in the Catholic *Christlicher
Gewerkverein*—which was nominally interdenominational and in
the summer of 1905 dropped from its statutes the clause by
which a member defined himself as an "enemy of Social Democratic principles and endeavors"[55]—and 2 percent in the newly
established *Polnischer Berufsverein,* the one destined to show the
most rapid growth in subsequent years. By 1911 the total
number of miners had gone up from about 270,000 to over
350,000 and 71 percent of these were now organized, an indication of very considerable success in attracting the unorganized.
But *Der Alte Verband* showed the smallest rate of growth with its
share rising to only 34 percent. That of the Catholic union went
up from 16 to 24 percent, while the Polish Union shot up from 2
to 13 percent. The newly organized workers were evidently
flowing much more rapidly into unions with an ethnic and religious flavor than into the one loosely identified with socialism.[56]

At this point, the zenith of their efforts at organization and
collective action, we may take leave of the coal miners. The big
strike of 1912 was an anticlimax. Ostensibly over wages, and the
only one of the major prewar strikes where wage rates constituted the central issue, the strike failed to gather much support
and soon collapsed. Actually the strike appears to have been
primarily a diplomatic move by *Der Alte Verband* to discredit the
Catholic Union and absorb its membership. As a riposte, and to
avoid joining in the wake of *Der Alte Verband,* the Catholic Union
resorted to an appeal to patriotism, pointing out that the threat
of a strike in England at that moment might give Germany a
good opportunity to seize more of the market if production
could continue. In this instance, as in others, patriotism coincided with the workers' interest in their jobs. Such is the stuff of
trade-union politics. After only eight days the leaders broke off
the strike. This behavior discredited union leaders and led to a

---

[55] Koch, *Bergarbeiterbewegung,* 110.

[56] Percentages computed from the table in Adelmann, "Betriebsverfassung," 118.

substantial loss in membership.[57] By that time, however, unions all over Germany were in trouble. What the strike shows, I suggest, is that the miners' successes in creating instruments of collective action had begun to generate new problems and intensify some older cleavages. Before long, however, the war was to inflict wounds that overshadowed, though they did not obliterate, these issues.

In looking back over the historical record of the miners' efforts to establish a collective identity and effective political presence, four interrelated factors stand out as having contributed in a decisive fashion to the result. First of all, the expansion of the output of the coal mines came about mainly through an expansion of the labor force. That was perhaps the most important of all the factors at work in the situation. It meant that the miner with his pick remained a key factor in the productive process. Second, the situation favored the preservation of social relationships and traditions inherited from the past, specifically, the *Gedinge* as a primitive method of collective bargaining and the *Knappschaften* as a primitive arrangement for security against the hazards of the occupation. A third factor was the tradition of government supervision over mining operations. Even if this supervision diminished drastically with the advent of liberal legislation, it did not disappear completely. The *Berggesetz* provided a standard to which appeal was possible and made protest against specific grievances something distinct from subversion of good order. It facilitated collective protest at the same time it helped to limit the objectives of such protest.

The fourth factor was the flood of immigrants into mining, in itself a consequence of the expansion of output through increasing the number of workers. In most accounts immigration appears as something that contributed to cultural and religious divisions among the miners, and hence as a factor inhibiting collective identity and collective action. Undoubtedly that is an important part of the truth. Still there are reasons for doubting that it constitutes the most important part of the truth. The role of the unattached and the unorganized as a source of angry discontent forcing the leaders to take militant action recurs as a major theme in the history of the miners' struggles. The unorganized, perhaps even the unorganizable, it appears, were predominantly though not exclusively new recruits to mining. Without this leaven of militant discontent it is unlikely that the

[57]Koch, *Bergarbeiterbewegung*, 121–129, 146; Gladen, "Streiks der Bergarbeiter," 141–148.

struggles would have taken place at all. Social arrangements and traditions inherited from the past, and perpetuated by the requirements of an industry that could not yet alter the fundamental technology of production, provided the pattern for miners' efforts to resist and soften the impact of the new bureaucratic discipline directed toward increased production for the market. Yet without a fire under them from "irresponsible" social elements freed from the inhibitions of tradition, organized miners would have been far less active. Thus it was this fusion of limited preservation *and* destruction of their collective past that both helped and forced the miners to create a new collective identity.

3. The iron and steelworkers

In any attempt to catch glimpses of the real life of the "toiling masses" in the ironworks, blast furnaces, and rolling mills of the Ruhr before 1914 one has to cope somehow not only with the mists of rhetoric but also with the obliteration of evidence that time and unconcern have produced. It is not even easy to answer the elementary question: how big were these toiling masses? As pointed out earlier, the occupational census of 1907 yields a total of 135,000 foundry workers and iron pourers, no more than 11 percent of the industrial workers in the Ruhr (1,258,000). By 1914 there were undoubtedly a great many more. A publication of the German Metalworkers Union that appeared in 1912 lists the big firms in the Ruhr together with the number of workers employed in each.[58] Adding them up yields a rough total of 180,000 workers. Many of these firms, however, conducted operations outside the Ruhr, and their workers inflate the total by an amount impossible to determine. If we put together the data from the 1907 census, the Metalworkers' list, and allow something for growth, by 1914 there were almost certainly not as many as 200,000, but no fewer than 150,000. That is as close an estimate as I can make. Probably we would not be far from the mark if we thought of only one Ruhr worker in eight as a servant of the new giants.

[58]*Die Schwereisenindustrie*, issued by the Executive of the Metalworkers Union, 194–234. I have made a guess of 5,000 workers for the Mülheim division of the Deutsch-Luxemburgische Bergwerks und Hütten-Aktiengesellschaft (204–205) where no figure was given, and another guess of 10,000 for the Westfälische Stahlwerke (233–234) for the same reason. In a few other cases where the total was reported as "officers and workers" I have deducted one-twelfth in accord with the general ratios between "administrative staff" and workers shown in Table 6.

The political character of the iron and steelworkers appears from scattered sources to have been almost exactly the opposite of the coal miners. As we have just seen, the coal miners were quite receptive to union organization and, more significantly, forced their leaders into the biggest labor disturbances that rumbled through German society before 1914. Ironworkers and steelworkers in the Ruhr did nothing of the kind. They were the despair of one of the biggest and most powerful unions in prewar Germany, the Metalworkers, who were almost totally unable to organize them. Not necessarily contented, they were, at least outwardly, very docile.

That of course is one reason why there is so much less evidence about them. The most visible marks that the lower classes have left on the historical record come from the troubles they have made for their superiors. There is also at times a fainter impress where they have failed to respond to the efforts of those from within and outside their own ranks who have tried to help them. Such is the kind of evidence available for the steelworkers. It suggests very strongly that for some reasons the steelworkers down to 1914 and beyond remained in a state of political and economic apathy or helplessness. Before searching for what the reasons might be for their inertness about their own fate, it will be prudent to review the evidence for its existence.

The most useful as well as the most striking piece of evidence comes from some travel notes that Otto Hue, who knew his coal miners, published in 1908 in the *Metallarbeiter-Zeitung*, the organ of the Metalworkers Union, on the occasion of one of his visits to a large foundry and rolling-mill district. There, he reported, the foundry magnates ruled autocratically over huge masses of workers. His comments on the workers themselves, despite or perhaps even because of their elitist overtones, deserve reporting in his own words: "And the mass of the workers lives with the viewpoint that this is the way it's got to be 'because that's the way it's always been.' Regular twelve-hour shifts in a red-hot shop; when business is good, if the shop setup allows it, a twenty-four shift at the end of the week; at times (like now) when the market drops after an extravagant production push, off and on there will be one or two shifts a week canceled without pay. The very idea that regulation in everybody's interest ought to take hold never enters the head of the vast mass of the proletariat that we see here, dragging themselves exhausted down the street after the end of a shift." Hue continues with some comments on the miserable housing in which this mass "vegetates in dumb endurance of its lot, bows its head in reverence before 'Sir, my Lord' and only too often finds forgetfulness in the most miserable kind of alcohol. The encouraging news about the power of worker solidarity and trade-union organization to raise the level of culture is just terribly necessary for these tens and tens of thousands of people."[59]

The somewhat earnest and even priggish sense of moral superiority, quite characteristic of the Social Democrats at that time, suffuses these comments. I suspect that this attitude may have blinded Hue to a rough-and-ready lustiness, a capacity to grasp the pleasures of the moment in a way that makes life bearable. Vigorous males engaged in hard and dangerous physical work often display these qualities. But beyond the slighting reference to alcohol I have no evidence in this case. Furthermore to smile at Hue's priggishness in our superior modern way could make us miss the point. However boisterous these workers may or may not have been among themselves, there is no reason to challenge Hue's report that they were docile and obsequious to their employers. On that score Hue was reporting facts that were unpleasant for him and his trade-union audience to contemplate, with serious consequences for union strategy. In turn he traces this docility to an illusion of inevitability somehow perpetuated and sustained by the conditions under which these workers were living.

Though there is a fair amount of additional evidence, by and large it corroborates Hue's thesis without providing much in the way of explanatory clues. For an earlier period there are glimpses of Alfred Krupp (d. 1887) as a rather tyrannical patriarch who managed to gain the loyalty of at least some of his more skilled workmen. A very different image emerges from trade-union descriptions of working conditions a decade and a half after his death. By then the patriarchal attitudes and corresponding loyalties are no longer visible. All that is left is the tyranny of a drive for production and profit. Putting these fragments of information together, we can infer with some confidence that employers had adopted a patriarchal and paternalist attitude in the early days, seeking and to a considerable extent obtaining from their workers a sense of loyalty to the industry and to the firm. With the expansion of the industry these attitudes evidently eroded, though they have by no means disappeared. Traces of them still exist today.[60]

[59] From a long verbatim extract in *Fünfundsiebzig Jahre Industriegewerkschaft 1891 bis 1966*, 134–138; portions quoted are on 134–135.

[60] See Pounds, *The Ruhr*, 115; and especially Klaus J. Mattheier, "Werkvereine und wirtschaftsfriedlich-nationale (gelbe) Arbeiterbewegung im Ruhrgebiet," in Reulecke,

To be sure, the workers did not take everything lying down, and by modern standards they had an astonishing amount of abuse to take. There are intermittent comments on the problem of insubordination in the sources that can be discussed in a more fruitful way later. On these matters the trade unions either could not or would not help. A detailed account of strikes and strike tactics in the 75th-anniversary volume of the Metalworkers Union passes over the Ruhr in silence.[61] By 1913 the union did have about 67,000 members in its administrative district which included the Ruhr, though the district was considerably larger than the Ruhr itself. Of these around 10,000, according to an occupational breakdown of the membership, were working in the big iron and steel plants.[62] That is a pathetic showing against a minimal estimate of some 150,000 iron and steelworkers in the Ruhr alone. Union politics too at this time took the form of equally pathetic vituperations and accusations among the powerless, as the local branch of the socialist Metalworkers Union exchanged accusations with its Catholic competitor and the Hirsch-Duncker union during a minor strike. Each union accused the other of bad faith and secret dealings with the employer.[63]

It is also symptomatic that a great deal of the brief flowering of the company unions between 1912 and 1914 took place in the foundries, chemical, and machine-tool plants of the Ruhr. Company unions were financed by the industrialists in the hope of encouraging old-fashioned loyalty to the plant. Though it is not easy to get accurate figures on their membership, there appear to have been at least 20,000 members in 1913, which would have put them well ahead of those in the Metalworkers Union.[64]

Arbeiterbewegung an Rhein und Ruhr, 177–178. Cf. in *Die Schwereisenindustrie,* 470 ff., the hostile union picture of Krupp and other large steelmaking firms. The German workers' identification with the firm (like early workers who were proud to call themselves "Kruppianer") recalls that of the Japanese workers so well portrayed in Ronald Dore, *British Factory—Japanese Factory.* Although Japanese habits and attitudes had indigenous roots, it is worth noticing that, according to Dore, one of the late nineteenth-century leaders in the Japanese movement to model the factory on the extended family claims to have found much of his inspiration in Krupp and the National Cash Register Corporation (395).

[61]See *Fünfundsiebzig Jahre Industriegewerkschaft,* 138–150.

[62]*Der Deutsche Metallarbeiter-Verband im Jahre 1913: Jahr- und Handbuch für Verbandsmitglieder,* Anhang, 98, 101.

[63]See *Der Deutsche Metallarbeiter-Verband 1913,* Anhang, 101–102, 111–116. The name of the Catholic union was the *Christlicher Metallarbeiter-Verband;* that of the Hirsch-Duncker union was the *Gewerkverein der deutschen Maschinenbau und Metallarbeiter.*

[64]Mattheier, "Werkvereine," 188–189, gives a total for 1913 of about 55,000, with 21,000 in the mines. Most of the 34,000 metalworkers were presumably in the foundries and

It would be misleading of course to portray the political complexion of all the iron and steelworkers in a few shades of dull, apathetic gray. There was more variation than that. Only a few in all likelihood were the models of patriotism, religious conviction, and loyalty to the firm that the employers would have liked to see as the predominant one. At the other end of the scale the workers in the metal industries of Düsseldorf apparently enjoyed a reputation for being solidly behind the class struggle.[65] In the end, however, it is behavior that counts. And on that score the testimony is unanimous and decisive. Before the war there were no labor troubles worth mentioning in the foundries, steel mills, or machine-tool plants.[66] That alone is enough to distinguish the iron and steelworkers sharply from the coal miners.

Before searching for the reasons for this distinction it will be well to pause to take stock of certain significant points that emerge from the evidence just discussed. The iron and steelworkers at the outbreak of the war had an elite of organized workers that was utterly fractured along several lines of potential cleavage: religious, national, economic and political. Shading off by degrees underneath this elite was a mass of unorganized and generally inert workers.

That is hardly the situation to be expected at the leading edge of technological change in the industrial heartland of what was then Europe's most economically advanced country. Furthermore the situation is inexplicable in terms of any conception of trade unions as *the* institutional mechanism that ties the new industrial workers to the status quo and renders the industrial working classes essentially conservative. The Ruhr iron and steelworkers were attached to the status quo and very conservative, at least in their behavior, without any such training or *dressage* of the soul from the unions. Obviously the unions were

---

machine tool plants. According to the *11. Sonderheft zum Reichs-Arbeitsblatte: Die Verbände ... 1913,* Zweiter Teil, 49, the *Werkvereine* had about 20,000 members scattered throughout the major cities of the Ruhr. This is the figure I have adopted in the text. The same publication (Erster Teil, 36) gives a table showing membership in these unions for several cities in the Ruhr and comparing that with membership in the socialist unions, which yields the much higher total of 39,000 for the company unions. I am unable to account for the discrepancy and have used the smaller figure. Though the comparison refers to *all* industries, not just iron and steel, it is of some interest. It shows the company unions to be running neck-and-neck or even surpassing the socialist unions in Essen, Gelsenkirchen, Bochum, and Oberhausen. But in Düsseldorf, Elberfeld-Barmen, and Dortmund the socialist unions heavily outnumbered the company ones, bringing their total membership up to 84,000, or more than twice that of the company unions.

[65]Reulecke, "Der Erste Weltkrieg," 209.

[66]Mattheier, "Werkvereine," 177.

too weak and busy quarreling with each other to provide any such service to capitalism. But the conservatism of these workers was very different from the kind that emerges in and through union organization under liberal capitalist regimes. The two types belong to two different historical epochs. The steel-workers' pre-trade-union conservatism looks like a mixture of patriarchal residues, blended with fear and apathy. There is not much in it—or at least not in the general situation—in the way of a vested interest in the status quo buttressed by busy activities and hope for something better if and when business improves, the essential mark of trade-union conservatism. These two forms of conservatism were to react quite differently under the strains of war and defeat. By and large the pre-trade-union type of loyal submission seems to have dissolved into a variety of radical currents whereas the newer one, based on the "sensible" workers with extensive union experience acquired during the war, became very much more conservative.

To return to the prewar situation, the essence of what requires explanation has already turned up in the observation that this sector of the proletariat—a term clearly more applicable to these workers than to the coal miners—took by modern standards an astonishing amount of abuse. They took it for the most part stolidly as though that were the natural order of the universe. For reasons to be ascertained later the metalworkers evidently failed to articulate standards of condemnation. A good deal of the evidence indicates that the standards simply did not exist. Certainly these workers failed to make them the effective bases for action to anything like the extent achieved by the coal miners.

At this point it is necessary to be as precise as the evidence permits. There is no claim that the miners' action as such was particularly effective. Nor is it necessary to claim that the steel-workers *felt* less badly about their situation than did the miners, though I strongly suspect that such was the case. All that the evidence permits one to assert is this: a large number of miners developed out of *their* life experiences a set of standards that enabled them to say they ought not to put up with specific abuses and that they ought to engage in collective action to change their situation. And they did exactly that, with at least some limited success. Among the iron and steelworkers there is practically no sign of any of this. Instead, the record shows no strikes, company unions rather than trade unions, and a work force described as utterly submissive. What factors account for the difference?

There may well have been differences in the organizational

skills that the unions brought to bear in each case. If that is in fact the main reason, the search for an explanation is nearly hopeless. If the secret could be discovered, it would have to be found in the archives of the unions, local government officials, and employers. The published record that I have been able to consult gives no clues that point in this direction.[67] On general grounds this type of explanation seems unpromising. Basically the same influences were at work on both the miners and those in the metalworking industries: mainly a variety of unions with different religious and political tintings and a set of authoritarian employers, actually in many instances the same employers for both sets of workers. Though it is impossible to rule out an explanation based on differing techniques of organization, on balance it seems an unpromising lead. We will do better to set this aspect aside and examine the situation of the workers themselves. Conceivably there may have been aspects of their situation that made or kept the workers in the foundry and rolling mill unresponsive to agitation and which also distinguished their situation from that prevailing in the coal mines.

On such straightforward material matters as hours of work, wages, and the physical hardships and dangers to which workers were exposed, there were some differences. Yet they hardly seem sufficient to account for the near absence of collective effort among the iron and steelworkers. Hours that were too long appear as the major grievance for both coal miners and steelworkers.[68] In regard to wages the main difference between the two occupations was that for workers in metalworking plants there was a substantially wider range of pay rates than for miners.[69] This distinction may well have had some effect in dividing steelworkers against each other. We shall return to this point shortly in a wider context. The Metalworkers Union certainly thought so. But union officers also noticed that the arrangement created many grievances because it seemed unfair and arbitrary to the workers. This aspect, one would think, could have provided an effective opening for efforts at organization.[70] Whether

[67] According to one local study the native miners in the Ruhr with their traditions close to the world of the artisans were the first to be receptive to organization by SPD organizers who were themselves overwhelmingly from an artisan background. See Koszyk, "Die Sozialdemokratische Arbeiterbewegung," 152–153. Such evidence, however, suggests that it was the workers' situation and traditions that made the difference, not techniques of organization.

[68] *Die Schwereisenindustrie*, 631, states flatly in its conclusion that this is the most important issue.

[69] Cf. Koch, *Bergarbeiterbewegung*, 141.

[70] *Die Schwereisenindustrie*, 331–333.

there was an overall advantage in take-home pay and on whose side it was is hard to determine. Since both coal miners and iron and steelworkers felt their wages to be inadequate, it is unlikely that complicated calculations would yield a conclusion that would be of great assistance in explaining why they behaved so differently.[71] It is also worth noticing that in the Ruhr, despite the reputation of its employers for being especially backward, wages in both coal mining and foundry working were the highest of any of Germany's main industrial and mining areas.[72]

In regard to danger and general physical demands of the job, insurance statistics do show a rate of fatalities in mining that runs nearly twice that for foundries and rolling mills.[73] On the other hand, it is improbable that many ordinary workers looked at the statistics, and the iron and steel plants were dangerous enough. The Metalworkers Union's study, without mentioning coal mining, labels this industry the most dangerous and physically demanding of any: "Nowhere else does death and mutilation menace the workers to so great an extent as in the heavy iron and steel industry." They report 125 fatalities and 943 permanent injuries a year for the near-quarter-century 1886–1909.[74] For at least a good many jobs in ironwork and steel, routine physical demands were certainly severe and possibly more so than in coal mining. Blast furnace operators worked a twelve-hour shift exposed to the weather; others were constantly bathed in sweat as they tended the ovens and rolling mills.[75]

Whatever their jobs, the iron and steelworkers in general faced rough and unsanitary conditions in regard to heat and cold, light, ventilation, drinking water, facilities for washing and dressing, eating rooms, and toilet facilities. (The toilets in one of the main sections of the Krupp plant sound like medieval torture instruments where in winter there was the additional danger of freezing tight to the iron seats.)[76] Since the evidence on all these

[71] Average wages in the Ruhr blast furnaces ran to over 1500 marks a year in 1910, according to *Die Schwereisenindustrie*, 326. According to Koch, *Bergarbeiterbewegung*, 150 the average wage in coal mining ranged from 1494 to 1586 marks a year between 1908 and 1912, dropping to 1382 in 1910. These figures are enough to indicate that many miners and steelworkers must have earned the same wages, though there must have also been many iron and steelworkers at the lower end of the wage scale who earned less than the miners.

[72] See Koch, *Bergarbeiterbewegung*, 79, and *Die Schwereisenindustrie*, 326.

[73] Koch, *Bergarbeiterbewegung*, 145.

[74] *Die Schwereisenindustrie*, 542, 553.

[75] *Die Schwereisenindustrie*, xii.

[76] *Die Schwereisenindustrie*, 508–523. The description of the facilities at the Krupp plant occurs on 523.

matters comes from the workers' own complaints as expressed in questionnaires distributed by the Metalworkers Union, it is unlikely that the workers didn't care about bad working conditions because they were used to them or had never known anything different—even if the union very likely drew the workers' attention to them.

To sum up so far, the evidence shows rather clearly that in these two crucial sectors of the economy the historical process known as the creation of a proletariat had indeed created very similar conditions in matters generally regarded as decisive for the workers: hours of work, wages, and the physical demands of the job. Yet the social and political response was very different in the two sectors. It will be necessary to look elsewhere for an explanation. This is not to say that such issues were unimportant to the workers. They were important, as the whole history of labor movements abundantly testifies. The evidence merely indicates that what moderns correctly regard as bad material conditions were not enough by themselves to trigger off a collective response aimed at changing the situation. There must have been other factors that facilitated such a response among coal miners and inhibited it among steelworkers.

More promising clues appear as soon as we examine the workers' relationships with each other and with their superiors in the plant. Compared with the miners, the iron and steelworkers were a diverse and divided lot, so much so that the growth of any form of cooperation and shared outlook faced severe obstacles. Foundry workers, the Metalworkers Union reported, generally knew nothing about work processes in other parts of the plant. On account of the system of compartmentalization and supervision they never left their own place of work.[77] In the light of the complex and rapidly changing technology of heavy metalworking, it is difficult to see how they could have moved about. For miners the situation was quite different. Despite variations in the character of a coal seam, presumably a competent miner could be sent just about anywhere. In contrast iron and steelworkers were quite specialized. A contemporary description of the way workers prepared the masses of material continuously consumed by a blast furnace includes nine different occupational categories ending with an "etc." A similar list of the categories of workers in a pipe rolling mill contains fourteen categories, likewise ending with an "etc."[78] Some tasks evidently

[77]*Die Schwereisenindustrie*, XIII.

[78]*Die Schwereisenindustrie*, 11, 22.

required enormous strength and endurance. Others might be performed by ordinary day laborers.[79]

Thus for purely technological reasons the organization of work in the heavy metalworking industries divided the workers from each other much more than was the case among the coal miners. That was also the reason for the wider range of pay scales. Presumably many groups of skilled and unskilled workers had to cooperate in order to carry through specific operations. In this way sentiments of mutual loyalty and small nuclei of solidarity may well have grown up. I, however, have found no description to indicate that such was definitely the case. In any event they would have had to appear in separate parts of separate plants, making coalescence around common experience difficult. I have come upon no trace of any arrangement that resembles the miners' *Gedinge*, the miners' team whose senior officer regularly struck a bargain with the supervisor about collective pay rates.

Relationships between the workers and their immediate superiors were notoriously bad in both occupations. According to the miners' complaints that surfaced in strikes, there was a plethora of personal abuse by superiors. In the iron and steel industries it could hardly have been much better. The Metalworkers Union asked about verbal abuse in their questionnaire study, covering about 760 firms, and compiled the results with meticulous care. Two pages of fine print list the various epithets hurled at workers in the various plants of the Ruhr and constitute an interesting addition to any foreigner's German vocabulary. A large proportion of the terms indicate that exasperated foremen often regarded the workers as stupid and lazy animals. In the same inquiry the workers were asked to grade their treatment into four classes: good, satisfactory, unsatisfactory, and bad. Even if the results require a skeptical attitude for proper interpretation, they are worth mentioning:

Good and satisfactory treatment	600
Unsatisfactory and bad treatment·	717

Thus more than half the workers were willing to report their treatment as unsatisfactory or worse, even by the standards of the time. Some indication of the nature of these standards appears in the replies to another question asking the workers to

---

[79]See the general descriptions in Pounds, *The Ruhr*, 105–120; *Die Schwereisenindustrie*, 6–23.

report on the presence or absence of outright physical abuse. The answers were:

No physical mistreatment	907
Physical abuse	256[80]

Even if we allow for crudeness in the questionnaire and the fact that the Metalworkers Union had an obvious interest in exaggerating bad treatment of the workers, it is safe to conclude once more that these workers did take considerable abuse by present-day standards.

In the big iron and steel plants foremen and minor supervisors were generally former workmen on a *Du* basis with their workers. The second person singular in German as in French, however, has an ambiguous connotation: it can imply the familiarity of intimacy and equality *or* that of superiority to the point of contempt. (The reader may recall that one of the demands of workers in 1848 was to be spoken to in the usual polite form among nonintimates, the second person plural, *Sie.*) Clearly the element of superiority predominated. Foremen possessed the immediate right to fire workers, and at that time there was, according to the union, *no* legal restriction on its use. A worker could be fired for just about any reason that occurred to a foreman. Many foremen apparently used their authority to vent on the workers all sorts of hatred, envy, and personal dislike.[81]

It is natural to ask: why did workers put up with such treatment? The Metalworkers Union answers the question very simply. There was nothing else they could do. Anyone who knew the situation at first hand, the union's publication remarked, was aware that the prime consideration, fear of losing his job and his bread, kept the worker's mouth shut. Any attempt to defend himself was likely to be taken as insubordination and a violation of the regulations decreed by the management. In effect the worker was told that if he didn't like the way he was treated he could get out and get out quickly; there were plenty of others ready to take his place.[82] Undoubtedly that was a major element in the situation, perhaps the most important one of all. Yet it

---

[80]*Die Schwereisenindustrie*, 488–490.

[81]*Die Schwereisenindustrie*, 500–501. The source appears inconsistent in its claim that there were no legal restrictions on discharges, since it also mentions that the use of bad language to a superior did not constitute technical insubordination and legal grounds for discharge. There apparently were *Gewerbegerichte* or trade courts before which such matters could be taken, but this source reports that workers seldom resorted to them.

[82]*Die Schwereisenindustrie*, 492.

could not have applied with equal force to all kinds of workers. It is hardly likely that a strong and skilled workman doing a key job in a complicated technical process could be replaced as easily as an ordinary day laborer.

From the standpoint of the individual worker the prospect of losing his job almost certainly constituted the most important weapon in the employer's arsenal of techniques to ensure a docile and dependable labor force. There were others too. One was the yellow or company unions, already discussed in another connection. Here it is worth noticing that the employers did not feel sufficiently threatened by competition for the allegiance of their workers to resort to this device until 1908.[83] The other device concerned pensions. Their main purpose, along with provisions for housing and arrangements for cheaper food, was to tie the workers to a particular firm. Thus they are an indication that labor mobility did concern the employers, and that the worker's freedom to leave the job was not an altogether negligible weapon in the hands of the labor force.

Pension plans were especially characteristic of the big iron and steel plants in the Ruhr. In prewar Germany the most important ones existed there. In the sample of about 122,000 workers that the Metalworkers Union studied, slightly over 65 percent belonged to a pension system. In most cases membership was obligatory. The worker paid an entrance fee on taking a job and dues while holding it. But on leaving the job the worker lost his pension rights. According to the Metalworkers Union it was common practice to fire workers after long years of service just before the time when they could collect their pensions. The Krupp firm is cited as one that engaged in this practice. The union also presents figures on one of the Krupp plants that ostensibly show the firm's contribution to be quite small while that of the workers in the form of entry fees, dues, and fines was much larger.[84]

---

[83]For the circumstances see Mattheier, "Werkvereine," 180. As the same author points out on 188, company unions in the mines had managed by 1914 to attract nearly 10 percent of the labor force. But there they had serious competitors who had already organized the bulk of the labor force. This was not at all the case in the iron and steel industries.

[84]*Die Schwereisenindustrie*, 524–529.

4. The consequences of different historical experiences

Pausing now to look back at the situation as a whole we can see that for every abuse that the Metalworkers Union complained about in the last years before the outbreak of the war there was a parallel in the coal mines. The fundamental grievances of both sets of workers come down to these: (1) lack of decent human treatment and respect; (2) bitter resentment against fines and deductions in their pay, deductions that they felt were unjust and arbitrary—after all, they had put in tremendous effort; (3) pay scales over which they had no control and which were arbitrary and unjust in the way they rewarded or failed to reward skill and effort, and which tended to pit workers against each other in relentless competition; (4) lack of security in their jobs and the prospect of being fired by an angry supervisor out of pure spite and malice. On these essential points their situation was similar. Yet the miners did a great deal about their situation, even if with limited results, and the metalworkers next to nothing.

The main difference between the workers in iron and steel and the miners was this: the miners had their *Gedinge*, their *Knappschaften*, and their *Berggesetz*, social arrangements that set miners off from other bodies of workers and played a major part in facilitating collective protest. Though a good deal of the steam behind this protest may have come from unorganized workers, the *Gedinge* and the *Knappschaften* served as models and nuclei for its expression while the *Berggesetz* contributed to its legitimacy. All three were the precipitates of past historical experience, perpetuated because mining expanded through an expansion of the labor force. Evidently the iron and steelworkers faced a generally similar situation by 1914, but came to this situation through a quite different set of historical experiences. This distinction emerges as the most probable solution to the puzzle of their different reactions. For reasons pointed out earlier there is unfortunately much less historical information about the workers in the giant metalworking plants than about the coal miners. But there is enough to sketch the character and probable impact of this set of experiences.

In contrast to coal mining the iron and steel industries expanded their output through a series of major technological advances that deserve the rather overworked label revolutionary. Iron was the first to expand. The replacement of charcoal by coke for smelting did not begin in the Ruhr until 1849. After that came the huge furnaces. In 1850 the average Prussian furnace produced 720 tons. By 1871 it produced more than 5,000. In iron, however, refining remained a bottleneck. The puddling furnace required men of enormous strength and endurance, capable of standing up to the heat for hours as they stirred the thick porridge of semiliquid metal and drew off blobs of what was to become wrought iron. Efforts to mechanize this part of the process failed. The eventual solution came with the discoveries of how to manufacture cheap steel and its substitution for wrought iron in most uses. These discoveries, associated with the names of Bessemer and Siemens-Martin, were not applied in Germany on a wide scale until well after 1870.[85]

Steel has important technical advantages over iron, which in the form of pig iron is hard but brittle, and in the form of wrought iron is soft and easy to work, but very susceptible to wear and tear. Steel, on the other hand, by its hardness and elasticity combines the advantages of both. Originally, due to the amount of labor and fuel required, it was a very costly commodity sold and used by the pound for such objects as razors, surgical tools, and the like.[86] The new technical advances changed all that. Iron continued to be used and its production continued to expand down to the outbreak of the war. But starting from much smaller beginnings, the production of steel expanded much more rapidly as it became widely used for railroads, battleships, and many other purposes. Below are the figures (in thousands of metric tons) for the output of pig iron and steel in Germany as a whole in selected years before the First World War. During each interval of time the production of iron approximately doubled while that of steel came close to tripling.

	Pig Iron	Steel
1880	2,729	624
1890	4,658	1,614
1900	8,521	6,646
1913	19,309	18,935[87]

The making of steel appears to have been a process more complicated than was the case of iron and requiring even

[85]Landes, *Unbound Prometheus*, 218–219, 264.

[86]Landes, *Unbound Prometheus*, 251–252.

[87]*Handwörterbuch der Staatswissenschaften*, Vol. 3, *s.v.*, "Eisen- und Stahlindustrie," 548, 556. For wrought iron in relation to steel see the comments in Landes, *Unbound Prometheus*, 260, where he draws a parallel between the continued use of wrought iron after the coming of steel with the development of the clipper ship after the introduction of the steamer.

more powerful machinery. We read of tiltable furnaces of 100–300-ton capacity, forges, rolling mills out of which finished metal rushed at forty to sixty miles an hour, flying shears for cutting, and the like. By the end of the nineteenth century German steel plants had the most advanced equipment in Europe.[88]

These powerful technological advances had several consequences that created sharp differences between the coal miners' general situation and that of the metalworkers. For one thing, the productivity of labor increased very considerably in heavy metalworking, whereas in coal mining, as pointed out earlier, it was largely static once new ways of working deeper seams had gone into effect. Though I have not been able to find usable statistics to demonstrate this rise in productivity, it is a matter on which standard sources agree,[89] and seems close to obvious from the history of techniques just recounted. Furthermore, with only something like half as many workers as in coal mining by 1913, those in the new giants aboveground were a much more diverse group. A smelter and a man who helped to operate the flying shears were not likely to have as much in common as the various grades of coal miners, making collective action much more difficult. Finally, and although this distinction is not, so far as I can see, directly traceable to differences in technology, in iron and steel workers had no continuing tradition of a benevolent state authority to which they had a right to appeal and which gave some color of legitimacy to their grievances. Originally some of them may well have had this sense, since up until 1861 the foundry workers were subject to the authority of the state's mining offices (*Bergbehörden*). In that year, as part of the liberal reforms of mining, and thus before the period of rapid growth in both heavy metalworking and mining, the foundry workers lost whatever protection their special status might have provided as new legislation transferred them from

[88]Landes, *Unbound Prometheus*, 263–269.

[89]Landes, *Unbound Prometheus*, 268, cites some statistics for steel but points out their contradictions. Wolfram Fischer, *Wirtschaft und Gesellschaft*, 181, observes that the nineteenth-century iron industry had one of the highest rates of increase in the productivity of labor. Helmut Croon, "Vom Werden des Ruhrgebiets," in Först, editor, *Rheinisch-Westfälische Rückblende*, 212, gives some scattered statistics to show that the labor force grew much more slowly in the iron and steel plants than in coal mining. His claim that working conditions were better in iron and steel than in coal seems to me, on the basis of evidence cited above, rather doubtful. On the other hand, his observation that there was less turnover of labor in the iron and steel plants makes sense. Coal mining was clearly voracious in its demand for labor. There must have been many who left the mines after a short trial, either forced out or leaving of their own accord.

the authority of the mining officials to that of the ordinary civil authorities.[90]

If the descent into the darkness of the mine had its mysterious and frightening aspects, against which, however, long-established traditions and customs provided some security, the first contact with the new Molochs above the earth must have been a truly terrifying experience for simple peasants and artisans. Unlike the coal miners, most of the metalworkers came from a western German artisan and worker background. There was also a contingent of east-European immigrants, as the existence of a Polish union demonstrates.[91] From their artisan and peasant backgrounds the iron and steelworkers could hardly have brought with them a common set of experiences and standards with which to assess their new situation. Particularly for those who had come from an artisan background the transition to blast furnace or rolling mill with its overwhelming technology must have been a vastly more traumatic experience than that which Carl Severing underwent as a young *Schlosser*. In many a small factory around 1900 the line between artisan and factory life was still blurred. An individual could go back and forth across it without being aware of the distinction. The situation in coal mining too, as we have had several occasions to notice, perpetuated certain characteristics and traditions of artisan life. Those who entered coal mining found a vigorous common culture upon which they could draw. For the iron and steelworkers there was nothing of the sort.

To sum up, the iron and steelworkers had no tradition of informal collective bargaining such as the *Gedinge*, nothing but the feeblest memory of a paternalist state formerly embodied in the authority of the *Berggesetz*, no rudimentary system of social insurance like the *Knappschaften* with a tradition that the miners should run it themselves. The iron and steelworkers were, so to speak, an historical creation from scratch—without customs, collective experience, or memory. Or more accurately, what customs they had were probably different one from another and obliterated in the course of the creation of the new plants that

---

[90]There they were subject to the *Gewerbeordnung* (trade regulations), which may have provided German industrial workers in general somewhat greater protection than was the case in liberal England. The transfer is mentioned in Wolfram Fischer, *Wirtschaft und Gesellschaft*, 152, 173–174.

[91]Mattheier, "Werkvereine," 176. The *11. Sonderheft zum Reichs-Arbeitsblatte . . . 1913*, Erster Teil, 49, mentions a Polish union of foundry workers with over 11,000 members. According to Wilhelm Brepohl, *Industrievolk: Im Wandel von der agraren zur industriellen Daseinsform dargestellt am Ruhrgebiet*, 202, local researches have shown that most immigrants to the Ruhr came from either a west German or east German rural background.

burgeoned in the 1880s. This lack put them at a tremendous disadvantage in any efforts at self-help, whether on their own or suggested to them by outsiders. There were other obstacles too. Since the great metal industries were technologically more advanced than coal mining, they generated and required a more diverse labor force with a wider range of pay scales and more varied skills. Workers, engaged in different processes, of which there was a great number, performed their daily tasks physically and socially isolated from each other in different parts of the plant. Together, the absence of shared traditions and social fragmentation in the place of work must have rendered very difficult any sense of a common fate as the basis for collective action. That, by way of tentative conclusion, emerges as the most persuasive reason why the steelworkers were so much less receptive to union organization than the coal miners, and why they were far less active in defending themselves.

Even if the coal miners were more active and had supported the greatest strikes in the history of the German working class prior to 1914, there is not the slightest hint that they were the carriers of revolutionary sentiments. The growth of big industry in the Ruhr had created a substantial industrial working class that one can with good reason call a proletariat. But the politically conscious elite of this sector was fractured along several fault lines, while the mass of the workers, when they stirred at all, impelled the leaders toward the pursuit of limited objectives. To call these merely bread-and-butter issues is to slander them. There was a powerful emotional charge behind them. Their central thrust was toward the acceptance of the workers as decent human beings in a more humane social order.

Whether that goal was attainable by peaceable or violent means, or some combination of the two, is quite another matter. In any case, among workers as a whole, the impulses toward that goal varied sharply from industry to industry, as this chapter has tried to demonstrate. Even where the impulse was strong, it reflected the situation in a particular industry. Coal miners had coal miners' grievances and did something about them. Iron and steelworkers had their grievances too, but were unable to do much about them. Would the shared trauma of war and defeat provide a common set of experiences to override these distinctions and fuse the industrial workers into a single revolutionary force that would usher in a new age? There were those in Germany who greatly feared this possibility and worked feverishly to prevent it, just as there were those who committed all their considerable energies and intelligence to bring it about. Both, as it turned out, failed. In the chapters that follow we shall try to understand why.

CHAPTER EIGHT

The reformist revolution 1918–1920

1. General background

The strains of the First World War, the shock of a defeat that destroyed the monarchy and temporarily discredited the dominant strata and institutions of German society—Junkers, military leaders, the civilian bureaucracy, big business—created conditions that enabled a diffuse revolutionary movement to surface in 1918. The reformist wing of the labor movement took power peacefully on November 9, 1918, partly because both the reformists and the leaders of the old regime were anxious to head off a radical upsurge. At this point those committed to a revolutionary transformation of the existing order were still a small minority. The leader of this movement was Rosa Luxemburg, who subsequently attained a worldwide reputation, though it would be hard to prove that she was the dominant figure at the time. A much larger group among those traditionally called radicals were unsure of what they did want and mainly agreed on what they did not want, a return to the status quo of 1914. These were the Independent Socialists, or USPD, from the German initials for Independent Socialist Party of Germany, who had broken off from the SPD in 1917. Still, revolutionary radicalism, which before the war had been mainly a ferment among left intellectuals, had begun by 1918 to acquire a mass basis. This mass basis grew very rapidly, partly because of the policies adopted by the SPD leaders and partly for other and more fundamental reasons. Whether the SPD could have handled the situation in a different manner, and with less disastrous results, is a difficult question, to be discussed after we have seen

275

what actually happened. Moderate and reformist elements among the industrial workers did manage to contain and defeat the radical impulse—or rather several radical thrusts which came at different times and from somewhat differing sources. But they bought this success at the price of an alliance with the conservative and antidemocratic forces in German society. The Pyrrhic and limited victory of the moderates created a legacy of bitterness within the industrial working class and a liberal capitalist regime with very few liberals. Within a decade and a half that regime succumbed to Hitler.

In capsule form that is the historical tale that forms the framework for the remaining historical portion of this book. This chapter and the next will analyze certain aspects of the part played by the workers in this major tragedy of modern civilization.

The war and its aftermath thoroughly disrupted the ordinary daily routines of life for practically every industrial worker in Germany, as it did no doubt in the rest of Europe. This fact by itself goes a long way toward explaining the political turmoil of the immediate postwar period. A huge number of workers changed jobs. Others joined the armed forces, many of whom became casualties. Women and children did men's work but left the labor force at war's end. For those men who stayed in the same job the conditions of work changed markedly. Taken together, these changes meant that the familiar social networks and sanctions that had tied individuals to the status quo underwent severe strains and had to be re-created—or else broke down altogether.

The occupational statistics give some indication of the major dimensions of the changes. Tables 10 and 10a present them in summary form.[1]

---

[1]The tables are based on the reports of the *Gewerbeaufsicht* or Factory Inspection Service (which covered firms with ten employees or more), as cited in *Statistisches Jahrbuch für das Deutsche Reich,* Vol. 42 (1921/22), 96–97. For 1913 the report included about 7.4 million workers. Since there were about 8.5 million workers in 1907, the date of the last occupational census, in 1913 there must have been more than a million workers not covered by the Factory Inspection Service. There appears to be no way of filling this gap in the data. A new occupational census was not taken until 1925. During the war and indeed up until 1922 the *Statistisches Jahrbuch* blandly continued to report occupational data from the 1907 census. Since the Factory Inspection Service was hard pressed with other duties and undermanned, and by no means enjoyed full cooperation from employers in gaining access to company records, it is unlikely that its records could have been very precise. Though these defects should be kept in mind, they do not destroy the value of the data altogether. Our interest is in workers in the larger plants that were usually covered by the Factory Inspection Service, and it is hardly likely that the service's statistics are so inaccurate as to misrepresent the general direction of changes. As rough approximations the figures still remain very revealing.

Table 10.

Industrial Workers, as Reported by the Factory Inspection Service

(in thousands)

Industrial categories	1913				1918				1920			
	(1) Males	(2) Females & youth under 16	(3) Total no. of workers	(4) Col. (2) as % of (3)	(1) Males	(2) Females & youth under 16	(3) Total no. of workers	(4) Col. (2) as % of (3)	(1) Males	(2) Females & youth under 16	(3) Total no. of workers	(4) Col. (2) as % of (3)
WAR INDUSTRIES												
III. Mining	1134	63	1197	05	955	180	1135	16	1227	100	1327	08
V. Metalworking	521	159	680	23	405	328	734	45	503	196	699	28
VI. Machines	1008	165	1173	14	1097	654	1751	37	1151	269	1420	19
VII. Chemicals	146	35	181	19	256	231	488	47	208	52	259	20
VIII. Oils, etc.	70	12	82	15	54	23	77	30	82	16	98	16
Totals	2879	434	3313	13	2767	1416	4185	34	3171	633	3803	17
INTERMEDIATE												
IV. Stone, clay	537	111	648	17	180	84	264	32	343	93	435	21
X. Paper	115	84	199	42	60	98	158	62	103	84	188	45
XI. Leather	92	29	121	24	51	49	100	49	71	29	101	29
XII. Wood	383	71	454	16	323*	92*	415*	22	353	92	446	21
XVI. Building	263	14	277	05	106	13	119	11	178	11	189	06
Miscellaneous	15	3	18	17	12	11	23	48	15	6	21	29
Totals	1405	312	1717	18	732	347	1079	32	1063	315	1380	23
CIVILIAN												
IX. Textiles	400	556	956	58	98	305	403	76	233	400	634	63
XIII. Food	468	246	714	34	258	286	544	53	330	243	573	42
XIV. Clothing	112	319	431	74	52	242	294	82	93	263	356	74
XV. Cleaning	13	43	56	77	7	37	44	84	9	33	42	79
XVII. Printing	134	66	200	33	70	68	138	49	116	65	181	36
Totals	1127	1230	2357	52	485	938	1423	66	781	1004	1786	56
Grand totals	5411	1976	7387	27	3984	2701	6687	40	5015	1952	6969	28

Table 10a.

Changes from 1913 in Numbers of Industrial Workers

(in thousands)

Industrial categories	1918 vs. 1913		1920 vs. 1913	
	Number of workers	Percentage change	Number of workers	Percentage change
WAR INDUSTRIES				
III. Mining	−62	−05	+130	+11
V. Metalworking	+54	+08	+19	+03
VI. Machines	+578	+49	+247	+21
VII. Chemicals	+307	+170	+78	+43
VIII. Oils, etc.	−5	−06	+16	+20
Totals	+872	+26	+490	+15
INTERMEDIATE				
IV. Stone, clay	−384	−59	−213	−33
X. Paper	−41	−21	−11	−06
XI. Leather	−21	−17	−20	−17
XII. Wood	−39*	−09	−8	−02
XVI. Building	−158	−57	−88	−32
Miscellaneous	+5	+28	+3	+17
Totals	−638	−37	−337	−20
CIVILIAN				
IX. Textiles	−553	−58	−322	−34
XIII. Food	−170	−24	−141	−20
XIV. Clothing	−137	−32	−75	−17
XV. Cleaning	−12	−21	−14	−25
XVII. Printing	−62	−31	−19	−10
Totals	−934	−40	−571	−24
Grand totals	−700	−09	−418	−06

SOURCES: For 1913, 1919 (where used) and 1920, *Statistisches Jahrbuch für das Deutsche Reich*, Vol. 42 (1921/22), 96–97; for 1918 see Waldemar Zimmermann, "Die Veränderung der Einkommens- und Lebensverhältnisse der deutschen Arbeiter durch den Krieg," in Rudolf Meerwarth et al., *Die Einwirkungen des Krieges auf die Bevölkerungsbewegungen und Lebenshaltung in Deutschland*, 351. In Table 10 figures for column 2 represent the difference between columns 3 and 1.

NOTE: The Factory Inspection Service reported only on establishments with 10 or more employees.

*1919 figures used instead of 1918 figures since Zimmermann's total for male woodworkers merely repeats the 1913 total, an entry I regard as an unfortunate error all too easy to let slip in.

At first glance it might appear that the war had greatly accelerated the trend toward the making of a modern industrial proletariat and in this fashion created the social basis for postwar "proletarian" upsurges. The war industries—from mining to chemicals—are those most characteristic of a modern industrial economy. The total number of workers in this sector increased by 26 percent between 1913 and 1918. Meanwhile the intermediate category of industries lost 37 percent of its workers and the civilian category 40 percent. On closer inspection this plausible hypothesis loses most of its force. Even in the war industries the number of males declined, as the composition of the labor force changed sharply. The proportion of females and youths rose from 13 percent in 1913 to 34 percent in 1918. As 112,000 men left the war industries, presumably for the trenches, 982,000 women and youths streamed in to create the increase in workers in this sector of the economy.

Between 1918 and 1920 most of these dropped out of the work force and could hardly have been a source of radicalization. Indeed it is worth noticing that by 1920 the proportion of women and youthful workers under 16 returned to one very similar to that of 1913 in all three sectors. In 1913 it was 13 percent in the war industries, 18 percent in the intermediate sector, and 52 percent in the civilian sector. By 1920 the respective proportions were 17 percent, 23 percent, and 56 percent.

After the war, to be sure, in 1920 the wartime sector still had a net gain in employment of 15 percent, with machines (group VI) showing the largest absolute gain of any occupational category by the addition of 247,000 workers. Hence an explanation of radicalism in terms of the growth of the sector most characteristic of a modern industrial sector is not to be discarded out of hand. But, as the rest of the table shows and as I have already suggested, the basic fact of industrial life was not by any means just growth. Instead, it was wild fluctuation in the type and conditions of employment. Hence it will be more useful to notice what some of the major changes were in specific industries, especially because the overall total for industrial workers and even the subtotals in the wartime, intermediate, and civilian sectors mask such changes.

The industries that gained workers between 1913 and 1918 were in the war sector (except for the insignificant group "Miscellaneous"):

Industrial Category	Increase in No. of Workers	Percentage Gain
V. Metals	54,000	08
VI. Machinery	578,000	49
VII. Chemicals	307,000	170

Those making gains over the entire period 1913 to 1920, again excluding "Miscellaneous," were:

Industrial Category	Increase in No. of Workers	Percentage Gain
III. Mining	130,000	11
V. Metals	19,000	03
VI. Machinery	247,000	21
VII. Chemicals	78,000	43
VIII. Oils, etc.	16,000	20

Except for the catch-all category of "Miscellaneous," all these gains were in the advanced industrial sector.[2] And it was also in this sector, particularly in mining, that the most severe turmoil and upheaval were to occur between 1918 and 1920. In large measure the radical thrust took the form of a rejection of the leadership of the SPD unions in metals and machinery, and in mining.

The occupational categories that suffered the sharpest losses, on the other hand, were relatively tranquil, at least in the sense that whatever happened there had little or no political repercussion on the national scene and failed to leave any marked traces in detailed histories of the period. The following industries lost more than 100,000 workers between 1913 and 1918:

Industrial Category	No. of Workers Lost	Percentage Change
IV. Stone and clay	384,000	−59
XVI. Building	158,000	−57
XIII. Food	170,000	−24
XIV. Clothing	137,000	−32
IX. Textiles	553,000	−58

At the war's end in 1918, with more than half the workers gone in the industry that made cooking ware and household crockery, in construction and textiles, and very severe cuts in food and clothing, the supply of civilian goods must have been extremely tight. That in turn meant severe physical hardship for many and a widespread disruption of daily routines—the best

[2]Workers classified as "Miscellaneous" increased by 17 percent by 1920, but since the original number in this group was small in 1913, amounting to 18,000, and their diverse tasks not essential to the economy, I am omitting them at this point.

possible recipe for social upheaval. In 1920 severe damage to this sector remained, as shown by the industries that still showed a loss of more than 100,000 workers:

Industrial Category	No. of Workers Lost	Percentage Change
IV. Stone and clay	213,000	–33
XIII. Food	141,000	–20
IX. Textiles	322,000	–34

It is worthwhile drawing attention to the implications of the occupational shifts between 1913 and 1920 for the SPD unions, since these unions were on balance a significant mechanism for social integration and stability. Before the war the SPD had mass unions, that is, unions with more than 100,000 members, among the metalworkers, miners, woodworkers, and construction workers.[3] There were no dramatic numerical changes by 1920 in the number of workers in metalworking and woodworking, though there were changes in working conditions to be discussed in a moment. There were, however, sharp fluctuations in mining, which lost 62,000 workers during the war but by 1920 was 130,000 higher than in 1913. Construction and textiles experienced heavier losses during the war that were only partly made up in the first two postwar years. Thus the occupational figures reveal two severe sources of strain on union organizations. In occupations such as mining, which made gains between 1913 and 1920, the unions were flooded by new members unfamiliar with union habits and discipline. In those occupations such as construction and textiles, where total employment declined, the exactly opposite situation prevailed: the traditional base of union membership had eroded.

One further aspect of Table 10 and 10a deserves attention, the marked drift back to "normalcy" between 1918 and 1920. As already noted, by 1920 the distribution between adult males and auxiliaries returned, after a wartime surge, to quite close to that of 1913. In terms of total employment, wartime industries had gained 26 percent in 1918 and the intermediate and civilian sectors had lost 37 percent and 40 percent. But by 1920 the respective changes were down to a gain of 15 percent for the war industries and losses of 20 percent and 24 percent for the other

[3]There was also a large union of factory workers with 211,000 members in 1913. Presumably its members were scattered in various occupational categories. Hence they are impossible to trace by means of these data. The union of transport workers with 230,000 members in 1913 also remains beyond the net cast by the Factory Inspection Service. During the postwar upheavals the railroad workers played an important part, sometimes on one side, sometimes on the other.

two. Actually this period of a return to "normalcy" was one of repeated political crises and very serious social upheavals. At the same time this tendency to revert to older structural relationships probably helped the moderates to gain the upper hand in the end.

The war generated strains not only in the pattern of occupational choices open to workers but also to the social contract governing the just reward for labor. What happened to the notion of an extra reward for skill is quite revealing. This moral assumption came into conflict with other moral assumptions, as well as the imperatives of a war economy. If these imperatives were at bottom the imperatives of the dominant classes, they were also to a degree shared by the workers until the sacrifices made by workingmen began to seem to them unfair. In several sectors of the economy—notably railways, construction in certain cities, and in several Bavarian industries—there is evidence to support the familiar claim that wage differentials between skilled and unskilled workers declined. Severe rises in the cost of living created the "necessity" to protect the lower-paid workers in these sectors. This "necessity" evidently reflects not only upperclass concern about disorder but also popular beliefs to the effect that there should be some sort of a minimum or living wage along with differential rewards for skill and effort.

The leveling of wages was also due to the influx of new and less skilled workers, mainly women and younger workers, shown in Table 10. On the other hand, in the war industries, where the proportionate rise in women and younger workers was greatest, the wage rates of unskilled workers increased *less* than did those of their fellow workers. In this sector of the economy the scarcity of such skilled persons as the precision workers in metals and machinery served, together with the requirements of the war, to keep their wages high.[4] There is something intriguing in the fact that the wave of "proletarian" radicalism began precisely among these highly privileged workers. Shortly we shall take a closer look at their situation.

With these observations it is time to raise some questions about the significance of straightforward material hardship in the whole upheaval. There is no reason to doubt that there was very severe material hardship among many workers toward the end of the war and during the chaotic years that followed. In some areas there was outright starvation. Real wage rates for selected occupations show declines of 25 to 50 percent between

[4]Gerhard Bry, *Wages in Germany 1871–1945*, 202–203, 283–284.

1913 and 1917. In 1918 and 1919 there was a surprising recovery that brought some real wages to levels higher than in 1913, but with severe fluctuations to follow between 1919 and 1923. During that time there were drops of as much as 50 percent. The figures suggest a world of very unstable expectations—if indeed it made sense to have *any* expectations—and fortunes that rapidly changed for reasons completely beyond the control of any individual worker. On the other hand, in the series reported, real wage rates for the unskilled held up better during declines and rose higher during recoveries than did the rates for skilled workers. In this sense, then, there was some cushioning to the dizzying lurches of the wheel of fortune.

There are also data[5] on average daily real earnings for male and female workers in the main industrial categories. Taking March, 1914, as 100, the rates in September, 1918, or shortly before the mutinies and workers' uprisings that followed defeat, were as follows:

	Males	Females
War industries	77.4	87.9
Intermediate industries	64.2	71.1
Civilian industries	55.5	61.9

One striking aspect of this evidence is the fact that real wages for females declined substantially less than did those of males. This fact is significant for several reasons. For most workers what really mattered was family earnings, not just the wages of the male breadwinner. One way of coping with lower wages and higher prices was for another member of the family—wife, son, or daughter—to get a job. If the father had to join the military forces, the only way to pull through a very tight situation was for someone else in the family to get a job. Unfortunately there is no way to obtain a quantitative measure of the female contribution to family income, because there is no information to show how many women in the labor force were wives or daughters in the households of working husbands.[6] On the other hand, the increases in the auxiliary labor force reported in Table 10 show quite clearly that worker families sought—or were forced to seek—this solution on a very wide scale during the war, but

[5] All data on wage rates from Bry, *Wages in Germany*, 210–212.

[6] Waldemar Zimmermann, "Die Veränderung der Einkommens- und Lebensverhältnisse der deutschen Arbeiter durch den Krieg," in Rudolf Meerwarth *et al.*, *Die Einwirkung des Krieges*, 468.

abandoned it as soon as possible otherwise, despite continuing severe hardship.[7]

Despite extraordinarily long hours of work and wages that failed to keep up with prices, always excepting some highly favored workers in munitions industries, material hardship was something one felt as a consumer rather than as a worker. Or to put the point more concretely, it was something that hurt more after work than the work itself, even if that hurt too. Again it is hard to pin this point down in meaningful quantitative terms. But we have already seen evidence that the industries producing consumer necessities were starved for manpower. They were also very short of raw materials, including of course food. To judge from scattered reports, including those on the political atmosphere among the workers put out by the Factory Inspection Service, the rationing system worked in a way that was surprisingly erratic for a German bureaucratic creation. It is important to remember, however, that this was the first war to require the mobilization of the civilian economy and civilian population on such a scale. Workers widely resented the fact that they had to supplement their diet from the black market where, it seemed, the rich could buy what they wanted when they wanted it.[8]

To sum up what material hardship meant, and did *not* mean, in political terms, three points stand out clearly enough to deserve emphasis. The data on changes in real wages demonstrate that periods of increasing material hardship do not coincide closely with periods of political upheaval. Real wages were lower in 1917 than in 1918. Material hardships are a very necessary but quite insufficient cause for social upheavals. Secondly, those at the bottom of the economic heap, the unskilled, were not by and large the ones that suffered the most. Finally, the radical thrust from the "masses," a questionable but occasionally usable term, originated in its most privileged sector, the Berlin metalworkers.

---

[7]Otherwise it would be necessary to believe that this huge influx of women and youths came from outside the industrial working class. Since peasant women were busy trying to keep the farms going and bourgeois German women would not have done this on any wide scale, this possibility seems most unlikely.

[8]Bry, *Wages in Germany,* 213; Jürgen Reulecke, "Der Erste Weltkrieg und die Arbeiterbewegung im rheinisch-westfälischen Industriegebiet," in Reulecke, *Arbeiterbewegung an Rhein und Ruhr,* 221–222.

2. The duel between the SPD and the radicals

What I have called here the Reformist Revolution of 1918–1920 was in fact a bitter duel for the allegiance of the industrial working classes, and control over them. The main contest was between the moderate and reformist leaders of the SPD and a heterogeneous series of opponents who shared little more than a common disillusionment with SPD policy during and immediately after the war. A third actor, and a very important one, in this tragic drama was the Army and its key officers. For the historian to state the issues before describing the contest is to risk a degree of falsification, because many of the contestants only became aware of the issues as the situation developed and choices had to be made to the sound of crackling rifles, rumbling trucks, or the roar of excited crowds. For this reason too it is necessary to present a fairly detailed chronological account of the main events. Nothing else can hope to do justice to this fascinating and tragic example of escalation and polarization as the contestants reached out for stronger and more effective weapons against their opponents.[9]

Still, if the reader keeps this risk constantly in mind, it is helpful to realize what the contestants could not always see: that the struggle was over the possibility (and desirability) of transforming Germany into a much more humane society by methods that remained within the framework of liberal traditions. By and large, the radicals became convinced that liberal and parliamentary methods and institutions were totally incompatible with this objective. Liberalism was something many radicals came to reject both as a means and as an end, partly because of what they saw was happening as the moderate socialists tried to behave and sound like liberals. Other radicals of course felt that liberalism was inevitably and inherently part of the capitalist system. They started out with an attitude of suspicion mixed with contempt. Long after the events themselves both moderates and revolutionaries have been inclined to argue from quite different postulates that each side followed a basically correct policy or the only one that was possible under the circumstances. In this

---

[9]It is a process that has occurred more than once. Thucydides describes its murderous course in the town of Corcyra in the early stages of the Peloponnesian War and reflects on it in a famous passage (BK. III, LXXX–LXXXV, espec. LXXXII–LXXXV) that remains even today one of the best arguments for political moderation.

manner they have imparted an air of inevitability that may actually have not been inherent in the events themselves. Only recently has a new generation of German historians begun to probe gingerly at this veil of inevitability. When the record is before us, we shall return to this issue.

Though only a narrative account can hope to recapture the way in which issues actually arose and appeared to the participants, there can be no such thing as a complete narrative. Even the most naïve chronicler is guided by principles of selection. In turn these principles are related to the problems to which one seeks answers. It will be both appropriate and helpful, therefore, to indicate very briefly what the questions are and the themes that govern the narrative. First of all, how could it happen that the socialist leadership concluded a working alliance with key sectors in the discredited dominant strata: the military, the administrative bureaucracy, and big business? On what assumptions and perceptions of the existing situation did the reformist strategy rest? In the second place, what was the radical challenge to the reformist strategy, and how did it fit into the larger context of both German and international politics? Finally, what kinds of support could the contestants muster? How and why did this support vary as the struggle proceeded?

The outbreak of the war had only temporarily and superficially healed the divisions within the SPD. Most socialist leaders did support the war. So for some time did an overwhelming majority of the industrial working classes, at least in the sense of providing willing services and not making trouble for the authorities. At first, disputes were limited to the leadership and to the theological issue of whether socialists could in good conscience support the German war effort, whether this effort was fundamentally a defense of the fatherland (which might permit at least some justifiable border rectifications and even a small dose of annexations for the sake of security), or something quite different. Leaders who opposed the war did manage to establish political organizations and distinct identities. The Spartacists did so as a small revolutionary group under the leadership of Rosa Luxemburg and Karl Liebknecht as early as January 1, 1916.[10] The Spartacists continued as an oppositional nucleus within the general framework of a larger and more moderate group, the Independent Social Democratic Party (USPD), which was set up on April 6, 1917, at a point when Germany's situation had begun to weaken visibly. The line between those willing to

---

[10]A. J. Ryder, *German Revolution of 1918,* 70, 94.

work for change within the prevailing order and those who sought to overthrow it ran through the USPD rather than between the USPD and the Spartacists. Actually it ran through the heads of some members of the USPD, who had great difficulty in making up their own minds in the turmoil of the times. Though the USPD attempted to become a mass political party after the end of the war, it failed to establish any very clear and effective political identity largely because its leaders, and very likely a large proportion of its following, could agree on very little beyond objecting to the policies of the majority socialists. Until the last year of the war all these leaders of the opposition remained generals without an army to follow them. When an army did put in an appearance in the form of open opposition to the war from significant sectors among the workers, the generals proved unable to command it.

To a considerable degree the workers developed their own leadership, organization, and methods of action. As early as the first year of the war a group of local officers in the Berlin Metalworkers Union, later known as the Revolutionary Shop Stewards, began their first attempts to organize. These were local union officials opposed to the union's official policy of economic and political truce during the hostilities, a policy followed in all the unions. At first they directed their efforts to the turners' branch of the union, made up of the most highly skilled workers. Later they gained control of almost the entire armaments industry in Berlin. This was of course the most privileged sector of the German economy. Richard Müller, a major leader of the Revolutionary Shop Stewards, emphasizes that the labor aristocracy of highly skilled workers was the driving force behind the radical movement at this time. There was little or no radicalism among the bottom strata of the workers. Indeed, the last elections to the Reichstag in 1918 demonstrated, according to Müller, that the mass of the workers had not broken away from reformist and democratic illusions. That was true even among Berlin workers, as shown by elections held there on October 15, 1918, less than a month before the outbreak of what I have called the Reformist Revolution.[11] On the other hand, these highly skilled workers were often willing to join battle not merely on behalf of their own interests but also in order to help those categories of workers whose position was weaker.[12] If that is so, it hints at the possibility of a sense of guilt among the

[11]Richard Müller, *Vom Kaiserreich zur Republik*, I, 131–132.
[12]Müller, *Kaiserreich*, I, 131–132.

privileged armament workers. There were other factors too behind their radicalism. If they were highly skilled and highly paid, they were also in other respects definitely proletarian. They worked in big plants such as AEG, Borsig, and Siemens. They were also thoroughly urbanized. In their case the bonds with a rural, petty-bourgeois, and artisan existence had dissolved.[13]

From 1916–1917 on, the Revolutionary Shop Stewards managed to extend their influence and connections outward in a rather loose manner throughout Germany. They had only very tenuous connections with the Spartacists because they did not trust the Spartacist inclinations toward a premature revolutionary putsch. They also distrusted the USPD for the opposite reason: its excessive reliance on parliamentary methods. The Revolutionary Shop Stewards were not a large group. Its core amounted to no more than fifty to eighty individuals with shared political views, confidence in one another, and strategic positions in a particular plant. Individuals in this core, on the other hand, cultivated connections with generally like-minded individuals similarly placed in other factories. In this informal manner they were able to exercise a very powerful influence as deteriorating conditions produced disenchantment with the war among wider sections of the workers.[14]

Even if a minor current within the working class as a whole, the Revolutionary Shop Stewards movement does represent an authentic expression of indigenous working-class radicalism. Since it arose among the labor aristocracy, we can leave to others the debate about whether or not it deserves to be called proletarian radicalism. It put in an appearance and gained mass support only as a consequence of the war. But it is impossible to argue that this form of radicalism was an accident or the result of something external to the development of modern industrial society unless one is prepared to believe that the war itself was an accident. (More precisely one would have to believe that, given the political and economic configurations of the early twentieth century, the prospects of peace were at least as good as those of global conflict—a proposition I find impossible to swallow.) To be sure, this was an inchoate and uncertain radicalism: the Revolutionary

[13]Fritz Opel, *Der Deutsche Metallarbeiter-Verband während des Ersten Weltkrieges und der Revolution*, 54–55. On this score their way of life presumably differed sharply from that of the industrial workers mentioned above, who had managed by very hard work to arrange their lives in a *gut bürgerlich* fashion.

[14]Peter von Oertzen, *Betriebsräte in der Novemberrevolution*, 72–75; Eberhard Kolb, *Die Arbeiterräte in der deutschen Innenpolitik 1918–1919*, 38–41.

Shop Stewards had few if any ideas about what should happen after the seizure of power.[15] Their main tactic was to put pressure on the government through strikes. In this they became increasingly successful, though they were able to mount a strike only when some specific event sparked latent discontent among the workers.

The first important strike occurred on June 28, 1916, when Karl Liebknecht was tried for treason. Then the turners stopped their machines. In Berlin 55,000 workers, it is claimed, came out on strike to express their solidarity. In April, 1917, a much larger strike followed when the government ordered the bread ration to be cut by one-quarter. By far the largest and most important of the wartime strikes, that of January, 1918, began for the same reason. That one started in Austria with a cut in the meager flour ration. From Austria it spread slowly to Germany. In Berlin perhaps 200,000 workers were out on strike by January 28, 1918. The political temper of the movement appears in the action committee that the strikers elected. There were eleven Revolutionary Shop Stewards, three representatives of the USPD, and, significantly, three members from the SPD, which was still officially very much in favor of continuing the war. The election of three members from the SPD indicates that even militant workers were still reluctant to cut their ties with their traditional leaders, an attitude that persisted after the end of the war. Characteristically the strike started with consumer grievances, reflecting experiences much more widely shared than those in the workplace which would vary from job to job and plant to plant, and quickly picked up very specific political demands from the immediate situation. The strike spread rapidly to several other German cities. Its major demands were the rapid conclusion of peace without annexations and indemnities on the basis of the Russian offer at Brest-Litovsk. Only in Berlin and Munich did the strike last for as long as a week. It ended when the government placed the armament factories in Berlin under martial law. It was also the only mass movement on a national scale until the outbreak of the November Revolution later in 1918.[16]

Meanwhile as unrest increased and the prospects of defeat replaced the hopes of victory, the dominant elements began to make concessions and even to seek a dam against disorder by making arrangements with "responsible" working-class leaders. As early as April 7, 1917, the day after the official formation of

---

[15]Kolb, *Arbeiterräte*, 41–42.

[16]F. L. Carsten, *Revolution in Central Europe 1918–1919*, 12–15.

the USPD, Kaiser Wilhelm issued an Easter decree promising reform after the war. His announcement that "there is no more room" for the three-class suffrage system amounted to a promise to grant one of the main prewar demands of the moderate socialists.[17] Up until October of 1918, on the other hand, the big employers had hoped for a military victory that would strengthen the authoritarian regime and hence their own position in relation to organized labor. By October the prospect of defeat was plain. Business leaders therefore abandoned, at least for the time being, their traditional connections with the Junkers and the authoritarian state to seek an arrangement with labor. At this point they were unwilling to terminate their support of yellow (company) unions, though they did agree to recognize the nominally socialist unions as representatives of labor, and the general notion of parity between labor and management. Precedents of a sort for such arrangements had already been established under government pressure during the war, though the power of labor representatives was slight. Toward the end of October, 1918, signs of dissolution were becoming ominous and included the prospect that the SPD might lose control over its own following.[18] Speed and further concessions by business would be necessary if business and the organized labor movement were to stem the tide. On November 2, 1918, both parties managed to agree on the demand for a demobilization office with extensive executive powers. In itself this agreement turned out to be more important as a symptom than anything else. By the next day a mutiny in Kiel was well under way. It ignited a spontaneous revolutionary movement that spread over most of Germany, taking on different forms and displaying different degrees of radical ardor in different parts of the country. On November 12, 1918, in the midst of this upheaval Hugo Stinnes, the industrialist, and Carl Legien, chief of the labor unions, did conclude a major formal bargain. The industrialists agreed to discontinue financial support for the yellow unions; they also accepted the application of the eight-hour day to all industries (but with overtime permitted) and the general introduction of collective wage agreements. In the Stinnes-Legien agreement organized labor achieved major goals that labor movements have sought in all countries. This is true even though the employers managed to protect themselves with ambiguous language and secret protocols, and were able to prevent any inter-

[17]Gerald D. Feldman, *Army, Industry, and Labor in Germany 1914–1918,* 336.
[18]According to von Oertzen, *Betriebsräte,* 64.

ference by organized labor in the operation of their plants or the conduct of business affairs.[19]

The pattern of events from the Kaiser's proclamation through the Stinnes-Legien agreement was not a new one in Germany. In the Stein-Hardenberg reforms, the limited constitutionalism of 1848, the partial democratization of 1918, and its extension in 1945, Germany experienced institutional changes that in other Western countries were the product of acute internal and even revolutionary struggles. In Germany, on the other hand, they were the consequence of bureaucratic reform from above, in a setting of defeat or abortive revolution or both. That is one important reason why there has been difficulty in making the reforms take hold or become an accepted part of German institutional life. The Stinnes-Legien agreement was not a sign of the unions' maturity or strength, but of their weakness in a time of turmoil and crisis. It did not represent the acceptance by labor and capital of methods for settling disputes within a larger framework of agreement on fundamental institutions. It was a temporary switching of alliances, more a diplomatic minuet amid the smoke of battle than an alliance, a flirtation rather than a marriage.

The Revolution of 1918 began with the mutiny of the sailors in Kiel. On October 28 the sailors had refused to obey admiralty orders to go to sea and fight the British. By November 3rd the mutiny had become a revolt and begun to spread to shore installations and to other cities. As it spread, those in revolt formed workers' and soldiers' councils. Though the names and the basic idea first appeared in Russia, these bodies were essentially a German response to German conditions.[20] Most were quite moderate, anxious mainly to cooperate with the military and civilian officials in maintaining order during a period of transition the outcome of which was highly uncertain. But not all were this way. On November 7th in Munich Kurt Eisner, at the head of USPD demonstrators who had seized arms, marched on military barracks. Their occupants hoisted the red flag and marched on the city. On November 8th a provisional workers', soldiers', and peasants' council proclaimed Bavaria a republic, with Eisner as president. At the same time the revolution led to a change of government in Württemberg, triggered by a strike of workers in the Daimler and other factories. On November 8th the revolution began in Saxony, which led on the 14th to the premature

[19]Feldman, *Army, Industry, and Labor,* 525–528.

[20]On this aspect see especially Kolb, *Arbeiterräte,* 56–60.

manifesto by the workers' and soldiers' councils of Dresden, Leipzig, and Chemnitz, announcing that capitalism had collapsed and that the revolutionary proletariat had seized power. Beginning later in Berlin than elsewhere, the revolutionary wave reached that city only on November 9, 1918. On that day the abdication of the Kaiser was announced and the Republic proclaimed by Philipp Scheidemann, a major SPD leader who had worked closely with government circles during the war.[21]

Though the proclamation of the Republic infuriated Friedrich Ebert, the SPD leader to whom the last Imperial Chancellor had formally and peacefully turned over the government, there are good reasons for believing that it prevented more radical actions. In Berlin by the end of October or the beginning of November, 1918, the Revolutionary Shop Stewards had at their disposal about 120,000 workers with military experience, of whom they believed about 75,000 were ready to strike at the word of command. On November 2, 1918, their executive committee worked out a detailed plan for the take-over of the city.[22] Even if Karl Liebknecht was to declare Germany a "free socialist republic" shortly after Scheidemann's proclamation, the transfer of power to Ebert and his colleagues forestalled any such move.

The old order was unraveling rapidly before everyone's eyes. With the deceptive vision of historical hindsight it is possible to make a strong claim for the thesis that the revolutionary forces were still essentially moderate at this stage in the unfolding of events. But the situation was fluid, and certainly not all of the revolutionary forces were moderate. To the participants, whether moderates with acute anxieties or radicals with high hopes, the revolution could hardly have seemed so moderate. The situation recalls the old tale about a man who was looking at a lion in a zoo where the cage was rather fragile. In an effort to reassure the spectator the keeper told him the lion was not really dangerous. "*You* know he's not dangerous," the visitor replied, "and *I* know it. But are you sure the lion knows it?"

Ebert at any rate was not going to take chances. By putting themselves at the head of the revolution, the SPD leaders had

---

[21]For these events I have filled out the sequence reported in William L. Langer, editor, *An Encyclopaedia of World History* with Ryder, *German Revolution,* 140, 145, 147; Carsten, *Revolution,* 35–38; *Schulthess' Europäischer Geschichtskalendar,* N.F., vol. 34 (1918), part 1, 406 ff., and the "Chronik" on 515 ff. of the *Illustrierte Geschichte der Deutschen Revolution.*

[22]Heinz Oeckel, *Die Revolutionäre Volkswehr 1918/19,* 39–40. According to Müller, *Kaiserreich,* I, 139, the date for the takeover was to be November 11. But there was also, as he shows clearly, a great deal of confusion and uncertainty about the wisdom of any attempt at all, especially since the reformist temper of workers in the provinces did not match the militance of urban workers.

forestalled the possibility that the wave of radicalism could sweep over the capital. As events turned out later, this move was crucial in breaking the whole force of the wave, such as it was. Nevertheless, the situation as of the day of the proclamation of the Republic was still volatile. The forces of moderation and orderly change felt themselves far from in control. In complex negotiations over the character of the new government the SPD had agreed to share power equally with the USPD. Three seats on the hastily formed provisional government, the Council of People's Representatives *(Rat der Volksbeauftragten)* went to the SPD; three to the USPD. Meanwhile the left had managed to gain a point. Workers' and soldiers' councils were to be elected in Berlin factories and barracks the next morning and assemble in the Circus Busch in the afternoon of the 10th to elect the provisional government. Thus there was at least the possibility of a refusal to grant popular legitimacy to Ebert's new government.

What emerged instead was a compromise arrangement that gave the SPD a substantial advantage. The Circus Busch meeting confirmed the Council of People's Representatives with the members agreed upon by the two parties. That was a key victory for Ebert and the moderates. What the left got, in addition to the symbolic gesture of sending fraternal greetings to the Soviet government with an expression of "admiration for Russian workers and soldiers who have opened the path to revolution, and its pride that the German workers and soldiers have followed them . . . ," was an Executive Council *(Vollzugsrat)* for the Berlin workers' and soldiers' councils that was to claim a controlling or supervisory authority over the actions of the Council of People's Representatives. That claim, however, the Executive Council was never able to make stick.[23]

Ebert's important victory at the Circus Busch was the consequence of popular support among the Berlin workers, though there were elements of manipulation, as there generally are, behind this local plebiscite. Müller, who was a leader of the Revolutionary Shop Stewards and participant in these events, provides a firsthand account that reveals a great deal about the workers' and soldiers' mood at this point. Workers in the factories, he reports, were wildly enthusiastic about the apparent end of socialist fratricide and the unity of the SPD and USPD. In

---

[23]Carsten, *Revolution*, 39–40, 47–49, 75; Kolb, *Arbeiterräte*, 114–137, treats in some detail the struggle between the *Rat der Volksbeauftragten* and the *Vollzugsrat* that emerged from the Circus Busch meeting. For a brief description of all the Councils and councils that came into existence during the period under discussion the reader may consult the note appended to this chapter.

factory meetings hastily called to elect delegates for the Circus Busch meeting, Revolutionary Shop Stewards had no success in their efforts to remind the workers about the SPD betrayal of the workers' economic interests and its collaboration with the Kaiser's government. In some plants SPD officials who would have been beaten up the day before because they would not join the general strike were elected members of the workers' council. It became plain to the leaders of the Revolutionary Shop Stewards that the Circus Busch meeting was almost certain to support a government in which right-wing socialists would dominate, that this government would break the power of the workers' councils, and move on to a National Assembly and a bourgeois-democratic republic. (In that estimate they were of course absolutely correct.) Hence these leaders decided to resort to a trick: to get the meeting to elect a leftist "action committee" with ill-defined powers that could serve as a counterweight to the government and provide some sort of revolutionary holding action. The soldiers at the meeting, among whom the SPD had been carrying out a great deal of agitation, according to Müller—though this seems hardly necessary—saw through the trick and raised a tumult that almost broke up the meeting. Meanwhile the workers simply sat still. It was Müller himself, ironically, who proposed the election of Ebert and his colleagues.[24]

After his return from the Circus Busch meeting Ebert received a telephone call from General Groener, Ludendorff's successor, Hindenburg's right-hand man, and also the army officer who during the war had had the most extensive dealings with organized labor. General Groener informed Ebert that the High Command put itself at the new government's disposal. In return the High Command expected the government to fight Bolshevism and support the officer corps in the maintenance of order and discipline in the army.[25] Ebert concealed his reply from his socialist colleagues in the government. At the same time he managed to get their support, including that of the USPD members and even of Emil Barth, the lone representative of the Revolutionary Shop Stewards, for meeting the essence of General Groener's demands.[26] Ebert's decision amounted to a continuation of wartime trade-union and SPD policy. By accepting the army's offer and terms under these new conditions Ebert had joined forces with the reactionaries, and had done so almost

[24]Müller, *Kaiserreich*, II, chap. 4, espec. 34, 36, 40.

[25]Carsten, *Revolution*, 55.

[26]Ryder, *German Revolution*, 160–163.

immediately after his power had been confirmed by the popular assembly in the Circus Busch. To the extent that there is *any* reason to take seriously the notion of a "stab in the back"—the phrase later given currency by Hindenburg as an expression of the reactionary thesis that the German Revolution had stabbed an allegedly undefeated army in the back and seized power by underhand means from honest German patriots—it is applicable here in reverse. Ebert's secret agreement with the General Staff was a stab in the back, not only for a socialist revolution, which for reasons to be set out in due course I do not think was a realistic possibility anyway, but even for a liberal revolution.

At eleven o'clock on the morning of the day after Ebert's telephone conversation with General Groener, or November 11, 1918, hostilities formally ceased on the Western front, and the next day the Stinnes-Legien agreement was signed. Though, curiously enough, neither event receives much if any attention even in detailed accounts of the period, both must have been very helpful to the traditional and moderate leaders of the working classes in their duel with those to their left. Peace after all was what the mass of the population, including the workers, yearned for so deeply. And, as already pointed out, the Stinnes-Legien agreement meant the achievement of long-standing and universal trade-union goals even if the achievement was hedged about with reservations and possible escape hatches for the employers.

At about the same time, on the other hand, there was a surge of new members into the unions that was to prove a very mixed blessing to the moderates. Immediately before the outbreak of the revolution the membership of the unions affiliated with the SPD stood at 1,453,000. At the end of 1918 the number had nearly doubled to 2,866,000. During the next three months almost 2,000,000 more joined. During 1919 the rush continued, to swell the total to the enormous figure of 7,338,000 by the end of the year. Most were newcomers, unused to union strategy,[27] and especially unfamiliar with the trade-union strategy of striking at just the right moment when profits looked promising and the labor market was tight for a particular plant or industry. By the middle of November, 1918, the atmosphere among the workers was a mixture of euphoria at the prospect of far-reaching changes—had not a "socialist" government just come to power?—and desperation due to dislocations, shortages, and fatigue from the war.

[27]Heinz Josef Varain, *Freie Gewerkschaften, Sozialdemokratie, und Staat*, 132–133.

This influx did not bode well for the efforts of the moderate SPD leadership. They were committed to getting production going again as rapidly as possible and the restoration of social order. Both policies implied further belt tightening and continued sacrifices by the workers. Ebert and his associates were trying to put into effect the characteristic program of a "realistic" postrevolutionary dictatorship, to consolidate the gains of a revolution that had not been much of a revolution. They were also trying to do this without having on hand the usual instruments of a revolutionary dictatorship: a powerful police force, willing executioners, a monopoly over the diffusion of ideas. Instead, they relied at first on what was left of the instruments of repression under the old regime and then botched the job of creating dependable ones of their own. Their failure to solve the problem of the army and the police—one can go further and say their astonishing inattention to these issues—was a decisive cause for their overall failure. Hence it is hardly a wonder that soon after their acceptance of power (it was *not* a seizure of power), radical waves reflecting popular disenchantment intermittently gathered force to break upon Ebert's government and its successors. With the failure of the radical attempts, the waves were to subside into a sullen current of organized rejection of the status quo: the German Communist Party.

The reformist SPD leaders did have a policy in the sense of a roughly agreed-on perception of the situation facing them and a strategy for coping with it. Unless one could take seriously the prospects of a worldwide revolution sweeping aside Clemenceau, Lloyd George, and Wilson, the outcome of the combined wishes of these men would inevitably set the outside limits for German policy. These limits were hardly likely to include many opportunities for experimenting with socialism. All this the SPD and union officials saw clearly. Their opponents on the extreme left did not.

Under these conditions it is hardly surprising that the main thrust of the SPD and union leadership's policy was to restore order, to get production going again as rapidly as possible, and to do both under the auspices of a liberal capitalist or parliamentary regime.[28] In their opinion it was impossible to socialize

---

[28] A brief and pungent expression of these policies may be found in Gustav Noske, *Von Kiel bis Kapp*, 130, 186. There is a more detailed exposition in the speech of Max Cohen to the first Congress of Workers' and Soldiers' Councils in *Allgemeiner Kongress der Arbeiter- und Soldatenräte Deutschlands . . . Stenographische Berichte*, cols. 209–224. The Congress took place December 16–21, 1918, and was dominated by the SPD for reasons to be discussed later. Hilferding's proposals to this Congress (cols. 312–321) constitute the

bankruptcy, the basic situation of the German postwar economy as they perceived it. For these leaders an important further justification for the acceptance of parliamentary democracy was their expectation that the SPD would receive a strong mandate at the polls that would enable it to put its major policies into effect. As events turned out, this calculation was quite mistaken. There were deeper considerations too that derived from a mixture of Marxist theory and humanist convictions.

Such considerations lay behind the rejection by the SPD and union leaders of two possible revolutionary policies. The leaders ruled out any solution along the line of workers' control or allowing the workers to take over the factories and operate them. Aside from the confusion and damage to overall production, they held that this policy would simply reproduce under socialism the anarchy of production that existed under capitalism and hurt the workers, especially workers in less favored industries, most of all.[29] They also ruled out the policy of a minority dictatorship similar to the one that Lenin was following. Humanitarian and ethical convictions probably played a role in this choice, though their significance is difficult to assess. Such convictions had not inhibited support of the German war effort. Nor did it inhibit the use of brutal and lawless policies in putting down enemies to their left. Even so it is legitimate to wonder just how much room for maneuver there was within the framework of this ethical commitment and the actual circumstances, a point to which we shall return in a later chapter. In any case there was much more than sheer hypocrisy in their sense of disillusionment and moral shock on the occasion of Lenin's forceful dissolution of the Russian Constituent Assembly.[30]

There were also quite immediate and practical reasons for avoiding too radical a course. If they were to try for socialism at once by either of these routes—the spontaneous one or through a minority dictatorship—the consequence would probably be a civil war in Germany. Most of the soldiers would be on the other side, despite the enthusiasm with which they had greeted the end of the war. Furthermore the Allies would simply march in. Any notion of international working-class solidarity to prevent the Allies from taking such a step was, they believed, sheer wishful

---

closest approach made to socialism. They amount to a retention by the government of control over key sectors in the economy—a sort of New Economic Policy three years before Lenin was to adopt such a strategy in Russia. The proposals never went into effect.

[29]Hilferding in *Kongress*, col. 313.

[30]Peter Lösche, *Der Bolschewismus im Urteil der Deutschen Sozialdemokratie 1903–1920*, 129–137, discusses the reaction to this crucial event.

thinking.[31] Self-serving considerations pointed in the same direction as more humanitarian ones. As bureaucrats and in many ways good German patriots, SPD and union leaders did not want starvation, disorder, and mass unemployment because the more such conditions spread, the more they would lose out to their radical competitors for the allegiance of the workers. At the same time the workers would also be the ones who would bear the brunt of any suffering, which would probably be much more intense in an integrated industrial economy such as Germany's than in a peasant society like Russia. As shrewd politicians, these leaders must also have been aware of a powerful undertow of yearning for a return to the stabilities and amenities of ordinary everyday existence, an end to the demands of "politics" and the public sphere which had dominated so much of even the workers' lives during the war. There are plenty of signs of this undertow, even if the historical record as usual highlights the manifestations of political excitement.[32]

From the SPD and union leaders' perspective anything that interfered with the restoration of order and getting the economy going smacked of sedition and Bolshevism. This was also the case, we may be fairly sure, with large segments of the population, including a great many industrial workers who had little taste for continued political excitement. Such was the environment in which movements for radical change in the social order had to work. It was also an atmosphere that contributed heavily to the hardening of political positions and to their polarization. The contempt and distrust of moderate working-class bureaucrats for what they felt were demagogic or dangerous appeals and actions made them drag their feet when faced with radical proposals. To those seeking to change the social order, foot-dragging looked like double-dealing and bad faith, which in some cases it definitely was. The consequence was even greater desperation in parts of the far left, and at certain

---

[31]Cf. the remarks of Carl Severing to a delegation of radicals from his Metalworkers Union in *Mein Lebensweg*, I, 232–234, and those of Max Cohen, *Kongress*, col. 220.

[32]The vivid, passionate complaints about the absence of revolutionary enthusiasm with which Ernst Däumig, a leader of the Revolutionary Shop Stewards, began his speech to the Congress of Workers' and Soldiers' Councils, provides one good clue among many. Toward the end of his speech he returned to the same theme but with greater emphasis on the puzzling German habit of obedience, which he did see as the consequence of historical experience and long training. The spirit of submission, he remarked, still stays embedded in the bones of the ordinary German, even in these days of revolution: "People want a supreme authority." (*Man will eine Obrigkeit haben*.) That he found strange among those who had during the war performed acts of incredible bravery. Nevertheless he concluded with emphasis: "This German Revolution has damn little self-confidence!" (*Diese deutsche Revolution sich selbst verflucht wenig zutraut!*) See *Kongress*, cols. 227, 234.

points a sharp rise in its appeal and constituency. That in turn made the SPD leaders and their allies dig their heels in even harder.

The test of Ebert's decision to rely on the army was not long in coming. A week after one of his secret telephone talks with General Groener, on November 17, 1918, the government created a Republican Defense Force (*Republikanische Soldatenwehr*) under the command of Otto Wels. Its essential purpose was to keep domestic order, and it numbered about 12,000 men. By means of soldiers' councils, radical groups were able to infiltrate the Republican Defense Force and neutralize its effectiveness as a weapon in the hands of the SPD, even though the majority of the troops remained loyal to the government.[33] Two days earlier, on November 15, 1918, the Spartacists had begun the organization of the Red Soldiers' League (*Der Rote Soldatenbund*) which reportedly reached a maximum of about 12,000 men, scattered over several cities. Though most of the units must have been tiny, the League is described as having been especially strong in Berlin.[34] On December 6, 1918, Otto Wels's Republican Defense Force put down a Spartacist demonstration at the cost of sixteen lives.[35] On the left there was suspicion that a counterrevolutionary plot was hatching; among the reformists, continuing fears of a radical putsch. Both sides were quite correct, and each regarded its own actions as a defense against the other. The government at this point decided to call on the army for help. High army officials decided to use the occasion to make Ebert temporary dictator and get rid of the workers' and soldiers' councils for good. Surviving army sources claim that Ebert knew about the plan and gave it his tacit assent. That seems highly likely but is not proven.[36] In any case the army's move was an utter failure. The troops under the command of General Lequis entered Berlin on December 10, 1918, in the guise of returning heroes. Ebert greeted them, telling them that they had "returned undefeated."[37] But as soon as the troops came in contact with the population, they simply melted away.[38]

[33]Oeckel, *Volkswehr*, 47–48.

[34]Oeckel, *Volkswehr*, 46.

[35]Ryder, *German Revolution*, 184–185.

[36]See Erich Matthias, editor, *Die Regierung der Volksbeauftragten 1918/19,* Erste Reihe, Bd. 6/I, 316–318 (document 51), and Bd. 6/II, 27–29 (document 69).

[37]See Ryder, *German Revolution*, photo 7a and p. 162.

[38]For further details on this complicated episode see F. L. Carsten, *The Reichswehr and Politics: 1918–1933*, 12–16. According to an older authority, Gordon A. Craig, *The Politics of the Prussian Army 1640–1945*, 351, on December 8th General Lequis had ten divisions

The episode is significant because it demonstrates that Ebert's decision to rely on the army was a failure. Hence it undercuts the standard SPD thesis that there were only two choices in the situation: radical revolution or a reliance on the forces of the old regime. The immediate consequence of the affair was to make the reformists clearly aware of their own powerlessness and to intensify greatly the suspicions of those who stood to the left of Ebert, including the moderate wing of the USPD whose representatives were still part of Ebert's government.

On December 12, 1918, two days after General Lequis's entry into Berlin, Ebert and his colleagues issued a decree calling for the formation of a People's Army (*Volkswehr*). This was to be a whole new army based on volunteers. The government never pushed this proposal, which remained a dead letter. The only effect was to create severe trouble between the government and the high command. Since the quarrel was intertwined with other events and disputes that cover the whole range of issues then facing Germany, it is necessary to look at these first.

By the middle of December, 1918, Ebert's government, the first workers' government in an advanced industrial country, was in a very curious position. It had some color of revolutionary legitimacy acquired from the meeting at the Circus Busch. It also had through the army a veneer of legitimacy from the old order. The two sources of authority were incompatible and neither was sufficient to give the government much effect. Yet the SPD still enjoyed a considerable reserve of goodwill among workers throughout Germany. In elections held in Dresden on November 24, 1918, the SPD had obtained fifteen times as many votes as the USPD. In Chemnitz, where all inhabitants above the age of eighteen were entitled to vote, the SPD polled twelve times as many votes as the USPD.[39] And so far the workers were the only politically active sector in the population. Momentarily the others were still stunned and inclined to lay low. The reformists badly needed to strengthen their popular legitimacy if they were to take hold as a government. This they managed to do at a

---

under his command, of which only about 1,000 men were left at the end of a week. Craig's brief account of these years (though now outdated and very sympathetic to Ebert) is a lucid and useful introduction to the problem of the SPD leaders' relations with the army. In Craig's account General Lequis appears at the gates of Berlin for no visible reason. But the reasons surfaced long after the publication of Craig's book. I have also consulted Harold J. Gordon, Jr., *The Reichswehr and the German Republic 1919–1926* but found it misleading in some details important to this inquiry.

[39]Carsten, *Revolution*, 162–163.

general, all-German Congress of Workers' and Soldiers' Councils, the first such gathering after the hastily assembled one at the Circus Busch whose delegates had come only from Berlin. The new all-German Congress met from December 16 to 21, 1918, in the capital city. The Congress itself constituted both the high point of the council movement and its abdication as a revolutionary or liberalizing force. Both the composition of the Congress and its decisions indicate that the temper of the working classes was still quite moderate at this time. Of the 490 delegates only 84 represented soldiers' councils, a reflection of how far demobilization had progressed. Of the more than 400 workers' councils represented, less than 100 belonged to the USPD. The Spartacists were still among these at this time. There were another 10 or so from extreme left organizations in Bremen and Hamburg. About 60 percent of the delegates were members of the SPD, who were able to control the proceedings in almost all respects from start to finish. Early in the meeting an indication of its temper appeared with the defeat by an overwhelming majority of a motion to admit Rosa Luxemburg and Karl Liebknecht with an advisory voice.[40]

It is impossible to show of course that the generally conservative tenor of this Congress accurately reflected public opinion even within the working class (to which its membership was mostly confined), in the way that a well-done public opinion poll with a carefully drawn sample might have done. The elections were conducted hastily and confined to whatever "sample" the workers' and soldiers' councils represented. It is a safe assumption, on the other hand, that these councils drew on the politically more active sector of the working classes, and that both the rest of the working classes and other sectors of the general population would have been even more conservative. Though 63 delegates failed to pass muster with the commission on credentials, this commission was made up of persons from all three political groupings and reached its decisions either unanimously or after businesslike discussion and votes which never went along party lines.[41]

As it was presented to the Congress, the main issue before Germany was whether to proceed gradually toward socialism under a form of liberal capitalism, which meant support for elections to a National Assembly that would write a new constitution, or whether to press on more rapidly on the basis of the

[40]Carsten, *Revolution*, 133.

[41]*Kongress*, cols. 193 ff. and p. 216, "Abgelegte Mandate."

workers' and soldiers' councils.[42] There was no real doubt about the outcome. The SPD wanted the elections as soon as possible. Though they may have sensed that they were losing ground to more militant competitors, their explicit argument was that early elections provided the best chance for a Social Democratic majority and hence a strong government committed to a program of vigorous reform. As we now know, this calculation was wrong. The USPD, more an umbrella group bringing together various forms and degrees of dissatisfaction with the SPD than an organized and effective political party, sought no more than a postponement of the elections to provide more time to get organized and convince the electorate. A large majority of the Congress rejected the dates of March 16, 1919, and then of February 16, to accept January 19, 1919, only four weeks after the end of the Congress' sessions. Another motion to create a Central Council of the workers' and soldiers' councils and give it an effective veto over parliamentary bills met overwhelming defeat too. In effect the idea of workers' and soldiers' councils as the basis for a new government was dead. The verdict of the coroner-historian can only be: suicide. After suffering defeat on these vital decisions, the USPD declared that they would not take part in the Congress' election of a Central Council (*Zentralrat*), the committee that was to be the German government until the National Assembly had written the constitution and established the Weimar Republic. The result was that the Congress voted in the SPD list. A new and completely SPD government now took power and responsibility for Germany's fate.[43]

The other major issue that faced the Congress was reform of the army. Because of the light the events during and immediately after the Congress shed on current attitudes, they deserve more detailed discussion. At this juncture there would have been powerful public support for thorough democratic reform of the German army, measures to make the army into a servant of the republic instead of a crucial instrument in the hands of reactionary and antidemocratic groups. In the later stages of the war and after the revolt in Kiel, the military and especially the officer corps appeared to large sectors of the population as the cause of all that was wrong: the source of both harsh discipline for those in the services and for civilians the source of disruption of their daily lives. The first and reformist phase of the German revolu-

[42]The main speech by Max Cohen was entitled "National Assembly or Council System." See *Kongress*, cols. 209–224.

[43]Carsten, *Revolution*, 134–135.

tion was much more an antimilitarist than an anticapitalist upheaval. Admittedly it would not have been easy to use the opportunity, because much of the antimilitarist sentiment was a visceral reaction against any form of hierarchy and discipline. Still a skilled leadership might have been able to draw on this sentiment for realistic ends. Ebert made no attempt to do this. Instead he just collapsed in the face of objections to reform from the representatives of the High Command.

Four days before the opening of the Congress, as the reader may recall, the government had issued its decree, destined to remain a dead letter, calling for the formation of a democratic People's Army. Meanwhile several radical groups had been trying to set up a series of red guard formations such as the Spartacist Red Soldiers' League for the defense and advance of the revolution. There were also quite spontaneous and politically ill-defined movements afoot. To say that the issue was on the public mind would be the height of academic understatement. On December 17, 1918, a group of soldiers claiming to represent 17 Berlin regiments burst into a session of the Congress and presented their demands, threatening violence if there were no immediate action. The Congress almost broke up in angry confusion at this point.[44] In the meantime Walter Lamp'l, a delegate from Hamburg, worked out, and obtained considerable support for, a somewhat milder set of reforms. Some time later Lamp'l was to reveal that his proposals were not intended as the basis for a socialist army. "For us," he said, "the main purpose was to get rid of the not altogether unjustified opposition of the leftist radicals."[45]

The Congress passed these milder proposals, hastily patched together, it appears, mainly as a way of fending off more radical demands from the streets. Nevertheless the Hamburg proposals, as they were known, were enough to infuriate the army command. The army's objections were by no means merely self-interested and reactionary fulminations. As General Groener pointed out in a powerful speech to a joint session of the Council of People's Representatives and the newly created Central Council on December 20, 1918, the proposals embodied principles, such as the election of officers by the men, which even the Bolsheviks had abandoned, and which, he asserted, were incompatible with the discipline needed in *any* army. Wilhelm

[44]*Kongress*, cols. 121–126.

[45]Eberhard Kolb and Reinhard Rürup, editors, *Der Zentralrat der Deutschen Sozialistischen Republik 19.12. 1918–8.4. 1919,* 124.

Dittmann, a moderate USPD and still a member of Ebert's cabinet, replied at once that meeting General Groener's objections meant suicide for the Central Council. (In effect it meant going back on the mandate of the Congress, the source of the government's badly needed popular legitimacy, though the proposals were obviously passed under threats.) But the session closed, as often happens when there is a dissident voice in a small group, with what looks like tacit agreement to meet General Groener's objections by backing away from putting the Hamburg points into effect.[46] Still the situation remained sufficiently ambiguous to permit moderates with hopes for progress to deceive themselves. At another joint session of these two governing bodies on December 28, 1918, Hugo Haase, likewise a moderate USPD leader still in Ebert's cabinet, in response to some sharp questioning, assured those present that the Cabinet (i.e., the Council of People's Representatives dominated by Ebert) would unquestionably pass *both* the Hamburg points and measures for socialization![47] Neither event took place. The reformist policy amounted to government by procrastination. Evading the issue at this time, the SPD leaders within a few weeks found themselves facing a much more dangerous situation—the Spartacist revolt. They resorted to an even more disastrous remedy, the creation of the armed adventurers of the *Freikorps*.[48]

During the rest of December, 1918, revolt continued to sputter in Berlin. On December 23, 1918, a mutinous band of sailors managed to take the government prisoner briefly, in what was essentially an effort to collect back pay. Once again regular troops proved useless in maintaining order. Mutual suspicions, intensified in the course of this complicated episode, put an end to the fragile remnants of collaboration between the SPD and the USPD.[49] For some time the Spartacists had been convinced that Ebert and Scheidemann were just as much counterrevolutionaries as Ludendorff and Wilhelm the Second. To judge by what the government had not done about the economy, the civil bureaucracy, and the army, their suspicions were sensible. From the Spartacist standpoint the only answer to counterrevolution was revolution itself. This is what they attempted

---

[46]For this episode see Matthias, *Regierung der Volksbeauftragten*, Erste Reihe, Bd. 6/II, 11–13 (document 62).

[47]See Kolb and Rürup, *Zentralrat*, 70–83 (document 11), espec. 83.

[48]For a good study see Robert G. L. Waite, *Vanguard of Nazism: The Free Corps Movement in Postwar Germany 1918–1923*, espec. chap. 3 on the organization and character of this body.

[49]Ryder, *German Revolution*, 188–191.

against the advice of their best leaders, Luxemburg and Lieb-knecht, and with fatal consequences for themselves and for Germany.

Beyond the banal assertion that the Spartacists were a small group attracted to Rosa Luxemburg and Karl Liebknecht and committed to the general idea of a proletarian revolution as the only feasible route to a genuine socialism, it is just about impossible to characterize them briefly, accurately, and fairly. Among themselves they were unable to agree on whether the proletarian revolution would occur in the very near future or at some more remote point after a protracted struggle. Luxemburg and Liebknecht were much less sanguine about the immediate future than their followers, but were overruled by them. Nor could the Spartacists agree among themselves on how to pursue the goal of a proletarian revolution. They realized the need for mass support, but were uneasy about organizing the masses through a political party of their own, or making tactical alliances with organized political movements that shared at least some of their views, such as the left wing of the USPD. There was admiration for Lenin's revolutionary decisiveness, and even for his willingness to shatter parliamentary illusions by dissolving the Russian Constituent Assembly. But there was likewise a current of deep distrust about Lenin's conception of a tightly disciplined party as the vanguard of the revolution. There was also a faith in the spontaneity of the masses—a sense that revolutions really cannot be produced artificially but occur only when the masses are both sufficiently educated by events—*and* made sufficiently angry by these events. Then they might overthrow a social order that had become historically obsolete.

The traditional leaders of the labor movement felt about the Spartacists roughly the same way as they had felt before the war about critical activists in their own ranks. Such persons might stir up the rank and file to rash actions that would only lead to defeat at the hands of the employers, at which point the disappointed masses would stream away and the labor movement be set back for years. But now the stakes were much higher and the workers' real enemy the Entente, who with the blockade could and did shut off Germany's food supply, or march in with its troops in the face of quixotic revolutionary adventurism. For the moderate leaders too the Spartacists provided a convenient explanation for the failure of their policies. If workers refused to tighten their belts and go back to work, it was easier to blame the Spartacists than the conditions of the time. In this fashion the SPD helped to inflate the reputation of the Spartacists at the same time that they tried to blacken it—with some success, thought Rosa Luxemburg, among the workers themselves.[50] The combination of circumstances led to the reformists' perception of the Spartacists as a dire threat, a menace with overtones of pollution, something to be rooted out. There was a vicious press campaign against the Spartacists, which in some ways foreshadows Nazi themes. Just how much responsibility the SPD had for this campaign is not clear. There is no doubt, on the other hand, that the reformist leaders would have liked to see the Spartacist movement disappear from the political scene. They may even have taken some actions to promote this desired event.[51]

Whether the course of events during December, 1918, and in early January, 1919, had actually generated a revolutionary mood among a substantial sector of the workers in Berlin is also difficult to determine. Two points are clear. Many Spartacists were riding a wave of revolutionary euphoria and believed that such a mood existed. Even many of the Revolutionary Shop Stewards, who had closer contact with workers and who dominated the big engineering plants, shared the belief. In the second place, there was one major event that could easily have made this belief seem far from absurd. On January 5, 1919, the largest mass demonstration that Berlin had ever seen gathered near the Brandenburg Gate. The huge gathering was a response to the discharge of the Berlin chief of police, Emil Eichhorn, a member of the USPD with a reputation of sympathy for the far left. After listening to fiery oratory, the crowd marched to police headquarters, and demonstrated for hours before dispersing. The SPD, it will be recalled, had just gained total control of the government (i.e., the Central Council), and were within their legal rights in dismissing Eichhorn. But to many on the far left this decision looked like one more step, and a decisive step, toward counterrevolution. The Revolutionary Shop Stewards and the USPD decided to back Eichhorn, and were joined by the Spartacists. (Actually at this point one should call them Communists, since they had founded the German Communist Party only a few days before at a conference in which they tried to broaden their base and decide upon their political identity and policies.) There was clear reason to believe then that a large sector of Berlin's population was very angry at the SPD leadership and ready to follow resolute leaders. This point deserves emphasis because

[50]Gilbert Badia, *Le Spartakisme*, 243.

[51]Badia, *Le Spartakisme*, 238–245, 247–248.

there has been a tendency to dismiss the Spartacists as carried away by their own rhetoric, against the counsel of Rosa Luxemburg and even Karl Liebknecht.

The existence of at least some semblance of a revolutionary mood was one major element in the uprising. The other ingredient was that the leaders found themselves caught in a situation from which there seemed to be no possibility of retreat that was compatible with revolutionary commitment. On the same day as the demonstration at the Brandenburg Gate, small, armed, radical detachments seized buildings belonging to newspapers, including that of the SPD paper *Vorwärts*, which in the opinion of the revolutionaries had been stolen from them during the war. It is possible that the initiative for this act came from *agents provocateurs*. In any case it caught the hastily established Revolutionary Committee by surprise and created a situation from which it seemed impossible to retreat. The uprising began on January 6, 1919.

On that day there occurred two episodes that shed a vivid light on German habits of obedience to authority. The revolutionaries sent a leader with three hundred armed men to occupy the War Ministry. Berlin was in a state of turmoil, and though there were to be other risings later that gathered a much larger following, one can claim that this day, and even this episode, was a significant peak of spontaneous revolutionary fervor in modern German history. One of the civilians in the revolutionary group showed the lieutenant who received them at the War Ministry a typed proclamation, which announced in fiery language that the Revolutionary Committee had provisionally taken over the government. The lieutenant demurred at yielding up the building on the grounds that the proclamation was only typed and not signed. The civilian revolutionary agreed to take the paper back to revolutionary headquarters and get the proper signatures, after which the building would be turned over to the new revolutionary authorities. (At a later trial that investigated the events, this lieutenant denied that his act was a ruse, and stated he was absolutely serious about handing over the building if the government were overthrown.) At the revolutionary headquarters only two of the necessary leaders were available for signatures. Karl Liebknecht signed both his own name and that of an absent member.

A similar episode occurred at a depot of the Republican Military Guard. This time a leader of the depot noticed that the proclamation was signed but not stamped. He told his men that because the document was not stamped it probably was not authentic. That evidently convinced his men, who protested sharply against the revolutionaries. After an angry exchange the latter had to beat a hasty retreat.[52] As Carsten remarks dryly, the good old ways of bureaucracy defeated revolutionaries who had forgotten the importance of stamps and signatures. Despite the irony in the situation the episodes reveal how difficult it can be even for committed revolutionaries—and in a time of crumbling authority and revolutionary euphoria—to make a clean break with respect for established authority.[53]

If an odor of *opéra bouffe* clings to these episodes, the rest of the uprising and its consequences were deadly serious. Everything went wrong for the rebels. Help promised from Spandau and Frankfurt did not arrive. The mutinous sailors declared their neutrality. The masses did not rise. Only a few hundred of the demonstrators joined in the actual fighting. It appears that the masses were willing to go on strike but not fight with arms.[54] On the other hand, the workers' and soldiers' council of Bremen, inspired by the Berlin events, proclaimed on January 10, 1919, a short-lived socialist republic.[55] The next day the workers' and soldiers' council of Essen, composed of all three socialist parties (SPD, USPD, KPD), in an effort to quiet matters in the Ruhr where more than 80,000 miners were on strike, proclaimed that the mines were to be socialized.[56]

Different as they were, these events coming together in this manner could scarcely have reassured the moderates in charge of the central government. On the day the uprising began, Noske had accepted the job of commander-in-chief for Berlin. Members of the first body of Freikorps troops were now to get their baptism of fire—and the taste for atrocities against rebels

[52]All the specific events mentioned in this discussion of the Spartacists are reported in Carsten, *Revolution*, 210–218, or Ryder, *German Revolution*, 193–207. The frontispiece of the latter book is a reproduction of the document shown at the War Ministry, evidently after Liebknecht had signed it.

[53]Careful investigation would, I suspect, turn up variations of revolutionary attitudes toward existing authority that are traceable to historically determined national cultures. It is hard to imagine Lenin or Trotsky signing such a document, or their followers being intimidated by demands for stamps and signatures. It is equally hard to imagine such behavior in the case of Robespierre and his successors in French revolutionary history. In neither France nor Tsarist Russia (very likely also Soviet Russia) did the bureaucracy manage to achieve the degree of awe and respect that it seems to have won in Wilhelmine Germany.

[54]Ryder, *German Revolution*, 201, citing Müller, *Kaiserreich*, II, 35, 49, 58. Badia, *Le Spartakisme*, devotes chap. 17 to the events of "the bloody week," but gives no indication of mass support for the uprising.

[55]Carsten, *Revolution*, 149.

[56]von Oertzen, *Betriebsräte*, 113.

—under official socialist auspices. In the recapture of the *Vorwärts* building (January 10–11th) they shot a number of prisoners and savagely mishandled others. A few days later they captured and then brutally murdered Karl Liebknecht and Rosa Luxemburg. The military were caught in obvious lies about the circumstances of their death, and a later official inquiry turned into an equally obvious whitewash. A wave of outrage swept over a large segment of the workers. Many persons who had little sympathy with Spartacist aims felt shock at the murder of the leaders.[57] If there had been any chance of a reconciliation between right and left socialists before the Spartacist uprising, there was vastly less now that these two had been murdered and the SPD was openly relying on miscellaneous generals and their motley volunteers to restore order in the name of a democratic republic.

This change in the political atmosphere appears, at least in retrospect, as the most significant consequence of the uprising, more important indeed than the temporary crushing and decapitation of the incipient revolutionary movement. There were bigger risings to come and to be suppressed likewise by Noske and his Freikorps. Unlike the Spartacist revolt they clearly deserve the appellation of mass risings by the workers. The Spartacist revolt marked the beginning of the radical upsurge, not its end. We shall examine these upheavals in more detail in the next chapter for the light they shed on how ordinary workers perceived and reacted to their own immediate circumstances and on their own sense of justice and injustice. Before doing that, however, it is necessary to sketch out the main political developments through the spring of 1920, in order to set the workers' demands and actions in their general political and social context. For a large portion of the industrial workers it was a context of mounting disappointment and frustration.

On January 19, 1919, four days after the murder of Rosa Luxemburg and Karl Liebknecht, there took place the elections to the National Assembly that was to draft the Weimar Constitution. The outcome was a severe blow to those SPD leaders who had counted on the party's gaining the preponderance of power through the electoral process and continuing the slow road to socialism under a liberalized capitalist regime. The outcome must also have been a rude awakening to any on the far left who believed they had the mass of the population behind them. The SPD won 42 seats against only 15 for the USPD. But 40 seats

[57]Ryder, *German Revolution*, 203–204.

went to the bourgeois parties.[58] Up to this point national politics had been mainly an internecine conflict among organizations and groups claiming to speak for the industrial working class, with the military hanging in the wings as the main tangible presence of the old order and the former dominant classes. The old elites, however, had been stunned rather than destroyed by defeat and the upsurge of popular movement. Even the workers' and soldiers' councils, partly because many were controlled by the SPD, rarely had inclinations to dismantle the institutional framework inherited from the past. The old elites remained quiescent but intact during the confusion and fratricide on the left. In the elections they came to the surface once more. The new electorate of 35 million, including women for the first time, gave no mandate to rule to anybody. Five million persons stayed away from the polls. Instead, the popular message to each political party was that it could *not* rule, at least not on its own. Either the political groups and parties could learn to get along with each other and hammer out a minimal consensus on policies and procedures—something possible only where the stakes are not a matter of political survival—or else they could succumb to the temptation to get their way by illegal, violent, and extra-parliamentary means.

In this tense situation there did occur a series of radical thrusts toward a new and different distribution of power and a new set of economic institutions, all based on the industrial workers. Though there were significant similarities from case to case, the revolts were in large measure local responses to local conditions or, perhaps more accurately, general conditions that became acute in different parts of Germany and displayed specific local peculiarities. There was no central coordination whatever to the revolts. If that is one reason for their failure, it is hard to see how at this time there could have been any coordination beyond a certain amount of mutual inspiration that did in fact exist.

Variations on the theme of workers' control as exemplified in the plant councils (*Betriebsräte*) played an important role. At issue too was the role of workers' councils (*Arbeiterräte*), essentially the successors to workers' and soldiers' councils after the demobilization of the army, which had sprung up spontaneously after the uprising in Kiel. In many areas the sentence of revolutionary suicide expressed by the SPD-dominated Congress of Workers' and Soldiers' Councils held in Berlin in mid-

[58]Carsten, *Revolution*, 163.

December, 1918, failed to take effect. After the suppression of the Spartacist uprising in Berlin in January, 1919, Noske and his Freikorps intervened in several parts of Germany where the workers' councils still took part in the government or attempted to seize and extend their power. Violent conflicts took place in the port cities of Hamburg and Bremen,[59] the industrial areas of central Germany, the Ruhr, and also in Bavaria.[60] With the conquest of Munich by government troops in May, 1919, the council movement went downhill, to become merely an issue of the internal distribution of authority within the plant. Nevertheless for some time it remained a matter of passionate concern. As late as January 13, 1920, there was a violent demonstration in Berlin against proposed national legislation on plant councils, in the course of which 42 persons were killed. A diluted residue of the movement for plant councils did find its way into the Weimar Constitution. Like proposals for socializing a part of industry it was destined to remain a dead letter.[61] By the summer of 1919 the Social Democrats had curbed by military force, at least for the time being, all active movements that smacked of socialism. But they had by no means destroyed them.

With the radical threat apparently under control, that sector of the respectable public which concerned itself with politics turned its attention to the form of the constitution and even more to the burning issue of the peace treaty. There was a storm of indignation in Germany over the alleged harshness of the treaty, an indignation in which both leading members of the SPD and many army officers shared. Responsible authorities gave serious consideration to the possibility of refusing to sign what became known as the *Diktat* of Versailles. The situation gave rightist groups an opportunity to abandon completely the storm cellars in which they had been hiding since the days of defeat and revolution and blow their patriotic trumpets. Meanwhile those with the responsibility to make the decision came to the conclusion that the refusal to sign represented an even worse alternative: it could mean full-scale occupation of Germany, even greater economic burdens, possibly even the dismemberment of the country and the destruction of very recent and hard-won unity. On June 22, 1919, the National Assembly accepted the peace conditions. From the beginning the Weimar Republic was sad-

---

[59]See Richard A. Comfort, *Revolutionary Hamburg*, 68–72.

[60]See Allan Mitchell, *Revolution in Bavaria 1918–1919*, 207–211, 223–230.

[61]Helmut Heiber, "Die Republik von Weimar," in *Deutsche Geschichte seit dem Ersten Weltkrieg*, I, 40, 42, 58.

dled with the burden of having capitulated to the *Diktat*. The economic sacrifices required for reparations, the heavy taxes, and inflation could all be blamed on democracy.

Early efforts by nationalist and military circles to discredit and destroy the republic culminated—for the time being—in the Kapp Putsch (March 13–17, 1920), a short-lived attempt to overthrow the government by a military coup. Both the Freikorps and units of the regular army (*Reichswehr*) were involved in the coup, and the regular army as such refused to defend the government. The government under Ebert, by this time President of the Republic, had to flee, first to Dresden and then to Stuttgart. Standard accounts of the putsch stress the role of the workers in defeating the uprising by their response to the government's call for a general strike. Certainly that aspect was very important. But it is also worth noticing that the civil servants in Berlin also struck, a unique occurrence in German history, and that the Reichsbank refused to honor drafts without a constitutionally authorized signature. (Stamps, signatures and legality once more! In due time they were to ease Hitler into the role of Chancellor.) Not even all the army would obey the "putschists." Left hanging in the air without a political apparatus that would obey them, they rapidly vanished.[62]

For the purpose of this inquiry two events that were the result of the putsch are more revealing than the putsch itself. In its immediate aftermath, Carl Legien, head of the German Confederation of Labor, the nationalist and gradualist leader *par excellence* of the labor movement (Ludendorff and Hindenburg had honored him frequently during the war, and he had demanded Liebknecht's expulsion from the SPD for breaking party discipline) realized where the moderates' alliance with the military had taken them and demanded an abrupt reversal of course. In a dramatic confrontation with the Ebert cabinet he demanded the elimination of Noske and other compromised ministers, the punishment of all collaborators with the putsch, and most important of all, the purging of anti-Republican and dubious elements from all Reich and *Länder* police troops.[63] If such a policy had been carried out much earlier, and had also been extended to the army and the bureaucracy, the Republic might have been able to survive. With its enemies on the right under control there would have been far less likelihood of creat-

[62]This sketch of events from the peace treaty to the Kapp Putsch follows Heiber, "Die Republik von Weimar," 47–48, 53–61.

[63]Ruth Fischer, *Stalin and German Communism*, 124–125.

ing such bitter hostility on the left. It is indeed significant that a man like Legien under crisis conditions came to at least a partial awareness of this constellation of forces. But if such a policy could have succeeded in 1918, by 1920 it was too late. All that Legien obtained was the sacrifice of Noske, not a real change in policy. The army went ahead to make itself a state within a state. The old officer corps was if anything relieved to see the rather dubious Freikorps discredited.

On the left the USPD and the Communists had not struck merely for the sake of putting the moderates back into power. This was especially true in the Rhineland and the Ruhr where many workers on the basis of recent experience had good reason to fear the combined forces of the regular army and the Freikorps. In 1919 the Freikorps troops had taken workers prisoner, led them through the town, spat on them, called them *Schweinehunde*, and shot them as they marched. In this area the call for a general strike in defense against the Kapp Putsch aroused the workers to arm themselves. They formed workers' battalions and called themselves the Red Ruhr Army.[64] Before the movement was finally crushed (March 30, 1920), the Red Army had reached the size of several divisions and gained control of several big cities.

The defeat of the Red Army marked the close of workers' revolts and disturbances that were essentially indigenous not only in their causes but also in their programs and leadership. Subsequent upheavals, the "March action" of 1921 and the abortive revolt of 1923, were primarily Communist and Russian attempts to fish in troubled waters. With the end of spontaneous upheavals we may break off the narrative to examine more closely some of the revolts themselves.

3. A note on Councils and councils 1918–1920

Since Councils proliferated upon councils at the national and local level during the German Revolution, and since all nouns in German are capitalized, the uninitiated reader may find useful a brief glossarylike sketch. At the all-German or national level there were three: (1) the Council of People's Representatives (*Rat der Volksbeauftragten*), of which Ebert was the leading

---

[64]Ruth Fischer, *Stalin and German Communism*, 126–127.

member, having taken over the chancellorship from Prince Max von Baden, last chancellor of the Imperial government. It came into existence on November 9, 1918, and received revolutionary legitimacy from the Circus Busch meeting on November 10, 1918. This was a gathering of workers' and soldiers' councils limited to the city of Berlin. The left wing here managed to establish (2) an Executive Council (*Vollzugsrat*) as part of an unsuccessful effort to checkmate Ebert and his colleagues in the more conservative Council of People's Representatives (*Rat der Volksbeauftragten*). On December 16, 1918, delegates from all over Germany met in Berlin for what presented itself as a revolutionary parliament of workers' and soldiers' councils, the *Allgemeiner Kongress der Arbeiter- und Soldatenräte Deutschlands* (referred to in the text as the Congress), whose sessions lasted until December 21, 1918. It created on December 16, 1918 (3) a Central Council (*Zentralrat*) which on December 21, 1918, absorbed the powers of the Executive Council (*Vollzugsrat*) that had been created at the Circus Busch meeting. This Central Council was something halfway between a parliament to which the Council of People's Representatives (*Rat der Volksbeauftragten*) was vaguely responsible and an executive body in its own right. By this point, however, the majority socialists in the SPD were in full charge. Formal parity no longer prevailed between the SPD and the USPD, and the SPD held all the seats on the Central Council (*Zentralrat*). Officially the radical revolution ended when the Congress voted overwhelmingly for the calling of elections to the National Assembly on January 19, 1919. Actually the main radical thrusts came *after* the Congress closed down on December 21, 1918, and partly in reaction to its decisions. There was a second and less important national gathering of workers' and soldiers' councils (or *Rätekongress*) on April 8, 1919. The Central Council (*Zentralrat*) remained in theory the chief governing authority in Germany until it turned over its powers to the National Assembly on February 4, 1919. In the meantime, however, the main executive power remained in the hands of Ebert and his associates in the Council of People's Representatives (*Rat der Volksbeauftragten*), which also relinquished its powers to the National Assembly. A convenient source for most of this information is the introduction to Kolb and Rürup, editors, *Der Zentralrat der Deutschen Sozialistischen Republik 19.12.1918–8.4.1919*, espec. pp. XI–XIII, XXIX, L, LV, which I have supplemented with the help of the index in Ryder, *The German Revolution of 1918* and Carsten, *Revolution in Central Europe 1918–1919*.

There were two main grass-roots or local forms of councils.

The first was the workers' and soldiers' councils (*Arbeiter- und Soldatenräte*) that sprang up and spread over most of Germany in late 1918. Not all of them combined workers and soldiers. Depending on local circumstances and timing—the soldiers' councils evaporated with the progress of demobilization—many appear as simply workers' councils or as soldiers' councils. In some parts of Germany there was even a brief and abortive effort to get peasants to participate. The other form consisted of factory councils (*Betriebsräte*). These were confined to industrial workers and became important mainly in the spring of 1919 as part of the second and more radical phase of the revolution. Essentially they were the expression of a movement for workers' control and decentralized socialism.

CHAPTER NINE

The radical thrust

1. General aspects

The failure of the Spartacist revolt introduced a new element into the workers' situation: massive and bloody repression of the left. It was only after January of 1919 when the revolt was crushed and after Noske and the *Freikorps* swung into action that the workers rose in massive ranks throughout the main industrial areas of Germany. The first wave of the revolution that had begun in Kiel in November, 1918, with the sailors' revolt had been predominantly a "people's" revolution, with limited liberal objectives. It was a general popular upheaval directed almost entirely against the military, the monarchy, and anything that smacked of the continuation of wartime discipline, suffering, and sacrifice. Though the workers played a major role, those who sought to turn the popular revolution into a radical or proletarian one were a small and scattered minority. Had not Ebert and his colleagues forestalled them by taking power in Berlin, they might have mounted a coup but hardly a revolution. The local workers' and soldiers' councils that sprang up spontaneously after the Kiel uprising might have become the organs of a popular democracy, or at least agents to break the institutional hold of the dominant classes—the Junkers, big business, the higher levels of the judiciary and the bureaucracy. But this did not happen. One obvious reason is that the reformist leadership of the SPD was afraid of letting it happen, lest the movement get out of hand and turn into a socialist revolution, which they believed would have disastrous consequences for all of Germany, including the industrial workers. Another reason why nothing resembling a democratic dictatorship emerged from the council movement is the fact that by and large the peasants would have nothing to do with the councils.

Thus the popular revolution failed to bring about any of the social transformations that have been part of the establishment of liberal democracies in England, France, and the USA. The second revolutionary wave that gathered force after the failure of the Spartacist revolt was very much a reaction against the shortcomings of the first wave—and they were shortcomings even by a liberal standard.[1] This second wave of the revolution was proletarian in the sense of being based on the industrial workers. Even rhetorically there was hardly any attempt to dress it up as a movement of the whole people. To put the point in a slightly different light, the articulate elements in the second wave saw or defined the industrial workers as the mass of the people. This was statistical nonsense. The census of 1925 shows the workers to have been only about 29 percent of the German population.[2] Even in the Ruhr the industrial workers were slightly less than a majority (48 percent), though they would have formed a slight majority by adding similar elements from commerce and transportation. That, however, hardly matters. Amid the euphoria and anger of the times neither revolutionaries nor their opponents could be expected to spend a great deal of time poring over statistics.

In terms of strict chronology the radical wave actually had its origins in the wartime factory strikes discussed in the preceding chapter. It continued alongside of, but was largely submerged by, the wider popular wave that began with the sailors' revolt in Kiel and overturned the Kaiser. Sometimes the two waves flowed together. But at least some of the leaders remained conscious throughout of conflicting objectives. The reformist, popular, or democratic revolution came to a halt when the first Congress of Workers' and Soldiers' Councils, December 16–21, 1918, decided on elections to a National Assembly at the earliest possible date and by this action wrote *finis* to this form of the council movement. By the time that Noske crushed the Spartacist rebellion a few weeks later the popular movement had already lost its revolutionary impetus. By having provoked repression instead

---

[1] The next chapter will examine more closely the reasons for this failure, and particularly the reformist claim that the radicals bear most of the responsibility for the failure of liberalism, in an effort to discover whether the SPD leaders could have done anything else.

[2] *Statistisches Jahrbuch für das Deutsche Reich,* vol. 46 (1927), 20–21 for summary of 1925 census; for data on the Ruhr see Chapter Seven, Table 6 (p. 229).

of revolution, from that point onward through 1919 and 1920 the radical thrust had a strong defensive component. It was defensive even though it acquired a much larger mass basis. Indeed, the fact that it *was* a defense against a resurgence of military force in the service of big business appears, as I read the evidence, as the main reason for mass support of what are loosely called radical movements at this time in Germany.

To sum up, the fundamental causes of the radical surge were these: Long-term change in the structure of the economy, evident already before the war, had begun to enlarge the burden placed on the main institutions for integrating the industrial workers into the capitalist order. The importance of crafts and small productive units in provincial cities, where the SPD and the unions had their firmest roots, had begun at long last to decline, while the importance of big factories and metropolitan life increased. The war gave a temporary spurt to these trends. It caused much hardship and a general disruption of traditional social bonds and familiar routines. The war was also the reason for the quite sudden appearance of huge concentrations of workers in certain plants and areas. In many parts of Germany the shortages of housing, fuel, clothing, and especially food—which occurred in such a way as to discredit the authorities and to emphasize the gulf between rich and poor—made industrial workers irritable and angry. Disappointment and abortive putsches, of which the Spartacist revolt was only the most dramatic and important, led to the use of troops to quell revolts. After the failure of the Spartacist uprising many workers lost hope in any form of political activity. They tended to fall back on their own devices, particularly the movement for plant councils (*Betriebsräte*), a mixture of workers' democracy and workers' supervision over plant operations to be discussed in more detail shortly. When these devices failed, or were encouraged to fail by suspicions and foot-dragging from above, or were used as the justification for direct government and military intervention, the protests turned into open revolt.

If these were the causal conditions, what types of workers were attracted to radical movements? Obviously not all of them were, and it will be best to begin with a few comments on these. With the important exception of the metalworkers, to be discussed in a moment, radical movements did not take hold in areas where the trade unions had established deep roots. Nor were they likely to occur where the traditions of the artisan were still strong, a notable contrast to the situation in 1848. Finally, the areas of textile mills with their large number of unskilled and female workers stayed aloof, though they were against the collaborationist policies of the unions during the war and later developed a strong Communist minority in their ranks. Since a sympathetic and very perceptive student of the movement for factory councils reports that it failed to appeal to the majority of German workers, it is a safe inference that very many workers even in big urban industries and in mining likewise resisted radical appeals.[3]

Where, then, did radicalism find favor? Different types of radicalism appealed to different types of workers. Starting at the bottom, the rejects of the social order—called variously *das Lumpenproletariat, die Unterschicht, die Ausgestossenen*—provided numerous recruits for various forms of utopian activism and terrorism. This stratum contained the unemployed and nearly unemployable, as well as casual labor. The harbor workers in Hamburg, who erupted on occasion into the political arena in a violent demonstration only to disappear into apparent apathy shortly afterward, constitute a good example. Such men were only superficially attracted to the council movement.[4]

In marked contrast the new workers, who entered new industries during and after the war, especially, for example, the chemical plants, and who lacked prior traditions and connections, flocked readily to the movement for plant councils. The same was true of several other sectors that had not been under union control before the war and into which new workers flooded during the war—railroad employees and state employees generally, also shop clerks.[5] Plant-council radicalism also gained a very powerful footing among miners and foundry workers. Aside from generally harsh working conditions the immediate predisposing factor appears to have been the workers' reaction to what they viewed as highly authoritarian and irrational forms of managerial authority.

The metalworkers, whose Revolutionary Shop Stewards played so important a role, constitute the last and perhaps the most instructive example. The metalworkers had a long and

[3]Peter von Oertzen, *Betriebsräte in der Novemberrevolution*, 277–278, 323.

[4]von Oertzen, *Betriebsräte*, 276, 292.

[5]von Oertzen, *Betriebsräte*, 277. The penetration of council ideas into the ranks of employees and shop clerks is particularly significant since this sector later provided masses of recruits for Nazism. What mattered to these people was the *threat* of proletarian status, rather than actual membership in the proletariat. Evidently the council idea could appeal in varying degrees to both those threatened by this fate and those actually subject to it. Possibly the same was true of others, such as the chemical workers just mentioned, since as a new type of worker their status must have been uncertain.

successful tradition of trade unionism (except in the heavy iron and steel industries in the Ruhr). They were also highly skilled and especially well paid during the war. Why then did demands for radical social change—with admittedly vague and fluctuating objectives—take such strong hold in their ranks? One possible reason is that the coming of the big factory meant that the possession of skill was much less a guarantee of security than it had been.[6] But other factors were probably more important. In the metalworkers' union the shop stewards were experienced trade-union officials whose job kept them on the shop floor in contact with rank-and-file workers. There appears to have been a crucial difference here, since in other unions minor leaders were generally drawn off into the union bureaucracy and hence subject to a much more conservative social network that favored a cautious approach to all problems. On the plant floor under wartime stress and early postwar conditions, on the other hand, the conflict between employer and worker appeared in its sharpest form. Therefore these men were daily exposed to experiences that could turn them in a radical direction.[7]

Hence *some* generally predisposing factors, which vary sharply from case to case, are apparent all through the working classes from the lowest ranks of the social rejects, up through the modern proletariat of unskilled workers in big cities and big factories, reaching up even to highly skilled and highly paid workers. The only area where radicalism seems to have had no appeal to speak of was in the small artisan shop. Very likely that was due to a situation where the employer was not sharply differentiated either in social status or economic function from the workers at the bench. In this situation the employers performed tasks that appeared to the workers as both inevitable and necessary, much as they would, say, in a small plumbing or machine shop in modern America.[8]

Two general observations about the underlying or predisposing causes of working-class radicalism are in order at this point. Both of them indicate the need for caution in making judgments about such causes. The different forms of radicalism all appear to have been a minority current among German workers most of the time. The true extent of freely given allegiance to radical

---

[6]On the general change in the implications of skill see von Oertzen, *Betriebsräte*, 316–318.

[7]See von Oertzen, *Betriebsräte*, 281–290.

[8]This point deserves fuller investigation in the specific German context. It is the situations where radicalism has taken hold, rather than where it has not, that have so far attracted scholarly attention.

movements is, on the other hand, extremely hard to judge. Where its overt expression is risky and dangerous due to repression by employers or the state, there can be a great deal of latent support for radicalism. The other side of the coin is the fact that in times of excitement and of shaky political authority, the opposite kind of situation is likely to prevail. Then there is liable to be a good deal of bullying by militants to force laggards into line and sustain the appearance of solidarity. Though some ordinary workers may spontaneously assume heroic risks, it is no more likely that the mass of ordinary workers is inclined in this direction than any other segment of the population. Ordinary soldiers in an army under fire require the social corset of military discipline even when they believe in their cause. Revolutionary bullying plays a somewhat similar role. Even if reactionaries and conservatives overstress this aspect of popular upheavals, there is no reason to doubt its significance under certain circumstances. This difficulty in judging the extent of freely given allegiance to militant and radical programs under conditions of both repression and deteriorating authority can create the illusion of a sudden burst of radical sentiment where in fact there has actually been very little change.

It is also necessary to be cautious about putting too much explanatory weight on general social and economic factors. As the sudden influx into militant and radical movements and the equally sudden exodus demonstrate, very immediate circumstances can make all the difference in the world—especially if the criterion of significance is political effectiveness.[9] By this point the reader hardly needs to be reminded that misery in some objective sense is quite insufficient to provoke a popular outbreak. But the development of standards of condemnation —a social explanation of misery and its moral rejection—are also not necessarily sufficient in themselves. For mass outbreaks or political action to take place there has to occur some precipitating incident in the form of a new, sudden, and intolerable outrage. (The definition of intolerable will also vary historically.) A cut in the food supply, or an act of peculiarly offensive or tactless injustice by someone in authority, or some "unreasonable" demand—such as the order to put to sea which produced the sailors' outbreak at Kiel—are examples of this kind of incident.

[9]To avoid misunderstanding it is necessary to point out that the acceptance of this criterion does not imply writing victors' history. One can try to find out why the losers failed and of course sympathize with them or not. Political effectiveness seems to me a criterion of significance that the very structure of the facts themselves imposes on a student of human affairs.

Then, as in a steep Alpine valley where winter snows have piled up in just the right way to generate tons of explosive pressure, the toss of a snowball can sometimes release a whirling blinding force that overwhelms every obstacle in its downward rush. These situations, however, are as rare as they are dramatic, and an explosive situation in one historical and cultural context may not be that at all in another time and place where human experiences, memories, judgments, and hopes are different.

With these expressions of diffidence about the causes of radical discontents we can now look at their main forms of expression in concrete behavior. From January, 1919, onward, radical discontents among the industrial workers found expression in four different forms: (1) intermittent but at times a sharp increase in electoral support for the USPD;[10] (2) strong rank-and-file movements in opposition to the entrenched leadership of the unions; (3) some minimal support for putsches, and much greater support for defensive (but hopeless) actions against Noske's Freikorps; (4) the movement for workers' democracy and workers' control through the plant councils (*Betriebsräte*). These councils had practically nothing in common with the workers' and soldiers' councils (*Arbeiter- und Soldatenräte*) which continued to exist on through 1919 with steadily diminishing importance. All that they shared was the word "council" in their title and a few leaders active in both movements. As we have seen, the workers' and soldiers' councils were, or had tried to be, popular democratic organs representing the "people" as a whole in a given area. The plant or factory councils were explicitly the organs of workers in a given plant or factory. Hence their class character was much more pronounced. Since it is in this movement that the concerns of ordinary rank-and-file workers find their clearest expression, the remaining general discussion will concentrate on them.

The movement for plant councils was not a pure working-class movement in the sense that all of its ideas came from the workers themselves and none from intellectuals or other outside sources. For that matter it is unlikely that a completely pure movement ever could have existed, since the workers have never been altogether isolated from intellectual currents flowing through the rest of the social order. The strategy came from outside. Its theoretical elaborations need not concern us here. From the standpoint of the present inquiry the significant as-

---

[10]Gerald D. Feldman *et al.*, "Die Massenbewegung der Arbeiterschaft in Deutschland am Ende des Ersten Weltkrieges (1917–1920)," 99–100, 104.

pects are these: when leaders from outside their immediate ranks told angry workers that they would have to take control of the process of production themselves if they were going to win any real improvements in their own situation, large numbers of workers responded enthusiastically. I would hazard the guess that this is what socialism generally meant to workers on the shop floor. Somewhat more concretely it meant more control over their own fate and a greater respect for human dignity. It was much closer to anarchism than to Marxist or centralized socialism.

Though developments in the Ruhr will be the subject of more detailed analysis later, it is appropriate to discuss the plant councils here, because the coal mines of the Ruhr became the area in which the movement secured, if briefly, its strongest foothold. In that area a number of spontaneous workers' movements sprang up in November of 1918 at the same time as the regional workers' and soldiers' councils, but, it appears, quite independently of them. Most of them presented standard miners' grievances, all of which—including objections to the arbitrary authority of the administration—had appeared in the course of the miners' prewar movement. The notion of trying to do something about these grievances through the mechanism of plant councils appears to have come from the outside. It was also based on wartime arrangements. An official from the Metalworkers Union, Heinrich Schliestedt, made an official visit to the Ruhr and then presented a brief but vigorous defense of the miners' militant behavior at the Berlin Congress of Workers' and Soldiers' Councils in December, 1918. He warned the assembled delegates to be serious about introducing socialism at least in the mines, and not to put it off until *Sankt Nimmerleinstag* (Saint Nobody's Day), which is what actually happened. But for him socialism was no general abstraction. "Now one more thing," he said toward the end of his speech, "what matters is that we have to work in the plants in an entirely different way from before, and that is what the National Assembly can't accomplish. What matters is *the management of the plants*. It can't go on so that the owners and their officers do the managing alone; instead we have to get *the workers* to share in it. . . . The management of the work must therefore be put into the hands of workers' committees or workers' councils."[11]

The effective message to the workers was roughly this: if you

---

[11]von Oertzen, *Betriebsräte*, 111–113; *Allgemeiner Kongress der Arbeiter- und Soldatenräte Deutschlands . . . Stenographische Berichte*, col. 333 (italics in original).

want to do something about your grievances you will have to have the government take over the mines, *and* you will have to have your own men in on management in order to put an end to arbitrary acts. This became the main thrust behind the demands of the miners. It was a new version of the age-old demand for "decent human treatment," a theme explicitly stressed in the council movement. On this occasion the workers' demands went beyond the usual ones for an improvement in their material and social conditions. If decent human treatment still seems the central one, only through a share in management did the more politicized and alert workers believe that they could attain this long-standing objective. Both socialization and the council system formed an indivisible unit in their diagnosis and remedy for their plight.[12]

During the spring of 1919 these demands aroused a powerful response among the miners. The details of the movement, which ended with blows from the armed fist of the Freikorps, need not be summarized here.[13] But certain points deserve to be brought out. Radical putschism in the Spartacist manner (just how big a role the Spartacists really played remains unclear) could not gain a hold among the workers as long as there seemed to be a prospect of winning these demands through the plant councils. In fact the strikes stopped at once when negotiations with the government appeared to promise this result. On the other hand, violence and mass participation increased as the government backed and filled, finally reaching a point where approximately three-quarters of the miners (or over 300,000) were out on strike in support of these demands. In the course of some of the strikes there were bloody conflicts. By the end of April, 1919, the strikes petered out under the impact of military threats and the intervention of Carl Severing. Socialization and the system of plant councils were both defeated. The miners' only gain was a reduction of the working day to seven (not six) hours.[14]

In Central Germany the council movement followed a

---

[12]von Oertzen, *Betriebsräte*, 127–128.

[13]For a full account see Peter von Oertzen, "Die Grossen Streiks der Ruhrbergarbeiterschaft im Frühjahr 1919," in Eberhard Kolb, *Vom Kaiserreich zur Weimarer Republik*, 185–217.

[14]The strike began in early April, 1919, with demands for a six-hour shift, recognition of the council system, disarming of the Freikorps, arming of the workers, and the restoring of German relations with Soviet Russia. (The last demand was very probably tacked on; the others correspond to the immediate situation.) See von Oertzen, *Betriebsräte*, 117. For a brief account see F. L. Carsten, *Revolution in Central Europe 1918–1919*, 153–155.

generally similar pattern. Amid the widespread political excitement and the mushrooming of workers' and soldiers' councils in 1918, plant councils also put in an appearance, again with quite concrete demands. In the great Leuna chemical works, a huge war industry that had literally sprung up out of the ground, the workers' council on November 9, 1918—the day of the revolution—put five demands to the management: (1) an eight-hour working day; (2) no more overtime and Sunday work; (3) the same meals for all persons in the plant; (4) decent human treatment *(anständige Behandlung)* by supervisors; (5) an end to military production.[15]

The Leuna works constituted a classic case of the partial radicalization of masses of new workers streaming into an unfamiliar and disagreeable situation. More intense there than elsewhere, this is a process that must have taken place to some degree all over Germany. In the case of the Leuna works too it is possible to catch a valuable glimpse of the competition among the workers between a reformist and a radical set of diagnoses and remedies for their actual situation. One of the former leaders of the movement for plant councils reports in his memoirs how the situation appeared to the radical leaders on the spot. From their standpoint the main task was to prevent the new workers from being "melted in" with the old organized workers. One way to accomplish this result was to go around the barracks from bed to bed, drumming up subscribers for the left opposition newspaper. In a few months they had more than a thousand subscribers in the barracks. Payday gave another opportunity for political agitation. That was the time when agitators went around to get subscription forms renewed, and there was usually plenty of time and opportunity for a good political discussion with the subscriber.[16]

In mining, also important in Central Germany, the situation resembled that in the Ruhr. The main grievance among the workers here was the arbitrary and unfair action of the management. In this part of Germany there were some cases of wildcat or spontaneous socialization by the plant council. Von Oertzen synthesizes four main demands from the variety of actions and statements by workers in February, 1919, that is, after the Spartacist uprising. These were (1) some form of "democratization" of the internal structure of the firm; (2) a

---

[15]von Oertzen, *Betriebsräte,* 134–135.

[16]Wilhelm Koenen, "Wir kämpften für die Rätemacht und den Sozialismus" in *Vorwärts und nicht Vergessen,* 378–380.

voice in the immediate social conditions affecting the job (e.g., safety measures), the setting of pay rates, and discharges; (3) access to all relevant records of the firm's operations; (4) a fair share (not further specified) of the firm's profits, along with a reduction of the large differences in property and income between owners and workers. In turn, the plant councils were to recognize that they had certain duties, particularly to care for the general interests of the firm.[17] Though some political outriders of the movement may have hoped for a revolutionary rising and a dictatorship of the proletariat, neither the leaders of the plant-council movement nor the workers themselves showed any inclination in this direction.[18] Nevertheless events followed essentially the same course as in the Ruhr. The government and the owners were somewhat sharper in their refusal of the workers' demands, but there were negotiations in which they made minor concessions. The workers became radicalized. There was a general strike on February 22, 1919, which was widespread and very effective. In March the troops under General Maercker marched in and disarmed the workers amid bloody struggles and numerous excesses on both sides.[19]

As one looks back over the record of the movement for factory and plant councils, certain points stand out with significant general implications. The source of the workers' anger was essentially a combination of two things: certain material deprivations and what they themselves called lack of decent human treatment. Lack of decent human treatment offended their sense of fairness. In their terms it apparently meant the failure to treat the worker as a human being in the course of ordinary routine contacts, such as excessive gruffness, failure to use polite forms of address, and the like. More important, it appears to have meant punishment for actions that the worker did not regard as his fault or for which he could not be responsible. Many workers evidently did retain a sense of obligation to do their work properly and according to certain customary standards, as appears from the explicit statement that they had obligations toward the firm. The arbitrary abuse of authority by management formed the ground for workers' demands for plant democracy, access to information about the plant's operations, a voice in discharges, etc. Socialism and plant councils, in other words, were the way to get decent human treatment. By

[17]von Oertzen, *Betriebsräte,* 139–140.

[18]von Oertzen, *Betriebsräte,* 147.

[19]von Oertzen, *Betriebsräte,* 140–144.

and large the way to get it appears to have been suggested to the workers from above. On the other hand, workers accepted the suggestion warmly and were willing to fight for it stubbornly and bravely. Without the combination of material deprivations and moral grievances it seems most unlikely that this mass political movement could have gained any footing. Even with these grievances, the workers were essentially nonrevolutionary and paid little or no attention to putschist agitators. This was evidently the case even in a time of general euphoria alternating with anger and despair. It took disappointment and the threat of force to drive these workers to the barricades.

In Germany in 1919, unlike Russia in late 1917, there was no opportunity to discover through experience the limitations inherent in workers' control over production. The experiment was crushed almost before it began. Full-scale control of the productive process cannot in any case exist at the level of the individual plant. In a modern industrial society with its complex exchange of goods and services among myriads of units of production and consumption it is out of the question for either management or the workers in an individual plant to make autonomous decisions about what the plant will produce and how machinery, raw materials, and labor will be combined to carry on production. The decisions of individual plants have to be coordinated with each other, as the Russians very quickly noticed when workers at several plants decided to produce what suited their fancy rather than what other producers and consumers required. There are only two basic mechanisms for producing this coordination: the free market or a centralized bureaucracy. Still these general imperatives of coordination and exchange leave a considerable range of choice in the making of concrete decisions at the level of the individual plant or firm. This range of choice includes how much purely technical efficiency a society as a whole may be willing to forego for the sake of other social objectives, such as some culturally defined decent standard of living and decent human treatment for the industrial workers. In their occasional statements about the need for responsibility to the firm, and even more in their willingness to hold off from militant actions while general issues were under negotiation, a good many of the most politically alert German workers showed an instinctive awareness of the limits imposed by the general imperatives of social coordination in industrial society. It will not do therefore to dismiss the movement for plant councils as utopian. Instead it was one more of human history's potentially liberating alternatives, crushed by stronger forces.

2. *The Ruhr from war to revolt*

At this point in the discussion it will be helpful to draw on the device of the old-fashioned detective story by telling the end of the story in order to show what requires explanation. The revolt in the Ruhr, in reaction to the Kapp Putsch, the abortive rightist coup of March 13–17, 1920, was the most significant uprising by industrial workers that has so far taken place in any modern industrial country. Within a few days the Ruhr workers managed to improvise a Red Army. With this army they managed to capture Dortmund and Essen, major cities in Germany's industrial heartland, and several smaller ones. At the height of its power the Red Army may have had somewhere between 80,000 and 120,000 men under arms.[20] Even if the figures are not to be taken literally, they are enough to indicate that this was a full-scale mass rising and no isolated putsch by a small band of *enragés*. There is also every indication that the rising was spontaneous, in the negative sense of not being the result of advance planning and careful organization. Here at least a large mass of modern industrial workers had become thoroughly angry to the point of violently attacking the existing regime. How and why did they reach this state? Why did they behave the way they did? What was the meaning of their own actions for ordinary workers who took part in the rebellion?

These are some of the questions we must try to answer. It is easy enough to draw a connection between the existence of the rebellion and the fact that the Ruhr was the continent's industrial heartland. But the links in this chain of causal connections have a way of dissolving or turning into puzzles as soon as one subjects them to careful inspection. In searching for an explanation a sociologist's first guess might be to the effect that the combination of the war and advancing industrialization had transformed the occupational structure of the area in such a way as to increase greatly the proportion of the proletariat. Though there are problems in their interpretation, the available occupational statistics fail to support this type of explanation. Instead they suggest a stability and continuity of social structure that is quite surprising.

Before trying to interpret the figures let us see what they are

[20]As reported in a source almost ludicrously hostile to the workers but which nevertheless reproduces some useful data from contemporary documents. See Hans Spethmann, *Zwölf Jahre Ruhrbergbau*, II, 143. An estimate of fifty to sixty thousand for the Red Army at its highest point is offered by Erhard Lucas, *Märzrevolution 1920*, II, 86.

and where they come from. The last prewar occupational census took place in 1907; the next one was not taken until 1925. Table 11 shows the distribution of the working population among the main economic categories for these two years.

Table 11.

Distribution of Gainfully Employed Persons in the Ruhr

(in thousands)

Major Occupational Categories	1907 No.	1907 %	1925 No.	1925 %	Change in Proportion 1907–1925 %
Agriculture	373	14	201	06	−08
Commerce, transportation	309	12	556	16	+04
Public service, professions	109	04	150	04	00
Health, social services	NA		67	02	NA
Other (servants, no occupation)	295	11	407	12	+01
Industry, mining, and constuction					
a. owners, managers	161	06	171	05	−01
b. administration	99	04	233	07	+03
c. workers	1258	48	1672	48	00
Total for industry, mining, and construction	1518	58	2076	60	+02
Grand total	2604	100	3457	100	

SOURCES: *Statistik des Deutschen Reichs*, N.F., Bd. 204, *Berufs- und Betriebszählung vom 12. Juni 1907*, Abt. III, 507 (Regierungsbezirk Düsseldorf); 442 (Regierungsbezirk Arnsberg); 411 (Regierungsbezirk Münster). *Statistik des Deutschen Reichs*, N.F., Bd. 404, *Volks-, Berufs-, Betriebszählung 1925*, Heft 16, 86 (Regierungsbezirk Düsseldorf); Heft 15, 90 (Regierungsbezirk Arnsberg); Heft 15, 72 (Regierungsbezirk Münster). Slight discrepancies are due to rounding.

Though there was a large increase in the working population of the area, from about 2.6 million to nearly 3.5 million, the occupational distribution remained very stable. The largest change, as might be expected, was in agriculture. But that dropped only by 8 percent.

More important for our purpose is the fact that there was no change at all in the proportion of industrial workers. Changes within the industrial working class are shown in Table 12.

Here too there were no great changes. The biggest one, an increase in iron mining, probably reflects a more general increase in the extraction *and* preparation of iron and steel—as well as a lag in the formulation of categories for the census— since the category directly labeled "iron and steel preparation"

Table 12.

Principal Occupations of Industrial Workers in the Ruhr

(in thousands)

Industrial Categories	1907 No.	1907 %	1925 No.	1925 %	Change in Proportion %
Coal mining, etc.	293	23	461	28	+05
Iron mining, etc.	8	01	253	15	+14
Iron and steel preparation	134	11	166	10	−01
Machines, apparatus	73	06	126*	08	+02
Textiles	144	11	147	09	−02
Clothing	59	05	82	05	00
Construction	163	13	166	10	−03
Other	220	17	271	16	−01
Subtotal 1907	1094	87	NA	NA	
Other skilled metal-workers, etc., 1907	164	13	NA	NA	
Totals for above groups	1258	100	1672	100	

SOURCES: *Statistik des Deutschen Reichs*, N.F., Bd. 204, *Berufs- und Betriebszählung vom 12. Juni 1907*, Abt. III, 507–512 (Regierungsbezirk Düsseldorf); 442–447 (Regierungsbezirk Arnsberg); 411–416 (Regierungsbezirk Münster). *Statistik des Deutschen Reichs*, N.F., Bd. 404, *Volks-, Berufs-, Betriebszählung 1925*, Heft 16, 86–90 (Regierungsbezirk Düsseldorf); Heft 15, 90–94 (Regierungsbezirk Arnsberg); Heft 15, 72–76 (Regierungsbezirk Münster). Slight discrepancies are due to rounding.
*Automobiles were included in this category in the 1925 report.

shows a small drop, which is rather hard to believe in the light of more general information about the importance of the iron and steel industries. The addition of automobiles to the 1925 census was not accompanied by any great increase in the proportion of workers engaged in the production of machines and apparatus. Again the impression that the census leaves is one of fundamental social stability. It almost seems as though the statistics were registering the growth of some huge organism where the size of the various parts and their structural relationships were governed by some mysterious or as yet undeciphered principle of social organization.

Could this impression be an illusion, indeed a dangerously deceptive delusion because it reinforces the self-confirming myth that human beings cannot possibly control their own destiny? Is this the modern version of the illusion of inevitability discussed at several other points in this book?

There are two reasons for suspecting that this might be the case. One is quite simple. Taken at these widely separated intervals of 1907 and 1925 the data cannot of course reflect whatever changes there were during and immediately after the war. From materials already discussed we know that in Germany as a whole there were large-scale movements into and out of different kinds of work and a general disruption of ordinary workers' lives with important political consequences. Shortly we shall see what happened in the Ruhr.

Nevertheless this objection does not dispose of the issue altogether. Even if the figures cannot register some obvious upheavals, there is still the problem of accounting for what can in this case indeed be conveniently labeled "a return to normalcy." The strong similarity between the division of labor in 1907 and 1925 can hardly be the result of sheer accident. But whose "normalcy" was this, and how did the situation come to be and remain "normal"? The most casual acquaintance with the history of the period is enough to show that there was a very powerful element of coercion behind this "normalcy." The occupational distribution of 1925 reflects the failure of attempts to redistribute political and economic power in Germany after the war. That is the second and more powerful reason for suspecting the existence of undisclosed social mechanisms controlling the division of labor.

These reflections lead to an awareness that the occupational structure is part of what requires explanation at least as much as a causal factor in its own right. The structure of incentives and disincentives that leads individuals into the jobs that they take and hold or fail to hold is part of the whole political order, and the deck of cards dealt out in the game of life has never been shuffled in such a way as to give each player a hand completely determined by chance. The most one can say about causes on the basis of the evidence in this particular instance—and it is indeed a significant point—is that the statistics demonstrate the absence of any inherent trends in the economy of the Ruhr that could override the existing constellation of forces and generate a larger and more powerful carrier of fundamental social changes. No technological or other changes appeared during this period to increase the proportion of the proletariat. The automatic march of history propelled by industrial advance, on which so many Marxists had counted before the war, seems to have come to at least a temporary stop, well before the guns of August, 1914, had begun to boom. The wheels kept on turning and changes kept on occurring, many of them traumatic for large groups of workers. But the economic machine had no built-in characteristics that would make it explode or turn into a different kind of machine if it just kept on running, or were made to keep on running. The invisible hand had never been one of its major moving parts, especially in the Ruhr, and the mailed fist could serve the same purpose quite effectively. That, as I read it, is the main message of the occupational statistics.

If there were no far-reaching structural changes in the economy of the area during the period, it becomes necessary to take a closer look at the workers' experiences during the war and especially in the immediate postwar period in order to find out just what made them turn to armed rebellion. Though the coal miners' strikes had been the largest labor disturbances in Germany's prewar history, they were, as we have seen, struggles to overcome grievances quite specific to coal mining. During the same prewar years the workers in the great iron and steel plants hardly stirred. By 1914 the Ruhr as a whole was anything but a hotbed of revolutionary ferment. What did happen, therefore, to make the situation change, and even more significantly, how deep did the changes run? Did the mass of the workers *ever* become revolutionary?

The chaos, confusion, moving about, rise and fall in individual fortunes that characterized the fate of the German working classes in general during the war appear to have been especially intense in the Ruhr.[21] In this connection it is important to remember that the First World War was also the first one in human experience where the ability to mobilize industrial resources counted decisively. The German military authorities originally hoped for a quick and decisive victory. Only when this was not forthcoming did they improvise general controls. Hence there was an enormous turnover in the industrial labor force as armament makers tried to expand their operations and other factories turned to war work.

The Krupp works in Essen grew from about 34,000 workers

---

[21]The only general statistics on this movement that I have been able to find come from a report on Düsseldorf by the *Gewerbe-Aufsichtsbeamten* (factory inspection officials) for the years 1913–1918. During this wartime period the number of adult male workers in all work categories fell from 423,000 to 379,000 while the total number of adult females shot up from 85,000 to 181,000. In mining and foundry work (a combined category not broken down in this report), the total number of workers, male and female, rose from 73,000 to 98,000; the change in the number of females was from zero to 14,000 in that category. On the other hand, in textiles, which was in 1913 by far the largest occupational group in the Düsseldorf district and one in which there were five women for every six men, by 1918 there was a decline in total employment from 124,000 to 43,000, with roughly two women for every male worker. See *Jahresberichte der Gewerbe-Aufsichtsbeamten und Bergbehörden für die Jahre 1914–1918*, vol. I, 950–951. Such data confirm the general impression that the examples cited in the text, while probably extreme, could hardly have been unique.

in 1913 to more than 100,000 in 1918. One heavy steel *(Gross-eisen)* plant lost 41 percent of its workers to the armed forces in the first few months of the war. Another major establishment gained 28,000 workers during the war but lost 21,000. The turnover in this case was so great that the number of workers lost was about ten times the minimum number employed at any one time (2,100 workers) and about double the maximum number employed (10,000). In other words, workers simply passed through this plant. The Factory Inspection Service reports that on the average each free worker spent no longer than a year in any one job. To cope with the shortage of workers, especially skilled workers and trained supervisors, the firms resorted to a variety of devices: the use of Russian, Polish, and Belgian civilian workers from occupied territories, war prisoners, German soldiers subject to military punishment, and especially the services of labor contractors who made considerable sums by rounding up shady characters (draft dodgers, and those trying to escape the long arm of the law for other reasons) and turning them over to prospective employers for a fee. To make up the difference employers often paid these workers higher wages for exactly the same work, a practice that could scarcely have contributed to the morale of the industrial labor force. Women and adolescents were also as elsewhere pulled into the arms factories in large numbers, while those factories that were not engaged in war work, most notably textiles, did their best with remarkable ingenuity to become war plants.[22]

Not all the consequences of this churning about were unfavorable to the workers. As the Factory Inspection Service noted, in the very tight labor market that developed by about 1916 a worker who got angry at his supervisor could afford to quit and get a better job—or just move on in search of higher wages—despite regulations on paper that were supposed to prevent such behavior. On the other hand, the sources claim that the more experienced workers, who could by and large be counted upon to act as a stabilizing force, were both drawn off from the labor force by the military, especially in the early days of the war, and then later swamped by newcomers. This occurred at a time when the workers were under intense strain. Despite the overall reduction in the number of workers by 1918, housing must have been a severe problem as firms in one locality expanded and others

---

[22]*Jahresberichte der Gewerbe-Aufsichtsbeamten 1914–1918*, I, 952–961. I have not found evidence of the same degree of overturn among the coal miners during the war itself, though war prisoners served underground and women replaced men wherever possible in work aboveground.

declined. Wages rose in terms of money but declined heavily in terms of purchasing power. Food shortages became acute during the winter of 1917 when the prospect of victory had also begun to seem very dubious. There were numerous strikes in the Ruhr and elsewhere in Germany during that winter because of food shortages, an ominous sign: revolutionary upheavals usually start with food and other consumer shortages, even if not all food shortages produce revolutions or even popular upheavals.[23] Hours of work were astonishingly long. In the early first years of the war there were some exceptional occasions when workers took on a Sunday shift and stayed on the job for 24 and even 36 hours. Such feats became impossible as the supply of food deteriorated. Yet even in the summer of 1918, when due to food shortage a large-scale movement developed among munition workers seeking a reduction of hours, the arbitration committees only reduced hours from an average of 59 a week to between 53½ and 54½. An attempt to reduce the usual 60-hour week in the big steel plants to 54 hours ran up against the combined opposition of employers and the military and failed.[24]

The industrialists in both coal as well as iron and steel were quite stiff-necked even by the standards of the time. In coal they refused to sign wage agreements with the miners' unions.[25] Generally the industrialists counted on the support of the mili-

---

[23]On the strikes and food situation in the winter of 1917 see Gerald D. Feldman, *Army, Industry, and Labor in Germany 1914–1918,* 326. There is some evidence to show that the coal miners may actually have been not too badly off. A comparison between annual earnings in the coal mines of Dortmund and the minimum cost of living in that area for the years 1909–1922 reports a steady rise in real earnings between 1909 and 1921. See Bruno Heymann and Karl Freudenberg, *Morbidität und Mortalität der Bergleute im Ruhrgebiet,* 32–33. I am skeptical about the accuracy of information about the prices that miners actually had to pay in their own neighborhoods. Nevertheless such data are not to be dismissed out of hand. Furthermore, miners received special rations during the war. Conceivably these strikes represent just one more indication of the miners' greater capacity for collective action in the face of adversity. They may not have been a response to a deteriorating "objective" situation.

At another point Feldman *(Army, Industry, and Labor,* 492–493, 506) presents some information on the situation in Germany as a whole in 1918 that shows very nicely how memories of the past and anticipations of the future can change the behavior that would be expected as a response to such "objective" conditions. In May and June of 1918 several conditions favored serious strikes. Efforts to achieve the long desired suffrage reform in Prussia had failed. Wages in the army's factories had been cut in March and again in May. Yet the unions opposed strikes, and the workers obeyed. One reason was the harsh way the government had suppressed the strikes in January of that year. Another reason was the prospect of victory from the last Ludendorff offensive. By late June this reason was ceasing to be effective. In July military disaster occurred with swiftly deflating effects on home-front morale, even though by this time the food situation had actually improved.

[24]*Jahresberichte der Gewerbe-Aufsichtsbeamten 1914–1918,* I, 963.

[25]The first wage agreement in the coal industry of the Ruhr was signed on October 25, 1919, according to Erhard Lucas, *Märzrevolution im Ruhrgebiet,* I, 52.

tary authorities for their conservative stance. But this support was not always forthcoming because the military officials feared labor disturbances that would interfere with badly needed military hardware.[26] In the later stages of the war the Ruhr industrialists reluctantly accepted workers' committees (*Arbeiterausschüsse*) with rather limited powers to present the workers' grievances. These committees also had on their hands the rather thankless task of allocating food rations among various categories of workers. Among rank-and-file workers these allocations were the cause of much complaint and grumbling.[27] Such experiences probably contributed to a strong current of suspicion about anything that smelled of worker-management collaboration, a current that is very noticeable in the early postwar period.

Meanwhile in the coal mines the unions played a double game of acting both as an official arm of the government and trying to increase their influence and membership among the miners. This they did by playing on and even at times deliberately fomenting the workers' discontent. Union officials were evidently aware that if they did not do this, they would lose ground to leftist and oppositional elements in their ranks.[28] Simultaneously, under the stress of the conditions just described, more and more workers came to feel that *both* the unions and the worker-management committees were, to put it mildly, less than sufficiently vigorous in pressing their justified complaints.

In the coal mines such sentiments foreshadowed the rank-and-file rebellion against union leaders that was so widespread in the years immediately following the war. During the war itself, on the other hand, the workers in the Ruhr did not take the lead in the strike movements that shook Germany in its later stages. The big food strikes of April, 1917, which rapidly acquired political overtones had been preceded by smaller ones in the Ruhr. But in April itself the strike centers were Berlin and Leipzig.[29] During the still more important and more explicitly political strikes in industrial areas in January of 1918, in the Ruhr there were only short coal miners' strikes, mainly concerning higher wages.[30] As was to happen later and as had happened

---

[26]Feldman, *Army, Industry, and Labor,* presents an excellent and detailed analysis of this complex and changing relationship; see, e.g., 379, 396, 418–419.

[27]*Jahresberichte der Gewerbe-Aufsichtsbeamten 1914–1918,* I, 965–966.

[28]Feldman, *Army, Industry, and Labor,* 131–135.

[29]Feldman, *Army, Industry, and Labor,* 337.

[30]Feldman, *Army, Industry, and Labor,* 451.

before, workers with somewhat different traditions and responding to local variations of the same general situation reached their political boiling points at different times. Then the authorities could cope with each one separately by using whatever mixture of repression and concessions that promised results.

Pausing for a moment to assess the workers' situation by the end of the war, we can see that by 1918 the proletariat in the Ruhr was in terms of its collective experiences and relationships to authority a very different body from the one that had entered the war. It had lost a good many of the key individuals in it—the "seasoned and sensible workers," to use the language of the authorities—who could be counted on to favor social stability. Mechanisms of political integration and the peaceful settlement of disputes had barely begun to put in an appearance before the war. The war had speeded up their development while as improvisations they had been subject to enormous strains. Food supplies had become hard to get, while to the workers the manner of their allocation appeared arbitrary and erratic. On the other hand, war profiteers could buy what they wanted on the black market. The injustices of the prevailing order were appearing in a new form as vivid aspects of daily experience. The pace of work was exhausting, the hours extraordinarily long. Then came the Kiel revolt of November, 1918, workers' and soldiers' councils, peace and defeat, a new socialist government, the sudden possibility of collective bargaining . . . It is not hard to sense that workers' tempers must have been getting very short, that hopes had been raised, and that if these hopes were to be disappointed, a radical explosion would very likely follow.

Indeed it is rather too easy to find an explanation. We have to keep in mind the many occasions on which the workers did not rise, even occasions in which both material conditions and subjective expectations might have been expected to produce this result. What then might be the missing ingredient? Before large numbers of workers would rise in revolt, I suggest, there would have to occur some event that would appear as a threat to *all* workers, some experience that would create a simultaneous boiling point in the generalized anger of individuals and groups whose experiences were still in many ways quite diverse. Then wider masses might follow the lead of those best equipped by *their* experience to take collective action, in this case the coal miners. This combination of circumstances did not occur until the aftermath of the Kapp Putsch in the spring of 1920.

For the years between the end of the war and the outbreak of the rebellion almost the only evidence I have been able to locate has to do with the miners. Since they were a leading group in the area and what happened to them must have had widespread repercussions, this limitation if unfortunate is not altogether crucial. Their bitter struggle for the socialization of mining and for plant councils has already been discussed in another connection. It ended in defeat in April of 1919, though the miners did win one victory: the introduction of the seven-hour shift. That this victory was of no small importance is indicated by a report that about 100,000 persons are reported to have immigrated into the Ruhr shortly afterward. The net increase would have amounted to more than a quarter of the original number of miners in the last year of peace, 395,000.[31] Though it is hardly likely that there would have been such an influx into mining if the material conditions were as bad as is frequently asserted, the newcomers could scarcely have been a source of peace and order.

After the defeat of the big strikes in April of 1919 there followed a series of small ones. In January of 1920 the movement for a further reduction in hours reappeared, stimulated it seems by gains that the railroad workers had just achieved. Again the miners demanded a six-hour shift. In the same month there was a serious uprising in Berlin in protest against the watered-down version of national legislation about plant councils. Forty-two persons were killed. In reaction to the uprising the central government proclaimed a state of emergency in several parts of the country. In the Ruhr the military authorities set to work to use the state of emergency to break the back of the movement for a six-hour shift.[32] As will appear in due course, this type of intervention was a decisive factor in bringing on the revolt.

With a bit of diligence it would be possible to add further details and paint the picture of developing repression in still darker hues to culminate in the tragedy of the bloody and defeated uprising. But that is not the way history necessarily happens. There are often contrary trends and suppressed possibilities that the wisdom of hindsight can easily obliterate. In this case there were enough signs of improvement and consolidation in the miners' position to suggest that if the Kapp Putsch had not intervened, there might just possibly have been a gradual development toward an uneasy class peace and the resolution of differences through collective bargaining.

[31] Heymann and Freudenberg, *Morbidität und Mortalität*, 28; cf. Max Jürgen Koch, *Die Bergarbeiterbewegung im Ruhrgebiet zur Zeit Wilhelms II. (1889–1914)*, 139.

[32] Lucas, *Märzrevolution*, I, 50–53.

The first wage agreements with the unions in the history of the mining industry had been signed on October 25, 1919. The general strike planned for February 2, 1920, did not come off as planned. An agreement was signed in Essen about overtime and increased pay during the same month—only a limited gain for the miners since they at that time wanted above all to reduce their time in the mines, but still a gain of sorts.[33]

To try to resolve these ambiguities in the evidence by measuring more precisely the degree of the miners' material misery would be to miss the point. The miners were not angry simply because they were hungry and poor, but because they felt they were not getting their rights. Villagers like Ulrich Bräker of Wattwil had often been hungry and poor, but did not get angry the way the miners became angry. The situation facing a Swiss peasant in the eighteenth century was not one that would lead him to put much blame for his misfortunes on human targets. Instead he blamed the weather, God—rather indirectly and reluctantly, to be sure—his luck, himself, and his creditors.

For the coal miners the situation was totally different. There were obvious human agents whom they could blame for their misfortunes. The cultural climate and their own experience provided at least some ready-made ways for dealing with the situation. Wartime experiences had made them redefine these rights upward in response to external pressures that had depressed them. The miners also perceived new ways of trying to get these rights, as in the movement for plant councils, and their failure to achieve these rights could hardly have made them well disposed to the prevailing social order. In fact the economic issues were seen as moral issues on *both* sides, which is what made the situation so explosive. Even socialists in the government saw coal as the lifeblood of the German economy, were aware that the sharp drop in production threatened catastrophe for all Germans, and regarded the demand for a six-hour shift as totally unreasonable. Their sense of the danger to Germany as a whole made them relatively blind to the exhaustion of both the mines and the miners as a result of the war.

If the situation was tense in Germany as a whole, it was even more so in the Ruhr itself. Under the state of siege, slightly eased in April of 1919, there was intermittent repression and arrest of political leaders, especially after the Berlin uprising. Von Lützow, a prominent conspirator behind the Kapp Putsch, came to

[33]Lucas, *Märzrevolution*, I, 51–52, 56.

the Ruhr in February of 1920.[34] The Freikorps was not, however, the main force, or at least not the largest, behind the maintenance of "order" in the Ruhr. By far the largest was the *Einwohnerwehr* (literally, inhabitants' defense force), the result of an attempt to create local security forces by obtaining volunteers from all classes and giving them arms. (There was also a third security force, the *Sicherheitspolizei* or *Sipo,* an all-German organization established on similar principles.) Perhaps the best clue to the climate of political opinion in the Ruhr comes from Carl Severing's opposition to the establishment of the *Einwohnerwehr.* In many parts of the Ruhr, he argued, class antagonisms had become so intense that it would be impossible to set up security forces drawn from all sections of the population. Instead there would come into existence either purely bourgeois defense forces or purely worker ones. That in turn would intensify hostilities even further.[35] His prediction was not quite correct. In some cities workers did join the security forces in substantial numbers and fought hard against other workers in the insurrection that followed.[36]

Even if it is impossible to rule out altogether the possibility of a peaceful development, it is obvious that intense hatreds lay just below the surface. For the workers the objects of this hatred were the police and the military, the visible enforcers of rules and regulations they felt as unjust and oppressive. That the hatred was reciprocated by the officers of Freikorps goes without saying. In their case there is no doubt that they wanted to destroy the Republic for the sake of law and order and German honor.

In any case the course of events was far from peaceful and the putsch *did* occur. I shall not try to give a full account but will instead concentrate on what can be learned about the feelings and behavior of ordinary workers.[37] At this point it will be useful to point out the most puzzling and significant aspect of this behavior. By March 17, 1920, the Kapp Putsch was over, and Ebert's government had regained its powers. Yet it was only *after*

[34]Lucas, *Märzrevolution,* I, 65, 75.

[35]Lucas, *Märzrevolution,* I, 67. For a description of the military and police forces in the Ruhr before the outbreak of the revolt see 64–68.

[36]This was the case in Dortmund and Essen, according to Spethmann, *Zwölf Jahre Ruhrbergbau,* II, 121, 130. It is apparent that these workers, as might be expected, were drawn from what was on the local scene the right wing of working-class opinion, the SPD and the Christian unions. Lucas, *Märzrevolution,* I, 60 reports the decline of the SPD in the Ruhr and the rise of the USPD. In 1919 the USPD had become the strongest party in the area.

[37]For a general study see Johannes Erger, *Der Kapp-Lüttwitz-Putsch: Ein Beitrag zur deutschen Innenpolitik 1919/20.*

that date that the most severe fighting and the real insurrection took place. Why did the workers in the Ruhr go on from actions in defense of the Republic to a revolutionary offensive against the Republic? Was it really a revolutionary offensive, and *can* one distinguish clearly between the defensive and offensive aspects in this particular case?

The reasons for keeping on fighting are to be found partly in the way the workers' movement developed and the forms it took in its original response to the news of the putsch, partly in unfulfilled demands at the time the putsch collapsed, and most of all in severe local provocations by the Freikorps stationed in the Ruhr. All this and other matters we shall go into shortly. But it will be well to state the conclusion that in my judgment has to be drawn from this evidence. The mass of the workers were not at any point in a revolutionary frame of mind. They were very angry. But they had limited and specific targets. They did not want to establish a new social order. Circumstances beyond their control forced them into revolutionary actions. They saw revolution—to the extent that they saw it at all—as the only defensive move open to them in a very threatening situation.

Now let us look more closely at details. The short-lived Kapp coup took place in Berlin on March 13th. An official announcement from the Kapp government confirmed the army's commanding general in the Ruhr, von Watter, in his post. General von Watter was to remain in his post as the commanding general who restored order and put down the insurrection at the behest of Ebert's government when it regained power, working closely, though not without some friction, with Carl Severing, the Social Democratic leader who had plenipotentiary powers from the Republic. The general was a shrewd trimmer and at once issued an ambiguous proclamation that avoided any statement of allegiance to either the putschists or the legal government, but called for the maintenance of law and order, asked all officials to remain at their posts, and asserted that he would stand up for all the rights guaranteed to German citizens.[38] If still somewhat ambiguous, it was clear that General von Watter's position leaned heavily toward the putschists. There was no ambiguity about the commanding officers of several Freikorps units under his command. With parades through the towns and official statements they came out flatly in support of the coup. The *Sicherheitspolizei* and *Einwohnerwehr* indicated their support in a less explicit fashion.

[38]Lucas, *Märzrevolution*, I, 99.

The *Arbeitsgemeinschaft,* an umbrella organization of industrialists and trade-union leaders in the area, did not meet until
the next day, March 14th, to deliberate the proper stand to be
taken. Hugo Stinnes presented to union leaders the draft of a
statement rejecting the coup and calling for a return to constitutional government because the coup might lead to separatist
movements and the disintegration of Germany. With that the
union officials were able to agree. But they could not agree with
his call for workers to stay on their jobs and maintain order. Such
a step went directly against the proposed general strike, the legal
government's main weapon against Kapp and his followers. For
this reason there was no agreement and the meeting came to
nothing.[39] The heads of the four coal miners' unions had managed to meet on the afternoon of the day of the putsch. But they
were unable to agree on anything beyond the most innocuous
proclamation repeating their earlier opposition to a dictatorship
from the left, announcing their firm opposition to a dictatorship
from the right. On this basis they asked the workers to remain
calm, keep faith in their organizations, and await further instructions as soon as circumstances could be clarified.[40]

Within a few exciting hours the workers had learned of the
putsch, had seen the local security forces come out in support of
a military dictatorship whose consequences for their own lives
they knew well enough on the basis of their own bitter experiences, and had seen their own trade-union leaders waffle or keep
silent in the face of the crisis. The dominant social organization
had turned against them; a main part of their own social organization had failed them. For their own defense they would have to
create new social forms from scratch, and make do with whatever was left in the way of functioning organizations of their
own, mainly local unions and political party organizations, bend-
ing them to their purposes. That is the way the more militant
workers evidently perceived the situation and began to act on it,
almost at once.

As the news came in from Berlin on the 13th, a Saturday, it
stirred up a great deal of talk among the miners. Presumably

[39]Lucas, *Märzrevolution,* I, 104–108, 114–115. Erger, *Der Kapp-Lüttwitz-Putsch,* 197,
points out that in fact *none* of the socialist parties justified the strike in terms of a defense
of the constitution and the legal government. The SPD's central committee *(Vorstand)* was
willing to let the existing government fall by the wayside; its proclamation was couched
not in the language of loyalty to the constitution, but in more leftist terms of loyalty to the
Revolution of 1918 and "preventing the return of Wilhelm II." Erger could have added
that the SPD's own policies had made a major contribution to the prospect of losing what
had been gained in 1918.

[40]Lucas, *Märzrevolution,* I, 120.

they were discussing among themselves what they ought to do. That afternoon work stopped in quite a few shafts, though by and large, according to Spethmann, the crews did not lay down their tools of their own accord. Threats were necessary in order to get the workers to stop. It is clear from Spethmann's account, on the other hand, that the threats, which were sometimes quite violent, were directed against minor supervisory personnel in charge of the workers. The workers may well have been quite happy to drop their tools but afraid of the supervisors and unwilling to act until *force majeure* removed this obstacle. In some areas wandering groups of armed men, reputed to be strangers, forced shutdowns. In one instance at least there is a clear indication of workers persuading other workers to lay down tools: a large part of one shift went over to the shaft to make the afternoon shift leave early. A spontaneous and uncoordinated search for arms likewise began on the same day. The fact that the workers, in this case under the leadership of a minor supervisor (the attitudes and actions of minor supervisors, as might be expected from their position between two fires, varied considerably) broke into the director's house to look for arms, reveals a good deal about the tense atmosphere in the area.[41]

Since there were a few cases of what looks like revolutionary bullying to create solidarity, it is appropriate to set this form of behavior in its general context in this type of situation. To stop ordinary work is an important negative response to a crisis produced by an attack from those who hold the levers of power. If enough people cease the ordinary routines of life, the whole mechanism that sustains the authority and power of the dominant groups grinds to a halt, leaving them hanging powerless in the air. But this step is only a negative one. By itself it is not enough. Furthermore, in an industrial society it is very costly to the participants. In an industrial society it is extremely difficult to go over to the next step of organizing guerilla enclaves where the rebels produce enough food and services to sustain a separate economy. Therefore if the rebels (it is important to remember that they may *become* rebels against their intentions due to the power holders' offensive) are to change the situation to their advantage, they will have to create social mechanisms for active defense and, in the hope of defeating or checking their oppressors, political demands that can be the basis for a settlement of the conflict. The creation of those mechanisms is of course not a single act but a continuous process, marked by a

[41]Spethmann, *Zwölf Jahre Ruhrbergbau*, II, 102, 103, 106–112.

great deal of trial and error, checking back with constituents to verify and drum up support, revolutionary bullying, etc., that goes on for the duration of the conflict. Thus revolutionary bullying, something no more pleasant to contemplate than any other form of bullying, appears as an unavoidable human reaction to crisis. When a fire starts in a crowded house, the occupants rushing about to put out the flames are unlikely to adhere to the rules of polite persuasion in their behavior toward apparent laggards who do not take the situation seriously.

In the Ruhr the workers developed three types of social mechanisms for these purposes: crowds, mass meetings, and action committees. The last were gatherings of local leftist political party leaders. Sometimes they got together behind closed doors to hammer out and agree on policies and slogans—if indeed they could agree. At other times the meetings of action committees were large and open affairs. Crowds were the most spontaneous and loosely organized form of all, the clearest example of collective behavior, which some social psychologists define as the form of group action that arises in the interstices between organized institutional behavior and *against* the existing institutions. Crowds of workers in this case attempted to take immediate action of a kind that makes very good sense for the circumstances. Generally they sought two objectives: arms for the workers and the release of political prisoners. These were limited, concrete, yet very useful objectives. The release of prisoners they sought not only out of sympathy and solidarity, though that played a part. Political prisoners were likely to be former activists and valuable leaders in the events to come, as some indeed turned out to be. That there were threats of violence and some actual roughness is hardly surprising. If anything, the small amount of violence is at this stage surprising. There is no indication of plundering or of vengeance taken on hated class enemies. In fact some of the crowds drew not only workers but even some followers of middle-class parties.[42] Later on, after both sides had tasted blood, the situation changed sharply.

Mass meetings were more organized affairs. Such gatherings have to be announced in advance and people have to go to them. To point out that they serve expressive purposes by allowing people to blow off steam and enjoy a sense of solidarity is not

[42]This was the case in Hagen according to Lucas, *Märzrevolution*, I, 154. For further instances of crowd behavior see 156–161. Gerhard Colm, *Beitrag zur Geschichte und Soziologie des Ruhraufstandes vom März–April 1920*, 25–26, however, reports a clash between police and workers in search of arms that cost eighteen lives.

enough. In this case they served more strictly political purposes. They gave ordinary workers an opportunity to set the boundaries for general lines of policy and to choose, or at least confer a mandate upon, their leaders. Those present at a meeting did this by applause or hooting—positive or negative acclamation of the speakers. The speakers were usually local spokesmen for the SPD, the USPD, or the Communists (KPD), the latter at that time a small but slowly growing body rent with internal quarrels that were even more severe than in the USPD. Workers who did not attend a mass meeting in effect disfranchised themselves. Probably these were a large majority. It would be a mistake to regard them as apathetic; very many may well have felt that the situation called for acts, not talk.

Where the workers did create and use these opportunities for political expression, the main message that they conveyed to the leaders was that they had little or no patience for, or understanding of, the principles that divided the political parties, nor the varying diagnoses and remedies for the current situation that the political leaders offered. Unity in the crisis for the sake of struggle against reaction was what the workers wanted. All over the Ruhr they responded most warmly to a three-party appeal that included (after much bargaining behind closed doors with the SPD leader who later confessed that he had made an error) a clause about the "achievement of political power through dictatorship of the proletariat until the victory of socialism based on the council system."[43] When the KPD's Essen section tried to attack both the SPD and this rather dubious unity, the workers gave them a very chilly response. In addition to party unity the workers generally agreed on the tactic of a general strike for March 15th. Beyond party unity and a general strike the workers did not go. Since they refused to condemn the SPD, it is unlikely that the phrases about socialism and the dictatorship of the proletariat had much meaning for them. In most cities the main demands reached at these meetings boiled down to freeing political prisoners and the acceptance of a large proportion of organized workers into the local defense forces.[44] The fact that the workers even thought of being accepted into the security forces indicates that they did not see the situation as a revolutionary one. In a revolution one storms the police station; one does not volunteer for the police force.

Among rank-and-file workers there was evidently a division

---

[43]Lucas, *Märzrevolution*, I, 127.

[44]Colm, *Geschichte des Ruhraufstandes*, 26.

of opinion about whether to take arms by force or whether to join the police, just as among the leaders in the action committees there was a division between those who advised an armed uprising and those who thought such action hopeless. In such a situation the persons who take concrete action, even if they are a minority, can determine the subsequent course of events. Within a few days the workers had managed to obtain a respectable number of weapons from the police, from segments of the *Einwohnerwehr* that were made up of workers or were fooled into giving up their weapons (as in the case of one *Einwohnerwehr* unit made up mainly of peasants), as well as from private individuals and para-military clubs. The existence of so many weapons in the hands of the workers disturbed Severing, and may have furnished the military authorities with the pretext for action that they wanted. In any case the atmosphere became much more tense, and the slightest disturbance or rumor of one could set off an explosion.

Monday the 15th of March was the first full working day after the proclamation of the putsch. In response to the general strike all work in the Ruhr stopped except for the most essential services,[45] as it did throughout much of the rest of Germany. It was also the day on which open conflict broke out in the Ruhr.

There was a plan afoot for the workers to gather on that day in the town of Hagen where the leaders were to distribute weapons and establish a security force. Instead a small detachment of the Freikorps marched into the nearby town of Wetter on the basis of a report, denied by the local *Bürgermeister* when the troops appeared, that disorders and plans to set up a revolutionary republic (*Räterepublik*) existed there. Word that the Freikorps was marching into Wetter was enough to send masses of armed workers rushing to the scene. When the Freikorps unit arrived in Wetter, the local action committee and the Bürgermeister asked the officer in charge on whose authority he came, and what his political stand was in relation to the putsch in Berlin. The officer, a certain Captain Hasenklever, threw powder on the fire by his reply: that he came on the authority of General von Watter to restore order and that he stood "on the ground of Lieutenant General von Lüttwitz," one of the chief conspirators, who had come to the Ruhr in February. During these parleys, workers had mingled with the troops and persuaded some twenty or thirty to change sides. The workers also got possession of a machine gun. Hasenklever's reply, which

---

[45]Colm, *Geschichte des Ruhraufstandes*, 25.

rapidly spread over the whole of the Ruhr, infuriated the workers and confirmed their worst suspicions. Fighting broke out almost instantly. The workers evidently outnumbered the small Freikorps unit and had the advantage of high terrain around the railroad station. The small band of troops defended themselves but were defeated with sixty-four dead including Captain Hasenklever, as against only seven killed among the workers. Winning this battle and similar ones that followed it, the workers rapidly increased their stock of arms.[46] In this way the Red Army came into existence.

In its structure and operations the Red Army resembled revolutionary guerilla organizations that sprang up in many rural parts of the world twenty to thirty years later. But the differences derived from its setting of an industrial working class in a modern industrial state were more important and contributed to its rapid defeat. A variety of local units formed the basic cells of the army. Often they were political party districts. In a few cases whole mine crews might form companies. Bachelor dormitories also contributed units. Local commanders generally decided who was to take command of the unit at the front. No fully effective central command came into existence. There was a "central organization" in Hagen, that appears to have been the creation of a local KPD, USPD, and surprisingly also a local SPD leader. There was also a General Headquarters in the automobile of the teacher, Stemmer, who tried to take charge of day-to-day military operations. Stemmer and the Hagen "central organization" worked together reasonably well. But they were unable to extend effective authority over the western area of the revolt where an indigenous leadership had grown up with a different political base, primarily KPD and Syndicalist. Even in the heat of battle, proletarian unity was evidently a myth; the reality was still sectarian political struggle. As is usually the case with guerilla armies, the supply of weapons came from the enemy, that is, military and police units. Among its weapons the Red Army possessed a few cannons, mine throwers, and even two airplanes. In contrast to weapons, food supplies, as might be expected in an industrial area, presented severe problems: the line between requisitioning and plunder was not easy to draw. The inability to solve this problem soon alienated the supporting population and created, as we shall see shortly, demoralizing chaos.[47] To sum up, loosely shared political passions were not in

[46]My account follows Colm, *Geschichte des Ruhraufstandes*, 27–34.

[47]Colm, *Geschichte des Ruhraufstandes*, 60–66. Unfortunately what might have been the

themselves enough to create a durably effective military organization, an observation that both George Washington and Leon Trotsky might well endorse on the basis of their own practical experiences.

What the workers did and did not do with their power once they had taken over a town or city, sheds a revealing light on the character of the insurrection, even though their tenure was very brief. There was considerable local variety. The most radical regimes were those in places where union organization was most recent or where pro-employer unions had dominated. Rank-and-file workers by and large, however, played a very small role. They let party and trade-union functionaries take control of the city. They in turn established executive committees (*Vollzugsräte*). Originally at least, the KPD had generally demanded that workers' councils be elected to take over the administration of the city. Such elections did not take place, partly because they would have taken too much time. Evidently the usual German notion that there *always* had to be some sort of legal government was deeply rooted among the workers as well. The opposite type of reason prevailed in some cities such as Dortmund, however; there the radicals feared that elections would not produce a sufficiently radical political leadership because all the workers, including those in the Christian unions, would participate in the vote. For this combination of reasons most of the executive committees were made up of party and union secretaries, editors, and the like. There was, it seems, only one case of a radical opposition to this essentially traditional leadership. Even in this instance the opposition appears to have been confined to two Communists who felt that the executive committee was not supporting the Red Army with sufficient energy and resources.[48]

After the takeover of a city the executive committee always declared that it had assumed supreme power. In fact it generally contented itself with exercising a moderate supervision over the preexisting administration. Thus the earlier experience of the workers' and soldiers' councils repeated itself. In several places the executive committees placed "on leave" those officials whom the local workers particularly disliked. In some cases the committee's first act was to relieve the local police of their duties, only to call them back again shortly afterward, asking them, however, to

---

most instructive portion of this very useful sociological study by a student of Max Weber, an examination of why men joined the Red Army (50–56), presents mainly a rehash of speculations by Simmel and Le Bon. More data, available to me too late to use, are in Lucas, *Märzrevolution*, II.

[48]See Colm, *Geschichte des Ruhraufstandes*, 84–89.

serve without their uniforms because of the ugly feeling among the workers. In many cases in which executive committees did try to take over the management of urban services (security, social welfare, food supply, transportation, etc.) on their own, they only became mired in the details of administration and lost sight of larger issues. By and large, however, the executive committees reached a *modus vivendi* with the prior administrative authorities. A major reason, according to Colm, was that the executive committees either did not believe in the possible success of the "second revolution" or did not even interpret the movement as a revolutionary one. Though there were exceptions,[49] the most striking aspect in all these developments is the lack of any effective pressure from below to push the executive committees in a more radical direction. By itself this fact tells a great deal about the ordinary workers' attitudes and degree of "class consciousness" at the height of an acute struggle.

On March 16, 1920, the day after the general strike, the mine owners and the unions called for a return to work. On the 17th the government in Berlin called off the strike after the collapse of the putsch. But the workers' capture of Essen took place on the 19th.[50] By that time the putschist military forces had been driven out of the industrial sections of the Ruhr, and the Ebert government restored. At this point the "central organization" of the Red military called off the general strike. But the main fighting continued until March 23, 1920, at which time negotiations, about which there will be more to say later, began with Severing and the army.

As we asked earlier, why did the insurrection continue after the Ebert government had been restored? Does not the fact that it did continue demonstrate the essentially revolutionary character of the whole enterprise?[51] Had not the Kapp Putsch torn the veil of illusion that draped the murderous policy of collaboration between the SPD and military reaction—a policy for which Noske, deeply compromised in the putsch, was no more than a cutting

[49]See Colm, *Geschichte des Ruhraufstandes*, 96–97. Duisberg was the most important exception, where the main result was evidently the strong use of requisitions and an attempt to arrest leaders of the moderate workers. These acts produced many bitter quarrels; see 99–103.

[50]See Lucas, *Märzrevolution*, I, 248; on Essen see 283–289 and Colm, *Geschichte des Ruhraufstandes*, 40.

[51]*Illustrierte Geschichte der Deutschen Revolution*, 499–504. This is an early Communist work of collective authorship, already very stilted in its manner of presentation, but with many references to original documents.

tool—and finally driven Germany's proletarian heartland into a last desperate revolutionary surge?

Enough material about the behavior of the workers has already turned up to cast considerable doubt on such an interpretation. As soon as the Red Army had come into existence and begun operations it had acquired a momentum and purpose of its own. Workers under arms could hardly be expected to drop their weapons and obey a back-to-work call. In some places too, notably Düsseldorf, rough and provocative actions by military and police forces gave those who wanted to continue the strike the upper hand. At the Krupp firm in Essen, there was a sharp debate in the plant councils over continuation of the strike. Significantly the reasons given by the left-wing speakers (USPD-KPD) for continuing the strike were all concerned with quite local and concrete issues. They said nothing about socialism. Included in their list of unfulfilled objectives were: reconstituting the *Einwohnerwehr* or local defense force by bringing in more workers (i.e., joining the police instead of overthrowing it); release of political prisoners; support for the survivors of those killed by the *Sicherheitspolizei* or security police two days before; permission for the reappearance of the USPD newspaper that had been banned for ten days. On the last point the speaker for the trade union announced that a telegram had been sent to Severing asking for the lifting of the prohibition. Even more significantly the plant council decided for a return to work on the basis of the prohibition's being lifted.[52]

In Essen and its environs the workers went back to their jobs even though the forces of the Red Army were nearby, and the news of the capture of Dortmund had already reached them. In other cities, such as Hagen, Hörde, and Barmen, where the workers had driven out the military and police forces, the local action committees called for a return to work on the grounds that this was a matter of life and death for the proletariat, a further indication of the difficulties facing sustained military opposition in an urban setting. The only place where the call was not heeded was Elberfeld. There the workers insisted on staying off the job until there had been a proper funeral for those killed in the recent battles. Lucas calls this episode one of the rare acts of "disobedient solidarity" in the history of the German labor movement. In still other cities, however, the workers simply returned to their jobs *without* any orders to do so from the action

[52]Lucas, *Märzrevolution*, I, 249–250.

committees.[53] In this distinction between the workers who kept on under arms and those who returned to work there appeared still another division that was to prove far more serious later on when the disintegrating Red forces accused the cities of betrayal and turned to plunder on a large scale.

The insurrection reached the height of its power on March 20th, by which time the decisive first military phase ended.[54] On the same day and from then on, von Watter was able to bring in military reinforcements from Württemberg and Bavaria.[55] Then the inherent weaknesses of the insurrection came to the surface. They included the threat of severe hunger in the Westphalian section of the Ruhr; inadequate supplies of food, clothing, and ammunition for the Red forces; and the failure of any workers' rising to take place elsewhere in Germany, as well as absence of support from party leaders in Berlin.[56] For this combination of reasons negotiations between the insurgents and the representatives of the central government began in Bielefeld on March 23rd. Carl Severing's tactic in the negotiations was to detach the trade unions, adherents of the Center Party, Democrats, and SPD from the workers' army. Basically this tactic was successful, another good clue to currents of opinion in the area.

One consequence of Severing's success, on the other hand, was further radicalization as the moderates withdrew from the Red forces.[57] Another cause of radicalization was von Watter's action in adding "armistice conditions" that were impossible to carry out in the brief time his ultimatum allowed, and which greatly angered the Red forces. It was at this point that the members of the Red Army felt themselves completely betrayed by their home cities. Short of money, supplies, threatened by von Watter's troops, they turned in desperation to plunder and called it revolution. Even Communist leaders condemned the anarchic behavior that ensued. The situation deteriorated so far that a Communist leader in Dortmund is reported to have telephoned a request for the entry of Reichswehr troops because he was unable to control the armed bands in the city.[58']

---

[53]Lucas, *Märzrevolution*, I, 250–255. In the light of the concrete examples that he gives and which have been cited here it is hard to accept Lucas's claim (248) that probably the majority of the workers in the Ruhr, in any case many more than those organized in leftist groups, did not heed the call to end the strike.

[54]Colm, *Geschichte des Ruhraufstandes*, 111.

[55]Lucas, *Märzrevolution*, I, 272.

[56]Colm, *Geschichte des Ruhraufstandes*, 113.

[57]Severing, *Mein Lebensweg*, I, 262–263, 266.

[58]Colm, *Geschichte des Ruhraufstandes*, 125–130.

Finally on April 3, 1920, as Severing puts it in his memoirs, the Reichswehr troops marched in and restored order "relatively easily and without serious loss of life." The *Illustrierte Geschichte* tells a different story of brutality and revenge, literally a white terror. Vengeful troops hauled workers out of their houses and shot them, along with women and children. It reports one case of the butchering of 65 canal workers, another of a mass grave holding more than 90 victims. Large numbers of workers fled into territories occupied by the Allies. Persuaded to return by promises of amnesty, they were snatched off the trains by government troops and thrown into prison camps. Many received long prison sentences. Those on the right who had provoked the uprising by their putsch in Berlin got off, on the other hand, very lightly. Of the 540 officers who played a leading part in the Kapp rising, only one received punishment, and that to only a term of five years' imprisonment.[59] In this bloody tragedy ended the closest approximation to a spontaneous proletarian revolution that has taken place in a modern industrial state.

Could it have succeeded? Was it a revolution? We can see matters more clearly by answering the second question first. Over and over again the evidence reveals that the mass of the workers was not revolutionary. They did not want to overturn the existing social order and replace it with something else, least of all one where ordinary workers would be in charge. They were, however, very angry. They were backed into a corner and fought in self-defense. The defense turned rather unexpectedly into a brief offensive. Even then it is clear that very many of those workers who were not under arms had no interest in turning the struggle into a revolution. The revolutionary ingredient, such as it was in the whole struggle, was something that only a minority of the local political leaders tried to impose on the whole movement.

Yet even if one grants all these points, from the standpoint of political consequences they do not really matter. Revolutionary objectives are generally imposed by leaders on an angry mass that serves to dynamite the old order when other conditions make it possible. Indeed I would hazard the suggestion that in any of the great revolutions that have succeeded, the mass of the followers has not consciously willed an overturn of the social order. I define success here in the very limited and inadequate sense of taking and exercising power.

To the extent that angry little people want something new, it

[59]*Illustrierte Geschichte,* 505–508.

generally amounts to their perception of the old order minus the disagreeable and oppressive features that affect them. We have seen this at numerous points in the examination of German history, and we shall see still another version with a different social base in the case of the Nazi movement. And that is not a revolution. Conceivably in some cases the new order might be something better, though it certainly was not in the case of the Nazis. To the extent that abuses and oppression are a structural consequence of the old order, such hopes are also utopian. It is hardly necessary to add that modern professional revolutionaries have not been very successful in imposing their supposedly better founded views of reality on mass movements through the device of revolutionary parties in such a way as to transcend the limitations of popular utopianism and still create less oppressive societies.

If we agree provisionally that a revolutionary mass is not by itself an indispensable ingredient for a successful revolution, we are left with the first question: could this uprising have turned into a successful revolution? At a preliminary level of analysis it is reasonably clear that without "dependable" military forces, the government might have fallen. That these forces were not really dependable, in the sense of being loyal to this particular government, is too obvious to require further extended comment. More specifically and concretely, radical risings occurred separately, and those in the capital were either headed off (as in November, 1918) or had too little support (the Spartacist attempt of January, 1919). Thus the government was able to use the troops nominally at its disposal to put down, one by one, revolts that were partly the consequence of its own policies. These occurred, as we know, mainly in the Ruhr, Saxony, and Bavaria during the winter of 1918 and spring of 1919. Though the most serious and violent, the one we have just examined in some detail was essentially the last flicker of its type.

Here too, however, to put the emphasis on timing and the possibility of military suppression misses the most important point. It is not enough to say with the Social Democrats that the uprising had to become a civil war and that in a civil war even armed workers cannot be a match for regular troops. For one thing, regular troops at an early phase in Berlin merely melted away when sent against the workers, just as they had in Russia. The fact that there *was* a regular army of sorts is the one that requires explanation.

Despite the initial shock of defeat in 1918 the old regime had by no means lost all of its appeal and legitimacy. The existence of an army, made up at first of picked volunteers, shows that there was a substantial number of men who *wanted* to get out and fight for the restoration of something like the old order. In the early, crucial phases Ebert had done nothing to neutralize this body and in fact had turned to it immediately for assistance. Yet there is more to the situation than Ebert's policy, disastrous though that proved to be. The old order was temporarily defeated and discredited. But it was not completely rotten—not *morsch*, to use the apt German expression—as it had become by 1917 in Russia. In Germany, the peasants, the urban middle classes, and even large segments of the industrial workers had turned on their leaders for losing the war, not for reasons that had much to do with domestic policies. Among these strata the right could find its recruits. The far left was just enough of a threat to swell their numbers. Before long the right would cease to be monarchist and noble, and take on for its own uses a populist and egalitarian hue. With that mutation the Nazis were on the road to power.

PART THREE

General Perspectives

CHAPTER TEN

The German and Russian revolutions: some comparisons

With the collapse and suppression of the revolt in the Ruhr, we have reached the end of our history of German workers, though for the next two chapters we shall continue drawing on German social history in order to analyze major theoretical issues. The ascent toward "pure" theory will be gradual. Remaining within the context of German history, the next two chapters will discuss how it might be possible to ascertain objectively the existence of a liberating historical alternative and assess moral responsibility for its suppression, and the distinctions as well as similarities between liberating and repressive forms of popular moral anger. From there we can proceed to more general issues of moral relativism, rational and irrational forms of authority, and the ways in which inevitable evils can be culturally redefined as intolerable abuses. At the present juncture we have just observed some of the reasons for the failure of the most important radical thrust to date that was based on the industrial workers in an advanced industrial country. But what is the meaning of this failure? Do not the Russian revolutions of 1905 and 1917 vindicate the conception of a proletarian revolution, even if in a sense quite different from that originally envisaged by Marx?

If by proletarian revolution one means a revolution based primarily on the industrial workers, the answer to this question, as I read the evidence, remains negative. To be sure, in all three of the Russian revolutions (in 1905, and in February and October, 1917) the industrial workers in the big cities did play a significant and perhaps even indispensable role. Furthermore a party that claimed to speak for what was by November, 1917, a thoroughly radicalized majority of these workers did take and keep power. Nevertheless there were much more important

357

reasons for the revolutionary transformation. These were (1) peasant rebellions and land seizures in a country whose population was still 80 percent peasant and hostile to existing property relationships; (2) the alienation and dismay by 1917 of nearly all influential sectors of the population in the face of Tsarist incompetence and weakness as revealed by the strains of the war; and finally (3) the disintegration under these strains of the main instruments of repression, the army, and police forces. This disintegration was decisive. It was not the power of the revolutionary explosion that brought down the Tsarist edifice. It was the collapse of its defenders. Both in February (March by the new calendar) and October (November), 1917, the revolutionaries merely trampled through an open door rotting crazily on its hinges. That is the reason there was so little bloodshed in the revolutions themselves. Bloodshed came later with a vengeance, as the "dictatorship of the proletariat" struggled to establish itself as a minority elite based in the cities, endeavoring to rule and then transform a peasant society.[1]

All this was, of course, very different from what took place in Germany. Rather than engage in further debate about whether the concept of proletarian revolution does or does not fit Russian revolutionary experience, it will be more profitable to ascertain some of the reasons why the Russian workers behaved as they did and to assess somewhat more closely their actual role in the revolutionary process.

The Russian industrial working class grew up in an historical setting very different from its German counterpart. The Tsarist bureaucracy was a decisive element, perhaps *the* decisive element in this setting. Its policies heavily influenced the rate and character of Russian industrial growth. Tsarist policies were also in great measure responsible for the radicalization of Russian industrial workers prior to 1914, though other forces were also at work that in time might possibly have led to results closer to the degree of integration apparent in Germany. Tsarist policies were again heavily responsible for the disintegration of Russian military and police forces. After the February revolution the Provisional Government was unwilling or unable to reverse the process of disintegration and find for itself a new social base.

[1]In the discussion that follows I have not been able to draw on two important books that appeared just as this one was about to go to press: John L. H. Keep, *The Russian Revolution* and Alexander Rabinowitch, *The Bolsheviks Come to Power*. The first, a general analytical treatment, emphasizes the role of both the workers and the peasants; the second is a detailed account of events in Petrograd in 1917.

In both their social composition and institutions the Russian industrial workers were also a very recent historical creation, the consequence of Russia's rapid industrial growth before the First World War. Here are some figures on the number of industrial workers for selected prewar years:

1863	358,000
1890	720,000
1897	1,124,000
1900	2,278,000
1914	2,700,000[2]

In sharp contrast to Germany a very large proportion of these workers, nearly 50 percent by 1902, were employed in giant establishments of 1,000 and more workers.[3] Again, unlike Germany, the factories sprang up in the larger cities. In less than three and a half decades Riga, Kiev, Odessa, and Rostov tripled or quadrupled their populations while Baku, Tsaritsyn, and others grew by factors from five to eight.[4] Eventually the concentration of workers was to be especially important in the capital, Petrograd as it was known in 1917, where there were almost 400,000 workers; 60 percent of these were employed in metal industries which were by then almost exclusively producing war matériel.[5] The population of Petrograd in 1914 was 2,119,000.[6] By 1914 Moscow had a population of 1,700,000 with a factory population in 1912 of 159,000.[7] Since less than half of the total population of each city was made up of adult males and most of the workers were men, these proportions are considerably larger than appear at first glance. If the physically active males—the kind that could show up for political demonstrations—were about a third of the population in each city, the workers would have been a clear majority of these males in Petrograd and over a quarter in Moscow.

Nevertheless it would be unwise to conclude that industrial-

[2] Woldemar Koch, *Die bol'sevistischen Gewerkschaften*, 2–3. The figures can only be taken as approximations, since the definitions of the category "worker" vary. Thus the figure for 1900 includes, for the first time, miners (672,000) and branches of industry subject to the excise tax (243,000), while that for 1914 is an underestimate, being limited to the territory of what was to become the USSR.

[3] Koch, *Die bol'sevistischen Gewerkschaften*, 4.

[4] Teddy J. Uldricks, "The 'Crowd' in the Russian Revolution: Towards Reassessing the Nature of Revolutionary Leadership," 401.

[5] Paul H. Avrich, "Russian Factory Committees in 1917," 163 and note 14.

[6] Victoria E. Bonnell, "The Politics of Labor in Pre-Revolutionary Russia: Moscow Workers' Organizations 1905–1914," 34, note 3.

[7] Bonnell, "The Politics of Labor," 2, 4.

ization by itself created in Russia, unlike Germany, a mass of social tinder liable to explode at the first spark. Legacies of the past left their inhibitions in the form of fear of those in authority —more concretely, fear of Cossacks galloping through a crowd, cracking their long whips—apathy, socially enforced patterns of deference to superiors, faith in the benevolence of the Autocrat. On top of these, industrialism itself created the inhibitions we have seen elsewhere: sheer exhaustion from long hours of work in noisy establishments where it was often impossible to talk with other workers. Then too there was the widespread preference for individual solutions and hanging onto one's job at low risk over sacrifice for distant collective goals, not to mention the beginnings of a bread-and-butter trade unionism about which there will be more to say in a moment. All these obstacles would have to shrink, or else the workers would somehow have to overcome them before they would behave in a revolutionary fashion.

The important point is that all these things *did* happen, and what is even more important, were likely to happen, given the character of the Tsarist regime. Among the strong probabilities inherent in the general situation beginning about 1900 was that Russia would get itself involved in wars with more advanced countries for which it was ill prepared. Russia, if a weak power, much weaker than some of its rulers realized, was still a world power with interests to defend or promote in Europe, the Middle East, and Asia. Nevertheless not all elements in the situation pointed toward inevitable revolution. There were some forces of capitalist integration at work both in the countryside and in the cities, as well as precapitalist bonds inherited from the past, even if these were rapidly eroding. Paradoxically, Lenin's writings provide as good evidence as we need of their existence. His voluminous prerevolutionary output amounts to a sustained and in many ways fearful polemic against the forces of integration and "spontaneous" social tendencies that could inhibit or pervert the revolution he so eagerly sought.

To analyze properly all these contradictory tendencies would require a book in its own right. Here I will confine myself to a few comments on the workers' attempts to organize and promote their own interests. On this score it would be hard to imagine a sharper contrast with Wilhelmine Germany and its powerful trade-union and Social Democratic Party bureaucracies. In Germany as early as 1848, as Stephan Born's memoirs demonstrate, there existed, at least for a brief period, a considerable degree of de facto toleration of workers' efforts to organize and bargain with their employers over wages.[8] In practice Tsarist autocracy had not yet reached this stage by 1914.

The prewar history of the Russian labor movement is mainly a record of workers' attempts to organize themselves for limited economic and social objectives, intermittent Tsarist moves to control or suppress these efforts, and generally ineffective maneuvers by quarreling radical intellectuals to take control of the labor movement for their own purposes. We can begin the relevant parts of the story in 1896 when Russia's first major industrial spurt was drawing to a close. In that year the textile workers of St. Petersburg astounded literate opinion in much of Russia and Europe by carrying out a remarkably disciplined strike that lasted for more than two weeks. At this point quarreling sectors among Russia's radical intelligentsia were still casting about for a suitable agent and set of techniques—be they terror, peasants, workers, or some combination among them—for far-reaching social and institutional changes. Among them a group of Marxists had hit upon the device of finding out what the factory workers actually objected to in factory life and then distributing leaflets based on these concrete grievances. Such leaflets apparently helped to stir up the St. Petersburg textile workers. The workers themselves spread the strike, however, through roving bands who used pleas, shouts, and hails of stone to persuade other factories to shut down.[9] This strike appears to have marked the high point of any direct link between the Marxists and concrete workers' grievances—a tenuous link at best. Its very success led to the heresy of "Economism," the pursuit of limited bread-and-butter interests, which Lenin was to anathematize.[10] Subsequently the link eroded from friction between the intelligentsia and the workers, while the intelligentsia turned to quarrels of its own. The Mensheviks became interested in establishing workers' organizations along Western European lines but had next to no opportunity under Tsarist conditions to put these ideas into practice. The Bolsheviks generally remained suspicious of such efforts, though when they had what they thought was a good opportunity to get control of workers' organizations and put them to their own use, they did not hesitate to make the attempt. These efforts were of little importance until just

[8]See above Chapter Five, Section 5 and P. H. Noyes, *Organization and Revolution: Working-Class Associations in the German Revolutions of 1848–1849*, 70–72, 83–90.

[9]Allan K. Wildman, *The Making of a Workers' Revolution: Russian Social Democracy, 1891–1903*, 48–50, 61–68, 73–74.

[10]Wildman, *Workers' Revolution*, 55–56.

before the outbreak of the war in 1914. Meanwhile the workers drifted back toward more traditionalist forms of organization. One of these forms was Tsarist "police socialism."[11] Though police socialism attracted the workers sufficiently to cause very considerable anxiety among the Marxists, this attempt at integration came to an abrupt end when Tsarist troops fired on Father Gapon's unarmed procession of thousands of workers and some curiosity seekers, many bearing ikons and portraits of the Tsar and singing religious and patriotic songs, as they headed for the Winter Palace to present a petition asking the Tsar to redress workers' grievances. It was Sunday, January 22, 1905, when several hundred defenseless persons were killed or wounded by the Tsarist troops. Bloody Sunday marked the final break of the people's naïve but perhaps gradually dwindling faith in the Tsar as their father-protector.[12]

Countless workers afterward destroyed the picture of the Tsar in their rooms, saying: "We have no Tsar any more!" There were other events to destroy the nimbus of patriarchal authority for far wider segments of the population. Bloody Sunday occurred about three weeks after the fall of Port Arthur in the Russo-Japanese War. Begun as a deliberate attempt to unify Russia and conceal its smoldering discontents through a patriotic upsurge, the war with its defeats produced insurrection from Siberia to Poland.

Again in 1905 the workers acted mainly on their own. On October 20th a railroad strike began over a question of pension rights. It spread rapidly over the country and brought rail traffic to a standstill. Soon the strike took on a political character. The demands, it is worth noticing, were liberal and not socialist: free elections, a constituent assembly, and amnesty for political prisoners. By October 24th the railroad strike had turned into a general strike that paralyzed the whole country. This was the high point of the 1905 revolution, a wave of violence that extorted limited constitutional reforms from the autocracy.[13] Though the Russian Social Democrats were able to ride the revolutionary tiger once it was out of the cage, they appear to have had little if any part in releasing the beast. The outbreak of

[11]Wildman, *Workers' Revolution*, 90, 251 (note 58).

[12]For the Marxists' concerns see Solomon M. Schwarz, *The Russian Revolution of 1905*, 58–74; for an account of the event see Valentin Gitermann, *Geschichte Russlands*, III, 389–391. See also Daniel Field, *Rebels in the Name of the Tsar*, 20–21, on ordinary people's attitude toward the Tsar.

[13]William Henry Chamberlin, *The Russian Revolution: 1917–1921*, I, 51. See also Gitermann, *Geschichte Russlands,* III, 407–410.

the most important strikes in October found them utterly surprised and confused about what advice to give the workers.[14]

Among the workers, labor unions had sprung up during the Revolution of 1905. In March of 1906, as part of the semiconstitutional and liberal reforms granted by the autocracy, they received their first legal authorization in Russian history. For a brief period lasting only until 1907 there did appear some grounds for anticipating a development along German lines. Mensheviks and Bolsheviks competed with each other in organizing unions, with the former predominating. Between them they managed in the city of Moscow to organize about a tenth of the labor force.[15] Though that proportion compares unfavorably with the near half of the German labor force organized into unions in 1914—with about one worker in three in a nominally Marxist union—it did mean that thousands of Russian workers for the first time gained some experience in organizing unions and collective bargaining with their employers. The standard problems of Western labor movements, such as craft versus industrial unions and the closed shop, put in their appearance. While the Mensheviks hoped to create organizations that would enable the workers to educate and eventually liberate themselves in the course of an extended and undefined time period, the Bolsheviks were more interested in quick revolutionary results. Contrary to what one might expect and what later Bolshevik historians have claimed, Bolshevik organizational successes were mainly in the artisan sector of the Muscovite economy, *not* in the big plants with large numbers of workers.[16]

Whatever prospects there may have been for a reformist integration largely disappeared with the repressive turn in Tsarist policy between 1907 and 1912. During these years the unions were put out of action. After that they enjoyed two more years of relatively unfettered existence, making a total of only four years of such experiences before the outbreak of the war. To expect reformism to have taken hold under such conditions and in such a brief time span may seem a bit odd. Compared with the

---

[14]For details on this aspect, based partly on the author's personal experience, see Schwarz, *Revolution of 1905*, 138–143.

[15]In addition to Bonnell, "The Politics of Labor," which concentrates on Moscow, I have drawn on A. El'nitskii, *Istoriia Rabochego Dvizheniia v Rossi*, chap. 13, which on 288–289 gives some interesting information on widespread worker participation in elections to the second Duma. Both accounts agree insofar as they report how Tsarist repression deflected reformist tendencies in a radical direction.

[16]Bonnell, "The Politics of Labor," iv, vi, vii, for general information; on Bolshevik sources of support, xiv, xv, 84; for more detail on union activities, 85–100.

first phase of activity, the 1912 revival was weak. If after 1906 many workers turned to unionism out of disillusionment with revolutionary attempts, from 1912 onward there was disillusion for the opposite reason: experience showed that *both* the Tsarist regime and the employers were intransigently opposed to the workers. Hence it is hardly surprising that Bolsheviks edged out Mensheviks in the leadership of the unions during this second phase.[17] Rather than a preparation for gradualism the Tsarist experience with its mixture of stop-and-go legality and opposition by both the government and the employers would seem to provide a reasonably good formula for rebellion. If the German government allowed large-scale mediating organizations with a considerable interest in the status quo to grow up against its will, the Tsarist regime had under different conditions managed to prevent their putting in more than a token appearance. The difference was important, but by itself far from the main cause of the revolution.

As one can see from a study of the sequence of events, workers' grievances—more concretely, their grievances as factory workers—were hardly the chief cause of Tsarism's collapse in 1917. In 1905 the government had been able to suppress the rebellion without great difficulty because the army was still dependable. By the third winter of the First World War this essential prop had begun to disintegrate.[18] Behind this disintegration lay the slaughter of a peasant army by a technologically superior enemy. Once traditional bonds of loyalty and nationalism snapped, peasants had no great desire to support a regime run by and for landowners whose land many of them coveted. A second and closely related factor was the strain on an inadequate system of transportation. This meant that arms, when they

[17]Bonnell, "The Politics of Labor," chaps. 4–6. For a more general attempt to describe rank-and-file worker sentiment see Leopold H. Haimson, "The Problems of Social Stability in Urban Russia 1905–1917," parts one and two. Haimson points out that the small, reasonably well acclimated urban proletariat developing by 1914 was continually inundated by waves of migration from the countryside. Many peasants brought with them a spirit of elemental rebelliousness, *buntarstvo*. On the other hand, I think that the habit of moving back and forth between the city and the village must have acted as an economic safety valve for those at the bottom of the heap in both places. Hence the political effect is very hard to assess. Presumably with elemental rebelliousness and mobility would have made such workers hard to organize. In the Ruhr the reader may recall, the "Polacken" or rural immigrants to the mining areas were culturally rough but politically docile at first. Later, as a mass of unorganized and volatile workers they served as a powerful stimulus to union militancy. Under Russian conditions from about 1900 onward one might expect similar but much more pronounced swings of mood.

[18]On weaknesses in the army see E. N. Burdzhalov, *Vtoraiia Russkaiia Revoliutsiia*, II, 90–91. The bread ration had been reduced and fast-days introduced; discipline had begun to weaken.

existed, could not get to the front, and more important for social peace, supplies of food and other necessities could not get to the big cities. The main apparatus of repression was breaking down at the same time that consumer grievances were rising, an ominous combination for any established order.

By the beginning of 1917 the crisis in supplies was general throughout the country. Supplies to Petrograd in January scarcely met half of the established norms.[19] Nevertheless when the uprising occurred that overthrew the old regime, it surprised everyone, not least of all the participants. A demonstration on the 10th of February had been a fizzle due to the confused appeals of quarreling Social Democrats and the fact that the preceding day was the beginning of the pre-Lenten carnival week.[20] But amid bread shortages and freezing cold the situation was highly volatile. In the long lines of women, children, and old men there was much grumbling about why there was no bread to be had, who was guilty for the people's suffering, who got something out of the war (komy nuzhna voina). The Petrograd police wrote that the bread lines had all the effects of revolutionary meetings with tens of thousands of revolutionary leaflets. The customary routines of daily life which in ordinary times hold society together were breaking down into severe consumer grievances, and the consumers saw authority as guilty of breaking the social contract. The street had turned into a revolutionàry club. Women were especially hard hit because the men were at the front, leaving them to cope with a job, children, and food shortages.[21]

The revolution itself broke out on International Women's Day, February 23 (March 8), 1917. The main area of the uprising at first was not the great Putilov metalworks, but the textile area of Vyborg that employed many women. The day before, however, a lockout at the Putilov works had put some twenty thousand workers on the loose, which could scarcely have calmed the situation.[22] At this point many or most of the mounted police were still willing to ride into the crowds with saber and whip. Others were reluctant and turned back when facing a crowd led by women. That in turn gave the crowds hope

[19]Burdzhalov, *Vtoraiia Russkaiia Revoliutsiia,* I, 81–82.

[20]Burdzhalov, *Vtoraiia Russkaiia Revoliutsiia,* I, 107–108. Another demonstration on the 14th was bigger but not much more successful.

[21]Burdzhalov, *Vtoraiia Russkaiia Revoliutsiia,* I, 116–119.

[22]Burdzhalov, *Vtoraiia Russkaiia Revoliutsiia,* I, 116, 119–120. Cf. Gitermann, *Geschichte Russlands,* III, 477, who attributes more importance to the Putilov workers.

and courage. Still, the forces of order had been able to put down the uprisings of February 10th and 14th.[23] Again on February 26th the Tsarist forces opened fire on the workers as they tried to reach the central part of the city. Many workers thought the uprising was at an end: an unarmed demonstration cannot oppose a government willing to take decisive measures. On this day the soldiers by and large behaved in a disciplined manner, refused to fraternize with the crowds, and fired upon them. The authorities were satisfied.[24]

The mood of the Petrograd garrison was to be decisive for the whole uprising. Though stiffened by some reliable forces, the garrison was made up mainly of reserve troops. There was a high proportion of local workers newly called to the colors and of evacuated squadrons: men who had been at the front, wounded, and returned to the ranks. These men knew life in the trenches and had no desire to return.[25]

The news that the army had fired on the people horrified some of the soldiers in the garrison. On the same day that the troops opened fire, one small group went over to the revolution. Those sent against it refused at the last moment to open fire. The next day, February 27th, the workers, following a strategy urged by the Bolshevik leaders desperately trying to assume leadership, stood around the gates of the barracks trying to talk with the guards and in general to break down the barrier between the troops and the populace.[26] It is unlikely that these efforts could have had a great deal of effect. What was taking place among the soldiers themselves in the way of arguments and discussions, about which we unfortunately lack information, was probably much more important. The situation itself is, on the other hand, obvious: the soldiers would either have to fire on their own people in a massive way or else break the oath of discipline— something that their subsequent behavior shows they were very frightened of doing.

At six o'clock on the morning of February 27th four hundred soldiers of a guards unit had drawn up on the parade ground and greeted their officer with a normal salute. Then by prearrangement they drowned out the officer's voice with hurrahs when he tried to read the Tsar's order to repress the uprising. Next they went to other barracks to call out fellow soldiers.

[23]Burdzhalov, *Vtoraiia Russkaiia Revoliutsiia,* I, 107, 129–130.

[24]Burdzhalov, *Vtoraiia Russkaiia Revoliutsiia,* I, 172–173.

[25]Burdzhalov, *Vtoraiia Russkaiia Revoliutsiia,* I, 104.

[26]Burdzhalov, *Vtoraiia Russkaiia Revoliutsiia,* I, 177–178, 184.

These in turn hesitated and then streamed out of the barracks. Soon the streets were full of soldiers running about in disorganized and uneasy groups. As soon as a stray officer joined up and took command on the side of the revolution, they followed enthusiastically. Desertions snowballed. On the evening of the 26th six hundred had deserted; by the next morning there were 10,200, by the afternoon of the 27th 25,700, and by evening 66,700. The main action of the mingled soldiers and workers was to release prisoners, some 7,600 of them.[27] This action in turn provided new leadership for the revolutionary forces. Finally, the soldiers streamed spontaneously to the Tauride palace, where the Duma, the symbol of continuing legality, remained. To protect themselves for having broken their oath of loyalty they sought the blessing of continuing authority. The Bolsheviks tried to oppose this flight to legality, which now included all sorts of people, and establish a revolutionary center at the Finland station. That turned out to be impossible. But with the posting of military guards at key points in the city the revolution itself was secured.

I have dwelt on these aspects of the February upheaval in some detail because they shed important light on some general revolutionary processes. The decay of obedience among the soldiers was the crucial aspect of the revolt. Until decay overtakes the apparatus of repression no revolutionary movement stands a chance.[28] In the case of the Petrograd garrison the record allows us to discern once again the decisive role of social support in disobedience as well as some of the classic obstacles to the break with legitimate authority. On the side of the revolutionaries the grievances of the industrial workers did play a part. But the workers were quite hard to bring to the proper pitch of revolutionary heat and convert into a revolutionary crowd—by itself helpless against resolute armed force as one episode showed—until and unless the factories themselves were shut. Working conditions, bad as they undoubtedly were, evidently remained insufficient to produce this effect as long as the workers were in the social setting of a going concern. Inside shut-down factories, on the other hand, with the workers still all crowded together, agitators were able to get results. It is a safe guess that the more peaceably inclined and "responsible" workers—and there must have been some though far fewer in the Russian setting than in

---

[27]Burdzhalov, *Vtoraia Russkaia Revoliutsiia*, I, 185–187; 190 on release of prisoners; 193 on desertions.

[28]On this aspect see Katharine Chorley, *Armies and the Art of Revolution.*

the German—were overwhelmed by their more excitable colleagues, and to some extent dragged and bullied into joining the revolutionary crowd.[29] Rather than the specific discontents of the workers, the whole collapse of ordinary daily routines on account of consumer shortages, in turn traceable to the breakdown of the transportation system, was the factor that created a specifically revolutionary atmosphere. In this connection the role of the women in both leading the first stages of the revolt and in effect disarming the forces of repression comes strikingly to the fore—and not for the first time in a revolutionary upheaval.[30]

From the February Revolution onward the rest of the story is epilogue, at least from the standpoint of a comparison with Germany. Unlike Germany, Russian society, for reasons already discussed, had failed to generate a moderate labor movement to whom power could be transferred. The peasants were a source of increasing revolutionary agitation instead of a brake on the revolutionary process, and the Russian capitalist bourgeoisie was far weaker than its German counterpart. Thus the process of radicalization could continue to destroy the existing set of social relationships until a resolute party was able and willing to take power and attempt the tremendous task of revolutionary reconstruction. More factories would shut down due to worse shortages. The army would disintegrate into a nearly helpless mass.

Two aspects of this process, however, still deserve our attention. What sort of demands did the workers themselves put forth in this process? The end of Tsarist controls provide a unique opportunity to gain some insight into the mentality of ordinary workers and their perceptions of what was taking place around them. The other question of general interest is this: what was the role of revolutionary planning and organization in the Bolshevik seizure of power? The February (March) Revolution was, as even Soviet authorities are now able to recognize, a spontaneous and unplanned affair. How different was the next one? Could it be that all that has been written in the East and the West on the importance of a revolutionary party and organization, using this event as an archetype, is mainly an exercise in social mythology?

The best information about what the workers themselves wanted comes from the statements of the committees that

---

[29]Burdzhalov, *Vtoraiia Russkaiia Revoliutsiia*, I, 122–123 gives a vivid account of the discussions inside the factories.

[30]On the role of women in the French Revolution see Olwen H. Hufton, "Women in Revolution 1789–1796," 90–108.

sprang up in individual factories immediately after the February revolution. Apparently the workers organized these committees to a great extent on their own, though Menshevik and Social Revolutionary agitators contributed. At first there were few if any Bolsheviks. Starting in Petrograd immediately after the February revolution, the factory committees spread swiftly to every industrial center of European Russia.[31] Even if they were undoubtedly dominated by the articulate and politically advanced —circumstances soon led to their domination by the Bolsheviks —the committees were in close touch with the workers and, especially at first, reflected their spontaneous desires and feelings. Fortunately the French historian Marc Ferro provides a useful summary of a large number of their requests and communications, which poured in from all over Russia.

Nearly all the demands that surfaced with the end of Tsarism had to do with wages and working conditions. Far and away the most popular one was for the eight-hour day. There was widespread opposition to piecework. Instead they wanted to be paid by the day, with wages to be paid once a week and two weeks' pay in case of dismissal. Like the German workers they were not at all egalitarian. They had definite ideas about the rates of pay appropriate for different levels of skill. Again like German workers they wanted a floor under wages in the form of a definite minimum. Requests for raises began after the end of March, but were mainly due to inflation. In some respects the Russians were ahead of German workers in asking for the abolition of child labor and the end of discrimination by sex.

As to conditions in the workplace there was the equivalent of the German demand for decent human treatment: management should be polite to the workers. From several places there were objections to arbitrary deductions from wages in the form of fines. Other demands were very simple and concrete: that management should supply boiling water for meals, install canteen and toilet facilities, and supply tools instead of making workers supply their own.[32]

On political issues the workers were at first diffident and divided about continuing the war. Support for the new Provisional Government was reluctant at best. The workers perceived the fall of Nicholas II as settling the issue of the general form of government, which was to be some sort of a republic. Though many workers wanted to hasten the calling of the Constituent

---

[31]Avrich, "Russian Factory Committees," 161–165.

[32]All of the above from Marc Ferro, *The Russian Revolution of February 1917*, 113–115.

Assembly, they did not see the task of this body as determining the general forms of the new political order. Rather it was to set up the rules and institutions under which it should work.[33] In general the whole thrust of these demands, as Marc Ferro observes, was to improve working conditions, not to change them. Once again we see that the workers' idea of a good society—an idea by no means confined to workers—is the present order with its most disagreeable features softened or eliminated. But in the characteristic euphoria of a revolution's first phase, when everything suddenly seems within reach and the aura of inevitability has suddenly evaporated, the Russian workers were hardly in a mood to wait. Their demands were limited and concrete. But they had to be met, completely and without delay.[34] In the prevailing circumstances of chaos and destruction, disappointment and further radicalization were more than likely.

The factory committees also put forward one demand that at this stage of history, and especially in the context of a revolutionary upheaval, did transcend the framework of the established order. In Petrograd very soon after the uprising, factory committees demanded that management recognize the committee and give it the right to control the hiring and firing of workers as well as other aspects of internal factory discipline. The workers' main motive, especially at first, seems to have been job security: they wanted to keep the factories operating and control hiring and firing for the sake of protecting their own jobs.[35] In present-day American factories the control of discipline and personnel is shared between management and unions. It is a touchy issue, but one that can now be settled within the general framework of a capitalist economy. In revolutionary Russia of 1917 the situation was very different. Management saw such demands as an intolerable intrusion upon its prerogatives. On the workers' side there were justifiable suspicions that management harbored counterrevolutionary intentions.

The workers' fears of factory shutdowns were not imaginary. Between the outbreak of the February uprising and July, 568 enterprises closed down, putting 100,000 workers out of work. By the time of the Bolshevik Revolution there were to be 800 closures.[36] Workers' committees and management groups blamed each other for this situation, one fundamentally due to

---

[33]Ferro, *Russian Revolution*, 117–119.

[34]Ferro, *Russian Revolution*, 121.

[35]Ferro, *Russian Revolution*, 116–117; Avrich, "Russian Factory Committees," 162–164.

[36]Avrich, "Russian Factory Committees," 170.

the continuing war. Meanwhile each side maneuvered to gain the advantages of a power that was simply ceasing to exist. In a number of cases after a brief dispute the factory committees ejected the employers and technical directors and carted them off the premises in a wheelbarrow. Then they tried to operate the plant themselves, sending delegates to brother committees in other enterprises in search of fuel, raw materials, and financial aid. Though some committees boasted of maintaining or even in a few cases raising the existing level of production, the general effect was to intensify the anarchy of production already created by the war and the continuing collapse of transportation.[37] Quite apart from their own inadequate technical and administrative knowledge, the individual factory committees could not have organized production. There was no way to coordinate the activities of individual factories in the absence of effective incentives from the market or of centralized bureaucratic controls. This form of workers' control was bound to produce chaos. But chaos and the smashing of what was left of the capitalist system was exactly what Lenin sought to promote after his return to Russia in April of 1917. As the situation deteriorated, the Bolshevik Party was the gainer, not only in increasing its own membership but also in obtaining control of the factory committees. Lenin came to regard them as "the organs of the insurrection" that was to come no later than September or October.[38]

Thus even though the mood of the workers in March had been a long way from one that would support a second and socialist revolution, their defensively oriented behavior had contributed to an atmosphere of insurrection. All this had happened in Germany too, but within a very different balance of political forces. Meanwhile the Bolsheviks were the only party overtly committed to a socialist revolution. Well before October they had won widespread influence among the workers. Furthermore they prided themselves on their discipline and organization, their capacity to lead and orchestrate a revolution whenever a favorable situation might occur. The situation was favorable, and we know they succeeded. But how important to their success was their vaunted capacity for organization?

If one looks carefully at the sequence of events, one can only conclude that this capacity played only a minimal role if indeed it played any at all. Even Lenin's personal role was limited to forcing a decision to attempt insurrection on a somewhat reluc-

[37] Avrich, "Russian Factory Committees," 171–172.
[38] Avrich, "Russian Factory Committees," 173–174.

tant leadership, who departed from his strategy on crucial points. During an important part of the insurrection he was completely out of touch with those who were leading it. In short the organizational weapon at this juncture was mainly a myth.

So far as it can be measured, the movement of opinion in the big cities favored the Bolsheviks. By the summer of 1917 the Bolsheviks had outpaced the Mensheviks and become the first party.[39] In September the Bolsheviks won a majority in the Petrograd soviet. Shortly afterward Trotsky became its chairman.[40] In Moscow elections to ward councils showed a startling rise from 11 to 51 percent between July and October for the Bolsheviks, while the Mensheviks dropped from 12 to 4 percent.[41]

By the end of July, that is, even before the upsurge in Bolshevik strength had become apparent, Lenin had concluded that the Bolshevik Party must take power by force. At this time he discarded the soviets as organs for the attainment of proletarian power, mainly because the Petrograd soviet had recently supported reprisals against the Bolsheviks for a premature and apparently spontaneous uprising earlier that month.[42] From this point on, through the successful October (November 7) uprising Lenin was to maintain an attitude of hostile impatience toward the soviets, arguing repeatedly that it was the task of the Bolsheviks to take power as the vanguard of the proletariat. Presented with the fact of a successful proletarian takeover, Lenin insisted, the soviets would happily endorse and support the vanguard. Perhaps fortunately for the Bolshevik cause, Trotsky, who played a more active role in making concrete decisions during the course of the uprising, followed a different policy of trying to make the insurrection appear as a defense of the soviets against reactionary plans.[43] Though the differences between such outstanding leaders as Lenin and Trotsky hardly confirm the notion of a monolithic and disciplined revolutionary organi-

[39]Robert V. Daniels, *Red October: The Bolshevik Revolution of 1917,* 34.

[40]Leonard Schapiro, *The Origin of the Communist Autocracy,* 54.

[41]Chamberlin, *Russian Revolution: 1917–1921,* I, 279.

[42]Schapiro, *Communist Autocracy,* 48–49; for the earlier rising, 41–42.

[43]Schapiro, *Communist Autocracy,* 52–53; Daniels, *Red October,* 101–103. Neither Lenin nor Trotsky followed this policy with complete rigidity. Later Lenin briefly revived the slogan of "all power to the soviets" as a slogan for immediate insurrection. See Schapiro, *Communist Autocracy,* 58–59. Trotsky's position is somewhat harder to determine. It is reasonably plain that in opposition to Lenin he wanted to delay the insurrection until the Congress of Soviets could vote itself into power. Later, in the course of his struggle against Stalin, he tried to present himself as a Leninist, claiming that his talk about waiting for the Congress of Soviets was merely a cover to deceive the enemies of the Party. See Daniels, *Red October,* 104.

tion, at least they appear to have helped the Bolsheviks attain their goal. That was not true of other disputes within the top leadership.

Lenin began his campaign for an active insurrection from Helsingfors, where he was in hiding, with letters to the Central Committee. They reached Petrograd on September 15 (28). The effect on the Central Committee was astonishment and consternation.[44] Though Lenin did manage in time to convince enough members of the Central Committee to vote resolutions in favor of insurrection, the resolutions remained on paper. The meeting that, according to many accounts, finally decided on the uprising took place on October 10 (23) after Lenin had returned to Petrograd and found a hiding place there. From the dry protocol of the meeting it is plain that Lenin still had an uphill fight to persuade his colleagues to adopt the principle of insurrection in the immediate future. That battle he did win by a vote of ten to two. Much to Lenin's fury the opposition of Kamenev and Zinoviev soon leaked out and became a matter of public polemics in the press. In any case, according to Trotsky, "no practical plan of insurrection, even tentative, was sketched out in the session of October 10th."[45] This was indeed an odd conspiracy in which the conspirators could not agree among themselves, could not keep their own secrets, and could not make concrete plans for what they intended to do.

There were further inconclusive meetings of the Bolshevik leadership on October 15 (28) and 16 (29), whose details I pass over except to mention that reports on the revolutionary morale and state of preparedness from various parts of Petrograd were far from reassuring.[46] As late as October 17 (30) the Bolsheviks had made no real preparations for an uprising. In this sense Lenin had apparently failed to achieve his goal. Trotsky visited him on the 18th (31st). After that, so far as the record shows, no one came to see him. He remained in his apartment far from the center of the city and out of touch with events for a whole week.[47] When he emerged once more to take command, the insurrection was at its height, and the Bolsheviks already had most of the city under

[44]Daniels, *Red October*, 53–54.

[45]Daniels, *Red October*, 74–79, giving most of the protocol of the meeting and 97–99 on the leak; a briefer account including the leak to the press in Schapiro, *Communist Autocracy*, 59–61.

[46]Daniels, *Red October*, 92–96; fuller details of the reports in Schapiro, *Communist Autocracy*, 55.

[47]Daniels, *Red October*, 98, 106. The author may be stretching the evidence in claiming that Lenin had fallen into a deep depression.

their control.[48] Only then, in the early hours of October 25th (November 7th) did the insurrection pass over to the offensive.[49]

With so much reluctance and confusion, not to say outright bungling, it is reasonable to wonder how the insurrection ever got started, far less succeeded. The detailed record of events, given most fully by Daniels, yields, I suggest, these answers. The insurrection started as a defensive move against a preemptive attack by Kerensky and the Provisional Government, who could read about the prospect of a Bolshevik coup in the newspapers even if they were unaware from other sources. The insurrection succeeded mainly because there was no longer any effective force on the side of the Provisional Government. To be sure there had been at least a limited degree of preparation. Trotsky had obtained arms for the Red Guards—workers with an absolute minimum of military training—and managed to ensure the neutrality of the Petrograd garrison through a mixture of soviet legality and playing on fears that the troops would be sent to the front.[50] But that was relatively easy, at least in comparison with the February uprising. The sailors, who were also to play a part, hardly needed any persuasion. Far more important than the strength or organization of the Bolshevik side was the weakness of the Provisional Government. This weakness was due to its inability or unwillingness to end the war, settle the land question, and get supplies moving into the cities, as well as more immediate events such as the recent fiasco of an attempted right-wing military coup under General Kornilov, which alienated what moderate support the government still had.

In this connection it is important to recognize that the insurrection did not take the form of crowds of workers streaming forth—either armed or unarmed—to attack the government's strong points. What it amounted to instead was just a changing of the guards in front of a series of public buildings, usually with some arguments or a bit of token resistance.[51] Except for the attack on the Winter Palace, there appears to have been only one

---

[48]It is revealing that Lenin had to ask permission twice to leave his apartment and join the leaders in the Smolny Institute. After two refusals he just went on his own with one bodyguard by streetcar and on foot. Aside from any danger to Lenin, the leaders in Smolny may have feared he would upset their plan of waiting for the Congress of Soviets. See Daniels, *Red October*, 157–158, 161–162.

[49]Daniels, *Red October*, 156, 161.

[50]Daniels, *Red October*, 111, 128–131.

[51]Daniels, *Red October*, 162–164, 177. In his justly celebrated firsthand notes and impressions, N. N. Sukhanov, *Zapiski o Revoliutsii*, VII, 224, the author remarks on how little there was in the way of street action or mass uprising. As he saw it, there was almost nothing for the workers and soliders to do.

episode of active struggle.[52] By the time of the attack on the Winter Palace, the last refuge of the Provisional Government, the rest of the city was in Bolshevik hands and the issue decided. Even that attack produced only a few casualties, and its outcome was really the consequence of the defenders' giving up a cause that had clearly become hopeless.

What Lenin did—and this was very important—was first of all to force through the general idea of insurrection. Then when he reached the revolutionary headquarters at Smolny on the day of the insurrection, he forced the movement onto the offensive and saw to it that it was carried through to a conclusion, that the guards were changed at remaining strong points. All that was revolutionary strategy and tactics of a sort, though hardly the kind pictured by historians and students of revolution both sympathetic and hostile to the Communist cause. Over the years Lenin may have created the groundwork for revolutionary organization. It was left to later generations of revolutionaries to put the idea to the test—and to change it beyond anything Lenin could have recognized. If the significance of a revolutionary party turns out to be so dubious in Russia at this time, it appears even less likely that the absence of a well-organized revolutionary party in the Germany of 1918 was an important cause of that revolution's failure.

To conclude, the industrial workers did in Russia provide a major urban base for the victory of the revolutionary forces. That is true even though the workers were in many places but a minority of the urban population. (In Moscow, where they were a minority, about a quarter of the city's population, there was a brief and bloody battle at the time of the Bolshevik uprising.) If the urban enemies of the revolution had been able to unite and organize themselves, they might have defeated or crushed the revolution in the cities. But at some point they would have had to come to terms with the peasant revolution. The same is true the other way around. Subsequent revolutionary experience in China, Vietnam, and Cuba shows that a revolution with its main social base in the countryside cannot impose a revolutionary policy on the whole society until and unless it can gain control of the cities, something it may have to do with an army rather than a revolutionary party. It is the state of the army, of competing armies, not of the working class, that has determined the fate of twentieth-century revolutions.

---

[52]Chamberlin, *Russian Revolution: 1917–1921*, I, 315–316.

CHAPTER ELEVEN

The suppression of historical alternatives: Germany 1918–1920

1. Some general considerations

At various points in this book the suggestion has surfaced that particular historical events need not have turned out the way they did: that history may often contain suppressed possibilities and alternatives obscured or obliterated by the deceptive wisdom of hindsight. There have been occasional if less frequent observations on the limits of determinism in sociology and other ways of studying human affairs. By now the discussion has reached a point where it is high time to confront these issues directly. Since the notion of suppressed historical possibilities, with its overtones of moral responsibility for missed opportunities to create a less cruel and repressive social order, brings the issues together in a reasonably satisfactory fashion, we may stick to that. If this notion is to be more than a rhetorical device to trigger off suitable moral emotions (e.g., condemnation of all existing social institutions, romantic glorification of any violent struggle against authority), it ought to be possible to show in some concrete historical situation just what was possible and why. That means marshaling evidence, creating and testing an argument, in the same way one goes about explaining any form of human behavior.

Thus the enterprise requires an effort to analyze a segment of history in order to explain why something did *not* happen, and to assess the significance of the cause or set of causes. This is the area we are about to enter: one, as the saying goes, where many tracks enter and few come out. For those who are strongly skeptical about the whole enterprise there is little to offer in the way of general justification. There is not much use debating the logical and ontological status of a camel with someone who has severe doubts about the animal's existence: it is better to show the skeptic a real camel. In this case, however, that is impossible. One cannot provide irrefutable proof of the existence of a suppressed historical possibility. On the other hand, it is equally impossible to prove that any given situation had to turn out in exactly the way it did. There is plenty of room in between for serious discussion whose outcome has very serious consequences for real life.

The historian's reluctance to engage in debate about why something did not happen is quite understandable. Historians justifiably feel that they have enough work to do in explaining what did happen. But any explanation of what actually took place connotes an explanation of why something else failed to occur. If revolutionaries failed to win power, there must be reasons why they failed and evidence in support of these reasons. Hence, so far as I can see, historians have to use some conception of suppressed historical possibilities whether they choose to or not. By itself this consideration seems to me enough to make the enterprise intellectually respectable, though I have no intention of throwing the burden on other shoulders.

Another useful reflection comes from considering the working habits and practices of historians. To the extent that suppressed historical alternatives exist at all, they evidently have different degrees of existence. Though that sounds philosophically deep and puzzling, I do not think it really is. To speak to the case we are about to examine, not even the most vigorous opponent of historical inevitability would be likely to claim that German society in 1918 could have returned to the ways of medieval knights and serfdom. But the possibility of a breakthrough to some variant of socialism or liberal capitalism, more stable and humane than the sequence of the Weimar Republic and the Nazi regime, is not so easy to exclude. Existing facts quite obviously limit the range of possible alternatives. Thus suppressed alternatives have to be concrete alternatives and specific to concrete situations. A big part of the task of any empirical investigation would be to determine the extent to which any given situation actually *was* open: more precisely what facts limited the range of options open to those men and women whose behavior strongly influenced the course of events.

The word "determine" has unavoidably crept into the discussion. What can it really mean? The answer can hardly be a matter of grammar and ordinary English usage. Instead, it requires explicating, however briefly, a position on the famous and thorny issues of determinism and moral or political responsibility. To put the issue very simply, how can an historical actor—great or small, a single individual or a whole group such as the German workers—be politically responsible for its actions if it is also true that such actions have definite causes? The concept of causation must be complete and consistent. The notions of determinism and responsibility cannot be brought in and out of a discussion simply to support a predetermined conclusion. As Max Weber remarked, in discussing Marxist determinism, it is not a taxi one can take and then get out of whenever one pleases. Hence it seems that moral responsibility is incompatible with determinism.[1]

Let us take up the concept of determinism first. So far as I can see, the thesis that everything in the universe has causes or a set of causes is unprovable because the proof presupposes omniscience. Scientists and scholars do not really need this assumption as a presupposition for their investigations. All that they need is a hunch that there might be some connection among the materials they are about to examine and then set out to discover whether such a connection actually exists and what it may be. It is just as important to keep in mind that there may not be any connection or a very weak one. (Here we may recall the highly charged issues of the role of race and inherited intelligence.) After all it is possible to find "evidence" for almost any explanation. By itself theory provides no way out of this trap. It is possible for the fertile human imagination to invent theories quite freely. Thus in the actual process of inquiry the general concept of determinism plays a rather secondary role, if indeed it plays any at all. As such it does not seem to be a bar to the type of inquiry proposed here.

In order to keep the notion of moral and political responsibility it does not, however, appear necessary to drop the concept of determinism or, as I prefer, universal causation. Here, too, the issues impress me as primarily factual, though I have encountered strong disagreement with this point of view. Universal causation does not exclude the idea that some causes can be more important than others and that the relative significance of causes can change. It is reasonably plain that the results of human intelligence and human effort have been continually entering

---

[1]Robert Paul Wolff, *The Autonomy of Reason: A Commentary on Kant's Groundwork of the Metaphysic of Morals*, presents in the last two chapters an uncompromising statement of this dilemma and concludes that Kant's famous resolution is untenable.

and transforming the stream of historical causation as far back as the record goes. The history of technology and/or ideas provides sufficient factual testimony for this familiar point of view. Though we understand the process very imperfectly, there are evidently reasons why particular ideas enter the stream when they do, or why they fail to make an entry. But that is what the investigator tries to find out, not what he should assume in advance. Thus the idea of moral or political responsibility merely means that the application of human effort and intelligence can make a difference in human affairs. What difference we have to find out. Such responsibility, to put the point in a slightly different way, can have both causes and consequences. The task in any given case is to find out what they were.

Though hardly likely to be universally persuasive, this effort to combine the general idea of personal and group responsibility with notions of determinate causation will have to suffice for working purposes. Furthermore if moral responsibility is to have any meaning, it must indicate that human beings are responsible for those consequences of acts and decisions that in the actual circumstances of the time these persons should have been able to foresee. Thus moral responsibility has to be made historically specific and include an assessment of the level of knowledge and judgment available to specific historical actors. Clearly that will be an important aspect of the investigation on which we are about to embark.

These considerations lead back to the conception of suppressed historical possibilities and the central question that will evidently require an answer: who are the people who do the suppressing and why do they do it?[2]

In the rest of this chapter I shall explore the thesis that in Germany immediately after the First World War, conditions may have existed that rendered possible some sort of a liberal breakthrough resulting in a regime more stable than the one that in a decade and a half was to succumb to Adolf Hitler. It is a thesis suggested though not systematically developed in recent German historical work critical of the standard SPD apology: that in 1918 the only choice was between an oppressive revolutionary dictatorship of the proletariat or an alliance with the old order.

---

[2]This is a recurring theme in the justly celebrated book by E. P. Thompson, *The Making of the English Working Class*, to my knowledge the only major work by a modern historian that is both rich in factual evidence and takes the idea of historical alternatives seriously. Though explicit, the theme is not systematically developed. That is scarcely a criticism, since other valuable qualities in this book would have disappeared had the author added this labor to his already large burdens.

Though a critical analysis of this thesis provides a useful set of questions around which to organize much of the material, the demolition of this thesis—or indeed of any thesis—is not the object of the inquiry.

Instead there are two positive objectives. The first is to search for the *kinds* of arguments that might sustain the thesis that the liberal alternative was a viable one. This will not be an exercise in abstract logic. There will also be an examination of relevant evidence, though the examination can hardly be an exhaustive one. An authority on German history may easily notice important aspects that I have overlooked or misinterpreted. That would be all to the good since it would mean that concrete evidence was relevant to the discussion. Through the device of exploring these arguments, it may be possible—and this is the second objective—to shed new light on the capacities and limitations of German industrial workers in their efforts to establish a more just and humane society at this important historical juncture.

The choice of a liberal over a socialist alternative rests on the view that the liberal one was both closer to the actual possibilities at that point in time and, as a set of institutional arrangements, held somewhat greater promise for a less repressive social order than that which had just come to grief with the collapse of the Imperial system. There is no reason to make a secret of the fact that my general political inclinations run in the same general direction for the same general reasons. But if one starts with a socialist alternative, the technique of investigation remains the same. The questions to ask are fundamentally the same: they include: (1) In these specific circumstances what concrete steps would such a policy imply? (2) What were the obstacles to carrying it out? Were they real or imaginary obstacles? How can we tell? (3) On what resources in the existing social order could such a policy draw? What do we know about the working or nonworking of institutional arrangements, and the situation and predispositions of various sectors of the population during this period that would enable us to draw tenable inferences about this policy? (4) If there should be enough evidence to support the view that the policy was indeed feasible, why then did it fail of adoption? Did nobody in power think of it, and if that is the case, what are the reasons for this apparent failure? If those removed from the levers of power did think of such a policy, why was their position so weak?

There is of course a risk of tailoring the evidence to suit preconceptions, a risk that exists in all forms of inquiry. In this particular case the main risk may be that of making radical and revolutionary movements seem puny and "manageable" at some points in time, and very formidable at others. But fortunately the political preconceptions and preferences of investigators differ. The conclusions that they reach can be checked against evidence. The factual component in the answers to the questions just mentioned is sufficiently large to impose in due course a wide area of agreement. Historians can and in fact already do agree on a great deal more than just dates and raw events. After all, the situation in Germany between 1918 and 1920 was what it was no matter what a liberal, socialist, or reactionary historian now wishes it had been.

These preliminary observations are, I hope, sufficient to establish the intellectual legitimacy of the task on which we are about to embark. To go into the issues more thoroughly runs the risk of engaging in empty polemical speculation. In any case some of them will crop up again in the course of interpreting concrete events, where it will be easier to clarify their import. To avoid possible misunderstanding it is necessary to state explicitly one more limitation on the nature of the task attempted here. It is not that of proving a point. Anyone seriously interested in the history of Germany during this period would very likely require detailed evidence about which I am ignorant and whose presentation would be impossible within the framework of this book. Rather it is an effort to explore what sort of an argument *could* be constructed on the basis of readily available evidence, most of which has been presented in preceding chapters: to see where the argument appears tenable and where it might break down, and through this procedure learn more about the political limitations and possibilities inherent in an historically decisive instance of popular moral outrage. The effort requires constructing the argument in such a way that disproof is possible through resort to evidence. Since rigorous proof is in any case impossible, the more modest objective may, I hope, turn out to be attainable and useful.

2. A crucial non-decision: the SPD and the army

The first task of any government is to govern, especially that of a brand-new government. In November, 1918, Ebert's new government began trying to use the moral authority of the SPD to bridge the gap between two incompatible sources of legitimacy, the crumbling authority of the Imperial regime and an upsurge of popular protest. Under any conditions it would not be an easy task. It would be an impossible one if the government did not have some reliable force at its disposal. If the military problem, in effect a police problem at that point even more than a military one, could not be solved in some way favorable to the eventual establishment of a liberal regime, there was no prospect of solving the others. A government that cannot command obedience is no government at all and rapidly vanishes from the scene. A government that does not consider the way it will obtain and use force forfeits the opportunity to determine its own policies.

As has often been pointed out, Ebert's government did next to nothing about reforming or controlling the bureaucracy and the judicial system. In both of these, antirepublican and reactionary sentiments were to have a powerful impact on policy. The SPD tactic of acquiescence, in the name of law and order and the restoration of the economy,[3] prevailed generally across the board. In that sense military policy was no exception. But if there were to be a more vigorous policy, it would have to start with the military and succeed. Otherwise nothing else could work. To antagonize the civil bureaucracy and leave the officer corps intact would be an obviously infallible formula for the success of counterrevolutionary plots. But if the army were well in hand, other elements would have to think twice about undue delay in the execution of government policies, especially if there were strong signs that the new government enjoyed widespread popular support, as was the case in early November, 1918. If the SPD leaders really could not have done anything more than they actually did—which in effect was nothing—about taking control of the army, there was nothing else they could have accomplished.

From the standpoint of the reformist leadership a double imperative required an alliance with the General Staff. One aspect was the danger from the left. Modern historians are inclined to minimize this danger. In Chapter Eight, recounting the duel between the reformists and the radicals, I have presented evidence in support of the view that the danger of at least a coup was quite real but that, on the other hand, the old army was just about totally ineffective as a force for order. Indeed, the attempts to use it may have made the situation worse. An impera-

[3]For a good account see especially sections 3, 4, and 5 (II–LXXII) in the introduction by Erich Matthias to the collection of documents *Die Regierung der Volksbeauftragten 1918/19*.

tive that fails to work when put into practice is hardly a real imperative. The other aspect was the requirement of an orderly demobilization. That prong of the alleged imperatives inherent in the situation requires closer examination.

Again from the standpoint of SPD objectives, as orderly a demobilization as possible was certainly most desirable. Masses of soldiers were utterly sick of the war and just wanted to get home. To bring the men home was one of the strongest demands of the moment. No government that claimed to have popular support could afford to be dilatory. At the same time Germany's armies were still mainly on foreign soil. (What business they had being there in the first place was not, so far as I have noticed, a question that came up in discussions between the SPD and the General Staff.) On the Eastern frontiers and beyond, sporadic fighting was to continue for some time. The technical problems must have looked enormous. The potential consequences of failure to solve them rapidly and satisfactorily must also have looked like a slide into anarchy and disaster for the German population as a whole. The General Staff had powerful and apparently realistic arguments to present. Millions of men had to be brought back across the front. It was necessary to find trains to transport them. Next it was necessary to find supplies to feed them. Then it was necessary to disarm them in an orderly fashion. Otherwise there was the risk of masses of hungry soldiers foraging and plundering on their own, a savage and angry *Soldateska* such as the one that had ravaged town and country in the Thirty Years' War. For all these reasons, the General Staff's arguments continued, it was necessary to maintain centralized control over the military apparatus and authority in the country as a whole. To do their job the military needed the maintenance of discipline in their own ranks, which meant no interference from soldiers' councils, and no nonsense about the election of officers by the soldiers.

These arguments[4] must have sounded impressive to Ebert and some of his colleagues, who were at heart solid German citizens anxious to do right by their country. That was of course part of the trouble. But how valid were the arguments? Was there a way of getting the soldiers back in a more or less orderly fashion without the degree of reliance that the SPD placed on

[4] I have reconstructed them from memory after following through military affairs with the help of the index in these published records: Matthias, *Regierung der Volksbeauftragten* and Eberhard Kolb and Reinhard Rürup, editors, *Der Zentralrat der Deutschen Sozialistischen Republik 19.12. 1918–8.4. 1919.* Some of the most important highlights culled from this exercise appear in Chapter Eight above.

the General Staff? Austrian experience suggests that there was.

There the whole demobilization, which was expected to last for about two years, took place in about three weeks. It was a spontaneous and somewhat disorderly process in which the high command played very little role, partly because the Austrian armies were at the time of the armistice in a state of demoralization and decomposition much more advanced than the German armies were. In Austria there were fears of plunder, if only for the sake of food, but they never materialized on more than a very local scale. The devotion of the railway authorities and the workers kept the trains running. According to one eyewitness report, soldiers simply left the front and their officers, rushed the train, broke the windows to get in and even piled onto the roofs. Large numbers of these were knocked down and killed, as the trains passed through tunnels. In most places there was just enough organization of a local sort to disarm the soldiers and supply food and clothing, which kept looting down to a manageable and temporary form. Even the prisoner-of-war camps failed to become the cause of major disturbances. When the guards went home, the camps just emptied themselves.[5]

To be sure Austria was not Germany. Carsten's assertion that "there can be little doubt that the German armies would have marched back safely from France and Belgium even if this move had not been directed by the military authorities" may be open to challenge. That challenge, however, would have to point to elements in the German situation that made the Austrian solution, or something similar to it, out of the question.[6] As matters stand, the Austrian experience constitutes strong evidence for the thesis that a different solution, and not necessarily a revolutionary one, would have been possible for Germany.

To sum up the argument so far, there is enough evidence to present a strong challenge to the thesis that Ebert and those who followed his lead had no choice but to rely on the old officer corps for the sake of orderly demobilization and necessary

[5] F. L. Carsten, *Revolution in Central Europe 1918–1919*, 23–26.

[6] Carsten's statement occurs on p. 26. As he recognizes, the situation on the Eastern front was different. By the end of 1918 this fact was to provide a welcome reason for speeding up the call for volunteers. On this point the minutes of a joint meeting of the Executive Committee and the Council of People's Representatives are especially revealing. See Kolb and Rürup, *Zentralrat*, document 28, January 3, 1919, espec. 193, where Robert Leinert remarks: "We should not let ourselves be pushed around by such a low-standing people as the Poles and permit the destruction of the great achievements that the workers have created and that are reaching their peak in the great victory of the revolution." Polish forces were then encroaching on the Silesian mining areas. But the question of the Eastern frontier was not acute in the earlier stages.

minimum of domestic tranquility.[7] It is not hard to see how and why these leaders *felt* the way they apparently did, and even to feel considerable human sympathy for them as well as their opponents. But that is something very different from an acceptance of the proposition that circumstances were such that they could do nothing else. If we reject that proposition on the basis of the evidence just sketched, we have grounds for asking what kind of a policy might have had some chance of succeeding.

3. Was a different policy possible?

For the reformist leaders the problem of keeping order and hanging on to power was crucial in the sense that if they failed on that score they could not do anything else anyway. In fact they nearly did fail before they managed to put together an instrument of repression in the *Freikorps*. Nevertheless the problem of domestic order and relationships with the army was by no means the only issue Ebert and his associates had to decide. It was part of a whole series of related issues. Together they added up to a decision about what kind of a society the SPD wanted to create amid the conditions facing them and how they would go about trying to establish it. Hence a more vigorous policy toward the old officer corps would have required a quite different political and economic policy. The whole strategy would have had to be different from the one actually pursued.

Let us therefore raise the question of what general strategy might have been suitable to the circumstances and compatible with liberal rather than revolutionary objectives and assumptions. By liberal I intend no more than to stress the importance of rights of free expression and protection against the abuses of authority. There is a sense in which the distinction between liberal and revolutionary tends to evaporate, because revolutionaries of almost all persuasions generally assert that liberalism in practice has been a fraud which is now historically antiquated, and that their revolution is in any case the only way to attain the objectives liberals pretend they want. There is no reason to enter

[7]One curious aspect of the whole situation is that no responsible leader appears to have thought of the possibility of creating a national police force instead of using the army. Such a proposal would of course have clashed head-on with the particularist traditions of the individual German states, especially Bavaria. But the government did not hesitate to use what military force it could muster to put down radical movements in the several states in 1919 and 1920.

this debate here except to remind the reader that the historical experience since 1918 which colors so much of the present debate still lay over the horizon for those who were deeply concerned about the issue at that time. The problem before us is a related but distinct one: whether in fact a "third way" was possible somewhere between a de facto alliance with the old order and revolutionary dictatorship. One way to find out more about the problem is to state what such a policy would have amounted to in practice. Then and only then does it become possible to perceive some of the elements in the situation that could have favored the execution of such a policy as well as the obstacles it would have encountered.

If the SPD moderates were to have established themselves without heavy reliance on the army and other pillars of the old order, they would have had to adopt economic policies to undercut the radicals on their left and still draw some support from moderates to their right. That meant getting the economic wheels to turn, and more besides, in a situation of defeat and disorganization with the Allies looming in the background and holding many of the decisive keys to their future, as well as a revolutionary government in Russia which at that point exerted immense powers of attraction. It is necessary to concede at once that the obstacles to any such policy were enormous and that no government, no matter how able, imaginative, and energetic, might have overcome them successfully.

In pursuit of this general strategy the government would, I suggest, have had to take the following measures. It would have been necessary to intervene decisively in the affairs of the army and the bureaucracy by putting its own men in key positions to control policy. In the army that would have meant using and influencing the soldiers' councils as well as sending representatives with broad plenary powers to the High Command.[8]

Intervention alone could of course be no more than a preliminary stopgap, even if it was essential. For that matter there

---

[8]One episode in the negotiations of November 9, 1918, between the SPD leaders and the government of the last Imperial Chancellor, Max von Baden, over the transfer of power to the SPD demonstrates vividly how little was the inclination of the reformist leaders to press this issue. At one point Philipp Scheidemann said that one of the conditions of the transfer would have to be that the post of war minister go to a Social Democrat. Scheüch, Max von Baden's war minister, at once refused, saying that he had to stay at his post to take care of the armistice negotiations. That settled the matter. Neither Ebert nor Scheidemann insisted. According to one version of the record, Ebert even thanked the war minister for his willingness to continue serving. See Matthias, *Regierung der Volksbeauftragten*, I, 6, 12 (documents 1a and 1c). Though the record is imperfect, there is no doubt about the essentials of the exchange.

was intervention in the administrative bureaucracy, though it was weak and ineffective.[9] There are good grounds for holding that the forces of order, with the emphasis on the police rather than the military, would have had to be constructed on the basis of traditional forms of discipline, that is, without the election of officers but with other means to assure loyalty to the government and its general principles. It would also have been necessary to find ways to protect the citizenry against abuses of authority that had been far from rare under the Imperial regime. *Some* liberal governments have faced these issues fairly successfully, though not to be sure under conditions like those the reformists faced in 1918 and 1919. The effort would almost certainly have required starting from scratch to create new organizations at the same time that the old ones were being dismantled. It is easy enough to agree that the task was formidable. But it is also quite clear from the historical record that the SPD did precious little about these matters—that in fact they hardly realized the problem existed —and that their failure to act vigorously contributed powerfully to the suspicions and disenchantments among the industrial workers. If this failure did not create radicalism among the industrial workers, it certainly intensified this mood to the point where the SPD could only control it by force.

In economic and social policy it would have been necessary for the government to take control of some key sectors of the economy—mining is an obvious candidate where the promise that this might happen sufficed to quiet the miners temporarily at a high point of radical turmoil—and give the workers additional influence over conditions in the pit and on the shop floor. It would not, I suggest, have been necessary to give the workers a voice in the basic decisions about investment and marketing along the lines of full-scale workers' control. The government, presumably responsive to popular pressures, could have kept some levers in this area, and the workers would have gained influence too over these decisions indirectly, through what they could do about working conditions. There are many indications that such policies, sketched here in the barest possible outline, would have greatly undercut the support for a radical solution.[10]

[9] For a detailed account of what happened see Matthias, introduction to *Regierung der Volksbeauftragten*, I, LXVII–LXXII. The effect was to shield the traditional bureaucrats from interference from the intrusions of workers' and soldiers' councils, a policy on which there appears to have been tacit agreement all around, including USPD representatives.

[10] To anyone who firmly believes that radical or revolutionary solutions to the problems of a capitalist society were and are the only desirable ones, these observations will appear as the rankest form of suggested manipulation. There are two points one might make in

In the situation at the time when the Social Democrats half accepted and half took power there were several factors favorable to such a policy, or that at the very least provided more room for maneuver than Ebert and his associates exploited. The spontaneous revolt spreading out from Kiel and the army's call for an armistice stunned the traditional supporters of the old order. Army officers complained bitterly about the spinelessness of the middle classes, complaints that were to continue well into 1919. If pursued vigorously from the very beginning, a policy along the lines of the one just sketched could hardly have run much risk of provoking a counterrevolutionary coup from the right. The army itself, as events recounted earlier show, was at that point a paper tiger: the soldiers would not obey counterrevolutionary orders.[11] Without effective military support no counterrevolution could have hoped to succeed. By their policies Ebert and his colleagues *created* in the Freikorps and parts of the old army the necessary instrument for counterrevolution of the old prefascist model (i.e., without massive popular support) and handed it to the right on a steel platter. At least some old-fashioned union leaders like Carl Legien realized this at the time of the Kapp Putsch, when it was much too late.

Thus the old order was temporarily out of action. For the most part the "respectable" elements in society tried to keep out of sight and carry on, which was one of the ways they managed to hang on and survive. The middle classes seem to vanish from the political arena until about the time of the elections to the National Assembly in January, 1919, while the workers and their quarrels swarm into the center of the historical stage. This of course is partly an optical illusion, now being corrected by recent research. In middle-class circles the feeling was quite widespread that sharp structural changes in the economic and social order were inevitable, and that they would be in the general direction of giving more power to the lower classes. Though many in the middle classes must have feared this prospect, there was a substantial sector for whom it seemed desirable. In the first weeks

---

reply. First, all forms of social behavior, including revolution, require manipulation of some sort, and the case that revolution brings about better results is far from established. Second and more important in this connection, the issue under discussion is whether or not a left-liberal policy *could* have succeeded. Whether one admires or detests such a policy really has no bearing on such an estimate.

[11]The High Command knew this too. Before the Kaiser's abdication it had come to the conclusion that even frontline troops would be of no use in putting down domestic disorders and no longer stood behind the Kaiser. See on this point Matthias, *Regierung der Volksbeauftragten*, I, 13 (document 1c). Evidently the High Command needed the Social Democrats even more than the Social Democrats needed the army.

following the proclamation of the Republic a number of influential bourgeois leaders, mostly professionals but including such figures from the world of big business as Hjalmar Schacht, impressed by the new regime's support for property, legality, and civil liberties, publicly expressed acceptance of the new order and even of socialization as appropriate for the monopolized sector of industry.[12] To be sure, such statements require considerable discount as a manifestation of the confusion and euphoria that often appears in the early stages of a revolutionary upheaval. Nevertheless they are also part of the general fluidity of such situations that a determined and acute political leadership can use to make important policy decisions. Thus this evidence further supports the view that Ebert and his fellow reformists had more room for maneuver than they used or even wanted to use.

A vigorous policy along the lines just indicated might have drawn enough support from the middle classes to give it a fighting chance. From the creation of a new military and police force they would have had nothing to lose and some things to gain. It would have meant pushing the Junkers aside. Even if the German middle classes had too much awe of the aristocracy to perform this "bourgeois" historical task on their own, they might not—and at that point could not—object very effectively if workers did it for them. As long as there were clear limits to the socialization of industry, admittedly a very difficult condition to establish in the light of what socialists had been saying for a long time, there would probably have been grudging toleration of the new regime in some middle-class quarters and considerable support in others. Influential segments from the professions, light industry, and the export trade were, as we have seen, inclined to support the new regime out of opposition to the autocratic features of the departed empire, while big business showed inclinations to come to terms out of fear lest more radical currents gain the upper hand. Certainly there would have been severe struggles later. But these happened anyway, and a government with a vigorous policy at the beginning would have been in a much stronger position to cope with them effectively.

The main source of support would have had to come from the industrial workers. There can be little doubt that they would have welcomed policies to the left of those actually pursued. The

---

[12]See Matthias, introduction to *Regierung der Volksbeauftragten*, I, cxxv, and for more detail Lothar Albertin, *Liberalismus und Demokratie am Anfang der Weimarer Republik*, 25–32, 54–59.

essentially moderate Congress of Workers' and Soldiers' Councils, held in Berlin December 16–21, 1918, passed resolutions on military and economic issues distinctly to the left of those suggested here as feasible.[13] Ebert subjected these resolutions to euthanasia by procrastinations. It is a fair inference that even quite moderate workers lost their faith in reformist socialism. As pointed out in the two preceding chapters, the government's policies gravely weakened its most powerful asset, its moral authority among the industrial workers.

With a strategy less conservative than that Ebert and his associates adopted, revolutionary radicalism might never have acquired the resonance that it did attain. In the absence of the radical thrust the extreme right would have lost its main excuse for existing. In fairness to the moderates it is necessary to point out that they did not create left radicalism out of whole cloth: the war created the social conditions in which it could flourish. There are grounds for holding that it posed a real threat just before the government took power, an issue inevitably subject to debate. What is beyond dispute is that the really powerful radical thrust, with mass support behind it, did not begin until *after* the government had been in power for about two months. It did not reach its most threatening point until the armed revolt in the Ruhr in the spring of 1920. For this upsurge the government's policies were mainly responsible; more accurately it was the lack of policy, and especially the lack of independent military policy, that did so much to create the radical revolt.

Now let us turn to the obstacles and difficulties any such policy would necessarily have faced from the circumstances of the time. Would the Allies have tolerated any steps toward the creation of a regular army before the signing of the peace treaty, even if such an army were under strong democratic controls? Would they have tolerated even a minor degree of socialization in an atmosphere where Communism had not yet revealed its ugliest potential and exerted a powerful popular attraction? Just raising these questions is enough to suggest some of the more formidable obstacles. Even if the internal situation in Germany had been highly favorable, which it was not, a more leftist policy could easily have come to grief for these reasons.

If international problems *had* turned out to be soluble, there remains the question of whether a new German government with the policies just sketched could have carried the rest of the

[13]*Allgemeiner Kongress der Arbeiter- und Soldatenräte Deutschlands . . . Stenographische Berichte*, 181–182.

country with it. The industrial working class was still a minority of the working population and the government could scarcely have counted on its undivided support. To survive and be effective it would have had to seek allies to its right and keep the far right quiescent. To make its writ run throughout Germany it would have had to fly in the face of federalist and particularist traditions with roots in local economic interests. (The Bavarian separatist movement might with some justice be considered a premature and badly led movement for national liberation with not enough attention given to peasant interests.) Above all, such a government would have had to overcome scruples about presenting the National Assembly with a set of *faits accomplis*, something a policy of strong controls over the army and limited socialization of the economy would surely have done.

In any case the significance of these liberal and legalistic scruples is open to serious doubt. This is not a matter of judging intentions or probing the recesses of Ebert's mind, at least not entirely. It is also a matter of noticing what actually happened. The decisions to rely on the army and then on the Freikorps, as well as to postpone socialization, did in fact present the National Assembly with *faits accomplis*. Noske showed no scruples about shooting down rebellious workers in defense of liberal democracy. All deviations from a purist and probably impossible conception of liberalism, one that seeks the resolution of all social conflict through discussion and rational persuasion, were deviations to the right. The reformist leaders showed almost no awareness of the consideration that in order to give democracy and constitutional government a chance to survive (even as a necessary prelude to socialism) it might be necessary to do something about the power of those groups and institutions whose behavior had long proved them to be convinced and effective enemies of these principles. That is odd for even the most nominal Marxist.

4. Why was such a policy not attempted?

The analysis has turned up several reasons for concluding that the situation when Ebert took power was not as compelling as it is often made out to be. In order to move toward a more stable liberal democracy, I have suggested, the government would have had to set to work at once to take control of the armed forces, the administrative bureaucracy, and the judiciary, remolding them as instruments loyal to the Republic. It would have had to adopt an economic policy that included a degree of government control over certain areas of heavy industry, with some concessions to the workers over conditions on the shop floor. In doing all that, the government would have had to be willing to forestall the National Assembly by taking a series of essentially irreversible decisions necessary as the foundation for a liberal and democratic version of capitalism. Such a policy might not have succeeded. For the purpose of the present discussion that is not really very relevant. The important point is that it was not even attempted. Why? The search for a satisfactory answer leads back not only to German history but to general principles of historical analysis.

One answer that readily comes to mind is that to do all these things is close to saying that the dominant members of the new government would have had to stop being Social Democratic officials and turn into something else. The objection is an important one and worth pursuing to see where it might lead us.

The policy of military reform and limited socialization of industry suggested here as a possible alternative to what Ebert actually did is not very different from what the moderate wing of the USPD wanted.[14] This is an important fact from two points of view. It demonstrates that the ideas discussed in the previous section were indeed current intellectual coin, that it was not somehow historically "too early" for them to exist. In the second place, we know what happened to the moderate wing of the USPD, how little support they could muster, not only among the workers but in the country as a whole. With this evidence at hand, does not the hypothesis that the SPD leaders could either adopt or execute such a policy turn out to be somehow both sociologically and historically naïve?

Was not the very structure and dynamics of the SPD and its place in German society such that it was almost certain to generate leaders very similar to Ebert and his colleagues? Is it realistic to expect them even to have *thought* of a policy fundamentally different from the one they actually pursued? Is not what Ebert and the others did perfectly explicable as a consequence of historical trends in the German working class: the trade-union and political organizations that sprang up and took root during the prewar years, the experiences that these leaders faced and the imprint of these experiences on the leaders? Ebert's govern-

[14]See Dittmann's report to the Congress of Workers' and Soldiers' Councils on December 16, 1918, in *Kongress*, 19–24, cols. 37–48, where Dittmann, speaking as a member of Ebert's government, clearly took the proposals for military reform and socialization quite seriously.

ment, an astute observer said, tried to run Germany like a big trade union.

From this standpoint the whole story begins to look like a confirmation of the saying that nothing fails like success. The failure of the left opposition and the radical impulse likewise have their historical and sociological causes. But the issue is broader than one of working-class history. Was not the failure of the working class at this point in German history—if we can agree to call it failure—a structural consequence not only of the experience and history of the different parts of the industrial working class but of German society as a whole: the stunted political development of the middle classes, the failure of liberalism, the survival of the bureaucracy and the aristocracy, a complex of forces that generated both war and defeat?

Doubts about this line of reasoning surface at this point, if not earlier. Obviously it is impossible to stop with German society as such. Especially at this point in history it is necessary to consider the German situation in its international setting. But the international setting was important not only in 1918. It was an important element in Bismarck's policies, the failure of liberalism, and all the other aspects of German history just mentioned. With this type of reasoning, before long it becomes necessary to bring in all of world history merely to explain the behavior of some mediocre working-class leaders. Weber's quip about determinism not being a taxicab again comes to mind. This kind of grand historical determinism provides no clear guide on how to assess different forms and degrees of causation. By explaining everything we end up by understanding nothing.

It makes far better sense to adopt the position that not all links in a chain of historical causation are equally solid. Since each link is actually a contest among opposing forces, it would be even better to drop the metaphor of a link and find a better one. A series of switching points with forces pushing in several directions conveys the real situation more accurately. The relative strength of the forces at work also varies from situation to situation. Circumstances are what human beings respond to, but the way they respond makes a difference, sometimes a very big difference. From this standpoint political will and political intelligence can make a powerful difference in the outcome even if, as pointed out earlier, this degree of leverage has its own set of causes. An accurate understanding of these causes can contribute to the effectiveness of political will and intelligence in the future, while an inaccurate one can perpetuate and even increase stultification.

Where does this brief excursion into and retreat from a more general sociological explanation of the failure of a liberal alternative leave us? If there is no need to abandon the conception of suppressed historical alternatives, there still remains the obligation of ascertaining who suppressed this particular one and why. One plausible answer at this stage of the discussion might read: Ebert and his immediate associates did it because they were characteristic products of the SPD at this point in time. The Social Democrats in 1918 had a choice and an opportunity. They neither saw nor took it because their historical experience had rendered them incapable of doing so.

This is hardly a novel conclusion, though it is one more likely to be applied to the alternative of revolutionary socialism than to the liberal variant. It is also not a very satisfactory one. It has to put a great deal of weight on the forces integrating the SPD into the social order. Here it is important to recall that these forces could operate freely for no more than a short period of time, between 1890 and 1914. Before that the party was illegal if tolerated. Even after legalization it was subject to many forms of rejection and suspicion. To weigh these contradictory pulls is not an appropriate task at this point, especially since they have in any case been the focus of a great deal of scholarly attention.[15] It is enough to observe that the sociological impossibility of generating a vigorous and astute leadership with a policy resembling the one just described is far from proven. Ebert's dominance, or that of leaders like him, does not seem altogether inevitable. Somewhere and somehow the German working class might conceivably have thrown more critical leaders to the top even if an Ebert, we can easily agree, was bound to be a powerful contestant.

These considerations indicate that we ought to look again at the struggle within the working class. Perhaps this struggle had a dynamic of its own that was highly significant for the outcome. If the answer (or at least an important part of it) lies somewhere in this area, that implies a shift in the type of causation and explanatory methods brought to bear on the problem. As a first step in pursuing this line of thought it is useful to set the struggle within the German working class in a much wider historical context.

---

[15]The most recent and basic study is Dieter Groh, *Negative Integration und revolutionärer Attentismus*, although it does not offer rich material on ordinary workers. Works closer to our problem include Vernon L. Lidtke, *The Outlawed Party: Social Democracy in Germany, 1878–1890*; Guenther Roth, *The Social Democrats in Imperial Germany*; Gerhard A. Ritter, *Die Arbeiterbewegung im Wilhelminischen Reich*; and Hedwig Wachenheim, *Die deutsche Arbeiterbewegung 1844 bis 1914*. As a piece of analytical history Carl F. Schorske, *German Social Democracy 1905–1917*, is so truly outstanding that it leaves me uneasy for reaching somewhat different conclusions.

In the most acute phases of the long series of conflicts that were part of the establishment of liberal society—the Revolt of the Netherlands, the Puritan Revolution, the French Revolution, and the American Civil War, radical thrusts with a mass following did a great deal of the dirty work of making liberal regimes possible, through the damage they inflicted on the institutions and representatives of the old order. Regicide in the Puritan and French Revolutions was only the most spectacular aspect of this whole complicated process, which, when looked at closely, does not provide much support for the more inspiring myths of either moderates or radicals. There was too much brutality and bloodshed for that. In the German Revolution from 1918 to 1920, though there was plenty of brutality and bloodshed, the popular thrust from below—by this time derived from industrial workers instead of journeymen, artisans, and peasants—accomplished nothing of the sort.

This is all the more surprising since, if the preceding analysis is anywhere near the mark, there was not a great deal of dirty work to be done. The shock of defeat may have done enough. In the euphoria of disaster much of the old order was ready to "stand on the ground of the facts," as many members of the respectable classes put it at the time or, in other words, just cave in.

A combination of reasons, no one of which is sufficient by itself and whose sequence over time is important, may account for the different character and consequence of the radical thrust in the German Revolution. There were only pockets of mass support for revolutionary change, and these pockets did not become sizable until provoked. Furthermore, the pockets were in the wrong places, that is, not in the capital (except for a close call at the beginning), but in the Ruhr and other industrial splotches on the map of Germany. These aspects were due, in great part, to historical trends discussed at some length in this book. It is unlikely that anyone could have done anything about them or used them in a different way.

Other factors in the situation were of a more contingent nature in the sense that they stemmed more from the acts and personalities of individual leaders. One very important one was the relative ease of the transformation from Empire to Republic. If the old elites had chosen to put up more of a fight from the very beginning, quarrels on the left would have been less severe. In this connection it is probably important that the splintering of the left, a characteristic revolutionary process, had already reached an advanced stage during the war and thus well *before* the collapse of the Imperial regime. With the leaders of the industrial working class justifiably suspicious of each other on the basis of wartime experience, and with no obviously powerful enemies to contend with on their right, the quarreling and polarization could gather momentum until they fatally damaged the whole left and rendered powerless those between Ebert and the Spartacists. Hence the old order in this largely abortive revolution was able to rely on the "responsible" moderates to do *its* dirty work, that of suppressing radicalism. Relatively slight changes in timing and tactics in this fluid situation could, I suggest, have brought about quite different consequences. With slightly different changes in leadership and tactics all around, it is not too hard to envisage a situation in which rather less "responsible" moderates than Ebert forced far greater concessions from the old elites by means of threatening that, if the concessions were not granted, revolutionary radicals would take power. Had that happened, not only Germany but the rest of the world might have been spared enormous tragedies.

This form of explanation retains the notion of Ebert's moral responsibility but puts it in a different context in such a way as to make it much less the consequence of long-term trends in German society and much more the result of a specific political dynamic that once started did indeed carry its own momentum. Likewise this form of explanation distributes the blame among Ebert and his rivals. But it is not the moral judgments that are at stake here so much as the accuracy of the analysis. A disproof could take the form of demonstrating more clearly the limitations on the behavior of the various actors imposed by the legacy of the past and by pointing out flaws in the analysis of the dynamic of polarization, showing that the changes in leadership or in tactics suggested were improbable.

Another victim of the constellation of circumstances and actions just mentioned was the socialist alternative. I have not explored it because the impulse behind it was much weaker and the forces arrayed against it much stronger at that particular juncture. There is also the reason that in practice the revolutionary socialist alternative has not turned out to be a humane one. Since the liberal one has scarcely turned out to have an attractive record on that score, it is appropriate to mention briefly some reasons for thinking that the suppression of the socialist alternative too was one of the tragedies of the German revolution. They involve a speculative leap even more dangerous and less controlled by possible evidence than any risked so far. Still it is fair to ask what might have happened in the world at large had a socialist revolution occurred in Germany soon after defeat. Would socialism in *both* Germany and Russia have eased the strains on socialist modernization in such a way as to avert the horrors of Stalinism? Would the Allies have been willing and able to stop its triumphant march?

That too we can never know. Instead we do know what actually happened. In Germany the institutional obstacles to parliamentary and capitalist democracy did in time succumb to the successive onslaughts of Adolf Hitler, the Second World War, and the Soviet occupation of the Junker domains. As these events were taking place, there was no one to ask the millions of victims if the results could be worth the cost.

CHAPTER TWELVE

Repressive aspects of moral outrage: the Nazi example

1. The issue

Until now this study has focused almost entirely on the liberating and humane aspects of popular and lower-class conceptions of injustice. This emphasis has been the fruit of a deliberate choice in posing the questions central to this book: under what circumstances have human beings accepted, or at times chosen, lives marked by misery and oppression? And under what circumstances have people arrived at a moral rejection of misery, embracing forms of behavior new to them in their efforts to resist and change the social order?

But at this point we must consider another set of historical facts that will force us to deepen and darken how we shall ask and try to answer our central questions. The Nazi period in Germany, and more broadly the worldwide twentieth-century phenomenon of fascism, demonstrate beyond any doubt that popular movements can and do have at times a very cruel and repressive component. Indeed, fascism has revived the age-old conservative tradition that sees in demagoguery and the masses generally the central threat to liberty and a humane social order. To disregard this issue would falsify the entire analysis.

Against this revival of a conservative tradition that reaches back at least as far as Plato, modern writers on the left have mounted a defense of popular movements based on a variety of empirical and theoretical considerations. Several studies of popular movements have shown that support for authoritarian trends came mainly from "respectable" and conservative elements in modern industrial societies while working and lower-class movements have generally taken the form of rational responses to legitimate economic grievances.[1] Though these investigations have pointed to some mistaken conceptions of modern mass movements, they have not made the issues vanish. There is no way to deny the plain fact that fascist movements have enjoyed or created enough popular support to make them hideously dangerous. As we shall see, the popular basis of fascism included only a tiny proportion of the industrial workers. Nevertheless among all such movements German fascism almost certainly enjoyed the most enthusiastic and widest range of popular support. For that very reason it was the most dangerous manifestation of a worldwide trend.

A more general and theoretical argument would, if it were acceptable, justify the exclusion of fascist movements from the subject matter of any book that purported to be about moral outrage and the sense of injustice, whether popular or not. From this standpoint, fascist beliefs and sentiments have nothing to do with morality and justice. The social and political objectives of fascism are aggressive and oppressive, the exact opposite of the liberating and humane objectives of revolutionary mass movements. The fact that both resort to violence means nothing, since violence directed against the oppressor by his victim is something very different from the oppressor's violence directed against the victim.

The world we live in would be at least morally much more manageable if this argument were completely convincing and the distinctions it draws in theory more obvious in practice. Unfortunately the violence of the oppressed has often become the new violence of the oppressor, and the moment of transition from one to the other has been both fleeting and hard to detect. The stated purposes and objectives of political movements have no more to do with their actual behavior and consequences than is the case with individuals. The Sermon on the Mount can be a step on the road to the Inquisition, and the dream of a world without oppression become the justification for a terrorist secret police. Though the connection is not necessarily an inevitable one, a denial of the connection will not help human beings to avoid a repetition of such experiences in their continuing search for a world with less cruelty and oppression. Then, too, the

[1]See Michael Paul Rogin, *The Intellectuals and McCarthy;* Richard F. Hamilton, *Affluence and the French Worker in the Fourth Republic.* Maurice Zeitlin, *Revolutionary Politics and the Cuban Working Class,* gives useful evidence on the Cuban workers' generally favorable attitude toward civil liberties during the sixties, while a more somber light appears in Carmelo Mesa-Lago, *Cuba in the 1970s.*

sentiments of moral anger at felt injustices have been a powerful component in mass support of fascist movements. Finally and most significantly, even if this line of argument were convincing, it would reveal nothing about the causes of popular movements with a powerful component of cruelty and aggression.

We have glimpsed some of these frightening possibilities in the discussion in Part One of how and why oppressive forms of authority gain acceptance and why human beings at times inflict suffering on themselves and even seem to enjoy doing it. In this chapter I shall pursue this theme further by using the National Socialist movement in Germany as a paradigm to uncover some of the causes and social roots of this streak of cruelty in popular movements.

2. Who were the Nazis?

The first question to ask about such a movement is what kinds of people joined it. More precisely we want to learn what we can about the circumstances of their daily lives that helped to produce the savage resentment against the world around them so characteristic of the Nazis. Immediate circumstances alone will not adequately explain their feelings and behavior. It will also be necessary to understand as much as possible about the ways people who were or became Nazis saw and interpreted their own circumstances, ways that were in large measure due to the imprint and residue of still earlier experiences. These included the defeat and turmoil of 1918 and subsequent years, the catastrophic inflation of 1923, the deceptive years of prosperity, and then the Great Depression that began in 1929 and was still raging like an epidemic when Adolf Hitler took power in 1933. To these perceptions we will turn later after an attempt to sketch the Nazi movement in its social setting.

For this purpose there happens to exist a pair of sources that so far as I have been able to discover have not been carefully explored, or at least not together, and which taken together reveal much that is useful about the Nazi movement and its appeal to different segments of the German population. One is a study of the social composition of the Nazi party (NSDAP from the German initials for National Socialist German Workers' Party) carried out secretly by the Party leadership in 1935 and which became available after the end of the Second World War.

For one thing this document, the *Parteistatistik*,[2] enables us to see fairly precisely the extent to which the NSDAP was a workers' party and the extent to which it drew on other sources such as those often identified as the lower middle class. The other source is an occupational census taken at the same time as a general census in June, 1933, or about five months after Hitler had come to power (January 30, 1933). At least up to this time the Nazis do not appear to have interfered seriously with the central statistical services responsible for the census which had behind them a long and distinguished bureaucratic tradition. The census is very full and detailed, free of Nazi jargon, written and executed in the manner of previous censuses. Where information is lacking, it is lacking for the same reasons as in earlier censuses. Thus a full list of female occupations fails to list prostitutes, and more significantly it is still impossible to distinguish, as the census itself points out, an industrial tycoon from the owner of a tiny store. Both fall into the old category of "self-employed property owners."

Nevertheless it is possible on the basis of the census and the *Parteistatistik* to determine the proportion of NSDAP members in several of the major occupational groupings in German society at about the time of the Nazi takeover. That in turn reveals a great deal about variations in susceptibility to the Nazi appeal.[3] Since the NSDAP was very much a man's party—94.5 percent of the members were men[4]—and since the target of their recruitment effort was almost exclusively males, I have, where possible, located the number of males in each occupational category.

This aspect has an important bearing on the interpretation of the statistics. Thus the NSDAP has often been characterized as having a special appeal for the white-collar workers spawned by advanced industrial society, due to their insecure position as employees just as dependent on management for their salaries as

[2]*Parteistatistik, Stand 1: Januar 1935,* issued by the Reichsorganisationsleiter of the NSDAP. The three volumes were printed in typescript with a notice that the information contained therein was not to be given to anyone except the inner staff of the Reichsleiter's office without written permission and that the volumes were to be kept in a secure place.

[3]Election returns furnish valuable information too. Their interpretation is often very difficult, however, since the returns refer only to geographical units and it is necessary to make the sociological and political inferences on the basis of whatever may be known about the social character of these units. Furthermore for the issues under discussion here it is more important to identify the sort of people who joined the Party rather than those who voted for it. I have, therefore, set election returns aside. For varying interpretations of these data see Seymour Martin Lipset, *Political Man,* 131–152; Rudolf Heberle, *Social Movements,* 222–237; and Richard Hamilton, *The Bases of National Socialism.*

[4]*Parteistatistik,* I, 41.

workers on the shop floor are for their wages. Yet at the same time white-collar workers do "clean" or nonmanual work in an office that brings them closer to management and encourages a tendency to look down on, as well as fear, the industrial workers. In the 1930s, as today, a large proportion of the white-collar workers were women working as stenographers, typists, etc. If one includes the women, the proportion of NSDAP members among white-collar workers would make it the *least* Nazified of the nonmanual occupations. At first glance the result seems a surprise that contradicts the predominant interpretation of National Socialism, and indeed fascism generally, as a revolt of the petty bourgeoisie. That aspect will require further discussion shortly. All that it is necessary to notice now is that the paradox vanishes when one considers only *male* white-collar workers as the target of NSDAP recruitment. Then this occupational group ranks third in terms of the proportion of Nazi members, but is numerically the largest in Group 1 in Table 13 below, a distinction which is clear in the table, where I have ranked occupational categories by the proportion of Nazi membership in them.

An alert reader may wonder at this point whether the results might be distorted by the phenomenon of opportunism. Might not the Party's social composition have changed very markedly two years after Hitler had come to power? Fortunately the Party leaders were themselves very much concerned about this possibility. At various points the *Parteistatistik* uses the expression *Konjunkturritter* (literally, knights of a rising market) to characterize the opportunists. It is highly likely that this was the Party's main reason for compiling the data, which include information enabling us to assess this objection as of little importance.

The elections of September 14, 1930, were the first ones in which the Nazis increased their vote to the point where there seemed to be a good chance that they might be a winning Party, either legally or illegally. Party members who joined before that date were unlikely to have done so for opportunist reasons. The *Parteistatistik* provides data on their occupational distribution as well as that of the total membership in 1935. A comparison of the percentage of all Party members in different occupations in 1935 with the corresponding distribution of Party stalwarts, as we may label those whose membership antedates 1930, reveals surprisingly little difference. The proportion of industrial workers and agricultural laborers (not distinguishable for this calculation in the NSDAP) rose by 4 percent; that of white-collar workers dropped by 4.6 percent. All other occupational categories show smaller changes.[5]

In interpreting Table 13 the first point to take into account is the fact that as a supernationalist party, the NSDAP tried to recruit Germans from all segments of the population. In their propaganda they made a great deal of the notion of a "people's community" and the obliteration of class alignments. The Party's total membership of 2,493,890 works out to 7.7 percent of the labor force *(Erwerbspersonen),* which was 32,296,496. Of these, slightly less than two-thirds or 20,817,033 were males.[6] Taking males as the main Nazi recruiting target, one can estimate that Party membership represented about 12 percent of the labor force. Hence if Party membership had been distributed equally among all occupations, the Nazi "quota" would have been roughly 12 percent in each of them.

Instead Table 13 breaks down naturally into three types of occupations. Group 1 contains mainly a series of lower-middle-class occupations, a term to be analyzed more carefully in a moment. In this series the NSDAP's power of attraction varied from a shade over their "quota" to more than three times this amount. Group 2 contains manual workers in the city and the countryside. For these the NSDAP appeal dropped off to between two-thirds and one-half of their "quota." The members of Group 3 were essentially outside the economy. For these the Nazi appeal was minimal. Let us now look more closely at each segment in turn.

In Group 1 we find a large contingent of small property owners facing difficulties in disposing of their wares in the market. There are the small retail merchants in rank 2 who faced competition from the mail-order houses. As rural property owners many peasants faced problems of mortgage debt, as well as in marketing their produce. The self-employed craftsmen, such as carpenters, shoemakers, and watchmakers, possessed painfully acquired skills for which the market somehow seemed to provide no demand in a world that was out of joint. Taken together, these owners of limited property and manual skills

[5]See *Parteistatistik,* I, table on p. 70. Since the number of Party stalwarts was so small as to have yielded only fractions of a percent in most cases, I have used the 1935 membership figures for comparison with the census. While the Nazi table also provides data on less stalwart members who joined between September 15, 1930, and January 30, 1933, and after January 30, 1933, we can afford to disregard these data. Hence if we ignore any difference of less than 5 percent, a procedure advisable due to other probable sources of error as well, we can use Table 13 as a first approximation toward an assessment of the Nazis' popular appeal to different occupational groupings.

[6]Census figures are in SDR, Band 453, Heft 2, 6.

Table 13.

Selected Occupational Groups Ranked by Proportion of NSDAP Members, Based on 1935 Party Figures and Official Census Reports

(in thousands)

Occupation	No. of NSDAP Members in		Total No. in Occupation		No. of Males in		Unemployment rate for				Proportion of Nazis to		
							Males		Occup.		Males		Occup.
	Sub-group	Group	Sub-group	Group	Sub-group	Group	Sub-group	Group	Sub-group	Group	Sub-group	Group	Group
GROUP 1													
1. Teachers		84		307		212						.40	
2. Self-employed small merchants		188		1000 (est.)		750 (est.)						.25	
3. White-collar employees (total) of which		484		3916		2385		.24		.22		.20	
a) technical & others	197		1203		817		.23		.20		.24		
b) sales, office	287		2713		1568		.24		.21		.18		
4. Students		34		334		187						.18	
5. Officials		223		1464		1336						.17	
6. Self-employed craftsmen		208		1279									.16
7. Peasants		255		2005		1805				varied from .03 to .61		.14	
8. Free professions		79		716		622						.13	
GROUP 2													
9. Workers in industry & crafts (total) of which		662		9939		7982		.42		.39		.08	
a) skilled metal	155		9989		9156					.39		.07	

c) unskilled	162									
d) miners	22									
10. Agricultural laborers	94	446	446	446	2530	1672	.37	.15	.12	.05
GROUP 3										
11. Rentiers & pensioners	38	5822								.06
12. Housewives	65	9901		2786					.01	.006

SOURCES: From the Nazi *Parteistatistik*, I, 55, 68, 70, 72, one can compute separate figures for most occupational groups, although this source lumps together members within a category (see *Arbeiter*), concealing some social aspects. The main data for the number of persons in occupational categories come from *Statistik des Deutschen Reichs* (SDR), Bd., 453, Heft 2, 22–24, 52; on unemployment *ibid.*, 9, 12–13, 15, 25–26. Percentages for unemployment and proportion of Nazis in occupations are my calculations. In addition for specific occupations I have used SDR, Bde. 458, 459, and 461; also *Statistisches Jahrbuch für das Deutsche Reich* (1934); and *Das Grosse Brockhaus* (15th ed.) for definitions of occupational groups. Sources used for each group in Table 13 are listed below.

(1) *Teachers*: SDR, Bd. 453, Heft 2, 23, where I totaled persons in census categories Nos. 356–360.

(2) *Self-employed small merchants*: SDR, Bd. 458, 35, where I totaled persons in categories Wz 414, 442, 411, 451, amounting to 1,133,000 persons. To exclude owners of large department stores, etc., I have simply reduced this total to 1,000,000. This sum is probably low, since bakeries, tailoring shops, etc., which produce as well as sell goods occur elsewhere in the census as self-employed craftsmen (SDR, Bd. 453, Heft 2, 17). Since ¾ of the small merchants were males, for males alone I offer an estimate of 750,000 (see *ibid.*, 52).

(3) *White-collar workers*: SDR, Bd. 453, Heft 2, 52, where I totaled nonmanagerial employees in categories W.-Abt. 2/3, 4, and 5. Agricultural and domestic employees are excluded.

(4) *Students*: *Statistisches Jahrbuch* (1934), 529–535, where I have totaled persons from the 10th through 12th years of primary school, from middle schools, and universities.

(5) *Officials*: SDR, Bd. 453, Heft 2, 14–15, 52.

(6) *Self-employed craftsmen*: SDR, Bd. 453, Heft 2, 16, 17.

(7) *Peasants*: the figure for peasants in the general population given by the *Parteistatistik*, I, 53, is 6,699,000, a total that is highly inflated, most probably by including working family members; cf. SDR, Bd. 453, Heft 2, 52. One can estimate a more realistic figure for peasants who own and/or work the land by using the definition of peasants as those working between 2 and 100 hectares of land, with 90 percent of these owner-operators. See SDR, Bd. 459, Heft 1, 54, 55. In this range another census volume reports a total of 2,005,000 *Inhaber* or holders, who might be owners, renters, or hold by still other forms of tenure. See SDR, Bd. 461, Heft 1, 12. If then we consider as peasant proprietors 90 percent of these *Inhaber*, we arrive at a total of 1,805,000—or 27 percent of the Nazi figure.

(8) *Free professions*: the German definition of *freie Berufe* is broader than that usual in English; for a definition I have used *Der Grosse Brockhaus* (15th edition), Vol. 7, 100, *s.v.* "Geistesarbeiter," and Vol. 6, 563, *s.v.* "Freie Berufe." On that basis I have added up census categories nos. 167, 171, 271, 361–365, 370, 373, 381, 383–384 (engineers and technicians, chemists, architects and master builders, editors and writers, artists, lawyers, patent lawyers, legal consultants, singers and voice teachers, actors, physicians, dental surgeons, dentists, and dental technicians), in SDR, Bd. 453, Heft 2, 22–24.

(9) *Workers*: SDR, Bd. 453, Heft 2, 52. In *ibid.*, 22, for skilled metalworkers I have totaled males from census categories 141–166, deducting owners as well as women. Miners: *ibid.*, 22, where no women appear, although some were of course employed as aboveground workers.

(10) *Agricultural laborers*: *ibid.*, 52; see also 22, 12, 19.

(11) *Rentiers and pensioners*: SDR, Bd. 453, Heft 2, 5, 6.

(12) *Housewives*: SDR, Bd. 453, Heft 2, 5, 6.

constitute what is widely known as the old middle class, the historical precipitate of an earlier phase of capitalism. It is too much to claim that they were doomed to extinction under advanced capitalism. But in depression-ridden Germany they were indeed in trouble.

The new middle class was the offspring of the rise of big government and big industry. Its main elements were salaried employees and administrators in business and government. Teachers, the occupation with the highest proportion of NSDAP members, belong in this category. Many of the Party members were probably elementary-school teachers. There are signs of a connection here between a limited degree of education, that is, a mental skill acquired with some effort and whose results were not readily marketable, and the Party's power of attraction. Among the white-collar employees the proportion of NSDAP members in the technical sector was substantially higher than in the sales and office sector, even though the unemployment rates were almost identical. The same is true of the professions. As a German census category the term *freie Berufe* or free professions included segments of both the old middle class, such as lawyers and doctors, and the new, such as engineers and a variety of technicians. It was a heterogeneous group united by the necessity to find both a market outlet and some degree of social approval for acquired skills. The rate of failure to find such an outlet, as measured by the unemployment statistics, varied enormously from one profession to another. It was 16 percent for chemists, 33 percent for engineers and for technicians in metalworking, 61 percent for actors, and less than 3 percent for physicians. Thus the overall proportion of NSDAP members, 13 percent or approximately the "quota" in this sector, must conceal wide variations from one profession to another.

All in all, the social characteristics of Group 1 confirm the familiar if intermittently challenged thesis that the NSDAP appealed most strongly to the lower middle classes. The resentments that according to this evidence nourished the Nazi movement were those of the "little man" angry at the injustices of a social order that threatened or failed to reward the virtues of hard work and self-denial as these personal efforts became crystallized in the merchant's store, the peasant's plot, the craftsman's manual skill, the white-collar job, and the technician's and journalist's gifts. Here was one possible outcome of the labor theory of value.

Though there is a distinct drop in the proportion of Nazis in Group 2, composed of manual workers, it is not enough to

sustain the thesis that *industrial* workers, despite the truly catastrophic rate of unemployment, were immune to the Nazi appeal. With 12 percent (actually 11.7) as their "quota" the NSDAP
apparently managed, with an 8 percent recruitment rate, to
attract something like two-thirds of their expected "quota" from
the industrial workers. Even allowing for the unreliability of the
statistics and an uncertain portion of nominal members, their
success here represents an effective and sinister performance.
The skilled metalworkers, the reader may recall, were a major
source of the militant and even revolutionary impulse in 1918.
Though the data show that they had not swung over to Nazism in
any large number even by 1935, the Nazis were able to make
inroads here up to more than half their "quota." The rate among
the miners, the closest we can come to a segment of the "pure"
industrial proletariat with the available data, turns out, on the
other hand, to be the lowest of any group of manual workers.

The members of Group 3 share the common characteristic of
being in a status that is marginal to or outside the economy and to
a considerable extent the rest of society's institutions. It was also
marginal and outside in a sense different from unemployment,
though for pensioners the economic effect must have been the
same in many cases, if not more hopeless. A housewife could of
course take a job *if* she could find one at a time of disastrous
unemployment. Though both recipients of pensions and
housewives had socially acceptable statuses, many must have
been economically trapped and strapped. "Objective" considerations could easily lead to the conclusion that these groups too
were full of rather hopeless resentment. If that is so, and I rather
think it is, it must have been a very different form of resentment
from that found in Group 1. Where the persons in Group 1
contributed at least their "quota" of Nazi members, this form of
marginal resentment served to produce only one-twelfth of the
"quota" among male rentiers and pensioners and even less
among housewives.

The differences between the groups may be due to frustrated
or unrewarded effort. There have been several occasions to draw
attention to the resentment that hard work without reward can
produce. All of the people in Group 1 were in one way or another
subject to this type of frustrating experience. Those in Group 3,
on the other hand, were in social positions freeing them from
the obligation to work. The workers in Group 2 were in still a
different situation. Huge numbers of them could not *find* work.

To the extent that there is any central explanatory key to the
fascist form of resentment that these data suggest, it seems to lie

407

in the different forms of moral outrage that are generated by frustrating human beings able and willing to work very hard. A vigorous work ethic may be the necessary historical precursor for this kind of a cruel and reactionary popular movement. It is a clue worth pursuing.[7]

How about the social makeup of the NSDAP itself? As a highly organized and disciplined party, both the core and the inspiration for the kind of resentment and moral outrage under discussion, it had a life of its own. This aspect I will discuss only tangentially as we see its effect on ordinary members. And at this point we are interested only in what we can learn from statistical sources about what kinds of people they were. Table 14 presents the membership categorized in accord with certain familiar yet useful contemporary social distinctions. One is that between manual and nonmanual labor. Within the category of nonmanual labor there is the further distinction between white-collar employees performing routine tasks along with the retail shopowner, on the one hand, and larger property owners,[8] doctors, lawyers, administrators and government officials, on the other hand. Persons in this stratum generally exercise considerable control and influence over the lives of other people. For the sake of convenience we can refer to these three major groupings as working class, lower middle class, and upper middle class, although in the table I prefer to use the more neutral term social category, a device that permits a variety of combinations for making estimates of the Party's composition in terms of social class.

With the available data there is no great difficulty in distinguishing the manual workers and some of the major components of the lower middle class. But there are greater difficulties in specifying what proportion of the NSDAP came from the upper middle class. Where, for example, should one place the teachers? In order to make possible both a minimum as well as a maximum estimate of the lower-middle-class component in the NSDAP I have put all possible members of the upper middle class in the "Mixed" category No. 4. But first let us take a more general look at the results.

---

[7]For Japan the suggestion makes good sense on the basis of my limited information. Italian fascism may have been a mixture of the frustrated work ethic and an attempt to impose a work ethic. In this Mediterranean culture "getting the trains to run on time" had some of the aspects of what Marxists regard as the disciplining of the labor force, an historical process carried out in Russia by the Communist Party. There is a fascinating field for serious research here.

[8]These are not identifiable either in census statistics or those provided by the NSDAP. I have refrained from even guessing at their proportion in the Party since our primary concern is with popular and plebeian movements.

Table 14.

Social Composition of NSDAP in 1935   *(in thousands)*

Occupations	No. of Members in		Percent of Total NSDAP Membership in	
	Occupation	Social Category	Occupation	Social Category
1. *Manual*				
Workers in industry and mines	662		26.5	
Agricultural laborers	94		3.8	
Peasants (*Erbhofbauern* & others)	255		10.2	
Total		1011		40.5
2. *Manual, lower middle class*				
Self-employed craftsmen	208	208	8.3	8.3
3. *Non-manual, lower middle class*				
White-collar employees	484		19.4	
Self-employed small merchants	188		7.5	
Total		672		26.9
4. *Mixed lower middle to upper middle class*				
Officials	223		8.9	
Teachers	84		3.3	
Free professions	79		3.2	
Total		387		15.5
5. *Miscellaneous*	80	80	3.2	3.2
6. *No occupation*				
Rentiers, pensioners	38		1.5	
Housewives	65		2.6	
Students	34		1.3	
Total		136		5.5
Grand total (1 to 6)	2494	2494	100	100

SOURCE: *Parteistatistik*, I, 55, 63, 64, 68, 70.
NOTE: Discrepancies are due to rounding.

In a rough and preliminary sense the social composition of the NSDAP in Table 14 presents a pattern that is a mirror image of that revealed by the rank-ordering of Nazified occupations presented in Table 13. Adding together those who worked with their hands in categories 1 and 2 yields 1,219,000 representing

48.8 percent, or nearly half, of the Party membership. Those who are clearly lower middle class, category 3, come to a little over a quarter or 26.9 percent. By this interpretation the NSDAP consisted mainly of people for whom the Party exerted a minimal attraction. In other words, the weakest area of the Nazi magnetic field attracted the most members due to the specific demographic structure of German society in which manual workers outnumbered white-collar workers. In 1933 white-collar workers and officials made up 17.1 percent of the work force, and workers (including here agricultural laborers), 46.3 percent.[9] In a moment I shall present a different interpretation. But it is necessary to agree that the Party's appeal did effectively cross class lines and that it was a popular or populist party made up mainly of "little people." Well over three-quarters of its membership belonged to this fluid yet still meaningful category.

Looking more closely at Table 14, we can see that the workers in industry and mining with 26.5 percent of the NSDAP membership and the most clearly lower-middle-class elements, in category 3, with 26.9 percent constituted together slightly more than half (53.4 percent) of the membership. But it is obvious that category 3 represents too restricted a conception of the lower middle class. Others are tucked away in other categories. How many is a matter of judgment. To the 26.9 percent in category 3 I propose adding (1) all the self-employed craftsmen in category 2, or 8.3 percent; (2) from category 4 a little more than half, or 8 percent; and (3) from those without occupation in category 6 another 2 percent. The total of these still comes to less than half (45.2 percent) of the NSDAP.

In this manner we come to the somewhat surprising conclusion that the main organizational expression of lower-middle-class resentments probably drew no more than half of its membership from this stratum. On the other hand, this was the largest group in the Party, with the industrial workers making up slightly more than a quarter. The finding helps to explain the flexibility of Nazi strategy. That, however, is hardly its main meaning. Neither democratic nor authoritarian political movements are likely or able to pursue consistently the aims of those whose interests and aspirations they claim to embody. Instead, the finding suggests that in the search for the main structural setting and contours of National Socialism we have pushed a certain form of inquiry as far as it can go and still yield results. No amount of ingenuity in the manipulation of census data and

[9]SDR, Band 453, Heft 2, p. 7.

figures for Party membership can reveal how people actually felt and behaved: their fears, angers, and explanations of the world. To force German fascism into the sociological straitjacket of mere lower-middle-class resentment would be misleading and in the end reveal nothing. Structural data can provide indispensable information about what kinds of people were likely to have certain feelings, how many such people there may have been at certain points in time, and their place in a complicated and changing web of social relationships. But that is not enough. For what human beings felt as injustice and what they tried to do about their particular conception of injustice it is necessary to turn to quite different kinds of evidence.

3. Forms and sources of Nazi moral outrage

The fact that the NSDAP contained so many industrial or at least urban workers was a distinct political advantage. Even if the Party's appeal was most effective among the lower middle classes, this fact gave some color of truth to their claim to speak and act for all Germans, or better, all patriotic Germans. After they had gained power, their policies of conquest and plunder did in fact bring benefits to most Germans—as long as it was successful. Rearmament ended the scourge of unemployment and helped to generate profits for business. After the war there were a good many Germans who remarked bitterly that Hitler had made only one mistake: he lost the war. It is necessary to remember too that in any country a nationalist appeal has some basis in fact, that amid the turmoil of the last years of the Republic there was a sense in which all Germans shared a common historical legacy and were in the same boat because they were the inhabitants of the same state.

Even if with widely varying degrees of success, therefore, the Nazis could and did appeal to practically all strata of the population. Where they succeeded, they evidently managed to find resonances among individuals with a certain set of shared experiences and a certain cast of mind, or at least a set of prior inclinations. Both the experiences and the way of interpreting them were themselves historical and social products which we must now investigate. For this purpose the autobiographical

411

accounts of rank-and-file Nazis, collected by Theodore Abel in 1934, provide valuable information.[10]

One striking feature in the autobiographies is the conventional morality and outlook on life that these individuals report as the consequence of their upbringing. There is a recurring stress on hard work, honesty, loyal obedience to duly constituted authority,[11] patriotism, and the virtues of being a good family man as the recipe for a contented and useful life. The autobiographies generally describe parents in an idealized fashion along these lines, even in the case of working-class families where the father was a Social Democrat. In such instances, however, there may be signs of differences between the mother and father over religion. While the atmosphere sounds strict, there is room for the indulgence of boyish pranks and exuberance. This indulgence is consistent with the strict demarcation of sex roles and the emphasis on the virtues of manliness, also very noticeable in the accounts.

This morality is common to men from quite different occupational backgrounds and does not appear to be specific to any particular social class. It represents the precipitate of several converging historical influences. At points there are strong echoes of the simple moral earnestness that was a conspicuous current among the artisans as far back as 1848, without, however, the strong religious overtones. It is also easy to recognize this whole complex of virtues as the ideals of early competitive capitalism.

That institutional complex, on the other hand, never took firm hold in Germany: Concurrenz (competition), as we know, was evil. Hence, as will become clearer later, there are contradictions: the individual is expected to make his own way in life through his own exertions but somehow not in competition with others. Then there are several detectable influences that are much more recent and come down to indoctrination by the upper classes n patriotism and obedience. The educational system, the army, and daily experiences of contact with those in authority evidently did their work well upon a substantial portion of the underlying population. The whole complex is conventional, representing the imprint of specific historical experiences and an amalgam of these. It is petty bourgeois rather than bourgeois (and hardly

---

[10]See Abel, *The Nazi Movement: Why Hitler Came to Power*. For a statistical analysis of the Abel data see Peter H. Merkl, *Political Violence under the Swastika: 581 Early Nazis*.

[11]Merkl, *Political Violence*, 489–491, 691, however, reports and discusses the 76 cases out of 581 who displayed a generalized hostility toward all authority.

patrician: there is no sense of being accustomed to receive deference) with a strong overlay of both bureaucratic and even feudal features. The bureaucratic ones take the form of emphasis on the importance of performing a limited task in a disciplined manner; the feudal ones appear as a sense of personal honor and diffuse loyalty to superiors. The whole combination as such is specifically German.[12] Yet it would be an error to overemphasize the strictly German aspects. Fascism, I have argued elsewhere, was a worldwide historical phenomenon, even if it reached its most virulently destructive form in Germany. Generally similar causes, including a similar morality and outlook on life, existed as dominant or subordinate trends in many parts of the globe.[13]

Equipped with this way of perceiving and judging the world, a way that was quite widespread but by no means universal in Germany after 1918, these young men underwent a series of disillusioning and threatening experiences. For many a soldier the return to the revolutionary homeland of 1918 was a bitter shock and challenge to which he responded in punitive fashion in the manner reported by this one:

> Troops were once again returning to the Fatherland, yet a disgusting sight met their eyes. Beardless boys, dissolute deserters and whores tore off the shoulder bands of our front-line fighters and spat upon their field gray uniforms. At the same time they muttered something about liberty, equality, and fraternity. Poor, deluded people! Was this liberty and fraternity? People who never saw a battle field, who had never heard the whine of a bullet, openly insulted men who through four and a half years had defied the world in arms, who had risked their lives in innumerable battles, with the sole desire to guard the country against this horror.
>
> For the first time I began to feel a burning hatred for this human scum that trod everything pure and clean underfoot.[14]

Others who were also to become Nazis referred to similar experiences as a "slap in the face of every decent German," a situation where "heroism had become cowardice, truth a lie, loyalty was rewarded by dastardliness." One who was too young to fight told about wearing the monarchist red, white, and black cockade

---

[12]For an excellent historical study of the interplay of feudal and bureaucratic features see Hans Rosenberg, *Bureaucracy, Aristocracy and Autocracy: The Prussian Experience, 1660–1815.* Rosenberg shows that forms of blind and amoral obedience, which some writers regard as the product of advanced industrial society, appeared in full bloom in Germany long before the industrial revolution.

[13]See *Social Origins of Dictatorship and Democracy,* chap. 8.

[14]Abel, *Nazi Movement,* 24.

as a choir student while walking on the streets of Berlin on the day of the revolution. Two men approached him, tore the cap from his head, and boxed his ears. "I went on in tears," he continued in his account, "not so much because I had lost my cockade, but because those fellows had been mean enough to attack a child. The bitter resentment of that moment made a lasting impression on me."[15]

Even sharper shocks struck many a man who discovered that the traditional virtues of thrift and hard work—or at least their attempts to put these virtues into practice—were no route to contentment and economic security in postwar Germany. Many of the accounts report either the fact of going downhill in the world or painful fears at the prospect. What aroused the most acute resentment was that other people, especially Jews, seemed to succeed without any investment of hard work, and indeed in ways that struck these Nazis as parasitic. In this way the widespread taboo on the dog in the manger discussed in an earlier chapter makes its reappearance in an ominous fashion. So does resentment at effort without reward. Here is a characteristic tale:

My most urgent task in 1919 was to make my business a going concern once more. This was the more difficult since throughout the long years of the war no one had had the time to concern himself with it.

After much effort I finally succeeded in getting some orders. All my hopes, however, were dashed. The inflation put an end to my endeavours. . . . Hunger and privation once more held sway in my home. I cursed the government that sanctioned such misery. For I was convinced at the time that the inflation was not necessary on the scale on which it had been carried out. But it had served its purpose: the middle class, which still had some funds, and which had steadily opposed Marxism without actually combating it, was completely wiped out.

[This man goes on to report that he declined the invitation of friends to join one of the numerous reactionary movements of the day] since, there too I should have been an outsider. The only way out of our misery was to find a man who might succeed in uniting all Germans who still had some regard for honor.[16]

The inflation that reached astronomical proportions in 1923 and wiped out cash savings was for many a traumatic experience. Here is the way a man who wandered from job to job to become a government clerk saw the situation in recollection:

[15] Abel, *Nazi Movement*, 25–27.
[16] Abel, *Nazi Movement*, 122.

Momentarily there was the false boom of the inflation, the greatest swindle ever perpetrated on a decent, thrifty people. The world turned upside down. Diligence was penalized, while profiteers waxed rich. Public houses stocked with strumpets sprang up everywhere. All sluices of indecency were thrown wide open. The front-line fighter and the decent part of the population waged a hopeless battle against this defilement. Parliamentarianism celebrated veritable orgies. Some thirty-five parties arose to confuse the people, a very Witches' Sabbath. Devoid of political training, sick of body and soul, the German people reeled giddily after the different will o' the wisps.[17]

Like many others this man perceived an economic issue in moral terms and reacted by sensing an immoral conspiracy that formed a source of pollution that would have to be rooted out. This is an age-old reaction to economic disaster. It was a reaction too that included hostility to the dominant classes, not by any means just the newly rich, but also the traditional ruling classes because of their apparent aloofness, security, and unwillingness to help. Together with anticapitalist sentiments this current of class hostility gave the Nazi movement its radical veneer prior to the seizure of power.

In one of the autobiographies reproduced in full, the son of a mason recalls the bitter impression left from contact with the upper classes during his school years:

We went to school barefoot. Though our clothes were clean and whole, the sons of middle-class families appeared with collars and shoes. Only too often I was made to feel that this gave them an advantage, though such superiority was not justified by achievements or capacities.[18]

When he had grown up, he

. . . saw only too often the honest working man being exploited by the supporters of capitalism. I felt most bitter about the way the puffed-up bourgeois passed by the fellow German, who was only a workman with matter of fact gestures. My own view of life and my own observations of life led me to see that the class struggle was not a condition brought about by the working group. The middle class created the prerequisites for it, while on the other side false prophets found it only too easy to drive the wedge so fatefully amid the German people.[19]

[17]Abel, *Nazi Movement*, 123–124.

[18]Abel, *Nazi Movement*, 247.

[19]Abel, *Nazi Movement*, 248.

After a series of ups and downs, and the total loss of his young wife's inheritance in the inflation, this man enlisted in the SS. There he claims to have found what he had been looking for—in effect a resurrection of the traditional virtues—"the expression of steadfastness, manliness, honesty, simplicity, modesty." In the last lines of the autobiography he refers to the Blood Purge of 1934, the end of Nazi "radicalism," when Hitler ordered the SS to execute Roehm, the leader of the brownshirted SA, and other potential rivals. "We saw June 30, 1934 coming. Again destiny has compressed the consciousness of life in one final formula: The Leader is calling, gun in hand. And everything else falls away."[20]

In its mixture of class resentment and abdication of reason, masquerading as manliness that culminates in murder, this career epitomizes the radical component in National Socialism and fascism generally. Other accounts provide variations and amplifications on similar themes. Another speaks in more stilted and stereotyped terms of Junkers who used their whips on working men around the manor, the businessman cutting coupons and making "this terrestrial existence as pleasant as possible for his 'lady' and his spoiled only child," of the contempt of big business for the workers, to conclude with a burst of rhetoric about the people's community that should put an end to such hostilities.[21]

One last account worth mentioning briefly describes the disenchantment of a white-collar worker with the *Deutschnationale Volkspartei*, a reactionary monarchist Party that drew its support from Junkers and big industry. Their solution to the problem of unemployment, as this man saw it, was general improvement in economic conditions to absorb the unemployed. This policy, as he saw, implied

... years of bayonet rule to deal with the desperation bound to follow. How different from this was the daring proposition that sprang from Hitler's warm sympathetic heart! His idea was not to use the resources of the state to help industrialists and land owners, but to take advantage of them immediately to relieve the misery of millions of unemployed Germans![22]

[20]Abel, *Nazi Movement*, 259, 262.

[21]Abel, *Nazi Movement*, 140–141.

[22]Abel, *Nazi Movement*, 129.

The remark reveals another side of the emotional currents among the less fortunate classes: a desire to have the benefits of revolution without the costs in conflict and suffering. This hope the Nazis shared with many forms of statist liberalism, from Franklin Roosevelt onward. But there is a significant difference. Even the statist version of liberalism presupposes the continuation of group conflict whereas the Nazis' view looked forward to the dissolution of conflict within the boundaries of the "people's community" as part of an intensified struggle on an international scale with liberalism and Marxism.

By this point it is, I hope, clear enough that the Nazis did draw their popular support from people who felt morally outraged by the social order around them.[23] They felt themselves to be the persecuted victims of the liberal capitalist Republic of Weimar. If anything, this sense of persecution increased for those who took the step of joining the Nazi Party. According to Abel, several hundred National Socialists were stoned, shot, or knifed to death in street brawls with organized leftist groups between 1930 and 1932.[24] Though the courts were generally very lenient with Nazi and other rightists who resorted to violence, local police forces did at times crack down severely on the Storm Troopers.[25] The effect of physical persecution was merely to intensify loyalty to Hitler and the cause.

Rank-and-file party members evidently perceived and explained the shocks they received at the hands of a society in upheaval in very simplified moral terms. Since most saw themselves as strictly moral and hard-working, the catastrophes and threats of catastrophe in their own lives *had* to come from an

---

[23]Merkl's statistical study concludes that for a majority of Abel's respondents the experiences of comradeship in the trenches, defeat, the revolution, exposure to foreign occupation and the situation in border areas appear to have been the decisive precipitating factors in their adhesion to Nazism. To this he adds as a distinct and crucial factor the political youth revolt of a younger generation "which gave the war-motivated movement the staying power to triumph in 1933." See *Political Violence*, 711. For this younger generation, comradeship in struggle, embodied in the notion of the *Volksgemeinschaft*, appears to have been important in its own right. Though the youngest of this contingent do not appear to have been directly affected by the depression, as youngsters they did witness what the older generation experienced more directly. On these aspects see *Political Violence*, 413, 420, 423–424, 443.

[24]*Nazi Movement*, 105.

[25]For some examples as seen by the Nazis, see Abel, *Nazi Movement*, 95–110. Sometimes the tone of the accounts raises the suspicion that their authors were emphasizing their virtues as old-time fighters for Hitler against others who had sought and found soft berths, a burning issue at the time of the Blood Purge, which occurred when the autobiographies were being collected. Hence the theme of loyalty steeled through struggle may be overemphasized. That this syndrome existed is, on the other hand, quite clear.

external source that was evil. If effort did not lead to reward in the way traditionally expected, something must be radically wrong and immoral. (At other times and places human beings can be trained and have been trained not to expect much reward.) This something was partly conspiracy and partly a radical defect in the whole social order. Rank-and-file Nazis did generalize. If anything, they generalized too much. There is practically no concrete social and economic analysis in their popular diagnosis of the social order. Instead there was a pervading sense of evil and pollution. Root out the pollution in a manly "old-fashioned" way, and the unpolluted could live happily every afterward in a "people's community." Such were the essential elements in this popular diagnosis and remedy for suffering.[26]

The Nazi conception of people's community[27] was a response to quite varied experiences and frustrations. The main content of the notion has its roots in an idealized recollection of life in the trenches, contrasted with the disappointments of civilian existence. Life in the trenches purportedly was one of comradeship and mutual support, not one of anonymity and cutthroat individualist competition. By a somewhat contradictory twist of recollection a man in the trenches was judged, they thought, for what he really was and what he could do. Thus performance alone counted, as it does in competitive situations. But no "external" qualities supposedly entered in: a man was what he was, independently of education and social background. And the ties formed between men stripped to their essentials in the face of shared danger were felt to be somehow deeper and more

---

[26]In *Mein Kampf* Hitler frequently asserted that the struggle would have to continue on an international scale after the NSDAP had won power in Germany. But in the long quotations from the Abel autobiographies there is very little talk about a coming international struggle. To me the anti-Semitic motif also seemed muted in comparison with Hitler's official propaganda. Abel, *Nazi Movement*, 164 and note 14, reports that 60 percent of the respondents made no reference to show that they held anti-Semitic attitudes, which might, however, have been held tacitly, in varying degrees, by all who joined the NSDAP. Using the same autobiographies, Merkl, *Political Violence*, 499, found only 25 percent with no evidence of anti-Semitism. Without access to the documents we must question the reliability of quantitative measures like these, where honest men's results show such a huge discrepancy. One must, therefore, treat with reserve one of Merkl's suggestive findings: that those who reveal physical aggressiveness show the least verbal prejudice (466, 489). This inverse relationship, Merkl proposes, may reflect an equivalence in psychological function between violent action and symbolically violent speech. As we know, however, the consequences for other people are very different. Furthermore, violent language and fantasies may be a psychological preparation for destructive behavior.

[27]For a somewhat different treatment of this issue see Merkl, *Political Violence*, 96–118. We agree on essentials: that it was a key concept for Party members (101), derived in large measure from the experience of comradeship in the trenches (98).

genuine. In this sense the notion of community was an egalitarian weapon against the class distinctions—new and old—that rankled and festered under the Weimar Republic. Life was to be a permanent camping trip *after* the arrival of *Der Tag*.

This utopia appears mainly as a camping trip for men only, as was life in the trenches. With its overtones of ritual and rebirth, and equality in the face of a hostile environment, the people's community, like the Nazi Party itself, shows significant resemblances to the *Männerbünde*, organizations of adult males which anthropologists have found in many nonliterate societies.

But it is hardly necessary to go that far afield in order to recognize in the conception of people's community the reflection of pains and desires that occur in many other societies including our own, and that may indeed be nearly pan-human. In an idealized and not very veiled form the people's community amounts to an imaginary return to the security of the family, of childhood if not even the womb. One obvious source of this fantasy is fear of the atomizing and selfish tendencies (noticeable in reports of concentration camps) that can set in whenever customary goods and services become scarce and individuals start to scramble for them at each other's expense. The forceful reassertion of the social bond is one common and more or less natural defense against this tendency. Because the capitalist order is an attempt to emphasize and institutionalize competition, all its critics have stressed some conception of community or tried to invent a new one. In the ideal community all the quarrels, pains, and uncertainty that are a part of life in every society about which we have records will, it is hoped, vanish to be replaced by the comradeship of affectionate, trusting relationships. This is an ancient and probably perpetual human dream.[28]

Neither the Nazis nor the modern romantic advocates of community show much awareness that in real communities,[29] as they have existed in peasant villages or most nonliterate societies, there are suffocating sanctions against deviance from the community's norms. In practice these small groupings are dominated by the *coq du paroisse*, or a petty oligarchy. Mrs. Grundy in male or female form is usually the real power behind the throne in what amounts to a petty autocracy where there is hardly any refuge from the disapproving eye of the upholders of tradition.

[28]For an instructive general study see Roger Mucchielli, *Le Mythe de la cité idéale*.

[29]We may define community as a relatively autonomous group of people small enough for all individuals to know each other well but large enough to take care of most of the group's economic needs with a simple division of labor.

It is no place for those who really "want to do their own thing," another tendency that is pan-human if it means simply to satisfy one's own desires whenever and however they occur. That too is, of course, ultimately impossible. But those who seek to change the frequently indefensible barriers between human beings in modern society would do well to consider the possibility that by and large the destruction of community may be the most valuable achievement of modern industrial civilization.

4. "Right" and "left" radicalism: similarities and differences

With the discussion of community we have already broached the issue of similarities and differences between the Nazi variant of radicalism and other forms commonly if not universally regarded as left liberating versions. On this score the most important observation, and one that should be made at the outset, is that National Socialism, like other variants of fascism, soon turned out in practice to be pseudo-radical. Populist and radical elements in the original fascist program either dropped out or receded into the background as the movement began to take political responsibility seriously. Though the reasons varied from case to case, the main one was the necessity of coming to terms with the industrialists and higher military leaders for a policy of conquest and expansion. Behind that necessity in turn lay the impossibility of reorganizing the society, with or without revolutionary violence, along peaceful and constructive lines. Of that fascism was incapable. More accurately, fascists were just not interested in a humane social order. For them that was an effeminate and contemptible goal.

If fascism was structually incapable of contributing to anything that could be called human liberation, if the cruel and repressive traits were both obvious and predominant from the very beginning, there may seem to be no reason at all to seek for any comparison with leftist movements. The issue just vanishes. But is that really true? It would be true only if both revolutionary movements and liberal regimes had not also developed savagely repressive characteristics. Yet advances have occurred in the course of human history and some of them are traceable to revolutions—unless one is willing to abandon any conception of causal connection in history that falls short of mathematical certainty. No matter how one tries to exorcise it, the issue of similarities between repressive and liberating popular movements of social protest remains—to the discomfort of those on the left, the ignorantly complacent satisfaction of those at the center of the political spectrum, and the grim glee of those on the right.

As a basis for some brief comparative observations we may consider European revolutionary movements from the time of the *sansculottes* down to the present day. That leaves out Puritanism and the Puritan Revolution, where the similarities are even more noticeable. On the other hand, there are enough reasons for doubts and reservations about the liberating intentions or consequences of Puritanism to avoid complicating matters further by the consideration of this case. In the emotional tone, content, and origin of the programmatic demands there are enough striking similarities if we start with the *sansculottes*. As before, the discussion will concentrate on popular notions and the ideas of the rank and file,[30] so far as they are known to us, not on official doctrines elaborated by professional thinkers.

In leftist movements there has often been the same rage at unrewarded effort and the same hostility to those who seem to obtain the good things of this earth without working for them as existed among the Nazis. The concept of frustrated or useless effort as the source of punitive moral sentiments might well be widened to include the effort that goes into the control of socially disapproved desires. To use George Homans' terms, an investment in self-control that turns out to be futile is liable to seem grossly unfair in a way that makes people seethe with resentment. At times of extreme political tension such sentiments can become a generalized punitive rage at unjust treatment by those in authority, symbolized, for example, by the guillotine, which the *sansculottes* saw as an effective weapon against speculators and hoarders as well as the aristocracy generally. Like the Nazis, though on different grounds, leftist movements see their enemies as morally evil and a source of pollution that must be destroyed, though there may be a somewhat stronger tendency on the left to believe in the possibility of regenerating opponents by appropriate treatment. Still on both sides there is a firm belief in the existence of an irreconcilable core of opposition that will have to be destroyed before the final victory and the introduction of a new social order. Among themselves there

---

[30]For such information about the *sansculottes* see the detailed analysis in Albert Soboul, *Les Sans-culottes parisiens en l'an II*, 407–677.

exists on the left as on the right the same ethos of comradeship and the same hostility to privacy as a potential source of deviance and backsliding. These characteristics are especially prominent in Communist movements, but existed among the *sansculottes* as well.

In the attitude toward leaders differences begin to appear along with some striking similarities. In some leftist movements there is the same demand for a single supreme authority to set the world aright as existed among the Nazis. The fundamental source is probably the same in both cases: a sense of individual powerlessness and inability to control a world that appears evil and oppressive. On the other hand, anarchists reject this attitude outright. There are also reasons for doubting whether the affection and even adoration for a leader that does occur in leftist oppositional movements has in it the same degree of self-abasement and abdication of reason that the Nazis displayed. By and large, the left tries to mobilize around a program for specific changes in social institutions and at the very least an appeal to some form of self-interest, especially in the phase preceding the capture of power. I would hazard the generalization that on the left it is only *after* the seizure of power that there has occurred the same kind of self-abasement that is so prominent in the Nazi movement. Then, as in the case of Stalin and Mao, despite their very significant differences, the leadership cult is organized from above mainly as a weapon in internal policy disputes. By that point too the left has changed its character enough to render its claims to be a liberating force highly suspect.

Are there then any sharp qualitative differences? I suggest the following: The anger of leftist movements finds its expression in terms of principles supposedly applicable to all of humanity. Brotherhood, solidarity, comradeship, fraternity, equality are at least potentially open to all other human beings in the same situation of oppression. This is not to deny that what gives many an oppositionist movement its staying power is a stubborn pursuit of fairly narrow group interests and quite narrowly perceived grievances. The German coal miners provided as good a case of that as we need. Nor is this a denial of the fact that group interests among the less fortunate frequently clash very sharply. The hostility of many a workman to the competition of foreign immigrants is the sole reminder needed on that score. The most one can claim, therefore, is that many spontaneous expressions of lower-class rage *do* take an open form of generally applicable principles—partly out of an awareness of shared fate and the need for allies. The objective is a new social order for the whole world, not a "New Germany." Even after leftist movements have taken power, the universal appeal can remain a useful weapon in the diplomatic and even the military armory of the new regime. This has been clear enough in the cases of China and the Soviet Union; it was true as far back as Napoleon.

There are also discernible distinctions between right and left popular movements in the stance toward the use of force and violence, or in punitive attitudes generally. This is a very difficult terrain that would require a book by itself for adequate exploration. Again I shall offer only a very preliminary reconnaissance. At first glance it is tempting to assert that for leftist movements both the attitude toward violence and the targets differ sharply from rightist popular movements like Nazism. For the left, one might claim, violence is not generally an end in itself, but rather something necessary to achieve political and social objectives. Leftist anger is not generally directed toward the weak and the powerless. Its targets are not the Jews and the gypsies of the Nazis, nor the helpless blacks of angry Southern lynch mobs in the United States. Its method is not the pogrom. Instead, popular leftist anger chooses as its targets the symbols and embodiment of oppressive power: kings, aristocrats, government officials, men of power and substance generally.

It would also be much more tempting to believe these assertions if they were really true. They are much too comforting, at least for those on the left, to be that true. At best they represent, like the claim of liberal regimes to be able to resolve social conflicts peacefully and fairly, an ideal and a tendency that have on more than one occasion been approached in practice. Leftist claims are closest to the truth in characterizing their enemy, fascist movements. These *do* glorify violence and force, though it will be necessary to enter some qualifications and distinctions on this score in a moment, and they do display a strong tendency to select weak targets—or in plainer language, to destroy the weak and the helpless.

But a brief examination of the famous episode of the September Massacres during the French Revolution is enough to destroy the illusion that such claims can be part of any general characterization of popular uprisings. As this case along with much other evidence shows, surges of popular moral outrage can take either liberating or oppressive forms and pass rapidly from one form to the other, depending on circumstances. Where such a transformation does occur, it is, as far as I am aware, only in one direction: toward vindictive and oppressive behavior. Lynching mobs do not turn into revolutionary uprisings, while something like the reverse has happened frequently. Since the September Massacres have attracted the attention of distinguished historians and reveal some of the essential processes, it will be useful to look more closely at this evidence.

In a very loose sense it is true that the target of the mob in the September Massacres was a set of figures who *had* held authority. The trigger for the uprising was a rumor to the effect that the massive departure of good revolutionaries under arms to the front would empty Paris of the revolution's supporters and thereby provide the occasion for a counterrevolutionary rising with its center in the prisons. Several of these were then full of persons who had been on the losing side of the defense of the Tuileries on August 10, 1792, the occasion when the King gave his order to the Swiss Guard to hold their fire. But the plain fact of the matter was that roving mobs in the course of several days massacred more than a thousand helpless prisoners.[31]

Jules Michelet, writing in the 1850s and with access to archives, some of which perished in 1871, provides the most usefully detailed account that I have been able to find. Only two of the forty-eight sections into which the "little people" of Paris were organized actually voted for the massacre.[32] This limitation, however, had hardly any practical effect. There were enough angry and excited people to perform these grisly acts. Among them were the *boutiquiers*, small shop owners forced to close down due to the confusion and dislocation of the times. Michelet's comment on them sheds an interesting light on their historical affinity with the Nazis, even if he is mistaken about their attitude being a strictly French characteristic:

L'ouvrier supporte souvent mieux la faim que le boutiquier la faillite. Çela tient à bien des causes, à une surtout dont il faut tenir compte; c'est qu'en France la faillite n'est pas un simple malheur (comme en Angleterre et en Amérique), mais la perte de l'honneur. *Faire honneur à ses affaires* est un proverbe français et qui n'existe qu'en France. Le boutiquier en faillite, ici, devient très-féroce.[33]

---

[31]Pierre Caron, *Les Massacres de septembre*, 95, on the basis of surviving archival evidence gives the number of victims as falling between 1,090 and 1,395.

[32]Jules Michelet, *Histoire de la Révolution française*, V, 52.

[33]Michelet, *Révolution française*, V, 63 (Italics in original). (The worker often tolerates hunger better than the small shopkeeper bankruptcy. That is due to many causes, above all to one that one must take into account: this is that in France bankruptcy is not a simple misfortune (as in England and in America) but the loss of one's honor. "*Hold high the honor of one's business*" is a French proverb—and it exists only in France. Hence the small shopkeeper in a state of bankruptcy becomes terribly ferocious.)

The *boutiquiers* were joined by all sorts of apprentices, butcher boys, and the floating population in which Paris abounded. As each prisoner left the door of the prison, the mob set upon the victim with pikes.

Here and there the mob did employ a drumhead justice in the selection of victims, at times sparing, for example, those imprisoned for debt, or those who for some reason caught their fancy.[34] There is also some doubt about reported acts of mutilation and sexual assault on the bodies of female victims.[35] With these minor exceptions and reservations the crowds behaved with indiscriminate fury and brutality.

From Michelet's account it is clear that there was a progressive relaxation of the inhibitions on aggression. When the slaughter broke out on September 2, 1792, the crowds showed some signs of diffidence. Barefoot members were not yet ready to help themselves to the shoes of dead aristocrats. By the next day the murdering had become a pleasure.[36] The worst episode occurred on September 4th. Crowds went out to attack the chateau of Bicêtre, a huge storage depot of the old regime for miscellaneous social rejects and unfortunates, including lunatics, orphans, abandoned apprentices, and servants imprisoned at a word from their master. Bicêtre was similar to the Bastille except that this time the castle was full and the crowd came to kill instead of to liberate. Only a relatively small number got that far because many in the crowd stopped off along the way to attack the chateau of the Salpêtrière, a similar institution for females, including prostitutes. There they killed some thirty-five women, thirty of them prostitutes. At Bicêtre the crowd somehow stumbled upon a group of abandoned and abused small boys and killed about thirty. Somewhat earlier another crowd slaughtered persons condemned to the galleys at still another prison, the Bernardins.[37]

Throughout the slaughter the leaders of the revolution made no serious effort to intervene or to put a stop to it. Both

---

[34]This aspect appears in the account by Jean Jaurès, *Histoire socialiste de la Révolution française*, IV, 232–243. On 234 Jaurès shows he was not impressed: "Je n'aime pas les plaidoyers hypocrites des contemporains qui s'extasient sur 'l'esprit de justice' du peuple parce qu'il a épargné et élargi les prisonniers pour dettes."

[35]Mentioned by Jaurès, but see Caron, *Massacres de septembre*, 61–62, 65. This kind of behavior does occur, however, and is not the product of prurient imagination. For an example see the material on an orgiastic feast of victory among New Guinea highlanders in Ronald M. Berndt, *Excess and Restraint*, 282–284.

[36]Michelet, *Révolution française*, V, 88.

[37]Michelet, *Révolution française*, V, 108–112. Caron, *Massacres de septembre*, 6–7, 148–150, in general confirms Michelet, and adds the case of those condemned to the galleys.

Danton and Robespierre used the occasion to advance factional interests. In the judgment of some modern historians Danton through shrewd inaction bears a heavy degree of responsibility for the event. Though Marat talked in bloodthirsty terms at the time, it is doubtful that he had any real influence or contributed significantly to the movement.[38] Revolutionary contemporary opinion, to the extent it is revealed in newspapers and surviving fragments of correspondence, was generally favorable or apologetic. Sharp criticism did not surface for about three weeks, though it may have been felt beforehand. Later on through much of the nineteenth century the epithet *septembriseur*, put into circulation by counterrevolutionary propaganda, gained widespread currency as an expression for the brutal side of revolutionary extremism.[39] For sensitive moderns the worst aspect is the slaughter of the defenseless.

Up to this point we have been discussing popular mass movements that are either largely spontaneous and leaderless or if organized, as the Nazi movement certainly was, do have a mass following. There are several other types of situations where the attitudes of large numbers of people toward force and cruelty come to the surface in a way that makes possible some further comparisons between radical and reactionary movements.[40] One important type is the terrorist movement that enjoys widespread support among the population. Guerilla movements in their early stages belong in this class. Both terrorist and guerilla movements may, of course, lack or fail to gain any support from the population. These can be set aside as not relevant for the issues at hand. Concrete contemporary and recent examples of those that are relevant are the nationalist bands that proliferated and carried out numerous murders under the Weimar Republic, the OAS in Algeria and France, the Irish Republican Army, the Palestine Liberation Organization, and others.

The purpose of this form of terror is not to seize power, at least not in the short run. In that sense it differs from the armed conspiracy. The purpose rather is to disorganize the existing government, to undermine its legitimacy and the apparent inevitability of its authority, and to publicize grievances—all

---

[38]On these aspects see the account by Jaurès, *Histoire socialiste*, IV, 251–255, 262, and Louis R. Gottschalk, *Jean Paul Marat: A Study in Radicalism*, 124–128.

[39]Caron, *Massacres de septembre*, 8, 121–153, 167–168.

[40]As in the case of right and left, the attitude toward social equality provides a usable criterion for distinguishing between radical and reactionary movements. A pogrom is clearly reactionary since it seeks to perpetuate and intensify an existing inequality or even to eliminate its victims from human society altogether.

through acts of terror, such as assassinations and bombings. They are extremist acts intended to mobilize and to create a sense of both desperation and hope in a sector of the underlying population. Without this sense of despair in the underlying population, which can come from frustrated feelings of national identity, economic and social grievances, or a combination of these, the terrorist organization is unable to take root and liable to wither. Sometimes, as in the case of the OAS in Algeria, the terrorist organization can also count on a degree of tacit tolerance among segments of those in power, who try to use it as a weapon in their own quarrels. This factor can help the group attain more or less legitimate authority or at least a degree of political respectability, as was true of the NSDAP in Germany. Originally just one of several competing nationalist sects, it managed to become a mass party and then to capture power in all of Germany. Partly by playing on differences among the Arab countries, the PLO managed by 1974 to have its spokesman deliver a speech from a podium of the United Nations, the cachet of at least partial political respectability.

A podium in the United Nations is, on the other hand, hardly comparable to the German Chancellorship and, as the fate of the OAS demonstrates, a terrorist organization can fade away if its dominant opponents settle their differences at its expense and that of its followers. Though liberal regimes may suffer an especial handicap in coping with terrorist opposition because they cannot resort to effective police measures without undermining their own legitimacy and further publicizing grievances, they are not necessarily helpless. Terrorists can alienate their own supporters and arouse the fierce antagonism of other segments of the population through strategic and tactical miscalculations. Governments can use effective mixtures of force and concessions. The simplified liberal formula of giving in completely to each and every social demand, merely because it is expressed in loud rhetoric and somehow sounds justified, probably would not work even if it were ever tried. Desperate emotions generally resist satisfaction, and there is such a thing as a political appetite that increases with the eating. There can also be such a thing as a defensible scale of social priorities that commands widespread public support and at least a rough-and-ready rational allocation of a society's limited resources to the pursuit of these objectives. Where that situation prevails, terrorism is unlikely to become more than a minor police problem.

Characteristically enough, leftist terrorism has been directed toward figures of authority, either local ones on the spot—as seems to be more characteristic of modern peasant guerillas—or symbolic figures at the center that appear to be favorites for more romantic movements with far less support.[41] The distinction here is that rightist movements select as victims prominent figures who symbolize opposition to their policies, *both* among those in authority and potential leaders on the left. Thus the victims of rightist terror in Weimar Germany include—to mention only the most famous—Karl Liebknecht and Rosa Luxemburg, on the one hand, Walther Rathenau and Matthias Erzberger, on the other.

As Michael Walzer, who is presently engaged in some research on terrorism, pointed out to me in conversation, however, this kind of distinction may be breaking down with the rise of indiscriminate attacks on individuals and groups who have little or no connection with the policies that are the source of grievance, and certainly no responsibility for creating or executing these policies. They are the "civilians" in this kind of warfare and to many in the general public appear simply as innocent bystanders. Many such cases have been reported in newspaper accounts of the struggle in Northern Ireland, but they are by no means confined to that part of the world. The earliest instance known to me of this indiscriminate form of terrorism occurred in 1894. In that year a young anarchist intellectual, Émile Henry, put a bomb in a cafe near the Gare Saint-Lazare where a large crowd of modest shopkeepers, clerks, and workers were quietly drinking and listening to the band. The explosion did much damage, wounding twenty persons, of whom one died. When reproached with killing innocent people Émile Henry simply replied, "Il n'y a pas d'innocents."[42] Henry apparently meant that anyone who lived as an ordinary citizen, paying taxes, holding a job, etc., in the bourgeois society he so passionately hated necessarily contributed to the ordinary functioning of that society and therefore shared in its general guilt. It is, of course, a viewpoint that through its rigid determinism obliterates both any possible conception of degrees of moral responsibility and

[41]Now that the Vietcong has won in Vietnam, it is useful to recall that they did use systematic terror, even if the consequences of American terror were worse and employed on behalf of a corrupt and reactionary regime. For a sober analysis based partly on firsthand observation see Douglas Pike, *Viet Cong*, espec. 244–252, and Robert L. Sansom, *The Economics of Insurgency in the Mekong Delta of Vietnam*, 238–245. Sansom's analysis is in my judgment much superior because he puts the use of terror in its social and economic context of popular grievances. But the facts of terror itself look alike in both accounts.

[42]James Joll, *The Anarchists*, 137.

perfectly plain factual distinctions in degrees of influence and control over social and political policy.

As such this outlook is neither new nor leftist. One finds it as far back as the superpatriot Cato's cry of "Carthago delenda est." It has passed into our language with the term "Carthaginian peace" to describe deliberate policies of utter destruction. Cato, however, was a member of a ruling elite. We have very little reliable information about how rank-and-file sympathizers with terrorist movements feel about policies of indiscriminate slaughter. In Peter Merkl's study of 581 rank-and-file Nazis, he found 155 autobiographies that revealed realistic or romantic acceptance of violence with or without actual involvement, and 187 reports of actual involvement in violent acts.[43] Even if it is impossible to take the figures as such at face value, they are enough to reveal plenty of latent sentiment that could be turned to massively destructive purposes. On the other hand, there is the well-known fact that the Nazi leaders felt it necessary to conceal their genocidal policies and machinery from the mass of the German population. In the end, however, these distinctions hardly matter. It is only too easy to find enough people who are willing to execute grisly policies, even if they had no such aggressive inclinations to begin with. For those unwilling to carry them out, once a terrorist regime is in power there is next to nothing short of suicide open to an individual or even a brave group.

Enthusiasm for the act of violence as somehow redeeming and therapeutic for the victim as well as for the victimized society does not appear to be a prominent current among ordinary members of subordinate or oppressed groups.[44] For one thing it is often just too dangerous. In the second place, it can bring reprisals on the whole group. As has been pointed out earlier, the group often tends to protect itself by punishing the protester. To be sure, these sanctions do not always work. Occasionally slaves did murder their masters in the American South. To the slaveholders the pattern and motivation of these individual acts seem to have been inexplicable.[45] Individual acts of this sort, whatever their motive, are not the same thing as a cultural and moral climate stressing the virtues of violence and actions against the social order. This climate, which reaches an extreme man-

---

[43]Merkl, *Political Violence*, 542.

[44]Violence as therapy runs through the writings of Georges Sorel and in more recent times shows up in Frantz Fanon, *Les Damnés de la terre,* with its approving preface by Jean Paul Sartre.

[45]See Eugene D. Genovese, *Roll, Jordan, Roll*, 361–363.

ifestation in experiments with the idea of motiveless murder, appears mainly as the plaything of intellectuals repelled and bored by the apparent regularity, monotony, and philistinism of bourgeois society.[46] In recent years it has become a major theme in mass entertainment in the United States, along with pre-occupation with massive disasters. As a mood it has no specific political content and can turn either to the right or to the left. Mussolini's career from militant leftist to fascist leader exem-plifies the switch from one to the other nicely.

But on this score, too, it is necessary to make careful distinc-tions. Anger at the regularity and philistinism of bourgeois soci-ety was not a general characteristic of rank-and-file National Socialists. The evidence from Abel shows the NSDAP to have been a wrenching upheaval in favor of the restoration of tradi-tional bourgeois virtues so that hard work and overall impulse control would again receive their deserved reward in the new collective context of the people's community. Nazi propaganda and art were also thoroughly "healthy," cozy, and reassuring. This thrust in favor of the restoration of traditional virtues sharply distinguishes the Nazi movement from the student re-bellions and the upsurge of the youth culture during the 1960s. Revolutionary socialist movements in the backward countries likewise stress the virtues of hard work in a collective context, and try to stamp out "morbid" social interests and preoccupa-tions with the self. They demand art forms as "healthy," reassur-ing, and banal as the Nazis. On this score the distinction between revolutionary socialism and fascism is not so obvious at first sight. Both are very "square" and conventional, morally and culturally. Again the difference rests in the context within which the gen-eral control over impulses and the focusing of aggression for collective purposes take place. Socialist movements have made extensive efforts to overhaul their social and political institutions in order to reduce social inequalities and the institutional sources of aggression. In so doing some of them have engaged in massive cruelty. Whether the end result will be an eventual historical transformation to more humane social arrangements is by no means as clear to me as it is to the revolutionaries and their sympathizers. Nevertheless they have made the attempt and are still engaged in it. Thus the purpose and social function of the revival of generalized impulse control and self-discipline is quite different on the left from on the right.

[46] As a witness to man's perennial interest in sadism and its artistic expression, see Mario Praz, *The Romantic Agony.*

Attempts to draw a distinction do, it appears, continually fall back on some aspect of intentions, hopes, and possibilities for the future. Still the argument *may* find firmer ground insofar as it stresses institutional capacities, tendencies, and historical directions rather than programs, doctrines, and individual hopes. The assertion that fascism could not possibly have developed in a humane direction, that its violence had to be purely destructive seems quite tenable. The claim that leftist forms of destruction are part of some creative historical process is one that only the future can verify. The twentieth-century portion of the record is far from encouraging.

Two other general types of situations deserve attention in this preliminary reconnaissance of popular attitudes and behavior in regard to force and violence, especially violence against the relatively weak and helpless. The first is a situation of general breakdown of political and social authority, a *sauve-qui-peut*, such as was reported in parts of South Vietnam just before the capture of Saigon by North Vietnamese troops. A second type is a deliberate and temporary lifting of some aspect of government authority, as in official encouragement of a pogrom, or in the notorious slaughter of French Protestants in the St. Bartholomew's Day Massacres.[47] It produces similar and perhaps worse results. The basic features appear to be two: one is the release and perhaps intensification of whatever pent-up aggressions exist in a population, due to the lifting of the taboo on its expression and its replacement by the luxury of socially sanctioned aggression. This level will in turn be the result of quite specific conditions together with the legacy of recent history. There is no reason to assume that the result will always be equally horrible. On the other hand, this kind of "liberation" is hardly likely to occur in very favorable circumstances. The second feature is the severe competition for scarce goods and even for life itself that can occur with the temporary withdrawal or collapse of authority, especially an unpopular one. By itself this sort of competition can turn the most civilized human beings into savages almost instantly. People shed the veneer, restraints and inhibitions acquired from and sustained through living in organized society, to claw at each other for a tiny but crucial advantage, provided they do not perceive or define the situation as utterly hopeless. The situation is at its worst where there is no regular and dependable way of allocating what people want—

[47]On this and similar events see the analysis by Natalie Zemon Davis, "The Rites of Violence: Religious Riot in Sixteenth-Century France," 51–91.

such as escape—as well as an inadequate supply. If the victims are able to improvise their own system of allocation, there may be much less vindictiveness, competition, and even slaughter.

A semi-anarchical situation does not appear to have characteristics that would identify it with any part of the traditional political spectrum. In connection with this type of breakdown the terms left, moderate, conservative, and reactionary do not shed much light. Though rare so far, it is a situation that can occur under any type of regime.[48]

At the opposite end of the scale from the *sauve-qui-peut* of near anarchy there is the instrumental terror of a regime seeking to establish or consolidate a shaky authority. Ordinary speech distinguishes between a red terror and a white terror, with the implication that white terrors have been the work of attempts at counterrevolutionary monarchist restorations. That is not true. One of the bloodiest white terrors occurred with the suppression of the Paris Commune and the beginnings of the Third Republic.[49] It is a reasonably safe inference that a majority of French citizens, at that time still small property owners in town and countryside, heartily approved the slaughter.

The degree and kind of mass support for red and white terrors is, on the other hand, hardly the most important feature. Nor does it make much sense to count up the number of victims of red and white terrors to decide which one has been worse. This kind of moral arithmetic is somehow obtuse. There is something wrong with a person who could feel satisfaction with the totals on either side of the ledger no matter how they turned out. Furthermore they would not prove anything about the nature of popular sentiments. Such sentiments provide only part of the original impulse behind official terrors, red and white. Then officialdom, in one form or another, takes over with its card files and categories of victims. Older proscriptions may have lacked card files, but they still worked with categories. The terrifying aspect here is the human capacity to obey orders believed to be just and appropriate. Stanley Milgram's experiments, discussed earlier, beautifully demonstrate this capacity, and also reveal some of the conditions under which it does break down.

[48]The most one might say is that a liberal regime firmly committed to the rule of law would be the least liable to exploit it for its own purposes by lifting the taboo on aggression. But how many liberal regimes can or do remain committed to the rule of law when faced with a crisis threatening a general social breakdown?

[49]See Frank Jellinek, *The Paris Commune of 1871*, 338–387. For a more recent discussion see Henri Lefebvre, *La Proclamation de la Commune: 26 mars 1871*, espec. part 4, 173–233.

Toward the end of his book Milgram comments on this capacity for obedience: "This is a fatal flaw nature has designed into us, and which in the long run gives our species only a modest chance for survival." Still later in a footnote he points out correctly that the elimination of authority proposed by the anarchists constitutes no solution at all.[50] But the choice is not between anarchy and irrational obedience. It is between more and less rational forms of authority. There is nothing wrong in obeying an authority that pursues humane objectives and has special competence or skill relevant for the pursuit of these objectives. There are troubles enough for humanity without creating unnecessarily apocalyptic dilemmas. In the end the choice between right and left is less meaningful than between more and less rational forms of authority.

[50]Stanley Milgram, *Obedience to Authority*, 188, 212 (note 30). Some persons may be inclined to assert that we needed no demonstration of this terrible capacity; recent history had already provided enough. But a variety of presumably intelligent laymen and experts when asked to estimate the degree of obedience that the experiments might turn up greatly underestimated the results, which astonished the experimenters themselves. On this point see Chapter Three.

CHAPTER THIRTEEN

Moral relativism

1. Evaluative and descriptive aspects

Only in recent times has a fairly large number of educated people come to realize that there is not and cannot be any source of moral authority except human beings themselves. Even among educated people the realization is far from universal. With the decline of divine sanctions some influential thinkers for a time tried to substitute collective reifications with a teleological twist, such as Natural Law, History, and Progress. These, too, failed to provide an objective standard for moral approval and condemnation.

Historical and social analysis can provide powerful insights into what kinds of morality are probable and feasible under specific circumstances. Such analysis can also tell us about the costs in human suffering of different types of morality and who bears these costs. This knowledge is indispensable for informed moral judgment. But it is no guarantee by itself of correct moral judgment. Only too easily can it become a mixture of advice to swim with the tides of history and a justification for every cruelty recorded by history.

With the disappearance of traditional certainties and the failure of new ones many intelligent people came to doubt that there was or could be any such thing as correct moral judgments. That is one possible if extreme meaning of moral relativism. To elaborate slightly, it is impossible to make valid moral distinctions and moral judgments because it is presumably impossible to establish any valid distinction or independent criterion that would enable us to make these judgments. Fascists have their moral codes, liberals and radicals their codes, and that is all there is to be said. This is the evaluative side of moral relativism.

There is also a purely descriptive or factual side to moral relativism. This viewpoint merely stresses the enormous variety of moral codes to which human beings at different points in time and space have given passionate allegiance and asserts that there is no way to connect up this variety with any worthwhile generalizations. Different moral codes constitute different ways by which human beings have tried to live together under a large variety of circumstances described by anthropologists, historians, and other social scientists. The explanation of the connection between a given moral code and a specific set of circumstances is all that any intelligent person can ask for under this descriptive variant of moral relativism.

So far as I can see, there is no logical reason why the descriptive and evaluative forms of moral relativism should go together, though they usually do.[1] For example, it would be possible to claim that all past and existing codes of morality except our own were not really moral. To a great extent that is the moral chauvinism and provincialism of ordinary men and women against which moral relativism has been a reaction. In its historicized relativism the Marxist position displays a similar chauvinism: all past moralities are both historically necessary for and historically superseded by the revolutionary morality that will lead to liberation. A morality that justifies all crimes, including Stalinism, forfeits any claim to be taken seriously. In the West at any rate this combination of an awareness of variety in moral codes and the adherence to a single standard of judgment has been quite rare. The more influential varieties of moral relativism have stressed both the variety of moral behaviors and the futility or moral provincialism of efforts to pass judgment on these differences from the outside. "To every country its own concentration camps" would be a satirical but by no means inaccurate epitome of the moral relativism that has governed much if not most serious writing about human affairs during a large part of the twentieth century.

Like Marxism, and to some extent along with Marxism, this form of moral relativism has powerful achievements to its credit in liberating the human mind from cramping and dangerous illusions. Again, like and along with Marxism it can leave a residue of its own dangerous illusions. During the twentieth

---

[1]The tension between the two is quite apparent in at least one major classic of moral relativism, William Graham Sumner, *Folkways*.

435

century there has been both a rapid disintegration of traditional moral standards and a sharp increase in conflicts that have a powerful moral component. Conventional forms of moral relativism strike many thoughtful people as somehow an inadequate stance from which to face such issues. Some of the attempts to find new bases for moral judgment are retreats from reason. Occasionally they are quite explicitly that. As familiar grounds for security give way, people still flounder and toss in troubled search for the right to obey forms of authority that cannot possibly exist.

In any given case, morality and ethics amount to the rules that specific human beings have created and persuaded or forced each other to accept in order to work and live together. Poorly equipped for survival by their purely biological endowment, with the decisive exception of their brains, human beings are so constituted that they must cooperate somehow merely in order to stay alive. Survival, on the other hand, is no more than the absolutely minimal prerequisite for the other collective purposes served by moral rules. Apart from these purposes and the effectiveness or ineffectiveness that a moral code may have in both selecting and sustaining them, I see no criterion with which to pass judgment on any given form of morality.

Nevertheless this criterion of adequacy in meeting a series of biological needs and social imperatives, and their respective conflicts, may yield a method of judgment superior to decaying moral absolutisms and prevailing forms of relativism. It is a theme worth exploring, partly on the basis of ground covered in this book, partly with the help of considerations that have not yet come to the surface. Before discussing further the evaluative aspect of moral relativism it will be better to turn to descriptive and factual aspects. Though moral judgments, and more especially judgments of other people's morality, are the source of vital passions that play an immensely important role in human affairs—both capitalism and socialism came into the world on tidal waves of revulsion against the existing social order—the arousal of moral passion is relatively light work in comparison with accurate description and causal analysis.

There are myriads of possible collective purposes. Some of them are quite trivial in the sense that they have very little to do with human survival, happiness, or unhappiness. In such cases the element of moral judgment in the rules that people create may be rather slight, though there is likely to be a touch of it in any collective endeavor. The rules governing poker, bridge, and other games have no purpose except to provide pleasure through skill and luck. The rules could be different; new games and variations on old ones are invented intermittently. Nevertheless there is considerable moral outrage vented against those who cheat at cards or deliberately violate the rules of any game. At the other end of the scale are moral rules that are essential, or are believed to be essential, for group survival or the pursuit of goals that the group may regard as even more important than survival. These collective purposes are themselves ethical goals such as honor, independence, salvation. On this score there is obviously a great deal of variation.

At this juncture, therefore, we encounter the central factual issue in moral relativism. What observable agreement, if any, exists on the principles of social justice? To the extent that variation exists, as it certainly does, what are its causes? By way of preliminary observation it is necessary to point out that no single scholar, in fact not even several scholars working together, can possibly know all the various moral codes that human beings have at some time or other established for themselves. Therefore some exceptions are bound to turn up that will refute any but the most banal universal propositions about the human sense of justice. In some remote corner of the world an anthropologist may still come upon forms of morality that lead to collective suicide.[2] To dismiss such discoveries as mere curiosities would be a serious error because such extreme variations often reveal a great deal about the nature of similar but more widespread types of morality. It requires no great erudition to recognize that a moral code which may be suitable for one set of historical circumstances can become suicidal or at least totally unsuited to a later set of circumstances. Don Quixote stands as the paradigm for this sort of transformation. Thus the most an attempt at generalization could hope to establish would be the existence of widely recurring tendencies.

Such tendencies are more likely to arise out of the shared unpleasant experiences of the lower strata in many forms of human society than they are from the experiences of the dominant strata, because the dominant strata have more room and resources with which to vary the tenor of their lives.[3]

In the search for recurring tendencies, as pointed out in Chapter One, it is best to begin by looking for some universal problems that all human societies must resolve in order to

[2]For such a case see Jules Henry, *Jungle People*, 59, 108–110.

[3]There are noticeable recurring features among these too: art, erotic intrigue, and ceremonial techniques for the expression of social solidarity and aggression.

exist and perpetuate themselves. Among these issues are those of authority, and the production and distribution of goods and services. For the purpose at hand we can regard this set as a single problem: that of the division of labor, or somewhat more precisely, the coordination of the various activities that each individual pursues in order to make this aggregation of individuals into a society. Without such coordination there is no society. The division of labor usually involves the extraction of an economic surplus by dominant groups or individuals for the creation of certain goods and services, though in nonliterate societies the surplus may be quite small and the element of domination minimal. Whatever arrangements exist have powerful moral sanctions behind them. On the other hand, the degree to which these sanctions are accepted by an underlying population will vary considerably. Furthermore at least some detailed aspects of the division of labor are subject to continual and even daily renegotiation as people decide among themselves how to go about the day's work. This is the informal social contract at its minimum level. There are moral sanctions behind this contract as well, though not so powerful and distinct as those governing the general pattern of a society's division of labor.

The first chapter drew attention to several recurring features in the resolution of these issues, which I shall not repeat here. If human beings had been able to produce only one kind of society and one moral code, the species would have rapidly become extinct. Variability is an essential element in the adaptation to different and changing circumstances. Again one source of variability is biological: the human capacity to *withstand* pain and suffering. It is not necessary to teach people to feel pain. But it is possible—and to a modern sensitive product of Western culture it sometimes seems astonishingly easy—to teach human beings to withstand and even ignore pain and one's own suffering. People can and do put up with just about anything, though there are undoubtedly wide individual differences in this ability. The main reasons come down to two. Either they are unable to conceive of a different way of life, or if they do imagine one, they are unable to do anything about it. Generally both reasons operate simultaneously. There are two more major sources of social and moral variation and change. One is the choice made, voluntarily or forced upon people, between reciprocal and predatory solutions to the issue of the division of labor. This choice occurs at all historical stages while taking somewhat different forms in each stage. The other source comes from the historically developing capacity to solve the problems of scarcity, toil, and disease. It is therefore intimately connected with the choice between reciprocal and predatory solutions.

This capacity has two main components. One is technology, or tools for the control of the natural environment as well as knowledge about how to use these tools. For this component human history provides clear evidence of progress, though certainly not uninterrupted progress. The evidence reaches back through recorded history, as far into that distant past as the archaeological record will take us. Whether progress can or will continue is of course another question for which we can have no certain answer. The other component is social and cultural. It consists of the social arrangements and the body of knowledge through and with which human beings make use of technological changes, distributing their benefits among themselves. If by progress in this area we mean a reduction in socially produced misery, the evidence for its existence is pathetically slim. To judge from what we know about a few scattered and isolated primitive tribes, human beings had the capacity to supply themselves with sufficient food and shelter to live in certain favorable environments without the scourges of war, hunger, disease, and oppression at a very early stage of technological development, roughly by the time they had learned how to control fire and make a few simple implements for hunting and gathering. If we define a decent society as one without these scourges, humanity attained the capacity to create decent societies almost at the dawn of history. But except in a few isolated parts of the globe, human beings did not do that. Competition with other societies prevented them by encouraging and sanctioning predatory and aggressive qualities, which if not instinctual are nevertheless terrifyingly easy to arouse. There are also some clues from contemporary anthropological evidence to the effect that human beings may not have been particularly happy with what I have labeled a decent society. Aside from intermittent complaints about their lot, which we should perhaps discount somewhat as no more than inevitable grousing about *any* degree or form of frustration, there are signs that these people *are* easily tempted by the fruits of civilization and on occasion obtain them by methods short of very hard labor—such as, for example, theft.[4] Thus both the imperatives produced by competition with other human societies and the temptations of "higher" civilization have for a long time pushed human societies away from reciprocal forms of social organization and toward predatory

---

[4]Colin M. Turnbull, *Wayward Servants*, 40, 42–43.

ones. That has been rather steadily the case despite any increase in the human capacity to control and understand the physical and social environment.

2. *Rational and predatory authority*

Predatory solutions we shall come to shortly. First, let us look more closely at one aspect of reciprocal relations, rational authority, in order to distinguish it from domination or predatory authority. There is all the more reason to do this because there has been a noticeable tendency of late to regard any and all forms of authority as somehow irrational and illegitimate. In any complex society with a complicated division of labor where not everybody can do absolutely everything—in other words, any society that claims to be civilized—many forms of authority are unavoidable. And it is better that such authority be rational rather than irrational and oppressive. Rational authority is equitable even if it is sometimes painful. But how is it possible to tell if authority really *is* rational?

The claim that purely rational authority has never existed is quite plausible. Nevertheless there are enough rational elements in such familiar forms of authority as that of a gifted doctor, the pilot of an airplane, the commander of a revolutionary army, and, yes, even the skilled administrator of a far-flung industrial enterprise, to enable us to discern the basic features. Rational authority is a way of advancing individual or collective purpose by granting certain persons the right and in some cases even the obligation to execute specific tasks and give orders to other people in the course of so doing. For such authority to be rational the individual and collective aims must themselves be rational.

I will define as rational any form of activity for which in a given state of knowledge there are good reasons to suppose that it will diminish human suffering or contribute to human·happiness without making other human beings miserable. The last stipulation is necessary in order to exclude predatory forms of authority, which are often quite rational from the standpoint of those who profit from them, but not at all rational from the standpoint of the victims. According to a distinguished intellectual tradition it is impossible to apply the term rational to ultimate human purposes. From this standpoint one can only speak of rationality in connection with means and methods. I do not think it is necessary to enter this debate, though it may avoid some unnecessary confusion to indicate more explicitly the position taken here. About instrumental rationality there is little to discuss at this moment, though I would like to emphasize that it should take human and psychological costs into account. As for values and ends, it does *not* make sense to regard the cruder forms of suffering such as hunger, disease, wounds—or for that matter any form of pain and suffering—as ends in themselves.

In some forms of rational authority, skill in the execution of a difficult task is the most important feature, while giving orders to other people is no more than incidental. It is true of the doctor and the airplane pilot, though it is worth noticing that where other people's lives are at stake, moral codes give this form of authority the right to expect prompt obedience. This form of rational authority is confined to strictly defined activities and social relationships even if in practice, most noticeably in the case of medical authority, there is a tendency for it to spill over into other areas. There are other forms of rational authority where the main element is simply that of telling other people what to do. The control tower at a busy airport is a good example of this variety. In such situations the purpose of granting authority is to coordinate the action of a large number of persons so that each one can gain his or her objective with a minimum of risk and inconvenience. It doesn't matter who the holders of authority are. In cases where little or no skill is necessary, such as the traffic policeman in a busy city, the authority can be handed over to machines. In an increasingly crowded world we are liable to see more and more of this kind of authority, which is a far from pleasant prospect. But there is no claim here that rational authority is always pleasant—only that it is less unpleasant than disorder or irrational authority.

It is, I think, impossible to argue that rational authority always has to be freely chosen authority, because there can from time to time be situations where prompt obedience is absolutely essential and where some individuals may be reluctant or slow to obey out of ignorance, momentary absent-mindedness, or just sheer cantankerousness. When the captain of a cruise ship in a storm has to order the portholes closed and the promenade deck out of bounds, he cannot be expected to spend an hour convincing some stubbornly self-willed passenger that the order is necessary. He has other things to do. Admittedly that is an emergency situation, though none the less important for that reason. This type of situation, on the other hand, is not confined to emergencies. In any large society that is less than perfect there are bound to be at least some adults who cannot or will not listen to reason, who insist on smoking in bed or throwing their garbage into the gutter, and who regard regulations against such practices as manifestations of tyranny.

To put the matter still more generally, not every rational form of authority can possibly suit everybody. There has to be an element of compulsion. For those subject to it therefore there must always be ways to recognize just what rational authority is. Otherwise rational authority turns into domination. This is a perpetual problem whose character continually changes with developments in human capacity to resolve existing issues and create new ones. Rational authority is one thing among loose bands of hunters, something else again in a settled agricultural society, and very different again in an advanced industrial society. If rational authority cannot be altogether freely chosen, the element of free, rational, and deliberate submission has to be clearly predominant in this form of authority.

What, then, can be the basis or criterion upon which a mature and intelligent human being decides to obey the orders or suggestions of another person? If the elements of stress, danger, and need for speed are absent, rational authority can and should at some point take the form of discussion and suggestion rather than command. In either type of situation the rational considerations behind submission and obedience involve judgments about (1) the social importance of the activity to be carried out—such as supplying medical care, or providing any set of goods and services from automobile tires to safety pins; (2) the best ways of performing these activities; and (3) above all, the competence of certain individuals to fill certain demanding roles in carrying them out.

Here some of the main obstacles to the extension of rational authority come clearly into view. The more complex a society is, the more differentiated the activities it carries out, the less likely it is that every adult citizen can know enough to pass intelligent judgment on these matters. The members of each occupation are liable to regard their own contribution as somehow indispensable and to make increasing claims for it at the expense of everybody else. This is not a novel situation. But by the mid-1970s it was very noticeable in formally open societies. It was also quite visible not far below the surface in formally mobilized and authoritarian ones, such as China. Just how this obstacle can be surmounted, if indeed it can be at all, I do not pretend to know. Increasing leisure may or may not provide the basis for wider understanding of how society works—and why it so often fails to do so. With increasing specialization the delegation of authority upward in pseudo-democratic forms such as Communist demo-cratic centralism (or, one hopes, more genuine variants) is also unavoidable.

One last observation. The negative effects of increasing knowledge and specialization, though real enough, are often exaggerated in a way that conceals more important social issues. Today the knowledge necessary for informed and humane social policy is vastly better in terms of both quality and quantity *and* more accessible than it was in the times of a Colbert. Incompe-tent and vicious authority is not merely a matter of ignorance.

It is now time to take a closer look at the key element in rational authority: judgments of competence. Quite clearly the character of such judgments will vary historically with the state of productive arts and social knowledge generally. Likewise the character of the problems to be faced alters over time. It is in this sense that rationality is an essentially historical and time-bound concept. One cannot consider irrational such acts as dances to make the rains come and the crops grow if carried out when the sciences of meteorology and agronomy had not yet come into existence. They were just useless for that purpose, though probably quite helpful for morale. All this is fairly obvious.

The real problem in establishing rational forms of authority is to find ways of testing the competence of those in authority by ways that are both effective and fair. By and large, the only way open to the ordinary citizen is to judge by results. Airplanes that fall down and doctors whose patients die and washing machines that break down two days after the expiration of the guarantee are plainly enough inferior to products and services that do not display these characteristics. To be sure, the links between results and causes are often numerous, complex, and obscure. Fur-thermore they are continually changing. Nevertheless these connections are by no means altogether mysterious. With the general and quite justified disintegration of the mystical and shamanistic trappings of authority in modern societies, the way things work or fail to work does become accessible to those with energy, ingenuity, and a dose of angry curiosity. Their conclu-sions then get passed along to others and become, in the course of contest with other interpretations, part of influential public opinion. The process works very imperfectly even in open societies. But it is only in open societies that the credentials and competence of authority can be checked at all. From this it follows that rational authority is only possible—to the degree that it is possible at all—in open and informed societies.

A few comments on elitism will serve to conclude this brief discussion of rational authority. There are justified and unjustified forms of elitism. They depend on the criteria upon which the distinctions are based. An elite based on knowledge and skills that are useful to the society, and which are difficult to acquire and hard to practice, is perfectly justified up to the point where the distinctions serve as spurs to acquire these skills. That point, however, is very hard to determine. There is no need to overreward people for the accident of innate talents that they would develop and use without rewards. The psychological rewards of social respect and honor are probably even more effective for this purpose than strictly material ones.

Unjustified elitism exists wherever socially harmful activities receive prestige or where the prestige is based on false or inappropriate criteria. Intellectual snobbishness based on knowledge that is merely recondite is one form. So is the acclaim granted to a popular entertainer or the sports celebrity who merely panders to the prejudices of the public. The intellectual snob has contempt for both of these, but lacks any better claim for distinction. All criteria for excellence change over time and with the requirements of the social order in which they exist. The Chinese scholar-gentleman may have served some useful purpose in helping to maintain peace and order. By the middle of the nineteenth century he and the society to which he belonged had become historically obsolete. Classical literary skills, combined with political acumen of a rather limited and traditional variety, were insufficient on the threshold of an industrial age with predatory powers eager to squeeze what they could out of China. One cannot consider the prestige and authority of priests and magicians irrational—though in many cases they may well have been socially harmful—before the knowledge arose that could demonstrate that their rituals were hocus-pocus. For people to believe in such things today, and even to seek out the strangest and most exotic forms they can find, is something else again. If the terms cultural and moral pathology are more than ethnocentric epithets, as I have come to believe they are, they apply to such deliberate abdications of human reason.

As human knowledge and the power of rational judgment and distinction have advanced over time—by no means always steadily—so too have the complexity of the division of labor and the issues with which human reason has had to cope. It is hardly a wonder that rational authority has displayed little more than a stunted growth. Although it is the only equitable form of authority because it is based on the exchange of equivalent goods and services, there are, of course, many other kinds of authority. Here I want to discuss only predatory authority.

Basically there are three ways by which human beings can get what they want in the way of goods and services. (Services here can include the satisfaction of psychological needs and wants.) First of all, people can make what goods they want themselves either individually or collectively. Of course people cannot "make" admiration or distinction themselves. Other people have to grant it. But this is possible on rational grounds in a variety of collective undertakings. The other two ways for people to get what they want is to steal it, or else force other people to make it for them. Where either of these two ways becomes a regular way of life for a set of human beings we have domination and predatory authority. Strictly speaking, predatory authority exists only in the third situation where somebody forces other people to create goods and services, and where the victims accept this relationship as at least a partly legitimate and moral one. By definition, stealing is not legitimate and without legitimacy there is no authority. There is merely domination.

Along with domination, predatory authority has played a major role at many points in all of the world's civilizations and is by no means rare in nonliterate societies. Obviously it works. Just as obviously instrumental rationality plays a big part in making it work. The predatory ruler who ceases to use the most effective methods to control his or her subjects may sooner or later cease to have any subjects and therefore cease to be both a ruler and predator. This observation was plain enough to Thucydides when he wrote the Melian Dialogue, though about two thousand years later Machiavelli found it necessary to remind people about it.

In any concrete case it is essential to be careful about determining the extent to which the elite really is or has been predatory. In and by itself the extraction of a surplus does not prove the existence of predatory rule. It is wise to remember further that in human history poverty and anarchy have often formed the base line from which social evolution began[5]—with many a repetition of past experience. Thus a truly predatory elite is one

[5]About the remote starting point or points we know next to nothing. Some of the simplest primitive societies do not suffer from either material want or social disorder. Many others suffer severely from one or the other or both—and did so in their pristine state before the white intrusion. So far as I can see, there is no way of telling which one of these two extreme situations predominated at the dawn of human history, if indeed either of them did. Recorded history, on the other hand, provides all the evidence about repeated periods of widespread hunger and social disorder.

that renders very few services to the underlying population and extracts for its own purposes a big enough surplus to create poverty on a massive scale that would not exist if the subordinate population were left to its own devices. Plantation slavery is a reasonably clear example. In other cases a series of energetic and even occasionally cruel leaders can over time create islands of relative peace and order amid a sea of general misery. One cannot deny a considerable measure of rationality to such achievements. Such, we are told, was the history of French royal absolutism at various points in its development toward a system in which by the time of Louis XIV predatory aspects did come to predominate.

These considerations boil down to the conclusion that there is a distinction between rational and predatory authority, even if the distinction is not as easy to make as the partisan critics of a given system of authority may at times lead us to think. The distinction impresses me as clear enough to reject any thesis to the effect that political preferences can be nothing more than matters of opinion, subjective whim, or personal values. Simply put, in terms of the misery they can cause, there *are* better and worse moralities, better and worse social systems and collective purposes. Whether one calls them rational and predatory does not really matter a great deal.

In other words, there is such a thing as meaningful moral criticism. Pure moral relativism is an untenable position if one cares about human suffering. And the victims beyond a certain point of possible conditioning cannot help caring. Moral criticism is also politically very significant, though it has limitations I shall try to point out in a moment. In every major social and political transformation for some two thousand years the old order has, as de Maistre observed, suffered a moral defeat and the erosion of its legitimacy well before the political changes took place. That was true of the triumph of Christianity over paganism. It was also true of the great revolutionary movements, from the Revolt of the Netherlands, the Puritan Revolution, the French Revolution, the American Civil War, the Russian and Chinese Revolutions. In each case the old order ceased to make moral sense for influential sectors of the population before it was overthrown. Economic and social changes may have made the old order cease to make moral sense. But without the concurrent development of new standards of condemnation, and new goals for the future, the results of economic and other transformations would have been very different, and quite likely sheer chaos. In each case too the new morality claimed to express the feelings and aspirations of a wider segment of humanity. There has been more than a touch of hypocrisy in all such changes, as the new moralities served to justify the infliction of their own forms of cruelty and suffering, by no means always completely novel ones. Still the world has moved. . . .

Do these considerations support the conclusion that predatory moralities and social systems can in some objective sense be considered pathological? Despite the rejection of moral relativism the answer to this question may remain ambiguous. In some political situations, while it may be possible to make an accurate diagnosis of pathology, the diagnosis is neither necessary nor helpful. In other situations moral judgments, with or without a judgment of pathology, can be totally inappropriate because they imply the asking of inappropriate questions about the nature and causes of the situation. Before exploring these issues it will be well to clarify briefly the meaning of pathology.

The concept of pathology implies some corresponding state of health subject to empirical observation and objective determination. To make sense, the state of health has to be appropriate to the organism under consideration. A horse that lacks wings is not in a pathological state. A bird that lacks them is. Pathology is a process or condition harmful to a particular organism. The causes for the process may be internal to the organism or external to it, as in the case of a wound produced by a blow. Some pathologies with internal causes, such as aging, can be normal for particular organisms. Human societies are not biological organisms. Nevertheless they do suffer from internal and external processes that are harmful and destructive. The extent to which historical processes of decay may repeat themselves in such a way as to make them amenable to firm diagnosis is of course highly problematic. That decay does occur sooner or later is, on the other hand, reasonably certain. Furthermore decay is not the only form of harmful process to which human societies are subject. On these grounds the concept of pathology seems at first quite promising, perhaps even necessary. Possibly we do not use it because it might reveal something disagreeable about our own society.

Further reflection soon reveals important considerations that restrict the usefulness of the concept for social analysis. One major difficulty is that of determining the original, healthy state. If a predatory animal suffers from a disease that prevents it from behaving in a predatory fashion, one would conclude that it was suffering from a pathology. Would not the same argument apply to a predatory human society? As long as it succeeded in being predatory, would we not have to admit that it was perfectly healthy? After all, there have been numerous warrior societies organized for predatory purposes.

As already pointed out, it might be possible to answer this objection and get around this difficulty with empirical arguments to the effect that predatory societies have caused a great deal of misery. Should we not therefore conclude that they are themselves a form of pathology? Let us assume for the moment that the argument is logically and factually correct though I shall soon give some reasons for rejecting it. What difference would it make? Suppose someone had tried to tell Hitler and the Nazis that their morality was pathological—as in fact many critics of National Socialism did assert either explicitly or implicitly. What could be expected to happen? The Nazi leaders might just possibly have been interested if they had learned that their version of the warrior ethic was becoming subject to an internal decay for which a social scientist could devise appropriate administrative therapies. Indeed there are several indications, including the secret study of their own membership cited in the preceding chapter, which demonstrate that such fears were quite strong. But nothing except coarse laughter and abusive epithets would have greeted any attempt to inform them that Nazi morality as a whole was pathological.

If someone rejects the reduction of misery and suffering as a goal, there is no external authority to which one can effectively appeal in order to make that person, group, or state desist from dangerous acts. Neither God, nor the alleged forces of history, nor some presumably rational structure of the universe, can serve as effective arguments or sanctions. Even if it were possible to demonstrate with mathematical certainty that a certain form of predatory morality and society would lead to the extermination of all humanity, a cruel and romantic egotist could still snap his fingers in disdain and lead the march on to Armageddon, firmly believing that humanity deserved no better than destruction. Force and force alone can restrain such madness. And the use of force even for strictly defensive or "socially constructive" purposes gives a powerful impulse to the establishment of predatory institutions and habits.

At a less apocalyptic level of discourse it is necessary to point out that the temptation for groups and individuals to resort to predatory social arrangements, and predatory moralities to justify them, is a powerful and recurring one. The temptation is likely to remain powerful as long as there is no universally satisfactory solution to the problem of the division of labor within and among human societies. Even if such a solution were found, there are good reasons to suspect it could not be permanent since different parts of the world would still be likely to change in different ways at different rates.

If one accepts the temptations of predatory social arrangements and the consequent necessity for defense against them as probably permanent features of the human scene, it becomes difficult to take seriously the notion of predatory morality as universally pathological.[6] Where a certain form of behavior is just about inevitable, it is impossible to be morally serious about condemning it. Hence it is not enough to assert that humanity is responsible for its own morality and its own fate, that the goal of rational authority has to be deliberately affirmed and chosen. Human beings would also have to create the basic conditions that make rational authority feasible and turn predatory forms of authority into a pathological rather than normal state of affairs.

There are good reasons for doubting that this change can or will occur on a global scale in any foreseeable future. National sovereignty and indeed all forms of collective egoism would have to come to an end. There are even better reasons to avoid expending a great deal of energy in lamenting this state of affairs. The lamentation turns very easily into a form of self-indulgence that diverts attention from other important problems. It is not necessary to have the goal of eliminating *all* forms of socially produced suffering, or even all forms of predatory authority. Doctors do not give up trying to cure and prevent different kinds of illness just because they cannot prescribe pills for immortality.

3. Principles of distribution

For reasons mentioned above I have postponed a discussion of popular attitudes toward the distribution of the social product until other relevant considerations had emerged. Notions about who should get what and why are the most important aspect of popular conceptions of justice. If the evidence shows no set of popular principles that could serve as ways of settling disputes in

---

[6]Perhaps one should talk about "the pathology of the normal." But that strikes me as mainly a clever pose. As such, the phrase explains nothing. Nor can the concept of a just war serve as a general formula to resolve the dilemma. The easier it seems to apply the concept, the more suspicious we ought to be of self-serving rationalizations. That some distinctions remain possible goes without saying.

more than one society, that would be a vindication for the most extreme form of moral relativism. In its most significant form, moral relativism does not deny the possibility of discovering recurrences and even uniformities. It simply denies that any uniformity or recurrence that does or may exist can possibly serve as a basis for settling disputes. Human beings do not, as Homans, for example, has argued, quarrel about the principles of social justice. What they fight about is the application of these principles.

The best way to begin is to try to set down in some sort of order the main ways in which different people have actually tried to cope with the issue of distributing goods and services. As I read the evidence, there is variation, and therefore the possibility of disagreement and conflict, both in what principles to apply and in some cases what the principles ought to mean in concrete cases. But this variety does not necessarily mean that there are no preferred resolutions, or that no resolution is possible at all.

One way that turns up from time to time in the anthropological materials, but also occurs elsewhere, is to try to deemphasize and defuse the whole issue. "Don't worry, don't haggle, don't be too particular about getting what you need; eventually your turn will come around. Then you will get what you want or at least what you need." Such seems to be the moral message that some groups try to inculcate in their members. It is an appropriate solution where the supply of goods is uncertain, as among hunting tribes, as well as among those groups like the early Christians who seek both to escape and insulate themselves from social and moral pressures generated by the surrounding society. This solution is enshrined in the famous New Testament admonition to take comfort from those nonhuman forms of life which "toil not, neither do they spin." Like the other principles it is suitable to only a limited range of circumstances.

Closely related to the device of deemphasizing the whole issue is the principle of equality in the distribution of goods and services. There is no need to point out its recurrent appeal. Its application means that those who presently have nothing will get something, which is enough to account for the appeal, though insufficient to explain the moral passion behind it. The principle of equality is more than a demagogic sop to envy where it is combined, as it often is, with some notion to the effect that all human beings as such share precious common qualities and a common fate. The principle has two distinct advantages in sustaining the existence of a group. It is a good form of social insurance against disasters that may strike individual members of the group. It is also for the most part free from ambiguity in its application. Under the principle of equality there can be no argument about how much a person deserves or why. Shares are equal, and that is that. The disputes that can arise, provided there is real agreement on the principle itself, concern goods or services that by their nature are difficult or impossible to divide up equally. What theater can have equally good seats for all the spectators?

So far no society sufficiently complex to make use of a written language, and very few of the others, have chosen to organize distribution around the principle of equality or by deemphasizing the whole issue. By itself this fact does not prove that such arrangements are impossible, though it does prove the existence of powerful obstacles, a point that need not be pursued here. Taking a written language as a rough empirical index to the existence of social arrangements called civilization, we can say that all civilized societies and very many others have organized themselves around one or more principles of social inequality reflected in their ways of distributing goods and services. For the purposes of the present discussion these systems can be boiled down to two polar types. In those where social mobility exists the distribution of goods and services (including esteem and distinction) depends in some fashion on an individual's actual performance during his or her own lifetime. Legitimate performances are those generally deemed to be in some fashion a contribution to the social good. Illegitimate ones are deemed socially harmful. In either case it is performance that counts. Which performances to reward and which ones to penalize, and in what ways and by how much, are an obvious source of potential disagreement and conflict. Such a society is inherently unstable. But the emphasis on performance means that things get done. What gets done can vary all the way from predatory to equitable objectives. The opposite type is one where principles of distribution depend on inherited social status. In a sense they represent frozen performance, or that of preceding generations. Hence kinship and descent play a decisive role in the workings of the principles of distribution, and the unit of consumption is not just the individual. For this reason too, more than mere performance comes into play: distribution takes place in accord with imputed general human qualities alleged to be characteristic of specific castes or estates in the social order, each with its own function and form of social honor or, in many cases, social dishonor. An approach to this type is only possible in a static society existing in a static environment.

Looking now more closely at the sources of disagreement and conflict, we can easily recognize the connection between the rise of modern industry and titanic struggles between principles of allocation based primarily on inherited status and those based on performance. The erosion of customary systems of inequality based on status and social honor, whose degree of acceptance by the underlying population varied greatly from case to case and almost certainly was never as great as that described in sources that reflect mainly the concerns and doings of dominant strata, allowed a variety of group egoisms to surface. Forms of group egoism and the pursuit of selfish interest are not far below the surface anyway in any good-sized and moderately complex society—not to mention even many simpler and smaller ones. But what does the pursuit of selfish interest really mean? In most discourse it merely characterizes what one's opponents and competitors are doing. Is it then no more than an epithet, an emotive term devoid of ascertainable factual content? The grounds for a claim that these words can have a genuine factual component are, so far as I can see, the following ones. They have an important bearing on the whole issue of moral relativism.

In any given concrete case it is possible for a reasonably detached observer to assess and distinguish the relative contribution to the well-being of the social order—again in its immediate and concrete circumstances—of any specific collective undertaking from, let us say, collecting the garbage, through the provision of medical care, to the provision of a common defense. For the argument to stand, it is not necessary that these assessments and evaluations be very precise. Rough judgments as to relative ranking order and equivalents will do. Nor is it necessary for the validity of the argument that there be universal agreement on these judgments. Indeed, if one wishes to take the argument seriously, it is better to assume the existence of lively and passionate debate about these matters. But it is necessary to assume that the debates can be conducted intelligently and that there exists or can be found a rational conclusion to the discussion. Without the possibility of some objective standard, there is indeed no possibility of labeling any form of collective behavior selfish or antisocial.

Merely to state these prerequisites is enough to show how far modern societies are from meeting them, be they communist, capitalist, or anything else. Those who argue that these prerequisites cannot possibly be met under any conceivable conditions, or that the issues underlying social distribution are inherently insoluble by rational means, have a plausible case. The best answer that I can see makes the following points. Since social allocation has to take place somehow, it is better that it should take place on rational grounds to the extent that is possible. Otherwise, human relationships can never be anything but chaos brought under partial control by the right of the stronger, based on force and fraud. *Some* rationality is obviously possible and more of it is better than less. We can make distinctions among collective activities on the basis of the amount of harm and suffering they cause in relation to the benefits they purportedly produce. Food does not have to be poisonous (as on occasion it is), and post offices do not have to "lose" large amounts of mail unless it can be clearly demonstrated that the delivery of the mails on time and the production of food free from poison would require socially unacceptable costs for the general population. Perfect performance in any collective undertaking would very likely entail prohibitive costs.[7] That is no a priori reason for accepting any situation the way it is. Finally, the meaning of social rationality, despite any common core, changes over time with changing historical circumstances.

These considerations imply that society needs competent and indeed gifted individuals able to explore the meaning and applications of rationality without let or hindrance from official and unofficial taboos. Reasonableness in human relationships has always faced enormous obstacles. The intellectual obstacle of deciding just what rationality amounts to and what it entails is not necessarily the most important one. In itself disagreement about this fundamental issue is not by any means a mortal threat to the human enterprise. Instead it can be a sign of vitality and a prelude to growth and discovery. But it could be a mortal threat if human beings came to believe quite generally that rationality itself was a delusion and gave up the search altogether.

Whatever position one adopts on this issue of objective judgment, it is easy enough to see that the principle of distributing goods and services to the members of a society in accord with their performance raises far more perplexities than do the principles of equality, allotment in accord with traditional status and conceptions of social honor, or just dodging and muting the whole issue.

Even if considerably de-emphasized, some sort of a connection between performance and share in the social product is likely to be a part of actual practice, whatever the principles of

---

[7] It is necessary to be very clear in answering the question: prohibitive to whom and for what reasons? Otherwise there is a return to a struggle among various group egoisms.

inequality. As the historical materials show, particularly in the case of the German miners, the transition from the status of an estate with corporate traditions that enjoys the benefits of considerable paternalist protection and considerable social esteem to one based on individual performance creates all sorts of strains. Some benefit under the new arrangement, and others lose out. It takes time and new shared collective experiences to create a new identity in the form of unions and political movements. Such social devices represent a reluctant adaptation to the performance principle, an attempt to play the performance principle for what it is worth as well as to protect the workers against the efforts of owners and managers to turn the new situation to their advantage. In the earlier stages of industrialization businessmen are inclined to be uneasy on noting signs that the labor force is learning about the performance principle. They prefer a docile body of workers who accept the importance of hard work as an aspect of social honor and who de-emphasize secular and material rewards—in other words, certain kinds of preindustrial status groups. Except under socialism, where the ethic of revolutionary construction imposes similar attitudes, this kind of a labor force is becoming harder and harder to find. Both socialism and capitalism constitute attempts to change the accepted social definition of the relationship between collective and individual performance and shares in the social product.

Is there then any meaningful core of agreement behind the various social definitions of a just or proper system of distribution? In consideriing this issue it is important to recognize that *any* principle of distribution will work to *some* people's disadvantage *some* of the time. Human beings in any society have to be trained to put up with such consequences. It is quite clearly possible to do that, indeed perhaps alarmingly easy.

It is also reasonably clear that no single principle is likely to be a suitable arrangement for all possible circumstances. On the other hand, it is also reasonably clear that different principles are suitable to different sets of circumstances: suitable in the sense that their operation minimizes socially produced misery. Playing down the issue of distribution, or furthering moves toward equal distribution, or favoring distribution according to inherited social status are all ways of creating a sense of security and damping down social rivalries. Distribution according to inherited social status requires a good deal of social training and at least a regular and dependable supply of food and shelter if it is to bring about this result. Distribution in accord with performance is, on the other hand, a way to accomplish things, especially new things in a changing social order. It is also the only way by which individuals can improve their own situation. As Marx emphasized, any system of distribution depends very heavily on what the members of a society (and not necessarily all members) want to produce.

What makes human beings angry, then, is a change in the social principles to which they have been accustomed, or the application of principles that are not suited to a particular kind of activity and set of circumstances. The history of industrialization and modernization is full of these moral conflicts. The principle of reward according to merit, as measured by price in the market, conflicted with the principle of reward according to inherited social status. The triumph of the newer principle was a triumph for the bourgeoisie and its way of organizing human affairs. Politically significant moral anger comes then from the application of a new principle that works to the disadvantage of substantial numbers of people, and particularly when the new principle deprives them of the results of hard work. It is not the objective suffering that is the main cause of moral anger; it is the apparent social cause. To perceive the causes as human is a necessary first step toward doing something about human misery and injustice.

4. Exploitation

All of the above issues come together in connection with the vexing concept of exploitation. To the extent that the term can have an objective meaning it designates nonreciprocal social relationships. Some people get more out of the relationship than their contribution warrants and others get less. Thus the concept presupposes the possibility of an objective assessment of the value of social activities and the contribution of each party. Presumably the workers receive wages that do not cover their contribution to the productive process while the factory owners take home more than their contribution warrants. Priests frighten the population into paying tithes without rendering adequate services in return. The list can be extended at will.

The absence of reciprocity can refer to social relationships in the institutional areas of authority and social coordination, production, and distribution, or more commonly in all three. Any claim that exploitation exists has to take into account all relevant exchanges. It is not enough to demonstrate that a dominant class or caste consumes more material goods than it produces. It is also necessary to show that the other services it provides, such as coordinating the various economic and noneconomic activities of the society, rendering justice, providing defense against common enemies, are services that it fails to provide adequately, or that the social functions themselves have for some reason become less valuable than they were.

All such judgments depend for their validity on the possibility of constructing objective criteria for assessing social performance. It is not necessary to discuss the difficulties in constructing such criteria, because there are other and more serious limitations on the explanatory value of the concept of exploitation that have led me to make very little use of the notion in this book. These limitations will appear in a moment. But it is important to notice that the mere fact of human disagreements about the worth of certain activities, and by extension the worth of people who perform these tasks, does not by itself disqualify exploitation as an impartial scientific term. Impartial, incidentally, does not mean neutral; an impartial judgment can condemn somebody or something. The acceptance of a low estimate on the value of one's work and general social contribution is for low-status groups generally the result in large measure of social conditioning. The social conditioning itself can therefore be a result of exploitation, and it is exploitation itself that accounts for many variations in social evaluations. The fact that large numbers of blacks and females have taken for granted lower rates of pay for work identical with that performed by white males can hardly be used to demonstrate that exploitation is a purely arbitrary and subjective notion.

At the same time there are areas where social decisions are both unavoidable and for which it is impossible to construct criteria that yield clear-cut decisions. In any concrete case how serious is the threat from foreign enemies? Very few human societies have had the luxury of being able to disregard this question. Most of them must consider how much emphasis to place on military virtues and how much in resources to devote to military conflict. Nobody can have a completely accurate measure of the intentions and capabilities of potential military opponents. Since an underestimate is more dangerous than an overestimate, much of human history has been an unavoidable search for a self-defeating margin of security.

In a rough-and-ready sense the limits of certainty coincide with the boundaries of feasible social control as they exist for a particular society at a particular point in time. The capacity of human societies to recognize and do something about the

sources of human misery changes over time and helps to produce changes in the principles of social inequality or the evalua-
tion of different social tasks and functions. In this sense exploitation is an historical category and a recurring historical discovery.
It comes into existence at the point when human beings become
able and willing to ask certain questions about their own society:
Is this social activity—that of priests, fighters, cultivators, artisans, etc.—necessary? Necessary for whom and why? What may
happen if we change or cease this activity? What material resources are necessary for it, and who should get them? Every
society develops collective answers to these questions whether or
not any of its members ever stops to think about them. It would
be presumptuous optimism to claim that unambiguous answers
are always possible, and even more foolish to hope that the
existence of clear answers would by itself put an end to violence,
cruelty, and injustice. Without better answers, on the other hand,
without the recognition of exploitation, it is impossible to move
in that direction.

Furthermore, the presence or absence of exploitation as
determined by some supposedly impartial observer by itself
makes very little difference in human feelings and human behavior. It is always necessary to find out how people themselves
judge their situation. To label a social institution "exploitative"
tells us very little about how the persons concerned will react.
That has been my main reason for refraining from any extended
use of the concept in this book. There are too many potent social
and psychological mechanisms that can prevent human beings
not only from expressing moral outrage at their situation but
sometimes even from feeling it. There is no guarantee that
exploitation, or just plain human misery, will somehow secrete its
own antidote.

Human beings have to create their own moral standards of
condemnation and their own forms of collective action in order
to change such situations. As already noted, there is nothing in
the structure of the universe, or History with a capital H, that
guarantees success in the endeavor, or even that the endeavor
will occur. But such attempts have taken place repeatedly. In the
next chapter we shall try to disentangle the main factors that
produce and sustain them.

CHAPTER FOURTEEN

Inevitability and the sense of injustice

1. Introductory observations

As we approach the end of a long journey I would like to return with the reader to concerns that have impelled us to make the journey together. What is moral outrage? Under what conditions does it occur? When and why does it not occur? Is it something natural to all human beings? If so, what does "natural" really mean? Is not the apparent absence of a sense of injustice even more significant than its appearance? Though the book has explored these questions, its author does not pretend to have provided definitive answers if definitive implies the kind of answer that will persuade and satisfy everybody. Nor do I intend to present in conventional capsule form here what has been discussed at greater length throughout the book. Instead I propose to explore once again how the sense of injustice does make its appearance, drawing on the material we have covered together and whatever considerations I myself can contribute.

Let us begin by asking if there might be some common themes that appear in the behavior of Hindu Untouchables, steelworkers in the Ruhr before 1914, Ulrich Bräker's inability to get angry at the patron who sold him as a mercenary to the armies of Frederick the Great, the awe of the Spartacists before stamps and signatures, the self-inflicted tortures of ascetics, and the reactions of human beings upon whom the Nazis inflicted the trauma of the concentration camps. In varying degrees and in different ways all these people felt that their sufferings were unavoidable. For some victims such suffering appeared to a degree inevitable and legitimate. People are evidently inclined to grant legitimacy to anything that is or seems inevitable no matter how painful it may be. Otherwise the pain might be intolerable. The conquest of this sense of inevitability is essential to the development of politically effective moral outrage. For this to happen, people must perceive and define their situation as the consequence of human injustice: a situation that they need not, cannot, and ought not to endure. By itself of course such a perception, be it a novel awakening or the content of hallowed tradition, is no guarantee of political and social changes to come. But without some very considerable surge of moral anger such changes do not occur.[1]

It is tempting to posit a straightforward reaction of pain and anger at the blows inflicted by the physical and social environment, as the beginning of all human attempts to "do something" about whatever hurts. Undoubtedly the pain is there and an indispensable spur to action. There may even be an almost automatic angry response that is independent of whatever cultural conditioning and social standards the individual has acquired. Did anyone have to tell Thersites that soldiering for Agamemnon was no fun? Homer didn't think it was necessary to explain how he came to feel that way. The reaction of a poor foot soldier, dragged into a campaign in which he had no interest, was presumably as understandable to a Greek three thousand years ago as it is to us. What was remarkable to Homer's audience, and to us, is that Thersites had the audacity to stand up before Agamemnon and say to his fellow soldiers "Let us go back home in our ships, and leave this man here by himself in Troy. . . ." Such daring is indeed out of the ordinary.

Essentially our problem is to state what conditions may make such audacity possible—and effective. But we are not even safe in assuming that a person in the boots of Thersites or someone like him will even *feel* the anger, far less speak his mind about it. The notion that there is some indomitable spirit of revolt in all human beings is, I fear, sheer myth. As the material from the concentration camps shows, it is possible to destroy any such spirit and even the will to survive. Admittedly, that is an extreme case, and not all inmates by any means responded in this fashion. Still the evidence there is enough to show that any inclination

---

[1]Even fantasies of liberation and revenge can help to preserve domination through dissipating collective energies in relatively harmless rhetoric and ritual. For the dominant group such a phenomenon has the further advantage of justifying alertness, keeping the tools of repression in good working order and their own supporters in line. Among the leaders of both oppressors and oppressed there can be a tacit understanding that this is the way the system is supposed to work, that this is the form the social contract takes.

toward anger, and even the capacity to feel pain, can vary over a wide range to the point of complete extinction.

The most that one can assert with considerable confidence is that suffering in the forms of hunger, physical abuse, or deprivation of the fruits of hard work is indeed objectively painful for human beings. They do not seek suffering for its own sake. Even ascetics impose suffering on themselves for the sake of other goals, such as salvation, release from social obligations, or control of the universe. In the objective quality of suffering our search does reach a point that can serve as a firm basis for departure. If no culture makes suffering an end in itself and all cultures treat certain forms of suffering as inherently painful, we are justified in considering the absence of felt pain as due to some form of moral and psychological anesthesia. From this standpoint the assertion that there is no indomitable spirit of revolt takes on a different meaning. It means that under certain specifiable sociological and psychological conditions the anesthesia can be terribly effective.

How does the introduction of an historical perspective alter our understanding of social anesthesia? Historical analysis brings into the center of our vision the importance of improving capacities to control the natural and social environment along with the apparently endless chain of new causes of human suffering that this improvement produces, and the related changes in the principles of social inequality. It will be necessary to return to these issues again. It is a perspective that raises the question of whether we can legitimately speak of historically necessary forms of anesthesia. These could be connected with aspects of human suffering for which human society generally had not yet developed adequate techniques to control or eliminate. The control of diseases seems to be the clearest example. For historically necessary forms of suffering then there is nothing human beings can do but endure the pain or resort to such forms of cultural anesthesia as magic and religion. At any given stage of human development there would also be historically unnecessary—or historically futile—forms of suffering, that is, those that people could eliminate but fail to do so, presumably due to the opposition of vested interests. Thus in any concrete case we would have to ask, historically necessary for whom and why?

There are potentially dangerous pitfalls in the use of the concept of historical necessity, some of which have turned up in earlier chapters. Others it will be better to defer to a more appropriate context. By asking to whom the necessity applies and who gets what out of its application, it is possible to avoid the pitfalls and retain the kernel of anti-utopian truth: not every-thing is possible all of the time.

That will do as a preliminary outline of the theoretical dangers. The task at hand is to determine how human beings awake from anesthesia, how they overcome the sense of inevitability and how a sense of injustice may take its place. The situation of the Hindu Untouchables, one of maximum acceptance of servile status with a minimum of force, may serve to illustrate the type of starting point in which we are mainly interested. In milder forms the same feelings and social relationships are quite plain in the case of Ulrich Bräker, the steelworkers of the Ruhr and countless others. On further inspection and reflection they cease to seem in any way bizarre. Instead they are instances of responses to one of the oldest and commonest of human experiences, generalized patriarchal authority. In this prototypical experience the young person *wants* to please the father, even if hatred may also exist. There is an exchange of dependence, services, and childlike trusting adoration in return for care, protection, and another type of affection. In daily life one can see the essence of the relationship in the behavior of a dog toward its master.

I do not know whether dogs can develop a rudimentary sense of injustice if their masters mistreat them. Quite possibly experimental psychologists have demonstrated something of the sort. Quite obviously human beings can and do develop it. In this process of growth and emancipation one can discern three distinguishable but related processes. At the level of the individual human personality it is necessary to overcome certain forms of dependence on others and acquire or strengthen controls over impulses. This dependence and lack of control, to the extent that it actually exists and is not merely a rationalization for the authority of the dominant strata, is likely to be one aspect of psychological adaptation to the fact of subordination and powerlessness. In effect, people have to grow up.

At the level of social organization they also have to overcome dependence. Here the historical component becomes more obvious, due to the ways in which economic and political forms (in Europe, for example: city-state, feudalism, royal absolutism, capitalism, state socialism) have succeeded each other. As part of the process of overcoming dependence there may be the creation of new forms of solidarity and new networks of cooperation if the subordinate group was composed of atomized units. If, on the other hand, it was already a cohesive unit with a high degree of internal cooperation and sentiments of solidarity, this solidarity may require redirection. Instead of working in cooperation

461

with and support of the dominant groups, it will be necessary to find ways to turn it against these groups. Instead of solidarity in adopting heroic gestures that endanger the group, it will be necessary to find ways to support effective resistance. Finally, at the level of cultural norms and shared perceptions it will be necessary to overcome the illusion that the present state of affairs is just, permanent, and inevitable. The historical component is crucial in this area too. What is an illusion at one point in time will not have been an illusion at an earlier point. Economic and social trends have to develop to a point where possibilities change, where what was reality becomes illusion. It is vastly easier for historians to explain the illusion convincingly after the event[2] than for social prophets to proclaim the event convincingly before it happens. It is harder still to tell exactly whose reasoning is correct.

The conquest of the illusion of inevitability is not confined to dramatic political revolutions. It has been part of the whole transformation that we call modernization and industrialization, one that has been going on ever since the rise of commercial cities in the later phase of European feudalism. There was an earlier burst in a different form that began before the pre-Socratics and petered out about the time of Alexander the Great. Though specialists on the history of other societies and cultures will surely challenge the claim, so far as I can see the conquest of the illusion of inevitability has until quite recent times been mainly a process within Western culture. Behind this process, as we recognize more clearly from an historical perspective, are changes in a society's capacity to solve the traditional problems of hunger and disease—thereby generating new issues—and associated changes in the principles of social inequality. Now that the process as a whole has come into sight, it will be useful to step back and comment further on the psychological, sociological, and cultural aspects.

2. Individual personality

Starting with the individual human being, it is easy to see that it is very difficult not to feel inferior when one *is* inferior and nearly all social pressures work to remind one of it. The case of the

[2]Who could have been certain that France under Louis XVI coming to the aid of the American Revolution was much closer to collapse than France at the death of Louis XIV?

Untouchables is only an extreme example of the way these pressures work. A secure but lowly status is much easier to bear than no position at all. In a lowly status the individual can trade obedience and loyalty for security if the relationship has some color of justice and affection.

Both Freudian psychology and theories of conditioning that hark back to Pavlov shed considerable light on how submission and dependence arise and are maintained, as well as how some ties may be broken. They show why it is so terribly hard to believe that long-established authority is not essentially benevolent. It is the source of awe, conscience, and rewards, as well as punishments and frustrations. Erratic rewards rather than consistent ones, according to some indications from experimental psychology, are more effective spurs to learning, and hence presumably to implanting attitudes and even feelings. That may be why inferiors so often prefer premodern forms of authority, those that appear to them as gruff, unpredictable, but protective of all their concerns, to modern bureaucratic forms with their machinelike consistency applied to one narrow segment of life. In popular conceptions patriarchal justice, whose erratic character contains a perpetual hint of possible loopholes and even the prospect of some sharp plea bargaining, is preferable to perfect justice. The latter is, like nemesis, somehow fearful. Rational authority is hardly the poor man's first choice.

Practically by definition, authority implies some degree of frustration for those subject to it. Otherwise how could it be authority and how would the subject know it existed? The idea of freedom as the rational person's completely free acceptance of rational law may or may not be good philosophy. But it runs directly counter to common observation as well as whatever psychology and sociology this writer has learned. Where there is frustration there is also the possibility of anger. The range of variation in the amount and form of anger is on the other hand very wide. Hence to say that all attitudes toward authority are ambivialent is not very helpful. In a society where the system of authority has functioned in the same way for as long as anyone can remember and one that is sufficiently isolated so that inferiors have no possibility of learning about anything else, it seems possible to impose considerable frustration without creating much anger. Again the Untouchables come to mind. Possibly the anger is directed inward in self-destructive ways, though that seems to me doubtful: the personalities are by no means *that* pathological by any definition of the term.

The opposite kind of situation occurs in cases of conquest

and slavery. In such instances the oppressed bring with them into the new situation standards of condemnation in the form of recollections of their own past. Even plantation slavery, it has been pointed out, was not a total institution like the concentration camp.[3] It was possible for slaves to create and sustain a subsociety and a subculture of their own. That is probably why the relationship between master and slave contained such a potential for anger. It was not due to the deprivation and degradation, or rather not to these alone, as they can kill the will to resist. With this mixture of anger and dependence—very likely also anger at dependence—the relationship could often be a highly ambivalent one, changing from rage to dependence and even affection quite rapidly, according to momentary circumstances and expectations.

Sambo was real, and so was the slave who slit the master's throat in the night. They might be the same person. Which was mask and which was real? To the extent that it occurs in response to the promptings, cajolings, threats, or rewards of other people any and practically all behavior is a mask. And it is very difficult to act a mask or a role continually without acquiring the character that goes with the role. We know it is true of oppressors who are often, to begin with, quite ordinary persons, changed and marked by circumstances. It is hard to believe that the same processes do not occur among the oppressed.[4]

For audacity to occur and become effective—that is, for it to be more than an occasional flare-up of hopeless rage, important changes are necessary in the human character produced by poverty and oppression. Roughly the same changes appear to be necessary (1) for effective political resistance, (2) for adapting to the new discipline of the machine, and (3) for individual efforts to struggle up a rung or two on the social ladder. They amount to a strengthening of the ego at the expense of the id, the taming of natural impulses, and the deferral of present gratifications for the sake of a better future.

To be sure, there is an odor of hypocrisy in much current talk about characteristic personalities among the poor and oppressed. It scarcely behooves those who profit most from the social order to preach renunciation and self-discipline to the poor. Furthermore there is plenty of evidence to show that just as

---

[3]For that matter the concentration camp is not a total institution either. The term is an exaggeration but useful for certain limited purposes.

[4]For a good discussion that shows the variety among both masters and slaves see John W. Blassingame, *The Slave Community*, espec. chap. 11. Variety is a recurring theme all through Eugene D. Genovese, *Roll, Jordan, Roll*.

the victims of the social order will be slouchers on the job when other persons appropriate the results of their labor, they will work in a very self-disciplined manner on self-chosen tasks or on those that promise personal gains. Slaves who scrimp and accumulate to buy their freedom are one example. So are the collective farmers under Russian socialism, who are very indifferent producers on the collective farms because the state takes most of the benefits. On their own small private plots, on the other hand, they lavish energy and care to the point where this private sector of the economy has long been indispensable for the supply of food under socialism. Similarly there is good evidence to show the extraordinary fortitude and adaptability of many characteristic lower-class individuals in the face of overwhelming misfortune, even when they find it impossible to organize their lives in such a way as to prevent the misfortunes from happening.[5]

What this evidence also shows is that life-situations and prospects to a great degree determine behavior—as much among the victims of the social order as its beneficiaries. For the victims the delay of gratification can be an unrealistic policy, though this is a complicated matter where more dispassionate investigation is necessary. In our own society, for example, it is often claimed that working extra hard and being a good boy or girl is unrealistic because the occupational structure contains relatively few tasks that are rewarding anyway. Furthermore our society allegedly reserves most of the rewarding ones to persons from privileged backgrounds through a series of formal and informal devices.[6] On the other hand, no inconsiderable number of persons do manage to "make it" into more responsible jobs through effort and self-discipline. Is the "realistic" adaptation of preferring immediate gratification to hard work therefore no more than a self-fulfilling prophecy, a rationalization for failure within the prevailing system? That too is part of the truth. To assess its significance one would have to find out just what proportion of the lower classes did try hard to achieve upward mobility but failed, as well as the reasons for failure. To my limited knowledge dependable studies of this sort do not yet exist.

In the meantime one significant aspect stands out as reasonably well established. For blacks the reluctance to work hard for

---

[5]See Oscar Lewis, *La Vida: A Puerto Rican Family in the Culture of Poverty*, for valuable raw material on this point.

[6]For some data see *Work in America*, Report of a Special Task Force to the Secretary of Health, Education, and Welfare.

whites is an historical legacy. Without doubt it was a realistic adaptation for them, and for many other subordinate and oppressed strata.[7] To overcome this legacy on any massive scale, to set up an effective and fundamentally noncoercive set of incentives that really takes hold, is a task that neither capitalism nor the Russian variant of socialism has solved. Chinese claims to have solved it—starting from a situation where a traditional work ethic did exist—await serious and impartial scrutiny.[8]

To return now to the starting point, in a hierarchical society dependency of some sort is the major fact of life for the lower strata, and the human personality adapts to this fact. This broad similarity in situations helps to explain why the same exhortations to abstention from the pleasures of the world, the same calls for self-control, come as much from those who seek to help the downtrodden and to change their lives as from those who profit from their labors. From Saint Paul to Lenin the themes and exhortations are very similar. The priggish and prudish attitudes of the German working-class elite toward the rest of the workers before the First World War are cut from the same cloth. They were a response to the same problem of trying to instill a new morality into those for whom fleeting gratifications helped to make a harsh existence bearable.[9] Evidently there is a great deal more to the need for rational mastery of the impulses and desires than mere bourgeois preaching. Gaining control over their own impulses is part of the way in which human beings learn to resist oppressive authority and fight against both the physical and moral aspects of a harsh and degrading environment. It is part of learning to resist the moral authority of the oppressor, to say

[7]But by no means all. Both Chinese and Japanese peasants have long had a reputation for being very hard workers, while most Indian peasants are described as indifferent cultivators. Though I have tried to account for some of these differences in my *Social Origins*, the whole issue of the cultural distribution and historical origins of the work ethic remains, so far as I can see, wide open. It is by no means clear whether Max Weber's famous contribution in *The Protestant Ethic and the Spirit of Capitalism* constituted an important breakthrough or a blind alley.

[8]By 1975 one important point stood out. The surging campaigns to establish a new set of socialist motivations, the Great Leap Forward and the Great Proletarian Cultural Revolution, were also periods of very considerable deterioration in the material welfare of both workers and peasants. These facts come through clearly in the highly sympathetic but honest study by Charles Hoffmann, *The Chinese Worker*, 158–168.

[9]By and large the student rebels of the 1960s were the first revolutionary hedonists. Conceivably the change marks a new historical departure not possible until now, a theme that may be picked up and intensified at some future date. But there are grounds for skepticism. The student revolts were hardly movements *of* the oppressed, nor even *for* the oppressed in their consequences.

to themselves that the oppressor's punishments are undeserved. The creation of new moral standards and their incorporation into the personality of the oppressed is part of the whole process. As every revolutionary recognizes, the victims have to put iron in their souls. The tragedies occur when revolutionary leaders use the iron in their own souls to require the sacrifice of their followers.

As we saw in Chapter Three, psychologists can tell us something about how iron enters the human soul, though few psychologists would be likely to use this language. In any case iron in the soul does not determine the direction and consequences of a political movement. It is merely a necessary ingredient in political trends, from the most revolutionary to the most repressive (and can help the former turn into the latter), including movements for self-help and social uplift. It is well to remember that the iron in Socrates' soul, his own guardian spirit that he referred to in the *Apology*, told him both to resist and question the moral standards and judgments of the Athenians, and to accept the proffered hemlock with expressions of love for the city of Athens and loyal obedience to its laws.[10] To understand where newly focused and perhaps even newly created psychic energies may turn or, in other words, help to shape the formation of standards of condemnation, it is necessary to look beyond what takes place in the human personality, and very often beyond what is happening among the poor and the oppressed.

Once again the historical perspective is helpful and salutary. By no means is all poverty due to oppression. Poverty is after all the starting line from which humanity has departed. If we define poverty very roughly as an insufficient and irregular supply of food, combined with shelter inadequate for protection against severe physical discomfort, the starting line is barely two centuries behind us for the bulk of the population in even the most economically advanced countries. Whether the physical resources exist for eliminating this kind of poverty in a world inhabited by more than two billion people is a question I shall not attempt to answer. It is enough to remind ourselves that the .dimensions and perceptions of the issue have altered beyond recognition in a brief span of time and in a way that must have brought a variety of new forces to bear on the individual sufferer. Only relatively recently has it been both possible and necessary for new standards of condemnation and new principles of social

[10]For the latter aspect see the *Crito*.

organization to take hold. Whether they will take hold is another matter, especially since even very intelligent and well-informed people are in passionate disagreement about just what these standards and principles should be.

3. Social aspects

Let us now therefore focus on the social and economic aspects of how a social order that appears more or less inevitable to the underlying population may lose all or part of this aura. Once again, but with attention directed to different variables and processes, the task is to understand how standards of condemnation arise and through what kinds of social organization human beings put them into effect. I shall concentrate almost entirely on urban populations, drawing only occasionally on agrarian experiences for comparative purposes.

The first essential ingredient for the whole process is a rather rapid improvement in a society's capacity to produce goods and services, enough to make it appear possible to "solve" the problem of poverty as it has been traditionally defined. One could go further and assert that the improvement must be enough to make poverty appear as a *problem* and not part of the natural order of the universe. Such a transformation, it is worth emphasizing again, has occurred only once on this scale in human history and only very recently.

It is possible to imagine an improvement in a society's capacity to produce and exchange goods and services taking place in such a way that all sectors of the population make equal gains and therefore without generating any pressures for institutional changes. Conceivably that could happen somewhere in the future. But it has not happened anywhere yet, and is highly unlikely because any such improvement is almost certain to bring in its train significant changes in the division of labor and hence in systems of authority, as well as in the procedures for distributing goods and services among the population. That is one reason why Marxists regard changes in economic structure as over the long haul the basic causes of other social changes, including moral standards.

There is another good reason behind the Marxist position. Changes in ideas and ideals will not be feasible until and unless there are changes in a society's capacity to reduce its level of socially necessary misery, based on an increase in productivity.

Without this increase in economic potential, ideas of liberation can be no more than intellectual dreams and playthings for a limited number of people. The same may not be necessarily true for repressive notions about how to intensify subjection and submission, though on this score too advancing technology has made available new and alarming possibilities.

Nevertheless the Marxist position is open to serious criticism when it asserts, as Marx himself occasionally did,[11] that economic changes necessarily *cause* intellectual and social changes. Sometimes they may and sometimes not, and the causation can also run in the opposite direction. Economic institutions have often been adapted to military, political, and even religious considerations. Systems of ideas and cultural meanings also display a dynamic of change quite on their own that may have very significant consequences for economic institutions. That changes in economic arrangements are a necessary condition for successful change in, say, law, morals, and religious beliefs is not the same thing as asserting that economic changes are always the causes for the latter. Universal propositions about the primacy of economic changes, even when qualified by the useful escape clause "in the long run," are to be rejected out of hand.

Granting and even emphasizing that ideas cannot become effective without economic (and other) changes, there is still an important positive point to be made. Without strong moral feelings and indignation, human beings will not act against the social order. In this sense moral convictions become an equally necessary element for changing the social order, along with alterations in the economic structure. The history of every major political struggle reflects the clash of passions, convictions, and systems of belief. That is plain as far back as the historical record will take us, back to the Hebrew prophets, back even to the struggles of Ikhnaton, beyond which the record begins to fade. Convictions are also probably necessary for a society to continue to work along customary lines, though that is harder to demonstrate. People may be able to continue to behave according to familiar routines in a rather cynical and desultory fashion with only small cues from their associates to indicate what is expected from them. In a crisis or novel situation, on the other hand, their

---

[11]Cf. Marx' famous remarks in "The Poverty of Philosophy" (355):

> In acquiring new productive forces men change their mode of production; and in changing their mode of production they change their way of earning their living— they change all their social relations. . . . The same men who establish their social relations in conformity with their material productivity, produce also principles, ideas and categories, in conformity with their social relations.

reactions are liable to be unpredictable, at which point collapse and chaos may set in.[12]

For reasons mentioned a moment ago it is highly unlikely that the benefits of a rise in productive capacity will benefit all sectors of a society equally. A rise in productive capacity is not the same thing as a change in a society's capacity to solve its own problems—or again more accurately to make long-standing causes of human suffering *become* problems. It is only one indispensable contribution to this capacity. For the desire to make use of this potential, or for standards of condemnation to arise and take hold, other things have to happen, and often do happen.

The next ingredient, which appears to be an indispensable as well as a frequently observed one, is a marked increase in the suffering of the lower strata. For standards of condemnation to take hold, the suffering has to increase rapidly enough so that people do not have time to become accustomed to it. It will be necessary to go into this aspect more thoroughly later. It is important that the apparent causes of the suffering be new and unfamiliar, traceable to the acts of concrete easily identified persons. That such judgments have often been mistaken goes without saying. It is the consequences that matter from the standpoint of this inquiry.

In this form of suffering the disruption of the social organization is probably more significant in its political consequences than straightforward material deprivation, painful though the latter undoubtedly is. For the individual the disruption means the collapse or at least partial breakdown of familiar daily routines. Artisans and sellers lose their customers; new forms of "unfair" competition appear; others start hoarding; it becomes hard to find food, or to pay for it if it can be found. Crop failures in an economy still vulnerable to them can greatly intensify the disruption.

By itself disruption may cause nothing more than apathy,

[12]On the significance of moral convictions I adopt Max Weber's position. A strict behaviorist might object that we know nothing about the feelings of other people; all we can observe is their behavior. It is necessary to grant that we cannot observe other people's feelings, only their behavior as manifested in speech, gesture, facial expression, and much else. There is also a risk in using introspection to assert how people feel on the basis of such evidence. But the risk should not be exaggerated just for the sake of preserving the chastity of scientific method. Human responses are sufficiently alike for observers who are not socially deaf, dumb, or blind to be able to tell when those they observe are angry, sad, or happy. In any case most historical evidence consists of reports about what people said and did. Thus the purists can limit their correlations, inferences, and deductions to strictly behavioral data, and delete all references to feelings if they prefer to. The deletions are unlikely to do more than slightly impoverish any significant historical or political theses.

confusion, and despair. If it is liable to make a population more malleable, it can make it malleable to new and oppressive forms of authority. We have seen that happen in the case of the Nazis, and something of the sort apparently played a part in the submission of the German iron and steelworkers to their fate. The destruction of the social framework supporting traditional morality and expectations does not automatically mean that better ones will take their place. In fact the complete destruction of existing institutions and habits of cooperation may make resistance impossible, indeed unthinkable, by destroying the basis from which it can start.

For changes that will reduce human suffering, other things have to happen. The disruption has to spread to the dominant classes and split them in such a way that alliances can be formed between elements in both the dominant and subordinate classes. One reason the Revolution of 1848 in Germany produced so few results is that this realignment did not occur. At the same time, for standards of condemnation to take form, some elements in the dominant classes must appear as parasitic to the lower classes, as making no contribution to the workings of the social order and hence as violating the implicit social contract. In this connection it would be enlightening to investigate more carefully the historical development of popular attitudes toward effort—the intensity of work rather than work itself—to see if there has not been up until quite recent times a steadily increasing value put upon this quality.

Where the causes of misery appear to the sufferers as due to the acts of identifiable superiors, such as employers or prominent officials, in the early stages these acts are likely to appear too as violations of established rights and norms, again a breaking of the established social contract. Petitions for redress, addressed to still higher authority, are therefore a characteristic first response. The supreme authority appears as a benevolent paternal figure who needs only to hear about injustice in order to correct it. This reaction was widespread in Germany, but by no means confined to that country or cultural milieu.[13] In other situations there may be blind outbursts of rage at the violation of norms of conduct and reward that human beings always create in the course of antagonistic cooperation in the place of work. The final cry of poor Karl Fischer, "There is no order here!"

[13]In Chapter Ten, p. 362 we saw the strength of naïve monarchist beliefs in the strong support Father Gapon mustered in his march in 1905 to petition the Tsar to relieve workers' sufferings. Bloody Sunday dealt a severe blow to those beliefs, as the Tsar's troops gave their answer.

comes to mind as a sad, vivid example. For such persons the world has gotten out of joint—it is a cry against essential unfairness.

For large numbers of people the world does get out of joint in the sense that they lose any regular respected and moderately secure status in it, even if their services in the form of brute physical labor power remain necessary. Though it is important to avoid romanticizing the security of the lower classes in premodern times, there is no reason to doubt that this process of atomization and degradation has taken place on a very wide scale. While the process may create some additional raw material for urban riots, its consequences for the social order do not by themselves appear to be very significant. Riots can be controlled by disciplined troops relatively easily. Indeed I would hazard the generalization that the formation of a large body of semi-outsiders, or proletariat, constitutes one of the least politically effective forms of human misery, as well as possibly the most painful. To be sure, the mere presence of this kind of a pre-factory proletariat can and did frighten the upper classes all over Europe in the early stages of industrialization. De Tocqueville in his *Souvenirs* reveals the horror and revulsion that many in the upper classes must have felt at this apparition from the depths during the rising in Paris in 1848. That rising on the other hand came to nothing, and General Cavaignac, perhaps the first of a sinister line of modern saviors of civilization, brutally stamped out its last flames a few months later. After 1848 the danger was past. The Russian Revolution was to come from quite a different constellation of forces: the grievances of land-short peasants and industrial workers in big factories in a few key cities.

Once a critical mass of potentially discontented people has come into existence through the working out of large-scale in-stitutional forces the stage is set for the appearance of "outside agitators." It is important to recognize the crucial significance of their role because social critics are inclined to minimize it for fear of carrying water to the mills of conservatism and reaction. Since the time of the Apostles, and perhaps earlier, no social move-ment has been without its army of preachers and militants to spread the good tidings of escape from the pains and evils of this world. It is always an activist minority that promotes and pro-mulgates new standards of condemnation. They are an indis-pensable if insufficient cause of major social transformations, peaceful and gradualist as well as violent or revolutionary. Generally they are relatively young and unencumbered by social ties and obligations. That is one more indication of the importance of social and cultural space, to be discussed shortly. Very frequently they are outsiders to the locality in which they serve. Their task is to find and articulate latent grievances, to challenge the dominant mythology, to organize for a contest with the dominant forces around them. The outside agitators do the hard work of undermining the old sense of inevitability. They are also the traveling salesmen for the new inevitability. In human affairs it requires tremendous effort to produce the inevitable, new or old, and no one is quite sure of what the new one will look like until after it has already happened. By then it is generally too late.[14]

The weakness of any collective consciousness and social organization beyond the narrow confines of neighborhood and occupation in the Paris of 1848 may have contributed to the failure of that uprising.[15] Be that as it may, the point to be emphasized is that the new forms of collective action that grow up in an urban context, revolutionary parties and trade unions, display a strong tendency to come to terms with the status quo.

One clear reason for this widespread turn to a gradualist and reformist strategy is the experience of defeat in revolutionary uprisings. Gradualism, reformism, and the techniques of legitimate opposition do not arise out of some innate process of maturing or even out of situations where there gets to be so much to go around that fighting ceases to be attractive and worthwhile. An increase in the size of the social product to be divided up may indeed be a helpful ingredient in domestic tranquillity. But the historical record shows that even in England, and still more so on the continent, suppression prepared the way for negotiation and bargaining. For the weaker contestants gradualism was not the virtue in its own right that it became for the dominant classes; it was a virtue forced upon them by necessity.

By this observation I do not mean to imply that even in this early stage of development there was among the lower strata in the cities any powerful revolutionary impulse that was somehow stifled and diverted. Both the liberal and the Marxist models of characteristic working-class development seem to me misleading

---

[14] Among leaders and led, militance can also be an intermittent escape from boredom and routine obligations. For some acute observations on this aspect of late nineteenth-century strikes in France see Michelle Perrot, *Les ouvriers en grève: France 1871–1890*, II, 547–568. With their policy of bread and circuses Roman rulers long ago recognized the importance of keeping control over ways to escape from boredom in their own hands. Is there a negative correlation between public holidays and public disturbances?

[15] According to Peter H. Amann, *Revolution and Mass Democracy*, the main attempt at organization was a dismal failure.

because they are too schematic and fail to capture the most important variables. According to the liberal view, the trauma of industrialization in its early phase is liable to create more or less irrational radical demands. With the passage of time and rising productivity the workers learn the virtue of collective bargaining and democratic pressure-group tactics and thus become peaceably incorporated into a system of liberal capitalism. There follows the demise of ideology. According to the Marxist scheme, the workers start from a generally inert situation, capable at most of occasional acts of instinctive revolt. Through the experience of industrialization, which brings them together in huge factories to impose upon them a common fate, they acquire a revolutionary class consciousness. This form of consciousness amounts to an awareness of their crucial role in the whole historical process as perceived and outlined by Marx, and a willingness to act on this awareness at the crucial historical moment. Though in Lenin's variant the awareness would not come of itself but had to be brought to the workers from the outside by intellectuals who had turned into professional revolutionaries, the experience of factory life under capitalism was a necessary prerequisite for the masses to undergo this *prise de conscience* with the help of the intellectuals.[16]

The German evidence made it necessary to reject both the Leninist interpretation and one that looks toward an independent capacity among industrial workers for general solutions to the problems of industrial society. To the extent that it is possible to discern mass reactions and attitudes, there is very little indication of a desire to overhaul the society. There can be at times a very large stockpile of anger. But this anger will not necessarily, and in fact in Germany did not, turn into a desire to make the world over, even in the form of quite simple egalitarian notions or a desire to have rich and poor change places. Certainly it did not turn into massive support for socialism, even at the height of the revolt in the Ruhr in 1920.

[16]It may be appropriate to mention that when I began this inquiry I felt that both approaches were too intellectual. In Leninism especially, both the condescending attitude toward the workers' capacity to find their own solutions to their problems and the smugly arrogant faith in the intellectuals' capacity—only Bolshevik intellectuals of course—to find the right answers to everything, had for a long time impressed me as peculiarly repulsive. Influenced by the work of E. P. Thompson, I had to some extent expected to come upon indications that industrial workers were capable of developing through their own experiences their own diagnosis and remedy for the ills that afflicted them. This diagnosis and remedy, I thought, might turn out to be rather more sensible and feasible than intellectuals had been inclined to grant, but that the workers had never gained enough power to try it out. Here, it seemed to me, might be one of history's suppressed alternatives.

Insofar as the rank-and-file participants were concerned the revolt in the Ruhr was primarily a defensive spasm against the threat from rapidly reviving rightist forces. This strictly defensive aspect has been a major component in popular support for other revolutionary movements. In the Russian Revolution the workers' demands that surfaced after the Tsarist collapse were essentially defensive: they were not for a new social order, even if they helped to bring one about. And in China, in order to mobilize peasant support the Chinese Communists had to soft-pedal their revolutionary objectives and stress limited peasant grievances. These were objections to "bad" landlords, that is, those who failed to adhere to patriarchal standards of behavior and charged rents exceeding traditional norms. Communists generally are likely to claim that more radical demands were stifled under the weight of the traditional village structure dominated by more well-to-do peasants. But that is highly doubtful. In any case it is nonsense to consider modern revolutionary regimes as expressing the spontaneous feelings of the mass of the oppressed population. In both Russia and China the overwhelming mass of the population was, of course, peasants. The really revolutionary changes, the collectivization of agriculture, came about against the will of this mass. On this score the difference between Russia and China is one of degree. It is not a qualitative distinction.[17]

What spontaneous general notions there were about the reordering of German society cropped up mainly among the artisans of 1848. Among the proletariat of that time there appears to have been nothing: they were inarticulate. Among the workers in the latter part of the nineteenth century, and down to the First World War, the reasons they gave for their anger and the remedies they sought were very specific to their own circumstances within specific industries. This industry-specific character and some of the general reasons for it appear very clearly from the contrast between the responses of the coal miners and the steelworkers to the experiences of industrialization. The experiences were broadly similar, the reactions very different and dependent on the social organization in the workplace and traditions about the nature of authority. The miners had their *Gedinge* and their *Berggesetz* and became very active. Lacking the cooperative relationships and norms emerging from teamwork in the *Gedinge*, and lacking the source of tradi-

[17]See the excellent study by Thomas Paul Bernstein, *Leadership and Mobilization in the Collectivization of Agriculture in China and Russia: A Comparison.*

tional legitimation for their grievances in the *Berggesetz*, the iron and steelworkers meekly accepted the authority of the employers. The standards of condemnation that workers develop spontaneously and the means that they use to put them into effect, it appears from this evidence, reflect the structure of cooperation or lack of it in the workplace, together with standards of legitimacy that also derive from experience but are considerably influenced by factors operating outside of the workers' own milieu.

To sum up provisionally, spontaneous conceptions among pre-factory workers, factory workers, and modern revolutionary peasants have been mainly backward looking. They have been attempts to revive a social contract that had been violated. Most frequently they were efforts to remedy specific and concrete grievances in their particular occupation. The tremendous diversity in the forms of daily life created through modern industry has almost certainly been a major obstacle to collective action by industrial workers, an obstacle only rarely and briefly overcome during periods of intense crisis, such as defeat in war, that disrupt the daily routines of an entire population. Conceptions of justice and injustice appear as generalizations from daily experience without the features that would be painful for any human being not continually conditioned and reconditioned to put up with them. It is hard to see how people who have to devote most of their time and strength to their work—and on this score industrial society has been changing and promises to change further—could develop very different ideas. In this light the powerful defensive component in insurrection and revolution also becomes quite comprehensible. At the same time these considerations point to the need to be wary about talking in terms of the creation or discovery of new standards of condemnation—within or by the masses—to say nothing of revolutions of rising expectations. What is apparent here is rather the emergence to the surface of latent standards. Some are deeply embedded in a specific historical experience and set of institutions. Others appear to be more pan-human reactions that surface with the prospect that a long familiar system of domination may be breaking up. These latent standards are new only in the sense that human beings have become newly aware of them.

In other contexts, however, experience can lead to new reactions that do amount to novel standards of condemnation. Over time a substantial number of German workers did pass through the stages of appeals to paternalist authority, through organizing to defend and advance their own interests in unions, to participation in revolutionary movements. The key factor here is rather clearly disappointment: as each strategy failed to bring about the hoped-for results, the workers changed their strategy. Meanwhile the context within which they had to apply their strategy was of course changing. There are also changes in standards that come from increasing satisfaction. French nineteenth-century workers had no idea of annual paid vacations. For them such a prospect was almost certainly beyond imagining.[18] Nowadays the sudden cancellation of vacations by the employers would appear as the acme of arbitrary injustice. And what group of workers in modern capitalist industry would put up with the long hours, arbitrary discipline, lack of procedure for the expression and settling of grievances, the absence of provisions for unemployment and other forms of social security, all of which were commonplace before the First World War?

Ideas about a new social order arose mainly among dissident intellectuals. In this sense the evidence, as I read it, fully supports the Leninist thesis that industrial workers on their own do not create anything except pure trade unionism. But it does not support the corollary that a vanguard party based on the workers can bring about either revolution or liberation. German intellectuals did establish a revolutionary party. Then pressure from the workers transformed it into a reformist one. As mentioned above, this happened partly because nothing else seemed possible. But it also happened because there was no pressure, at least none before 1914, from the advanced sector of the industrial proletariat to make it revolutionary. Industrialism killed the kind of revolutionary impetus that had existed in 1848. The miners were militant enough, especially the unorganized sector, but had essentially limited and very concrete demands. The steelworkers were inert. To be sure, the reformist character of other unions can often be traced to the survival of craft traditions and practices and the conservative, small-town atmosphere still widely characteristic of German industry and especially industry where the unions took hold. Nevertheless the situation in the Ruhr constitutes decisive evidence against the thesis that there was a substantial reservoir of revolutionary discontent waiting for the right leaders to tap it.

After the war there were mass uprisings in the more industrialized parts of Germany, as well as in Bavaria, which on the surface do look like massive support for revolutionary socialism. Certainly there were enough vocal spokesmen, enemies and

[18]Perrot, *Les ouvriers en grève*, I, 293.

leaders of these movements, who proclaimed that such was the case. Nevertheless the appearance dissolves on closer examination. The uprisings did not start on a wide scale until after January of 1919 and were in large measure a defensive response to justified fears of the return of the bad old days, or worse—a return to the old regime under the auspices of the SPD leaders in a de facto coalition with the military and support from right-wing business circles. In this sense the experiences of the war had indeed created, if not a clear desire for a new society, a definite unwillingness to return to the old one. The standards of condemnation had changed, but the change was, however, mainly negatively expressed: the workers knew what they did *not* want, far more than what they *did* want. Except for a limited degree of socialization, the demands of rank-and-file workers, so far as they can be ascertained, were mainly defensive in character (such as the disarming of the *Freikorps*) or else had to do with immediate and local grievances.

Looking at the process as a whole, we can see that the workers took what ideas and organizational help they wanted from the intellectuals and turned it to their own purposes. Unions were generally started up with outside help. On the other hand, if unions did not serve the workers' purposes, they soon withered and died. There was a process of interaction between workers and intellectuals in which the ideas of the intellectuals about changing the social order as a whole became transformed. Workers in the course of upward mobility in the unions and the Socialist Party became intellectuals of a new type, essentially pragmatic bureaucratic politicians. These did develop a vision of society considerably wider than that of the workers at the bench. At the same time this process of organization produced a split between organized and unorganized workers, with the latter a constant danger to the former. In the whole process there was a strong element of straightforward group egoism. The interests of certain workers within the body of those in a particular trade or occupation tended to set the political tone. The political strategy did not reflect the interest of all the workers in the trade, certainly not all industrial workers, and even more certainly not that of society as a whole.

To assert that the workers took over and modified the ideas of the intellectuals is not to minimize the role of the latter. The existence of the SPD and even the unions is hard to imagine without the contribution of the intellectuals. These organizations had an influence on working-class lives far beyond the ways in which they affected dues-paying members. Intellectuals have had a very powerful influence on the standards of condemnation developed within the working class and the ways in which these standards were put into effect, even if this influence has been very different from that hoped for and at times claimed by revolutionary intellectuals. It was the intellectuals who brought to the workers the conception that human society *did* have a capacity to solve its own problems and who suggested the main ways of doing it. If the workers refused some of the suggestions, and by and large displayed a reluctance to become revolutionary cannon fodder for the sake of ideals they had not created out of their own experience, who can blame them for that?

Nor does the fact that factory workers so far have shown little inclination, and perhaps even little capacity, for generating wide-ranging answers for the problems that plague humanity mean that answers or important contributions to the answers can never come from that quarter. Educational levels are rising along with exposure to other currents in modern culture. Workers may become a conservative force similar to nineteenth-century peasants[19] in Western Europe, anxiously clinging to the limited gains they have achieved at great cost, and fearful of forces in the modern world that threaten them. As long as capitalism works tolerably well, that could be the predominant trend. But there is no guarantee that capitalism will continue to work that way. In response to new and severe strains, equipped with a wider cultural horizon, industrial workers could generate a surge of popular inventiveness culminating in a wholly new diagnosis and remedy for social ills.

During the past few hundred years workers and townsmen generally have created three levers for forcing the changes they have wanted: the trade union, "revolutionary" political parties, and the revolutionary crowd or mob. The last of these is of course much older than the industrial working class. The contradiction between trade unions and "revolutionary" political parties has been the subject of much discussion. Is there not just as much of an inherent contradiction between the nature of a revolutionary party and a revolutionary crowd?

The essence of a revolutionary party is to be the conscious vanguard and strategist for a mass following presumed to be at least potentially revolutionary. In a society that permits considerable freedom to form oppositional political organizations the vanguard, as everyone knows, has to come to terms with the dominant groups. In so doing it is very likely to lose much of its

---

[19] I owe this observation to my student Mark Gould.

commitment to revolution. Even in an autocratic society, as Russian experience prior to 1917 demonstrates, the same tendency exists though on a reduced scale. Lenin had to devote a formidable amount of energy and printers' ink to keeping the Russian socialists on a revolutionary course.

A revolutionary crowd is something very different from a revolutionary party. Where the party is enduring, or tries to be, the crowd is ephemeral. Where the party is tightly organized and disciplined, the revolutionary crowd is very loosely organized. Crowds in general are forms of collective human behavior that arise outside of the normal institutional structure, the usual ties of political obedience, obligations to work, and the like. They are holidays from normal society. Like holidays and any form of euphoria (or acute unhappiness), they cannot last. Very soon the imperatives of ordinary life, getting food, exchanging at least some goods and services, reassert themselves. In an urban society it is impossible for each individual to take care of his or her own requirements without the help of others. For that reason the imperatives of cooperation reassert themselves rapidly, and the holiday comes to an end. There may in the meantime be significant changes: a government overthrown and a new one installed in its place. As a form of collective behavior outside normal routines the crowd constitutes a very important adaptive device for altering some of these routines.[20] If the revolutionary crowd does not succeed in effecting decisive changes during its brief period of existence, a crucial opportunity for a revolutionary breakthrough may pass without recurring for a long time, if at all.

A major purpose of the revolutionary party is of course to serve as a strategic avant-garde at the moment of crisis, to lead the crowd to strategic targets at the right moment. But it is exactly at this moment that the inherent structural contradictions between party and crowd are most likely to surface. As a form of collective behavior outside the prevailing institutions,

---

[20]There are of course other kinds of crowds that also take the form of holidays from routine daily existence and which serve to support the existing social order. Religious and patriotic festivals are the clearest examples. It is misleading, I think, to stress with Durkheim the function of such festivals in reaffirming the basic values of the society unless one is careful to explain what the reaffirmation amounts to. Very often religious and patriotic festivals amount to a restatement and bracketing off of these values because the mass of the population cannot live up to them even though it may still want to believe in them. The symbolism and the oratory reassure the spectators that the gods and goals of their fathers still exist. But they exist in a separate and sacred compartment of existence that need not put undue strains on the affairs of daily life. Such collective exercises in self-deception are evidently necessary to keep societies going as well as to change them.

the crowd is highly likely to create its own leaders. Studies demonstrate that collective behavior in crowds can be quite rational.[21] Crowds throw up their own leaders, gather their own information, decide on their own actions, all in a way that one might call instant democracy. While the crowd lasts, it displays a high degree of autonomy. A leader from the outside with an acute feel for the sentiments of the audience can persuade and sway a crowd, suggest new targets, and the like. (It may be much harder to persuade an angry crowd not to attack safe but trivial targets, especially if the target has symbolic value.) On the other hand, such a powerful leader generally has to share most of the crowd's sentiments and is therefore as much its prisoner as its leader. The longer the revolutionary party has been able to act under legal conditions, the more probable are strategic and temperamental differences between the leaders of the crowd and the party. If the party becomes bureaucratized, either in opposition or as the leader of a postrevolutionary regime, it is likely to fear mass uprisings. That happened to the Bolsheviks under Stalin. It also happened in China, with the significant distinction that Mao resorted to mass uprisings in the Cultural Revolution in order to get his way in opposition to the party.

For those who can believe in an infallibly sound "revolutionary instinct" among the masses, the problem of course disappears. The revolutionary party becomes superfluous the day the revolution breaks out, if not earlier. Such a belief is hardly any more warranted than the arrogantly elitist thesis that a revolutionary party is inherently infallible due to its nature as the avant-garde of historically inevitable revolution. Both parties and crowds are subject to distorted perceptions of social realities due to their structural forms, even if the reasons are not the same in each case.

Furthermore there is no guarantee that a revolutionary crowd will make its appearance on the historical stage at exactly the right moment—assuming that it is possible to determine exactly what that moment is. Both advocates and opponents of revolutionary change, as well as those professedly neutral, have devoted a great deal of time, energy, and ink to analyzing just how and why a revolutionary temper comes into existence among the masses. The answers run all the way from rising expectations, through relative deprivation, to certain processes thought to be at work in the structure of capitalist society. Certainly not all of this work has been wasted. Yet in my judgment

---

[21]See Ralph H. Turner, "Collective Behavior" in Robert E. L. Faris, editor, *Handbook of Modern Sociology*, 382–425, espec. 390–392, 418–423.

there has not been an adequate realization of the brief and fragile nature of revolutionary upsurges, especially in urban populations, nor of the variety of circumstances that have to come together to make it possible. Even when all "objective" circumstances are favorable, the rising may not occur due to popular memories of a recent defeat. Urban uprisings have a way of breaking out when neither friends nor enemies expect them. That happened in 1848, the February (1917) Revolution in Russia, not to mention the May "events" of 1968 in France. Conversely, widely anticipated risings may not occur, as in England in 1830 when there were widespread fears of a repetition of the overturn in France. The contradiction between planning for a revolution and actually making one is likely to remain as long as revolution itself continues to be a major way of realigning social institutions with social capacities.

For any social and moral transformation to get underway there appears to be one prerequisite that underlies all those so far discussed: social and cultural space within the prevailing order.[22] A society with social and cultural space provides more or less protected enclaves within·which dissatisfied or oppressed groups have some room to develop distinctive social arrangements, cultural traditions, and explanations of the world around them. Social and cultural space implies room to experiment with making the future. The medieval city provided this kind of room in a military and agrarian society. The use of social space is not just a matter of playing with alternative life-styles. For institutional changes to take place those who inhabit the space have to accumulate, intentionally or unintentionally, sufficient force for a challenge to the prevailing hegemony. This aspect is plain enough not only in the cases already mentioned but also in such diverse examples as the triumph of Christianity as well as guerilla and revolutionary movements. Not all challenges involve violence, certainly not all of the time. But sooner or later the distribution of power becomes decisive.

[22]Because alternative routes to the same goal are often possible, and because experience has so often revealed functional substitutes for supposedly necessary social arrangments, I resort to the term prerequisite with hesitation. On this issue I strongly commend the penetrating and iconoclastic essay by Albert O. Hirschman, *Exit, Voice, and Loyalty: Responses to Decline in Firms, Organizations, and States.* Here, on the other hand, the term does seem appropriate since it does not raise one particular sequence of historical development to the level of necessity, and covers a rather wide range of historical experience. In comparison with the theocratic societies of the ancient Near East, for example, the Greek communities that grew up on the basis of farming, piracy, trade, and fighting offered a great deal of social and cultural space. This fact does not "explain" the Greek polis and its intellectual achievements, but they would hardly have been possible without it.

As Gaetano Mosca has pointed out,[23] the significant feature in accounting for the triumph of new social forms is not their capacity to resist fierce persecution, but the relatively lax and intermittent character of the persecution they faced. In our terms the innovators enjoyed and used social space. Intermittent persecution created martyrs and myths that served to advance rather than crush the movement. Where persecution has been thorough and enjoyed popular support, as Mosca points out was the case with the Japanese persecution of Christians in the seventeenth century, it has succeeded in obliterating the challenge to authority. The notion that force can never destroy an idea is no more than a comforting myth. Revolutionaries have often proclaimed the myth before they took power. Afterward they have discarded the myth in their efforts to establish a system of prefabricated virtue, an effort that has required as much cruelty or more than that under which the revolutionaries themselves suffered.[24]

In this connection the distinction between totalitarian societies and nontotalitarian ones does become meaningful. The term totalitarian did not emerge as part of American self-serving mythology for the Cold War. To be sure, the distinction is not absolute. But a totalitarian society is one where a small ruling elite controls the means of coercion and persuasion and in the name of some ideal uses police and propaganda to stamp out dissent and reduce social and cultural space to an absolute minimum.[25] In a totalitarian society there is literally no room to experiment with the future, or for that matter with the past. The nature of both past and present is defined through continually shifting decrees that nevertheless maintain a permanent taboo on unofficial experimentation. We have yet to see whether such

---

[23]*The Ruling Class,* 190–192.

[24]In Mao's China there are no official or firm figures available on the number of deaths due to famine or politically induced suffering in cities, labor camps, etc., even though the world knew that violence had accompanied such well-publicized events as the Great Leap Forward (1958–1960) and the Cultural Revolution (1965–1968). For unconfirmable and varying estimates by foreign scholars see Ezra F. Vogel, *Canton Under Communism,* 254, on starvation in one poor county during the Cultural Revolution; Jürgen Domes, *The Internal Politics of China 1949–1972,* 115, where he quotes a huge figure for deaths as a consequence of the Great Leap Forward. On Chinese suffering during a famine in 1952 see Bernstein, *Leadership and Mobilization in the Collectivization of Agriculture,* 293, and Bao Ruo-Wang and Rudolph Chelminski, *Prisoner of Mao,* 10–11, 22, 185, 192, 248, 272, for personal impressions by a labor-camp inmate who witnessed some deaths firsthand.

[25]See Robert Jay Lifton, *Thought Reform and the Psychology of Totalism,* espec. part 3, for effects on Chinese intellectuals. Lifton's general analysis (part 4) spells out the main psychological processes and their limitations, which, as he suggests would almost certainly apply to any population.

societies based on permanent mobilization of the underlying population can sustain this mobilization well beyond the lifetime of leaders with actual experience of the revolutionary struggles that formed them.

4. The problem of national identity

There remains one final aspect of the relationship between social structures and the formation of standards of condemnation: the role of nationalism. Because of its protean nature I have deliberately left it to the last, hoping that clarification of other aspects of the process would aid our understanding of this one. In modern times nationalism has constituted the most widespread and pervasive standard by which human beings condemn or approve their social surroundings.

If we look first at the negative aspect, a nationalism that condemns one or more other nations, we may notice at once that it can be a prominent feature of reactionary as well as revolutionary movements. Nationalism was an important component in monarchist conservatism in nineteenth-century Prussia and in a much more virulent form in modern times in National Socialism as well as other forms of fascism. Yet nationalism has also provided, as it did in the French Revolution, much of the emotional fervor behind the revolutionary struggles of China, North Vietnam, and movements of national liberation generally in economically backward areas. Evidently the nation-state is a vessel into which it is possible to pour wildly differing contents. We also know that, despite the official proscription of the Social Democratic Party as an unpatriotic and subversive organization, a proscription that had ended formally in 1890 but remained an influential premise of respectable politics afterwards, German workers in 1914 followed the lead of that party in joining the carnival of slaughter. Finally, it might be observed that nationalist and separatist movements have enjoyed many successes in the past fifty-odd years, and that the number and fervor of their supporters is probably much larger than that behind any movement based on revolutionary working-class consciousness. Here then are puzzling and important facts that cry out for explanation. To use nationalism as an explanation in its own right will not do. That amounts to circular reasoning or worse: a resort to word magic. We need to understand why these feelings are powerful.

As any oppressed or suffering group seeks to come to terms with its fate, its members, and more especially its leaders and spokesmen, seek an explanation for that fate. *Homo sapiens* might be characterized as the explaining mammal. In the course of seeking this explanation, the group defines itself in relation to its enemies. Thus the foreign enemy is part of the group's self-definition achieved through its explanation of who and what are the causes for its suffering. In turn the character of this explanation will depend upon the circumstances of daily life as interpreted through the precipitate of past experiences which constitutes the culture or traditions of the group.

For the lower strata the available materials with which to construct an explanation and self-definition are likely to contain some elements from the upper classes. Not all of these ideas will of course be acceptable, and the harsher the rule of those in power, the fewer may be the upper-class traditions accepted by those underneath. Nevertheless, short of a revolutionary break, and perhaps even then, there will always be some influence from above. If under ordinary circumstances, free of crises, the dominant strata are nationalistic and use patriotic slogans to get more work out of the lower classes, the latter are likely to be suspicious. That was to a considerable extent the case in Germany before 1914. Quite a number of factory workers who responded to the Levenstein inquiry of 1907–1911 expressed what sounds like very spontaneous resentment against the employers' patriotic appeals. Unless I have missed some evidence despite several readings, there are no expressions of the contrary view. That, on the other hand, is only part of the evidence. The workers Levenstein chose to quote were relatively "advanced"; they had come somewhere near the point of defining themselves in opposition to the capitalists. SPD statements of the period are full of concern about that mass of workers who had not reached that point of self-definition. They include quite a scattering of complaints about chauvinistic currents among their followers. On this basis it seems safe to infer that there was in Germany before World War I a large body of workers who accepted the self-definition current in the rest of the society.

With these observations in mind it is worthwhile to pause and examine the general advantages of nationalism as a popular explanation for suffering. In the first place, it is simple, which Marxism certainly is not. Nationalism puts the blame for whatever is painful in one's own society squarely on an easily identified group: the outsiders, the foreign enemy. There is no need for nuances and complicated causal links. Class consciousness, on the other hand, runs counter to many obvious facts from daily experience. It is hard to put domestic power-holders in the same emotional and intellectual category as foreign ones, when every day's news brings evidence of conflict between "our" leaders and those of other states. It is also not so easy to make a steelworker believe that he has a great deal in common with a brewery worker if the price of beer goes up. (In Germany at times this was a thorny issue because worker meetings were often held in beer halls.) The foreign enemy is also a relatively safe target for day-to-day symbolic aggression. Retaliation is far less likely than in the case of an attack on local power-holders. For that reason too the attack is much more likely to attract diverse social support. To sum up, nationalism conceals divisions and weaknesses in one's own ranks—conservative *or* radical—and can attract a heterogeneous collection of allies who would be repelled by an out-and-out declaration of one's own interests.

As an appeal, nationalism works best in states that have recently been defeated in war, especially when enemy occupation follows defeat. Still it is quite serviceable in other situations. Any group's perception of itself comes out of its relationships with other groups. It creates its identity out of these relationships, something that exists over and against other groups. The identity has fluid and uncertain boundaries to the extent that daily social relationships are fluctuating and ambiguous. For the individual this fluidity and uncertainty is often a source of strain and even anxiety, perhaps especially so in complex modern societies. Is the newcomer in the neighborhood or at the place of work to be an ally or a threat? To what degree and in which situations? Will he or she be with us or against us, and exactly who are we here anyway? Thus nationalism as a form of self-definition is merely one facet of a much larger social process. It is an attempt to make the self-definition correspond with the boundaries of the largest units of continuous peaceful social behavior that human beings have so far created.

Like other social identities, national identity has its fluid and uncertain boundaries. For it to continue in existence, concrete individuals have to create and re-create this identity in continually changing historical circumstances. If we look again at the situation of the German industrial workers just prior to the outbreak of the First World War, we can see how the process works, noticing also some aspects that the discussion has not yet brought out with sufficient emphasis.

With the wisdom of hindsight, that insidious and inescapable enemy of rigorous analysis, it is not difficult to list the forces integrating German workers into the larger society. There was a common language and many elements of shared national experience. There was the strong influence of the educational system and compulsory military service. There were the forms of social insurance provided by the state, though Social Democrats made a point of keeping the shortcomings of the legislation before the public. In the fact that employers had to prosper in order to provide jobs there was an obvious degree of shared interest. By 1890 the worst barriers against political and economic action by the workers had fallen. Despite some threats of a reversal, there was the prospect that careful application of tactics whose virtues experience had demonstrated would continue to work in the future. At least that is what many of their leaders told the workers.

For some comparative illumination on what was happening to the German workers and to industrial workers generally we will do well to glance at the situation in France in the latter part of the nineteenth century. There were two important contrasts with that in Germany. In France the legacy of the revolution evidently facilitated the workers' identification with the Third Republic, especially at first. (Disillusionment with the bourgeois republic did set in later as the workers encountered employer intransigence supported by the state.[26]) That was very different from Wilhelmine Germany, a state created out of the defeat of the popular upheaval of 1848 and against the will of a substantial part of the population. In France, in the second place, there were many large pockets of foreign immigration where foreign workers competed with native Frenchmen for jobs. There were, as we have seen, numerous foreign workers in the Ruhr too. But there the voracious appetite of coal mining for labor apparently damped down the antagonisms. In France the antagonisms became virulent. In response to the threat to their jobs a powerful current of xenophobia and chauvinism swept through French industrial workers. In vain French socialists tried to instill internationalist sentiments and to ignore as bourgeois the symbolism of France's revolutionary past. Rank-and-file French workers by and large would have none of this. Instead they mobilized on their own the resources of French national history in order to defend their right to work in what they saw as a limited national market. The defense was far more than symbolic. There were numerous violent outbreaks against the foreigners. By 1884, a time of depressed economic conditions, the French workers

[26]Perrot, *Les ouvriers en grève*, I, 196–197.

had come to regard the foreigner as the source of all the troubles that afflicted them.[27] In this manner nationalism became the basic popular diagnosis and remedy for their plight, a spontaneous one that arose against the will of nominal working-class leaders.

Thus, differing national experiences and the economic situation facing ordinary workers exert a powerful effect on the way workers perceive their own state. But it would be misleading and fruitless to seek for an explanation of nationalism in strictly economic terms. As already indicated, an Hegelian notion of the struggle for identity in and through opposing forces accounts for the facts rather better than an analysis limited to the economic situation.

There are signs of an important psychological component in this play of opposing forces: relief and security in belonging to a group with a cause. Membership in a group can save the individual from the anxieties of carving out his or her own meaningful place in the world, especially when the realistic chances of doing so are tiny. Then there is the thrill of having an enemy for whom one can have contempt, fear, and respect all at once. Has brotherhood ever existed without the threat of real or imagined enemies?[28]

To return to the German situation, are the integrating forces discussed above enough to explain why the SPD leaders voted for the war credits and the workers flocked to the colors in 1914 amid the sounds of martial music? I think not, at least not by themselves. We have said nothing so far about the fact that the dominant classes controlled the levers of power, the heavy sanctions they could apply against rank-and-file workers along with dazzling rewards for the "sensible" cooperation of the leaders, the force of an excited public opinion, and patriotic sentiments running through other classes. For the working-class leader in 1914 the choice was between going along with the nationalist tide or risking the destruction of an organization to which he owed

---

[27]Perrot, *Les ouvriers en grève*, I, 170–174, 178–179.

[28]The pygmies as described by Colin Turnbull in *Wayward Servants* come to mind as a possible contrary example. They have no human enemies and in the rain forest a secure environment they treat with reverence. Cooperative social relationships are necessary for their form of hunting and permeate much of their lives. But, as Turnbull repeatedly stresses, the bands are continually breaking up and re-forming. This process of fission and fusion he regards as essential to the maintenance of their way of life. Continual splitting has an economic basis. Otherwise the bands would become too large to support themselves by hunting. It is also a way of avoiding and evading the explosive build-up of personal antagonisms. This society is possible only because of the size of the territory they inhabit. Once again we come upon the significance of social space.

his status and for which he had devoted his energy and intelligence since childhood. For the rank-and-file worker the choice was between going to jail or joining the colors. For both of them the decision to resist the patriotic upsurge meant disgrace and insult at the hands of fellow Germans; the opposite meant acceptance in a euphoric if ephemeral brotherhood. The social system to which the workers belonged—and here the factors of integration just listed do enter the explanation—essentially the party and the unions, was neither strong enough nor sufficiently inclusive to provide effective social support for the individual who wanted to stand aside from the flag-wavers. The boundaries of working-class society were fluid and permeable, penetrated by the searching roots growing out from interests shared with other classes. An individual act of heroic defiance threatened danger for the group as a whole and all who belonged to it (as in the concentration camps and in prisons). Only in the war and afterward, when the advantages of membership in the SPD or the union seemed problematic, and the prospects of resistance higher and the anger to fuel it more powerful, would defiance become widespread.

To put the point bluntly, straightforward bullying looks like one decisive factor in the adherence of German workers, such as it was, to nationalism. It is a significant aspect of the creation of any form of group loyalty and identity. No doubt its importance varies from case to case. Its significance is liable to escape the investigator's eye in cases for which one feels strong moral approval, and to appear salient in those where one feels a strong moral aversion. Nevertheless, bullying is liable to be a crucial aspect in the formation of loyalties where conflict is severe and the risk of allegiance high, that is, in any significant struggle. For the individual victims, bullying is not necessarily more pleasant in a good cause than in a bad one. Indeed, the rebel can have the worst of both worlds, taking the blows of those in authority along with recriminations and further blows from fellow rebels. No wonder so few choose the role deliberately.

5. Cultural definitions of the inevitable

By this point an alert reader will have noticed that the discussion has overflowed its conceptual dikes insofar as it has been necessary to refer to cultural conceptions of the inevitable while analyzing aspects of personality and social structure. Here I want to sketch some of the permutations of the general notion of inevitability.

In the modern world, and apart from any meaning it may have in specialized philosophical and theological discourse, the word "inevitable" generally characterizes something painful or unpleasant like death and taxes about which human beings supposedly can do little or nothing. People put up with the inevitable as best they can, shrugging their shoulders, gritting their teeth, or steeling themselves to face a tragic event. When something is defined as inevitable, such as occasional bouts of bad weather, there may be some sense to making at least limited preparations and taking some precautions. At the same time the definition rules out any serious struggle, or at least any serious struggle with a prospect of victory. The notion of inevitability implies a conception of the universe ruled at least in part by blind forces of fates ultimately not responsive to human will and action.

This attempt to take a detached look at our own cultural definition of inevitability yields two problems worth pursuing here. In the first place it is quite apparent that the concept of inevitability has contained different things for different reasons at different points in history. What then have been the grounds for labeling certain forms of suffering inevitable and how have these grounds and methods of labeling altered? The second query is a more fundamental one. Do all human cultures have the category inevitability, but apply it to different things depending on their capacity to manage their natural and social environment? Or does the concept of inevitability itself, with its overtones of law and regularity, constitute some form of major historical breakthrough and cultural discovery?

In attempting to answer the second question first, let us take hunger and disease as concrete examples of suffering. Modern educated Westerners who possess a secular explanation and remedy for these misfortunes and disasters are disinclined to treat them as inevitable. Early human cultures, so far as we can make legitimate inferences about them from anthropological evidence—something that appears quite safe in this connection though not by any means in all—were much less inclined to use such principles for the simple reason that they had much less in the way of knowledge and resources at their disposal. Simple secular explanations were not of course completely lacking. Nonliterate peoples, for example, know that crops will not grow without planting seeds, that animals they hunt for food can generally be found in some places and seldom or never in others.

Such peoples are often extremely acute at observing the natural environment and its meaning. They know that a broken twig means that game or a dangerous animal has passed that way recently, and can make many correct inferences of this sort that escape the literate man. They have to. But the resources for the application of secular rationality even in their own familiar environment are generally meager.

Where these fail them, they resort, as moderns do, to magic, incantation, and religion. Disease is the consequence of sorcery. Crop failure may be due to the inadequacy of the ruler. For that, as Fraser pointed out, it may be necessary and legitimate to kill the ruler. In these circumstances there is reason to doubt that such people had any concept of the inevitable at all. Where there is a magical remedy for every misfortune, it is hard to see how a general conception such as inevitability could arise. Though there might be at least rudimentary notions of cause and effect, the world would appear as subject to a series of ad hoc controls. If one of them fails to work, there is always the excuse that something went wrong in the attempt to apply the magic, or that someone used more powerful counter-magic.

Thus it appears that the concept of inevitability is itself the product of a long historical evolution. While there is evidence for a secular and commonsense root at a later point, myth and religion, as Alfred North Whitehead pointed out in *Science and the Modern World*, had earlier made an indispensable contribution. From them came the idea of the working-out of overwhelming forces over long periods of time, though the capricious aspect by no means disappeared. To Whitehead's derivation of the concept of causality from Hebrew religion and Greek mythology one might add that a conception of causality both strengthens and undermines cultural definitions of inevitability: when one can learn about causes, there arises the possibility of changing and mastering trends and events. Myth and religion also seem to have intensified the connection between notions of causality, inevitability, and moral judgments. Here, too, as in the case of causality and inevitability an element of tension remained, insofar as moral condemnation implied the possibility that a human actor could have acted otherwise and therefore somehow had escaped from the chain of causality. These perplexities have by no means altogether vanished today, and the notion of inevitability still carries moral overtones. In their very different ways both conservatives and revolutionaries use the notion to buttress their own hopes for the future.

In preindustrial civilizations the moral aspect has always

been decisive. Ordinary suffering of a chronic sort, the kind to which human beings teach themselves to adapt because it does seem unavoidable, is in such societies likely to appear as a fate that the individual deserves, one that is just and proper. At least the dominant strata will try to make it appear that way. In a stratified society the principles of social inequality, generally systematized by priests, explain and justify the more prevalent and routine forms of suffering. Since these principles also constitute the basic terms of the implicit or explicit social contract, there will be certain forms of suffering that both dominant and subordinate strata define as unjust and improper. Even in cases where force and fraud have played a major role in determining the respective roles of ruler and ruled, as in plantation slavery, there is a strong tendency for the social contract to reappear in actual practice. In these situations, therefore, there is a considerable moral component in the explanation of suffering. The challenge to this morality and this inevitability becomes a major political act. As the history of the iron and steelworkers in the Ruhr before 1914 suggests, human beings may have to be taught what their rights are. From this perspective, moral outrage becomes an historically acquired taste, one acquired in severe political struggles. Such struggles have been the major political fact of modern times. Hence it is worthwhile to stand back from the details once more in order to perceive the main features.

In eighteenth-century Europe and Asia social inequality took the form of estates or orders, ranked according to the esteem or social honor attributed to the social function of the males. There were of course many variations. Usually the warriors and the priests were the only ones marked off in a distinct fashion. The rest were mainly a residual category or series of residual categories, though the ranking might be more distinct again at the bottom, as in the outcastes of Japan. Only in India was there an attempt by the priests to order the whole society by ranks.

Practice did not correspond to this theory; everywhere in Europe and Asia the ranking was hereditary either in practice or in theory. Some degree of mobility was also possible everywhere. In China membership in the mandarinate was theoretically open and achieved by passing the examinations. In practice economic barriers to learning made the mandarinate an hereditary stratum. In Europe the individual was *born* a member of the Church, but one *became* a bishop, or even a parish priest. There too economic barriers to education limited access to the higher ranks. For each estate there was a prescribed style of life, indicated by rules of etiquette, dress, and by other means. The purpose of economic activity was a moral one: to enable each estate to live according to its appropriate style. The lower orders were expected to provide the higher ones with the means for so living, while at the same time retaining enough from their efforts to maintain their own social honor. It is doubtful that this happened very frequently, and the definition of what peasants, the overwhelming majority of the population, ought to have was, to say the least, ambiguous.

For each estate or order the prescribed style of life specified a distinct and appropriate moral code, even in many cases a specific kind of personality. The warrior was expected to be brave and usually generous, the priest gentle, the artisan diligent. Naturally there were in practice many deviations from both the ideal personality and the ideal morality for each order. On the other hand, there were also strong social sanctions to prevent individuals from adopting a way of life inappropriate to their station, either in an upward or downward direction. Morality was explicitly socially determined, and though these systems were by no means totally inflexible, an air of permanence and inevitability did permeate them. Moral anger arose mainly from violations of the social contract, particularly against individuals who did not act in accord with the requirements of their status. But here and there, especially in the European heretical movements that drew on real or alleged memories of equality among the early Christians, there were stirrings of doubt about the terms of the contract itself.

Wherever it became possible to acquire wealth in a novel fashion, the consequence was to undermine the old principles of social inequality and the old assumptions of inevitability. The older elites appropriated wealth of course in a variety of ways. But where new methods became possible, at first mainly in commerce, they enabled upstarts to short-circuit the older arrangements. The newly rich could simply buy necessary perquisites for the manner of existence that had been the privilege of the dominant strata. As modernization gathered momentum and turned into the industrial revolution, the old principles disintegrated at certain points amid the smoke and fire of revolution. The principles and practices of inequality that had at one time appeared necessary and inevitable became the source of open mockery, first among intellectuals, later among wide sections of the populace. In a famous passage de Tocqueville captured the political meaning of this metamorphosis of the inevitable into a series of abuses:

Only a great genius could save a ruler who tries to relieve his subjects after a long oppression. The evil suffered patiently as inevitable seems unendurable as soon as one conceives the idea of escaping from it. All of the abuses that have been removed seem only to delineate better those that remain and to make one's feelings more bitter. The evil, it is true, has become less, but one's sensibility is more acute.[29]

The rising commercial and industrial leaders in the towns did not make the series of revolutionary surges, which, beginning with the Revolt of the Netherlands, destroyed the older conception of the inevitable. The economically active sectors of the bourgeoisie were too busy making money, often in a parasitic fashion in the interstices of the old regimes, to "make" a revolution that in fact frequently frightened many of them. By and large they were quite content to let other people do the fighting and thinking for them. Once the dust had settled they were the main beneficiaries of the political changes that were the result of these revolutions. Furthermore, commercial and manufacturing interests were also the main agents of the economic changes without which it would have been impossible to apply the new ideas in practice.

The new principles were egalitarian only in the sense that they were directed against older forms of privilege. Both in their intent and their consequences they were still principles of social inequality. The rewards of society were to be distributed according to "merit," mainly merit as demonstrated by success in the marketplace. No longer was any individual or group supposed to be able to count on a secure economic underpinning appropriate to the function it performed in and for the social order. Theoretically the race was to the swift while few concerned themselves overmuch about straightening out the starting line.

During the nineteenth century the new principles spread unevenly through Europe from West to East, encountering resistance from old elites, as well as those driven from their niches much lower down in the social order. Together the economic and moral changes created new classes and new conflicts over what weights each could throw on the scales of Justice, a goddess who in the form of *Concurrenz* or the automatic workings of the market often appeared more blind than ever before.

In Germany, as mentioned earlier, the industrial workers did not create out of their own experience any new principles of social equality or inequality with which to combat the new ones.

[29]*Ancien Régime et la Révolution*, 223.

It was the intellectuals who brought to the industrial workers diagnoses of their ills and suggested the remedies. Marx was only one of these, and his ideas for a long time made only slow headway against competing products. Much as his name came to dominate the intellectual scenery for the German workers by the late nineteenth century, the working principles and strategy of the German labor movement were hardly his alone.

In the famous principle of to each according to his (now presumably also her) needs, and from each according to his (and again her) abilities, Marxism still allows for human inequalities. But it is a principle that completely rejects the market as a device for measuring human worth. So far of course no society has reached this objective, and there are reasons for continuing skepticism about its feasibility.

Under pressure from their followers in search of more immediate benefits, European labor movements, and not only those in Germany, stopped short of this goal in their working principles, if not always in their rhetoric about the future. But they did take into their working principles at least part of the goal insofar as they rejected the link between merit and the marketplace as the *sole* determinant of human worth. The workers' own experience was probably a more important component in this rejection than what Marx had to say, though Marxism may well have put faith and fire into what workers wanted to believe for other reasons. Conservatives too had rejected this linkage for their own and quite different reasons. They, however, generally proved rare and untrustworthy allies for the workers. With the help of a few dissident intellectuals the workers created their own organizations for collective defense against the unfettered workings of the market.

The general direction of labor-movement pressures as they were shaped by the obstacles they encountered was still toward a society organized in and through the market, that is, still a capitalist society. Meanwhile, even before the First World War the market had begun to show symptoms suggesting that it might not be the most satisfactory all-around device for organizing human society. Even at its height it had scarcely won universal allegiance in practice from those who had the task of seeing that governments actually worked and stayed in power. After the war the troubles became worse instead of better, and the pressures to revise the social contract both in theory and in practice became stronger. These pressures came from many sources besides the industrial working classes and converged on one point: society had a definite responsibility for the welfare of the individual. More concretely, there was an obligation on society to find ways to protect the individual against the ravages of the invisible hand of fate working through the market.

The ways in which different societies tried to respond to the new imperative, the classes and groups they have tried to protect and the ones upon whom the costs of protection have been thrown, have varied enormously over the past half century and more since the issue became acute. Liberal capitalist democracy, fascism, communism, movements of national liberation in the backward countries have all been responses to this issue. In their internal conflicts and conflicts with each other they have been attempts to set the terms of a new social contract rendered necessary by the loosening of tremendous new productive forces. Meanwhile mankind has used these forces for destruction on a scale without parallel in human history. In holding the state responsible for human welfare we seem to be back to killing the king in earnest. That, roughly speaking, is revolutionary violence. But the kings new and old abide by no contract with their subjects. They kill their own subjects, each other's subjects, and on occasion each other. And they all do it in the name of a "public interest," a "welfare" about which there is no agreement and which threatens to turn into a nightmare. One can only hope that the nightmare itself may be part of the universal illusion of a permanent present.

6. *Time and the sense of injustice*

This sketch of changing cultural definitions of the inevitable reveals, I hope, significant aspects of what has happened with the passage of time to the sense of what is just and unjust and what human beings feel they can and ought to do about injustice. The sketch makes no claim to cover all significant aspects. Its structure leaves two very important issues in the shadow. One issue appears from the way in which the passage of time by itself can apparently impart to some human arrangements a nimbus of justice and authority. Many institutions at many times and places have received their sanction from the supposed fact that they have the sanction of the ancestors, and have existed from time immemorial, or at least as long as the oldest inhabitants can remember. An ironical expression of the same general body of facts is that time obliterates all crimes. Now time itself does nothing; people do things. What is it they are doing and why?

In the second issue, time, so to speak, enters rational moral judgments in such a way as to make them seem insoluble. In that sense the effect of time is the opposite of the case in the first issue, because it is *future* time. A dilemma that faces all serious revolutionists is how many sacrifices, if any, can one justifiably impose on living human beings for the sake of those not yet born? In this form it is only an extreme version of a choice that all people inevitably make since merely continuing to live the way we do inevitably imposes some sacrifices on future generations.

The illusion that the mere passage of time can justify forms of human behavior presents, I find, the more complex problem. Is it altogether an illusion? What has satisfied at least some people in the past is after all quite likely to satisfy them again. The recipients of tribute can hardly object to receiving it at regular intervals. And human beings do forget the original basis on which tribute was exacted. Stability and predictability in human relationships have some advantages even for the disadvantaged. If there is an attempt to increase the tribute, to add to the obligations of the *corvée*, those subject to it can object that it violates custom established since time out of mind. Finally, if the subjects have no other experiences that could suggest different standards or provide standards of condemnation, that is, if the relationship is a closed and isolated one, on what basis could they be expected to change it?

Both Freudian and neo-Pavlovian psychologies shed considerable light on the mechanisms through which the mere passage of time under stable social conditions apparently justifies prevailing social relationships. Parents bring up their children in such a way as to make the values and moral judgments of the preceding generation to an important extent those of the next generation as well. The superego is the internalization of the past. In turn the series of rewards and sanctions that human beings impose upon each other in social life can teach people both to accept and value existing social relationships in such a manner that, once conditioned, human beings will have a strong tendency to perpetuate these relationships.

The notion of the just price comes to mind in this connection. People still make similar moral judgments about prices today. Popular ideas now may not be very different from what they were in the Middle Ages, a matter about which we know very little. What do people mean when they say for example that meat costs "too much"? Surely a large part of the meaning is that meat costs more than it used to. The just price is really the customary price as people get used to it and invest this particular social exchange with an aura of legitimacy. A modern market economy, where price changes continually reflect fluctuations in supply and demand, perpetually upsets the system of exchanges to which people become accustomed and tend to regard as just. That is one major reason why the spread of market relationships into traditional economies has generally created an outcry about its immoral effects.

The effects *are* immoral by the standards argued in the preceding chapter when they produce and sustain exchanges whereby one set of people continually makes huge gains and others suffer severe losses. This has happened very frequently as capitalism spread throughout the world and has provided modern socialists with one of their most effective arguments. But does the difficulty lie in the institution of the market, or is it something deeper? Both the transition to industrialism and a dynamic industrial society involve continuous and rapid change whether social coordination takes place mainly through the market or through centralized bureaucratic control, that is, socialism. The latter's record is hardly impressive, even if the traumatic aspects have been considerably less in China than the Soviet Union. Still it is naïve to expect ruthless and committed bureaucrats to be overly squeamish about the victims of what they consider progress. As long as change occurs in human society, it seems likely that there will be large amounts of suffering from felt and real injustices—and compelling reasons to protest these injustices.

These considerations lead us to the issues of future time and future sufferings. According to some revolutionary theories of social change the concept of historical necessity links past and future sufferings.[30] The painful struggles of each historical stage are a necessary part of mankind's progress toward the next higher stage. Slavery, serfdom, the disciplining of the labor force under early capitalism have in turn been historically necessary prerequisites for the degree of freedom from suffering that liberal capitalist society has attained. The sufferings of contemporary revolutionary struggles and those of the future are equally necessary. They include not only victims among the ranks of the revolutionaries but also the victims of the victorious revolution itself. These raise the most burning issues of all. By

---

[30]Within the Marxist tradition these are controversial issues that I shall not try to untangle. The problem at hand is not one in intellectual history. Rather it is to analyze a theoretical position. Who argued the position or whether anyone has expressed the viewpoint in quite this fashion are therefore inconsequential matters, important though they may be in other contexts.

what right can a revolutionary dictator uproot and destroy the lives of the present generation for the sake of future benefits? But does any less suffering occur if the responsibility for decisions (and the suffering they cause) is diffused among the myriads of individual decisions that take place through the market?

It is highly unlikely that there are solutions to such problems which can eliminate all suffering. That is no reason to stop looking for ways to reduce pain and suffering, including new ways of thinking. To repeat, medical science does not abandon the search for ways to prevent or cure specific illness because there is no prospect of immortality. Doubts about perfect solutions can be the beginnings of wisdom in the social sciences too, as long as they are not a plea for a narrowly complacent empiricism that confines itself to trivialities.

To address the radical tradition first, we have already seen that this use of the concept of historical necessity implies a determinist view that is untenable as well as unnecessary because it implies omniscience. Twentieth-century history has provided more than enough tragic evidence about the suffering that claims to omniscience can produce. In a more or less rationally ordered society no person or group can have the power or authority to impose huge sacrifices on a subordinate population for the sake of uncertain future benefits in which the victims will have no share. The more uncertain the benefits are and the more distant they are in time the weaker is the justification for imposing them.

On the other hand, it is necessary to draw attention to the formidable inconsistencies and obstacles in the arguments for a decentralized approach with maximum popular participation in the resolution of major political issues. These arguments, it is worth noticing, start from premises that range from reactionary through liberal to neo-anarchist. What they share is hostility to *both* bureaucracy and the market. Many economic and social problems are insoluble on a small territorial basis because what people do in one area can have adverse effects on the inhabitants of other areas. Irrigation schemes and industrial pollution are by now familiar examples. It is perfectly reasonable to insist on and indeed enforce sacrifices where there are strong reasons to anticipate large and widely distributed benefits in the fairly near future. All kinds of human societies have done and continue to do these things in matters large and small. It is not tyranny to stop someone from striking a match in the presence of gasoline fumes. The trouble is that we have not been able to devise good ways to cut short vastly more serious dangers. Nor is it always possible to apply the rule that the persons most affected by proposed changes are the ones who ought to have the most to say about them. Quite aside from matters of vested material interests—and the smaller the stake the more tenaciously and bitterly human beings will cling to it—there is merit in the radical contention that all supposedly free choices are tainted by whatever irrationalities and built-in forms of superfluous sufferings exist in the prevailing order. The real problem is to be reasonably sure of not getting something worse.

In trying to get a theoretical perspective on such matters, and see how the different parts of human society hang together, we would do well to drop any determinist assumptions about what the connections have to be. At this juncture it seems to me that skeptical reserve is the most appropriate stance toward economic determinism, idealist determinism in terms of values, functional relationships, historical necessity, and all the rest. It might be useful to drop any and all determinist notions and try to think mainly in terms of the contradictory forces that produce specific situations. Not so long ago going to the moon and seeing the other side of the moon were common metaphors for the inherently impossible, for something ruled out by determinist principles. Experience has taught otherwise. In social affairs when we say something is possible or impossible, likely or unlikely, we have to specify as carefully as we can the relevant forces at work, the possibilities of intelligent intervention, and the costs in human suffering. This intellectual liberation from the inevitable may be one of the most important next steps we have to take.

7. The expropriation of moral outrage

Though I have no intention of ending this discussion by adding one more elegy to the decline of spontaneity in contemporary society, there do seem to be important structural changes that have affected moral feelings and expression. We may call them the expropriation of moral outrage in analogy to the expropriation of the means of production that has taken place in both capitalist and socialist societies. To be sure, the phenomenon is neither altogether novel nor limited to modern industrial societies. Over the centuries the Catholic Church has had considerable success in expropriating guilt. It has achieved this by helping to create the sense of guilt and then providing the bureaucratic mechanisms for alleviating it. As an economist might put the point, the Catholic Church managed to create much of the demand and most of the supply.

But guilt is not the same thing as moral outrage, even if the two on occasion display a close connection. Furthermore with the rise of mass production, the mass market in capitalist societies, government control of the economy in socialist ones, and huge powerful bureaucracies in both of them, the whole context has changed in which moral anger can arise and find expression. To these elements in the modern situation it is necessary to add that of sheer numbers. The more people there are, the less any single individual's feeling can count, even if there may be greater social power due to a more complex division of labor. The consequence has been, I suggest, to produce a synthetic and indirect quality in moral outrage. Nowadays visceral moral anger may be much rarer or more difficult to express openly than it was a few generations ago, partly because for any single individual its expression may seem rather futile. Instead, opinion leaders of various stripes turn the moral current on and off as best they can in accord with larger considerations, or else smell out the shifting currents of public sentiment as forces they can use to propel their intellectual and commercial products in the direction of greater influence and profit. The upheavals of the late sixties and seventies both in China and in the West were efforts to restore gut reactions to a place of honor, efforts that the prevailing social apparatus for the most part managed to absorb or deflect.

The transformations wrought by the growth of modern bureaucracy and modern industry have by no means everywhere reduced individual freedom to express moral likes and dislikes. For the moderately prosperous sector within Western societies there may even be a considerable increase in the freedom of moral choices and a substantial decrease in the burdens of anxiety in making these choices. Sorting through the day's mail one can decide whether or not to express moral outrage about political prisoners in Chile or the Soviet Union, black or Spanish-speaking victims of racial injustice in American cities, the plight of farm laborers in California or that of whales in the Pacific Ocean. It is even possible to gauge very nicely the intensity of one's moral outrage by the size of the check. It is also possible to select a congenial color from the political spectrum by choosing one organization among several promoting the same general cause as the group to which one will mail the check. The system allocates society's store of moral outrage in exactly the same way as the market allocates the supply of fruit juices or canned potatoes. Those who need the product most may not get it because they lack the resources for expression through the mechanism of the market, and new suppliers can have trouble breaking into a crowded market. But these obstacles can be exaggerated in connection with such a commodity as moral outrage. The causes for the expression of such sentiments come and go ceaselessly as the market swiftly and impersonally allocates resources, growth, and fame to some producers and a slow withering extinction to others.

For the workers, as has been apparent at many points in this book, the expropriation and rationalization of moral outrage has been a major part of the capitalist experience. In the early phase of industrialization in western Europe the workers' protest took two main forms. One was the brief flare-up in the form of a strike over some apparent injustice by the employer: the sudden announcement of a wage cut or the firing of a fellow worker. The other was participation along with journeymen, artisans, some small proprietors, and even at times peasants in raggedly organized movements for social change. These ranged from the Chartists in England to the popular upheavals on the continent in 1848. Afterward came the organizational revolution as the workers acquired greater self-discipline, the techniques of union organization and carefully timed strikes that would yield an increase in wages. In his comparative study of working-class history Peter Stearns has emphasized the degree to which the workers' acceptance of organizational imperatives left them with a big residue of complaints arising out of the work situation.[31]

Under socialism, of course, all these matters are arranged very differently, even if many of the results turn out to be similar. Instead of depending on the vagaries of the market for its supply of moral outrage and the uses to which it will be put, a socialist society plans the production and allocation of this commodity in much the same way as it decides on the production and distribution of steel and electricity. (Since socialist societies do not produce very many relatively frivolous and wasteful items like fruit juices and canned potatoes, it is better to use different examples.) In this way it is possible, some authorities tell us, to deter-

[31]Peter N. Stearns, *Lives of Labor*, 300, 310, 322–323, 349. Scattered throughout Perrot, *Les ouvriers en grève* are numerous reports and acute observations on the contrasts between the old-fashioned, "spontaneous" strike—that often included a good deal of secret informal planning and discussion among the workers beforehand—and the modern carefully orchestrated strike and public demonstration. See espec. I, 120–124; II, 419, 425, 553–559. In Germany worker resistance to the "organizational imperative," one that the worker elite imposed on others, contributed to the explosive situation in 1918 and subsequently.

mine with some precision the society's priorities in moral outrage and exactly how angry the citizenry should be about each
offense against socialist morality, which represents, they tell us,
a higher stage of historical development than bourgeois morality.
As soon as the planners have agreed upon the list of enemies of
the people appropriate to the political, social, and economic
configuration of the moment, they can pull the levers that set in
motion the enormous machinery of a socialist state.

People's organizations, loudspeakers, newspapers, the secret
police, and the courts all swing into action and the campaign is
off. A reasonably intelligent person, particularly the educated
product of Chinese civilization that for centuries has stressed the
nuances of moral indignation in a setting of intrigue and
bureaucratic protocol,[32] will know at once just how to adjust
facial expressions and tones of voice in expressing the correct
degree of indignation for each degree on the official set of
priorities that ranks all possible varieties of the execrable behavior of the enemies of the people. A poor peasant or worker
cannot be expected to do as well. Worse still, a peasant or a
worker may have trouble understanding why this year's enemies
of the people include some of last year's heroes, and why it is
necessary to have another exhausting campaign so soon if the
last one was as successful as everybody said it was. But since
socialism is a workers' and peasants' state that belongs to the
people, there are lots of people to explain such matters to workers and peasants and indeed to everybody who cares to listen.
Furthermore just about everybody must care to listen. Woe to the
person who stubbornly refuses to listen to the right noises or to
try to make the right noises under socialism, since a socialist state
is very efficient in its allocation of human as well as material
resources. It sends human beings who prefer peace and quiet
and thinking for themselves to listening to and making the right
noises off to camps for reform through labor.

All this looks like a very efficient way of coping with the need
for moral anger and moral outrage. At least to sympathetic
foreigners watching the parade of enthusiastic demonstrators
marching through the great square of the capital carrying their
series of carefully worded slogans for the occasion—and who
never see camps for reform through labor—it all seems much
more efficient, equitable, and morally inspiring than do the
workings of the market and political contests or pseudo-contests

---

[32] For an instructive study of this configuration during the T'ang dynasty see Howard J.
Wechsler, *Mirror to the Son of Heaven: Wei Cheng at the Court of T'ang T'ai-tsung*.

under liberal capitalism. But is it really more efficient and more equitable in the sense of focusing moral anger in ways that are more effective for the whole society and more satisfying for the individual concerned?[33] The socialist society, for all its obviously stifling side effects, might just possibly have the edge on this score if those who drew up its moral priorities proceeded in as rational and informed a way as possible, listening carefully and sympathetically to the plaints of its citizenry. But that is hardly what happens. The moral priorities[34] are drawn up intermittently by the Wisest Man in the world and reflect mainly the thought of the Wisest Man in the world. He makes his decisions in his capacity as chairman of a Committee of the Next Wisest Men. The Next Wisest Men are the loyal advisers and helpers of the Wisest Man, but also his rivals and potential successors. The policy that is presented to the public as the outcome of rational discussion is actually very much the product of the system of rivalries, hostilities, and shifting clique relationships among these figures at the apex of the system and their institutional supporters lower down in the competing bureaucratic hierarchies. When the Wisest Man in the world dies, as evidently happens from time to time, the rivalry becomes all the more intense. Decisions about what to produce and what to be angry about are as much weapons in Byzantine bureaucratic intrigues as they are adaptations to the demands of a wider situation.

In the importance of bureaucratic and personal rivalries socialist and liberal capitalist systems approach one another. To speak of the expropriation of moral outrage under these conditions does not of course tell the whole story of the transformation that has taken place in modern times. But the notion may reveal significant historical trends and distinctions. In any event the situation now is hardly what it was when Ulrich Bräker could not even get angry at the noble patron who sold him into the armies of Frederick the Great or when poor Karl Fischer at long last thundered out his judgment of the factory director who fired workers whom he didn't even know. Both men didn't know what to do with their sense of outrage and injustice. But they did not know, and probably could not know, for historical reasons that differ sharply in their own two cases and are again very different from those prevailing today. Yet the historian who tries to avoid

---

[33]These two criteria are unlikely to be altogether compatible in any society. But any society where they are totally incompatible is probably headed for trouble.

[34]Economic priorities are also moral priorities.

both nostalgia about the past and cheap optimism about the future may pause with a disturbed wonder at the way different historical causes can produce such similar forms of human helplessness and unhappiness.

CHAPTER FIFTEEN

Epilogue: reciprocity as fact, ideology, and ideal

Without the concept of reciprocity—or better, mutual obligation, a term that does *not* imply equality of burdens or
obligations—it becomes impossible to interpret human society as
the consequence of anything other than perpetual force and
fraud. Great as has been the importance of these twin forces
throughout the record of human history, such an interpretation
would be a manifest exaggeration.

If perfect reciprocity existed, human society would be held
together by a network of related obligations whose performances would be equal in value according to universally accepted criteria. Those in authority would perform certain tasks
of social coordination and provide protection for the subjects,
giving services whose value would equal that of the subjects'
obligations in loyalty, obedience, taxes, military service, etc. The
division of labor and the allocation of goods and services within
the society would also take place through the exchange of goods
and services whose values were equivalent. Quite obviously no
society works this way, nor does it seem very likely that any
society ever will work in this way. Aside from the obvious
difficulty of agreeing upon criteria for evaluating each type of
contribution, a difficulty that in my judgment has been somewhat exaggerated (it is not *that* difficult for human beings to see
when they have been very badly abused), there is a further
obstacle: human beings, according to abundant evidence, don't
want that kind of society. More precisely, they often want for
themselves and their immediate associates a situation better than
that which reciprocity would produce. Others of course learn to
put up with considerably less.

Viewed somewhat differently, the point I am trying to make is that reciprocity, and social cooperation generally, do not flow inexorably from some innate tendency in human nature. Earlier we have noticed that moral rules whose violation arouses an anger that seems almost instinctive are not necessarily due to frustration of innate human tendencies by unjust or oppressive social arrangements. Rather the rules are the consequence of human nature in a painfully constricted social situation; to put the matter a bit too cynically, the consequence of an effort to make the best of a bad situation with considerable anger against those persons whose apparent lack of self-control threatens to make the situation even worse.

Reciprocity and cooperation do not develop spontaneously, except perhaps on a limited basis among small groups in fairly continuous personal contact. Otherwise there is a continual tendency for selfish individual and group interests to break through. According to more or less official ideology, medieval craft guilds were supposed to serve the city; the purpose of their rules was to ensure the quality of the product. But in practice the rules were used, and twisted, to advance the selfish interests of guild members against those of the city as a whole, and of course other guilds. Similar tendencies can be found in bureaucracies, where subdivisions fight against the interests of the bureaucracy as a whole, in military and ecclesiastical organizations, regional interests in a larger polity, and endless others. These fissiparous tendencies exist in all societies and cultures of any size.[1] Whatever there is in the way of social cooperation or coordination (of which reciprocity is only one form) is under continual threat from such tendencies. Where cooperation exists, it has to be created and continually re-created. Specific and identifiable human beings have to perform this act of creation and re-creation. That is true of even so impersonal a mechanism as the modern capitalist competitive market.

To conceive of the rule of reciprocity as some sort of automatic tendency to restore a social equilibrium based on fair exchange would be a gross idealization of what actually takes place. In practice, violations of reciprocity are commonplace at all "levels" of civilization. There are societies about which it seems fair to say that the social institutions themselves are too weak to enforce reciprocity; there are no effective sanctions. Either nothing much at all happens when an individual refuses to play his reciprocal part, or an injured individual may rage around

[1] It is therefore romantic nonsense to attribute them to the alienation of human beings from each other, allegedly produced by modern capitalism or industrial society generally.

507

ineffectually, especially if that person has a higher status. In such cases patterns of reciprocity may actually trigger off conflict by raising unrequited expectations.[2] In societies with more highly developed systems of authority, but by no means only in these, the right of the stronger prevails a great deal of the time in practice, and the injured party has to swallow his or her indignation.[3] Nevertheless, what is important for our purposes is that signs of indignation do occur very widely.

Compulsion, fraud, and force play an overwhelming role in this whole process. The citizens of the Roman Republic did not sit down and write a social compact about how the inhabitants of Italy would live together. They conquered the other tribes of the peninsula and forced them into submission. Nor was it some spontaneously developed reciprocity that sent women and children into the steaming, roaring mills of the nineteenth century or that now sends men forth to labor under the blazing sun or in the deep sunless shaft of a mine in order that men and women may enjoy a coffee break or quaff beer from a can.

On the other hand, the kings, statesmen, proconsuls, captains of industry, and others who create new forms of domination and division of labor, generally justify their acts in the language of reciprocity. Kings call their subjects "my" people, or "our" people. What ruler has ever denied that he had the obligation to serve and protect his or her people? Imperialism finds its justification in the burdens and responsibilities of power to create a more "efficient" division of labor between metropolitan and dependent areas. In general, rulers and dominant groups talk in terms of reciprocity (though they may not use the expression) to stress *their* contribution to the social units they head, and to praise the virtues and necessities of harmonious social relationships therein. In this fashion the notion of reciprocity readily becomes a form of mystification, an ideological cover for exploitation.[4] Yet the mere fact of its use as ideological rhetoric constitutes significant evidence for its central role in the universal code. As a familiar saying has it, hypocrisy is the tribute vice pays to virtue. The rhetorical and ideological use of the conception of

---

[2]Morton H. Fried, *Evolution of Political Society*, 72–75, surveys a variety of reactions culled from the anthropological literature.

[3]Leopold Pospisil, *Kapauku Papuans and their Law*, 178, 180, 183, 184, gives concrete examples from a society with very little in the way of organized authority, but a set of recognized "rules" about property.

[4]As maintained elsewhere I hold that exploitation can be an objective term to describe any relationship which gives to one or more participants systematically and continually much greater advantages and benefits than to others.

reciprocity testifies to its widespread appeal, to its possible role as the fundamental idea behind popular conceptions of justice and injustice, fairness and unfairness.

In many different times and places popular criticism of authority has been to the effect that authority has not lived up to its obligation to take care of its subjects, that it has oppressed and plundered where it should have cherished and protected. And the classic objection to the division of labor and the allocation of society's resources and products has held that "crooked judgments" have enabled the mighty to avoid laboring in the heat of the day while they have arrogated to themselves the best of the fruits of the earth. In a word they exploit, because they take without giving. By this I do not mean to imply that popular conceptions of reciprocity work in terms of exact equivalences rendered uniformly in the manner of a Manchester economist. In many a nonliterate society quite the contrary is the case: the obligation to render an equivalent is often tempered with what seems to the modern Westerner an undue compassion for human frailties. The notion of quantity may be vague, that of time imprecise, and up to a point the intention may take the place of the act.[5] Other forms of exchange are exact and detailed—perhaps after bargaining as in the case of bride price or dowry—to the point of punctiliousness. That, however, is the exactness of ritual and the delicate adjustment of one individual status to another. It is an exactness closer to eighteenth-century diplomatic protocol than to the calculations of the counting-house. Behind all these variations, nevertheless, it is possible to perceive a general ground plan, a conception of what social relationships ought to be. It is a conception that by no means excludes hierarchy and authority, where exceptional qualities and defects can be the source of enormous admiration and awe. At the same time it is one where services and favors, trust and affection, in the course of mutual exchanges are ideally expected to find some rough balancing out.

Under appropriate circumstances these conceptions can and do have a critical cutting edge. The king has failed in his obligation of protection, the relationship between this sovereign and his subjects has been broken, the implicit social contract has temporarily come to an end. Nations and cultures as different as England and China have gone through this experience. It was

---

[5]See Eileen J. Krige and J. O. Krige, *The Realm of a Rain Queen: A Study of the Pattern of Lovedu Society,* 56, 182, 184, 288, 293, 297. See also Raymond Firth, *Primitive Polynesian Economy,* 300–304, 306, 313, 338–344.

one component too, though a lesser one, in the French Revolution. Anger at the failure of authority to live up to its obligations, to keep its word and faith with the subjects, can be among the most potent of human emotions and topple thrones.

At the same time there are inherent limitations upon the subversive lengths to which this traditionalist form of criticism can go. Essentially it accepts the existence of hierarchy and authority while attempting to make it conform to an idealized pattern of how it should behave. Obligations are accepted but should be reciprocal in nature: for the obligations of the subject there should be corresponding obligations for the ruler, and the whole should redound to the benefit of the community. This appears to be by far the more common and widespread form which the conception of reciprocity has taken.

The really subversive form of criticism begins when people ask whether a specific social function needs to be performed at all, whether kings, priests, capitalists, or even revolutionary bureaucrats may not be something human society could do without. This form of criticism has a very ancient pedigree in human history, though as far as I have been able to determine it does not occur in nonliterate societies.[6] With this form of criticism one could claim that a "pure" form of reciprocity—and hence of the universal code—came into its own, since the only basis of human society could be freely accepted reciprocal obligations once all forms of authority were removed. That, however, is also "pure" speculation. So far in human history, forms of authority have simply succeeded each other; new ones have substituted quite effectively for those that have become historically obsolete. Whether there will be some qualitative leap into a very different future is an issue that an empirical inquiry like this can at present safely set aside.

[6]Possibly a detailed analysis of nonliterate mythologies would turn up traces of this outlook.

References cited

Abel, Theodore, *The Nazi Movement: Why Hitler Came Into Power*. 1938, reprinted, New York, 1966.

Abraham, Karl, *Der Strukturwandel im Handwerk in der ersten Hälfte des 19. Jahrhunderts und seine Bedeutung für die Berufserziehung*. Köln, 1955.

Adelmann, Gerhard, "Die soziale Betriebsverfassung des Ruhrbergbaus vom Anfang des 19. Jahrhunderts bis zum Ersten Weltkrieg, unter besonderer Berücksichtigung des Industrie- und Handelskammerbezirks Essen," *Rheinishes Archiv*, Nr. 56 (1962), 7–208.

Adler, Hans Günther, *Theresienstadt 1941–1945: Das Antlitz einer Zwangsgemeinschaft*. Geschichte—Soziologie—Psychologie. 2nd edition, Tübingen, 1960.

Adorno, T. W. *et al.*, *The Authoritarian Personality*. New York, 1950.

Albertin, Lothar, *Liberalismus und Demokratie am Anfang der Weimarer Republik*. Beiträge zur Geschichte des Parlamentarismus und der politischen Parteien, vol. 45. Düsseldorf, 1972.

Allgemeiner Kongress der Arbeiter- und Soldatenräte Deutschlands: Vom 16. bis 21. Dezember 1918 im Abgeordnetenhause zu Berlin. Stenographische Berichte. Published by the Zentralrat der sozialistischen Republik Deutschlands, Berlin, [1919].

Amann, Peter H., *Revolution and Mass Democracy: The Paris Club Movement in 1848*. Princeton, 1975.

Aronfreed, Justin, *Conduct and Conscience: The Socialization of Internalized Control over Behavior*. New York, 1968.

Asch, S. E., "Effects of Group Pressure upon the Modification and Distortion of Judgments," in Harold Guetzkow, editor, *Groups, Leadership and Men: Research in Judgment* (Pittsburgh, 1951), 177–190.

Ashton, Patricia Teague, "Cross-Cultural Piagetian Research: An Experimental Perspective," *Harvard Educational Review*, vol. 45, no. 4 (November, 1975), 475–506.

Avrich, Paul H., "Russian Factory Committees in 1917," *Jahrbücher für Geschichte Osteuropas*, Band 11, Heft 2 (1963), 161–182.

Badia, Gilbert, *Le Spartakisme: Les dernières années de Rosa Luxemburg et de Karl Liebknecht 1914–1919*. Paris, 1967.

Banfield, Thomas Charles, *Industry of the Rhine: Series II, Manufactures*. London, 1848.

Bao Ruo-Wang (Jean Pasqualini), and Chelminski, Rudolph, *Prisoner of Mao*. New York, 1973.

Barkun, Michael, *Law without Sanctions: Order in Primitive Societies and the World Community*. New Haven, 1968.

Basham, A. L., *The Wonder That Was India: A Survey of the Culture of the Indian Sub-continent before the Coming of the Muslims*. 1954, reprinted, New York, 1959.

Bebel, August, *August Bebels Briefwechsel mit Friedrich Engels*, edited by Werner Blumenberg. The Hague, 1965.

———, *Aus meinem Leben*. 3 vols. Stuttgart, 1910–1914.

———, *Die Frau und der Sozialismus*. Zürich, 1879.

Bernays, Marie, "Berufswahl und Berufsschicksal," part 1, *Archiv für Sozialwissenschaft und Sozialpolitik*, vol. XXXV, no. 1 (Juli 1912), 123–176; part 2, *ibid.*, vol. XXXVI, no. 3 (Mai 1913), 884–915.

Berndt, Ronald M., *Excess and Restraint: Social Control among a New Guinea Mountain People*. Chicago, 1962.

Bernstein, Thomas Paul, *Leadership and Mobilization in the Collectivization of Agriculture in China and Russia: A Comparison*. Doctoral dissertation, Columbia University, 1970. University Microfilms, Ann Arbor, 1971.

Beschlüsse des allgemeinen deutschen Arbeiterkongresses zu Frankfurt am Main, gefasst in den Monaten Juli, August, und September, 1848. Reprinted as Anhang I in Biermann, *Karl Georg Winkelblech (Karl Marlo)*, II, 441–456.

Bettelheim, Bruno, *The Informed Heart: Autonomy in a Mass Age*. Glencoe, 1960.

Biermann, Wilhelm Eduard, *Karl Georg Winkelblech (Karl Marlo): Sein Leben und sein Werk*. 2 vols. Leipzig, 1909.

Blassingame, John W., *The Slave Community: Plantation Life in the Antebellum South*. New York, 1972.

Bol'shaia Sovetskaia Entsiklopediia. 51 vols. 2nd edition, Moscow, 1949–58.

Bonnell, Victoria E., "The Politics of Labor in Pre-Revolutionary

Russia: Moscow Workers' Organizations 1905–1914." Unpublished doctoral thesis, Harvard University, 1975.

Born, Stephan, *Erinnerungen eines Achtundvierziger*. Leipzig, 1898.

Bräker, Ulrich, *Der Arme Mann im Tockenburg*. Reclam edition, Stuttgart, 1965. Originally published as *Lebensgeschichte und natürliche Ebentheuer des Armen Mannes im Tockenburg* (Zürich, 1789).

Braun, Rudolf, *Industrialisierung und Volksleben: Die Veränderungen der Lebensformen in einem ländlichen Industriegebiet vor 1800*. Erlenbach-Zürich, 1960.

Brepohl, Wilhelm, *Industrievolk: Im Wandel von der agraren zur industriellen Daseinsform dargestellt am Ruhrgebiet*. Tübingen, 1957.

Briggs, George W., *The Chamars*. London, 1920.

Bromme, Moritz Th. W., *Lebensgeschichte eines modernen Fabrikarbeiters*, edited by Paul Göhre. Jena, 1910.

Broszat, Martin, "Der Staat Hitlers," in *Deutsche Geschichte seit dem Ersten Weltkrieg*, vol. 1 (Stuttgart, 1971), 501–844.

Bry, Gerhard, *Wages in Germany 1871–1945*. Princeton, 1960.

Burdzhalov, E. N., *Vtoraiia Russkaiia Revoliutsiia*. Vol. I: *Vosstanie v Petrograde*. Moscow, 1967. Vol. II: *Moskva—Front—Periferiia*. Moscow, 1971.

Cahn, Edmond, "Justice," in *International Encyclopedia of the Social Sciences*, vol. 8 (New York, 1968), 341–347.

Caron, Pierre, *Les Massacres de septembre*. Paris, 1935.

Carsten, F. L., *The Reichswehr and Politics: 1918–1933*. Oxford, 1966.

———, *Revolution in Central Europe 1918–1919*. London, 1972.

Chagnon, Napoleon A., *Yąnomamö: The Fierce People*. New York, 1968.

Chamberlin, William Henry, *The Russian Revolution: 1917–1921*. 2 vols. New York, 1935.

Chesneaux, Jean, "Les Traditions égalitaires et utopiques en Orient," *Diogène*, no. 62 (avril-juin, 1968), 87–115.

Chinoy, Ely, *Automobile Workers and the American Dream*. 1955, reprinted, Boston, 1965.

Chorley, Katharine, *Armies and the Art of Revolution*. 2nd edition, Boston, 1973.

Cohen, Elie A., *Human Behavior in the Concentration Camp*. Translated from the Dutch by M. H. Braaksma. New York, 1953.

Cole, Michael, and Bruner, Jerome S., "Cultural Differences and Inferences about Psychological Processes," *American Psychologist*, vol. 26, no. 10 (October, 1971), 867–876.

Coles, Robert, *Children of Crisis: A Study of Courage and Fear.* Boston, 1967.

Colm, Gerhard, *Beitrag zur Geschichte und Soziologie des Ruhraufstandes vom März–April 1920.* Essen, 1921.

Comfort, Richard A., *Revolutionary Hamburg: Labor Politics in the Early Weimar Republic.* Stanford, 1966.

Conze, Werner, "Vom 'Pöbel' zum 'Proletariat': Sozialgeschichtliche Voraussetzungen für den Sozialismus in Deutschland," in Wehler, ed., *Moderne deutsche Sozialgeschichte,* 111–136.

Conze, Werner, and Groh, Dieter, *Die Arbeiterbewegung in der nationalen Bewegung: Die deutsche Sozialdemokratie vor, während und nach der Reichsgründung.* Stuttgart, 1966.

Craig, Gordon A., *The Politics of the Prussian Army: 1640–1945.* Oxford, 1955.

Croon, Helmuth, *"Vom Werden des Ruhrgebiets,"* in Först, editor, *Rheinisch-Westfälische Rückblende,* 175–220.

—— and Utermann, Kurt, *Zeche und Gemeinde: Untersuchungen über den Strukturwandel einer Zechengemeinde im nördlichen Ruhrgebiet.* Tübingen, 1958.

Daniels, Robert V., *Red October: The Bolshevik Revolution of 1917.* New York, 1967.

Davis, Natalie Zemon, "The Rites of Violence: Religious Riot in Sixteenth-Century France," *Past and Present,* no. 59 (May, 1973), 51–91.

Dentan, Robert Knox, *The Semai: A Nonviolent People of Malaya.* New York, 1968.

Der Deutsche Metallarbeiter-Verband im Jahre 1913: Jahr- und Handbuch für Verbandsmitglieder. Compiled by the Vorstand des Deutschen Metallarbeiter-Verbandes. Stuttgart, 1914.

Der Deutsche Metallarbeiter-Verband im Jahre 1916: Jahr- und Handbuch für Verbandsmitglieder. Compiled by the Vorstand des Deutschen Metallarbeiter-Verbandes. Stuttgart, 1917.

Deutsche Geschichte seit dem Ersten Weltkrieg. Publication of the Institut für Zeitgeschichte. 3 vols. Stuttgart, 1971–1973.

Dieterici, F. W. C., editor, *Mittheilungen des statistischen Bureau's in Berlin,* vol. I (1848), vol. II (1849). Berlin, 1849.

Dohna, Herrmann Graf zu, "Über das Los der freien Arbeiter," in Jantke and Hilger, eds., *Die Eigentumslosen,* 244–255. Original source: *Die freien Arbeiter im Preussischen Staate* (Leipzig, 1847), 34–75.

Domes, Jürgen, *The Internal Politics of China 1949–1972.* Translated by Rüdiger Machetzki. New York, 1973.

Dore, Ronald, *British Factory—Japanese Factory: The Origins of National Diversity in Industrial Relations.* Berkeley, 1973.

Douglas, Mary, *Purity and Danger: An Analysis of Concepts of Pollution and Taboo.* New York, 1966.

Drekmeier, Charles, *Kingship and Community in Early India.* Stanford, 1962.

Droz, Jacques, and Ayçoberry, Pierre, "Structures sociales et courants idéologiques dans l'Allemagne prérévolutionnaire 1835–1847," Istituto Giangiacomo Feltrinelli, *Annali,* vol. VI (1963), 164–236.

Elkins, Stanley M., *Slavery: A Problem in American Institutional and Intellectual Life.* 1959, reprinted New York, 1963.

El'nitskii, A., *Istoriia Rabochego Dvizheniia v Rossii.* 4th edition, Moscow, 1925.

Encyclopedia of Religion and Ethics, edited by James Hastings. 12 vols. New York, 1908–1927.

Entwurf einer allgemeinen Handwerker- und Gewerbe-Ordnung für Deutschland. Berathen und beschlossen von dem deutschen Handwerker- und Gewerbe-Congress zu Frankfurt am Main in den Monaten Juli und August 1848. [Frankfurt am Main, 1848].

Erger, Johannes, *Der Kapp-Lüttwitz-Putsch: Ein Beitrag zur deutschen Innenpolitik 1919/20.* Düsseldorf, 1967.

Erikson, Erik H., *Childhood and Society.* New York, 1950.

———, *Young Man Luther: A Study in Psychoanalysis and History.* New York, 1958.

Fanon, Frantz, *Les Damnés de la terre.* Preface by Jean Paul Sartre. Paris, 1961.

Feldman, Gerald D., *Army, Industry, and Labor in Germany, 1914–1918.* Princeton, 1966.

———; Kolb, Eberhard; and Rürup, Reinhard; "Die Massenbewegung der Arbeiterschaft in Deutschland am Ende des Ersten Weltkrieges (1917–1920)," *Politische Vierteljahresschrift,* vol. 13 (August, 1972), 84–105.

Ferro, Marc, *The Russian Revolution of February 1917.* Translated from the French by J. L. Richards. Englewood Cliffs, 1972.

Field, Daniel, *Rebels in the Name of the Tsar.* Boston, 1976.

Firth, Raymond, *Primitive Economics of the New Zealand Maori.* London, 1929.

———, *Primitive Polynesian Economy.* 2nd edition, London, 1965.

Fischer, Franz Louis, *Arbeiterschicksale.* Berlin, 1906.

Fischer, Karl, *Denkwürdigkeiten und Erinnerungen eines Arbeiters.* Leipzig, 1903.

Fischer, Ruth, *Stalin and German Communism: A Study in the Origins of the State Party.* Cambridge, Ma., 1948.

Fischer, Wolfram, *Handwerksrecht und Handwerkswirtschaft um 1800: Studien zur Sozial- und Wirtschaftsverfassung vor der industriellen Revolution*. Berlin, 1955.

———, "Soziale Unterschichten im Zeitalter der Frühindustrialisierung," *International Review of Social History*, vol. VIII (1963), 415–435.

———, *Wirtschaft und Gesellschaft im Zeitalter der Industrialisierung: Aufsätze—Studien—Vorträge*. Kritische Studien zur Geschichtswissenschaft, 1. Göttingen, 1972.

Först, Walter, editor, *Rheinisch-Westfälische Rückblende*. Köln, 1967.

Freud, Anna, *Das Ich und die Abwehrmechanismen*. London, 1946.

Fried, Morton H., *The Evolution of Political Society: An Essay in Political Anthropology*. New York, 1967.

Friedländer, Ludwig, *Roman Life and Manners under the Early Empire*. Authorized translation of the 7th edition of the *Sittengeschichte Roms* by J. H. Freese and L. A. Magnus. 4 vols. London, 1928.

Fünfundsiebzig Jahre Industriegewerkschaft 1891 bis 1966: Vom Deutschen Metallarbeiter-Verband zur Industriegewerkschaft Metall. Frankfurt am Main, 1966.

Genovese, Eugene D., *Roll, Jordan, Roll: The World the Slaves Made*. New York, 1974.

Ghurye, G. S., *Caste, Class and Occupation*. 4th edition, Bombay, 1961.

Gitermann, Valentin, *Geschichte Russlands*. 3 vols. Zürich, 1949.

Gladen, Albin, "Die Streiks der Bergarbeiter im Ruhrgebiet in den Jahren 1889, 1905 und 1912," in Reulecke, editor, *Arbeiterbewegung an Rhein und Ruhr*, 111–148.

Gluckman, Max, *The Ideas in Barotse Jurisprudence*. New Haven, 1965.

Göhre, Paul, *Drei Monate Fabrikarbeiter und Handwerksbursche: Eine praktische Studie*. 2nd edition, Leipzig, 1891.

Goffman, Erving, *Asylums: Essays on the Social Situation of Mental Patients and Other Inmates*. New York, 1961.

Gordon, Harold J., Jr., *The Reichswehr and the German Republic 1919–1926*. Princeton, 1957.

Goslin, David A., editor, *Handbook of Socialization Theory and Research*. Chicago, 1969.

Gottschalk, Louis R., *Jean Paul Marat: A Study in Radicalism*. 1927, reprinted, Chicago, 1967.

Goubert, Pierre, *Louis XIV et vingt millions de Français*. Paris, 1966.

Groh, Dieter, *Negative Integration und revolutionärer Attentismus:*

Die deutsche Sozialdemokratie am Vorabend des Ersten Weltkrieges. Frankfurt am Main, 1973.

Der Grosse Brockhaus: Wissenschafts-lexikon. 20 vols. 15th edition, Leipzig, 1928–1935.

Guetzkow, Harold, editor, *Groups, Leadership and Men: Research in Judgment.* Pittsburgh, 1951.

Haimson, Leopold H., "The Problems of Social Stability in Urban Russia, 1905–1917," part one, *Slavic Review*, vol. XXIII, no. 4 (December, 1964), 619–642 and *ibid.*, part two, vol. XXIV, no. 1 (March, 1965), 1–22.

Hamilton, Richard F., *Affluence and the French Worker in the Fourth Republic.* Princeton, 1967.

———, *The Bases of National Socialism: The Electoral Support for Hitler: 1924–1932.* Forthcoming.

Handwörterbuch der Staatswissenschaften, edited by Ludwig Elster *et al.* 8 vols. 4th revised edition, Jena, 1923–1928.

Harper, Edward B., "Social Consequences of an 'Unsuccessful' Low Caste Movement," in James Silverberg, editor, *Social Mobility in the Caste System in India: An Interdisciplinary Symposium* (Comparative Studies in Society and History, Supplement III), 37–65. The Hague, 1968.

Hazari, *Untouchable: The Autobiography of an Indian Outcaste.* New York, 1969.

Heberle, Rudolf, *Social Movements: An Introduction to Political Sociology.* New York, 1951.

Heiber, Helmut, "Die Republik von Weimar," in *Deutsche Geschichte seit dem Ersten Weltkrieg,* vol. I (Stuttgart, 1971), 13–211.

Henry, Jules, *Jungle People: A Kaingáng Tribe of the Highlands of Brazil.* 1941, reprinted, New York, 1964.

Heymann, Bruno, and Freudenberg, Karl, *Morbidität und Mortalität der Bergleute im Ruhrgebiet.* Essen, 1925.

Hirschman, Albert O., *Exit, Voice, and Loyalty: Responses to Decline in Firms, Organizations, and States.* 1970, reprinted, Cambridge, 1972.

Hitler, Adolf, *Mein Kampf.* 2 vols. in one. München, 1935.

Hobsbawm, Eric J., "Peasants and Politics," *Journal of Peasant Studies,* vol. I, no. 1 (October, 1973), 1–22.

———, *Primitive Rebels: Studies in Archaic Forms of Social Movement in the 19th and 20th Centuries.* 1959, reprinted, New York, 1965.

Hoffmann, Charles, *The Chinese Worker.* Albany, 1974.

Hofstadter, Richard, and Wallace, Michael, editors, *American Violence: A Documentary History.* New York, 1970.

Holmberg, Allan R., *Nomads of the Long Bow: The Siriono of Eastern Bolivia.* 1950, 2nd edition, New York, 1969.

Homans, George Caspar, *Social Behavior: Its Elementary Forms.* 1961, 2nd revised edition, New York, 1974.

Hue, Otto, *Die Bergarbeiter.* 2 vols. Stuttgart, 1910–1913.

Hufton, Olwen H., "Women in Revolution 1789–1796," *Past and Present,* no. 53 (November, 1971), 90–108.

Illustrierte Geschichte der Deutschen Revolution. Berlin [1929].

Isaacs, Harold R., *India's Ex-Untouchables.* New York [1965].

Jahresberichte der Gewerbe-Aufsichtsbeamten und Bergbehörden für die Jahre 1914–1918. Band I: Preussen. Reichsministerium des Innern, Amtliche Ausgabe. Berlin, 1919.

Jantke, Carl, editor, *Bergmann und Zeche: Die sozialen Arbeitsverhältnisse einer Schachtanlage des nördlichen Ruhrgebiets in der Sicht der Bergleute.* Soziale Forschung und Praxis, vol. 11. Tübingen, 1953.

――― and Hilger, Dietrich, editors, *Die Eigentumslosen: Der deutsche Pauperismus und die Emanzipationskrise in Darstellungen und Deutungen der zeitgenössischen Literatur.* München, 1965.

Jaurès, Jean, *Histoire socialiste de la Révolution Française.* 8 vols. Édition révue par A. Mathiez. Paris, 1922–1924.

Jellinek, Frank, *The Paris Commune of 1871.* New York, 1937.

Joll, James, *The Anarchists.* 1964, reprinted, New York, 1966.

Die Jugendgeschichte einer Arbeiterin: Von ihr selbst erzählt. Introduction by August Bebel. München, 1909.

Keep, John L. H., *The Russian Revolution: A Study in Mass Mobilization.* New York, 1976.

Keniston, Kenneth, *The Uncommitted: Alienated Youth in American Society.* New York, 1965.

―――, *Young Radicals: Notes on Committed Youth.* New York, 1968.

Koch, Max Jürgen, *Die Bergarbeiterbewegung im Ruhrgebiet zur Zeit Wilhelms II. (1889–1914).* Düsseldorf, 1954.

Koch, Woldemar, *Die bol'ševistischen Gewerkschaften: Eine herrschaftssoziologische Studie.* Jena, 1932.

Koenen, Wilhelm, "Wir kämpften für die Rätemacht und den Sozialismus," in *Vorwärts und nicht Vergessen,* 378–380.

Kogon, Eugen, *Der SS-Staat: Das System der deutschen Konzentrationslager.* 1946, revised edition, Frankfurt am Main, 1965.

Kohlberg, Lawrence, "Stage and Sequence: The Cognitive-Developmental Approach to Socialization," in Goslin, editor, *Handbook of Socialization Theory and Research,* 347–480.

Kolb, Eberhard, *Die Arbeiterräte in der deutschen Innenpolitik 1918–1919.* Beiträge zur Geschichte des Parlamentarismus und der politischen Parteien, vol. 23. Düsseldorf, 1962.
———, editor, *Vom Kaiserreich zur Weimarer Republik.* Köln, 1972.
——— and Rürup, Reinhard, editors, *Der Zentralrat der Deutschen Sozialistischen Republik 19.12. 1918–8.4. 1919: Vom Ersten zum Zweiten Rätekongress.* Quellen zur Geschichte der Rätebewegung in Deutschland 1918–1919 . . . , vol. I. Leiden, 1968.
Kolenda, Pauline Mahar, "Toward a Model of the Hindu Jajmani System," *Human Organizations,* vol. XXII, no. 1 (Spring 1963), 11–31.
Koszyk, Kurt, "Die Sozialdemokratische Arbeiterbewegung, 1890 bis 1914," in Reulecke, editor, *Arbeiterbewegung an Rhein und Ruhr,* 149–172.
Krige, Eileen J., and Krige, J. O., *The Realm of a Rain Queen: A Study of the Pattern of Lovedu Society.* London, 1943.
Landes, David S., *The Unbound Prometheus: Technological Change and Industrial Development in Western Europe from 1750 to the Present.* Cambridge, 1969.
Landtmann, Gunnar, *The Origin of the Inequality of the Social Classes.* London, 1938.
Lane, Robert E., *Political Ideology: Why the American Common Man Believes What He Does.* New York, 1962.
Langer, William L., editor, *An Encyclopedia of World History: Ancient, Medieval, and Modern, Chronologically Arranged.* 3rd revised edition, Boston, 1956.
Lefebvre, Henri, *La proclamation de la Commune: 26 mars 1871. Trente journées qui ont fait la France.* Paris, 1965.
Le Play, Pierre Guillaume Frederic, *Les Ouvriers européens.* Études sur les travaux, La vie domestique et la condition morale des populations ouvrières de l'Europe. 6 vols. 2nd edition, Paris, 1877–79.
Levenstein, Adolf, *Die Arbeiterfrage: Mit besonderer Berücksichtigung der sozialpsychologischen Seite des modernen Grossbetriebes und der psycho-physischen Einwirkungen auf die Arbeiter.* München, 1912.
Lewis, Oscar, *La Vida: A Puerto Rican Family in the Culture of Poverty.* New York, 1966.
Lex, Barbara W., "Voodoo Death: New Thoughts on an Old Explanation," *American Anthropologist,* vol. 76, no. 4 (December, 1974), 818–823.
Lidtke, Vernon L., *The Outlawed Party: Social Democracy in Germany, 1878–1890.* Princeton, 1966.

Liebow, Elliot, *Tally's Corner: A Study of Negro Streetcorner Men*. Boston, 1967.

Lifton, Robert Jay, *Thought Reform and the Psychology of Totalism: A Study of "Brainwashing" in China*. New York, 1961.

Lindzey, Gardner, and Aronson, Elliott, editors, *Handbook of Social Psychology*. 5 vols. 2nd ed., Reading, Ma., 1968–1969.

Lipset, Seymour Martin, *Political Man: The Social Bases of Politics*. Garden City, 1960.

Lösche, Peter, *Der Bolschewismus im Urteil der Deutschen Sozialdemokratie 1903–1920*. Berlin, 1967.

Lottin, Alain, *Vie et mentalité d'un Lillois sous Louis XIV*. Lille, 1968.

Lucas, Erhard, *Märzrevolution im Ruhrgebiet*. Vol 1: *Vom Generalstreik gegen den Militärputsch zum bewaffneten Arbeiteraufstand, März-April 1920*. Frankfurt, 1970.

———, *Märzrevolution 1920*. Vol. II: *Der bewaffnete Arbeiteraufstand im Ruhrgebiet in seiner inneren Struktur und in seinem Verhältnis zu den Klassenkämpfen in den verschiedenen Regionen des Reiches*. Frankfurt am Main, 1973.

McGuire, William J., "The Nature of Attitudes and Attitude Change," in Lindzey and Aronson, editors, *Handbook of Social Psychology*, III, 136–314.

Maehl, William, "The Triumph of Nationalism in the German Socialist Party on the Eve of the First World War," *Journal of Modern History*, vol. XXIV, no. 1 (March, 1952), 15–41.

Mantell, David Mark, *True Americanism: Green Berets and War Resisters: A Study of Commitment*. New York, 1974.

Maquet, J. J., *The Premise of Inequality in Ruanda: A Study of Political Relations in a Central African Kingdom*. London, 1961.

Marx, Karl, "The Poverty of Philosophy," in Emile Burns, compiler, *A Handbook of Marxism* (New York, [n.d.]), 348–370.

Mathiesen, Thomas, *The Defences of the Weak: A Sociological Study of a Norwegian Correctional Institution*. London, 1965.

Mathiez, Albert, *La vie chère et le mouvement social sous la Terreur*. Paris, 1927.

Mattheier, Klaus J., "Werkvereine und wirtschaftsfriedlich-nationale (gelbe) Arbeiterbewegung im Ruhrgebiet," in Reulecke, ed., *Arbeiterbewegung an Rhein und Ruhr*, 173–204.

Matthias, Erich, editor, *Die Regierung der Volksbeauftragten 1918/19*. Quellen zur Geschichte des Parlamentarismus und der politischen Parteien, First Series, vol. 6/1 and vol. 6/2. Düsseldorf, 1969.

Meerwarth, Rudolf; Günther, Adolf; and Zimmermann, Waldemar; *Die Einwirkungen des Krieges auf die Bevölkerungsbewegungen und Lebenshaltung in Deutschland*. Stuttgart, 1932.

Melzack, Ronald, *The Puzzle of Pain.* New York, 1973.

Merkl, Peter H., *Political Violence under the Swastika: 581 Early Nazis.* Princeton, 1975.

Mesa-Lago, Carmelo, *Cuba in the 1970s: Pragmatism and Institutionalization.* Albuquerque, 1974.

Meyers Lexikon. 12 vols. 7th edition, Leipzig, 1924–1930.

Michelet, Jules, *Histoire de la Révolution française.* 9 vols. Revised edition, Paris, 1868.

Milgram, Stanley, *Obedience to Authority: An Experimental View.* New York, 1974.

Mitchell, Allan, *Revolution in Bavaria 1918–1919: The Eisner Regime and the Soviet Republic.* Princeton, 1965.

Mitscherlich, Alexander, *Auf dem Weg zur vaterlosen Gesellschaft: Ideen zur Sozialpsychologie.* München, [1965].

Moore, Barrington, Jr., *Social Origins of Dictatorship and Democracy: Lord and Peasant in the Making of the Modern World.* Boston, 1966.

Mosca, Gaetano, *The Ruling Class.* Translated by Hannah D. Kahn. New York, 1939.

Mucchielli, Roger, *Le Mythe de la cité idéale.* Paris, 1960.

Müller, Richard, *Der Bürgerkrieg in Deutschland: Geburtswehen der Republik.* Berlin, 1925.

————, *Vom Kaiserreich zur Republik.* Vol. I: *Ein Beitrag zur Geschichte der revolutionären Arbeiterbewegung während des Weltkrieges.* Vienna, 1924. Vol. II: *Die Novemberrevolution,* Vienna, 1925.

Nagel, Peter, *Die Motivierung der Askese in der Alten Kirche und der Ursprung des Mönchtums.* [East] Berlin, 1966.

Noske, Gustav, *Von Kiel bis Kapp: Zur Geschichte der deutschen Revolution.* Berlin, 1920.

Noyes, P. H., *Organization and Revolution: Working-Class Associations in the German Revolutions of 1848–1849.* Princeton, 1966.

Obermann, Karl, *Die deutschen Arbeiter in der Revolution von 1848.* 2nd revised edition, Berlin, 1953.

Oeckel, Heinz, *Die Revolutionäre Volkswehr 1918/19: Die deutsche Arbeiterklasse im Kampfe um die Revolutionäre Volkswehr (November 1918 bis Mai 1919).* [East] Berlin, 1968.

Oertzen, Peter von, *Betriebsräte in der Novemberrevolution: Eine politikwissenschaftliche Untersuchung über Ideengehalt und Struktur der betrieblichen und wirtschaftlichen Arbeiterräte in der deutschen Revolution 1918/19.* Düsseldorf, 1963.

————, "Die grossen Streiks der Ruhrbergarbeiterschaft im Frühjahr 1919," in Kolb, ed., *Vom Kaiserreich zur Weimarer*

Republik, 185–217. Reprinted from *Vierteljahrsheft für Zeitgeschichte*, vol. 6 (1958), 231–262.

O'Malley, L. S. S., *Popular Hinduism: The Religion of the Masses*. Cambridge, 1935.

Oman, John Campbell, *The Mystics, Ascetics, and Saints of India: A Study of Sadhuism with an Account of the Yogis, Sanyosis, Bairagis, and Other Strange Hindu Sectarians*. London, 1903.

Opel, Fritz, *Der Deutsche Metallarbeiter-Verband während des ersten Weltkrieges und der Revolution*. Schriftenreihe des Instituts für wissenschaftliche Politik in Marburg/Lahn, Nr. 4. Hannover, 1957.

Parteistatistik, Stand 1: Januar, 1935. Issued by the Reichsorganisationsleiter of the NSDAP. 3 vols., München, 1935.

Peck, Robert F.; Havighurst, Robert J.; et al.; *The Psychology of Character Development*. New York, 1960.

Perrot, Michelle, *Les ouvriers en grève: France 1871–1890*. 2 vols. Paris, 1974.

Pike, Douglas, *Viet Cong: The Organization and Techniques of the National Liberation Front of South Vietnam*. Cambridge, Ma., 1966.

Pospisil, Leopold, *Kapauku Papuan Political Economy*. Yale University Publications in Anthropology, no. 67. New Haven, 1963.

———, *Kapauku Papuans and their Law*. Yale University Publications in Anthropology, no. 54. New Haven, 1958.

Pounds, Norman J. G., *The Ruhr: A Study in Historical and Economic Geography*. Bloomington, 1952.

Praz, Mario, *The Romantic Agony*. Translated from the Italian by Angus Davidson. 2nd edition, London, 1970.

Protokoll über die Verhandlungen des Parteitages der Sozialdemokratischen Partei Deutschlands. Abgehalten in Jena vom 14. bis 20. September 1913. Berlin, 1913.

Rabinowitch, Alexander, *The Bolsheviks Come to Power: The Revolution of 1917 in Petrograd*. New York, 1976.

Radin, Paul, *Primitive Religion: Its Nature and Origin*. 1937, reprinted, New York, 1957.

Rainwater, Lee, *Behind Ghetto Walls: Family Life in a Federal Slum*. Chicago, 1970.

Ranulf, Svend, *Moral Indignation and Middle Class Psychology*. 1938, reprinted, New York, 1964.

Rawls, John, *A Theory of Justice*. Cambridge, Ma., 1971.

Redl, Fritz, and Wineman, David, *Children Who Hate: The Disorganization and Breakdown of Behavior Controls*. 1951, 2nd edition, New York, 1962.

Reulecke, Jürgen, editor, *Arbeiterbewegung an Rhein und Ruhr: Beiträge zur Geschichte der Arbeiterbewegung in Rheinland-Westfalen.* Wuppertal, 1974.

———, "Der Erste Weltkrieg und die Arbeiterbewegung im rheinisch-westfälischen Industriegebiet," in Reulecke, ed., *Arbeiterbewegung an Rhein und Ruhr,* 205–239.

Rimlinger, Gaston V., "The Legitimation of Protest: A Comparative Study in Labor History," *Comparative Studies in Society and History,* vol. II, no. 3 (April, 1960), 329–343.

Ritter, Gerhard A., *Die Arbeiterbewegung im Wilhelminischen Reich: Die Sozialdemokratische Partei und die Freien Gewerkschaften 1890–1900.* Studien zur Europäischen Geschichte aus dem Friedrich-Meinecke-Institut der Freien Universität Berlin, vol. III. 2nd edition, Berlin, 1963.

Rogin, Michael Paul, *The Intellectuals and McCarthy: The Radical Specter.* Cambridge, Ma., 1967.

Rohrscheidt, Kurt von, *Vom Zunftzwang zur Gewerbefreiheit.* Berlin, 1898.

Rosenberg, Hans, *Bureaucracy, Aristocracy and Autocracy: The Prussian Experience, 1660–1815.* Cambridge, Ma., 1958.

Roth, Guenther, *The Social Democrats in Imperial Germany: A Study in Working-Class Isolation and National Integration.* Totowa, N.J., 1963.

Ryder, A. J., *The German Revolution of 1918: A Study of German Socialism in War and Revolt.* Cambridge, 1967.

Sahlins, Marshall, *Stone Age Economics.* 1972, reprinted, Chicago, 1974.

Sansom, Robert L., *The Economics of Insurgency in the Mekong Delta of Vietnam.* Cambridge, Ma., 1970.

Sass, Friedrich, *Berlin in seiner neuesten Zeit und Entwicklung.* Leipzig, 1846.

Schapiro, Leonard, *The Origin of the Communist Autocracy: Political Opposition in the Soviet State—First Phase 1917–1922.* London, 1955.

Schein, Edgar H.; Schneier, Inge; and Barker, Curtis; *Coercive Persuasion: A Socio-Psychological Analysis of the "Brainwashing" of American Civilian Prisoners by the Chinese Communists.* New York, 1961.

Schorske, Carl E., *German Social Democracy 1905–1917: The Development of the Great Schism.* 1955, reprinted, New York, 1972.

Schulthess' Europäischer Geschichtskalender. Neue Folge, several vols. Nördlingen and München, 1885–1936 ff.

Schulz, Ursula, editor, *Die Deutsche Arbeiterbewegung 1848–1919 in Augenzeugenberichten.* Düsseldorf, 1968.

Schurz, Carl, *Lebenserinnerungen.* 2 vols. Berlin, 1906–1907.

Schwarz, Solomon M., *The Russian Revolution of 1905: The Workers' Movement and the Formation of Bolshevism and Menshevism.* Translated by Gertrude Vakar. Chicago, 1967.

Die Schwereisenindustrie im deutschen Zollgebiet, ihre Entwicklung und ihre Arbeiter. Compiled and issued by the Vorstand des Deutschen Metallarbeiter-Verbandes. Stuttgart, 1912.

Scott, John Finley, *Internalization of Norms: A Sociological Theory of Moral Commitment.* Englewood Cliffs, 1971.

Sears, David O., "Political Behavior," in Lindzey and Aronson, eds., *Handbook of Social Psychology,* V, 315–458.

Seidmann, Peter, *Der Mensch im Widerstand: Studien zur anthropologischen Psychologie.* Bern, 1974.

Severing, Carl, *Mein Lebensweg.* Vol. I: *Vom Schlosser zum Minister.* Vol. II: *Im, auf und ab der Republik.* Köln, 1950.

Shih, Vincent Y. C., "Some Chinese Rebel Ideologies," *T'oung Pao,* vol. 44 (1956), 150–226.

Silverberg, James, editor, *Social Mobility in the Caste System in India: An Interdisciplinary Symposium.* Comparative Studies in Society and History, Supplement III. The Hague, 1968.

Soboul, Albert, *Les Sans-culottes parisiens en l'an II: Mouvement populaire et gouvernement révolutionnaire 2 juin 1793–9 thermidor an II.* Paris, 1962.

Solomon, Richard H., *Mao's Revolution and the Chinese Political Culture.* Berkeley, 1971.

11. Sonderheft zum Reichs-Arbeitsblatte: Die Verbände der Arbeitgeber, Angestellten und Arbeiter im Jahre 1913. Bearbeitet im Kaiserlichen Statistischen Amte, Abteilung für Arbeiterstatistik. Berlin, 1915.

25. Sonderheft zum Reichs-Arbeitsblatte: Jahrbuch der Berufsverbände im Deutschen Reiche. Jahrgang 1922. Berlin, 1922.

Spencer, Elaine Glovka, "Between Capital and Labor: Supervisory Personnel in Ruhr Heavy Industry before 1914," *Journal of Social History,* vol. 9, no. 2 (Winter, 1975), 178–192.

Spencer, Robert F., *The North Alaskan Eskimo: A Study in Ecology and Society.* Smithsonian Institution, Bureau of American Ethnology, Bulletin 171. Washington, D.C., 1959.

Spethmann, Hans, *Zwölf Jahre Ruhrbergbau aus seiner Geschichte von Kriegsanfang bis zum Franzosenabmarsch, 1914–1925.* 5 vols. Berlin, [1928–1931].

Springer, August, *Der Andere das bist Du: Lebensgeschichte eines reichen armen Mannes.* Tübingen, 1954.

Stadelmann, Rudolf, and Fischer, Wolfram, *Die Bildungswelt des deutschen Handwerkers um 1800: Studien zur Soziologie des Kleinbürgers im Zeitalter Goethes*. Berlin, 1955.

Statistik des Deutschen Reichs. Neue Folge, Band 204: Berufs- und Betriebszählung vom 12. Juni 1907. Abteilung III: Bevölkerung Preussens nach Haupt- und Nebenberuf. Berlin, 1909.

———. Band 211: Berufs- und Betriebszählung vom 12. Juni 1907. Abteilung X: Die berufliche und soziale Gliederung des deutschen Volkes. Berlin, 1913.

———. Band 217: Berufs- und Betriebszählung vom 12. Juni 1907. Gewerbliche Betriebsstatistik. Heft 1, Abteilung V: Grossstädte. Berlin, 1909.

———. Band 220/221: Berufs- und Betriebszählung vom 12. Juni 1907. Gewerbliche Betriebsstatistik. Abteilung VIII: Gliederung und Verteilung der Gewerbebetriebe im Deutschen Reiche. Berlin, 1914.

———. Band 404: Volks-, Berufs- und Betriebszählung 1925. Die berufliche und soziale Gliederung der Bevölkerung in den Ländern und Landesteilen. Heft 15: Provinz Westfalen and Heft 16: Rheinprovinz. Berlin, 1929.

———. Band 453: Volks-, Berufs- und Betriebszählung vom 16. Juni 1933. Berufszählung: Die berufliche und soziale Gliederung der Bevölkerung des Deutschen Reichs. Heft 2: Die Erwerbstätigkeit der Reichsbevölkerung. Berlin, 1936.

———. Band 458: Volks-, Berufs- und Betriebszählung vom 16. Juni 1933. Berufszählung: Die berufliche und soziale Gliederung des Deutschen Volkes. Textliche Darstellung der Ergebnisse. Berlin, 1937.

———. Band 459: Volks-, Berufs- und Betriebszählung vom 16. Juni 1933. Heft 1: Landwirtschaftliche Betriebszählung. Einführung, Zahl und Fläche der Betriebe, Besitzverhältnisse. Berlin, 1936.

———. Band 461: Volks-, Berufs- und Betriebszählung vom 16. Juni 1933. Heft 1: Landwirtschaftliche Betriebszählung. Das Personal der land- und forstwirtschaftlichen Betriebe. Berlin, 1937.

Statistisches Jahrbuch für das Deutsche Reich, vol. 35 (1914). Berlin, 1914.

———, vol. 42 (1921/22). Berlin, 1922.

———, vol. 46 (1927). Berlin, 1927.

———, vol. 53 (1934). Berlin, 1934.

Stearns, Peter N., *Lives of Labor: Work in a Maturing Industrial Society*. New York, 1975.

Steinberg, Hans-Josef, *Sozialismus und deutscher Sozialdemokratie:*

Zur Ideologie der Partei vor dem Ersten Weltkrieg. Hannover, 1967.

Strauss, Rudolph, *Die Lage und die Bewegung der Chemnitzer Arbeiter in der ersten Hälfte des 19. Jahrhunderts.* Berlin, 1960.

Sukhanov, N. N., *Zapiski o Revoliutsii.* 7 vols. Berlin-Moscow, 1922–1923.

Sumner, William Graham, *Folkways: A Study of the Sociological Importance of Usages, Manners, Customs, Mores and Morals.* Boston, 1906.

Sykes, Gresham M., *The Society of Captives: A Study of a Maximum Security Prison.* 1958, reprinted, Princeton, 1971.

Thompson, E. P., *The Making of the English Working Class.* London, 1963.

————, "The Moral Economy of the English Crowd in the Eighteenth Century," *Past and Present,* no. 50 (February, 1971), 76–136.

Tilly, Charles, Louise, and Richard, *The Rebellious Century 1830–1930.* Cambridge, Ma., 1975.

Tocqueville, Alexis de, *L'Ancien Régime et la Révolution.* Paris, 1952.

Turnbull, Colin M., *The Mountain People.* New York, 1972.

————, *Wayward Servants: The Two Worlds of the African Pygmies.* Garden City, 1965.

Turner, Ralph H., "Collective Behavior," in Robert E. L. Faris, editor, *Handbook of Modern Sociology* (Chicago, 1964), 382–425.

Uldricks, Teddy J., "The 'Crowd' in the Russian Revolution: Towards Reassessing the Nature of Revolutionary Leadership," *Politics and Society,* vol. 4, no. 3 (1974), 397–413.

Valentin, Veit, *Frankfurt am Main und die Revolution von 1848/49.* Stuttgart, 1908.

————, *Geschichte der deutschen Revolution von 1848/49.* 2 vols. Berlin, 1930–1931.

Varain, Heinz Josef, *Freie Gewerkschaften, Sozialdemokratie, und Staat: Die Politik der Generalkommission unter der Führung Carl Legiens (1890–1920).* Düsseldorf, 1956.

Verhandlungen des ersten deutschen Handwerker- und Gewerbe-Congresses gehalten zu Frankfurt a. M., vom 14. Juli bis 18. August 1848. Edited by G. Schirges, Protokollführer. Darmstadt, 1848.

Vogel, Ezra F., *Canton under Communism: Programs and Politics in a Provincial Capital, 1949–1968.* Cambridge, Ma., 1969.

Vorwärts und nicht Vergessen: Erlebnisberichte aktiver Teilnehmer der Novemberrevolution 1918/1919. Institut für Marxismus-

Leninismus beim Zentralkomitee der Sozialistischen Einheitspartei Deutschlands. [East] Berlin, 1958.

Wachenheim, Hedwig, *Die deutsche Arbeiterbewegung 1844 bis 1914*. 2nd edition, Opladen, 1971.

Waite, Robert G. L., *Vanguard of Nazism: The Free Corps Movement in Postwar Germany 1918–1923*. 2nd edition, New York, 1969.

Walker, Mack, *German Home Towns: Community, State and General Estate 1648–1871*. Ithaca, 1971.

———, *Germany and the Emigration 1816–1885*. Cambridge, Ma., 1964.

Walter, Eugene Victor, *Terror and Resistance: A Study of Political Violence*. New York, 1969.

Weber, Alfred, "Das Berufsschicksal der Industriearbeiter: Ein Vortrag," *Archiv für Sozialwissenschaft und Sozialpolitik*, vol. XXXIV, no. 2 (March, 1912), 377–405.

Weber, Max, *The Protestant Ethic and the Spirit of Capitalism*. Translated by Talcott Parsons. New York, 1958.

Wechsler, Howard J., *Mirror to the Son of Heaven: Wei Cheng at the Court of T'ang T'ai-tsung*. New Haven, 1974.

Wehler, Hans-Ulrich, editor, *Moderne deutsche Sozialgeschichte*. 3rd edition, Köln, 1970.

———, "Die Polen im Ruhrgebiet bis 1918," in Wehler, editor, *Moderne deutsche Sozialgeschichte*, 437–455.

Weiss, Walter, "Effects of the Mass Media on Communication," in Lindzey and Aronson, editors, *Handbook of Social Psychology*, V, 77–195.

Weissberg, Alexander, *Conspiracy of Silence*. Translated by Edward Fitzgerald. London, 1952.

Westermarck, Edward, *The Origin and Development of the Moral Ideas*. 2 vols. 2nd edition, London, 1917.

Whyte, William Foote, *Street Corner Society: The Social Structure of an Italian Slum*. Chicago, 1943.

Wildman, Allan K., *The Making of a Workers' Revolution: Russian Social Democracy, 1891–1903*. Chicago, 1967.

Wilkinson, Paul, *Political Terrorism*. New York, 1974.

Winkler, Heinrich August, *Mittelstand, Demokratie, und Nationalsozialismus*. Köln, 1972.

Wolfe, Bertram D., *Three Who Made a Revolution: A Biographical History*. New York, 1948.

Wolfenstein, E. Victor, *The Revolutionary Personality: Lenin, Trotsky, Gandhi*. Princeton, 1967.

Wolff, Robert Paul, *The Autonomy of Reason: A Commentary on Kant's Groundwork of the Metaphysic of Morals*. New York, 1973.

Wolff, Wilhelm, *Gesammelte Schriften*. Berlin, 1909.
Work in America, Report of a Special Task Force to the Secretary of Health, Education, and Welfare. Foreword by Elliot L. Richardson. Cambridge, Ma., [1973].
Yuchtman, Ephraim, "Reward Distribution and Work-Role Attractiveness in the Kibbutz—Reflections on Equity Theory," *American Sociological Review,* vol. 37, no. 5 (October, 1972), 581–595.
Zeitlin, Maurice, *Revolutionary Politics and the Cuban Working Class.* Princeton, 1967.
Zimmer, Heinrich, *Philosophies of India,* edited by Joseph Campbell. 1951, reprinted, New York, 1956.
Zimmermann, Waldemar, "Die Veränderung der Einkommens- und Lebensverhältnisse der deutschen Arbeiter durch den Krieg," in Meerwarth *et al., Die Einwirkung des Krieges auf die Bevölkerungsbewegung, Einkommen und Lebenshaltung in Deutschland,* 281–474.

Index

A

Abel, Theodore, 412, 414, 417 and
    n.23, 418 n.26, 430
Abraham, Karl, 133 nn.8 and 9, 138
Achilles, 29
Adelmann, Gerhard, 235 n.5, 239
    n.14, 247 n.32, 251 n.46, 252
    n.49, 255 n.56
Adler, Hans Günther, 69
Adorno, T. W., 106 n.28
Africa, Africans, 20 n.11, 33, 35, 42,
    66 n.40, 106 n.27
Agamemnon, 459
Albertin, Lothar, 389 n.12
Alexander the Great, 462
Algeria, 426, 427
*Allgemeiner Kongress der Arbeiter- und
    Soldatenräte Deutschlands.* *See*
    Congress of Workers' and Sol-
    diers' Councils
Amann, Peter H., 473 n.15
American Civil War, 395, 446
American Revolution, 462 n.2
Americans. *See* United States
Anti-Italian Riot (New Orleans), 237
    n.13
Apostles, the Twelve, 246, 472
Arbeiterverein, 170
Aristotle, 15

Aronfreed, Justin, 107
Asch, S. E., 93 and n.8, 100
Ashton, Patricia Teague, 108 n.36
Asia, 14, 33, 360, 492
Athens (ancient), 12, 213 n.73, 467
Austria, 131, 169, 289, 384
Austro-Hungarian Empire, 80
Australia, 99 n.17

B

Baden, Max von, 314, 386 n.8
Baden, 164
Badia, Gilbert, 308 n.54
Baku, 359
Bantu, 22
Bao Ruo-Wang, 483 n.24
Barmen, 261 n.64, 349
Barotse, 18–19 n.9, 20 n.11, 23 n.15,
    27 n.18, 34 n.25
Barth, Emil, 294
Bathsheba, 26
Bauernkrieg, 161 n.61
Bavaria, 192, 196, 282, 291, 311,
    350, 352, 385 n.7, 391, 477
Bebel, August, 183, 184 n.14, 190
    n.23, 198 n.37, 210, 222
Belgium, Belgians, 333, 384

Berlin, 133, 134 and n.10, 137, 138, 148, 154, 156, 159, 160, 162, 163, 164, 165, 179, 195, 208, 284, 287, 289, 292, 293, 299, 300 n.38, 301, 303, 304, 306, 307, 308, 310–311, 312, 314, 316, 335, 337, 338, 340, 341, 345, 348, 350, 351
Berlin Congress (August 1848), 161 n.60, 163 n.70
Berlin Metalworkers Union, 287
Bernays, Marie, 201 n.44, 206 n.56, 207–208 n.59, 211 n.68
Berndt, Ronald M., 425 n.35
Bernstein, Thomas Paul, 483 n.24
Bessemer, 270
Bettelheim, Bruno, 67, 68, 70, 72, 73, 74, 75, 76
Bicêtre, 425
Bielefeld, 350
Bismarck, Otto von, 221, 222, 393
Blassingame, John W., 464 n.4
Blood Purge of 1934 (Germany), 416, 417 n.25
Bloody Sunday (Russia, 1905), 362, 471 n.13
Bochum, 261 n.64
Bohemia, 224
Bolivia, 38
Bolshevik, Bolshevism, 294, 298, 303, 361, 363 and n.16, 364, 365, 366, 367, 369, 371, 372–373, 374, 375, 474 n.16, 481
Bolshevik (October) Revolution, 370, 372. See also February Revolution
Bonnell, Victoria E., 363 nn.15, 16
Born, Stephan, 148, 150, 153–154, 158, 159, 360
Borsig, 288
Brahmans, 40, 57, 61
Bräker, Ulrich, 120–125, 338, 458, 461, 504
Brandenburg Gate demonstrations, 306
Braun, Rudolf, 121
Bremen, 301, 308, 311
Brepohl, Wilhelm, 272 n.91

Brest-Litovsk, 289
Briggs, George W., 57 n.19
British. See Great Britain
British Empire, 172
Bromme, Moritz Th. W., 198 n.37, 200 n.42, 218 n.77, 222
Bruner, Jerome S., 108 n.37
Bry, Gerhard, 177 n.4
Buchenwald, 68, 71
Buddhism, 19 n.9
Burdzhalov, E. N., 364 n.18, 368 n.29

C

Cahn, Edmond, 39
California, 501
Caron, Pierre, 424 n.31, 425 n.37
Carsten, F. L., 308 and n.52, 314, 384 and n.6
Castro, Fidel, 246
Catholic Church, 492, 500–501
Catholics, 101, 181, 230, 241, 246, 247, 248, 249 n.39, 255, 260 and n.63
Cato, 429
Cavaignac, Louis Eugène, 472
Center Party (Germany), 230 and table, 241, 350
Central Council (Zentralrat), 302, 303, 304, 306, 314. See also Congress of Workers' and Soldiers' Councils
Central Europe, 126
Central Germany, 324–325
Chagnon, Napoleon A., 82 n.1
Chamars, 56, 57 n.19
Charles I, of England, 20
Chartists, 502
Chelminski, Rudolph, 483 n.24
Chemnitz, 164, 165, 166 n.78, 171, 195, 223–224, 292, 300
Chesneaux, Jean, 22 n.13
Chile, 501
China, 14, 20, 21 n.12, 22 n.13, 25 and n.17, 26–27, 28, 33, 43, 423, 442, 444, 466 and nn.7, 8, 475, 492, 509

Ch'in dynasty, 21 n.12

Chinese Communists and Revolution, 172, 375, 446, 475, 481, 483 nn.24, 25, 484, 498, 501, 503

Christianity, Christians, 50, 51, 52, 53 and n.14, 54, 172, 181, 339, 347, 446, 450, 482, 483, 493. *See also* Catholics; Protestantism

Christlicher Gewerkverein, 255

Christlicher Metallarbeiter-Verband, 260 n.63. *See also* German Metalworkers Union

Circus Busch meeting, 293 and n.23, 294, 295, 300, 301, 314

Clemenceau, Georges, 296

Cohen, Elie Aron, 65 n.36, 66 and nn.38, 40

Cohen, Max, 296 n.28, 302 n.42

Colbert, Jean Baptiste, 443

Cold War, 483

Cole, Michael, 108 n.37

Coles, Robert, 111 n.44, 112–113, 114, 115

Colm, Gerhard, 343 n.42, 346–347 n.47, 348

Cologne, 162, 165

Committee of the United Mining People of Essen and Vicinity, 242

Communism, Communists, 70, 72, 74, 101, 154, 306, 313, 319, 347, 348 n.51, 350, 375, 390, 422, 443, 475. *See also* Chinese Communists; German Communist Party; Russian Communists

Congress of German Artisans (1848), 144, 145–146

Congress of German Workmen (1848), 148 and n.32

Congress of Social Democrats (1913), 199, 217 n.76

Congress of Soviets, 372 n.43, 374 n.48

Congress of Workers' and Soldiers' Councils (Germany, 1918), 296 n.28, 298 n.32, 301–302, 303, 304, 306, 314, 317, 323, 390, 392 n.14

Congress party (India), 62

Constituent Assembly (Russia, 1917), 297, 305, 369–370

Conze, Werner, 136 n.16, 138, 221 n.84

Corcyra, 285 n.9

Cossacks, 360

Council of People's Representatives (Germany, 1918), 293 and n.23, 303, 304, 313–314, 384 n.6

Craig, Gordon A., 299–300 n.38

Croon, Helmut, 271 n.89

Cuba, 375, 399 n.1

Cultural P volution (China). *See* Great Proletarian Cultural Revolution

Czechoslovakians, 67, 224

D

Dahomey, 33

Daimler factory, 206, 291

Daniels, Robert V., 373 nn.45, 47, 374

Dante, 211 n.59

Danton, 426

Däumig, Ernst, 298 n.32

David, King of Israel, 26

Denmark, 168

Dentan, Robert Knox, 16 n.7

Der Alte Verband, 247–248, 255

Deutschnationale Volkspartei, 416

Dieterici, F. W. C., 132, 133 nn.8, 9, 134 n.10, 135 and n.12, 137, 138, 139 and n.22, 151 n.39

Dittmann, Wilhelm, 304, 392 n.14

Dohna, Herrmann Graf zu, 140, 141, 142

Domes, Jürgen, 483 n.24

Dore, Ronald, 260 n.60

Dortmund, 236, 261 n.64, 328, 334 n.23, 339 n.36, 347, 349, 350

Drekmeier, Charles, 19 n.9

Dresden, 165, 179, 292, 300, 312

Droz, Jacques, 163 n.66

Duisberg, 348
Duma, 363 n.15, 367
Durkheim, Emile, 27 n.18, 143, 480
    n.20
Düsseldorf, 165, 261 and n.64, 333
    n.21, 349

E

Eastern Europe, 236, 272
East Prussia, 236
Ebert, Friedrich, 292, 293, 294–295,
    296, 299, 300 and n.38, 303,
    304, 312, 313, 314, 316, 317,
    339, 340, 348, 353, 381, 382,
    383, 384, 385, 386 n.8, 388,
    389, 390, 391, 392 and n.14,
    394, 396
Eichhorn, Emil, 306
Eisner, Kurt, 291
Elberfeld, 165, 261 n.64, 349
Elkins, Stanley M., 64
El'nitskii, A., 363
Engels, Friedrich, 183, 184 n.14,
    221 n.83
England, English, 20, 32, 41, 51,
    103, 131, 133, 136, 156, 168,
    173, 190, 209, 228, 255, 317,
    377, 424 n.33, 473, 482, 502,
    509. See also Great Britain
Erasmus, 109 n.39
Erger, Johannes, 341 n.39
Erikson, Erik H., 110
Erzberger, Matthias, 428
Eskimo, 36
Essen, 242, 261 n.64, 308, 328, 332,
    339 n.36, 344, 348, 349
Eta, 56
Eumaios, 32
Europe, Europeans, 14, 22 n.13, 24
    n.16, 25, 33, 42, 43, 120, 126,
    149, 170, 171, 172, 179, 183,
    228, 249, 261, 271, 278, 360,
    361, 421, 461, 462, 472, 492,
    494, 495, 502
Executive Council (Vollzugsrat), 293
    and n.23, 314, 347

F

Factory Inspection Service, 175,
    177, 178 table, 276 n.1, 277–
    278 tables, 281 n.3, 284, 333
Fang-La, 27
Fanon, Frantz, 429 n.44
February Revolution (Russia, 1917),
    357, 358, 365–369, 370, 374,
    482. See also Russian Revolution
    of 1917
Feldman, Gerald D., 334 n.23
Ferro, Marc, 369, 370
Field, Daniel, 362 n.12
First World War, 88, 120, 173, 175,
    177, 180, 184, 188, 192 n.25,
    218, 227, 270, 275, 332, 335,
    359, 364, 379, 466, 475, 477,
    485, 486, 495
Firth, Raymond, 11 n.3
Fischer, Franz Louis, 198 n.37, 202
    n.46, 251 n.47
Fischer, Karl, 187 n.17, 198, 202
    nn.46, 47, 203–205, 212, 222,
    471, 504
Fischer, Wolfram, 121 n.1, 140 n.23,
    251 n.45, 271 n.89
Först, Walter, 271 n.89
Florence, 86
Fourth Estate, 134
France, French, 22 n.13, 126, 128,
    131, 149, 152, 155, 156, 160,
    162, 173, 211, 220 n.82, 222,
    308 n.53, 317, 384, 424 n.33,
    426, 431, 432, 446, 462 n.2,
    477, 482, 487. See also French
    Revolution
Francis of Assisi, 53, 54
Franco-Prussian War, 221 n.84, 236
Frank, Anne, 68
Frankfurt, 144, 148, 169–170, 308
Frankfurt Assembly (1848), 144,
    146, 164, 165, 168–169, 170
Frederick II the Great, 120, 121,
    123, 124, 125, 458, 504
Frederick William IV, 162, 165
Free Trade Unions, 181–183
Freikorps, 304, 308–309, 311, 312,

Freikorps (cont.)
313, 316, 322, 324 and n.14, 339, 340, 345, 346, 385, 388, 391, 478
French Revolution, 42, 88, 123, 131, 153 n.40, 170, 172, 211 n.59, 308 n.53, 368 n.30, 395, 423–426, 446, 484, 510
Freud, Anna, 50 n.1
Freud, Freudian, 8, 103, 104 and n.24, 109, 463, 497
Freudenberg, Karl, 334, n.23
Fried, Morton H., 34 n.25, 508 n.2
Friedländer, Ludwig, 41 n.40

G

Gapon, Father, 362, 471 n.13
Gelsenkirchen, 261 n.64
Genovese, Eugene D., 464 n.4
German Army, 285, 294, 295, 299, 303, 382, 383–384, 386, 388 n.11. *See also* Reichswehr
German Communist Party (KPD), 296, 306, 308, 344, 346, 349. *See also* Communism
German Confederation of Labor, 312
German Empire, 135, 136, 137, 175, 218 n.77, 221–226, 245, 314, 382, 386 n.8, 387, 395. *See also* Germany
German Independent Socialist Party. *See* Independent Socialist Party of Germany
German Metalworkers Union, 187 n.19, 190, 257 and n.58, 258, 260, 263, 264, 265, 266, 267, 268, 269, 323
German National Assembly (1919), 301, 302, 309, 311, 314, 317, 323, 388, 391, 392
German Social Democratic Party. *See* Social Democratic Party of Germany
Germany, Germans, 22 n.13, 67, 68, 73–74, 77, 78, 90, 96, 112, 119,

120, 121 n.2, 125, 126ff., 173ff., 227ff., 275ff., 316ff., 357ff., 376ff., 398ff., 454, 466, 471, 474, 475, 476, 477, 484, 485, 486–487, 488–489, 494–495, 502 n.31
Gestapo, 75
Gewerkverein christlicher Bergarbeiter, 247, 248
Gewerkverein der deutschen Maschinenbau und Metallarbeiter, 260 n.63
Gitermann, Valentin, 365 n.22
Glarus, 123
Gluckman, Max, 18–19 n.9, 20 n.11, 23 n.15, 26 n.18, 34 n.25
God, 141, 196, 204, 338, 448
Goffman, Erving, 65 n.37, 70 n.53
Göhre, Paul, 195, 202 and n.46, 203 n.48, 206 and n.55, 223
Graeco-Judaic tradition, 26
Gould, Mark, 479 n.19
Great Britain, British, 172, 228, 237, 291. *See also* England
Great Depression, 200, 400
Great Leap Forward (China), 466 n.8, 483 n.2
Great Proletarian Cultural Revolution (China), 466 n.8, 481, 483 n.24
Great Wall of China, 21 n.12
Greece (ancient), 12, 15, 19 n.9, 32, 42, 88, 213 n.73, 459, 482 n.22, 491
Groener, Wilhelm, 294, 295, 299, 303, 304
Groh, Dieter, 185 table, 221 n. 84, 394 n.15
Guevara, Ernesto "Che," 246

H

Haase, Hugo, 304
Haenisch, Konrad, 226 n.96
Hagen, 343 n.42, 345, 346, 349
Haimson, Leopold, 160 n.58, 364 n.17
Hamburg, 179, 301, 303, 304, 311, 319

Harijans, 55 n.16. *See also* Untouchables

Harper, Edward B., 60 n.28

Hasenklever, Capt., 345–346

Hastings, James, 58 n.23

Hauptmann, Gerhart, 192

Hazari, 57 n.19, 59 and n.26, 60, 61

Hebrew, 469, 491

Hector, 30

Heine, Heinrich, 192

Helsingfors (Helsinki), 373

Henry, Emile, 428

Hesiod, 35

Heymann, Bruno, 334 n.23

Hilferding, Rudolf, 296 n.28

Hilger, Dietrich, 135 n.11, 140 n.23

Hindenburg, Paul von, 294, 295, 312

Hinduism, Hindus, 19 n.9, 34, 50, 52, 53 and n.11, 55 n.17, 56, 57, 59, 61, 62, 63, 78, 79, 112, 458, 461, 463. *See also* Untouchables

Hirsch-Duncker unions, 181, 260 and n.63

Hirschman, Albert O., 482 n.22

Hitler, Adolf, 74, 109 n.39, 173, 276, 312, 379, 397, 400, 401, 402, 411, 416, 417 and n.25, 418 n.26, 448

Hoboken, 237 n.13

Hobsbawm, Eric J., 23 n.13, 187 n.18

Hoffmann, Charles, 466 n.8

Hofstadter, Richard, 237 n.13

Hohenzollerns, 161 n.61, 223

Homans, George C., 43, 45, 421

Homer, 19 n.9, 29, 32, 459

Hue, Otto, 239 n.14, 248, 249, 258–259

Hufton, Olwen H., 368 n.30

I

Ikhnaton, 469

Iks, 106 n.27

Incan, 33

Independent Socialist Party of Germany (USPD), 275, 286–287, 288, 289, 290, 291, 293, 294, 300, 301, 302, 304, 305, 306, 308, 309, 310, 313, 314, 322, 339 n.46, 344, 346, 349, 387 n.9, 392

India, 14, 19 n.9, 36, 40, 41, 50–52, 53 n.12, 55–56, 58–59, 61, 62, 466 n.7, 492. *See also* Hinduism

Indra, 53

Inquisition, 399

Irish, 237

Irish Republican Army, 426

Isaacs, Harold R., 61–62, 63

Iserlohn, 165

Italy, Italians, 237 n.13, 408 n.7, 508

Ithaca (ancient), 32

J

Jacobin, 88

Jantke, Carl, 135 n.11, 140 n.23, 240 n.16

Japan, Japanese, 56 n.17, 66 n.38, 89, 260 n.60, 408 n.7, 466 n.7, 483, 492

Jaurès, Jean, 425 n.34

Jehovah's Witnesses, 69

Jena, 231

Jesus, 91

Jews, 67, 68, 73–74, 123, 154, 161, 414, 423

Job, 24

Junkers, 131, 161 n.61, 224, 275, 316, 389, 397, 416

K

Kamenev, L. B., 373

Kant, Immanuel, 378 n.1

Kapauku Papuans, 28–29, 36, 38 n.33, 40

Kapp Putsch, 312, 313, 328, 336, 337, 338, 339, 340, 341, 348, 351, 388

Kautsky, Karl, 249

Keep, John L. H., 358 n.1

Keniston, Kenneth, 111 n.44

Kennedy, John F., 101

Kerensky, Alexander Feodorovich, 374

Kiel, 290, 291, 302, 310, 316, 317, 321, 336, 388

Kiev, 259

Koch, Max Jürgen, 235 table, 243 n. 20, 246 nn.30, 31, 249 and n.39, 252, 264 n.71

Kogon, Eugen, 65 n.36, 71

Kohlberg, Lawrence, 104 and nn.24, 25, 105 n.26, 107–108

Kolb, Eberhard, 293 n.23, 314, 384 n.6

Kolenda, Pauline Mahar, 60 n.28

Korea, 75

Kornilov, L. G., 374

KPD. See German Communists

Krige, Eileen J., 35 n.26

Krige, J. O., 35 n.26

Krupp firm, 259, 260 n.60, 264, 268, 332, 349

L

Lamp'l, Walter, 303

Landes, David S., 270 n.87, 271 n.89

Landtmann, Gunnar, 11 n.3

Lane, Robert E., 101 n.20

Lassalle, Ferdinand, 222

Laws of Manu, 50, 52, 58 n.23

Le Bon, Gustav, 347 n.47

Legien, Carl, 290, 312, 313, 388

Leinert, Robert, 384 n.6

Leipzig, 171, 179, 292, 335

Lenin, V. I., 110 and n.41, 297 and n.28, 305, 308 n.53, 360, 361, 371–373, 374 n.48, 375, 466, 480

Leninism, 166, 372 n.43, 474 and n.16, 477

Le Play, Pierre Guillaume Frederic, 162 n.65, 233

Lequis, Arnold, 299–300 and n.38

Leuna, 325

Levenstein, Adolf, 193, 194 and n.29, 196, 201 and n.44, 206, 207, 208 and n.59, 209, 210,

212 and n.71, 213, 215, 485

Lex, Barbara W., 69 n.52

Liebknecht, Karl, 222, 286, 289, 292, 301, 305, 307, 308 n.52, 309, 312, 428

Liebow, Elliot, 191 n.24

Lifton, Robert J., 483 n.24

Li Tzu-cheng, 25 n.17

Lloyd George, David, 296

Lobositz, 124

Lösche, Peter, 297 n.30

Louis XIV, 462 n.2, 446

Louis XVI, 424, 462 n.2

Louis Philippe, 156

Louisville (Kentucky) riots, 237 n.13

Lovedu, 22, 35, 44

Lucas, Erhard, 328 n.20, 334 n.25, 339 nn.35, 36, 343 n.42, 349, 350 n.53

Ludendorff, Erich Friedrich Wilhelm, 294, 304, 312, 334 n.23

Luther, Martin, 91

Lüttwitz, Walther von, 345

Lützow, Gen. von, 338

Luxemburg, Rosa, 249, 275, 286, 301, 305, 306, 307, 309, 428

M

Macaulay, Thomas, 157

McGuire, William J., 101 n.20

Machiavelli, 445

Maercker, Georg, 326

Maistre, Joseph Marie de, 446

Malay Peninsula, 37

Malinovsky, Roman, 110 n.41

Malinowski, Bronislaw, 85

Malmö, Truce of, 168–169, 170 and n.89

Mantell, David Mark, 106 n.28

Manu. See Laws of Manu

Maori, 38

Mao Tse-tung, 246, 422, 481, 483 n.24

Maquet, J. J., 24 n.16

Marat, Jean Paul, 426

March Days of 1848, 162, 163

Marx, Karl, 9, 82, 135, 148, 154, 155, 161, 176 n.3, 221 n.83, 222, 357, 455, 469 and n.11, 474, 495

Marxism, Marxists, 82, 84 n.3, 148, 155, 176 n.3, 183, 192, 205, 225 n.94, 249, 297, 323, 331, 361, 362 and n.12, 363, 378, 391, 408 n.7, 414, 417, 435, 455, 468–469, 473–474, 485, 495, 498 n.30

Mathiesen, Thomas, 67 n.42

Mathiez, Albert, 42 n.43

Mattheier, Klaus J., 260 n.64, 268 n.83, 272 n.91

Mecklenburg-Schwering, 164

Meerwarth, Rudolf, 278

Mensheviks, 361, 363, 364, 369, 372

Merkl, Peter H., 412 nn.10, 11, 417 n. 23, 418 nn.26, 27, 429

Metalworkers Union. See Christlicher Metallarbeiter-Verband; German Metalworkers Union

Michelet, Jules, 424 and n.33, 425 and n.37

Middle East, 360

Milgram, Stanley, 94 and n.9, 95, 96 and n.11, 97, 98, 99 and n.17, 100, 432–433 and n.50

Ming dynasty, 25 n.17

Moltke, Helmuth von, 222

Mosca, Gaetano, 84 n.2, 483

Moscow, 359, 363 and n.15, 372, 375

Mucchielli, Roger, 419 n.28

Mülheim, 257 n.58

Müller, Richard, 287, 292 n.22, 293, 294

Munich, 99 n.17, 179, 199, 289, 291, 311

Münzer, Thomas, 152

Mussolini, Benito, 430

N

Nagel, Peter, 53 n.14

Napoleon, 423

Napoleonic Empire, 172

Napoleonic Wars, 130

National Assembly. See Frankfurt Assembly (1848); German National Assembly (1919)

National Cash Register Corporation, 260 n.60

National Socialist German Workers' Party (NSDAP), 400–411, 417, 418 n.26, 419

Naziism (National Socialism), Nazis, 18, 63, 64, 69, 74, 76, 90, 96, 106 n.28, 306, 319 n.5, 352, 353, 377, 398ff., 448, 458, 471, 484

Near East, 482 n.22

Netherlands Revolt, 395, 446, 494

New Deal, 86, 147

New Guinea, 425 n.35

New Orleans riots (1871), 237 n.13

New York, 237 n.13

Nicholas II, Tsar, 362 and n.12, 366, 369, 471 n.13

Northern Ireland, 428

North Vietnam, 430, 484

Norway, 44–45, 67 n.42

Noske, Gustave, 308, 309, 311, 312, 313, 316, 317, 322, 348, 391

Noyes, P. H., 160, 161 and n.60, 165

O

OAS (Algeria), 426, 427

Oberhausen, 261 n.64

October (Bolshevik) Revolution, 370, 372. See also Russian Revolution of 1917

Odessa, 359

Odysseus, 32

Oertzen, Peter von, 323, 325

Oman, John Campbell, 51

Opel, Fritz, 288 n.13

Orange Riots, 237 n.13

P

Palestine Liberation Organization, 426, 427

Papacy, 172

Papuans. *See* Kapauku
Paris, 153 n.40, 156, 159, 163, 247, 424–425, 472, 473
Paris Commune, 221 and n.84, 223, 248, 432
Patroclus, 30
Paul, Saint, 466
Pavlov, Ivan Petrovich, 463
Peck, Robert F., 104 nn.24, 25, 106 and n.28
Pecqueur, Constantin, 176 n.3
Peloponnesian War, 285 n.9
Pentecost Riot, 237 n.13
People's Army *(Volkswehr)*, 300, 303
Pericles, 41
Perrot, Michelle, 473 n.14, 502 n.31
Petrograd, 358 n.1, 359, 365, 366, 367, 369, 370, 372, 373, 374
Philadelphia Nativist Riots, 237 n.13
Piaget, Jean, 103, 104 and n.24, 107, 108
Pike, Douglas, 428 n.41
Plato, Platonic, 18, 398
Poland, Poles, 236, 333, 362, 364 n.17
Polnischer Berufsverein, 255, 272 and n.91
Port Arthur, 362
Pospisil, Leopold, 21 n.11, 28–29, 38 n.33, 40 and n.38, 508 n.3
Prater, 168
Praz, Mario, 430 n.46
Princeton, N.J., 99 n.17
Protestantism, Protestants, 193, 195, 431
Provisional Government. *See* Russian Provisional Government (1917)
Prussia, Prussians, 124, 128 n.2, 131, 132, 133, 136, 138, 151 n.39, 155, 156, 162, 165, 168, 169, 224, 235, 242, 270, 334 n.23, 484
Puritan Revolution, 170, 395, 421, 446
Putilov, 356 and n.22

Q

Quixote, Don, 437

R

Rabinowitch, Alexander, 358 n.1
Radin, Paul, 11 n.3
Rainwater, Lee, 191 n.24
Ranulf, Svend, 35 n.27
Rathenau, Walther, 428
Red (Ruhr) Army, 227, 313, 328 and n.20, 346, 347 and n.47, 348, 349, 350
Red Guard (Russia), 374
Red Soldiers' League, 299, 303
Redl, Fritz, 105
Reichsbank, 312
Reichstag, 184 n.14, 222, 230, 231, 287
Reichswehr, 312, 350, 351
Republican Defense Force, 299
Republican Military Guard, 307
Revolt of the Netherlands, 395, 446, 494
Revolutionary Committee (Berlin, 1919), 307
Revolutionary Shop Stewards, 287, 288–298, 292, 293, 294, 298 n.32, 306, 319
Rhineland, 162, 163 n.66, 196, 230, 231, 244, 247, 313. *See also* Ruhr
Riga, 359
Robespierre, Maxilien de, 208 n.53, 426
Roehm, Ernst, 416
Rohrscheidt, Kurt von, 132 n.5
Rome (ancient), 26, 41 n.40, 473 n.14, 508
Rome (modern), 99 n.17
Roosevelt, Franklin, 417
Rosenberg, Hans, 128 n.2, 413 n.12
Rostov, 359
Ruanda, 24 n.16
Ruhr, 120, 177, 184, 188, 220, 227ff., 308, 311, 312, 317, 320, 323, 325, 326, 328ff., 357, 364 n.17, 390, 395, 450, 458, 461, 474–475, 477, 487, 492

Rürup, Reinhard, 314, 384 n.6
Russia, Russians, 43, 89, 160 n.58,
    168, 172, 225 n.94, 289, 291,
    293, 297 n.28, 298, 308 n.53,
    313, 327, 333, 353, 364 n.17,
    386, 397, 408 n.7, 465, 466,
    475, 480. See also Soviet Union
Russian Communists, 172, 373, 408
    n.7
Russian Constituent Assembly
    (1917), 297, 305, 369–370
Russian Duma, 363 n.15, 367
Russian Provisional Government
    (Feb. to Oct. 1917), 358, 369,
    374, 375
Russian Revolution of 1905, 357,
    358, 363
Russian Revolution of 1917, 160
    n.58, 357ff., 446, 472, 475. See
    also Bolshevik Revolution; Feb-
    ruary Revolution
Russian Social Democrats, 362
Russo-Japanese War, 362
Ryder, A. J., 314

S

SA (Sturmabteilung), 416, 417
Saigon, 431
Saint Bartholomew's Day Massacres,
    431
Saint Petersburg, 361
Salpêtrière, 425
Sansom, Robert L., 428 n.41
Sartre, Jean-Paul, 429 n.44
Sass, Friedrich, 134 n.10, 151
    n.39
Saxony, 157, 158, 251 n.47, 291,
    352
Schacht, Hjalmar, 389
Schapiro, Leonard, 372 n.43, 373
    n.45
Scheduled castes, 55 n.16, 62, 63. See
    also Untouchables
Scheidemann, Philipp, 217 n.76,
    222 n.85, 292, 304, 386 n.8
Scheüch, Heinrich, 386 n.8

Schiller, Friedrich von, 192
Schleswig-Holstein, 168, 172
Schliestedt, Heinrich, 323
Schorske, Carl F., 394 n.15
Schurz, Carl, 163 n.66, 165
Schwarz, Solomon M., 362 n.12, 363
    n.14
Scott, John Finley, 102 n.22
Sears, David O., 101 n.20
Second World War, 397, 400
Sedan, 220 n.82, 223
Seidmann, Peter, 109 n.39
Semai, 36, 48
September Massacres, 423–426
Severing, Carl, 219, 220 and n.82,
    223, 272, 324, 339, 340, 345,
    348, 349, 351
Shaka, 85
Shakespeare, 64
Shih-huang-ti, 21 n.12, 25 n.17
Siberia, 362
Sicherheitspolizei (Sipo), 339, 340,
    349
Siemens-Martin, 270, 288
Silesia, 143, 157
Simmel, Georg, 347 n.47
Singer Sewing Machines, 220
Siriono, 38
Siva, 50
Smith, Adam, 85, 128, 135 n.12
Smolny Institute, 374 n.48, 375
Soboul, Albert, 153 n.40, 421
    n.30
Social Democratic Party of Germany
    (SPD) and Social Democrats,
    174, 181–184, 189, 192–199,
    203, 206, 210–231, 241, 246–
    249, 255, 258, 263 n.67, 275,
    280, 281, 285–312, 314, 316,
    317 n.1, 318, 339 n.36, 340, 341
    n.39, 344, 346, 348, 350, 352,
    360, 365, 379, 381–385, 386
    and n.8, 387, 388 and n.11, 392,
    394, 412, 478, 484, 485, 487–
    489
Socialist Laws (1878–1890), 221
Socrates, 109 n.39, 467
Solomon, Richard H., 111 n.44

Sorel, Georges, 429 n.44
South Africa, 99 n.17
South Vietnam, 431
Soviet Union, 68 n.46, 101, 324 n.14, 397, 423, 498, 501. *See also* Russia
Spandau, 308
Spain, Spanish, 22 n.13, 55
Sparta, 12, 62
Spartacists, 286, 287, 288, 299, 301, 303, 304, 305–306, 309, 311, 316, 317, 318, 324, 325, 352, 396, 458
SPD. *See* Social Democratic Party of Germany
Spencer, Elaine Glovka, 240 n.15
Spencer, Herbert, 3, 85
Spengler, Oswald, 179
Spethmann, Hans, 328 n.20, 339 n.36, 342
Springer, August, 191–193 and n.25, 199, 202 n.46, 206, 211 n.69, 223, 226
SS (*Schutzstaffel*), 64–65, 66, 67, 68, 71, 72–73, 74–75, 76, 87, 416
Stadelmann, Rudolf, 121 n.1, 154 n.43
Stalin, Stalinism, 24, 220, 372 n.43, 397, 422, 435, 481
Stearns, Peter N., 502
Stein-Hardenberg reforms, 291
Stinnes, Hugo, 250, 290, 341
Stinnes-Legien agreement, 290–291, 295
Storm Troopers. *See* SA
Strauss, Rudolf, 139 n.22, 166 n.78, 171 n.90
Stuttgart, 225, 226, 312
Sudras, 52
Sukhanov, N. N., 374 n.51
Sumner, William Graham, 12, 85, 435 n.1
Sung dynasty, 25, 27
Sweden, 86
Swiss Guard, 424
Switzerland, Swiss, 121, 125, 155, 338

T

T'ang dynasty, 503 n.32
Theresienstadt, 67, 68
Thersites, 459
Third French Republic, 432, 487
Thirty Years' War, 25, 252, 383
Thompson, E. P., 379 n.2, 474 n.16
Thucydides, 285 n.9, 445
Timm, Joh., 200 n.41
Tockenburg, 121
Tocqueville, Alexis de, 472, 493–494
Trobriand Islands, 11
Trotsky, Leon, 308 n.53, 347, 372 and n.43, 373, 374
Troy (ancient), 30, 459
Truce of Malmö. *See* Malmö
Tsarists, 358, 360, 361, 362, 363 n.15, 364, 365, 368, 369
Tsaritsyn, 359
Turnbull, Colin M., 66 n.40, 105 n.27, 488 n.28

U

Union for the Protection and Advancement of Miners' Interests. *See Der Alte Verband*
United Nations, 427
United States, Americans, 4, 22, 28, 29, 30, 32, 38, 39, 49, 67, 73, 75, 80, 87, 92, 100–101, 112, 142, 146, 172, 236, 237 and n.13, 317, 320, 370, 395, 423, 424 n.33, 428 n.41, 429, 430, 446, 462 n.2, 483, 501
Untouchables, 34, 50, 55–64, 77, 112 n.46, 458, 461, 463
USPD. *See* Independent Socialist Party of Germany

V

Valentin, Veit, 169 and n.84, 170 nn.86, 89
Veblen, Thorstein, 39, 85
Venice, 86

Verbrüderung, 154, 158, 160
Versailles Treaty, 311, 312
Vienna, 163, 168
Vietcong, 428 n.41
Vietnam, 375, 428 n.41, 430, 431, 484
Vogel, Ezra F., 483 n.22
Vollzugsrat. See Executive Council
Vyborg, 365

W

Wachenheim, Hedwig, 226 n.96
Walker, Mack, 136, 157
Wallace, Michael, 237 n.13
Walter, Eugene Victor, 85, 100 n.19
Walzer, Michael, 428
Warsaw, 63
Washington, George, 347
Watter, Oskar von, 340, 345, 350
Wattwill, 120, 121 n.2, 122, 123, 124
Weber, Alfred, 194, 200, 201
Weber, Max, 347 n.47, 378, 393, 466 n.7, 470 n.12
Wechsler, Howard J., 503 n.32
Weimar Constitution, 309, 311
Weimar Republic, 90, 128, 292, 302, 311–312, 339, 340, 377, 389, 392, 417, 419, 426, 428
Weiss, Walter, 101 n.20
Weissberg, Alexander, 68 n.46
Weitling, Wilhelm, 154
Wels, Otto, 299
West, Western, 172, 212, 291, 363, 435, 438, 462, 490, 501, 509
Westermarck, Edward, 34 n.25
Western Europe, 126, 361, 479

Westfälische Stahlwerke, 257 n.58
Westphalia, 231, 247, 350
Wetter, 345
Whitehead, Alfred North, 491
White Rose group, 109 n.39
Whyte, William Foote, 191 n.24
Wilhelm I, King of Prussia, 242
Wilhelm II, German Kaiser, 166, 198 n.37, 221, 222, 223, 246, 290, 291, 292, 294, 304, 317, 341 n.39, 388 n.11
Wilson, Woodrow, 296
Wineman, David, 105
Winkler, Heinrich August, 132 n.5
Wolfe, Bertram D., 110
Wolfenstein, E. Victor, 109 n.38, 110 n.41
Wolff, Robert Paul, 378 n.1
Wolff, Wilhelm, 144 n.37
World War I. *See* First World War
World War II, 397, 400
Wrangel, Friedrich von, 165
Württemberg, 291, 350

Z

Zeitlin, Maurice, 399 n.1
Zimmer, Heinrich, 53 n.12
Zimmermann, Waldemar, 176 n.2, 278 table
Zinoviev, G. E., 373
Zionists, 67
Zola, Émile, 192
Zollverein, 136
Zulus, 85
Zürich, 121 n.1